THE
COLONIAL HISTORY
SERIES

General Editor
D. H. Simpson
Librarian of the Royal Commonwealth Society

AFRICAN QUESTIONS AT THE
PARIS PEACE CONFERENCE

AFRICAN QUESTIONS
AT THE
PARIS PEACE CONFERENCE

WITH PAPERS ON EGYPT, MESOPOTAMIA,
AND THE COLONIAL SETTLEMENT

BY

GEORGE LOUIS BEER

CHIEF OF THE COLONIAL DIVISION OF THE AMERICAN DELEGATION
TO NEGOTIATE PEACE, AND ALTERNATE MEMBER OF
THE COMMISSION ON MANDATES

EDITED WITH INTRODUCTION, ANNEXES,
AND ADDITIONAL NOTES
BY

LOUIS HERBERT GRAY

SECRETARY TO THE COLONIAL DIVISION

1968
DAWSONS OF PALL MALL
London

This edition is reprinted by arrangement with
The Macmillan Company, New York

First published and copyright by them in 1923

Reprinted 1968
Dawsons of Pall Mall
16 Pall Mall, London, S.W.1

SBN: 7129 0324 0

*Printed in Great Britain
by Photolithography
Unwin Brothers Limited
Woking and London*
(2229L)

EDITOR'S PREFACE

THE studies prepared for the American Commission of Inquiry by Mr. George Louis Beer, Colonial Expert to The Inquiry and subsequently Chief of the Colonial Section of the American Commission to Negotiate Peace, possess an importance which is not measured merely by the conditions which evoked them. They are a permanent contribution towards an understanding of the Colonial Problem, not only in Africa, but throughout the world, not simply for some one Power, but for all Powers. They are based on a minute, impartial, and scientific investigation of every factor involved; each point of view is given due consideration; and from the data thus gathered, certain conclusions are drawn for action henceforth advisable in guidance of those portions of the world which are as yet incapable of wisely directing their own destinies. If the essays are perfect by the canons of technical scholarship, they are also perfect in their applicability to practical statesmanship.

It was my privilege to be closely associated with Mr. Beer both in New York and in Paris; and it was, perhaps, for this reason that, shortly after his death, Mrs. Beer and Mr. James Shotwell suggested that I prepare for press the monographs which he had written for The Inquiry. The copy was almost ready for printing as Mr. Beer had left it, but it seemed advisable to do what he himself would doubtless have done, and to bring the entire volume, which had been finished early in 1918, up to the present time. The material which I have thus added is enclosed in brackets that it may clearly be distinguished from Mr. Beer's own work; and I have availed myself of this opportunity to indicate how closely the settlements actually made at Paris coincided with the recommendations which he had formulated before the Conference assembled. I am also responsible for the entire body of Annexes and for the Commercial Chart, which my friend, Mr. Craighill, kindly prepared for me while we were both attached to the United States Embassy at Paris.

I have not felt myself justified in excising any passage in the manuscript which Mr. Beer had not marked for deletion; and the reader may, consequently, observe a number of repetitions. In studies written at different times on kindred problems, occasional traversing of the same ground is almost inevitable; but each passage so repeated appeared to have its own justification, and reiteration seemed preferable to cross-reference.

In an Introduction to this volume, I have sought to give some account of Mr. Beer's work in Paris, taking care not to duplicate what will more fittingly be set forth in a Memorial Volume soon to appear.

My task has not been wholly easy. It is no small matter even to attempt to complete worthily the work of a true scholar and a dear friend when his counsel and his guidance may no more be sought. My debt to him and my affection for him were very great; the one I can never adequately repay, and the other I can never sufficiently express. But I have been helped by others who also knew and admired him, and though I may not yet record their names, they will be well aware of my gratitude to them.

May the volume aid in furthering the welfare of mankind whom George Louis Beer loved so well; and may it help to show that we who could only stand and wait through the dread years of war at least tried to serve!

LOUIS H. GRAY.

University of Nebraska, June 25, 1923.

CONTENTS

MAPS

INTRODUCTION

EDITOR'S INTRODUCTION

THE magnitude of the World War, and the principles and reasons underlying the conflict, made it obvious, almost from the beginning, that the termination of hostilities must be followed by political and economic changes of corresponding degree. Preparation for peace was as essential as preparation for war. Each belligerent Power realized this fact; and in the autumn of 1917, when it became evident that the Allies would win victory in the field, President Wilson requested Colonel House to create an American Commission of Inquiry to gather data—geographical, ethnological, political, legal, commercial, economic—regarding every problem that could possibly be discussed at the Peace Conference, and to study and report on each of these questions in all its bearings.

Among these matters, the Colonial Problem was recognized as one of the most important. It was only too clear that Germany's procedure in her colonies had been open to grave criticism, and that on moral grounds, as well as for political reasons, her retention of them could scarcely be justified. The question of their future was, therefore, urgent. Under such conditions, it was peculiarly fitting that George Louis Beer should be chosen as Colonial Expert on the Commission, of which he was one of the first members, both in time and in eminence.

For this work Mr. Beer possessed intellectual and technical abilities of very marked degree. He had studied minutely the history of the British colonial system, on which he had already written five volumes recognized as authoritative: "The Commercial Policy of England Toward the American Colonies" (1893); "Cromwell's Policy in Its Economic Aspects" (1902); "Origins of the British Colonial System, 1578-1660" (1908); and "The Old Colonial System, 1660-1754," Part I (2 volumes, 1912). His method throughout had been that which marks the true scholar in every line: unprejudiced, patient, and minute examination of every source of information; synthesis of the results of this examination into an ordered whole; deduction of principles and conclusions from that whole; and harmonization of the judgments thus reached with the complex of the *omne scibile*. All this Mr. Beer regarded, not as a counsel of perfection, but as a mere matter of course. Others might, for example, consider the Colonial Problem merely from the point of view of the individual Colony or individual Power possessing it; or from the relation of that Colony and Power to other Colonies and Powers; or in their historical and economic connections; or as pawns and knights on the diplomatic chessboard. He was wiser. To all these factors he assigned true value; but he also remembered that the Colonial Problem was only a part of the settlement which must be made, realizing that if the past lays the foundations of the present, the present, in conjunction with the past, conditions the future; and that the settlement, to be of real worth, must prepare the way for a practicable future better than past or present.

It was precisely here that Mr. Beer escaped a peril which often overwhelms one who is only a scholar, and against which he had consciously guarded himself. For ten years he had engaged in a business career, though for four years of this period he had also been a lecturer on European history at his *alma mater,* Columbia University. He thus received a practical training in addition to his scholastic education, so that he knew not only books, but men and conditions, not merely as they should be, but as they are.

These two aspects of Mr. Beer's character have been admirably summarized in a brief memoir in *The Round Table:* [1]

"A devouring reader of dry official documents, he possessed the extraordinary faculty of never forgetting the smallest details once read. His academic training had given him in a high degree the love of truth and scrupulous conscientiousness of a scholar. On the other hand, his ten years' business training enabled him to avoid the faults of a mere scholar when dealing with practical questions. He combined to an extraordinary degree the virtues of scholarship with those of a man of affairs."

From 1903 onwards, in the prosecution of his colonial studies, for which he was to receive, in 1913, the Loubat Prize from Columbia for the best works in English, during the preceding five years, on any subject of history, geography, or archæology relating to America, Mr. Beer spent much time in London, especially at the Record Office. Here he became acquainted with diplomatic procedure and with the group who were later to establish *The Round Table,* of which he was American correspondent, thus com-

[1] No. 40 (September, 1920), p. 934.

pleting the training which subsequently was to prove of such great value.

With this triple preparation in scholarship, practical life, and diplomacy, Mr. Beer entered in October, 1917, upon the work of The Inquiry, as the corps of experts, called together by Colonel House, was commonly termed. It was in connection with this committee that he prepared the studies which are collected in the present volume. These essays are of more than usual interest from several points of view. They are representative of the best type of the reports which the American Commission to Negotiate Peace had for their technical guidance; and they possess a further historical value when Mr. Beer's conclusions and recommendations are compared with the settlements actually made. In every matter of principle, and in almost every detail, it will be observed that, in so far as the colonial settlement was concerned, what he thought best to be done, was done. Nor is this all. They also show— and this is of more than mere historic worth—how scholarship may serve Government, not only in the exact collection of data, but also in the reasoned and impartial presentation of recommendations for a course to be pursued.

The three essays on the African Colonies present a purely inductive study which leads up to one of the most thoughtful suggestions for a major element in the League of Nations—the germ of the concept of international control which was later to be embodied in the Mandate Article of the Covenant of the League; and in this connection a special historical importance attaches to the brief study on Mesopotamia (dated January 1, 1918), in that it contains [2] the earliest use, so far as known either to Mr. Beer or to the writer, of the term "mandate" in which it is now technically employed. On this latter point, his colleague and close personal friend, Mr. James Shotwell, very pertinently remarks:[3]

"Yet it occurs in a most casual way in a sentence which bears no mark of special emphasis. For Mr. Beer had already matured the conception in his own mind, and developed it in discussion so that he did not stress the formula which expressed it. Subsequently he realized the importance of the formula, but it was typical of his scholarly approach to the problem that he himself was more interested in the content of the settlement than in the invention of a slogan for popular understanding even when he was the almost unconscious inventor. It was equally typical of his modesty that his associates on the Inquiry were for the most part ignorant of this and similar contributions."

An attentive reading of Mr. Beer's essays will reveal the principles which guided him in all his colonial studies. The first of these was that the colony must be administered primarily for the benefit of its native population; and that the material interests of the metropolitan Power must be given very minor consideration. The second was that the colonies which had been held by Germany must be placed under some system of international control. The former principle had long since received at least partial recognition, for the Signatories to the Berlin Act had declared themselves, in their Preamble, "concerned with the means of increasing the moral and material welfare of the

[2] P. 424.
[3] In his essay on the work of George Louis Beer at the Paris Peace Conference in the forthcoming Beer Memorial Volume.

native populations," and by Article 6 had undertaken "to
watch over the preservation of the native populations and
over the improvement of their moral and material conditions of existence"; while the various subsequent restrictions on slavery, arms, and liquor had been inspired by
the same high motives. Nevertheless, Mr. Beer realized
that this was only a beginning, and that, though the slave-
trade was dead, the traffic in arms and liquor required more
stringent measures. Further, there were the perils of
forced labor, of expropriation of native land, and of unwar-
ranted interference with native life and custom. Against
these evils he sought to provide, and—whether independently or not—the Mandates follow in all essentials the
lines which he had foreseen to be best.

The problem of international control was somewhat
more difficult. The system of the *condominium* has proved
open to grave objection, as is sufficiently shown by its
record in all past history, notably in the case of the New
Hebrides; the only successful surviving instance is Andorra.
Direct internationalization is equally perilous. Its most
effective application is undoubtedly that of the Commission
of the Danube; but the Peace Conference admitted this
régime only in the case of certain European rivers and
the Dardanelles.[4] In some other instances internationalization was suggested, but failed of adoption. The best solution was plainly that which Mr. Beer advocated—a dual
control whereby the direct administration should be exercised by the Powers immediately concerned in each particular territory, but with some system of international

[4] Treaty of Versailles, Articles 331-345; Treaty of Sèvres, Articles 38-61.

supervision by which the welfare of the native populations might be more effectively guarded and protection ensured against any possible abuse.[5]   But with this dual control, Mr. Beer, strongly opposed to any course which might tend to make the League of Nations a "Super-State," whether in reality or in appearance, clearly saw, and in private conversation repeatedly stressed, the necessity of safeguarding the sovereignty of each Mandatory Power, as of every State, Member of the League.   This requirement he had in mind throughout the Peace Conference; he expressed his convictions on the subject more than once during the sessions of the Commissions to which he was attached; and the Conventions which he helped draw up bear evidence of his firm, yet tactful, insistence on this vital point.

This brings us to a consideration of the somewhat brief study on the "Colonial Questions" (Part VI, pp. 429-458, of the present volume).   Here two points are of immediate interest.   In the first place, the memorandum is an excellent specimen of documents of its class, based on exhaustive preliminary research, but with its subject-matter condensed to the utmost practicable degree to serve as a basis for actual negotiation.   In the second place, its recommendations may be compared, point by point, with the settlements actually made; and thus one may perceive how expert advice had a very real influence on the decisions

---

[5] For some account of discussions of the problem by the Council of Ten see R. S. Baker, "Woodrow Wilson and World Settlement," I, pp. 254-275, Garden City, N. Y., 1922; cf. also Cioriceanu, "Les Mandats Internationaux," pp. 68-73; Antonelli, "L'Afrique et la Paix de Versailles," pp. 164-166, 176-178.

of the Plenipotentiaries. The charge has sometimes been made by opponents of the Conference that experts received insufficient consideration, but the writer feels himself to be in a position to state that the criticism lacks foundation.

Furthermore, the memorandum shows that Mr. Beer had by this time definitely adopted the mandate system, and that his recommendation was the one actually followed. So far as the territorial distribution was concerned, no prophetic gift had been needed. Any intelligent observer could foresee that the Powers and Dominions which had wrested the allogenous German and Turkish possessions from their former rulers would be extremely reluctant to part entirely with the lands for which they had been forced to pour forth blood and treasure. The arrangements made, during the war, for division of ex-enemy territories, as in the Anglo-French Accords of August 30, 1914 and March 4, 1916, regarding Togo and the Cameroons, or in the Anglo-Japanese Treaty of 1916 regarding the Pacific islands north of the Equator, were eminently reasonable in the pre-mandate period. The new element, however, which radically changed the status of these regions, was the Mandate. Of the intrinsic rightness of this combination Mr. Beer was firmly convinced, and his influence is traceable in the final decision.

Precisely here one may perceive a cardinal characteristic of Mr. Beer's mind and method. If it be possible to define this aspect of him in a word, he may be described as a "practical idealist." With his academic training corrected and supplemented by contact with actualities, and with realism held in its proper place by the refinement and breadth which deep study of the humanities brings, he could see at once the ideal and the real and, appreciating the viewpoints of others, bring them into harmony with his own. Perhaps, to take a concrete instance, he may have wished that Egypt might be a wholly sovereign State. Yet he clearly saw, as a reading of his "Egypt" (Part IV of this volume) will show, that this is as yet impossible in the best interests of the Egyptians themselves and for the protection of the foreign investor, if for no other reason; and he therefore advocated recognition of the British Protectorate.

But if Mr. Beer thus placed the welfare of the native populations of ex-German and ex-Turkish territories in the forefront, he did not forget the interests of the Powers, even of those who held no African possessions; he was a firm advocate, so far as local conditions would permit, of the policy of the "open door" and of equality of opportunity for the nationals of "all States, Members of the League of Nations." Another principle, brought out in his study on international control in Middle Africa, and introduced into the Arms Convention (Preamble, Paragraph 6) and into the Revision Convention (Article 15), was his strong belief in the necessity of conferences, restricted to definite subjects, at stated intervals for amendment, if necessary in the light of experience gained, of decisions and stipulations previously made.

With these views Mr. Beer was among those who accompanied President Wilson to the Peace Conference at Paris. There he was Chief of the Colonial Section of the American

Delegation, and sat, accordingly, on the Commissions for Morocco (March 31-April 5, 1919) and the German Colonies (April 24-25, 1919), the Convention for the Control of the Trade in Arms and Ammunition (July 8-25, 1919), the Convention relating to the Liquor Traffic in Africa (July 26-28, 1919), and the Convention revising the General Act of Berlin, February 26, 1885, and the General Act and Declaration of Brussels, July 2, 1890 (July 30-August 2, 1919), besides being an alternate to Colonel House on the Mandates Commission and aiding in the preparation of the Allied and Associated Reply to the German Observations on the Peace Conditions (Political Clauses relating to Countries outside Europe).

On the basis of the official *Procès-Verbaux* of the Commissions, in which all Mr. Beer's colleagues—British, French, Italian, Japanese, Belgian, and Portuguese—were, like him, animated with the single desire of furthering in every possible way the progress of backward peoples, it is now permissible to set forth in some detail his part in this work.

The first draft of the Morocco Clauses (Articles 141-146 of the Versailles Treaty) was prepared by French experts, and on March 28, 1919, the Supreme Council determined to create a Commission to examine these proposals, this work being performed in three sessions. In Article 141, the words, "Germany renounces all rights and privileges," are due to Mr. Beer; and, except for substitution of "The Sherifian Government" for "France," the first paragraph of the present Article 143 is the formula which was proposed by Mr. Beer to replace Article 5 of the French draft:

"In Morocco the German Government renounces maintenance of a Legation, possession of any public or private
establishment of general utility, such as post, telegraph
and telephone offices, schools and hospitals, and exercise
of protection there under any form whatever."

The Commission on African Colonies, created by the
Supreme Council on April 23, 1919, and holding two sessions, had before it a French and a British draft. In Article
126 (Article 10 of the French draft), already accepted in
essentials by the Council of Ministers for Foreign Affairs,
the words, "or some of them," were inserted as a result
of Mr. Beer's criticism that otherwise Germany was bound
to accept only stipulations unanimously adopted by the
Allied and Associated Powers. The French draft had
originally contained the following Article 6:

"Within three months from the coming into force of
the present Treaty the German Government will repatriate
at its own expense those of its European nationals who are
still actually resident in the German Colonies or who have
sought refuge in the Spanish Colonies in the Gulf of
Guinea. From the coming into force of the present Treaty
natives of the German Colonies who are now refugees in
the said Spanish Colonies will be free to return to their
original country without being subjected to any restriction
or hindrance in this respect by the German authorities."

This was, however, withdrawn in consequence of objections of Mr. Beer, supported by his British colleagues, Mr.
Payne and Sir Herbert Read, because of the danger of
infringement of Spanish rights of sovereignty. In Article
121, the words, "whatever be the form of Government
adopted for them," were substituted by Mr. Beer for the
passage in the British draft which had originally read:

"The provisions of Section   ,[6] Chapter I (Commercial relations) and Chapter IV (Property, rights and interests) shall apply in the case of a territory ceded by Germany to the Allied and Associated Powers, and the Government of which is entrusted by the latter to a mandatory, in the same way as in the case of a territory of an Allied or Associated Power."

In Article 120, Mr. Beer altered the original "mandatory" to "Government exercising authority," and he interchanged Articles 3 and 2 to their present sequence (Articles 120, 121). In Article 123, the opening words, "The provisions of Article 260 of Part IX (Financial Clauses) of the present Treaty shall apply," are due to his observation that this stipulation must be made to harmonize with the results reached by the other commissions; and in consequence he carried omission of the second paragraph of the original draft:

"The indemnities to be paid to German nationals in this connection shall be charged to the German Government after they have been fixed by local tribunals; the total sums thus disbursed by the State shall be deducted from the amount which Germany must pay in reparation of damage caused by the war."

In Article 124, Mr. Beer inserted the words, "and approved by the Reparation Commission"; and the present form of Article 125, except for editorial changes, was framed by him to replace Article 7 of the French draft:

"The Conventions governing the attribution of the territories formerly placed within the German zones of the African Continent being superseded by the stipulations of

*The *Procès-Verbal* has a blank space for the section-number, which was unknown.

the present Treaty, the German Government recognises that claims which might have been presented on the basis of clauses of those instruments are henceforth void. Deposits, credits, advances, etc., which would have been effected by virtue of these instruments in favour of the German Government are transferred to the Mandatory Powers.

"These Powers shall, further, have the right to fix the amount of the indemnities claimed by their nationals in consequence of the application of the Conventions aforesaid. The sum total of these indemnities shall be charged to the German Government."

On June 25, 1919, the Council of Ministers for Foreign Affairs determined to create a Commission to examine three draft Conventions, drawn up by the British and French representatives, to replace the General Acts of Berlin and Brussels and to deal respectively with control of the trade in arms and ammunition, the liquor traffic in Africa, and such other matters in those Acts as were of continued importance, but found no place in the other two Conventions. For all three, Anglo-French drafts had previously been prepared, and the Commission sat fourteen times between July 8 and September 8, 1919. Mr. Beer was represented at the first and second sessions by Captain Hornbeck, and at the final session by Mr. Woolsey. Seven sittings (July 8-25) were devoted to the Arms Convention, two (July 26-28) to the Liquor Convention, and four (July 30-August 2) to the Revision Convention, the fourteenth session (September 8), held after Mr. Beer had returned to the United States, being given to the few details which were still to be settled before the signature, which took place two days later.

The Commission first considered the "Convention for the Control of the Trade in Arms and Ammunition" (Annex E). For this, Mr. Beer had prepared a careful memorandum covering the entire first draft. This contains the germ of the third paragraph of Article 1 in the words:

"In the case of small-bore firearms and ammunition adapted for utilisation both for war and also for other purposes, the High Contracting Parties reserve to themselves the right to determine for what use each cargo is intended and to decide whether it falls within the scope of the stipulations of this Article";

but, despite the arguments of Captain Hornbeck, M. de Peretti de la Rocca considered it unnecessary and possibly provocative of confusion. It was, accordingly, reserved. In this memorandum, Mr. Beer also expressed the opinion that the original list of arms and ammunition whose export was prohibited by the first paragraph of Article 1—"machine-guns, bombs, grenades, small-bore firearms of every kind, whether complete or in parts, as well as ammunition for use with such arms"—was too restricted, and that "artillery and cannon of all kinds" should fall within the same category. It was, however, only at the fifth session (July 18) that an amendment to this effect, prepared by the Italian military experts, was presented by Count Marazzi; and the text was not finally adopted until the last revision by the Commission on July 25.

In Article 4, "State" was replaced by "country" on the basis of this memorandum, and the last paragraph of Article 5 was drawn unchanged (except for its original reading, "Each High Contracting Party agrees") from the same source. In like manner, the words, "or territory under mandate," were twice added in Article 7. In Article 10, where the final text reads, "Within the prohibited areas specified in Article 6, a State which is compelled to utilise," the original draft ran, "A State without access to the sea which, to reach it, is compelled to utilise." For this, Mr. Beer proposed, "A State within the prohibited area but without access to the sea which, to reach it, is compelled to utilise," the final phrasing being adopted, after further discussion, at the session of July 17.

When the third session of the Commission was held, on July 16, Mr. Beer was present. Strongly advocating the necessity of regular, periodical revisions "in the light of the experience gained," he now succeeded, after some debate, in incorporating a clause which he had already proposed in his memorandum and which is, in all essentials, the present sixth paragraph of the Preamble, its only noteworthy modifications being the extension of the revisional period from five to seven years, and its place in the Preamble instead of in Articles 1 and 25. In Article 6, the present form of the first paragraph is Mr. Beer's substitution for the original phrasing, "Importation and conveyance of the arms and ammunition specified in Articles 1 and 2 shall be prohibited in the following areas," which, after a long discussion, M. de Peretti de la Rocca had suggested should read, subject to the approval of the British and United States Delegates:

"The High Contracting Parties undertake, each as far as its own territory is concerned, to prohibit the importa-

tion and transportation of the arms and ammunition specified in Articles 1 and 2 into the following areas."

In the last paragraph of this Article, the concluding sentence reproduces essentially Mr. Beer's amendment of the
original draft, which read, "In this case, the highest possible import duty shall be levied on the arms and ammunition imported." In connection with this same Article, Mr.
Beer proposed, at the fourth session (July 17), an additional paragraph which he had already presented in germ
in his memorandum, and which he now couched as follows:

"In granting special licences in territories under mandate
and in territories in which commercial equality is guaranteed by international agreements, the local authorities shall
make no distinction whatever between subjects and citizens
of States, Members of the League of Nations, or between
arms and ammunition manufactured or imported by a
State, Member of the League of Nations."

The discussion which ensued was of unusual interest as
revealing a notable aspect of Mr. Beer's breadth of view.
He expressly declared his realization that this paragraph
was not absolutely necessary if the Mandate Clauses regarding commercial equality were applicable to the arms
traffic (as he knew they would be). Nevertheless, his proposed text would obviate all possibility of misunderstand-
ing, and might exercise on public opinion a happy impression of no negligible degree. His colleagues were, however, unable to see the force of his argument, and he
accordingly withdrew his proposal. At the following session,
he presented a revised formula, concluded in these terms:

"In issuing these special licences, the local authorities shall make no distinction whatever between subjects and citizens of States, Members of the League of Nations, or between arms and ammunition manufactured or imported by nationals of any one of these States."

In this, he was supported by the Belgian and Italian Delegates, but M. Merlin (France) objected that it involved a question of national sovereignty, while Colonel Norton de Mattos (Portugal) repeated his opinion, which he had advanced the day previous, that the matter belonged more properly to the Mandate problem; finally, the British Delegates were without instructions. The addition was, therefore, reserved; and at the seventh session (July 25) the Portuguese Delegation definitely rejected it. Since it had already been opposed strenuously by the French Delegates, it was withdrawn.

At the sixth session (July 22), Mr. Beer proposed to add to the present Article 11 the words, "Subject to any contrary provisions in special agreements already existing, or in future agreements"; and the entire Article was revised into the form in which it now appears, except for the addition of, "provided that in all cases such agreements comply with the provisions of the present Convention."

As regards the "Convention relating to the Liquor Traffic in Africa" (Annex F), the words, "and of beverages mixed with these spirits," were added to Article 2 by Mr. Beer, though he failed to secure a similar addition after "Articles 2 and 3" in Article 4; and the first paragraph of Article 7 (corresponding to the first paragraph of Article 5 of the Arms Convention) was due to his suggestion, supported by M. de Peretti de la Rocca.

The Commission next devoted attention to the "Convention revising the General Act of Berlin, February 26, 1885, and the General Act and Declaration of Brussels, July 2, 1890" (Annex G). Here Mr. Beer, who later added to the title its reference to the Declaration, criticized the original phrasing of the second paragraph of the Preamble:

"Whereas by the Brussels Declaration of July 2, 1890, it was found necessary to modify the commercial system established for twenty years by Article 4 of the said Act, and this system is now barred by limitation (*périmé*), and since that date no agreement has been entered into, contrary to the provisions of the said Article."

This, he held, was in contradiction both of history and of the principles of international law, for the system in question applied only to free imports, while it was inexact to say that it was now barred by limitation. After some further discussion, the paragraph was recast in its present form, while, at his suggestion, "sovereignties" was replaced, in the third paragraph, by "authorities" to provide for regions placed under mandate.

In the first Article, as well as in Articles 2, 3, and 11, Mr. Beer introduced the words, "and those of States, Members of the League of Nations, which may become parties to the present Convention." By Article 126 of the Versailles Treaty,

"Germany undertakes to accept and observe the agreements made or to be made by the Allied and Associated Powers or some of them with any other Power with regard to the trade in arms and spirits, and to the matters dealt with in the General Act of Berlin of February 26,

1885, and the General Act of Brussels of July 2, 1890; and the conventions completing or modifying the same."

Without the proposed addition, Germany might immediately enjoy all the advantages of the new General Act; with it, this could be only after she had become a member of the League of Nations. In view of this argument, the amendment was accepted; while, likewise at Mr. Beer's suggestion, it was decided to omit, as involving two diplomatic instruments applying to different areas, the second paragraph of the original draft:

"This provision will remain in force until June 13, 1929, the date when the Anglo-French Convention and Declaration of June 14, 1898, and March 21, 1899,[7] expire. Nevertheless, the High Contracting Parties reserve the right to introduce into the present Convention, by common agreement, such modifications as may appear to them to be necessary to bring it into harmony with stipulations of a general nature which may have been adopted elsewhere regarding commerce between the mother countries and their colonies."

In its original form, the concluding sentence of the third Article—"Each Power will, however, remain free to dispose of its private domain according to the laws in force in this respect in its possessions"—was the subject of much debate. At the tenth session (July 30), Mr. Beer considered it ill-placed, and he was supported in his criticism by Mr. Strachey (Great Britain) and M. Anzilotti (Italy). On the following day, MM. Duchêne (France) and Louwers (Belgium) presented a new draft: "Each Power will, however, retain the right to dispose freely of the

[7] For these documents see "Trattati . . . relativi all'Africa," pp. 594-599, 613-614.

property which it possesses and which permit of private appropriation"; and finally the amendment was transformed, except for minor editorial changes, into the present Article 4.

The present Article 5 (originally Article 4), taken up at the eleventh session (July 31), gave rise to long discussion, like those immediately following it. The Anglo-French draft ran:

"Subject to the provisions of the present chapter, the navigation of the Congo and Niger, as well as of all their branches and outlets, shall remain entirely free for merchant vessels and for the transport of goods and passengers.

"Craft of every kind belonging to the nationals of the High Contracting Parties shall be treated in all respects on a footing of perfect equality, as well for direct navigation from the open sea to interior ports, and *vice versa*, as for great and small coastwise navigation, and for navigation on the said rivers. No exclusive privilege of navigation shall be conceded to societies, corporations or associations of any kind or to private persons, each of the High Contracting Parties retaining the right of reserving for itself such monopoly as may seem to it expedient regarding navigation and transport by land, water or railway."

To this, the Belgian Delegation felt unable to agree, and they proposed, instead, to replace the first paragraph by:

"The navigation of the Niger, of its branches and outlets, as well as of all the rivers, and of their branches and outlets, within the territories specified in Article 1, shall, in the portions of their course serving more than one riparian State, be subject to the following provisions."

Retaining the second paragraph and modifying Article 7 (originally Article 6) to harmonize with Article 5, they also desired to add a new Article, which should read as follows:

"Subject to the provisions of the present chapter, navigation shall be entirely free for merchant vessels and for the transport of goods and passengers."

The question at stake was more grave than is perhaps apparent at first sight. By the original draft, based on Articles 13 and 26 of the Berlin Act, it was possible, Baron de Gaiffier and M. Louwers pointed out, for foreign Powers to construct and charter vessels flying their flag within territorial waters without navigable communication with their own dominions. This had notably been done by the Germans on reaches of the Congo cut off by cataracts from a direct course to the sea. Baron de Gaiffier maintained, moreover, that the conditions making a river international and open to free navigation should be twofold: (1) it must provide natural access to the sea; and (2) it must serve more than one State; but, in addition, he considered that the special situation of certain riparian States of the Congo and Niger rendered it advisable to extend freedom of navigation to all parts of these rivers which provided means of communication common to several States, even though they did not give immediate access to the sea. The *crux* was, therefore, the words, "in the portions of their course serving more than one riparian State." This would mean, M. Louwers declared, internationalization of the Congo from the ocean to the Ubangi, and of the Ubangi and M'Bomu along the Franco-Belgian frontier. The remainder of the Congo and the other rivers of the Conventional Basin, as well as the Niger, should be governed by the general law, and the Matadi-Léopoldville railway should be international. France, Japan, and Portugal sup-

ported the Belgian proposal; but the British, Italian, and
United States Delegates felt obliged to consult their Governments, Mr. Beer expressing the conviction that the
change marked a step backwards rather than forwards in
the path of internationalization pursued by all the world,
and adding that, in his judgment, Article 3 gave Belgium
all requisite rights of control. No agreement could, however, be reached; and the first paragraph of Article 5 was
reserved. At the following session (August 1), Mr. Beer
stated that he was not authorized to accept the Belgian
amendment; but on the next day, after a conference between him and M. Louwers, an agreement was happily
reached which proved acceptable to all. Article 5 was now
adopted (except for editorial changes) in its present form;
Articles 6, 7, and 8 (originally 5, 6, 7) were changed to the
reading which they now have; and a new Article (the
present ninth) was inserted.

In presenting the formula which was incorporated in
the final draft, M. Louwers pointed out that it would permit a Government exercising sole control over a portion of
one of the rivers of the Conventional Basin to close that
section if it were deemed advisable, as in time of scarcity
or in case of excessive exploitation, or if maintenance of
public order and security should seem to require it, the
only limitation on governmental action being the stipulation that it be applied simultaneously to nationals of all
the High Contracting Parties. The Belgian Delegation,
he added, did not desire to establish measures restrictive
to commercial equality, but sought only to place the Governments in a position to exercise, under the best condi-

tions, the authority for which they were responsible in the interests of their task of civilization.

The accord thus attained gave complete satisfaction to both sides and materially improved the whole Convention. Belgium gained the right for which she contended, and which Mr. Beer would have been the last to contest— sovereign control over her own colonies; and this was explicitly confirmed by the new Article 9, whereas the amendment proposed by M. Louwers had made no such direct affirmation, whatever might have been the implications that could have been derived from it. But, on the other hand, Mr. Beer gained precisely what he deemed necessary—an advance in the principle of internationalization except when and where special circumstance might render it inadvisable. The Belgian draft had been restrictive; the Article in its final form is inclusive, with limitations which might conceivably prove necessary appended as exceptions. Practically, perhaps, the result would have been the same whichever draft prevailed, but the underlying principles were radically divergent; and the principle for which Mr. Beer was here striving was that not merely of his Government, but of his own deep conviction.

Thus ended the only moments of tension during all the sessions of the Commission and the only conflict of principles which arose. It is not too much to say that it was solely Mr. Beer's tact which rendered possible the finding of a formula on which Belgians, French, Japanese, and Portuguese, on the one hand, and Americans, British, and Italians, on the other, could agree.

The opening paragraph of Article 14 (originally Article

11), taken almost verbally from Article 37 of the Berlin
Act, was also the subject of considerable debate. In its
first draft it ran: "The Powers who shall not have signed
the present Convention may adhere to its dispositions by
a separate Act"; but Mr. Strachey (Great Britain), at the
twelfth session (August 1), called attention to the fact
that, unlike the Arms and Liquor Conventions, this Convention could be enforced only by States holding territories
in the Conventional Basin, whence there was no reason to
expect adhesion of Powers which could undertake no
counter-engagements. Mr. Beer then proposed two for-
mulas, the first reading:

"The High Contracting Parties will endeavour to secure
the accession of other States, Members of the League of
Nations, which have interests involved in the Convention,"

and the second running:

"The High Contracting Parties will use their endeavours
to secure the accession to the present Convention of other
States, Members of the League of Nations, which were
parties to the Act of Berlin or to the Act of Brussels or
the Declaration annexed thereto, or which exercise their
authority over African territories."

The latter phrasing, he felt, had the disadvantage that
certain States, Members of the League of Nations, would
not benefit from the Convention, while, on the other hand,
it would permit the adhesion of interested States, such as
Abyssinia, which were not Members of the League. He
also suggested a new clause whereby all Members of the
League might adhere, subject to the approval of the League

Council (thus providing, for example, for Czecho-Slovakia); and M. de Peretti de la Rocca accordingly proposed to add the words:

"All other States, Members of the League of Nations, may be admitted to the privileges of this Convention at their request and with the approval of the Council of the League of Nations."

Certain Delegates felt, however, that it was unnecessary to invite the adhesion of uninterested Powers and that some States might profit without giving benefits in return; while M. Louwers expressed the opinion that the first formula respected the actual conditions, leaving each State with African territories free to reach understandings with other Powers. Mr. Beer, therefore, withdrew his second proposal, and the first was adopted. At the next session, the discussion was resumed, the result being an amalgamation of Mr. Beer's second formula with the original draft, and the Article thus assumed its final form. States which do not adhere remain bound, in virtue of Article 13, by the Berlin and Brussels Acts; while new States, Members of the League but not signatory to those Acts (as Czecho-Slovakia), may enjoy the advantages of the Convention in consequence of treaties between them and Powers signatory to the Convention.

The question of a Revision Clause, which the original draft did not contain, was the last which evoked noteworthy debate. The matter was brought up by M. de Peretti de la Rocca at the twelfth session, when he and Mr. Beer proposed to insert the ninth Article of the Liquor Convention, which had doubtless been influenced by

Articles 14 (last paragraph) and 36 of the Berlin Act, as well as by Article 97 of the Brussels Act. The phrase, "by common agreement," would imply that failure to secure unanimity would prevent any change in the Convention; but M. Louwers observed that here, unlike the case of the other two Conventions, political and economic interests were involved, adding that, if the Powers could not reach an agreement, it would be evident that the Convention was gravely unsatisfactory to some one of them. Mr. Beer proposed to require revision after a period of ten years "in the light of the experience gained, if the Council of the League of Nations, acting if need be by a majority, so recommends" (the phrase used in the Preamble to the Arms Convention). To this, the Belgian and French Delegates objected as giving control of Africa to the Council rather than to the Powers holding territory there; and M. de Peretti de la Rocca suggested the following text, which was acceptable to the Belgian Delegation:

"The present Convention will remain in force for a period of ten years from the exchange of ratifications. The High Contracting Parties reserve the right of introducing into the present Convention by common agreement after that period such modifications as may prove to be necessary."

Failure to reach agreement would make the situation identical with that under the Berlin and Brussels Acts: each Power would remain free to declare that it no longer considered itself bound by the Convention. Mr. Beer urged the importance of stipulating that the Convention should remain in force if accord could not be attained, and M. de Peretti de la Rocca therefore proposed to add the words:

"If agreement cannot be reached, the present Convention shall remain in force provisionally unless each State exercising rights of sovereignty in the Conventional Basin of the Congo is opposed to it."

To this the Belgian Delegation felt unable to agree; but Baron de Gaiffier was willing to accept a formula requiring reassembly for revision of the Convention and proposed the phrasing which now appears as Article 15, except for drafting changes and the addition of the words, "from the coming into force of the present Convention."

The influence which Mr. Beer exercised on the settlement of problems concerning the ex-German and ex-Turkish territories was far wider than the written records show. At Paris he quickly gained a position of distinction among his colleagues, both American, European, and Colonial; his rare personal charm won him firm friends; and his opinion was gladly sought on many questions other than those in which he was immediately concerned.

Thus he devoted much time and thought to the Liberian problem. The unfortunate economic and political position of this country was well known; and in virtue of arrangements of 1911 and 1912, France, Germany, and Great Britain had shared with the United States in the administration of Liberia's finances. By the Treaty of Versailles (Article 138), Germany renounced every right and privilege arising from these arrangements, "and particularly the right to nominate a German Receiver of Customs in Liberia," besides surrendering all claim "to participate in any measures whatsoever which may be adopted for the rehabilitation of Liberia."

Nor was it with Africa and Mesopotamia alone that he was concerned. Through his sympathy with Italy and his understanding of her needs and well-founded claims,[8] he had framed a solution of the Fiume problem which would have done justice to the wishes both of Italy and of Yugo-Slavia, and which would have avoided one of the most unhappy incidents of the entire Peace Conference; while if the Chinese Delegation had listened to his counsel to await a more favorable opportunity for stating their wishes regarding Shantung, a settlement less disturbing to many might have been made.

Very jealous of his country's honor and seeking her highest interests, he hoped, almost to his last days, that the United States would enter the League of Nations, performing the duties, as well as enjoying the rights, of the World-Power that she is. He very clearly realized that America's time of isolation is past; and that what may have been expedient, even necessary, for the struggling Thirteen Colonies is impossible and uncommendable for the United States. In particular, he felt that America should herself become a Mandatory Power, as of the Cameroons or of Liberia; and in this connection it may be observed that she had already held what was, in all but name, a self-appointed Mandate of the "A" class for Cuba.[9]

In the light of all that has been said, it was especially appropriate that, when the Secretariat of the League of Nations was organized, Mr. Beer should be selected as head

[8] See pp. 391-396, 451-452.
[9] Cf. Articles 1, 16 of the Hispano-American Treaty of December 10, 1898, and the Preamble to the Treaty between the United States and Cuba, May 22, 1903; Malloy, "Treaties," pp. 1691, 1695, 362-363.

of the Mandate Division. It was only from a sense of duty, and against his personal inclinations, that he accepted, for he desired the quiet life of the scholar rather than prestige and high position. Nevertheless, putting his own wishes aside, he commenced to plan for his new duties. He was no lover of mere administrative routine, and bureaucracy was abhorrent to him. Indeed, had his advice been heard, the Covenant of the League might have been even more elastic than it is. But at the same time, with his keen sense of practicality, he sought to provide for every contingency. He realized, for example, that, in addition to the annual report to be submitted to the Council of the League by each Mandatory with reference to the territory entrusted to its charge, actual tours of inspection would probably be advisable, thus anticipating a criticism recently advanced.[10] The present writer, who was to have been his secretary on the Mandate Division, is in a position to state this with authority, for he was directly informed by Mr. Beer that a considerable part of his secretarial duties would consist of such tours.

Shortly after the African Commissions had concluded their sessions, Mr. Beer returned to the United States. For many years he had suffered from ill-health, and the unremitting strain of the Conference had told heavily upon him. To this was now added mental pain, for he was to realize that the real foes of all that he had labored to do for America and the world were not the ex-Enemy Powers, still less the Allied Powers, but his own countrymen, misguided by specious leaders of reaction. There

[10] Cioriceanu, "Les Mandats Internationaux," pp. 91-92.

can be little doubt that his death, on March 15, 1920, at the early age of forty-eight, was hastened by the same sorrow which was, a little later, to bring Mr. Wilson to the verge of the grave.

George Louis Beer closed his eyes fearing lest he had striven in vain. In a sense, he was right, for the earthly lives of perhaps the majority of the truly great of History end in seeming failure. But in reality, he was victorious. The foundations which he helped lay stand firm, built upon Right; and on them the perfect structure shall surely rise. The obscurantists have their little night, denying what they would fain not see. *E pur si muove!*

PART I

THE GERMAN COLONIES IN AFRICA

(Written for THE INQUIRY, February 12-26, 1918.)

THE GERMAN COLONIES IN AFRICA

CHAPTER I

BEGINNINGS OF THE GERMAN COLONIAL MOVEMENT

Modern Imperialism.—The most far-reaching and fundamental fact in the history of the modern age has been the
gradual extension of European civilization over all the continents of the globe. In this prolonged process there have
been alternating periods of relative quiescence and of rapid
advance. Such a period of expansion set in around 1880,
after Italy and Germany had become unified states, after
the French Republic had been established, and after the
Balkan problem had been temporarily settled by the Congress of Berlin in 1878. For the time being, the Continent
of Europe was in a condition of stable equilibrium. As
their internal problems no longer demanded constant and
earnest attention, the European states had the opportunity
to look without and they sought for means to perpetuate
and to spread their special types of civilization. The prevailing nationalism was generally marked by a firm conviction on the part of each political group of the inherent
value and superior excellence of its distinctive civilization,
and this, in turn, led to the idea of a mission to uphold the
influence of these distinctive civilizations and to spread

3

them throughout the world. Imperialism was largely an expression of this new nationalism.

The English Example.—When these European states sought to pierce the veil that concealed the future, they began to realize the political and cultural significance of the English colonial movement from the days of Elizabeth on. It seemed clear to them that, unless they themselves deliberately and methodically embarked on a similar course, their future part in the world was destined to be relatively unimportant, in comparison with the seemingly assured destinies of the Russian and the English-speaking peoples who had spread themselves over vast areas. As Dr. P. S. Reinsch said:

"Suddenly the colonial wealth of England became an object of jealousy to her neighbors; they sought to mend their neglected fortunes by the rapid occupation of Africa, they endeavored to emulate her sea power, and sent out merchantmen to dispute with her the dominion of the world's trade. As formerly the political institutions of her national life, so now her methods of colonial expansion and of transmarine trade, became a model to other nations." [1]

The Political Factor in the German Colonial Movement. —In the German colonial movement this political motive was most marked. In her case it was reinforced by the fact

[1] Paul S. Reinsch, "Colonial Government," p. 9, New York, 1905. On the rise of this colonial movement, see John Fiske, "American Political Ideas," pp. 101 ff., New York, 1885; Alleyne Ireland, "Is Tropical Colonization Justifiable?", pp. 13-17, Philadelphia, 1899; J. A. Froude, "Short Studies in Great Subjects," 2d Series, 1890, pp. 149 ff., 280 ff., London, 1891; Paul Leroy-Beaulieu, "De la Colonisation chez les Peuples Modernes" (5th ed.), I, pp. xix, xx, Paris, 1902; Wilhelm Roscher and Robert Jannasch, "Kolonien, Kolonialpolitik und Auswanderung" (3d ed.), pp. 355 ff., Leipzig, 1885; Ramsay Muir, "The Expansion of Europe," pp. 135 ff., London, 1917; N. D. Harris, "Intervention and Colonization in Africa," pp. 1-17; J. H. Rose, "The Origins of the War," pp. 9-20, Cambridge, 1914.

that, in the early 'eighties, emigration suddenly increased at a most rapid pace. In 1878, the emigrants numbered only 46,371, but three years later their total was 247,332.[2] The predominant idea was well expressed by a distinguished German economist, Wilhelm Roscher, who contended that it was self-evident that in the long run a great and unified state could not look on indifferently while 100,000 to 200,000 emigrants annually left the Fatherland forever and not only were lost to its *Kultur*, but also added a considerable sum of technical strength and of social education and training to a competing foreign Power.[3]

The Economic Factor.—In addition, there were present certain persuasive economic motives. Germany was be-

[2] EMIGRATION FROM GERMANY

1878	46,371	1895	37,498
1879	51,763	1896	33,824
1880	149,769	1897	24,631
1881	247,332	1898	22,221
1882	231,943	1899	24,323
1883	201,314	1900	22,309
1884	149,065	1901	23,073
1885	110,119	1902	32,098
1886	83,225	1903	36,310
1887	104,787	1904	27,984
1888	103,951	1905	28,075
1889	96,070	1906	31,074
1890	97,103	1907	31,696
1891	120,089	1908	19,883
1892	116,339	1909	24,921
1893	87,677	1910	25,531
1894	40,964		

Wilhelm Roscher and Robert Jannasch, *op. cit.*, p. 373; W. Mönckmeier, "Die Deutsche Überseeische Auswanderung," p. 18, Jena, 1912. As illustrating the marked revival of German interest in colonization, it is worth pointing out that the former volume is a revised and enlarged edition of a work whose first and second editions had appeared respectively in 1848 and 1856. On the German colonial movement, see also A. G. Keller, "Colonization," pp. 535-539, Boston, 1908.

[3] Roscher and Jannasch, *op. cit.*, p. 375. In view of the present situation, it is especially interesting to note that Leroy-Beaulieu, the great French authority on colonization, took, at the time, the same view, claiming that it was a misfortune for the future of the world and a diminution of

coming increasingly industrialized. Manufacturing had been stimulated by the adoption of the protective system in 1879, and the need for oversea markets had been emphasized thereby. On the other hand, with the gain in population and the growth of industry, Germany was importing more and more foodstuffs and raw materials. As German political thought carried the theory of sovereignty to its logical extreme and had as its ultimate ideal complete independence, both economic and political, this situation was becoming increasingly irksome. Hence the demand both for fresh markets and for new sources of supply under the German flag became so insistent that Bismarck, though far from convinced, could not resist it. In 1884 and 1885 vast stretches of land in Africa were added to the German Empire.

Attitude of England.—Africa was the only continent where such vacant territory was obtainable. But, at practically every point, with the exception of the northwestern part, English commercial interests were then predominant. The Englishmen on the spot had for years been urging the annexation of what subsequently became German East and Southwest Africa, but the British Government steadfastly refused to assume such additional responsibilities. The entrance of Germany into the colonial field was, however, to this extent unwelcome in England, that it might endanger established British commercial interests in the areas placed under the German flag. As Germany had no fleet,

Germany's legitimate influence that 150,000 to 200,000 emigrants should yearly lose themselves among the 50,000,000 Anglo-Saxons of the United States. Paul Leroy-Beaulieu, *op. cit.,* I, pp. 306, 307; see also Henri Hauser, "Le Problème Colonial," p. 20, Paris, 1915.

England could have vetoed the entire proceeding. But instead of pursuing such a dog-in-the-manger policy, she confined her action to protecting her own vital interests, which, in turn, necessitated the annexation of vast regions to the British Empire, so as to prevent others from seizing them. Joseph Chamberlain, on January 5, 1885, described England's attitude in the following terms:

"If foreign nations are determined to pursue distant colonial enterprises, we have no right to prevent them. We cannot anticipate them in every case by proclaiming a universal protectorate in every unoccupied portion of the globe's surface which English enterprise has hitherto neglected." [4]

Two months later, on March 12, 1885, Gladstone spoke the following cordial words in the House of Commons:

"If Germany is to become a colonizing Power, all I can say is, God speed her. She becomes our ally and partner in the execution of the great purposes of Providence for the advantage of mankind."

In view of the general situation in Africa at the time, and of England's often expressed unwillingness to assume responsibility for the safety of German missionaries and merchants in some of the unoccupied regions and to extend her rule elsewhere, Germany's course was, on the whole, quite justified. It is unfortunate, however, that some of her proceedings were tainted by palpable trickery and deceit. As to England's attitude during this rather heated controversy, even so bitter a foe of that country as Reventlow has frankly and quite accurately admitted that "Great

[4] Joseph Chamberlain, "Speeches," I, pp. 135, 136, London, 1914.

Britain yielded either earlier or later, but virtually without exception." [5]

[5] Graf Ernst zu Reventlow, "Deutschlands Auswärtige Politik" (2d ed.), p. 26, Berlin, 1915. Another German author, whose interest is primarily in colonial problems, writes as follows: "In these acquisitions the most remarkable thing at all events is that England, which has been decried as so land-hungry, did not more energetically hinder Germany from taking possession of these territories; and, in order to understand this, one must know English colonial history. The English Government as such has never been anxious for a large territorial expansion of its colonial possessions, but has always, especially in Africa, been driven to such annexations by those directly interested therein." J. K. Vietor, "Geschichtliche und Kulturelle Entwickelung Unserer Schutzgebiete," pp. 1-2; see also É. Baillaud's Introduction to his "Politique Indigène de l'Angleterre en Afrique Orientale." Writing to Earl Granville on February 21, 1885, Sir Edward Malet describes the work of the Berlin Conference in allaying misunderstandings arising from territorial changes and acquisitions of France, Portugal, and the Congo Free State. "England has had no share in this distribution of territory, having confined herself to lending her aid to promote an amicable settlement between the parties interested. She entered the Conference as mistress of almost the entire coast-line from the western limit of her Gold Coast Colony to the Cameroons, and she had no desire to increase her responsibilities; she was indeed well pleased to see that other Powers were ready to undertake the charge of protecting the natives of the continent, and preventing the anarchy and lawlessness which must have resulted from the influx of traders of all nations into countries under no recognized form of government." Nevertheless, she had certain interests, and it was essential for her to obviate danger of discrimination against her commerce. *Africa*, No. 2 (1885), p. 6; Senate Executive Document, No. 196, 49th Congress, 1st Session, pp. 309-311.

CHAPTER II

Dominating Concepts.—Until very recently German colonial policy was completely dominated by two concepts, both of which were mistaken and greatly retarded the development of the colonies. On the one hand, the aim was to create in Africa a "New Germany" on the model of the "New Englands" that had grown up over the seas; on the other, the purpose was to free Germany from dependence upon foreign nations for colonial wares by producing them within her own African domain. The political motive was the compelling one with the people as a whole, and gained in strength as they became ever more and more indoctrinated with the creed of racial superiority and with a conviction of a mission to impress their "superior civilization" upon a decadent world.[1] At the outset, the Govern-

[1] "Various motives prevail with the different governments and nations, and the different classes among the respective peoples, in the matter of territorial expansion. Often the value attached to extended dominion is purely sentimental, inasmuch as many of the colonies hastily acquired by European nations will never make a material return to the people as a whole, for the outlay involved in their administration. Thus, while a policy of colonial expansion may be acceptable to individual capitalists as a means of profitable investment, to the common people, who are always swayed by the imaginary side of politics, it appeals as an extension of national prestige. Nothing will arouse greater enthusiasm in a popular meeting than an assurance that the national flag has been unfurled upon a distant island, where, perhaps, unregenerated savagery prevails; nor on the other hand, can any crime exceed in enormity the act of hauling down the flag where it has once been raised." Paul S. Reinsch, "World Politics," p. 10, New York, 1900.

ment was influenced more by the economic argument, but as time progressed, its objects as well became predominantly political.[2] The fundamental purpose of the colonies was to secure to Germany a position in the world commensurate with her military power and economic strength at home.[3] In so far as the attainment of these political and economic objects was concerned, the German colonial movement was a distinct failure. In 1913, there were in all the German African possessions only 22,405 white people, of whom 14,830 were in Southwest Africa.[4] At the same time,

[2] The predominant section of the colonial party in Germany before the war repudiated commerce as their object and had in view "the maintenance and extension of the German civilization." Its broad popular basis was derived from this idealistic purpose. "It is in the cult of Germanism that we trace the origin of the newer imperial policy which is not an outgrowth of the Bismarckian tradition, but a distinct negation of it. It repudiates the sordid motive of commercial gain as the mainspring of national policy. To prove that a proposed territory or province will not become profitable, is no deterrent. It is enough that it becomes German. The purpose of the German empire is not merely to make comfortable and secure the Germans of to-day, but to make them the leaven that shall leaven the lump." H. H. Powers, "The Things Men Fight For," pp. 219-222, New York, 1916.

[3] "We regard the founding of colonies and all measures for their development as having in view the object of strengthening the political and economic world-position of Germany." Dr. Paul Rohrbach, "Das Deutsche Kolonialwesen," p. 27.

[4] WHITE POPULATION OF GERMAN COLONIES IN 1913

	Total	Germans
East Africa	5,336	4,107
The Cameroons	1,871	1,643
Togo	368	320
Southwest Africa	14,830	12,292
	22,405	18,362

Statistisches Jahrbuch, 1915, p. 457. A very large proportion of these 18,362 Germans were members of the administrative and military staffs. Many others were temporarily employed in the colonies on railroad extensions. The number of actual German settlers was probably less than 10,000. John H. Harris, "Germany's Colonial Empire," in *The Nineteenth Century and After*, May, 1917, p. 1158.

these vast areas and the German islands in the Pacific
supplied Germany with only three per cent of the colonial
products which she required.[5] Of Germany's total foreign
commerce in 1913, less than five-tenths of one per cent was
with all her oversea territories.[6] Moreover, the lack of success in spreading the German language and civilization
among the natives was equally conspicuous.

Failure to Establish a "New Germany."—The failure to
establish a "New Germany" was by no means due solely
to the climatic and physical conditions of the African possessions. German Southwest Africa is primarily a white
man's country and, though its aridity will probably always
prevent it from supporting a dense population, there is
ample opportunity for several hundred thousand white
inhabitants. In addition, there are some possibilities of
white settlement in the northern parts of the Cameroons;
while, in East Africa, the suitable highlands have been estimated by Dr. Peters and other authorities to aggregate
about 50,000 square miles, which is equal to one-quarter
the area of [pre-war] Germany herself.[7] At the time of
their acquisition little was known even by the authorities
in Germany as to African conditions, and the difficulties of
white settlement were much underestimated. Moreover,
while the German has been an excellent settler in established
communities, his general lack of initiative prevents him

[5] In 1915, Dr. Solf, the Colonial Secretary, stated that the former German colonies could supply only about three per cent of this demand.
S. Grumbach, "Das Annexionistische Deutschland," p. 9.

[6] Germany's foreign trade in 1913 amounted to 22,500 million marks,
while her total trade with all the German protectorates, exclusive of
Kiaochow, amounted to only 110.5 million marks. *Statistisches Jahrbuch,*
1915, pp. 475, 480, 254.

[7] For the area of "white man's Africa," see map facing page 118.

from being a good pioneer. He is an admirable colonist, but a bad colonizer. Under African conditions there was no opportunity for the German peasant and the small farm. Some considerable capital was required by the settler. Development on a comparatively extensive scale, as well as capacity to manage the native races, was essential. Men of the type who had developed the British colonies had no inducement to leave Germany. There was a constant demand for them in the bureaucracy and army. Thus, Professor Moritz Bonn of Munich said in 1914:

"There was in Germany no necessity for exporting younger sons. To begin with, there was plenty of land in Germany, moreover, there were many situations awaiting them. The army counted 33,000 officers in 1907, and civil administration had posts for 55,000 civil servants of the higher division." [8]

In addition, the transfer to African soil of the Prussian militaristic and bureaucratic systems and the rigid stratification of the German social system deterred the immigrant,[9] while the free life of the United States and the British Dominions exerted a constant counter-attraction. Finally, towards the close of the last century, the movement of emigration from Germany slackened greatly and Germany gradually became a land of surplus immigration, like the United States, though on a smaller scale.[10]

[8] Professor M. Bonn, "German Colonial Policy," in *United Empire Magazine*, V (1914), pp. 131, 132.

[9] "Tradition proved too strong even for Prince Bismarck, and gradually the whole system of Prussian bureaucracy was introduced into each of the colonies, large and small, and Great Berlin at home was reproduced in a score of small Berlins in all parts of Africa and the Pacific." W. H. Dawson, "The Evolution of Modern Germany," p. 366.

[10] *Statistisches Jahrbuch*, 1915, pp. 11, 42, 416; I. A. Hourwich, "Immigration and Labor," pp. 180 ff.

Economic Blunders.—At the outset, also, there was no understanding of the economic possibilities of Africa. Much capital and energy were wasted in trying to produce the finer colonial staples, such as tobacco, coffee, and spices, for which Africa was not fitted. Instead of stimulating the native output of indigenous products, such as rubber and palm oil, unsuitable capitalistic undertakings were started with unfortunate results for all concerned. In addition, there was no appreciation of the fact that the wealth of Africa was not found chiefly in the coastal lowlands, but rather in the interior plateaus, and that these riches could be made available only by railroads. Bismarck was especially loath to burden the Imperial Treasury with colonial expenses and, with this object in view, he entrusted the administration of the oversea possessions to large companies with inadequate capital, to whom were granted vast territorial and mining privileges. The governmental functions of these associations had soon to be recalled and, while some of their proprietory rights were subsequently canceled, with or without compensation, they hampered the development of the colonies until the outbreak of the war in 1914. The same general parsimonious policy was pursued by Bismarck's successors until 1900, the era of Prince von Buelow.

Native Policy.—Another signal failure of these early years was an entire lack of comprehension of the fact that Africa's chief and indispensable asset is its native population and that for selfish reasons, if for no other, the colonizing state should make every effort to conserve and to increase it. For the first twenty years or so, there were constant conflicts with the natives in the Cameroons, East

Africa, and Southwest Africa. In the main, the trouble proceeded from a disregard of the native's right to the soil and a marked tendency on the part of the Germans to appropriate whatever lands they wanted. In Southwest Africa, this policy resulted in the Herero rebellion from 1904 to 1906. One area after another was acquired from the Hereros, who in dismay saw the time approaching when they would have no more territory for grazing purposes. They rose in revolt. This insurrection was due to bad policy and its suppression was marked not only by callous brutality, but by extreme unwisdom. Instead of trying to pacify the natives, Germany pursued a war of extermination, of which the final step was the enclosure of "the whole people in the arid desert with the result that one half died of thirst and starvation." [11]   As a consequence of this immense loss of life, says Dr. Paul Rohrbach, Southwest Africa has suffered and will continue to suffer from an irremediable scarcity of labor. Professor Bonn, likewise a recognized authority on German colonial policy, is in complete accord with this verdict. He states that Germany

[11] See Dr. Paul Rohrbach, "Das Deutsche Kolonialwesen," pp. 15-19. The number of Hereros who died as a result of this barbarously ruthless measure has been estimated by German authorities at from 12,000 to 15,000. When the rebellion broke out the Hereros numbered, according to the general view, 65,000. To-day, they have been reduced to less than one-third of that number; to be exact, to 21,611 in 1913. "Die Deutschen Schutzgebiete," *Statistischer Teil*, 1914, pp. 46, 47; W. H. Dawson, *op. cit.*, pp. 366, 393. [Between 1904 and 1911, the Damara population decreased from 30,000 to 13,000 and the Hottentots from 20,000 to 10,000. Antonelli, "L'Afrique et la Paix de Versailles," p. 72. "It is probable that the population of the African continent to-day is only half what it was a century ago. The entire absence of statistics forces the investigator to depend upon native tradition which throughout Africa is, however, consistent in its evidence that before contact with the white races Africa was comparatively well populated, although never so densely as the continent of Asia." John H. Harris, "Africa: Slave or Free?", pp. 61-62.]

started with a wrong conception of colonial possibilities and wanted to build up daughter-states by concentrating in Africa the emigrants she was losing in the 'eighties.

"We carried this idea," he says, "to its bitter end. We tried it in South-West Africa and produced a huge native rising, causing the loss of much treasure and many lives. We tried to assume to ourselves the functions of Providence, and we tried to exterminate a native race, whom our lack of wisdom had goaded into rebellion. We succeeded in breaking up the native tribes, but we have not yet succeeded in creating a new Germany." [12]

Bad Administration.—In addition, the type of official sent to the colonies, whether military or civilian, was in general not of the best. The celebrated explorer and administrator, Hermann von Wissmann, was not the only German to return home with a "white waistcoat"—to use Bismarck's expression—but far too often the oversea possessions were regarded as a dumping-ground for shady characters, family failures, and wrecked lives. The early record is one of noisome scandals and marked moral obliquity.[13]

The New Order under Stuebel and Dernburg.—The new order that was inaugurated with the appointment in 1900 of Stuebel as head of the Colonial Section of the Foreign Office marked a large measure of reform in many directions, and the administration improved considerably. The chief changes, however, were in securing grants from the Reichstag for building railroads in the colonies; and at the same time private capital was induced to invest in colonial under-

[12] M. Bonn, *op. cit.*, p. 133.
[13] P. Rohrbach, *op. cit.*, pp. 11, 12; W. H. Dawson, *op. cit.*, pp. 369-371.

takings. In general, Dr. Dernburg, who, in 1907, was appointed as first incumbent to the newly created office of Colonial Secretary, followed along Dr. Stuebel's lines, but, in addition, he was able to create a widespread enthusiasm for the colonial movement by active propaganda. Under the new order, the economic development of the colonies proceeded at a satisfactory pace.

CHAPTER III

General Description.—The African colonies comprised an area of 1,030,150 square miles, which was about five times the [pre-war] size of Germany herself and one third that of the United States. The white population in 1913 was only 22,405, but the natives numbered as many as thirteen millions and, according to other estimates, possibly more than fifteen millions.[1] Up to 1914, railroads of an aggregate length of 4,176 kilometers had been built and further extensions had been planned or were under construc-

[1] AREA AND NATIVE POPULATION OF THE AFRICAN COLONIES

	Square Miles	Square Kilometers	Native Population
German East Africa	384,000	995,000	7,646,000
The Cameroons	290,000	790,000	2,649,000
Togo	33,700	87,200	1,032,000
Southwest Africa	322,450	835,100	81,000
	1,030,150	2,707,300	11,408,000

To this table (*Statistisches Jahrbuch,* 1915, p. 457) must be added the 1,000,000 to 1,350,000 natives in that section of the Cameroons ceded by France in 1911 and also 150,000 to 200,000 natives in Ovamboland and the "Caprivizipfel" in Southwest Africa. Some authorities estimate the population of Togo at 1.5 millions and that of East Africa at 10 millions. *Statistisches Jahrbuch,* 1915, p. 457; Evans Lewin, "The Germans and Africa," p. 298; *The Statesman's Year-Book,* 1917, p. 936; A. F. Calvert, "The German African Empire," pp. 21, 22; Bruel, "L'Afrique Equatoriale Française," p. 353. [*Le Temps,* January 29, 1919, gives the population of Southwest Africa as only 300,000, and *The Statesman's Year-Book,* 1921, p. 239, as 190,000 (218,000 according to the same annual for 1922, p. 246), of whom 100,000 are in Ovamboland.]

17

tion.[2] Works of an important and substantial nature—roads, bridges, harbor facilities, telegraphs, telephones, wireless stations—had been successfully carried out. The public buildings in the chief ports, such as Lome, Duala, Swakopmund, Dar-es-Salaam, and Tanga, were of an exceptionally solid and imposing character. These cities were distinguished by order and cleanliness and, in so far as mere outward appearance was concerned, they generally compared more than favorably with similar ports in the British and French colonies. The volume of foreign trade was small from the European standpoint and it was even small in contrast with that of the flourishing British possessions. The exports of British West Africa alone were more than double that of all Germany's African colonies. But their trade was growing rapidly. The total foreign commerce of the German possessions had increased from 56 million marks in 1903 to 286 in 1913. The imports and exports were about equal. In order of value they included in 1912 diamonds (30.4 million marks), rubber (20.9), palm kernels and oil (10.8), sisal (7.4), copper (6.3), and cocoa (4.5).[3]

[2] END OF 1913

	In Operation Kilometers	Under Construction Kilometers
East Africa	1,435	167
The Cameroons	310	133
Togo	327	...
Southwest Africa	2,104	...
	4,176	300

Statistisches Jahrbuch, 1915, p. 459 [see also *infra,* pp. 158-166].

[3] FOREIGN TRADE OF THE AFRICAN COLONIES
(*in thousands of marks*)

1903	56,541	1909	155,624
1904	61,494	1910	202,043
1905	85,952	1911	211,710
1906	139,040	1912	232,226
1907	116,122	1913	286,100
1908	121,990		

Open Door Policy.—Although no preferential tariffs favored her wares, somewhat over two thirds of this trade was with Germany.[4] While it was a fundamental purpose of German policy that these colonies should serve German national ends,[5] no other course than the open door was

FOREIGN TRADE OF THE AFRICAN COLONIES IN 1913

(in millions of marks)

	Imports	Exports	Excess Imports	Total Trade
East Africa	53.4	35.6	17.8	89.
The Cameroons	34.6	29.1	5.5	63.7
Togo	10.6	9.1	1.5	19.7
Southwest Africa	43.4	70.3	— 26.9	113.7
	142.0	144.1	— 2.1	286.1

Statistisches Jahrbuch, 1915, p. 463. For full table of aggregate exports of all the German colonies, see "Die Deutschen Schutzgebiete," 1914, pp. 128, 129; for a similar summary of the exports of the African colonies, see Evans Lewin, "The Germans and Africa," pp. 300, 301. For full details, consult *Statistisches Jahrbuch,* 1915, pp. 464 ff. In 1913, the figures for exports were: diamonds, 58.9 million marks; rubber, 23.1; oil-palm products, 10.7; sisal, 10.3; copper ore, 7.7; cocoa, 5.7; hides and skins, 7; cotton, 3; copra, 2.3; ground nuts, 1.9; ivory, 1; coffee, 0.9. The foreign trade of British West Africa in 1913 was £30 millions. "Statistical Abstract of British Dominions," 1915, pp. 55, 61.

[4] FOREIGN TRADE IN 1912

(in millions of marks)

	Total Trade	Trade with Germany	Percentage
German East Africa	81.7	43.6	53.4
The Cameroons	57.6	47.	81.73
Togo	21.4	10.6	32.3
Southwest Africa	71.5	58.9	82.3
	232.2	160.1	69.

"Die Deutschen Schutzgebiete," 1914, p. xix.

[For the distribution and percentages in 1913, based on the *Statistisches Jahrbuch* for 1915, the pound reckoned at 20 marks, see the chart at end of this book.]

[5] Rohrbach says: "We hold it further to be a self-evident demand of national colonial policy that the relations between the Mother-land and the colonies should so develop that colonial production and the exchange of commodities between the metropolis and the oversea possessions should, above all else, serve the interests of Germany as a whole." "Das Deutsche Kolonialwesen," p. 27.

feasible, as it would probably have led to retaliation on the part of England, who was in a position to interfere by similar methods with Germany's very much more important commerce with the British possessions. The proportion of trade with Germany was, however, far larger than it would have been under entirely free conditions. In the first place, foreign merchants were disinclined to settle in the German colonies, whose rigid rule and stiff social system were uncongenial to them. In the second place, in some instances, Germany granted direct or indirect subsidies to German steamship lines,[6] which in consequence were virtually able to monopolize the carrying trade of the colonies and, in the process, naturally deflected trade to Germany.[7]

Southwest Africa.—Of the four oversea territories, Southwest Africa was quite distinct in nature and in prospects from those in the tropics. It is primarily a white man's land. Its climate is healthful and its native population is small. Unfortunately, there is a scarcity of rain, and hence agriculture on a large scale is out of the question. It is essentially a land for grazing and considerable progress

[6] In 1890, the German East African Line was added to those receiving subsidies and, by the agreement of 1900, it received 1,350,000 marks yearly. J. Grunzel, "Economic Protectionism," p. 236, London, 1916; W. Ross, "Die Entwicklung der Schiffahrt nach den Deutschen Kolonien," in *Weltverkehr*, 1914-15, pp. 88-90.

[7] MARITIME INTERCOURSE WITH THE GERMAN COLONIES IN 1912

(*net tonnage*)

	Total	German	Percentage
East Africa	1,811,107	1,771,997	97.8
The Cameroons	1,658,230	1,254,250	75.6
Togo	571,832	414,731	72.5
Southwest Africa	1,413,676	1,378,929	97.5
Total	5,454,845	4,819,907	88.36

Statistisches Jahrbuch, 1915, p. 460.

has been registered along these lines.   In addition, there are valuable copper mines in the Otavi district in the north of the colony, and very important diamond deposits have been developed in the desert coastal region to the south. The accidental discovery of these fields in 1908 by a native who had worked in the Kimberley mines, after they had been overlooked by experts who had been prospecting for years, not only put the economic life of the colony on a firm basis, but greatly stimulated German interest in the possessions as a whole.   The colonial government taxed this industry heavily and derived a very great proportion of its revenues from this source.[8]   In spite of this fact, the German Treasury had to spend yearly a considerable sum on the abnormally large military force maintained in this colony. As the life of these diamond fields is very limited— the estimates vary from fifteen to twenty years—the prosperity of the territory is bound to be temporary unless, in the interval before exhaustion, other industries, such as the production of wool and meat, become firmly established. Of this there is a good prospect and, in course of time, this land bids fair to be a prosperous community of white farmers, based upon native labor, like their neighbors in the Union of South Africa.[9]

[8] "Die Deutschen Diamanten und Ihre Gewinnung," pp. 39, 48, 76, 77, Berlin, 1914; Alfred Zimmermann, "Geschichte der Deutschen Kolonialpolitik," pp. 303-305; A. F. Calvert, "The German African Empire," pp. 67-105; Paul Rohrbach, "Die Deutschen Diamanten," in *Weltverkehr*, 1914-15, pp. 166 ff.; British Diplomatic and Consular Report (German Southwest Africa, 1913), pp. 11-18.

[9] Rohrbach estimated that there is sufficient suitable land for 5,000 individual farms of 10,000 hectares (about 25,000 acres) each. A. F. Calvert, *op. cit.*, pp. 43, 44. See also Dr. Paul Leutwein, "Siedelungs- und Plantagenkolonien," in *Weltverkehr*, 1914-15, p. 206; Dr. Karl Dove, "Die Grossen Wirtschaftsgebiete Afrikas," in *Weltwirtschaft*, V (1915), p. 162.

Togo.—Of the tropical [ex-German] possessions, the smallest and the most successful is Togo. It is in many respects a model colony, for not only have the difficulties with the natives been less here than elsewhere, but the expenditures and revenues of this region have balanced one another. Its scanty area (33,700 square miles) and its small native population, estimated variously from 1,000,000 to 1,500,000, are a bar to any very important future development. Its trade before the war amounted to only about twenty million marks, of which nearly one half was with Germany. Cotton textiles, of which over one half came from England, formed the most important item in the imports. Some small quantities of rubber and raw cotton were exported, but the chief outputs were palm kernels and palm oil.[10]

The Cameroons.—The other [ex-]German colony on the west coast, the Cameroons, has a far more extensive area and a native population possibly three times as numerous. Its trade is proportionately larger and has greater capacities of expansion. Development here was retarded by inadequate transportation facilities, by constant troubles with the natives, and by the adoption of a capitalistic system of exploitation. The chief items in the exports of 1913 were rubber, palm oil, palm kernels, and cocoa.[11]

[10] Of the 10.6 million marks of imports in 1913, 2.7 consisted of textiles and of the 9.1 million exports in the same year, palm kernels and palm oil contributed 3.1; raw cotton, 0.6, and rubber, 0.4. *Statistisches Jahrbuch*, 1915, p. 467. See also British Diplomatic and Consular Reports, No. 5147 (Togoland, 1913). [For a comprehensive survey see Report on the British Mandated Sphere of Togoland for 1920-21 (Cd. 1698).]

[11] Of the total exports of 29.1 million marks in 1913, rubber contributed 12.1; palm kernels, 6.2; palm oil, 1.96; cocoa, 5.7. *Statistisches Jahrbuch*, 1915, p. 465.

German East Africa.—Of all the [ex-]German colonies, East Africa is recognized to be the most valuable, not only on account of its large area and the general fertility of its soil, but mainly because it has a very considerable native population, whose numbers are not exactly known, but are variously estimated at from about eight to ten millions. As in the case of the Cameroons, a very considerable proportion of this colony had not been brought under German rule. In the northwestern section, in the region of Lakes Tanganyika and Kivu, are two large native states that are virtually autonomous, Urundi and Ruanda, whose inhabitants are estimated to number 1,000,000 and 2,000,000, respectively.[12] In contrast with the rest of the territory, the population in these two states is quite dense.[13] In a certain sense this is unfortunate, as this district is well suited for white settlement, although under the circumstances, it is of course out of the question here. In other parts of the colony, notably in the south near Lake Nyassa, in the Morogoro region to the west of Dar-es-Salaam, and in the Usambara-Kilimanjaro-Meru district in the northeast, considerable land is, however, available for white settlers. A number of flourishing communities have already been established.

Trade of East Africa.—The trade of the colony was growing rapidly, somewhat over one half being with Germany. As in the case of all these tropical possessions, the chief

[12 These two regions have been incorporated in the Belgian Congo; see *infra,* p. 440. For a general survey of the areas, see "Handbook of German East Africa," pp. 165-169, 337-340, 268-270, 195-196, 108-113.]
    13 "Die Deutschen Schutzgebiete," 1914, p. 36; M. Bonn, "German Colonial Policy," in *United Empire Magazine,* V (1914), pp. 127, 128.

item in a list of varied imports consisted of cotton textiles. In order of their value, the exports were sisal-hemp, rubber, hides, raw cotton, and copra.[14]   In East Africa, Germany was creating a mixed colony, planting in the highlands small white communities that are surrounded by a more or less dense native population.[15]   In the Cameroons and Togo were purely native societies with a few whites temporarily placed there to rule them and to develop their natural resources.   These two territories, in a general way, resembled British Nigeria and, on a very much smaller scale, British India.   Southwest Africa, on the other hand, was a distinctly European community with large estates and mining developments like the Union of South Africa. As has been aptly said, the European here was the lord of the manor and the African was his serf.

Cost of the Colonies to Germany.—What the colonies have cost Germany in the form of annual subventions, costs of wars and punitive expeditions, shipping and postal subsidies, and administrative expenses at home, has never been worked out in detail.[16]   At first, the Government was very loath to burden the Imperial Treasury with colonial expenses, but after 1900 the grants increased rapidly, and during the Herero War they rose to large sums.   The average colonial deficit for the five years 1904-08 was about

[14] Of the imports of 53.4 million marks in 1913, 17 consisted of textiles and clothing.   Among the 35.5 million exports, sisal amounted to 10.3; rubber to 6.6; hides and skins to 5.5; raw cotton to 2.4; and copra to 2.3. *Statistisches Jahrbuch,* 1915, pp. 464, 465.

[[15] For the distribution, occupation, nationality, etc., of the white population on January 1, 1912, see "Handbook of German East Africa," pp. 424-427.]

[16] See W. H. Dawson, "The Evolution of Modern Germany," pp. 364, 365.

160 million marks.[17]   Until the very outbreak of the war, yearly deficits had to be made good, the military expenses of the colonies had to be paid by the Imperial Treasury, and money had to be provided for railroads and other public services. During the five years preceding 1914, the average advances for such purposes in Africa were roughly 60 million marks yearly.[18] While a considerable part of these sums was for objects that gave fair promise of being ultimately reproductive, still it will be quite self-evident that, as a business venture, these colonies were from the standpoint of Germany as a whole a decided failure, considering that Germany's trade with them during this same period averaged only about 80 million marks yearly.[19]

[17] *Colonial Revenues*

	(in millions of marks)	*Colonial Expenses*
1904	12.7	133.8
1905	13.4	196.6
1906	16.5	161.
1907	21.7	167.4
1908	22.4	215.
	86.7	873.8

Paul Rohrbach, "Das Deutsche Kolonialwesen," p. 151.

[The expense incurred by Germany for her African colonies in 1913 is shown by the following table (in thousands of marks):

Colony	Revenue	Expenditure	Deficit
East Africa	13,489	20,078	6,589
The Cameroons	8,712	13,059	4,347
Togo	3,308	3,974	666
Southwest Africa	31,238	45,589	14,351
Total	56,747	82,700	25,953]

[18] *Statistisches Jahrbuch,* 1915, pp. 253, 462; "Die Deutschen Schutzgebiete," *Statistischer Teil,* 1914, p. 401; Paul Rohrbach, *op. cit.,* pp. 150-153; M. Bonn, *op. cit.,* p. 129; Zimmermann, *op. cit.,* pp. 307, 308.

[19] TRADE OF GERMANY WITH HER AFRICAN COLONIES

	(in millions of marks)
1909	61.8
1910	85.4
1911	82.2
1912	91.3
1913	94.6
	415.3

Statistisches Jahrbuch, 1915, p. 253. For obvious reasons, the German statistics cannot agree with those prepared in the colonies; but there is far more than the normal difference between the two sets. Thus, for 1912, the colonial statistics show an aggregate trade with Germany of 160.2, as opposed to a trade with them of only 91.3 according to the German statistics. *Ibid.,* pp. 253, 465-469, 475-480. Apart from unavoidable divergences because of different valuations, this large discrepancy arises predominantly from the fact that the figures of Germany's "Spezialhandel" do not include the *entrepôt* trade of such free ports as Hamburg. Thus, Manchester goods shipped *via* Hamburg to the German colonies figure in the colonial statistics as imports from Germany, but they do not appear in those of Germany's "Spezialhandel." *Ibid.,* p. 180.

CHAPTER IV

THE NATIVE QUESTION

The Native is Africa's Chief Asset.—While the material basis for a rapid economic development had been laid, the future depended entirely upon the labor situation. In 1914 there was a scarcity of labor in all the colonies, with the possible exception of Togo, where production was largely in the hands of the natives. This scarcity was, in part at least, the heritage of the persistent attempt to create a "New Germany" in Africa which led to a callous disregard of the negro's rights to the soil as well as to an open indifference to his general welfare. For the first twenty years there was practically no appreciation of the fact that all sound and permanent progress depended upon the conservation and elevation of the indigenous population. It was not only in Southwest Africa that the natives were deprived of their lands. The same course was pursued in the Cameroons, and to a less extent, also in East Africa.[1]

[1] In 1907, General von Puttkamer said: "The entire colonial policy is based upon the principle of Europeans depriving the inferior natives in foreign lands by main force of their land and maintaining our position there by force." Thus, as a result of an uprising, the Bakwiri were forced to surrender their desirable and fertile territories in the Cameroon mountain region, and these areas were sold to large plantation companies. J. K. Vietor, "Geschichtliche und Kulturelle Entwickelung Unserer Schutzgebiete," pp. 71, 72, 86, 87; W. H. Dawson, "The Evolution of Modern Germany," p. 372. In the British Gold Coast Colony, the negro is protected against improvident alienation of land. Transfers between natives are free, but those to Europeans are subject to careful inquiry and explicit sanction by the Concessions Court. J. du Plessis, "Thrice Through the Dark Continent," pp. 15, 16, London, 1917; cf. A. B. Keith, "West Africa," p. 231.

The German Plantation System.—The new order after 1900 somewhat remedied this land situation, but the system of developing the colonies by capitalistic exploitation was persisted in. Instead of trying to stimulate native production, the aim was to establish large European plantations on which the negro was to work as a hired laborer. Since the population was, in general, sparse, this necessitated the accumulation of natives in one center from more or less distant villages. But as their wants were few and were readily supplied by the bounties of tropical nature, the negroes had little inducement to leave their homes. Hence, there was for many years forced labor. This situation also has been somewhat improved. The recruiting of labor for the European plantations was before the war supervised by the Government and the grossest abuses had been remedied.

Evils of This System.—The general effect of drawing laborers from a distance was to disturb, and even to break up, tribal life. Furthermore, as many of the owners of large plantations in the Cameroons would not allow the laborers to bring their families with them, another result was extensive irregular sexual relations, with widespread syphilis which, in turn, was not only preventing an increase in the number of inhabitants, but was actually depopulating some sections of this region.[2] In 1913, Dr. Paul Rohrbach wrote: "It is hard to say the words, but thirty years after the proclamation of a German protectorate over Cameroon the hygienic conditions amongst the natives are in a large part of the colony worse than they were aforetime, and the population decreases instead of increasing." After visiting this

[2] J. K. Vietor, *op. cit.*, pp. 119-121.

territory, Dr. Solf, the Colonial Secretary, said: "It is a sad spectacle to see how the villages are depopulated of men. Family life is being ruined; parents, husband and wife, and children are separated." [3]

Native Production Discouraged.—At the same time, in order to secure an adequate supply of labor for this capitalistic system, native output was discouraged by the authorities. No greater contrast is possible than that between conditions in the Cameroons and those in the neighboring Gold Coast Colony. In 1912, the Cameroons produced 4,550 tons of cocoa, of which all but one seventh was grown on plantations owned by Europeans. In 1913, the British possession yielded 51,279 tons, which was about one fifth of the world's total crop. The Gold Coast Colony in that year surpassed all other single sources of supply, including São Thomé and Ecuador. This entire industry from its very inception, some ten years before this date, had been entirely in the hands of the natives and was a marked civilizing influence with them. [4] No sound progress is possible along the lines to which the Germans persistently adhered until just before the outbreak of the war. The inevitable result of a system in which the European plantation

[3] W. H. Dawson, "What Is Wrong with Germany?", pp. 190, 191, London, 1915.

[4] In 1899, Gold Coast Colony produced only 715,000 pounds; in 1905, 11 millions; in 1910, 50 millions; in 1913, 113 millions. "Statistical Abstract of British Dominions," 1915, p. 333. [In 1919, the output was 176,176 tons and in 1920, 124,773 tons. *The Statesman's Year-Book*, 1921, p. 249; 1922, p. 258.] See, for details, *Statistisches Jahrbuch*, 1915, p. 32*; Sir Harry H. Johnston, "The Black Man's Part in the War," pp. 35, 36; Sir Hugh Clifford, "Some Facts Concerning the Gold Coast," in *Journal of the African Society*, October, 1914, p. 22; J. K. Vietor, *op. cit.*, pp. 112, 113; W. A. Crabtree, "Economic Resources of the German Colonies," in *Journal of the African Society*, January, 1917, p. 129.

is predominant is to break up native society and in time to depopulate the country.

Forced Labor.—While these land and plantation policies have considerably disrupted the tribal life of those natives with whom the Germans came into intimate contact, the damage effected has fortunately not been so great as it might have been, primarily because they had not been able to extend their rule over large parts of their colonies. Similarly, their sanitary measures and their educational systems had reached only a small proportion of the total population. In all these activities there was a marked failure to understand native psychology. In fact, the negro was almost universally looked upon as a means to an end, never as an end in himself, and his welfare and that of the colony were completely subordinated to the interests of the German on the spot and to those of Germany as a whole. So liberal a thinker as Dr. Paul Rohrbach, while clearly recognizing the many evils of the past, as late as 1911 urged the necessity of forced labor, arguing that, when it was so difficult for people in all other continents to earn a livelihood, the Africans were not entitled to "a privilege of less work and more idleness." [5] Such a system of forced labor, by direct or by indirect means, for private or for governmental purposes, prevailed to the last in the German colonies.[6] It was based

[5] Paul Rohrbach, "Das Deutsche Kolonialwesen," pp. 33, 34. [On the general attitude of Germans towards their African subjects, see *Journal Officiel de la République Française,* November 8, 1918, p. 9631.]

[6] In 1908, Dr. Dernburg told the Budget Committee of the Reichstag that in East Africa "labourers were obtained under circumstances which could not be distinguished from slave hunts" and he further stated that "a young farmer came to him and told him that he had 'bought' 150 negroes." W. H. Dawson, "The Evolution of Modern Germany," p. 374. On forced labor in Southwest Africa at that time, see *ibid.,* p. 393. On

upon a desire of the European planter for quick results and was bound to have dire consequences. If the development of Africa is to be sound and healthy, the process must be relatively slow, for it is dependent upon the gradual elevation of the native.

The Liquor Question.—There was another evil in the German West African possessions which, however, was common to all along that coast. The high import fees on spirituous liquors which the signatories to the Acts of the Brussels Conferences agreed to impose on their respective colonies [7] proved ineffective. With increasing wealth, the natives were able to buy the low-grade poisonous liquors made in Holland and in Germany, despite these duties. This traffic was playing havoc with the negroes and was greatly decreasing their procreative powers.[8]

Attitude towards the Natives.—In general, the attitude both of the authorities and of the colonists towards the

March 17, 1914, Herr Erzberger, speaking in the Reichstag, condemned the abuses in colonial life and administration, "including the recognized system of forced labor, the frauds perpetrated on the natives, and the ill-treatment of laborers on the plantations." W. H. Dawson, "What Is Wrong with Germany?", pp. 190, 191. In addition, in the Cameroons and in Togo, the natives were obliged to work if they did not pay their taxes. There was considerable maltreatment and injustice in this system. In 1912, in Togo, there were 785,506 days of such work of which 410,789 were used for the construction and upkeep of roads, bridges, and market places, and 64,985 negroes paid this "Steuerarbeit." "Die Deutschen Schutzgebiete," *Statistischer Teil,* 1914, pp. 80, 409; Vietor, *op. cit.,* p. 111; A. G. Leonard, "Commercial Developments in German Kamerun," in *United Empire Magazine,* April, 1914, p. 331.

[7 Brussels Act, Arts. 92-93; Brussels Conventions of June 8, 1899, and November 3, 1906. "Trattati . . . relativi all'Africa," pp. 293-294, 618-621, 1247-1250.]

[8 Vietor, *op. cit.,* pp. 134-136. For details of importations in 1912, see "Die Deutschen Schutzgebiete," *Statistischer Teil,* 1914, pp. 228-230, 268-270. [Cf. also *infra,* pp. 174-175; for the measures taken to prevent this evil by the Convention of September 10, 1919, see pp. 176-178 and Annex F.]

aborigines was one of open contempt. The native was regarded as an inferior being, whose purpose was to serve the
ends of the white man. Sexual relations between white men
and black women were very frequent. Herr J. K. Vietor
of Bremen, who was a member of the Colonial Council
(Kolonialrat) and who had quite extensive interests in Togo
and the Cameroons, reports that, while the white population of Togo amounted to only 254 (of whom forty-two were
missionaries), there were 240 mulatto children. He states
that he knew one German who had fourteen mulatto
children and he further mentions the case of a German
official in one of the villages who had a special stone house
for his women. Yet in this small colony the relations between white and black were far more pleasant than elsewhere. In the Cameroons and in Southwest Africa, according to this same authority, the natives were treated "with
studied rudeness." No acknowledgment was made of any
salute or greeting from a negro. "He is allowed to stand as
long as possible before he is asked what he wants, and it is
very rare that he is offered a seat in case any business with
him is being transacted." In addition, no matter what
might be the age or standing of the native, he was invariably addressed by the pronoun of the second person
singular, which denotes inferiority. This was resented by
the educated negroes. Vietor further comments adversely
on the continual floggings administered to the natives for
trivial offenses, especially in the Cameroons.[9]

[9] J. K. Vietor, *op. cit.*, pp. 97-106. [Cf. also the Disciplinary Articles of
the German Chancellor's Decree of April 22, 1896, regarding Togo and
the Cameroons and the Instructions of October 15, 1901, translated in
Journal Officiel de la République Française, November 8, 1918, pp. 9631-
9632.]

Alienation of Natives.—Similar conditions prevailed in German East Africa. In 1908, Dr. Dernburg officially stated that in that colony "it makes a very unfavourable impression on one to see so many white men go about with negro whips. I even found one on the table of the principal pay office in Dar-es-Salaam; it is still the usual thing, and any one who has been there will confirm what I say." [10] These conditions were radically different from those in the neighboring British colonies, where the rule of law prevailed and where the colonist was kept to a large extent in check by its penalties. There is a definite significance in the fact that De Wet's rebellion in 1914 is partly attributed to the fact that he was fined a few shillings for an assault upon a native.[11] As a result of such practices, the negroes were distinctly hostile both to German rule and to *Deutschtum* itself. Herr Vietor reports that nowhere else in Africa did he see natives who looked at the Europeans so impertinently as did some of those in Duala, the port of the Cameroons; and that they did not remove their hats to greet the white man, as was generally customary in Togo. But even in that colony the negroes frequently refused to admit that they spoke German. He was often told that so and so in Togo knew only English, but when he addressed these people politely, they were immediately able to reply in German.

[10] W. H. Dawson, "The Evolution of Modern Germany," p. 374.
[11] *The Round Table*, March, 1915, pp. 465, 466. A Herero in British South Africa wrote to his kinsman under the German flag: "There is much work and much money, and your overseer does not beat you, or if he does, he breaks the law and is punished." W. H. Dawson, *op. cit.*, p. 373. It should be noted that the treatment of the natives is considerably better in those colonies that are under the control of the Colonial Office at London than in the Union of South Africa.

In this respect, Vietor further adds, the situation in the Cameroons was incredible. When he arrived there, he met a native employee, who immediately assumed an erect military attitude. Vietor asked him in German if he had been a soldier and the answer in English was, "Excuse me, Sir, I only talk English." Yet this man had served for ten years in the colonial military forces! During his four weeks in the Cameroons, Vietor heard scarcely a German word from the natives, though plenty of pidgin-English.[12] This is a sad climax to a movement whose larger and fundamentally idealistic aim was to spread German *Kultur!*

English Public Opinion Regarding Natives.—Ambassador Reinsch has quite accurately stated:

"England's greatness as a colonizing power is due to the fact that her foreign administration for the greater part of the nineteenth century has been subjected to the criticism of an enlightened public opinion at home, trained in judging and dealing intelligently with political affairs. It is the habit which the British people have acquired of watching and controlling their political agents that enables them to exercise a beneficial influence among inferior nations. Wherever a British officer or administrator has worked, he has felt himself responsible to a critical and alert public opinion, accustomed to dealing strictly with any lapses, breaches of trust, or offences against political morality." [13]

In this general connection, the Belgian socialist and statesman, Émile Vandervelde, has said:

"We do not know what is happening in the German colonies. There is not in Germany, as in England, a public

---

[12] J. K. Vietor, *op. cit.*, pp. 103-106. On pidgin-English in the Cameroons, see also Sir Harry H. Johnston, "The History of the Colonization of Africa by Alien Races," p. 448.

[13] Paul S. Reinsch, "World Politics," p. 352, New York, 1900. See also Ramsay Muir, "The Expansion of Europe," pp. 107 ff., London, 1917.

opinion on colonial questions that is anxious to reveal the abuses, the acts of violence and injustice of which the natives are the victims. The bourgeois parties there are in favor of the policy of the mailed fist. The socialists scarcely disguise under purely negative formulæ, the slight interest that they take in questions of native policy." [14]

German Public Opinion Developing.—A public opinion of this character was, however, gradually developing in Germany during the years just preceding the war. An organization patterned on the English "Anti-Slavery and Aborigenes' Protection Society" had been established and it was hoped that it would follow the example of its British model in furthering the welfare of the natives.[15] Moreover, the Government had seen the error of its ways and was beginning to safeguard the negroes. It had also officially adopted the course of stimulating native production in the Cameroons, which had hitherto been discouraged in the interests of the European plantations.[16] Yet as late as 1914, steps were being taken to effect a wholesale removal of the Duala tribe from their land! [17] The more enlightened policy had not definitely gained the day; there still remained considerable obscurantist opinion that clung to the disastrous aims of the past. Actually very little had

[14] Émile Vandervelde, "Belgian and British Interests in Africa," in *Journal of the African Society,* April, 1915, p. 267.

[15] Louis Hamilton, "The German Colonies," in *United Empire Magazine,* June, 1914, p. 493. One of the leaders of this organization was Professor D. Westermann and its organ was the *Koloniale Rundschau.* On his general attitude, see his article in Karl Schneider, *Jahrbuch über die Deutschen Kolonien,* 1912, pp. 76, 77, *et passim.*

[16] "Die Deutschen Schutzgebiete," 1914, p. xvii.

[17] *Journal of the African Society,* April, 1916, p. 280; W. A. Crabtree, "The German Colonies in Africa," *ibid.,* October, 1914, pp. 1-14; A. G. Leonard, "Commercial Developments in German Kamerun," in *United Empire Magazine,* April, 1914, p. 330; *L'Afrique Française,* Nos. 5 and 6, 1917, p. 181.

been accomplished. Thus Professor Bonn of Munich, one of Germany's foremost authorities on colonial policy, stated early in 1914:

"We are just entering the native states of Urundi and Ruanda [in German East Africa, with an estimated population of 3,500,000]. We have begun the delimitation of tribal frontiers, which is the basis of a stable native government. We have merely scratched the surface of the real colonial problem. . . . We have done a certain amount in native administration—though here, more than anywhere else, we are beginners—by spreading peace and sanitation, by teaching the natives in schools and in agriculture. But apart from Southwest Africa, where we solved the native problem by smashing tribal life and by creating a scarcity of labour, we are only just now beginning to understand it. . . . It is not merely a question how we are to rule them for where they are really numerous, we scarcely rule them to-day. . . . Only their numbers and their industry can make our Colonial Empire as useful and as necessary to us as it ought to be." [18]

The last sentence contains a thought which ran as a constant refrain throughout all German colonial literature. Oversea possessions were considered merely as subject communities that were to be useful and profitable to Germany. They were not, as in the British Commonwealth,

[18] M. Bonn, "German Colonial Policy," in *United Empire Magazine,* V (1914), pp. 129-134. Contrast the self-regarding, nationalistic tone of the last sentence with the following remarks of Lord Milner in introducing Professor Bonn to the Royal Colonial Institute, before which he made this address. Lord Milner said: "I think I may say that, in the rivalry of various European nations to develop their tropical possessions, the rivalry of our own people, the Germans and French and Dutch—in that rivalry that nation will, in the long run, be most successful which exhibits the greatest wisdom in its efforts to promote the welfare and progress and contentment of its subject peoples." *Ibid.,* p. 136. In his address on "The Future of Africa," on December 21, 1917, Dr. Solf himself stated that the Germans were just at the beginning of the reform development, but that Germany from the days of Dernburg had been on the right track. *Kölnische Zeitung,* December 22, 1917.

regarded as parts of one large political aggregate, each of which must be administered primarily in its own interest. Nor were they deemed components of an enlarged and expanded state, as is the tendency in France. The German doctrines of ascendancy that prevailed in Prussian Poland and in Alsace-Lorraine and forever condemned the conquered to an inferior status were predominant in the colonial sphere. The German possessions were virtually never regarded as ends in themselves, but merely as means to spread German *Kultur,* to reinforce German prestige and power, and to add to the wealth of Germany.

CHAPTER V

From the foregoing it is apparent that, whether the German Government's conversion to an enlightened native policy was sincere or half-hearted, practically nothing effective had been done up to the outbreak of the war to gain the sympathy and loyalty of their African subjects. The attitude of the negroes was inevitably determined by thirty years of more or less constant oppression, and it is not surprising that they generally welcomed the elimination of German rule.

Southwest Africa.—In Southwest Africa tribal life had been smashed and the native in the occupied districts was virtually the serf of the German overlord. The negroes are treated none too considerately in the adjoining Union of South Africa, but in the German possession matters were far worse.[1] Lieutenant-Colonel S. M. Pritchard, who was placed in charge of native affairs after the Anglo-Boer conquest of the German colony, reported that the employment of aborigines had never been satisfactorily supervised by the German authorities and that, as a result, the treatment

---

[1] The following statement by a South African Commission of Enquiry is unquestionably accurate. It says: "It is a matter of common knowledge that the German treatment of natives in the Protectorate, and their idea of what constitutes cruelty to natives, differ very widely from ideas prevailing in the Union." Papers Relating to German Atrocities, and Breaches of the Rules of War, in Africa, 1916 (Cd. 8306), p. 86.

of many laborers, especially on the farms, was only too often most cruel and unjust. He found many cases of negroes who had been employed for years (in one instance eleven years) without receiving any wages. For the slightest breach of discipline or for trivial offenses it was customary for the employer to send the delinquent either to the Native Commissioner or to the nearest Police Post with a request that the culprit should receive twenty-five lashes. "Assaults of the most serious nature on native men and women were matters of daily occurrence," he said; and he further added that several such cases, and even the shooting of negroes at sight, had been brought to his attention. Five of the most prominent German farmers were tried and found guilty of the murder of natives and they were sentenced with salutary effect to imprisonment for from two to five years.[2]

Ovamboland.—Although a considerable number of laborers had been derived from the northern section of the colony,[3] known as Ovamboland or Amboland, this region with an estimated negro population of 156,000 had never been brought under German rule.[4] Pritchard was also instructed to investigate conditions here and, in spite of the general opinion of the German settlers that such an expedition should be undertaken only when accompanied by a strong

[2] S. M. Pritchard, "Experiences in German South-West Africa," in *Journal of the African Society,* October, 1916, pp. 2, 3.
[3] According to the British Consular Report, the number of laborers that came from Ovamboland in search of work was, in 1911, 9,295; in 1912, 6,076; in 1913, 12,025. A. F. Calvert, "The German African Empire," p. 22; British Diplomatic and Consular Reports (German Southwest Africa, 1913), p. 7.
[4] S. M. Pritchard, "Report on Tour to Ovamboland," p. 11.

armed escort,[5] he was received in a very friendly manner
by the natives. Satisfactory relations with them 'were
established. Chief Martin of the Ovandonga tribe (60,000
people) frankly stated that they "had no love for the Germans, whose wars with the natives they had heard of, that
he and his people had always wished that the English would
come into their country." [6]

Togo.—In Togo the relations between the natives and
the Germans were far better than elsewhere, yet even here
the overthrow of German rule by the French and the British
was joyously acclaimed.[7] In part this may have been due
to the fact that ethnically two thirds of Togo belongs to
French Dahomey, its eastern, and one third to the Gold
Coast Colony, its western neighbor; but, in greater measure,
it was the nemesis of Germany's unsympathetic and con-
temptuous government. The following incident is signifi-

[5] In this connection Major Pritchard (such was then his rank) wrote:
"I mention this point in passing in order to take the opportunity of
remarking on the inherent feelings of excitability and fear which consume
many Germans in this country when faced with the necessity of moving
among natives unarmed or unsupported by force. I do not think it is
too much to say that to these very deficiencies of temperament, prompted,
as I believe they are, by the consciousness of the brutalities in their
treatment of natives, of which so many of them have been guilty, and
giving rise, as they so frequently do, to acts of frightfulness culminating
in serious assaults on, and even in the murder of, natives, that much of
the trouble between the Germans and the natives in this country can
fairly be attributed." *Idem,* "Report on Tour to Ovamboland," p. 1.

[6] *Ibid.,* p. 4. See also pp. 9, 10.

[7] *The Gold Coast Leader* of September 12, 1914, states: "The surrender
of Togoland has given rise to outbursts of joy and thankfulness among
natives throughout the Colony. In the Central and Western Provinces
women, dressed in white, their wrists and necks encircled with white
beads and their necks and chests rubbed with white chalk, for days on
end paraded the streets singing and chanting songs of praise and thankfulness for the victory of our soldiers." *Journal of the African Society,*
January, 1915, p. 207. For details, see Correspondence Relating to the
Military Operations in Togoland, 1915 (Cd. 7872), pp. 7, 8, 11, 22, 31, 33.

cant. One of the chiefs of western Togoland had asked in 1886 to be taken under British protection and, having been given a British flag just before his territory was brought under German rule, he hid it. When this was discovered by the Germans, he was exiled to the Cameroons and it was only after the capture of Duala in that colony in 1914 that he was enabled to return to his own country. Soon thereafter he addressed a most illuminating letter to the Governor of the Gold Coast in which, after offering a voluntary contribution of £101 10s. to the British Government, he said:

"It was my willing to give more than what I have done above, but on account of the Germans, and owing to their bad treatment giving, most of my village young men have removed from this land and entered into another calling for daily bread: also my land is very poor to-day. May God Almighty bless Great Britain to master the victory. I congratulate the Local and the Imperial Government and the District Political Officer, Mr. R. S. Rattray, who is treating us here very well and gentle. May he live long! And Mr. J. T. Furley, who is a best and good gentleman. May he live long! May God bless the English Government and prolong their power to be second to none. God save the King." [8]

The Cameroons.—As the northern part of Togo was beyond the area of effective German occupation, it is not possible to define the attitude of the colony as a whole or to make a summary statement that will apply to all the districts.[9] Such impossibility is even more obvious in the

[8] Sir Harry H. Johnston, "The Black Man's Part in the War," p. 29.
[9] G. M. Wrigley, "The Military Campaigns against Germany's African Colonies," in *The Geographical Review*, January, 1918, pp. 45, 46; Calvert, *op. cit.*, p. 222.

case of a large territory like the Cameroons, whose people
range from primitive cannibal tribes to highly organized
Mohammedan states, and where German administration
was restricted to only a small portion of the colony.   In
the Northern Cameroons, where many of the inhabitants
are Mohammedans and the Fula people are the leading
caste, the Germans succeeded in rallying to their cause
certain Fula sultans to whom they had left a large measure
of autonomy.   One of these rulers in the early days of the
war took the field with a train of mounted warriors on the
side of the Germans.[10] But in the Southern Cameroons,
where contact with German rule was very intimate, disaffection was rife.   Lieutenant Otto Wieneke, the German
District Commissioner at Duala, stated officially that "the
native population—the inhabitants of Duala—had proved
itself before and during the war uncertain, traitorous
and hostile to Germany." [11]   This people numbered only
91,808,[12] but they were among those who had been most
subjected to German influences.   One of the first steps of
the Germans on the outbreak of the war was to hang the
head chief of this tribe, Rudolf Bell, and several other
natives, on the pretext that they were friendly to the
British.[13]   A fervid German partisan, Dr. G. Lohringer,
describes the situation when the Anglo-French occupied the

[10] "The Times [London], History of the War," VIII, p. 281.
[11] Correspondence Relative to the Alleged Ill-Treatment of German Subjects Captured in the Cameroons, 1915 (Cd. 7974), p. 5.
[12] "Die Deutschen Schutzgebiete," *Statistischer Teil*, 1914, p. 41.
[13] *Journal of the African Society*, April, 1916, p. 280.   Rudolf Bell had
been educated in Germany.   John H. Harris, "Germany's Lost Colonial
Empire," in *Contemporary Review*, April, 1917, p. 466, and his book of
the same title, pp. 33-35.

town of Duala, shortly thereafter, in the following graphic
words:

"From that moment onwards Duala was actually in their
[British and French] power. What that meant was shown
first by the Duala tribe. Since the execution of Rudolf
Bell (Duala Manga) they had vanished. On this morning
it was as if the river-mouths and the basins spat Duala.
The sky rang again with an indescribable shout of scorn
and rejoicing." [14]

As a result of the disaffected spirit of the Duala and of
other coastal peoples, the Germans tried to intimidate them
from assisting the Anglo-French forces by the familiar
process of "frightfulness." Orders were issued "to treat
all the Duala natives and their intertrading compatriots on
the Mungo, Abo, and Dibombe rivers as combatants in the
war, and, in special cases, to treat them as rebels and
traitors." Every Duala village was ordered destroyed and
all Dualas carrying weapons were to be shot. Not only
men, but women and children also, were victims of brutal
atrocities—woundings, mutilations, and murders. A certain
advantage was gained by these methods, the British Commander, General Dobell, wrote, in that the natives were
terrified and afraid to give information as to German move-
ments.[15] But these proceedings have left a heritage of
hate as deep as that of the Hereros in Southwest Africa.

East Africa.—In German East Africa, a very considerable

[14] Cd. 7974 (1915), p. 35 [see also *Journal Officiel de la République
Française,* January 5, 1919, p. 178].

[15] Cd. 7974 (1915), p. 43. Papers Relating to German Atrocities, and
Breaches of the Rules of War, in Africa, 1916 (Cd. 8306), pp. 9-17 *et seq.*
See also the report of Colonel Brisset in Supplement 1 and 2 to *L'Afrique
Française,* 1917, pp. 45-47 [and cf. also *Journal Officiel de la République
Française,* January 5, 1919, pp. 179-180].

army was formed out of the German soldiers and civilians in the colony and its indigenous population. Thousands upon thousands of negroes were used either as troops or as carriers or porters. The soldiers, locally known as *askaris*, were drawn from very vigorous tribes, such as the Wahehe and the Wanyamwezi.[16] They were granted special privileges as regards the rest of the community and were generally well treated, though subject to the most rigid control. "For the slightest breach of discipline the native askaris were given twenty-five lashes with the kiboko, a long thick whip, usually made from hippopotamus hide."[17] On the whole, they were remarkably loyal. Many of these *askaris* and practically all the porters were impressed for service, being seized in their villages after the fashion of the former Arab slave-raiders. The porters were treated most brutally. They were often chained together and in many instances were literally worked to death's door, being shot down or bayoneted when they could walk no farther. Thus one of the German officers wrote in a private letter: "Our

[16] On these tribes, see Sir Harry H. Johnston, "The History of the Colonization of Africa by Alien Races," pp. 412, 413. The force was very mixed and included Sudanese, Somalis, Arabs, etc., from without the colony. The Wanyamwezi contributed largely to the German military forces and are, probably, the best fighters and porters in East Africa. "Immigrant Wanyamwezi, enlisted in British East Africa into our King's African Rifles, do not hesitate to fight against their blood brothers." R. V. Dolbey, "Sketches of the East Africa Campaign," pp. 22-23, London, 1918. [In September, 1915, the native troops in this colony numbered about 14,100. "Handbook of German East Africa," pp. 197-198; see also *infra*, p. 271. For the Wanyamwezi and Wahehe, see "Handbook of German East Africa," pp. 72-75, 98-101, 201-202; for conditions of service, treatment, equipment, and training, see *ibid.*, pp. 202-203.]

[17] Reports on the Treatment by the Germans of British Prisoners and Natives in German East Africa, 1917 (Cd. 8689), p. 10; see also p. 17. Cf. also R. V. Dolbey, *op. cit.*, pp. 134-135. For German brutality to natives see *ibid.*, pp. 35-36; to native chiefs, pp. 40-41; to Indian and British prisoners, pp. 135 ff.

road is paved with the corpses of the natives we have been obliged to kill." [18]   As the military pressure of the British and the Belgian forces increased, the German treatment of these porters and of the negro population as a whole became more and more ruthless and oppressive. The tribal chiefs were forced to furnish large supplies of corn; and natives were removed wholesale from regions threatened with occupation by the enemy. Entire areas were depopulated by the retreating German armies, which compelled women as well as men to act as carriers. As a consequence, German rule became increasingly and ever more widely unpopular, and disaffection spread even among those who had previously been loyal.[19]   According to the foremost living authority on Africa, Sir Harry H. Johnston, the general cry of the natives in German East Africa since the victories of the Allied troops has been: "The people of '15' have departed; may they never return." The "15" refers to the lowest number of lashes administered by the Germans for minor offenses. "The native," says this African expert, "would regard with terror any possibility of the return of the Germans." [20]

[18] Cd. 8689 (1917), p. 7; "The Times [London] History of the War," X, p. 132; XII, p. 80; XIII, pp. 418, 422.

[19] Cd. 8689 (1917), pp. 7, 16; J. B. Briggs, "German East Africa during the War," in *Journal of the African Society*, April, 1917, pp. 196-199; "The Times [London] History of the War," XIII, pp. 421, 422. The Germans had continual trouble with the natives and the situation was ten times worse than in British East Africa. They were in constant fear of an uprising as the German troops retreated. Dolbey, *op. cit.*, pp. 37-40.

[20] Sir H. H. Johnston, "The Black Man's Part in the War," pp. 68, 69. The war undermined white prestige and the restoration of East Africa to Germany would have wrought great harm to the prestige of Britain. Dolbey, *op. cit.*, pp. 42-43. [For a similar judgment regarding the Cameroons, see *Journal Officiel de la République Française*, January 5, 1919, p. 178.]

CHAPTER VI

GERMANY'S COLONIAL AIMS

Colonial Ambitions in 1914.—Throughout the years preceding the war, no secret was made of Germany's complete dissatisfaction with the political apportionment of the world's surface and the size of her own African domain. The prevailing thought was clearly expressed by General von Wrochem in 1913. "The longing for an eternal peace," he said, "was Utopian and enervating," and he further deplored the fact that, "at the division of the earth between the other Great Powers, Germany had gone almost empty away." [1] His country's openly expressed aim was to join her scattered and separated possessions on the eastern and western coasts into one compact mass, dominating Central Africa from the Indian to the Atlantic Ocean.

Anglo-German Agreements of 1914.—Shortly before the war, Germany had concluded with England an agreement which apparently made this project realizable.[2] The spirit

[1] William Archer, "Germs of German Thought," p. 52.
[2] Rohrbach, "Zum Weltvolk Hindurch!", pp. 47, 48, Stuttgart, 1914; *idem,* "Germany's Isolation," pp. 130, 131, Chicago, 1915; S. S. McClure, "Obstacles to Peace," pp. 9, 42, Boston, 1917. Considerable light has been thrown on this matter by the Memorandum of Prince Lichnowsky (ed. and tr. Munroe Smith, in *International Conciliation,* No. 127, June, 1918, pp. 58-65). In 1898 a secret treaty was signed by Count Hatzfeld and Mr. Balfour, "which divided the Portuguese colonies in Africa into economic-political spheres of influence as between us [Germany] and England. As the Portuguese government possessed neither the power nor the means to open up its extensive possessions or to administer them suitably, it had already at an earlier date entertained the idea of selling them and thereby putting its finances on a sound basis" [see *infra,*

46

in which Great Britain had conducted these negotiations—
which were part of a formal Anglo-German *rapprochement*
that had actually been consummated just prior to the out-

p. 108, and cf. A. Debidour, "Histoire Diplomatique de l'Europe, 1878-1904," p. 263]. "On its face, of course, this treaty was designed to secure the integrity and independence of the Portuguese realm, and the only purpose it expressed was to give to the Portuguese financial and economic assistance. In its wording, accordingly, it did not contravene the old Anglo-Portuguese alliance, dating from the fifteenth century, which was last renewed under Charles II" [in 1661. By Articles 16 and 17 of this Treaty, "if the King of Portugal shall be pressed in any extraordinary manner by the power of the enemies, all the King of Great Britain's ships which shall at any time be in the Mediterranean Sea or at Tangier shall have instructions in such cases to obey any orders they shall receive from the King of Portugal and shall betake themselves to his succour and relief"; while the King of Great Britain must "afford timely assistance of men and shipping according to the exigency of the circumstances, and proportionable to the necessity of the King of Portugal." On the inception of this Treaty, see Guernsey Jones, in *Annual Report of the American Historical Association* for 1916, I, pp. 405-418]. Nevertheless, at the instance of the Portuguese Ambassador to the Court of St. James, Marquis Soveral, a new treaty, the so-called Windsor Treaty, was concluded in 1899 between England and Portugal. Subsequent negotiations, begun, according to Herr von Jagow in his reply to Lichnowsky (*op. cit.*, p. 131), by Count Metternich and continued by Baron Marschall von Biberstein, were reopened by Prince Lichnowsky to amend the Treaty of 1898 as containing impracticable provisions, such as those regarding geographical delimitation. "Thanks to the conciliatory attitude of the British government, I [Lichnowsky] succeeded in giving to the new treaty a form which entirely corresponded to our wishes and interests." All Angola, as far as 20° East, was to pass to Germany, as were São Thomé and Principe which, lying north of the Equator, really belonged to the French sphere of influence—"a fact which caused my French colleague to enter energetic but unavailing protests." The portion of Mozambique north of the Licango was similarly to be transferred. "Originally, at the British suggestion, the Congo State also was to have been included in the treaty, which would have given us a right of preëmption and would have enabled us to penetrate it economically. But we refused this offer, out of alleged respect for Belgian sensibilities!" The real, though unexpressed purpose of the Treaty was "the actual partition at a later date of the Portuguese colonial possessions" and "provided that in certain cases we should be authorized to intervene in the territories assigned to us for the protection of our interests," these conditions being so broad that decision regarding them practically rested with Germany. The document was essentially complete in May, 1913. Some slight changes were introduced and it was initialed in August, but it was not until July, 1914, that Lichnowsky was

break of hostilities—was indicated by Sir Edward Grey in 1911, when he said:

"If Germany has friendly arrangements to negotiate with other countries with regard to Africa, we are not anxious to stand in her way any more than in theirs."

These "other countries" were Belgium and Portugal, for the German scheme depended upon the cession of more or less large parts, if not all, of the Belgian Congo and of Portuguese Angola. The attitude of Germany towards these small Powers was accurately defined as follows by the *Leipziger Tageblatt* in 1913:

"With all respect to the rights of foreign nations, it must be said that Germany has not as yet the colonies which it must have. . . . We are not an institute for lengthening the life of dying States. . . . Those half-States which owe their existence only to the aid of foreign weapons, money or knowledge, are hopelessly at the mercy of modern states." [3]

Angola and the Belgian Congo.—It is not yet publicly known whether Germany had actually commenced negotiations with Portugal,[4] but in the spring of 1914 the German

able to obtain Von Bethmann-Hollweg's consent to signature and publication. "The difficulty was that Sir Edward Grey was willing to sign only if the treaty were published, together with the two treaties of 1898 and 1899. England, he said, had no other secret treaties, and it was contrary to existing principles that binding agreements should be kept secret. He could therefore conclude no treaty without publishing it." The utmost concession that Lichnowsky could obtain was that publication must be made within one year, at latest, after signature. In any event, in the Prince's opinion, the contents both of the projected agreement and of the Treaty of 1898 were perfectly known to Portugal in view of her close association with Great Britain. Just after German consent had been gained, however, the Serbian crisis necessarily postponed execution of the document, which "too is one of the victims of this war" (*op. cit.,* pp. 59-69).

[3] William Archer, *op. cit.,* p. 318.

[4] Herbert Adams Gibbons, "The New Map of Africa," pp. 273, 274. Angel Marvaud, "La Situation Politique et Économique du Portugal," in *Questions Diplomatiques et Coloniales,* 37 (1914), pp. 86, 87.

Government sounded the French Ambassador in Berlin about the Belgian Congo. In the course of this conversation, the German Foreign Secretary, Herr von Jagow, stated to his unconvinced listener that only the Great Powers were in a position to colonize, and that the small nations could not in the future enjoy their former independent existence, in view of those changes in Europe which favored the large states that proceeded from economic forces and from improved means of communication. Such lesser peoples, he contended, "were destined to disappear or to gravitate into the orbit of the Great Powers." [5]

Present Aims Dependent upon Military Events.—These plans of 1914 are, however, not an infallible criterion for determining what Germany's colonial intentions now are, nor what they will be when the peace conference assembles.[6] It is a commonplace familiar to every student of history that concrete war aims develop out of the course of military events themselves and are modified with the changing fortunes of armies and navies. One thing alone seems to be certain, that the dominant spirit in Germany is well represented by Otto von Gierke of Berlin University, who complains that foreigners fail to understand the inner meaning of war. This distinguished jurist defines it for them as follows:

"War fulfils the world-historic task of pitilessly destroying decaying culture, worn-out law, degenerate freedom, in order, with native strength, to breed rejuvenated culture, a juster law and a more genuine freedom. They cannot

[5] "Royaume de Belgique, Correspondance Diplomatique," 1914-1915, II, No. 2, pp. 2, 3.
[6 See *infra*, pp. 274-275.]

understand that military power has the right to decide *(hat von Rechts wegen zu entscheiden)* the life or death of nations or States."[7]

Difficulty of Defining Present Aims.—It is to be assumed, and it were folly not to do so, that Germany will endeavor to retain as great a part of her European conquests as is possible, and also to get back her oversea possessions. It is not easy to determine what relative value is placed on these two areas and on different portions of them. The official attitude is no sure guide, for, in all direct and indirect peace negotiations, the skilled statesman or diplomat is prone to emphasize the worth of the things that he is prepared to abandon and to understate the importance of those that he wants to retain or to repossess. Current literature is also no reliable indication of Germany's present colonial aims. Certain facts seem, however, to be well established. In the first place, it is a fundamental principle of German policy that no sound oversea development is possible without an assured position in Europe. Secondly, the inability to defend the transmarine territories has led to a dampening of the colonial zeal, while the course of military events and Russia's disintegration have opened up vistas of unanticipated expansion in the eastern part of Europe.[8]

Germany's Continental Policy.—In 1913, Prince von Buelow stated the German point of view, as follows:

---

[7] Otto von Gierke, "Unsere Friedensziele," quoted in *The New Europe*, No. 59 (November 29, 1917), p. 220.

[8] See the very illuminating book of "W. Daya" (*nom de plume* of W. Karfunkelstein), "Der Aufmarsch im Osten," Dachau-bei-München, written shortly after the Treaty of Brest-Litovsk.]

"We must never forget that the consolidation of our position as a Great Power in Europe has made it possible for us to transform our industrial activity from a national into a world activity, and our Continental policy into a world policy. Our world policy is based upon the successes of our European policy. The moment the firm foundation constituted by Germany's position as a Great European Power begins to totter, the whole fabric of our world policy will collapse. . . . We can only pursue our world policy on the basis of our European policy." [9]

Since the war, Prince von Buelow has added to these lines the following significant words:

"Unless our position in Europe be assured and strengthened, we cannot profit by the acquisition of colonies." [10]

This is the cardinal maxim of German policy; and, as it is thoroughly sound from the German standpoint, it may be assumed that it will determine Germany's conduct, unless before the peace conference there should occur so complete a revolution as to involve a denial of the old gods.

Sea Power.—The validity of this continental principle is generally recognized, and so also is its corollary that even an absolutely unassailable position in Europe will not lead to world power unless sea power is acquired. Hence, the "Westerners" desire to strengthen Germany in Europe by annexing Belgium, with Antwerp as a "pistol pointed at England," thus contrasting with the "Easterners," who believe in rail power and aim at expansion towards the east—

[9] Von Buelow, "Imperial Germany" (ed. J. W. Headlam), pp. 51-52. See also General von Bissing's "Testament: A Study in German Ideals," p. 29, London [1917].

[10] On this fundamental maxim, see the petition of June 20, 1915, to the Chancellor signed by 1,341 men, chiefly professors, officials, judges, authors, etc., S. Grumbach, "Das Annexionistische Deutschland," p. 138 [English translation in "The Pan-German Programme," pp. 26-27, New York, 1918].

in Russia, Poland, and the Balkans. No one of these pro-
grams is exclusive of the others; none has been abandoned.
It is a question of priority and of securing from what is,
or may be, at present attainable that which will best afford
the means of gaining the others in some future conflict.

Reaction Against the Colonial Movement.—The lesson
of the war to the most realistic of German thinkers has been
that power in the oversea world must come after the laying
of the fundamental foundations on which alone it can rest
securely. In addition, as has already been noted, the virtually complete domination of the seas by the Entente navies
and the resulting inability of Germany to defend her transmarine possessions have resulted in a distinct reaction
against the colonial movement itself. These ambitions
have at the most been deferred or subordinated to what
seem to be more vital aims. Thus, in 1915, speaking of
Germany's future in Africa, Dr. Paul Rohrbach said that
if the World War did not lead to a decision, then in a few
years there would be a second Punic War.[11] In fact, there
is nowhere manifest any resignation to the loss of the
colonies—except possibly in the cases of Kiaochow, the
Pacific Islands, and Southwest Africa—and there is a widespread hope that there will be sufficient pawns to spare in
Europe to secure not alone a return, but an extension, of
the Mid-African possessions. So recently as December 22,
1917, the Colonial Secretary, Dr. Solf, spoke in this sense,
and Chancellor Hertling, on January 25, 1918, absolutely
demanded a reconstitution of the colonial world.[12]

[11] Grumbach, *op. cit.*, p. 174.
[[12] For the actual course of events, see *infra*, p. 274.]

Economic Argument.—Unofficial and official agencies have been keeping up their activities and demand a vast African empire. Great stress is laid upon the economic argument, on the need of Germany for raw materials. Superficially, this plea has been strengthened by the facts of the war and the effect of the blockade. But it is obvious that, even with a very large colonial empire, Germany would in this respect have been no better off, unless she had been able to secure command of the sea. On the other hand, this argument has derived some real cogency from the world-wide scarcity of raw materials, which for some time after the conclusion of peace will leave Germany dependent upon the good will of her former enemies, who control the bulk of these supplies.[13] As German thought rejects the idea of international solidarity, so it finds the economic inter-dependence of the modern world irksome. The German aim is to create a self-sufficient empire, after the model of those planned in the seventeenth and eighteenth centuries. Thus the Colonial Secretary, Dr. Solf, said in 1916 that a closer economic union of the Central Empires, including Turkey, however welcome it might be, could not compensate for the lack of colonies, because this confederation (*Staatenbund*) would have a continental character and would be in the same position as Germany regarding colonial raw materials. All the Great Powers, Germany included, must strive, the

---

[13] Edwyn Bevan, "The Method in the Madness," pp. 119-144; also his "The Great German Empire of Central Africa," three articles in the *Westminster Gazette,* February, 1918; Augustin Bernard, "Germany's Colonial Aims," in *Journal of the African Society,* July, 1917, pp. 306-313; René Thierry, "L'Afrique de Demain," in *L'Afrique Française,* 1917, pp. 167-175, 318-321.

argument continues, to be closed economic units and, therefore, must possess land in all the climatic zones.[14]

Its Fallacy.—Dr. Solf himself admitted that this goal
of economic self-sufficiency was not attainable and that all
that could be anticipated was such an increase in oversea
possessions as would supply a good share of the chief raw
materials. As, according to his own estimate, only three
per cent of the colonial imports came from the German
possessions before the war, it is patent that the most extensive territorial changes would have to be made to effect
even a partial realization of this dream.[15] The return of
the German colonies would not be an important step in this
direction; nor would even the cession to Germany of the
whole of tropical Africa. The entire argument is based
upon the illusion created by Africa's vast bulk, and shows
utter lack of appreciation of relative values. The foreign
trade of all Middle Africa is still quite insignificant and the
exports can be increased only gradually, if the native is
to be conserved and civilized. One of the principal products
of this region is the palm kernel, from which are derived
vegetable fats in the shape of oil and of cake for fodder.
Before the war this traffic centered in Germany, but the
imports of palm kernels there, in 1913, amounted to only
104 million marks, of which 91 came from British West
Africa.[16] In other words, this yearly trade, upon which

[14] S. Grumbach, *op. cit.*, p. 10. See also the resolution of the Colonial
Economic Committee (*ibid.*, pp. 143, 144) and the statements of Kuno
Waltemath and of Emil Zimmermann (*ibid.*, pp. 169, 185). Compare
further *ibid.*, pp. 171-173, 184, 190, 207, 236, 237, 250, 296, *et passim.*
[15] *Ibid.*, pp. 9, 10.
[16] It should be noted also that palm oil, manufactured from the kernels,
was exported in this year to the value of 25 million marks. *Statistisches*

so excessive a stress is now placed, was equivalent to less than the present daily expenditure of a number of the belligerent states.

The Argument of Power and Prestige.—The hollowness of this economic argument and its virtual lack of reality are recognized by many in Germany.[17] While it is prominently emphasized, it is merely a cloak used to cover broad imperialistic ambitions that are nurtured by the cult of power. The old idea of a "New Germany" beyond the seas has not been abandoned by all. It still hovers in the minds of publicists like Rohrbach.[18] The majority, however, men like Professor Hans Delbrück of Berlin and Dr. Paasche, the Vice-President of the Reichstag, are clearly aware of its impossibility and urge that a German India be created in Africa at the expense of France and the British Empire.[19]

Jahrbuch, 1915, pp. 184, 197. In an article in the *Vossische Zeitung* of December 22, 1917, on "Courland or Africa," Emil Zimmermann writes at length on Germany's future need of fodder for her cattle and argues in behalf of a Mid-African Empire on account of the vast number of oil palms available there. He favors a capitalistic exploitation of these resources from which the palm oil of commerce and the oil cakes for fodder are manufactured. See further *infra*, pp. 119-130.

[17] In the famous petition of June 20, 1915, to the Chancellor, it is stated that Middle Africa would, it is true, provide Germany with a vast domain, but not with proportionately large and adequate colonial supplies. S. Grumbach, *op. cit.*, p. 138 ["The Pan-German Programme," pp. 26-27].

[18] See views of Rohrbach and Rudolf Theuden, in S. Grumbach, *op. cit.*, pp. 301-304, 325-327.

[19] According to Delbrück, whose position as a publicist in Germany is similar to that of Charles W. Eliot in the United States and of Lord Bryce in England, the first and most important demand was for a German India, "so big that it is capable of conducting its own defense in case of war." This domain, according to him, was to consist of Germany's former African colonies, plus all the British, French, and Portuguese possessions in Africa south of the Sahara, and north of the Zambezi, including the islands off the coast, like Madagascar, the Azores, Madeira, and the Cape Verde Islands. To demand these territories, with a population estimated by him at over 100 millions, Delbrück claims "is not unjust and does not offend against the principle of equilibrium." Hans Del-

These men are thinking in terms of power and prestige.[20]
Thus, the champion of *Mittelafrika,* Emil Zimmermann,
points out that a compact empire in Africa reaching from
the Atlantic to the Pacific Ocean would enable Germany
to dominate some of the most important trade routes of the
world. *"Mittelafrika,"* he points out, "would lie at the very
centre of England's main arteries leading to South Africa,
Australia, and India; and, in German hands, it would con-
tribute towards crippling the British Empire." [21]

brück, "Bismarck's Erbe," pp. 202 ff., Berlin, 1915; and *Preussiche Jahr-
bücher,* quoted in "Conquest and Kultur," pp. 72-73, Washington, 1917.
The same idea is developed in the speech of Dr. Paasche, reported April
17, 1915, reproduced in S. Grumbach, *op. cit.,* pp. 72, 73. See also Edwyn
Bevan, *op. cit.,* pp. 121, 122, 302-306.

[20] In 1915, the founder of German East Africa, Dr. Karl Peters, said:
"Not to live and let live, but to live and determine the lives of others,
that is power." Grumbach, *op. cit.,* pp. 344, 345.

[21] *The New Europe,* No. 43 (August 9, 1917), pp. 122 ff. Cf. further
Professor Erich Brandenburg's views on Mittelafrika, *ibid.,* pp. 246 ff.
See also the lecture of J. E. Mackenzie at King's College, London, in
December, 1917, on "The Colonial Aspirations of Germany"; and General
J. C. Smuts's lecture on "East Africa" before the Royal Geographical
Society on January 28, 1918. [In Erzberger's memoir, addressed to Von
Bethmann-Hollweg and the General Staff in September, 1915, he depre-
cated German acquisition of Morocco as tending to a dissipation of
forces. On the other hand, he advocated annexation of Tunis by Italy
(especially as creating perpetual enmity between her and France) and of
Egypt by Austria. For Germany he demanded an empire stretching
from Dar-es-Salaam to Senegal, this involving annexation of the French
and Belgian Congos, Nigeria, Dahomey, and the French West Coast.
"By rounding out our colonial domain we are not scattered and we create
wide fields of activity for German interests. We do not need territories
for colonization since after the war emigration will be even more meager
than it was in the ten years preceding. . . . We must concentrate our
people" (quoted in *Le Temps,* April 30, 1920).]

CHAPTER VII

DISPOSITION OF THE GERMAN COLONIES

The Deciding Factors.—The question of the future of the German colonies must be considered both from the standpoint of pure justice and from that of political expediency. In all probability, considerations of the latter nature will prevail and the fate of Germany's conquered African empire will be determined by the dominant factors in the actual and prospective world-economic status and by the final military situation with its strategic possibilities on land and sea. These fluctuating conditions cannot now be foreseen. It would be futile to attempt to prophesy them. Even if force, both of an economic and military nature, be ultimately the determining element in the decision, still there is considerable practical value in studying this African problem as if it were an isolated one, apart from the inseparably connected factors in Europe and elsewhere. It is important to look at the situation from the standpoint of an impartial judge with plenary authority to render a verdict and to impose it.

Return to Germany.—1. *Native Standpoint.*—In such a judicial proceeding the question should be regarded primarily from the point of view of the natives of Africa, and secondarily from that of the neighboring civilized communities, such as the Union of South Africa and East India, that are vitally and directly concerned in these areas. The interests of Germany and those of the other colonizing powers and of the outside world should be treated as of subordinate importance. From the standpoint of the natives, there is no reason for the reëstablishment of German rule. Germany's record before and during the war was on balance distinctly bad. It is true that in his address of December 21, 1917, Dr. Solf emitted a note that had never before been heard in German colonial policy, when he said that the negroes have a right to be considered by the colonizing powers as an end in themselves and not merely as a means.[1] This is an isolated expression, which may or may not indicate a real change of heart. At best, it is a slender guarantee upon which to decide the fate of thirteen million people. In view of Germany's total failure to appreciate the duties of colonial trusteeship in the past, it affords scant assurance that in the future these colonies would be administered by her in the interests of the natives and of the world as a whole. Her stewardship hitherto has been quite accurately described by Professor Veblen, who writes:

"In the Imperial colonial policy colonies are conceived to stand to their Imperial guardian or master in a relation between that of a step-child and that of an indentured servant; to be dealt with summarily and at discretion and to be made use of without scruple." [2]

2. German Standpoint.—Nor would the loss of these possessions inflict any economic hardship upon Germany. Their maintenance was annually costing the German people

[1] *Kölnische Zeitung,* December 22, 1917.
[2] T. Veblen, "The Nature of Peace," p. 261, New York, 1917.

an amount which, though not large, was out of all proportion to German trade with these colonies. This traffic, moreover, was but a small fraction—less than .5 per cent—of Germany's entire foreign commerce. Furthermore, in comparison with Germany's total requirements, the amount of raw materials derived from these territories and those in the Pacific was quite insignificant, being only about three per cent of the whole.[3] Before the war, Germany had no difficulty in obtaining all the stocks that she needed on the same terms as did her competitors. In normal times, there is generally more anxiety on the side of the seller to dispose of his wares than there is on the part of the buyer to procure them. Germany, without physical and political control over these sources of supplies, can be assured the same equality in the future as she actually enjoyed in the past, provided the peace arrangements as a whole meet the views of the Allies. In the meanwhile, the control over raw materials and over the means of access to them is one of the most potent weapons to secure from Germany satisfactory terms and also to prevent any future aggression.

Germany's Wants.—While there is no real economic need for colonies, a strong desire for them is widely felt in Germany. This springs largely from the wish to play a great and influential part in the broad world. Moreover, the German oversea dominions have been hallowed for many Germans by the number of their fellows who have lost their lives in conquering and in defending them and who have found their graves in African soil. In the Herero rebellion alone, 1,411 Germans were killed or died of disease, and

[³ See *supra,* pp. 10-11.]

907 were wounded. "A country in which so many German sons have fallen and have been buried," General von Deimling said, some years before the war, "can no longer be a foreign land to us, but rather a piece of the homeland, to care for which is our sacred duty." [4] These feelings are strong and widespread. It is, however, a question whether, in the interest of world peace, it is not better to thwart these sentiments, even if a passing resentment be left in Germany, than to return colonies that will probably be used as points of vantage for future aggression. [5]

Southwest Africa.—In determining the fate of German Southwest Africa, the attitude of the adjoining Union of South Africa must be an important factor. British statesmen are well aware of the part that bitterness at the return of Louisbourg—New England's conquest—to France in 1748 played in bringing on the American Revolution, [6] and they will not lightly risk a renewed schism in the Commonwealth of Nations for such a cause. There is a distinct advantage, both as regards economic development and as regards native policy, in having virtually all of white man's Africa south of the Zambezi and Kunene under one administration. In addition, there is a strong and comprehensible desire in South Africa to eliminate an aggressive neighbor and to keep these areas out of the range of European poli-

[4] W. H. Dawson, "The Evolution of Modern Germany," pp. 366, 397, London, 1911. See also the same writer's "Problems of the Peace," p. 222, London, 1918.

[5] See the argument of Edwyn Bevan, "The Method in the Madness," pp. 305, 306, London, 1917. To give back the colonies "would not be to content Germany, but to keep up her appetite for colonial expansion: it would be to restore a condition of things essentially unstable."

[6] H. E. Egerton, "The Dominions and the Peace Settlement," in *United Empire Magazine,* June, 1915, p. 428.

tics.   An African Monroe Doctrine, based upon the same fundamental reasons as was its American prototype, is in process of formation.   Both Botha[7] and Smuts have expressed themselves clearly on this subject.   In this connection, General Smuts spoke the following pregnant words on January 28, 1918:

"The young nations who form the Dominions of the British Empire . . . should not be asked to consent to the restoration to a militant Germany of fresh footholds for militarism in the southern hemisphere, and thus endanger the future of their young and rising communities, who are developing the waste spaces of the earth.   They want a new Monroe Doctrine for the South, as there has been a Monroe Doctrine for the West, to protect it against European militarism."[8]

German East Africa.—East India, with a redundant population that is increasing most rapidly, has a somewhat different, but possibly equally legitimate, concern in East Africa.   A generation ago, Sir John Kirk, the guardian of British interests on the East African littoral, spoke of this region as "the America of the Hindu."[9]   In Zanzibar and along the entire coast, there are a fairly large number of Indians, and the retail trade in some sections is virtually altogether in their hands.   In German East Africa, there were domiciled the year before the war 8,780 Indians[10] and

[7] W. A. Crabtree, "Germans in East and West Africa," in *Journal of the African Society,* October, 1915, p. 4.

[8] Address before the Royal Geographical Society on January 28, 1918. See also Alfred Scholfield, "German South-West Africa and the Union," in *Contemporary Review,* July, 1915, pp. 62, 64.

[9] *Geographical Journal,* April, 1915, p. 287.

[10] "Die Deutschen Schutzgebiete," 1914, p. 11.   There has been considerable opposition to the presence of these Indians, but, on the whole, they have been well treated and have been protected by the authorities. J. K.

a relatively extensive commerce was carried on with India.[11]
Several British authorities have urged that German East
Africa be retained primarily as a colony for India's super-
abundant millions.[12] The influential Indian nationalist
leader, Gokhale, expressed this general wish in his testament. The self-governing white Dominions of the British
Commonwealth refuse to admit Indian immigrants. As in
the case of California, they fear that the lower standard of
Asiatic life will undermine their democratic institutions.
After referring to the feeling aroused in India by this attitude of South Africa, Canada, and Australasia, the Secretary
of State for India said, at the Imperial Conference of 1917:

"The unrestricted opening to Indian enterprise of any
territory acquired from the enemy in East Africa would, it
is believed, remove some of the bitterness which this controversy has engendered in the minds of Indian publicists
and politicians by the proof it would give that in the disposal of territories accruing to the Empire as a result of

Vietor, "Geschichtliche und Kulturelle Entwickelung unserer Schutzgebiete," pp. 131, 132; A. F. Calvert, "German African Empire," pp. 128, 129.
[11] In 1912, there were imported into German East Africa cotton textiles
to the value of 10 million marks, of which 1.2 came from England, 2.2
from Germany, 1.1 from Zanzibar, and 2.9 from India. "Die Deutschen
Schutzgebiete," Statistischer Teil, 1914, pp. 142-145. On the importations
of rice from India, see ibid., 1913, p. 11. Cf. likewise British Diplomatic
and Consular Reports, No. 5441 (German East Africa, 1912-13), pp. 5, 6,
8, 9, 18. [See also chart at end of this book.]
[12] Evans Lewin, "The Germans and Africa," p. 267; W. A. Crabtree,
"Economic Resources of German Colonies," in Journal of the African
Society, January, 1917, p. 132; Sir Harry H. Johnston, "The Political
Geography of Africa," in Geographical Journal, April, 1915, p. 287; A. J. S.
MacDonald, "Trade, Politics, and Christianity in Africa and the East," p.
41. Sir Harry H. Johnston writes: "In view of the loyalty which India
has displayed in this grave crisis in the history of the British Empire,
whatever dispositions take place in regard to German East Africa, it is
to be hoped that the claims of India for an outlet may here be satisfied."
"The German Colonies," in Edinburgh Review, October, 1914, p. 309. [See
also John H. Harris, "Africa: Slave or Free?", pp. 100-110.]

the War the needs of the Indian peoples have not been over-looked." [13]

Although it is not wholly clear that this proposal is feasible on an adequate scale, and while it is also not altogether plain why the addition of German East Africa to the British colonies in this region should be necessary for its success, the project has distinct merits from the standpoint of the needs of India and deserves thorough consideration.

[Since the foregoing lines were written, the problem on which they touch has come within the range of actualities. The Government of India, in a letter of October 21, 1920,[14] was unable to agree with Lord Milner's decisions of May, 1920, on various questions concerning the status of Indians in East Africa, dissenting particularly from his proposals for segregation of races and restrictions on Indian ownership of land, and disapproving of what it regarded as inadequate Indian representation on Legislative and Municipal Councils. His view that certain areas should be made a special reservation for Indian colonization likewise met with unfavorable criticism as being impracticable [15] and as preju-

---

[13] Imperial War Conference of 1917 (Cd. 8566), pp. 161, 162.

[14] Correspondence Regarding the Position of Indians in East Africa (Kenya and Uganda), 1921 (Cd. 1311), pp. 2-9.

[15] Report by Sir Benjamin Robertson, Dated 4th August 1920, Regarding the Proposed Settlement of Indian Agriculturists in Tanganyika Territory, and Letter from the Government of India to the Secretary of State for India, Dated 10th February 1921 (Cd. 1312), p. 2: "(1) There is no vacant land suitable for an Indian reserve. The land which is now vacant is generally vacant because it has some defect. That is, it is either sterile or dense bush or swamp or remote from the main lines of communication. In order, therefore, to obtain really good land for an Indian settlement it would be necessary either—

"(a) to expropriate the natives, or take land necessary for their natural expansion, which would be contrary to the principle of Article 22 of the Covenant of the League of Nations; or

dicial to the claims of Indians for equal rights elsewhere
within the Empire;[16] while, according to a letter from the
same Government to the Secretary of State for India, February 10, 1921, there was reason to doubt whether suitable types of agriculturists would be attracted from India
by the prospects for settlement.[17] The real point at issue
is that the Indians "appreciate the policy that the interests
of the natives should come first, and they expect no more
than equal opportunity with the nationals of other members of the League of Nations,"[18] a position which is sustained by the Government of India[19] and which may be
expected to prevail.]

"(b) to confiscate some of the privately-owned German plantations
which, under the economic clauses of the Peace Treaty, are to be
realised subject to the conditions of the original grant.
"(2) It is the view of the Administration that small settlers with only a
moderate amount of capital, whether white or coloured, face grave risk
of disaster in a country where capital for the employment of native labour
is essential."
[16] Letter from the President of the East Africa Indian National Congress
(Nairobi, November 15-16, 1919), quoted by Robertson (Cd. 1312, p. 3):
"It may not be out of place to mention here that on the advice of political
leaders from India and in the hope of sharing equal rights and responsibilities with the other fellow subjects of His Majesty the King in East
Africa, Uganda, Zanzibar, and ex-German East Africa Protectorates, my
Congress Committee has decided to refrain from asking any preferential
treatment for Indians and consequent reservation of ex-German East Africa
for Indian colonisation." Cf. also the letter from the Secretary of the
British East Africa Indian Association of January 19, 1920, cited ibid., p. 6:
"We feel that by claiming 'special' treatment in a particular place we
shall forfeit our claim for 'equal' treatment everywhere. What we want
is equal treatment in both East and West Africa, and in fact throughout
the British Empire. By asking for special treatment in German East
Africa we shall be violating the fundamental principle which we have
all along been fighting for, namely, that there shall be no differentiation in the treatment meted out to various sections of His Majesty's
subjects."
[17] Ibid., p. 5.
[18] Ibid., p. 4.
[19] Ibid., p. 6: "We agree with Sir Benjamin Robertson that the position

West Africa.—Most of the boundary lines in Africa are diplomatic in origin and, in very many instances, they are that abomination of scientific geographers, the straight line. These artificial frontiers cut across natural physical divisions and sever closely related tribes and peoples. This is conspicuously the case in West Africa. Part of German Togo belongs ethnically to French Dahomey, part to British Gold Coast.[20] The worst example of non-natural delimitation is to be found in the Cameroons, with its two prongs jutting into French territory and giving access to the Congo and Ubangi rivers. Under threat of war, France had been obliged in 1911 to cede to Germany these two projections, covering an area of one hundred thousand square miles. It was a distinct humiliation and aroused considerable resentment in France. As Count de Mun said at the time, "It was not only a question of national honor, but it meant the shattering of a splendid plan of African empire, that plan which

which the East African Indians have taken up is right, and we believe that it will be generally supported by public opinion throughout India. We have opposed, and will continue to oppose, unfair discrimination against our nationals overseas. We desire no discrimination in their favour. We ask for no more than equal rights. We can be satisfied with nothing less." Cf. also the Indian Government's letter of October 21, 1920, in Cd. 1311, pp. 2-10.

[20] On September 24, 1914, Sir Hugh Clifford, the Governor of the Gold Coast, wrote to the Secretary of State concerning the peaceful occupation of Yendi, the chief town of the Dagomba country, a district which was bisected when the Anglo-German boundary was determined. He added: "It should, I think, be noted for future reference that any attempt once more to divide the Dagomba country in a manner which is opposed to the ethnological distribution of the native population will be keenly resented by the chiefs and people both in the Northern Territories and in the Sansanne-Mangu district of Togoland. The foregoing remark applies with equal force to the feeling of the natives in the Peki and Misahöhe districts, and to the Awuna population in the Keta and Lomeland districts." Correspondence Relating to the Military Operations in Togoland, 1915 (Cd. 7872), pp. 31-32. [See insert map between pp. 66-67.]

offered to national pride the grand spectacle of a French Africa stretching without break from the Mediterranean to the mouth of the Congo." [21] France naturally desires to get back these lands and her colonial authorities have so expressed themselves.[22] Her wishes here have a distinct validity. In so far as the rest of the Cameroons is concerned—the colony as it existed before the Agadir crisis of 1911—and apart from the question whether Germany by her policy towards the natives and her militaristic aims has not forfeited her rights, neither France nor England would have any very strong claims. It has been suggested, on the one hand, that the United States should assume the task of introducing civilization here [23] and, on the other, that the German colonies be held by a future international association until Germany has reformed her ways.[24] Neither

[21] André Tardieu, "Le Mystère d'Agadir," pp. 519, 520, 577; Debidour, "Histoire Diplomatique de l'Europe," 1904-1916, pp. 151 ff.; for the text of the Treaty of November 4, 1911, see *ibid.*, pp. 336-341. [This Treaty, as well as the complementary Declaration of September 28, 1912, fixing the time-limit for the right of option by the natives of the territories in question and determining the régime of concessionary companies (cf. Debidour, p. 175, note 3), is abrogated by Article 125 of the Versailles Treaty, Germany undertaking "to pay to the French Government, in accordance with the estimate to be presented by that Government and approved by the Reparation Commission, all the deposits, credits, advances, etc., effected by virtue of these instruments in favour of Germany."]

[22] Baron Guillaume to M. Davignon, August 16, 1914. "First Belgian Grey Book," No. 74 ["Collected Diplomatic Documents Relating to the Outbreak of the European War," p. 341, London, 1915.]

[23] Evans Lewin, "The Germans and Africa," pp. 264-266.

[24] George Young has suggested forming a Council for the Allied Middle African Colonies which "would take charge of the German's share of the 'white man's burden' until the world was satisfied that he was 'a white man.'" *The New Europe*, No. 63 (December 27, 1917), pp. 334-336. It is significant that Mr. Young has abandoned his former argument in favor of international government for Middle Africa and now advocates international control. George Young, "Portugal Old and Young: An Historical Study," pp. 331, 332, Oxford, 1917. See also H. G. Wells, "The African Riddle," in *The New Republic*, February 23, 1918.

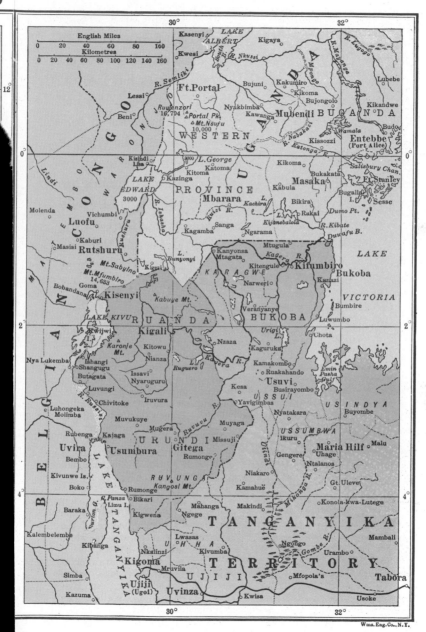

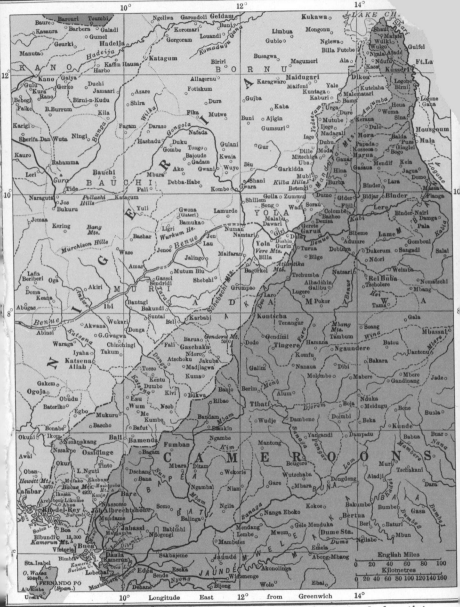

Areas which have changed hands are shown in darker tint

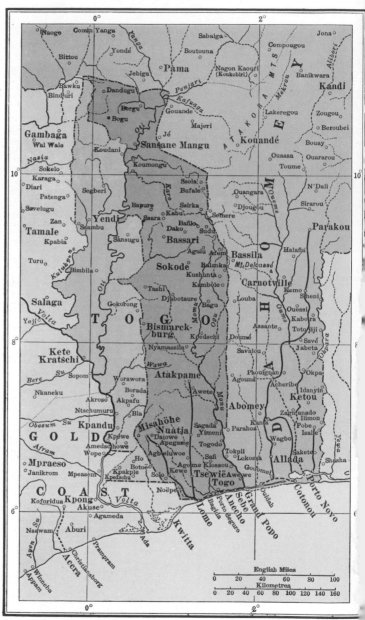

From "The Statesman's Year Book," 1920

proposal appears to be feasible. In that event, possibly the only solution is to assign part of the Cameroons to British Nigeria and part to French Equatorial Africa.[25] Provided there be effectively established a comprehensive system of international control, under which native rights will be fully maintained and the "open door" will always be kept wide open, and provided the mandatory of the Powers be wholly honest in his trusteeship and forego all purely national and imperialistic ends, it matters comparatively little to the world at large which flag flies in the Cameroons.

[25 For the final decision, see *infra,* p. 431.]

PART II

MIDDLE AFRICA: THE ECONOMIC ASPECTS OF THE PROBLEM

(Written for THE INQUIRY. Finished May 2, 1918.)

PART II: MIDDLE AFRICA: THE ECONOMIC ASPECTS OF THE PROBLEM

MIDDLE AFRICA: THE ECONOMIC ASPECTS OF
THE PROBLEM

INTRODUCTION

The Three Divisions of Africa.—1. The Mediterranean Littoral.—The vast continental mass of Africa is divided into three fairly well-defined regions by fundamental geographical, racial, economic, cultural, and political facts.[1] On the Mediterranean littoral in the north, shut off from the rest of the continent by the Atlas Mountains and by the Sahara and Libyan deserts, are a number of communities that are closely connected with Europe by many ties of varied nature. Though not completely separated from the Middle Africa of the negro, Egypt, Tripoli, Tunis, Algeria, and Morocco are by race, culture, history, and politics far more intimately bound up with Europe. Here are firmly established civilizations that can in all probability not be uprooted by the European, whose main function consists in guiding them along progressive lines.

2. White Man's Africa.—In the extreme south of the continent, beyond the Kunene and Zambezi rivers, lies

[1] Sir Harry H. Johnston, "The History of the Colonization of Africa by Alien Races," pp. 443 ff., and his article, "The Political Geography of Africa Before and After the War," in *Geographical Journal*, April, 1915, pp. 287, 288; Sir Thomas H. Holdich, "Political Frontiers and Boundary Making," pp. 227-229, London, 1916; H. Schurtz in H. F. Helmolt, "Weltgeschichte," III, pp. 392-400, Leipzig, 1901; F. Thorbecke, "Mittelafrika oder Tropisches Afrika," in *Petermann's Mitteilungen*, November, 1917, pp. 349, 350.

another of these three main divisions—white man's Africa—
where a distinctly European or Western type of civilization is developing subject to the adaptations necessitated
by local conditions, of which the most fundamental is the
presence of a large native population far outnumbering the
white settlers.

3. Middle Africa.—Between these two divisions lies the
huge area of Middle Africa, with its aboriginal peoples in
various degrees of development from the most primitive
savagery and cannibalism upwards. In the trading centers
on the West Coast, where intercourse with Europe has been
most close, in such colonies as Sierra Leone and the Gold
Coast, are to be found highly educated and civilized natives
—scholars, lawyers, doctors, planters, and merchants. But
these individuals are more or less scattered exceptions in
communities that, as a whole, are to a marked degree backward in comparison with progressive Europe and America.

This Division is Not Hard and Fast.—This tripartite
division of Africa is by no means hard and fast. There are
border regions in which the types merge and, in addition,
each division contains areas that differ radically from their
surroundings. Within the territorial confines of the Union
of South Africa, though politically not a part of this self-
governing Dominion, are purely native communities, such
as Basutoland, where European settlement is, in general,
prohibited.[2] Furthermore, the eastern coastal lowlands
to the south of the Zambezi are climatically unsuitable for
a white population. On the other hand, in the heart of
the continent are fairly extensive highlands where the white

[2] A. B. Keith, "South Africa," III, pp. 211-224.

man can thrive and establish his civilization. Furthermore, the Semitic and Hamitic peoples of the north have penetrated into tropical Africa and have brought with them their customs and usages, and, preëminently, their living and expanding religion, Mohammedanism. In addition, within each of the three great divisions are marked subdivisions. Egypt is in many respects quite distinct from Morocco, and so, in Middle Africa, is West Africa from the Congo Basin, as well as from the eastern shore.

Middle Africa as an Economic Entity.—Similar qualifications are also essential when we look upon Africa purely from the economic standpoint. Broadly speaking, the tropical portion of the continent forms an economic entity, but on its borders are a number of areas whose economic life tends to attach itself to one of the other two divisions of Africa. As Southern Mozambique depends upon the transit trade to and from the Union of South Africa, and as it is a recruiting ground for labor in the Transvaal gold mines, the economic problem of this section of Portuguese East Africa is in a number of aspects quite different from that of tropical Africa as a whole. Such factors as political relations and means of communication likewise exercise a centrifugal effect. Thus the Anglo-Egyptian Sudan's connection with Egypt and the fact that its commercial outlet is through the Red Sea detach it to a large extent from the Mid-African question. Abyssinia, Italian Eritrea, and the land of the Somalis under Italian, French, and British rule likewise look to the north. Similarly, while Northern Rhodesia is distinctly tropical, her connection with Southern Rhodesia and the growing white population there, the fact that the trade outlet is towards the southeast, and, finally, the political interest of the Union of South Africa in the destiny of this area link up all of Rhodesia in a measure with white man's Africa. These outlying regions have a dual economic aspect and thus present problems that are in some respects distinct from those of the typically central regions—West Africa, the Congo Basin, and the eastern shore.

The Two Sides of the Economic Problem.—Even when it is thus delimited, the economic problem of tropical Africa is one of a myriad facets, each of which presents its own difficulties. But regarded as a whole, the question has two distinct sides. On the one hand, it is the problem of civilizing the negro, which implies both the creation of new needs and the stimulation of those already existing, as well as the development of the natural resources of the country, so that the means to satisfy these requirements can be obtained by the native. From this aspect, the question is purely internal. It means the gradual creation of an African civilization with strong native roots. This side of the problem makes the paramount appeal to progressive thinkers, and gives an ethical basis to modern imperialism of the finer and sounder type. But as the negro is apparently incapable of advance by his own unaided efforts, foreign guidance was and is essential. With this tutelage has developed a measure of economic interdependence between tropical Africa and the advanced peoples of the world. They look to Africa to furnish them with part of the raw materials that their complex civilization requires and in exchange they send to Africa some of the products of their busy workshops. The vitally important side of the question is the development of a sound African civilization; the secondary side is Africa as a source of supply to the Western world and as a market for its finished wares. The problems arising from these interactions are not only of infinite complexity, but, as is true of all questions in which the human element is predominant, they do not admit of a definitive solution. At best, there is the prospect of temporary readjustments which, as new conditions develop, will lead to further questions demanding renewed settlement. The most essential thing is the determination of the lines of real progress and the rejection of all measures not in harmony with the welfare of the native, no matter how insistent be the demands of the outside world.

CHAPTER I

1. The Free Trade Area of 1885

Outside World as a Determining Factor in Africa's Economic Development.—Since the civilization of tropical Africa came from without, it followed inevitably that the economic development of the country was shaped in great measure by the requirements of the European peoples.[1] Just as their needs and wants have, in the past, largely determined what surplus commodities Africa should produce, so the future will be conditioned by those outside influences. Hence, the problem must first be analyzed from this aspect.

The Free Trade Provisions of the Berlin Act of 1885.— When, in the 'eighties of the last century, the modern colonial movement started with the rush that led to the partition of Africa during a scant decade, the chief economic argument advanced in its support by the colonizing Powers was the need of fresh sources of supply and of new markets under their exclusive national control. While each Power was taking what could be conveniently annexed, no one was willing to allow any of its rivals to appropriate the Congo Basin, whose potential riches had just been revealed to the world by the epoch-making discoveries of Stanley. It was

---

[1] On both this and the following section of this chapter, see also *infra,* pp. 195-205.

largely in order to stabilize the situation in this region and
to obviate commercial friction there that the Conference of
Berlin was called in 1884. One of the most important provisions of the General Act adopted by this assembly on
February 26, 1885, was to the effect that complete freedom
of trade should prevail and that no monopoly or favor of
any kind in matters of commerce should be established
within a carefully defined area embracing a very large part
of Middle Africa.[2] This region, generally known as the
Conventional Basin of the Congo, includes not alone the
Belgian Congo, but also a number of the other European
colonies. Within its borders on the West Coast were the
French Congo and a part of French Gabun, Portuguese
Cabinda with a section of Northern Angola, and a considerable part of the Cameroons. On the East Coast, this free-
trade area included British East Africa [now named
Kenya], Uganda, Nyasaland, and a part of Rhodesia, all
of German East Africa [now the Tanganyika Territory],
and the southern section of Italian Somaliland. The northern half of Mozambique is also actually in the Basin, but
Portugal in 1885 reserved to herself full freedom in fiscal
matters there. In the remainder of this vast area not only
were all differential customs dues prohibited, but all import

[2] Articles 1 to 5, Hertslet, "The Map of Africa by Treaty" (3d ed.), II,
pp. 468-486 ["Trattati . . . relativi all'Africa," pp. 104-120]; A. Debidour,
"Histoire Diplomatique de l'Europe, 1878-1904," pp. 301-315; H. W. Wack,
"The Story of the Congo Free State," pp. 530-544. For brief accounts of
this Conference, see J. Scott Keltie, "The Partition of Africa" (2d ed.),
pp. 208 ff.; J. Holland Rose, "The Development of the European Nations,
1870-1905," II, pp. 276 ff., London, 1905. For a *précis* of the proceedings,
see Sir E. M. Satow, "A Guide to Diplomatic Practice," II, pp. 138-144,
London, 1917. For a full account, see Senate Executive Document, No.
196, 49th Congress, 1st Session. On Portugal's reservation, see *ibid.*, pp.
66, 306; *Africa*, No. 2 (1885), p. 1.

duties whatsoever. As the Independent State of the Congo, which had come into existence by international recognition at the time of the Berlin Conference, was not able to finance itself without customs levies, the Conference of Brussels of 1890 modified this stringent prohibition and agreed to the imposition of import duties up to ten per cent *ad valorem*.[3] In addition, the Berlin Conference adopted elaborate regulations to secure equality to all in navigating the Congo and the Niger rivers.[4]

Comparative Ineffectiveness of This Provision.—It was the expectation of the Berlin Conference that a great stride forward in obviating international economic rivalry had been taken. Prince Bismarck clearly voiced this view when, at the concluding session, he said:

"The Resolutions which we are about to sanction formally secure to the trade of all nations free access to the interior of the African continent. The guarantees which will be provided for freedom of trade in the basin of the Congo, and the whole of the provisions which were embodied in the Acts relative to the navigation of the Congo and the Niger, are such as to afford the trade and industry of all nations the most favorable conditions for their development and security." [5]

[3] Hertslet, *op. cit.*, pp. 488-517.
[4] Berlin Act of 1885, Chapters IV and V, Articles 13 to 33.
[5] H. W. Wack, *op. cit.*, p. 94. On October 17, 1884, the American Secretary of State, F. T. Frelinghuysen, sent the following instructions to John A. Kasson, Envoy Extraordinary and Minister Plenipotentiary of the United States at Berlin: "So far as the administration of the Congo Valley is concerned, this Government has shown its preference for a neutral control, such as is promised by the Free States of the Congo, the nucleus of which has already been created through the organized efforts of the International Association. Whether the approaching Conference can give further shape and scope to this project of creating a great state in the heart of Western Africa, whose organization and administration shall afford a guarantee that it is to be held for all time, as it were, in

Unfortunately, the Conference failed to devise any means for securing the observance of these principles, such as periodic sessions for their interpretation and amplification and an international court with jurisdiction in disputes concerning them. Owing to the absence of such international organs, some of the interested parties disregarded the spirit of the Act and interpreted it liberally. This was especially the case in the Congo Basin proper where the free-trade provision was completely nullified by the system of economic exploitation adopted both by the Independent State and by France.

The Belgian Concessionaire System.—The Independent State of the Congo declared that all land not actually occupied by the natives, together with the india-rubber and other products thereof, was the property of the State. The Government itself proceeded to exploit these resources in extensive areas, and in other districts it granted the sole right of development to large concessionary companies. As a consequence of this system, the negro had nothing to sell to the private trader and, in turn, could not buy his wares. The Government and these privileged companies thus secured exclusive control of the entire traffic. Foreign merchants had absolutely no opportunity in the Belgian Congo and kept away.[6] Moreover, as a direct result of this system,

trust for the benefit of all peoples, remains to be seen" (Senate Executive Document, *op. cit.*, p. 14). For the expectations of Bismarck, see *ibid.*, pp. 282, 294.

[6] J. H. Rose, *op. cit.*, II, pp. 294-298; N. D. Harris, "Intervention and Colonization in Africa," pp. 40-46; E. D. Morel, "Africa and the Peace of Europe," pp. 89, 90; Sir H. H. Johnston, "The History of the Colonization of Africa by Alien Races," pp. 348-354. Under pretext of appropriating vacant lands, the State took all the forests, "malgré les droits d'usage que les communautés indigènes y exerçaient. Maître du sol, il se déclarait

the foreign commerce of the Independent State was virtually monopolized by Belgium. Of the 58 million francs of exports in 1906, 54 went to Belgium; and of the 21 million francs of imports, 15 came thence. Antwerp developed into a considerable mart for rubber and ivory.[7]

The Belgian Reforms.—In 1908, Belgium annexed the Independent State of the Congo, but Great Britain refused to recognize the validity of this course unless there was full compliance with the stipulations of the Berlin Act of 1885 as regards free trade and other matters. The British Government pointed out that the privileged companies covered about three fifths of the entire Congo State and represented eighty-five per cent of the exports and further claimed that "as long as the Concessions are worked upon the same conditions as at present, it is difficult to see how a complete freedom of trade, which is guaranteed under Article I of the Berlin Act, can possibly exist." Moreover, Sir Edward Grey insisted that the aborigines should be freed from excessive taxation, that sufficient land should be granted to them to obtain produce to enable them to buy and sell as in the other European colonies, and that traders of whatever nationality should be permitted to acquire land for the erection of factories "so as to enable them to establish direct trade relations with the natives."[8]   Such reforms

propriétaire des produits du sol. Et comme, dans ces conditions, les indigènes refusaient à travailler pour un salaire dérisoire, on les contraignait au travail, et, bien souvent, on sanctionnait cette contrainte en les terrorisant." Émile Vandervelde, "Belgian and British Interests in Africa," in *Journal of the African Society*, April, 1915, p. 268.

[7] Édouard Payen, "Belgique et Congo," pp. 29-32, 94, 95.

[8] *Africa*, No. 3 (1908), pp. 2, 3. Similar representations were made in 1908 and 1909 by the United States. *American Journal of International Law*, III, Supplement, pp. 94-96, 140-143.

were introduced and rapidly effected by the new régime.
The principle of the revised land system inaugurated in
1909 was that the negro had a claim and first title to the
soil, and important areas were reserved for his use.   In
addition, the privileges and rights of the concessionary companies were greatly curtailed and one region after another
was opened to free trade.   As a consequence, Great Britain
in 1913 formally recognized the annexation of 1908.[9]   There
are still vestiges of the old Leopoldian system, but the general situation was accurately described by Émile Vandervelde in 1915, when he said:

"The natives from now on have the right to the natural
products of the soil.   Forced labor is abolished.   The monopolies have been suppressed.   Freedom of commerce, complete and entire, exists throughout the whole extent of the
Congo." [10]

In 1916, the Belgian Colonial Minister, J. Renkin, admitted that at the outset Belgians had an economic advantage in the Congo, but he asserted that now "the Congo was
open to all without favor to anyone."   The old idea of
national privilege, he declared, had been abandoned and
foreign capital was welcome.[11]

[9] J. Renkin, "L'Avenir du Congo Belge," in *L'Afrique Française*, March,
1916, Supplement, pp. 62, 63; H. A. Gibbons, "The New Map of Africa,"
pp. 150-159; N. D. Harris, *op. cit.*, pp. 61, 62; British Diplomatic and
Consular Reports, No. 5260, p. 20; *L'Afrique Française*, 1913, pp. 88, 89,
245, 353-355, 414, 415.
[10] Émile Vandervelde, *loc. cit.*   See likewise the statement of the
German Consul-General at Boma, made in 1914.   *L'Afrique Française*,
1914, pp. 414, 415.   In 1917, M. Max Horn of the Belgian Colonial Office
stated that the old land system had been canceled and that all but three
of the concessions had been rescinded.   *Anti-Slavery Reporter*, July, 1917,
p. 25.   Yet of 54 million francs imports in 1912, 36 came from Belgium.
British Diplomatic and Consular Reports, No. 5260, pp. 5, 18, 19.
[11] J. Renkin, *op. cit.*, pp. 64-66.   M. Renkin in this address referred
specifically to the facilities granted to the British soap manufacturers,

The System in the French Congo.—In addition to her
more ancient coastal colony of Gabun, to the north of the
mouth of the Congo River, France has possessed since the
time of the Berlin Conference of 1884-85 a vast area on
the right bank of this river and that of the Ubangi, stretching far inland. For years French policy was concentrated
upon the interior region, with the object of cutting England
off from the lower Sudan and of preventing the physical
junction of that country with British Uganda. When this
avowed policy of *revanche* for Great Britain's continued
occupation of Egypt [12] was frustrated by the Fashoda incident of 1898, the French Government directed its attention
to the coastal districts, which had been sadly neglected
during the obstructive push towards the interior. Most
precipitately in one year, 1899, the major part of the
French Congo was divided up for colonization among a
number of companies, to which were granted exclusive
privileges like those of the Belgian *concessionaires.*

Virtually no reserves of land were retained for new ar-
rivals or for free commerce; practically all was alienated for
thirty years. As Leroy-Beaulieu wrote, "it was an orgy of
concessions." The same abuses followed as in the Belgian
Congo—forced labor and gross maltreatment of the natives,
together with the closed door to foreign trade.[13]

Lever Brothers of Port Sunlight, to develop the palm oil resources of the
Congo. On the extensive activities of this important concern, see Du
Plessis, "Thrice Through the Dark Continent," pp. 249, 250, 269, 270,
London, 1917, and *infra*, pp. 126, 129 [also "Manual of Belgian Congo," pp.
184-186; for commercial companies in the Belgian Congo, see *ibid.*, pp.
304-312].

[12] A. Debidour, *op. cit.*, pp. 193, 245-248.

[13] P. Leroy-Beaulieu, "De la Colonisation chez les Peuples Modernes"
(5th ed.), II, pp. 199, 200; Sir H. H. Johnston, *op. cit.*, pp. 230-234; H. A.

Anglo-French Controversy.—As these concessionary companies had the sole right to gather the produce of their vast domains, the established business of a number of British merchants trading with the natives for ebony, ivory, and rubber was ruined. The injured parties—notably the eminent African merchant, John Holt of Liverpool, and Hatton and Cookson—invoked the Berlin Act of 1885, but the colonial courts held that the prohibition of commercial monopolies by this Act was not pertinent, since the harvesting of nature's produce was not an act of commerce. The French Government took the same stand in answering the complaints of the British Foreign Office. A long controversy ensued, beginning in 1902 and running through the first Morocco crisis down to the eve of Agadir. Sir Edward Grey consistently opposed the theory of the French and Belgian concessionary companies, that the gathering of the products of the forest was not commerce, and refused to admit that the activities of the British merchants should be restricted to buying the meager products of native art and industry. He proposed to arbitrate the matter or to convoke an international conference to pass upon it. France, however, refused both offers and clung steadfastly to the letter of the Berlin Act, ignoring its spirit. It was contended that the French Government had acted within its sovereign rights in a matter in no way within the scope of the Berlin Act and that the question was purely a

Gibbons, *op. cit.,* pp. 342-350; A. Girault, "The Colonial Tariff Policy of France," p. 240; G. Bruel, "L'Afrique Équatoriale Française," pp. 428-435, 440-442; A. G. Leonard, "French Equatorial Africa," in *United Empire Magazine,* V (1914), pp. 238 ff.; E. D. Morel, "British Case in French Congo," and, also, his "Affairs of West Africa"; F. Challaye, "Le Congo Français: La Question Internationale du Congo."

domestic one, wholly inside the domain of internal sovereignty.[14]

French Reforms.—In 1906, possibly out of gratitude for Great Britain's support at Algeciras, France agreed to indemnify the injured British merchants, without, however, conceding the principle at stake.[15] Fresh disputes arose, lasting down to 1911.[16] In the meanwhile, the concessionary system was not proving a success and was evoking considerable hostility in France. The privileged companies were not developing the colony, and it was being realized that the policy was a blunder.[17] In 1910-11 the rights of these companies were greatly limited and a larger field was opened to the activities of French and foreign private traders.[18] The evils of the old system were, however, not completely eradicated.[19] The large tracts of land

[14] André Tardieu, "Le Mystère d'Agadir," pp. 209-245.

[15] *Ibid.*, pp. 255-257.

[16] *Ibid.*, pp. 260-285 *et seq.*

[17] Shortly after this, the Governor of French Equatorial Africa, M. Merlin, admitted that this policy had been a blunder. A. G. Leonard, *op. cit.*, pp. 239, 240. For details as to the development effected by these companies, see *ibid.*, pp. 242, 243.

[18] Tardieu, *op. cit.*, p. 348; A. Girault, *op. cit.*, p. 240. In 1910, new arrangements were made with the chief companies on the basis of the cultivation or development of the soil. The companies were permitted to select blocks of land of definite limits, but the title was to revert to them in 1920 only if they had systematically developed their holdings during the preceding decade. "All rubber concessions were to revert to the State in 1920, and after that time leases would be renewed yearly, subject to the production and conduct of the companies." Rights of the natives to their own villages and lands and to collect the forest produce from undeveloped lands were recognized. H. A. Gibbons, *op. cit.*, p. 350 n. For full details, see "Annuaire du Gouvernement Général de l'Afrique Équatoriale Française," 1912, II, pp. 223-322; Bruel, "L'Afrique Équatoriale Française," pp. 439-440.

[19] About the time of the outbreak of the war, the trade of the privileged companies in Gabun represented somewhat less than a third and in the Middle Congo more than a half of the external commerce of these two divisions of French Equatorial Africa. Girault, *op. cit.*, p. 241.

held by the concessionary companies worked against free trade and enabled them to control a large part of the commerce, especially in rubber, although the share of the private traders was increasing rapidly.[20]

[*Convention of 1919.*—During the Peace Conference a Commission was appointed to consider revision of the General Act of Berlin and the General Act and Declaration of Brussels. This Commission drew up three Conventions—one to control traffic in arms and ammunition; one for further restriction of the importation, manufacture, and sale of distilled beverages; [21] and one of a general character. All three were signed simultaneously with the Austrian Treaty, September 10, 1919. The general Convention [22] restricts equality of treatment of nationals, merchandise, vessels, missionaries, and scientists to "the nationals of the Signatory Powers, and to those of States, Members of the League of Nations, which may adhere to the present

[20] British Diplomatic and Consular Reports, No. 5249, pp. 4, 8; No. 5494, pp. 6, 7, 9. The proportional percentage of the shares of the concessionary companies in the special commerce from 1903 to 1911 was as follows (Bruel, *op. cit.*, p. 438):

	Imports	*Exports*	*Total*
1903	36	69	55
1904	38	80	59
1905	49	75	63
1906	49	68	60
1907	49	65	58
1908	41	76	63
1909	33	78	60
1910	28	72	57
1911	26	64	46

The decline in the percentage of exports in 1908-11 was due to the fact that the loan of 1909 and the military occupation led to the importation of considerable material for the account of the administration (*ibid.*, p. 437).

[21] See *infra*, pp. 170-171, 176-178.

[22] For the complete text of this Convention, see Annex G.

Convention," whereas the Berlin Act extends such equality to all nations. The Convention sets no time limit for ratification, which is to be "as soon as possible," whereas the maximum delay allowed by the Berlin and Brussels Acts is one year. Freedom of conscience and free exercise of all forms of religion "shall be subject," according to the Convention, "only to such restrictions as may be necessary for the maintenance of public security and order, or as may result from the enforcement of the constitutional law of any of the Powers exercising authority in African territories." The Berlin Act makes no such restrictions. In case of controversy between the High Contracting Parties, the Berlin Act requires mediation of "one or more friendly Powers"; the Convention states that such dispute "shall be submitted to an arbitral tribunal in conformity with the provisions of the League of Nations." The Berlin Act provides merely that the Signatory Powers reserve the right to make "subsequently, and by common consent," modifications or improvements which experience may show to be necessary; the Convention requires a conference at the expiration of ten years from the coming into force of the document for the introduction of modifications. The Convention also has several stipulations found neither in the Berlin nor in the Brussels Act. Subject to the provisions of equality already noted, "the States concerned reserve to themselves complete liberty as to the customs and navigation regulations and tariffs to be applied in their territories." Similarly, on condition of like equality of treatment, each State "reserves the right to dispose freely of its property and to grant concessions for the development of the natural

resources of the territory." Finally, all provisions of the
General Act of Berlin and of the General Act and Declaration of Brussels, with the exception of the delimitation of
the Conventional Basin of the Congo, are abrogated in so
far as binding between the High Contracting Parties signatory to the present Convention.[23]]

2. The Area Outside the Conventional Basin

Importance of This Area.—The area of Middle Africa
outside this Conventional Basin is very large and includes
some of the richest and most populous colonies. Such are:
British West Africa—Gambia, Sierra Leone, Gold Coast,
and Nigeria—covering 444,842 square miles and possessing
a population of 20 millions [24]; and French West Africa

[23] For the transactions of this Commission, see "Procès-Verbaux et
Rapport de la Commission pour la Révision des Actes Généraux de Berlin
et de Bruxelles," pp. 101-130, 132-136. The reasons for the divergencies
from the Berlin and Brussels Acts noted in the text (other than those
contained in the Anglo-French draft which formed the basis of the Commission's work) were as follows: The restriction of equality of treatment
to "the nationals of the Signatory Powers and to those of States, Members
of the League of Nations, which may adhere to the present Convention,"
was due, both here and elsewhere in this document, to Mr. Beer, the
representative of the United States on the Commission, in order that
Germany might not enjoy the privileges of the Convention without belonging to the League (pp. 103-104). To him was due also the setting
of a period of ten years as the date for the reassembly of the Signatory
Powers for introducing into the Convention "such modifications as experience may have shown to be necessary" (p. 128). The stipulation
governing concessions gave rise to some discussion (pp. 107, 113-115) during
which the clause was changed to its present form from its reading in the
original draft, "each Power will, however, remain free to dispose of its
private domain according to the laws in force in this respect in its possessions." The limitation of the free exercise of all forms of religion by
such restrictions "as may result from the enforcement of the constitutional law of any of the Powers exercising authority in African territories" was introduced by the Portuguese delegate, Colonel Norton de
Mattos, to ensure the exclusion from colonial territories of such religious
orders as might be prohibited in the mother-country (pp. 134-135).

[24] Census of 1911. "Statistical Abstract of the British Empire," 1915, p. 7,

with an expanse of 1,478,000 square miles and an estimated
population of 12½ millions.[25] Beyond the internationally
established free-trade area are also Togoland and the bulk
of the Cameroons, practically all of Portuguese East and
West Africa, the whole of Liberia and Spanish Rio Muni,
and a section of French Equatorial Africa.   The total for-

[25] *The Statesman's Year-Book*, 1917, p. 883. The estimates of popula-
tion, and of the area also, vary somewhat. See A. Girault, "The Colonial
Tariff Policy of France," p. 225; J. Saxon Mills, "The French Colonial
Empire," in *United Empire Magazine*, September, 1914, p. 715; N. D.
Harris, "Intervention and Colonization in Africa," p. 129; Sir H. H.
Johnston, "The History of the Colonization of Africa by Alien Races,"
pp. 209, 211; British Diplomatic and Consular Reports, No. 5423, p. 4.
Bruel ("L'Afrique Équatoriale Française," p. 480) gives the area of French
West Africa as 3,910,000 square kilometers and its population as 11,000,000,
while the area of French Equatorial Africa is estimated at 2,256,000
square kilometers and its population at 8,000,000.   He also records (p.
353) the following estimates of population for French Equatorial Africa,
though thinking that the figure is really 6,000,000 natives:

Colony	Before 1911	After the Cession to Germany, November 4, 1911
Chad Territory	1,650,000	350,000
Ubangi-Shari	1,350,000	240,000
Middle Congo	900,000	490,000
Gabun	1,050,000	250,000
Total	4,950,000	1,330,000

[According to the census of 1921, the approximate area and population of
French West Africa are as follows:

Colony	Area (square miles)	Non-African Races French	Non-African Races Foreign	African Races French	Total
Senegal	74,112	3,507	814	1,221,202	1,225,523
Guinea	95,218	751	606	1,874,639	1,875,996
Ivory Coast	121,976	728	107	1,544,845	1,545,680
Dahomey	42,460	470	68	841,705	842,243
French Sudan	617,600	843	140	2,473,606	2,474,589
Upper Volta	154,400	180	11	2,973,951	2,974,142
Mauritania	347,400	135	79	261,532	261,746
Territory of Niger	347,400	215	1	1,083,827	1,084,043
Total	1,800,566	6,829	1,826	12,275,307	12,283,962

The Statesman's Year-Book, 1922, p. 917.]

eign commerce of Middle Africa in 1913 amounted roughly
to 347 million dollars, of which about 97 millions belonged
to the Conventional Basin. Approximately two thirds of
this trade in the Basin was shared in equal parts by the
Belgian Congo and the British colonies. The foreign trade
of the area outside the Conventional Basin was in 1913
roughly 250 million dollars, of which the share of British
West Africa was 152 millions, that of French West Africa
55 millions, that of the Cameroons and Togoland 21 millions, and that of Portuguese Africa (excluding the cocoa
islands) 19½ millions.[26] Thus, commercially, this territory
is far more important than the Conventional Basin, where
free trade prevails according to international agreement.
In spite of the lack of such covenant covering this outside region, Great Britain and Germany have consistently
adhered to free trade. On the other hand, France and Portugal, as well as Spain,[27] still cling to the tenets of the mercantile system and discriminate against foreign trade with
their colonies.

[26] APPROXIMATE FOREIGN TRADE OF MIDDLE AFRICA, 1913

(in millions of dollars)

	Total	Within Basin	Outside Basin
British Colonies	183	31	152
French Colonies	67	12	55
German Colonies	43	22	21
Belgian Congo	32	32	..
Portuguese Colonies	19½	..	19½
Liberia	2½	..	2½
	347	97	250

It should be noted that there is some duplication in these figures resulting from intercolonial trade.

[27] In the Spanish territories in the Gulf of Guinea, there are different
schedules for foreign goods or for goods imported under a foreign flag,
and for Spanish products imported under the Spanish flag. Exports are
free if to a Spanish port under the Spanish flag, but are subject to duty

The French Fiscal System.—(a) Treaty Restrictions.— As regards fiscal policy, the French colonies are divided into three classes: first, those in which equality of trade prevails under international agreements; second, those which have been assimilated to the protective system of France and brought within her customs barriers; third, those with autonomous tariffs, but granting preferential treatment to French goods and receiving corresponding advantages for their products in the market of the metropolis. In addition to the Berlin Act of 1885, which prescribed absolute equality of commercial treatment in the part of French Equatorial Africa within the Conventional Basin, France is bound by the Nigerian Treaty of 1898. One clause thereof provides that for thirty years from the date of its ratification—that is, June 13, 1899—British and French persons and goods shall enjoy equality of treatment as regards river navigation, commerce, tariffs, and taxes in a carefully defined region of West Africa.[28] The French

if to a foreign port or under a foreign flag. Kelly's "Customs Tariffs of the World," 1918, p. 623.

[28] Article IX of the Anglo-French Treaty of June 14, 1898. Hertslet, "The Map of Africa by Treaty" (3d ed.), II, pp. 789, 790 ["Trattati . . . relativi all'Africa," p. 599]. In 1899 the limits of this region were extended to include the entire area south of 14° 20′ N. and north of 5° N., between 14° 20′ East of Greenwich and the course of the Upper Nile. Hertslet, *op. cit.*, p. 796 ["Trattati," pp. 613-614]; *Documents Diplomatiques, Correspondance Concernant la Déclaration Additionelle du 21 Mars 1899, passim,* Paris, 1899, and especially the annexed map.

By treaty, this equality also existed in the Shari Basin. In Article 3 of the Franco-German Convention of March 15, 1894 (Hertslet, *op. cit.,* II, pp. 658, 659), Germany and France agreed respectively concerning navigation of the Benue and its affluents within the sphere of influence of the former, and the navigation of the Mayo Kebbi and other tributaries of the Benue within the sphere of influence of the latter, to enforce the provisions of Articles 26, 27, 28, 29, 31, 32, and 33 of the Berlin Act of 1885, as well as the stipulations of the Brussels Act of 1890 regarding importation of arms and liquors. These provisions likewise held in refer-

colonies within this area are Dahomey and the Ivory Coast. Accordingly, in them there is no discrimination against foreign trade; and the customs duties, in general ten per cent *ad valorem*, are levied uniformly on all goods, no matter what be their origin.[29] As a result, these markets are wide open to foreign wares. Of total imports of textiles into Dahomey and the Ivory Coast amounting to 9 million francs in 1911, 7 million came from Great Britain. Of other imports, 9 million were French, 5 British, and 5 German.[30] This state of affairs has evoked considerable adverse comment in France, where the monopolistic principles of the old colonial system have still a strong hold.[31]

ence to the Shari and Logone, with their affluents. By Article 4 of this Convention, "les tarifs des taxes ou droits qui pourront être établis de part et d'autre ne comporteront, à l'égard des commerçants des deux pays, aucun traitement différentiel." By another Franco-German Convention of April 18, 1908 (Hertslet, *op. cit.*, III, pp. 1218, 1219), free navigation of the Benue, Mayo Kebbi, Shari, Logone, Sanga, and other affluents was to be governed by the above-mentioned Articles of the Berlin Act (Article 2). Article 3 was essentially the same as Article 4 of the former Convention, except that it was drawn "à l'égard des nationaux, sujets et protégés des deux pays." The Convention of 1894 established equal duties in the part of the Cameroons outside the Conventional Basin and it antedated the Anglo-French Treaty of 1898 regarding the Shari Basin on account of the favored-nation clause. No customhouse was established in the "Territoire du Tchad" and merchandise leaving or entering by the Benue, by Zinder or Kano, or by the frontiers north and east of the Chad were really free of duty. It was believed advisable, for the time being, to facilitate Central African commerce by these means, especially as the land frontiers with the Cameroons, the Egyptian Sudan, and Libya are too long (over 4,000 kilometers) to admit of watch and control of the commercial routes. Bruel, *op. cit.*, p. 425.

[29] Bruel, *op. cit.*, pp. 423, 424; Girault, *op. cit.*, pp. 112, 113.

[30] *Ibid.*, p. 232. In 1913, the total imports into the Ivory Coast were 18.2 million francs, of which France supplied 6.7, the United Kingdom 6.6, and Germany 2.9. British Diplomatic and Consular Reports, No. 5423, p. 27.

[31] Thus, shortly after his succession to William Ponty as Governor General of French West Africa, M. Clozel complained that the colony was burdened by a tariff system which had put more than thirty per cent of

(b) Assimilated Colonies.—The method in the French
assimilated colonies is essentially the same as that applied
in the case of Porto Rico, Hawaii, and the Philippines; they
are placed within the protective barriers of the Mother
Country. The French tariff prevails in the colony with
regard to foreign goods, while between the colony and
France there is free trade. In Middle Africa, the part of
Gabun outside the Conventional Basin alone came within
this category. In that section of French Equatorial Africa
—80,000 square miles out of a total of 660,000—the high
protective duties of France must be paid on foreign goods,
while in the rest of the colony, in accordance with the
Berlin and Brussels Acts, only revenue levies of ten per
cent, and in some cases even less, were assessed on all commodities alike.[32] The system was decidedly unsatisfactory.
The high duties led to considerable fraud and smuggling,
not only between the two parts of the French colony under
different tariffs, but also across the borders of the neighboring colonies.[33] Effective supervision over so long a frontier
in an unsettled country was out of the question. It was
clear that a uniform system for the entire French colony
was essential and also that tariff unification throughout
the whole area was highly advisable. No fully satisfactory
scheme was possible without international action and the
coöperation of the authorities in the adjacent Belgian, Ger-

the business of its southern parts into German hands. *L'Afrique Française,* 1916, pp. 54, 55.
[32] Girault, *op. cit.,* pp. 112, 113, 116, 117, 293, 294.
[33] With regard to Gabun, Bruel states (*op. cit.,* p. 424) that the decrees
of December 29, 1892, July 8, 1900, and December 31, 1903, "decreased
and suppressed the duties of the general tariff for certain articles."

man, Portuguese, and Spanish colonies.[34]   Not only did
the high duties divert trade from Gabun, but they did not
even prevent foreign goods from being legally imported on
a relatively considerable scale.   In 1913, out of 8.6 million
francs' imports into Gabun, 3.9 came from the foreign
countries.[35] It is true that the percentage of imports from
France was far larger than in the remainder of French
Equatorial Africa; still, the metropolis had by no means a
complete monopoly.

(c)   Tariff Autonomy.—An entirely different system
prevailed in French West Africa.   A part of this colony—

[34] Girault, *op. cit.*, pp. 236-239.
[35] Bruel (*op. cit.*, p. 427) gives the following figures, in millions of francs,
for imports in 1911:

CONVENTIONAL BASIN			GABUN			TOTAL		
French	*Foreign*	*Total*	*French*	*Foreign*	*Total*	*French*	*Foreign*	*Total*
4.8	5.	9.8	2.9	2.1	5.	7.7	7.1	14.8

Thus, the percentage of French imports into the Conventional Basin
was 49, and into Gabun 58.

The figures given by Girault (*op. cit.*, pp. 241-243) differ considerably.
The percentages for 1892-97 and for 1909-11 are as follows for French
imports (Bruel, p. 424):

	Conventional Basin	*Gabun*
1892	23.	40.
1893	23.	63.
1894	10.	42.
1895	12.	44.
1896	15.	43.
1897	12.	38.
1909	33.	59.
1910	41.	61.
1911	49.	58.

For 1913, the imports, in millions of francs, were:

	French Equatorial Africa	*Gabun*	*Middle Congo*
Total	21.2	8.6	12.6
From France	8.8	4.7	4.1

British Diplomatic and Consular Reports, No. 5494, pp. 9-14. See also
No. 5249, p. 7. It should be noted that the statistics of this colony are
very unreliable.

Dahomey and the Ivory Coast—was bound to equality of trade, but in the remainder, and by far the richest and largest section, a preferential schedule had been established.[36] In Senegal, French Guinea, and the French Sudan, imports paid customs of varying amounts and foreign goods a further surtax of considerable extent.[37] In addition, the products of these colonies on entering France were subject, as a general rule, to the minimum tariff, but in very many instances the customs were further lowered or they were exempted from all duties. Thus, coffee from French West Africa, and cocoa from French Guinea, Dahomey, and the Ivory Coast, were assessed only half the normal duties, while palm oil and woods were exempted from all payments.[38]   The net result was that the trade

[36] FOREIGN COMMERCE OF FRENCH WEST AFRICA, 1913
(in millions of francs)

Colony	Imports	Exports
Senegal	88.	72.9
Upper Senegal and Niger	10.8	3.7
French Guinea	19.4	16.6
Ivory Coast	18.2	16.4
Dahomey	15.2	16.5
	151.6	126.1

British Diplomatic and Consular Reports, No. 5423, p. 17.
[For 1918, 1919, and 1920 the figures were (*The Statesman's Year-Book*, 1921, p. 896; 1922, p. 918):

Colony	Imports			Exports		
	1918	1919	1920	1918	1919	1920
Senegal	295.8	198.2	443.9	215.2	202.2	428.7
French Guinea	23.	25.9	47.4	12.8	23.5	34.2
Ivory Coast	15.8	23.5	55.2	13.2	28.5	60.2
Dahomey	28.3	44.4	93.7	30.	70.1	63.6
Total	362.9	292.0	640.2	271.2	324.3	586.7]

[37] "Annuaire du Gouvernement Général de l'Afrique Occidentale Française," 1913-14, pp. 85-87.
[38] Girault, *op. cit.*, p. 117.

of the colony, both in its imports and its exports, tended to center in France. There was still room, however, for foreign competition, especially in textiles, which constituted about one third of the imports into French West Africa. Of the imports of cotton goods into Senegal, Guinea, and the Sudan in 1911, 16 million francs came from Great Britain, 12.5 from France and her colonies, and 1 million from Germany. On the other hand, of the imports exclusive of textiles, 16 million came from France, 10 from Great Britain, and 4.5 from Germany.[39] The French cotton manufacturers were greatly dissatisfied with this state of affairs and for years demanded increased protection. This was conceded shortly before the outbreak of the war. The new tariff changed the *ad valorem* duties into specific ones that were prohibitive as regards a considerable proportion of the cotton goods imported from Great Britain.[40] This monopolistic system was a marked feature of French colonial policy and had a strong hold upon mercantile and official classes in France.

The Portuguese Colonial System.—In the case of Portugal, this policy of monopolizing the colonial trade was even more accentuated. The method that prevailed was a direct survival of the practice of the seventeenth and eighteenth centuries. The fiscal arrangements differed in the various colonies, the greatest degree of discrimination prevailing in the cocoa islands São Thomé and Principe and the least in Portuguese Guinea. Naturally, there was

[39] Girault, *op. cit.*, pp. 231, 232.
[40] British Diplomatic and Consular Reports, No. 5423, p. 6. This decree of March 3, 1914, is in "Annuaire du Gouvernement Général de l'Afrique Occidentale Française," 1913-14, pp. 87, 90-93.

none in the Congo district within the Conventional Basin.
In general, Portuguese goods and those of foreign origin
imported through Portugal received marked preferential
treatment in the colonies. In return, the products of the
colonies were similarly favored in Portugal. In order to
make it doubly sure that these products would be shipped
there, a system of discriminating export duties was established in the cocoa islands and in Angola. In Angola, the
general rule was that goods shipped to Portugal paid three
per cent, as opposed to fifteen per cent if exported to
foreign markets. As a result of this comprehensive system,
the trade of Portuguese West Africa centered at Lisbon,
whence the colonial products were distributed. From here
also were shipped the great bulk of the supplies—Portuguese and foreign—needed by these colonies.[41]

3.   The Problem of the Open Door

Trade and the Flag.—If, as we have seen, the restrictive policy which was followed centered almost the entire
trade of Angola and of the Portuguese cocoa islands—São
Thomé and Principe—at Lisbon,[42] the commerce of the

---

[41] Kelly's "Customs Tariffs of the World," 1918, pp. 492-506; British
Diplomatic and Consular Reports, No. 5385, p. 8; No. 5402, pp. 12-14;
No. 5496, p. 4; No. 5497, pp. 10, 11; No. 5529, pp. 3, 4; George Young,
"Portugal Old and Young: An Historical Study," pp. 324-330, Oxford,
1917; Angel Marvaud, "La Situation Politique et Économique du Portu-
gal," in *Questions Diplomatiques et Coloniales*, 37 (1914), p. 87.

[42] For details, see "Annuário Colonial da 1916," pp. 233-236, 260, 292,
375-378. In Portuguese East Africa the situation was different, on account
of the fact that the major share of the trade of the southern part was
merely one of transit with the Transvaal, while Northern Mozambique
also had close commercial ties with British countries. Thus, of total
imports for local consumption into the Chinde District in 1913, amounting
to £198,040, £76,057 came from Portugal and her possessions, £95,601 from

Belgian Congo was in like manner confined to the Mother Country, notwithstanding the general reforms and the limitation of the privileges of the concessionary companies. In 1912, sixty-six per cent of the imports for consumption in the Belgian Congo came from the metropolis and ninety per cent of the colony's produce went there.[43] In French Equatorial Africa the proportion of French trade was considerably less than this. In 1913, about fifty per cent of the special commerce of this colony was with France.[44] This also was the approximate situation in French West Africa.[45]

British territories, £16,298 from German territories, and £10,084 from other sources. British Diplomatic and Consular Reports, No. 5484, p. 4. See also *ibid.,* No. 5306, p. 3. On this whole Section of the present chapter, cf. also *infra,* pp. 213-220.

[43] Special Commerce of the Belgian Congo 1912:

Imports, 53.9 million francs, of which 35.8 came from Belgium; exports, 59 million francs, of which 53.9 went to Belgium. *The Statesman's Year-Book,* 1915, p. 734; British Diplomatic and Consular Reports, No. 5260, pp. 5, 18, 19. In 1911, the corresponding proportions were 64 per cent and 88 per cent. *L'Afrique Française,* 1913, p. 207. For 1910-1912, the following figures, in millions of francs, are recorded in the "Annuaire Statistique de la Belgique et du Congo Belge," 1913, p. 520, Brussels, 1914:

	GENERAL				SPECIAL					
	IMPORTS		EXPORTS		IMPORTS		EXPORTS		*Total*	*Grand*
	Belgian	*Total*	*Belgian*	*Total*	*Belgian*	*Total*	*Belgian*	*Total*	*Belgian*	*Total*
1910	29.2	44	69.7	95.6	27.3	36.8	58.7	66.6	184.9	243.
1911	34.3	58.4	56.8	79.	31.4	48.6	47.6	54.1	170.1	240.1
1912	38.3	62.2	64.4	84.3	35.9	54.2	54.2	59.9	192.8	260.6

[Cf. also "Manual of Belgian Congo," pp. 273-274.]

[44] Bruel, "L'Afrique Équatoriale Française," pp. 452-464; British Diplomatic and Consular Reports, No. 5249, pp. 5, 11; No. 5494, pp. 8-14; A. Girault, "The Colonial Tariff Policy of France," pp. 239-242.

[45] British Diplomatic and Consular Reports, No. 5423, pp. 17, 25-43; Girault, *op. cit.,* pp. 227, 231-232. In 1913, the total commerce of the French territories under the Ministry of Colonies amounted to 1,445 million francs (imports, 680 millions; exports, 765 millions), an increase of 155 million francs over 1912, and of 278 million francs over the average for 1908-12. The share of France in this total was 588,470,000 francs, or 40.67 per cent (imports 284,255,000, or 41.70 per cent; exports 304,215,000,

But it was by no means only in the case of these Portuguese, Belgian, and French colonies, where freedom of trade had been or was in varying degrees restricted, that commerce followed the national flag. This condition was just as marked in the British and German colonies, where free trade prevailed. In the British colonies in 1913-14, sixty-two per cent of the imports had that destination. Of their total foreign trade, fifty-five per cent was with the metrop-

or 40 per cent); that of the French colonies themselves was only 2.48 per cent (imports 3 per cent, exports 2.45 per cent). "Statistique du Commerce des Colonies Françaises," 1913, I, p. 1, Paris, 1915. The statistics for the trade of the various colonies of French Africa in 1913, in millions of francs, were as follows (ibid., pp. 12-13, 43, 56-57, 227, 231-232, 275, 277, 291, 415, 422, 507, 634, 636; cf. also "Renseignements Généraux sur le Commerce des Colonies Françaises," 1914-1917, p. 8).

Colony	IMPORTS				EXPORTS				TOTAL			
	France	Colonies	Foreign	Total	France	Colonies	Foreign	Total	France	Colonies	Foreign	Total
French West Africa.....	66.54	2.3	82.11	150.95	66.3	.4	59.4	126.1	132.84	2.7	141.51	277.05
French Equatorial Africa	8.7	.08	12.4	21.18	14.4	....	22.3	36.7	23.1	.08	34.7	57.88
Madagascar...........	......	....	......	......	......	....	......	......	73.2	....	29.6	102.8
French Somaliland......	......	....	......	......	......	....	......	......	11.4	....	70.2	81.6
Senegal...............	42.	.8	45.5	88.3	44.4	.03	28.5	72.93	86.4	.83	74.	161.23
Upper Senegal & Niger..	7.	1.2	2.6	10.8	3.6	....	.01	3.61	10.6	1.2	2.61	14.41
French Guinea.........	7.9	....	11.5	19.4	7.7	....	8.9	16.6	15.6	....	20.4	36.
Ivory Coast...........	6.7	.04	11.46	18.2	6.6	....	9.8	16.4	13.3	.04	21.26	34.6
Dahomey..............	3.3	....	11.8	15.1	4.1	....	12.4	16.5	7.4	....	24.2	31.6
Total..............	142.14	4.42	177.37	323.93	147.1	.43	141.31	288.84	373.84	4.85	418.48	797.17

The percentages are as follows (cf. also "Renseignements Généraux sur le Commerce des Colonies Françaises," 1914-1917, pp. 10-11):

Colony	IMPORTS			EXPORTS			TOTAL		
	France	Colonies	Foreign	France	Colonies	Foreign	France	Colonies	Foreign
French West Africa.............	44.08	1.52	54.4	52.59	.33	47.08	47.95	.97	51.08
French Equatorial Africa........	41.08	.38	58.54	39.3	...	60.7	40.	.15	59.85
Madagascar...................	....	....	....	....	...	....	71.21	....	28.79
French Somaliland.............	....	....	....	....	...	....	13.97	....	86.03
Senegal......................	47.57	.9	51.53	60.88	.04	39.08	53.59	.51	45.9
Upper Senegal & Niger..........	64.82	11.11	24.07	99.72	...	.28	73.56	8.33	18.11
French Guinea.................	40.72	....	59.28	46.39	...	53.61	43.33	....	56.67
Ivory Coast...................	36.91	.21	62.88	40.24	...	59.76	38.21	.46	61.33
Dahomey.....................	21.85	....	78.15	24.85	...	75.15	23.42	....	76.58
Total....................	43.88	1.36	54.76	50.93	.15	48.92	46.9	.61	52.49

olis.[46] In the case of the German colonies, the proportion was greater, sixty-three per cent of their foreign commerce in 1912 being with Germany. For the Cameroons this figure was eighty-two per cent, which was even higher than the corresponding percentage for the Belgian Congo.[47] Only

[46] FOREIGN TRADE OF THE BRITISH COLONIES
(*in millions of pounds sterling*)

	Colony	Total Imports	From United Kingdom	Total Exports	To United Kingdom
1913-14	Nyasaland	0.2	0.15	0.3	0.2
1913-14	Uganda	1.	0.4	0.6	0.3
1913-14	East Africa	2.1	0.9	1.5	0.7
1913	Nigeria	7.2	4.9	7.4	3.7
1913	Gold Coast	5.	3.5	5.4	3.5
1913	Sierra Leone	1.8	1.1	1.7	0.2
1913	Gambia	1.	.4	0.9	0.06
		18.3	11.4 (62%)	17.8	8.7 (49%)

Total 36.1, of which 20.1, or 55 per cent, were with the United Kingdom; "Statistical Abstract of the British Empire," 1915, pp. 230-247.

[For 1919-20 the figures were (*The Statesman's Year-Book*, 1921, pp. xvii, xix):

Colony	Total Imports	From United Kingdom	Total Exports	To United Kingdom
Nyasaland	1.9	.5	2.4	.4
Uganda	3.4	1.6	2.5	1.3
East Africa (Kenya)	.5	..	.2	..
Nigeria	12.	10.4	14.7	..
Gold Coast	7.9	6.	10.8	4.9
Sierra Leone	2.1	1.4	2.1	1.4
Gambia	1.2	.7	1.5	1.1
Total	29.0	20.6 (71%)	34.2	9.1 (26.6%)]

[47] FOREIGN TRADE OF THE GERMAN COLONIES
(*in millions of marks*)

Colony	Total	With Germany	Percentage
German East Africa	81.7	43.6	53.4
Cameroons	57.6	47.	81.73
Togoland	21.4	10.6	49.69
	160.7	101.2	63.

"Die Deutschen Schutzgebiete," 1914, p. xix; *Statistisches Jahrbuch*, 1915, pp. 463-467.

to some extent was this situation the result of the industrial superiority of Britain and Germany. It was and is largely inherent in the colonial status itself. That trade tends to follow the flag is the resultant of many forces.

The Factor of Transportation.—One of these is the question of transportation. The political relations between colony and metropolis necessitate regular communications and these, in turn, facilitate the interchange of commodities. The shipping of the Mother Country tends to be predominant in the oversea possession. In view of British maritime primacy, such preponderance was not surprising in the case of the British colonies,[48] but the corresponding situation prevailed also in the Belgian Congo.[49] In some instances, furthermore, protective legislation and direct or indirect subsidies had established a virtual monopoly for ships flying the national flag. This was the case in the

[48] Vessels Entered and Cleared in 1913

	Total	British
Gross Tonnage British East Africa	3,201,939	1,460,916
Net Tonnage British West Africa	8,281,229	5,249,348

"Statistical Abstract of the British Empire," 1915, pp. 27, 29.

[49] Tonnage of Ocean Vessels Entered in the Belgian Congo in 1912

	At Banana	At Boma	At Matadi
Belgian	155,066	199,781	79,914
British	90,175	111,950	56,348
French	69,636	68,249	34,584
German	60,768	67,579	31,622

British Diplomatic and Consular Reports, No. 5260, pp. 16, 17.
[For 1913, the figures were ("Manual of Belgian Congo," pp. 257-258):

	At Banana	At Boma	At Matadi
Belgian	153,537	161,939	81,117
British	68,639	63,886	33,105
French	70,312	69,494	35,102
German	73,814	60,748	33,357
Portuguese	......	10,225	4,526

On the Congolese ports in general, see *ibid.*, pp. 253-260.]

Portuguese colonial trade.[50] Similarly, the German East Africa Line received a considerable subsidy from the Government,[51] which strengthened the monopolistic hold of German vessels on commerce with the colonies.[52] One

[50] In 1913, shipping of an aggregate of one million tons entered Angola. Of this amount, 710,512 was Portuguese. British Diplomatic and Consular Reports, No. 5402, p. 8. In São Thomé, of the entrances 353,259 tons were Portuguese, 35,740 British, and 28,298 German. *Ibid.*, No. 5496, p. 6. In addition to other protective devices, Portugal granted shipping subsidies. *Ibid.*, No. 5418, p. 5. See also "Annuário Colonial da 1916," p. 151.

[51] W. Ross, "Die Entwicklung der Schiffahrt nach den Deutschen Kolonien," in *Weltverkehr*, 1914-15, pp. 87-90.

[52] MARITIME INTERCOURSE IN 1912
(in tons)

Colony	Total	German
German Africa	1,811,107	1,771,997
Cameroons	1,658,230	1,254,250
Togoland	571,832	414,731

Statistisches Jahrbuch, 1915, p. 460. In the case of the French colonies, there was no such predominance of the national shipping. Of 4,864,961 tons entering the ports of those colonies in West Africa in 1912, only 1,628,412 were French. Supplement to "Bulletin de l'Office Colonial," No. 75, March, 1914. In 1913, the distribution of entering tonnage for ocean traffic and coasting trade was as follows ("Statistiques de la Navigation dans les Colonies Françaises," 1913, pp. 18-19, 22-23, Paris, 1915; for Gabun, see also Girault, *op. cit.*, p. 463):

Colony	OCEAN TRAFFIC			COASTING TRADE		
	French	Foreign	Total	French	Foreign	Total
Senegal	1,077,781	1,674,795	2,752,576	132,537	11,691	144,228
French Guinea	199,993	606,855	806,848	64,322	5,828	70,150
Ivory Coast	199,770	810,956	1,010,726	......	......	......
Dahomey	232,664	385,530	618,194	28,367	96,728	125,095
Gabun	112,272	325,907	438,179	197,839	207,891	405,730
Total	1,822,480	3,804,043	5,626,523	423,065	322,138	745,203

The total entering tonnage would, therefore, be:

Colony	French	Foreign	Total
Senegal	1,210,318	1,686,486	2,896,804
French Guinea	264,315	612,683	876,998
Ivory Coast	199,770	810,956	1,010,726
Dahomey	261,031	482,258	743,289
Gabun	310,111	533,798	843,909
Total	2,245,545	4,126,181	6,371,726

The number of vessels entering and clearing from ports in the territories under the control of the French Ministry of Colonies in the same year

direct consequence of this predominance of the national shipping in trade with the oversea territory was increased commercial interdependence of colony and metropolis.

Personal and National Factors.—Other factors were equally, if not more, important in establishing these closer ties. The personal equation enters largely into business relations. It was easier for a Frenchman to do business in a French colony than it was for a German and *vice versa*. Apart from all else, difference of language is a barrier and, besides, greater confidence is placed in a compatriot than in an alien. Moreover, the public authorities and those in charge of transportation and docking facilities are prone, at times purposely, but also at other times unconsciously, to favor their fellow citizens. No regulation or legislation can eliminate this factor of sympathy and prejudice, which must enter largely into the question of establishing the open door in dependent and backward countries. So long as there are distinct and sharply segregated nations and states, and men are primarily Americans, Englishmen, Frenchmen, and Germans, the full attainment of this goal is impossible. Until national prejudices are eradicated, and until the State is no longer regarded as carrying on trade through its individual members, commerce is bound to follow the flag to a more or less marked extent.

was, together with their tonnage ("Statistiques de la Navigation dans les Colonies Françaises," 1913, pp. 9-10):

OCEAN TRAFFIC			COASTING TRADE			TOTAL		
French	*Foreign*	*Total*	*French*	*Foreign*	*Total*	*French*	*Foreign*	*Total*
4,102	8,555	12,657	118,161	16,507	134,668	122,263	25,062	147,325
8 041,567	12,917,288	20,958,855	8,922,087	2,952,120	11,874,207	16,963,654	15,869,408	32,833,062

The Commercial Aspect of the Open Door.—On account of these fundamental facts, it is at present impossible to establish absolute equality of opportunity in the spheres of exploitation, investment, and commerce. In its commercial aspect, the open door means essentially that all individuals, regardless of nationality, should have equal opportunities in trade with backward countries. This implies three things:

First, that foreign merchants and traders should have unrestricted access to all dependent and backward countries and also the same freedom to settle there as anyone else enjoys; second, that goods of every origin and imported on any vessel should enter the colony on equal terms; and third, that colonial products may be freely shipped to any destination without discrimination.

The first can be secured only incompletely. It was notorious before the war that alien merchants were not welcomed in the French, Belgian, and Portuguese colonies.[53] Similarly, in the German possessions, the rigidly stratified social system and the bureaucratic and militaristic spirit kept foreigners away. There was no British trading firm in German East Africa and not a single British merchant was resident either in Tanga or Dar-es-Salaam.[54] In the British colonies, where there was most freedom of trade, a number of foreign merchants were established. But, as a general rule, the business of each possession was controlled

---

[53] J. H. Harris, "Dawn in Darkest Africa," pp. 87-97.
[54] A. F. Calvert, "The German African Empire," pp. 122, 123. In German West Africa, there were some British firms. In German Southwest Africa, according to Mr. Gorges, the administrator of this occupied territory, British settlement was distinctly discouraged.

by national firms. This is largely inevitable. It does not mean, however, that the imports into the colony and the exports thence must follow national trade routes. As a matter of fact, a very considerable proportion of the output from British West Africa went directly to Germany and France, and a marked share of the imports of cotton textiles into the German and French colonies came directly or indirectly from England. The open door in this sense can be adequately secured by international agreements, provided it should be deemed advisable.

Means of Securing This.—A decision on this point must be conditioned by many factors that are at present indefinite. In the first place, the nature of the peace—the extent to which the German menace has been eliminated—will determine to what degree German trade can be permitted to enjoy the same treatment as that of other nations. Apart from this, it is a comparatively simple matter to amplify the provisions of the Berlin Act of 1885 and to make them effective by including export duties within their scope and by prohibiting monopolies in exploitation.[55]

[55] The Treaty of January 24, 1891, ratified February 2, 1892, between the United States and the Independent State of the Congo is somewhat more explicit than is the Berlin Act. It contains, further, in Article XIII, an agreement to arbitrate any differences as to the validity, interpretation, application, or enforcement of the provisions of the treaty. [Malloy, "Treaties," pp. 328-333; "Trattati," Supplemento, pp. 22-28. In the Convention for a General Act Revising the Berlin and Brussels Acts, signed at Saint-Germain-en-Laye, September 10, 1919, it is provided by Article 2 that "no differential treatment shall be imposed upon the said merchandise [belonging to the nationals of the Signatory Powers, and to those of States, Members of the League of Nations, which may adhere to the present Convention] on importation or exportation, the transit remaining free from all duties, taxes or dues, other than those collected for services rendered." The Berlin Act, on the other hand, merely stipulates that "merchandise imported into these regions shall be exempt from all import and transit duties" (Article 4). The more difficult question of

The question of extending this free trade area beyond the Conventional Basin and of comprising within it all of Equatorial Africa must also be considered. There can be but little doubt as to the advisability of such an extension, but an attempt to effect it will probably raise the entire question of the open door in dependent countries. This may be very awkward for the United States, in view of the existing tariff arrangements in force in Hawaii, Porto Rico, and the Philippines and the preferential agreement with Cuba.[56]

The Financial Aspect of the Open Door.—In addition to commercial equality, the full open door further implies that all, irrespective of their nationality, shall have equal opportunity:

a. To secure contracts for public works and to furnish governmental supplies;

b. To obtain concessions for the development of the country's resources.

The first has to-day little actuality in so far as Middle Africa is concerned, but in time it will probably become of importance.[57] The Algeciras Act of 1906 provided that in

monopolies in exploitation receives the following solution in Article 4 of the Convention: "Each State reserves the right to dispose freely of its property and to grant concessions for the development of the natural resources of the territory, but no regulations on these matters shall admit of any differential treatment between the nationals of the Signatory Powers and of States, Members of the League of Nations, which may adhere to the present Convention." The provision of the Berlin Act (Article 5) was: "No Power that exercises or that shall hereafter exercise sovereign rights in the above-mentioned regions shall be allowed to grant therein a monopoly or favour of any kind in matters of trade."]

[56 The territory of the Conventional Basin is left unchanged by the Convention of September 10, 1919. For the Cuban Treaty of December 11, 1902, see Malloy, "Treaties," pp. 353-357.]

57 E. D. Morel, "Africa and the Peace of Europe," pp. 92-94.

Morocco such contracts should be awarded upon the basis of public international tender, and this principle was confirmed by the Franco-German Morocco Treaty of 1911.[58] In applying this method to Middle Africa, great care will have to be exercised that the colonial authorities are not hampered in their choice of the best mode of executing works of public utility,[59] and also that they are able to retain full control over them. Even then, there is grave danger that these economic rights will be used as a weapon of aggression and as a pretext for constant interference. They can be made an inexhaustible source of irritating diplomatic incidents. This was notoriously Germany's procedure towards France in the case of Morocco.[60] The only remedy against such abuse is vigilant and constant international control on a broad basis, with a permanent court for the adjudication of all disputes. Otherwise, a system of international tenders is apt to lead to more friction than it will allay.

Private Concessions.—The question of equal opportunity for all in securing concessions for the exploitation of Middle Africa's resources likewise bristles with difficulties. The problem would be comparatively simple could it be divorced

[58] Act of Algeciras, April 7, 1906, Chapter IV, Articles 105-119 ("Trattati," pp. 1178-1180; Malloy, "Treaties," pp. 2178-2180). Franco-German Morocco Agreement, November 4, 1911, Article VI (Debidour, "Histoire Diplomatique de l'Europe, 1904-1916," p. 333). On the significance of these clauses and on the Franco-German Consortium of 1909, see A. Tardieu, "Le Mystère d'Agadir," Chapters I and II, and pp. 483-487, 508-517, 565-576.

[59] For instance, in Nigeria, it was found that railways were built most expeditiously and cheaply by the Director of Public Works and Railways of the Colony. A. B. Keith, "West Africa," pp. 238-242.

[60] A. Tardieu, *op. cit.;* Louis Maurice, "La Politique Marocaine de l'Allemagne."

from its overshadowing political features. Indeed, the question is not primarily economic. The assumption that there was an active competition between the capitalists of different states for investment in backward countries is gross misrepresentation of the real facts. In the case of China, it was notorious that foreign loans frequently had political purposes, either aggressive or defensive.[61] It is also established that the Bagdad Railway was preëminently an imperialistic scheme and that German capital was not seeking an investment outlet there. In fact, one of Germany's bitterest complaints against England and France was that they would not coöperate in supplying the funds with which to carry out this enterprise.[62] Capital is proverbially timid and needs considerable cajoling and coaxing before it can be induced to venture into such a speculative field as Middle Africa. The important concession held by American interests in the Belgian Congo has never been extensively used. It took a number of years before Mr. Robert Williams could secure the funds with which to start the railway from Lobito Bay in Portuguese Angola to the Katanga mining district in the Belgian Congo.[63] Yet this is the most promising of the railroad enterprises under way in Africa. Germany's chagrin, when Mr. Williams secured this concession in 1902 without the knowledge of the Brit-

---

[61] S. K. Hornbeck, "Contemporary Politics in the Far East," pp. 392-395.
[62] See also the statements of the German Foreign Secretary, Kiderlen-Waechter, and of Dr. Helfferich. G. Bourdon, "The German Enigma," pp. 50, 51, 220, 221, London, 1914. See also the statement of Von Gwinner of the Deutsche Bank to Sir William Ramsay. *The New Europe,* No. 72 (February 28, 1918), p. 223.
[63] Robert Williams, "The Milestones of African Civilization," in *United Empire Magazine,* July, 1917, pp. 446-457.

ish Government, was not because a valuable economic prize had escaped her, but proceeded from the fact that this railroad would have enabled her to dominate the Belgian and Portuguese colonies. In the past, there has been constant dread on the part of the weaker colonizing Powers that foreign investments would lead to the loss of their possessions.[64] The problem in its present form would dis-

[64] Yet a number of the most important enterprises, such as this railroad and the chief company interested in the Katanga copper belt, were international in character. The Tanganyika Concessions Limited, a British corporation, owns 2,700,000 shares of the Benguella Railway Company, 98,000 shares of the Union Minière du Haut Katanga, and 557,264 shares of the Rhodesia-Katanga Junction Railway and Mineral Company. This represented respectively ninety per cent and seventy per cent of the outstanding stock of these railways. An affiliated British corporation, the Zambezia Exploring Company, likewise held 11,000 Union Minière shares and a large block of debentures of the Benguella Railway. It is quite true, as Mr. Robert Williams, the managing director of these two British companies, stated, that "neither the British Government of past days nor British banks would assist to finance any enterprise with the slightest commercial flavour about it, even though it might become of vital value to the Empire if successfully handled." German policy was just the reverse. Yet even in the British case, such purely private enterprises were bound to have their reflex action on policy. It is generally accepted that in 1898 Great Britain and Germany concluded a treaty for the eventual partition of Portugal's African colonies in case that country decided to dispose of them [see *supra*, pp. 46-48]. Since then, British capital has become heavily interested in the Benguella Railway Company and in the Nyassa Chartered Company of Northern Mozambique. In 1913, Sir Harry H. Johnston stated that "since 1898 various forms of British enterprise have become so established in Angola and Northern Mozambique that the effect of the 1898 agreement is considerably modified. Supposing that anything so improbable were to occur as the complete breaking-up of Portugal, it would be difficult now for the British Government to hand over Angola and Mozambique to the Germans, at least without making some reservations on behalf of very large investments of British money." It should be noted in this connection that, in the spring of 1914, the German banks secured control of the British Nyassa Consolidated Company. At this time also there were persistent rumors that the Anglo-German African Settlement of 1914 [see *supra*, pp. 46-48] gave Germany control of the Benguella Railway. Mr. Robert Williams has, however, made the following explicit statement: "Her banks offered to finance our Benguella Railway to completion on condition that they got full control of that railway—an offer which I may tell

appear if the boundary lines of Africa were definitely deter-mined and fully guaranteed internationally. Until Africa is secured from competing territorial ambitions, it would be unwise to oblige any state to open its colonies to economic penetration aimed at detaching them. Fears of such nature kept Portugal and Belgium from welcoming German capital in the past. There is no doubt that with restoration of the German tropical possessions there would be less opportunity for the investment of German funds in the Belgian and Portuguese colonies than if Germany should cease to be an African power. The crux of the prob-lem is to eliminate the political motive. That effected, the difficulty will not consist in giving equal opportunities to private capital of all nations, but in attracting it at all. This will be especially the case if the native is adequately protected from exploitation by effective labor laws.[65] As the railroads in Middle Africa will presumably continue to

you was at once refused, although the bribe was immense."—Addresses of Mr. Robert Williams before the Colonial Institute, May 8, 1917, and at the general meetings of the Tanganyika Concessions and Zambezia Exploring Company, December 12, 1917. The first address is printed in the *United Empire Magazine*, July, 1917. See also Sir Harry H. Johnston, "Common Sense in Foreign Policy," pp. 76-80, London. 1913; H. A. Gib-bons. "The New Map of Africa." p. 262 n; *L'Afrique Française*, 1913, pp. 317-319; *ibid.*, June and July, 1915, Supplement, pp. 127-130; Pierre Alype, "La Provocation Allemande aux Colonies." In his famous memorandum (ed. and tr. Munroe Smith, in *International Conciliation*, No. 127, June. 1918, p. 63), Prince Lichnowsky made a very interesting statement about this phase of the Anglo-German African agreement of 1914. It reads: "The sincerity of the British government in its effort to respect our rights was proved by the fact that, even before the treaty was completed or signed, English *entrepreneurs* who wished to invest capital in the districts assigned to us under the new treaty, and who desired British support for their undertaking, were referred by Sir Edward Grey to us, with the information that the enterprise in question belonged in our sphere of interest."

[65] See *infra*, pp. 252-255.

be in the main governmental undertakings, private capital and enterprise will be largely restricted to developing the mineral and agricultural resources. Such capitalistic exploitation cannot be wholly eliminated, but it should be carefully controlled. It is generally admitted that international agreements regarding the treatment of labor are essential. It will be exceedingly difficult to formulate them, largely because the international and local phases of the problem are intertwined.[66] But it will be even more difficult to provide for equal opportunities to all in securing concessions, granted that Middle Africa will be in such a stable state after the war that no political dangers are involved in the measure.

[66] See above, Note 55.

CHAPTER II

1. The Africa of Ivory and Rubber

Comparative Commercial Importance of Middle Africa.
—The illusion created by Africa's vast bulk has established
a false idea of the volume of Middle Africa's foreign trade.
In point of fact, this commerce was relatively, if not absolutely, insignificant, amounting in 1913 to approximately
350 million dollars. This sum would be somewhat reduced
could the duplication resulting from intercolonial trade be
accurately eliminated. Taking the statistics as they are,
this total may be advantageously compared with the foreign
trade of Cuba in 1913, amounting to 308 million dollars,[1]
and with that of Egypt in the same year, aggregating 298
millions.[2] Then, again, the imports and exports of Brazil,
in very many respects a similar area, were in 1913 almost
twice as large, amounting to 660 million dollars.[3] Looking
at the question from another standpoint, we find that the
trade of the United Kingdom of Great Britain with this
region in 1913 was only 107 million dollars out of her
aggregate foreign commerce of 7,018 millions.[4] The corresponding figures for Germany in the same year were 76 mil-

[1] *The Statesman's Year-Book,* 1915, p. 821.
[2] *Ibid.,* pp. 259, 260.
[3] *Ibid.,* p. 753.
[4] *Ibid.,* pp. 75-77.

lions and 5,216 millions.[5]   In both cases, the share was roughly one and a half per cent.   Even less important, naturally, was the trade of these two countries with their own African colonies.   In the case of Germany, it was one-third of one per cent of her foreign commerce, while it amounted to one per cent for the United Kingdom.   Essentially the same situation prevailed as regards France and Belgium. Except in the case of Portugal, where the cocoa islands contributed largely, the trade with Middle Africa played a very minor part in the economy of the colonizing Powers.[6]   The purely commercial value of these possessions was still further lessened by the fact that, as a general rule, annual grants-in-aid had to be made for improvements and to cover deficits.[7]   Moreover, entirely apart from these conditions, and with the exception of cocoa, palm oil, palm kernels, and groundnuts, Middle Africa does not yield any single product in such quantities as to fill an important rôle in the economic system of the world.   In practically every other instance, be it rubber, sisal, copra, cotton, or coffee, her contribution is but an insignificant fraction of the total supply.

The Part Played by Ivory and Rubber.—When, some thirty years ago, the European peoples began to penetrate the center of Africa, the chief commodities desired

---

[5] *Statistisches Jahrbuch,* 1915, pp. 253, 254.

[6] The reëxports of colonial goods from Portugal in 1912 amounted to nearly 16 million dollars, while Portugal's total foreign trade, exclusive of this amount, was only 123 millions.   British Diplomatic and Consular Reports, No. 5265, p. 3; *The Statesman's Year-Book,* 1915, p. 1238; George Young, "Portugal Old and Young: An Historical Study," pp. 330, 331, Oxford, 1917.

[7] For the Portuguese deficits, see *ibid.,* p. 317; British Diplomatic and Consular Reports, No. 5497, p. 6.

from what was then believed to be an inexhaustible new "El Dorado" were ivory and rubber. These resources were most ruthlessly plundered. The elephant herds were decimated; and, as a result, though still exported in appreciable quantities,[8] ivory is destined to play an ever less important part in African economic life. Rubber has maintained itself longer. Not only was this product the chief source of wealth in the early history of the Middle African colonies, but until the very outbreak of the war, it formed the principal export of nearly all of these possessions, with the exception of those attached to the British Empire. This was true of Portuguese Angola, of French Equatorial Africa, Guinea, and the Ivory Coast, of the German colonies as an

[8] British Diplomatic and Consular Reports, No. 5249 (French Equatorial Africa), p. 4; No. 5494 (do.), pp. 6, 7; No. 5260 (Belgian Congo), p. 19; No. 5493 (do.), *passim*; "Statistical Abstract of the British Empire," 1915, pp. 129, 133; *Statistisches Jahrbuch*, 1915, pp. 465-468. The value of the ivory exported from the Belgian Congo in 1910, 1911, and 1912 was 9,361,000, 9,237,000, and 9,358,000 francs respectively ("Annuaire Statistique de la Belgique et du Congo Belge," 1913, p. 521). [In 1915 and 1916, these figures had fallen to 4,588,798 and 7,929,196 francs respectively. *The Statesman's Year-Book*, 1919, p. 700. In 1917-18, the tonnage exported was 182; in 1918-19, 125. *Ibid.*, 1920, p. 695. In 1920 it rose to 336 tons, valued at 35,860,093 francs. *Ibid.*, 1922, p. 716. See also "Manual of Belgian Congo," pp. 267-268, 274-275.] According to Bruel ("L'Afrique Équatoriale Française," p. 364), the average exports from French Equatorial Africa in 1896-1910 were as follows:

	Tons	Francs
1896-1900	107	1,945,000
1901-1905	174	3,529,000
1906-1910	160	3,192,000

In 1910-11, 143 tons, valued at 3,067,000 francs, were exported, ivory constituting 20.5 per cent of the total exports.

[The value of the ivory exported from Tanganyika Territory (the former German East Africa) in 1918-19 was £11,000, and from Uganda, £37,918, as compared with £43,770 in the preceding year. *The Statesman's Year-Book*, 1920, pp. 181, 183. For 1919-20 the figures were £18,254 and £61,452 respectively. *Ibid.*, 1922, pp. 188, 190. For the statistics of 1905-11, see "Handbook of German East Africa," p. 246.]

aggregate, and of the Belgian Congo.[9] Of the total exports from the last possession in 1910, seventy-seven per cent were rubber; in 1911, sixty-four per cent, and in 1912, fifty-eight per cent.[10] The total exports of rubber from Middle Africa in 1913 were roughly 15,600 tons out of a world production of 108,000 tons.[11] The great bulk of African rubber was obtained from the wild vines and trees. The industry was in a markedly declining state, partly because the wild supply had been greatly diminished, but mainly be-

[9] A. W. Bloem, "Die Kautschukkrisis," in *Weltverkehr,* 1914-15, pp. 57, 58.

[10] British Diplomatic and Consular Reports, No. 5260, pp. 5, 19. In 1911, rubber constituted sixty-two per cent of the exports of French Equatorial Africa, *ibid.,* No. 5249, p. 2; G. Bruel, *op. cit.,* pp. 462, 361-364. [For the output from 1887 to 1916, see "Manual of Belgian Congo," pp. 263-264, and cf. *ibid.,* pp. 274-275.]

[11] APPROXIMATE EXPORTS OF RUBBER IN 1913, IN TONS

French Colonies	4,500
German Colonies	4,200
Belgian Colonies	3,500
Portuguese Colonies	2,200
British Colonies	1,200
Total	15,600

The exports from the French colonies in this year were divided as follows ("Renseignements Généraux sur le Commerce des Colonies Françaises," 1914-1917, p. 20):

Colony	Tons
Senegal	90
Upper Senegal and Niger	83
French Guinea	1,456
Ivory Coast	961
Gabun	228
Middle Congo and Ubangi-Shari-Chad	1,717
Total	4,535

[In 1918-19, 1,635 tons were exported from the Belgian Congo, and in 1920, 1,122 tons, valued at 5,396,397 francs, as compared with 2,600 tons in 1917-18. *The Statesman's Year-Book,* 1920, p. 695; 1922, p. 716. The value of the exports in 1918-19 from the Tanganyika Territory, Uganda, and the Gold Coast was £134,785, and from the Ivory Coast, £49,825. *Ibid.,* pp. 181, 183, 883.]

cause of the competition of plantation rubber that was being produced on a rapidly expanding scale in the Malay States and in Ceylon and, to a less extent, in the Dutch East Indies.

Competition of Eastern Plantation Rubber.—The rise of this British industry is one of the most important economic facts of the twentieth century, whose significance has been largely overlooked. In 1906, the total production of rubber in the world was 66,000 tons, of which the Eastern plantations furnished only 531. By 1911, the output of the latter had reached 14,000 tons; by 1913, 47,000 tons; and by 1915, 108,000 tons out of a total world production of 159,000. The value of the world output in 1915 was 215 million dollars, of which 155 was the share of the Eastern plantations.[12] Before this development had taken place, the great bulk of the rubber consumed had come, primarily, from the forests of Brazil and, secondarily, from those of

[12] RUBBER PRODUCTION

(in tons)

	Eastern Plantations	Brazil	Other Countries	Total
1906	531	36,000	29,500	66,031
1911	13,973	37,730	23,000	74,703
1912	28,518	42,410	28,000	98,928
1913	47,302	39,370	21,500	108,172
1914	71,959	37,000	12,000	120,959

Washington Daily and Consular Trade Reports, 1917, No. 292, p. 1013. While the production elsewhere remained stationary, that in the Eastern plantations increased rapidly, being in 1915, 107,867 tons; in 1916, 152,650; in 1917, 204,348. Of the shipments in 1917, 176,692 tons came from the Federated Malay States, the Straits Settlements, and Ceylon. On account of the accumulation of stocks and the ensuing fall in price due to this growing output and the scarcity of shipping, the British Rubber Growers' Association took steps in 1918 to restrict production to eighty per cent of the 1917 crop. W. H. Dickerson, "An Economic Study of the Rubber Industry"; New York *Tribune,* April 20, 1918.

Africa. Under the Leopoldian régime the rubber vines of
the Congo were most improvidently hacked to pieces, with
the result that this source of wealth has been greatly diminished.[13] There are still considerable areas of wild rubber
in the Belgian Congo, in French Equatorial and West
Africa, and in the Cameroons. But its cost of collection
is so high that it cannot successfully compete with the output from the Eastern plantations. For some time it had
been perceived that this source of wealth would ultimately
run dry; and accordingly, in 1899, King Leopold compelled
the natives to plant rubber trees. A very large number,
between twenty and thirty millions according to some estimates, were set out in the Congo, but the scheme was a distinct failure.[14] Similar plantations had been undertaken
by the Portuguese in Angola and by the Germans in the
Cameroons [15] and in East Africa. In the latter colony nineteen million trees had been planted, of which one half were
ready for tapping in 1913.[16] The industry both here and on
the West Coast was largely in this experimental state when
the price of rubber broke badly and a severe crisis occurred
in Africa.

[13] Thirty years ago the forests of the Congo were thick with mature
Landolphia vines. This species of rubber is of slow growth and probably
many of the vines were over a hundred years old. Scientifically tapped,
these vines would continue to-day to yield rubber in fairly large quantities. But nature was ruthlessly plundered. John H. Harris, "Dawn in
Darkest Africa," pp. vii, 204-208. [For the various sources of rubber in
this region, see "Manual of Belgian Congo," pp. 173-183.]

[14] J. H. Harris, op. cit., pp. 207, 216, 243-245.

[15] A. F. Calvert, "The Cameroons," pp. 26-30.

[16] British Diplomatic and Consular Reports, No. 5441, pp. 25 ff.; A. F.
Calvert, "The German African Empire," pp. 142-161; John H. Harris,
"Germany's Lost Colonial Empire," pp. 46, 47. In 1912, 1,017 metric tons
of plantation rubber, valued at £362,012, were exported from German East
Africa [see further "Handbook of German East Africa," pp. 234-235].

The Rubber Crisis of 1912-13.—As a result of the rapidly increasing output of the Malay States and Ceylon, the price of rubber declined precipitately; and in 1912 and 1913 a serious situation developed in all the Middle African colonies [17] except those of Great Britain, which, fortunately for themselves, had never extensively engaged in this industry. African rubber could not be sold at the same price as that of the East. With the growing scarcity of wild rubber in Africa and the fall in price, it no longer paid the natives to gather it. The cost of producing plantation rubber varied greatly in the different colonies, but in general it was much in excess of that of the Eastern plantations.[18] Apart from the fact that the East is favored by cheaper land transport, the fundamental fact is that the African native cannot compete with the more intelligent and industrious labor of the East, just as the latter cannot in other spheres rival the skilled labor and machinery of Western civilization.

Future of the Industry.—As the output of the Eastern plantations is steadily increasing, the African rubber industry seems destined to sudden or gradual extinction. Some relatively small quantities of wild rubber will probably continue to be exported, since it serves certain purposes for which the plantation product is not adapted.[19]   It is

[17] Governor-General Merlin, "La Crise du Caoutchouc," in *L'Afrique Française,* 1913, pp. 420 ff.; Édouard Payen, "La Crise du Caoutchouc," *ibid.,* 1914, pp. 58 ff.

[18] Calvert, *op. cit.,* pp. 144, 306; A. W. Bloem, *loc. cit.;* Alfred Wigglesworth, "Thirty Years of German Rule in East Africa," in *Contemporary Review,* April, 1916, p. 481.

[19] J. C. Willis, "Rubber," in F. W. Oliver, "The Exploitation of Plants," p. 73, London, 1917. The relative outputs, in tons, of plantation and wild

difficult to see, however, how the incipient African plantation industry, based, as it was, in the German and Belgian
colonies on hired labor and European supervision, can ever
effectively emerge from the experimental stage in which it
existed at the outbreak of the war. This system of capitalistic exploitation has never worked successfully in Africa.
Native hired labor, just because it is unwilling, is inefficient
and costly. Apparently, the most promising experiment is
that in British West Africa, where the natives some years
ago started on a small scale individual and communal rubber plantations under the guidance of government advisers.[20] But the success of this system even in Nigeria and
on the Gold Coast seems to be very problematical,[21] and
it is doubtful if its establishment elsewhere is feasible and
also if it would reduce the cost of production to the level
of that of the Eastern plantations. In the future, rubber
will, in all probability, play a more and more insignificant

rubber in 1909-18, together with the principal consumers, were as follows
(*The Statesman's Year-Book*, 1919, p. xxi):

	OUTPUT		CONSUMERS		
	Plantation	*Wild*	*United States*	*United Kingdom*	*Others*
1909	4,000	66,000	31,000	15,000	24,000
1910	8,000	62,000	32,000	20,000	18,000
1911	14,000	61,000	29,000	17,000	29,000
1912	29,000	70,000	50,000	19,000	30,000
1913	48,000	61,000	50,000	25,000	34,000
1914	71,000	49,000	61,000	19,000	40,000
1915	108,000	51,000	97,000	15,000	47,000
1916	153,000	49,000	116,000	27,000	59,000
1917	204,000	53,000	175,000	26,000	56,000
1918	240,000	50,000	187,000	24,000	27,000

[20] John H. Harris, "Dawn in Darkest Africa," p. 242; A. B. Keith, "West
Africa," pp. 251, 252.
[21] The production of rubber in Nigeria and the Gold Coast declined
greatly from 1899 to 1913. "Statistical Abstract of the British Empire,"
1915, p. 367. See also Cuthbert Christy, "The African Rubber Industry and
Funtumia Elastica."

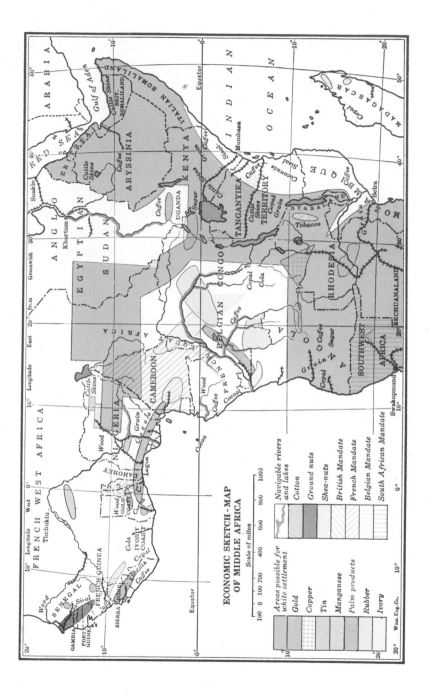

ECONOMIC SKETCH-MAP
OF MIDDLE AFRICA

Scale of miles

100   0   100 200   400   600   800   1000

100   0   100 200   400   600   800   1000

Areas possible for white settlement

Gold

Copper

Tin

Manganese

Palm products

Rubber

Ivory

Navigable rivers and lakes

Cotton

Ground nuts

Shea-nuts

British Mandate

French Mandate

Belgian Mandate

South African Mandate

Wm. Eng. Co.

part. The consequence must be that many of the colonies, practically all except the British, will have to change so fundamentally as almost to begin their economic life anew. They will not be able to prosper unless they diversify their products and restrict as much as possible the capitalistic system of exploitation. Apart from mineral resources, the most important and valuable products of Middle Africa are and for some time will continue to be vegetable fats and cocoa. It is fortunate also for a sound development of African civilization that these commodities have hitherto been by far most successfully produced by native industry, without the direct intervention of outside capital, management, or control.

2.   Vegetable Fats

Palm Oil.—For some time before the war there was a general and growing scarcity of animal fats, which was mainly manifest in Northern Europe. The Germans were already speaking of a "Fetthunger." This deficiency was being met by a constantly expanding production of oil from various seeds (linseed, cottonseed, rapeseed, sesame), nuts (coconuts, palm kernels, groundnuts), and beans (castor-oil, soya).[22] One of the most valuable sources of vegetable

[22] *Bulletin of the Imperial Institute,* 1909, p. 357; 1913, p. 206; 1914, p. 458; 1915, p. 470; 1917, p. 57; Report of Committee on Edible and Oil-producing Nuts and Seeds, Cd. 8247, 8248 (1916); Erwin W. Thompson, "Cottonseed Products and Their Competitors in Northern Europe," Part I (Cake and Meal), Part II (Edible Oils), Department of Commerce, Special Agents' Series, Nos. 84 and 89, Washington, 1914; Sir A. D. Steel-Maitland, "Oils and Fats in the British Empire," in A. P. Newton, "The Staple Trades of the Empire," pp. 9-31, London, 1917; R. E. Dennett, "British and German Trade in Nigeria," in *United Empire Magazine,* December, 1914; A. F. Calvert, "The German African Empire," pp. 234 ff.; J. H. Harris, "Germany's Lost Colonial Empire," pp. 39 ff.; A. H. Mil-

fat is the African oil palm—*Elaeis Guineensis*—which grows wild in extensive sections of West Africa, both in the coastal regions and for a very considerable distance inland. From the fruit of this tree is produced an oil, the palm oil of commerce, which was in great demand for various purposes. It was largely used in the manufacture of soaps, candles, lubricants, and metal polishes, and also to prevent oxidization in the manufacture of tin plates. Furthermore, it yields a considerable percentage of glycerine, which enters prominently into the preparation of explosives.[23] To a very much less extent this oil was made available for edible purposes, as an ingredient of the substitutes for natural butter known generally as margarine and oleomargarine. This relatively important industry was entirely native in character. It centered in British Nigeria and the bulk of the output—roughly three quarters—was shipped to the United Kingdom.[24]

Palm Kernels.—While the palm oil derived from the pericarp, or fleshy covering, of the nut is of considerable value,

bourne, "Palm Kernels from West Africa," in *Journal of the African Society,* January, 1916; Paul Leutwein, "Siedelungs- und Plantagenkolonien," in *Weltverkehr,* 1914-15, pp. 205, 206; Reports of Consul-General Skinner and Consul Hathaway in Washington Daily and Consular Trade Reports, 1916, Nos. 169 and 174; John H. Harris, "Dawn in Darkest Africa," pp. 225 ff. See also the Imperial Institute monograph of Wyndham R. Dunstan on "Oil Seeds and Feeding Cakes," Cd. 7260 (1914); A. Chevalier, "Documents sur le Palmier à l'Huile," Paris, 1910; Henri Jumelle, "Plantes Oléagineuses" (2d ed.), pp. 42-64, Paris, 1914.

[23] In the oils made from the unfermented fruit, known as Lagos and soft oils, the proportion of glycerine is from seven to ten per cent. During the war the exports of all oils and fats from the British Empire were carefully controlled. In some cases, arrangements were made with foreign countries to which exports of palm oil were licensed, by which they sent to Great Britain an equivalent percentage of glycerine in return. Steel-Maitland, *op. cit.,* p. 26.

[24] The exports from Nigeria in 1913 amounted to 83,089 tons, valued at

the kernels of the nuts themselves are even more important commercially. Before the war, these palm kernels were shipped in large quantities from West Africa to Europe. In round numbers, the total exports in 1913 were 335,000 tons, of an approximate value of 28 million dollars.[25]

This industry, likewise, had attained its greatest develop-

£1,854,384. "Statistical Abstract of the British Empire," 1915, p. 145. French West Africa produced to the value of about 10 million francs in 1912, but in all the other colonies the amounts were quite insignificant. A. Girault, "The Colonial Tariff Policy of France," p. 229.

[25] EXPORTS OF PALM KERNELS IN 1912

British West Africa	£3,802,472
French West Africa	680,618
German Colonies	389,278
Belgian Congo	110,835
	£4,983,203

Bulletin of the Imperial Institute, 1914, pp. 458, 459. Calvert, *op. cit.,* p. 243. This table is not absolutely complete, as it does not include the exports from Angola, the French Congo, and Liberia. In 1913, 4,500 tons, of an approximate value of £70,000, were exported from Angola. French Equatorial Africa exported 366 tons in 1912 and 575 tons in 1913. British Diplomatic and Consular Reports, No. 5529, p. 6; No. 5494, pp. 6, 7. In 1913, Germany imported from Liberia 1,952 tons. *Statistisches Jahrbuch,* 1915, p. 184. In 1913, the exports from British West Africa were as follows:

	Tons	Value Thousands of Pounds
Palm kernels	234,208	4,199
Palm oil	88,997	1,977
Palm-kernel oil	3,857	129
Palm-kernel cake	5,412	31
Total	332,474	6,336

The total trade in palm kernels for this year amounted to over £5,000,000, or more than half the exports of West Africa, by far the greater part of which came from the British possessions (Cd. 8247, p. 5; cf. also "Statistical Abstract of the British Empire," 1915, pp. 145, 149, 153, 155, according to which the exports of palm kernels—including shells, cake, and kernel oil—from British West Africa in 1913 amounted to 244,127 tons, valued at £4,361,156).

The output of palm kernels and oil from French West Africa in the years 1915-18 was as follows (*L'Afrique Française,* July-August, 1918, p. 158):

ment in British West Africa, primarily in Nigeria and
secondarily in Sierra Leone. The British colonies contributed about three quarters of the total supply, 244,000

	Palm Kernels (Tons)	Palm Oil (Tons)
1915	15,000	13,500
1916	15,000	14,500
1917-18	20,000	25,000

Both products were bought by the State and mainly went to Great
Britain, whereas in 1913 three quarters of the output from British West
Africa had been sent to Germany to be milled.

The output in tons of kernels and oil from the French African colonies
in 1913 was as follows ("Renseignements Généraux sur le Commerce des
Colonies Françaises," 1914-1917, p. 19).

Colony	Kernels	Oil
Senegal	1,901	....
Guinea	5,172	164
Ivory Coast	6,949	6,015
Dahomey	26,372	7,971
Gabun	575	119
Middle Congo and Ubangi-Shari-Chad	....	21
Total	40,969	14,290

The following figures for Dahomey for 1908-12 are also of interest in
this connection ("Statistique du Commerce des Colonies Françaises," 1913,
I, i, p. 515, Paris, 1915):

	KERNELS		OIL	
		Value		Value
	Tons	Millions of Francs	Tons	Millions of Francs
1908	23,000	5.6	9,500	4.6
1909	33,000	8.1	15,016	6.5
1910	34,783	9.979	14,628	6.4
1911	39,346	13.9	15,252	8.
1912	37,295	14.	11,916	6.4

The value (in francs) of the exports of palm kernels and palm oil from
the Belgian Congo in 1910-12 was ("Annuaire Statistique de la Belgique
et du Congo Belge," 1913, p. 521):

	Palm Kernels	Palm Oil	Total
1910	3,101,000	2,916,000	6,017,000
1911	3,504,000	2,032,000	5,536,000
1912	3 206,000	1,380,000	4,586,000
Total	9,811,000	6,328,000	16,139,000

[For the output during the years 1887-1916, see "Manual of Belgian
Congo," pp. 265-266. The values of these exports from part of West

tons out of 335,000.[26] The great bulk of these kernels, almost the exact equivalent of the total British production, was shipped to Germany. There the kernels were treated in the mills and yielded two products in somewhat unequal halves, palm-kernel oil and palm-kernel cake and meal.[27] The latter was highly esteemed as a fodder, especially for milch-cattle. Part of the oil was exported, but the remainder was used for industrial purposes and also in the manufacture of margarine.[28]

Africa in 1918 and 1919 were (*The Statesman's Year-Book*, 1920, pp. 241, 245, 883; 1921, pp. 245, 249, 899):

	Palm Kernels		Palm Oil	
Colony	1918	1919	1918	1919
Nigeria	£3,226,306	£4,947,955	£2,610,448	£4,245,893
Gold Coast	9,799	253,248	24,770	140,163
Ivory Coast	115,102	420,701	183,044	408,650
Dahomey	487,569	1,807,540	547,619	810,419

For 1920 the respective figures were: Nigeria, £5,717,981 and £4,677,445; Gold Coast, £222,468 and £114,084; Ivory Coast, £449,558 and £720,935 (*ibid.*, 1922, pp. 254, 258, 921). The exports from the Belgian Congo were, in tons (*ibid.*, 1920, p. 695; 1921, p. 702; 1922, p. 716):

	Palm Kernels	Palm Oil
1917	34,988	5,394
1918	31,362	5,126
1919	34,350	6,404
1920	39,457	7,624

In 1917 the values of the respective outputs in Sierra Leone were £842,508 and £62,375; in 1919, £1,191,607 and £115,515; and in 1920, £1,401,676 and £123,207 (*ibid.*, 1920, p. 247; 1921, p. 251; 1922, p. 261).

In 1917 the value of the exports of kernels from Eritrea was £43,580, and in 1919, £64,000 (*ibid.*, 1920, p. 1006; 1922, p. 1049) and from Uganda in 1919-20, £57,868 (*ibid.*, 1921, p. 185).]

[26] British, 244,000; French, 52,000; and German, Belgian, Portuguese, and Liberian together about 39,000 tons. The total output of kernels and oils from German West Africa in 1912 was 34,015 tons with a value of £532,000 (Cd. 8247, p. 6).

[27] In 1913, Germany imported 236,000 tons, valued at 104 million marks, of which 206,000 tons, valued at 91 million marks, came from British West Africa. *Statistisches Jahrbuch*, 1915, p. 184. The 261,408 tons imported in 1912 yielded 117,364 tons of oil and 138,816 tons of fodder. Thompson, *op. cit.*, No. 84, pp. 10, 11.

[28] The total quantity of margarine made in Germany was 250,000 tons;

The Proposed Export Duty of 1916.—The outbreak of the war in 1914 created a serious condition in British West Africa, as it deprived these colonies of their German market. Although the English farmer used large quantities of linseed and cottonseed cake as fodder,[29] he had no experience with palm-kernel meal or cake and could not be counted upon to purchase it. Besides, the British mills were not adapted to preparing the palm kernels. There were in Great Britain facilities for crushing only about 60,000 out of the 250,000 tons that needed a market. On the other hand, as a result of the general economic dislocation produced by the war, there set in gradually an increasing demand for the oil for edible purposes. The manufacturers were naturally timid about erecting mills especially adapted to crushing or dissolving palm kernels, unless they had some assurance that the industry would not revert to Germany immediately upon the conclusion of peace. Their fears were based upon the fact that in Germany an eager market was already established for this fodder, as a consequence of years of campaigning and education, while in Great Britain a demand had to be created gradually. In order to meet this obvious difficulty, the British Government in 1916 proposed to establish an export levy of not less than £2 per ton on all palm kernels shipped from Africa to any place but the United Kingdom. This duty was to remain in effect for five years after the conclusion of the war, but

in the Netherlands, 130,000; and in the United Kingdom, 100,000. Germany used but 25,000 tons of palm-kernel oil in the production of margarine. All told, of the 125,000 tons of palm-kernel oil manufactured, only 40,000 were made edible. Thompson, *op. cit.*, No. 89, pp. 7, 23.

[29] *Ibid.*, No. 84, pp. 49, 50.

was to be remitted on all kernels shipped to or crushed in any part of the British Empire.[30] This plan aroused vehement opposition in England, partly on the ground that it was a reversion to the old colonial system and a reversal of the policy of the open door which had been in effect for two generations, and partly because it was claimed that the native producer in Africa would be at the mercy of British purchasers, who might combine to keep the price of palm kernels down. Considerable hostility also manifested itself in the colonies and, accordingly, the project was quietly allowed to lapse.[31] In the meanwhile, the demand for margarine had greatly increased and the British farmer was being systematically taught the value of this fodder, learning his lesson all the more quickly as the cake and meal to which he was accustomed were rising markedly in price. As a result, virtually the whole colonial crop of palm kernels found a market in Great Britain.[32]

[30] Cd. 8247, p. 22.

[31] Hansard, House of Commons, August 3 and November 8, 1916; *Anti-Slavery Reporter*, January, 1917, pp. 81, 82; July, 1917, p. 29. On October 7, 1916, an export duty of £2 per ton on palm oil and one of £2 2s. 6d. per ton on palm kernels was imposed in Nigeria, but there was no discrimination in regard to the destination of the shipments. In the case of exports before April 1, 1917, only one-half of these duties was payable. On December 12, 1917, Sierra Leone placed export duties of 10s. a ton on palm kernels and of 10s. 5d. a ton on palm oil. On August 9, 1917, the Nigerian Government prohibited the export of palm oil to any place but the United Kingdom and on November 30, 1917, the British Food Ministry took control of all oil-seed supplies, including palm kernels. Washington Daily and Consular Trade Reports, 1917, Nos. 252, 291; *Board of Trade Journal*, January 10, 1918, p. 49; February 14, 1918, p. 196. For the preferential export duties on palm kernels from the Gold Coast and Sierra Leone, see *The Economist*, August 17, 1918.

[32] IMPORTS OF PALM KERNELS INTO THE UNITED KINGDOM

	Tons
1915	233,249
1916	241,501
1917	248,160

Future of the Industry.—The war has greatly intensified the previously existing scarcity of fats, and as this dearth will assuredly continue after the conclusion of peace, this African industry has, apparently, a large and prosperous future. Hitherto, it has in the main been confined to the British colonies, but the oil palm grows in profusion in the adjacent lands as well. It has been estimated that hitherto only one tenth of this wild fruit has been gathered. The Cameroons alone, according to some authorities, can yield as much as the British colonies.[33] The scarcity of ivory and the rubber crisis had even before the war made it imperative to diversify production and to develop fresh resources in these non-British possessions. The Belgian colonial authorities were fully aware of this necessity[34] and had granted a large concession in the Congo to the well known British soap-makers, Lever Brothers of Port Sunlight, who were actively developing the oil-palm industry on an extensive scale when the war broke out.[35] The French also were

[33 All but a small portion of the Cameroons has been placed by the Peace Conference under France as a Mandatory Power, the remainder being similarly assigned to Great Britain as holder of a like mandate; see *infra,* p. 431.]

[34] See the Address of the Belgian Colonial Minister, J. Renkin, of February 11, 1916, "L'Avenir du Congo Belge," in *L'Afrique Française,* March, 1916, Supplement, p. 64. For a discussion of this question, see "Bulletin de la Société Belge d'Études Coloniales," 1914, pp. 12 ff.

[35] This British undertaking, under the name of the Société des Huileries du Congo Belge, was actively engaged in developing these resources, having built a short railway, constructed factories, and established a flotilla of steamers. Thanks mainly to their enterprise, the exports of palm kernels from the Belgian Congo had increased from 7,200 tons in 1913 to 22,000 tons in 1916 and those of palm oil from 2,000 to 4,000 tons. British Diplomatic and Consular Reports, No. 5260, pp. 5, 19; No. 5493, p. 7, *et passim;* G. M. Wrigley, "The Military Campaign against Germany's African Colonies," in *The Geographical Review,* January, 1918, p. 59 n. ["Manual of Belgian Congo," pp. 184-186.]

alive to the situation and realized the possibilities of the oil palm.[36]   Although Germany was by far the largest consumer of palm kernels, only a very insignificant fraction of her supply came from the German colonies.[37]   But the blockade created a far greater scarcity of fats in Central Europe than anywhere else, and hence the future economic problem assumed there a grossly exaggerated aspect.   Emil Zimmermann, the chief champion of a German Mittel-Africa, advanced, as the main economic argument for this imperialistic project, Germany's need for fats, the fact that the African oil palm was the most valuable of oil plants, that hitherto it had been most inadequately exploited, and that its products were far more necessary to German agriculture than were the oleaginous seeds obtainable in what was Russia.   According to him, Germany's intensive agriculture would rest more securely on Mid-Africa with the oil palm than on the Slavonic East.[38]   In this connection, it should be noted that before the war Germany imported very large quantities of various kinds of oil-yielding material

[36] G. François, "L'Aide de l'Afrique Occidentale à la Métropole," in *L'Afrique Française*, May and June, 1917.

[37] IMPORT OF PALM KERNELS INTO GERMANY, 1913

	Tons	Value Thousands of Marks
Total	235,921	103,996
From:		
British West Africa	206,145	90,704
Cameroons	3,568	1,606
Togo	13,599	6,120
French West Africa	8,240	3,626
Liberia	1,952	878
Portuguese West Africa	1,835	807

Statistisches Jahrbuch, 1915, p. 184.

[38] E. Zimmermann, "The German Empire of Central Africa," pp. 40-41, 50-51.

and also of the prepared fodder. Less than one tenth of the
cake and meal which were used came from palm kernels.
Similarly, only about one seventh of the vegetable oils
consumed was palm-kernel oil.[39]

The Danger of Capitalistic Exploitation.—The oil palm
of Africa, it should always be remembered, is merely one of
very many sources of vegetable fats and enters into competition with the products of numerous widely separated
lands. The general situation has been well summarized by
Sir A. D. Steel-Maitland, who writes that, "for every use
enumerated, with but few exceptions, one oil is inter-
changeable with others under certain conditions of price,"
although the only two oils "which are mutually replaceable
for all purposes to which they are put, are coconut oil and
palm-kernel oil." Thus, while the African oil palm is
unique, Africa enjoys no more than a very limited monopoly. Yet oil-palm products were in constantly growing demand before the war and there is an almost absolute certainty that this requirement will in the future be much
more urgent. It is quite possible greatly to increase the
output of oil and of kernels. In the first place, only about
one third, or possibly one half, of the oil was extracted
from the pericarp surrounding the nut by the crude processes employed by the natives. A large proportion of this

[39] In 1912, Germany imported 1,443,447 tons of oil-yielding materials
valued at 109 million dollars, from which 525,643 tons of oil and 862,353
tons of fodder were manufactured. In addition, Germany imported
794,190 tons of cake and meal, valued at 28 million dollars. 263,623 tons
of this fodder were exported, leaving about 1,400,000 for domestic consumption, of which approximately 120,000 were made from palm kernels.
Thompson, *op. cit.*, No. 84, pp. 10-15. In 1913, Germany consumed
559,533 tons of vegetable oil, of which only 77,252 were palm-kernel oil.
Ibid., No. 89, pp. 8, 9.

waste might be eliminated and the quality of the product greatly improved. If so, palm oil would be a most useful hard fat in the manufacture of margarine. In the second place, each nut was generally broken separately by hand and the kernels were laboriously extracted by the natives. In the altogether probable event of satisfactory machinery being devised for this purpose—hitherto none has quite met the needs of the situation—the output should increase greatly.[40] If such a gain can be effected without fundamentally changing the native character of the industry as it is established in the British colonies, it would be a great boon to Africa and also a considerable advantage to the outside world. But, if Europe's need for vegetable fats should lead to an attempt to expand production by forced labor, open or disguised, it will be an unmixed evil and the oil palm may prove as great a curse to Africa as were the Congo rubber vines. It is a danger which cannot be ignored. It is true that Dr. Solf, the German Colonial Secretary, has publicly warned against such a course,[41] but the peril is inherent in German colonial practice. It will be the inevitable consequence of Emil Zimmermann's project, should it perchance ever be put into effect. This scheme is to plant the oil palm systematically and to exploit it capitalistically. The plantation method is opposed to the genius of the African people and has always led to most

[40] Since 1910, considerable progress has been made in the introduction of machinery into British West Africa for extracting palm oil and kernels (Imperial Institute Report on Oil-Seeds, Oils, Fats, and Waxes, p. 533 = Colonial Reports, Miscellaneous, No. 88 [Cd. 7260]). The machinery introduced by Lever Brothers is said to be entirely satisfactory; but the problem in the interior is unlike that on the Coast because of the transportation factor.

[41] *Kölnische Zeitung,* December 22, 1917.

unfortunate results, notoriously so in the cocoa industry of the Cameroons and the Portuguese islands. Any plan that involves concentration of labor and that takes the industry entirely out of the hands of the native, making him merely a contract laborer, is bound to be in the end disastrous. It disrupts tribal life and leads to depopulation. It will be very difficult wholly to eliminate this peril by international control and the harder the task, the more essential will it be to weigh these circumstances in deciding the fate of the conquered territories in Middle Africa.

Groundnuts.—In addition to the products of the oil palm, Africa has another valuable source of vegetable fats in groundnuts or peanuts. In 1913, roughly 670,000 tons of these were imported into Europe,[42] and of this quantity about forty-five per cent came from Africa, the bulk of the remainder being the output primarily of British India and secondarily of China. British India is by far the largest producer; her total crop was almost equal to the aggregate imports into Europe, although a considerable part was retained for home consumption.[43] Thus the African ground-

[42] IMPORTS OF GROUNDNUTS FOR CONSUMPTION, 1913

	Tons
France	493,467
Germany	98,085
Netherlands	67,428
Total	658,980

These were the main importing countries. Steel-Maitland, *op. cit.*, p. 20. See also Henri Jumelle, *op. cit.*, pp. 64-79.

[43] ESTIMATED CROP OF GROUNDNUTS IN BRITISH INDIA

	Tons
1903-4	94,419
1905-6	211,200
1907-8	352,500

nut does not enjoy even the limited monopoly that is the
portion of the palm kernel. In Africa, the groundnut was
produced in small quantities in a number of colonies, such
as Portuguese Guinea [44] and German East Africa,[45] but
virtually the entire African supply came from French Senegal and adjacent British Gambia. In 1913, Gambia exported 67,404 tons, worth roughly three million dollars,[46]
and French West Africa about 250,000 tons, valued at
twelve million dollars.[47] Not only does the African industry

	Tons
1909-10	459,300
1911-12	605,700
1912-13	631,400
1913-14	749,000

"Statistical Abstract of British India," 1915, p. 127; *Bulletin of the
Imperial Institute*, 1917, pp. 357, 359. In 1913-14, the exports were only
278,000 tons. [For 1917-18, 1918-19, 1919-20, and (provisional) 1920-21, the
crops were, in tons, 1,057,000; 626,000; 822,000, and 931,000. *The Statesman's Year-Book*, 1921, p. 138; 1922, p. 142.]
[44] The exports of groundnuts from Portuguese Guinea were:

	Tons
1910	1,694
1911	3,177
1912	6,000
1913	12,000

British Diplomatic and Consular Reports, No. 5418, pp. 4, 6.
[45] In 1913, the exports from German East Africa amounted to somewhat
under 2 million marks. *Statistisches Jahrbuch*, 1915, p. 465. [In 1919-20,
the Tanganyika Territory exported 16,485 cwts., valued at £18,000, and in
1920-21, 67,377 cwts., valued at £79,536. *The Statesman's Year-Book*, 1921,
p. 183; 1922, p. 188.]
[46] "Statistical Abstract of the British Empire," 1915, p. 157. In 1918, an
export duty of ten shillings per ton was imposed, without discrimination,
on groundnuts from Nigeria. *Board of Trade Journal*, January 10, 1918,
p. 49; February 21, 1918, p. 228.
[47] Of £2,395,661 exported in 1913, £2,291,150 came from Senegal. British
Diplomatic and Consular Reports, No. 5423, pp. 8, 9; G. François, *op.
cit.*, p. 195. The export of groundnuts from French West Africa in 1914
was 165,000 tons; in 1915, 236,000; in 1916, 150,000; and in 1917-18 (estimated), 300,000. The entire crop of 1917-18 was bought by the State. In
Senegal, decortization of the nuts has been begun, thus economizing tonnage and also permitting purchase of nuts at a greater distance from the

center in the French colonies, preëminently in Senegal, but of the total imports into Europe three quarters went to France. At Bordeaux and Marseilles, these nuts were manufactured into an excellent fodder, known as Rufisque from the Senegalese port of that name, and into edible oil,[48] widely used as a substitute for olive oil and also as a valuable ingredient in margarine. Its chief competitors in the manufacture of margarine are the soft oils made from cottonseed, sesame, and soya beans.[49] As the production of groundnuts in Africa can be considerably increased to meet the European need for fats,[50] this industry has an assured future, though unquestionably a considerably less extensive and important one than that in prospect for the oil palm.

Copra.—Various other oleaginous substances are produced in Middle Africa, such as the shea-nut of Northern

place of shipment. *L'Afrique Française*, July-August, 1918, p. 158. [The value of the exports of groundnuts from Nigeria in 1918 was £920,137; and from Gambia, £800,319, the figures for 1919 being £698,702 and £1,172,843 respectively, and for 1920, £1,119,688 and £2,398,444, while 250,000 tons were shipped from Senegal in 1918 and 247,672 tons in 1919. *The Statesman's Year-Book*, 1920, pp. 242, 244, 881; 1921, pp. 245, 248, 897; 1922, pp. 254, 257.]

[48] Germany and the Netherlands were, on a minor scale, also sharers in this industry.

GROUNDNUT IMPORTS INTO GERMANY, 1913

	Tons	Value Thousands of Marks
Total	98,085	28,162
From:		
British West Africa	23,874	7,401
German East Africa	3,231	1,115
French West Africa	30,960	7,895
Portuguese West Africa	5,019	1,154
British India, etc	21,505	6,021
China	9,883	3,360

Statistisches Jahrbuch, 1915, p. 184.

[49] Thompson, *op. cit.*, No. 84, pp. 29, 30; No. 89, pp. 14-19.

[50] The output of groundnuts, in tons, from the French African colonies

Nigeria and the coconut of the eastern littoral. Comparatively little attention had been given to developing the former,[51] but considerable efforts were made, especially by the Germans, to establish the coconut industry in East Africa. The dried flesh of this nut, commercially known as copra, was imported on a large and rapidly increasing scale into Europe, especially into Germany and France. From it were manufactured both meal for fodder and hard oil which is a very valuable ingredient of margarine. Practically the sole source of the European and American supply, about 550,000 tons in 1913, was the East—British India, Ceylon, and the Straits Settlements, the Dutch East Indies, the Philippines, and the South Sea Islands.[52] In 1913, Germany imported 196,598 tons, valued at 122 million marks, of which virtually all, ninety-five per cent, came from places under a foreign flag.[53] About 6.5 million marks' worth was received from Samoa and the German Pacific colonies. Africa supplied only a negligible quantity. In

in 1913-16 was as follows ("Renseignements Généraux sur le Commerce des Colonies Françaises," 1914-17, p. 18):

	Total	From Senegal	Shipped to France
1913	246,258	229,981	180,787
1914	285,549	280,527	161,902
1915	306,551	303,067	236,269
1916	125,435	124,142	100,041

In 1900, the exports from Senegal were only 140,000 tons. This was the chief output from French West Africa. Of total exports in 1913 of 126 million francs, 60 million were groundnuts. British Diplomatic and Consular Reports, No. 5423, p. 18.

[51] Thompson, op. cit., No. 89, p. 25. In 1913, the exports of shea products amounted to only £74,471. "Statistical Abstract of the British Empire," 1915, p. 145; Dennett, op. cit., p. 887.

[52] Thompson, op. cit., No. 84, pp. 11, 15, 31; No. 89, pp. 7, 22, 23; Steel-Maitland, op. cit., pp. 10 ff. [Cf. "Handbook of German East Africa," p. 237.]

[53] Statistisches Jahrbuch, 1915, pp. 184, 471, 475-480.

their East African colony, the Germans had, however, planted 784,458 coconut trees, of which 178,799 were capable of production in 1913. The amount exported was somewhat less than 2.5 million marks and a considerable part of it went to Zanzibar.[54] Unquestionably, the coconut thrives on this coast, but the infant industry faces two serious obstacles, labor scarcity and the competition of the East, with its expanding production.[55] Hence its future on a large scale is quite problematical.

3.   The Cocoa Industry

The Oil Palm and Cocoa Chiefly British Industries.— Unlike their neighbors, the British African colonies did not base their welfare upon ivory and rubber, and thus they were untouched by the sharp crisis of 1912-13 which resulted from the astoundingly rapid development of the rubber plantations of the British and Dutch East.   In some measure, this escape was due to a combination of good luck and business acumen; but, to an even greater extent,

[54] *Statistisches Jahrbuch*, 1915, pp. 465, 473; Calvert, *op. cit.*, pp. 162-164; J. H. Harris, *op. cit.*, p. 4.   [In 1918-19, 49,000 cwt., valued at £35,000, were exported (*The Statesman's Year-Book*, 1920, p. 181), these figures rising to 106,615 cwts. and £105,000 in 1919-20, but falling to 69,834 cwts. and £103,772 in 1920-21 (*ibid.*, 1921, p. 183; 1922, p. 188).]

[55] The exports of copra from British East Africa in 1913-14 amounted to only £35,587, but the industry was more firmly established in Zanzibar. In 1913, the imports of copra into that island amounted to £46,240, and the exports to £216,842. "Statistical Abstract of the British Empire," 1915, pp. 131, 461.   [The imports in 1918 amounted to £68,715 and the exports to £151,387; for 1919 the figures were £120,875 and £442,115 respectively; and for 1920, £167,007 and £535,434. *The Statesman's Year-Book*, 1921, p. 189; 1922, p. 193.]   On copra in Zanzibar, see A. R. Galbraith, "Zanzibar and its Possibilities," in *United Empire Magazine*, April, 1914, pp. 342-344; Norma Lorimer, "By the Waters of Africa," pp. 326-338; F. C. McClellan, "Agricultural Resources of the Zanzibar Protectorate," in *Bulletin of the Imperial Institute*, 1914, pp. 420-422.

it was the consequence of British colonial policy, whose main principle is one of local growth and not of systematic planning from a distant center. Downing Street does not try to determine the lines of economic development in accordance with the needs and interests of Great Britain, but the colony is considered an end in itself. As Bonar Law said with essential accuracy in the House of Commons on August 3, 1916:

"It is clearly one of the undoubted facts of our history in the government of any of these colonies that when you send officials out they look upon the interests of the colony to which they are sent as their business much more than the interests of the Mother Country from which they have come."

As a result of this decentralized policy, local economic forces and local initiative are largely allowed to decide the course of development, which consequently is likely to be along sound lines. Furthermore, the Colonial Office in London in coöperation with very influential private agencies—especially the Anti-Slavery and Aborigines' Protection Society—has consistently sought to guard the native against local exploitation. As a result of this combination of policy and circumstance, the economic life of the British colonies was on an exceptionally sound and solid basis. These possessions were the first to develop the oil palm and they were equally to the fore in establishing the cocoa industry on the African continent. The rapid evolution of this undertaking in the Gold Coast is one of the romances of recent economic history, and has radically changed the outlook as to the future of African civilization.

The Portuguese Cocoa Islands.—Until very recent times no significant quantity of cocoa came from the African continent. It was, however, grown on a considerable scale in the islands off the coast, chiefly on Portuguese São Thomé. It was produced there on large plantations owned by Europeans; and the labor system, though nominally one of long contracts, was in reality one of virtual slavery. The estates were scientifically run and the profits were large, but the conditions of life were execrable. They resembled those in the West Indian sugar plantations of the eighteenth century, where the mortality was so high that constant large purchases of slaves had to be made merely to maintain their numbers. Labor for the São Thomé cocoa plantations was recruited in Portuguese Angola on the mainland by methods which differed little, if at all, from slave raids. The recruiting agents did not confine themselves to Angola but went even into the Belgian Congo in quest of men. These abuses aroused remonstrances from the British Government and led to a boycott of the Portuguese product by some of the most prominent British manufacturers.[56] As a consequence of this action and also of a healthy public opinion in Portugal, which was greatly stimulated by the Revolution of 1910, many reforms have been introduced and conditions have improved very considerably. In 1917, Mr. Balfour stated officially that they were "entirely satisfactory."[57] They are, however, still far from being above

---

[56] H. W. Nevinson, "Modern Slavery," New York, 1906; W. A. Cadbury, "Labour in Portuguese West Africa"; E. D. Morel, "Africa and the Peace of Europe," p. 46; John H. Harris, "Dawn in Darkest Africa," pp. 134, 137, 161-166, 175-195; *idem,* "Portuguese Slavery: Britain's Dilemma."

[57] Cd. 8479 (Africa, 1917); *Anti-Slavery Reporter,* July, 1917, pp. 33-40; October, 1917, pp. 73, 74; George Young, "Portugal Old and Young: An

criticism, primarily because it is impossible to repatriate all the contract laborers of the old régime, since many of them have been on the island for decades and have in reality no other home. Time is the only remedy for this heritage of the past. But, in addition, it is questionable whether the plantation system can ever be wholly purged of labor abuses. It unquestionably tends to be subversive of native life. In the opinion of some, it is so fundamentally wrong in principle that in the end the São Thomé production is bound to succumb in competition with the native output in the Gold Coast.[58]

Rise of the Gold Coast Industry.—The Gold Coast industry is organized on a radically different basis. Here the cocoa is entirely the product of aboriginal enterprise. The natives own virtually all the farms, usually small ones of a

Historical Study," pp. 40, 318, 319, Oxford, 1917; Sir H. H. Johnston, "Common Sense in Foreign Policy," pp. 80, 81, London, 1913. In 1916, out of an estimated population of 68,220, 35,535 were contract laborers and 6,985 were child workers. It was estimated that of the old type laborers, the *serviçais*, or virtual slaves, 15,000 to 25,000 still remained in the islands. In 1914, 9,517 *serviçais* entered São Thomé, of whom 1,580 came from Angola, 7,893 from Mozambique, and 44 from the Cape Verde Islands; 5,922 adults and 1,158 minors were repatriated that year. "Annuário Colonial da 1916," p. 258.

[58] As yet, there are no marked indications of this. The Gold Coast industry is developing much more rapidly, but the São Thomé output is also increasing.

PRODUCTION OF COCOA IN SÃO THOMÉ AND PRINCIPE

(in sacks of 132 to 140 pounds)

1912	497,329
1913	535,808
1914	569,422
1915	471,024
1916	629,450

Washington Daily and Consular Trade Reports, 1917, No. 283, p. 878. See also British Diplomatic and Consular Reports, No. 5496, p. 3; "Annuário Colonial da 1916," pp. 257, 261.

few acres, and sell the output. No European capital is invested in it. In addition, there are in the colony many native merchants of considerable wealth and wide associations. According to some accounts, this industry was introduced as early as 1879,[59] but its real start dates from about 1899, when 715,000 pounds of cocoa were exported. The shipments grew at an astonishingly rapid rate until, in 1913, they reached 113 million pounds of a value of 12.5 million dollars.[60] This quantity was just equivalent to one fifth of the world's total production. In these few years the Gold Coast had become the largest single source of supply, surpassing Ecuador and Sao Thomé.[61] The fact that the native has been able by his own efforts to develop so important an industry is conclusive proof that he is capable of a far higher degree of civilization than he has as yet attained. It is the best augury for the future, and it has clearly indicated the line of real progress in Africa.[62] This lesson has not been wholly lost on the other colonizing Powers.

[59] *United Empire Magazine*, 1916, p. 298.

[60] EXPORTS OF COCOA FROM THE GOLD COAST

(in millions of pounds)

1908	28.6
1909	45.3
1910	50.7
1911	89.
1912	86.6
1913	113.2

"Statistical Abstract of the British Empire," 1915, pp. 332, 333, 149.

[61] The world's crop of cocoa in 1913 was 255,542 metric tons, of which the Gold Coast furnished 51,279, Ecuador 40,758, and São Thomé 35,900. *Statistisches Jahrbuch*, 1915, p. 32.

[62] On this Gold Coast industry, see John H. Harris, "Dawn in Darkest Africa," pp. 252-256; Sir Hugh Clifford, "Some Facts Concerning the Gold Coast," in *Journal of the African Society*, October, 1914, p. 22.

Future Prospects.—The future of the industry is bright. There is room for further expansion in the Gold Coast,[63] and another source of supply is developing in Nigeria, where the output has been rapidly increasing.[64] But apart from the British colonies, there is abundant suitable land with proper climatic conditions under other flags. In the Belgian Congo a very considerable area is available.[65] In the course of an address delivered in 1916, the Belgian Colonial Minister, M. J. Renkin, emphasized the need for diversification of production in the Congo. Rubber, ivory, and gum copal, he said, will lose their preëminence and the future must rest upon the methodical cultivation of oil-palm products, rice, cotton, coffee, sugar, and cocoa. He

[63] In 1915, the value of the exports of cocoa from the Gold Coast was 18 million dollars. *United Empire Magazine,* 1916, p. 298; *The Statesman's Year-Book,* 1917, p. 246. In 1914, the exports were 52,888 tons (£2,193,749); in 1915, 77,278 tons (£3,651,341), and, in 1916, 72,161 tons (£3,847,720). British Colonial Reports, Gold Coast, No. 948, p. 20; No. 894, p. 10. [In 1917, they were 90,964 tons (£3,146,851), in 1919, 176,176 tons (£8,278,554), and in 1920, 124,773 tons (£10,056,298). *The Statesman's Year-Book,* 1919, p. 240; 1921, p. 249; 1922, p. 258.]

[64] In 1913, Nigeria exported 8,111,920 pounds, valued at £157,480, as against 341,461 pounds in 1903. "Statistical Abstract of the British Empire," 1915, pp. 144, 145. [The value of the output was £499,004 in 1917, £235,870 in 1918, and £1,067,675 in 1919, and £1,237,538 in 1920. *The Statesman's Year-Book,* 1919, p. 237; 1920, p. 242; 1921, p. 245; 1922, p. 254.] On account of the dry season, cocoa does not thrive so well in Sierra Leone. W. Hopkins, "Agriculture in Sierra Leone," in *Journal of the African Society,* January, 1915, pp. 145, 146. Only a very small quantity, 114 tons, was exported from French West Africa in 1915. G. François, "L'Aide de l'Afrique Occidentale à la Métropole," in *L'Afrique Française,* May and June, 1917, p. 196. [The value of the cocoa exported from the Ivory Coast in 1918 was 556,298 francs; in 1919, 1,811,538 francs, and in 1920, 2,656,388 francs. *The Statesman's Year-Book,* 1920, p. 883; 1921, p. 899; 1922, p. 921.]

[65] John H. Harris, "Dawn in Darkest Africa," pp. 213-217, 249, 250. In 1912, the exports of cocoa from the Belgian Congo amounted to only a little more than one million francs. British Diplomatic and Consular Reports, No. 5260, p. 19. See also E. Leplac, "Agriculture in the Belgian Congo," in *Bulletin of the Imperial Institute,* 1914, pp. 60-75 [and cf. "Manual of Belgian Congo," pp. 189-192].

referred to the excellent results obtained by native output in Uganda, Nigeria, and the Gold Coast, and said that the future development could be along these lines or by means of large companies. While the latter method opens production, the former, he pointed out, increases it and leads to the civilization of the natives.[66] This lesson had been very incompletely learned by the Germans. For years they had been engaged in raising cocoa in the Cameroons but, instead of stimulating native initiative, they had discouraged it and had introduced the European plantation system. In fact, it was claimed that one of these cocoa plantations was the largest in the world.[67] But the total output of this colony, which far exceeds the Gold Coast in size and population, was in 1913 only about one tenth that of the British possession. Germany's consumption of cocoa was tenfold the production of her colonies.[68] The German Government had shortly before the war recognized the folly of discouraging native production and had reversed its policy, but the European planters were bitterly opposed to this change and it had not been effective.[69] Of the amount exported

[66] J. Renkin, "L'Avenir du Congo Belge." in *L'Afrique Française,* March, 1916, Supplement, p. 64. See also the discussion in the "Bulletin de la Société Belge d'Études Coloniales," 1914, pp. 12, 13, 235-243, 252, 253.

[67] J. K. Vietor, "Geschichtliche und Kulturelle Entwickelung Unserer Schutzgebiete," pp. 86, 87.

[68] *Statistisches Jahrbuch,* 1915, p. 32*.

[69] For instance, in the *Koloniale Monatsblätter* of July, 1914, Dr. Schulte stated his firm conviction "that it is a universal blessing to us here at home in Germany to know that the agricultural ventures led by Germans constitute the backbone of every single colony." *Journal of the African Society,* October, 1914, p. 48. The German planters realized that native production would ultimately mean the abolition of the system of forced labor upon which they depended. Thus, a writer in the *Kamerun Post* of May 2, 1914, asks: "What will become of this colony if the natives are not compelled to do any work? How shall export values be created, and how is it possible to increase the value of imports? What

from the Cameroons in 1912, about six sevenths was the product of the European plantations. With liberation of the Cameroons from German rule and eradication of the German system of large European plantations based upon forced labor, it may be possible to increase the output greatly. Even then there will be the difficulty of dispelling the effects of Germany's heavy hand and of stimulating a spirit of self-reliance and initiative among a downtrodden people. But if the plantation system, with its expensive European supervision, is maintained and if further the cost of production is raised by the establishment of decent labor conditions, in all probability the Cameroon industry will languish, if not disappear, in competition with its vigorous Gold Coast rival.

4.   Miscellaneous Products

Sisal-Hemp.—Ever since the European penetration of the African interior, experiments have been made with various agricultural products, such as cotton, coffee, sugar, tobacco, and sisal-hemp, all of which have thriven to a certain extent, but no one of which has reached an output of such dimensions as to figure at all prominently and influentially in the economy of the world. Climatic conditions were satisfactory and suitable land was available in plenty, but the great obstacle was the scarcity of labor. Of these

service is the native to us if he does not want to work?" Similarly, the editor of *Der Tropenpflanzer* said in 1912 that what was needed was a more liberal policy to enable Europeans to acquire further land and to obtain additional labor so as to warrant an extension of the cocoa plantations. He likewise claimed that what had been done in the Gold Coast with a suitable climate and intelligent natives could not be accomplished in the Cameroons with such material as Bakwiris and Dualas. John H. Harris, "Germany's Lost Colonial Empire," pp. 20-22.

products, one of the most promising is sisal-hemp, or henequen, which is used largely in the manufacture of cordage,
ropes, and twines. The chief source of the world's supply
is the State of Yucatan in Mexico, from whose port, Sisal,
the fiber derives its name.[70] This was virtually the sole
industry that the Germans introduced successfully into
Africa and it was the only commodity produced in their
colonies in sufficient quantities to meet the home demand.
In fact, German East Africa produced more sisal-hemp
than Germany consumed.[71] The plant was introduced into
that colony in 1893 from Florida. In 1901, fifteen tons of
the product were exported and since then the output has
increased very rapidly.[72] It is grown on the plantation system—62,000 acres were under cultivation in 1913; and the
industry is apparently not adapted to native production.[73]
Excellent machinery was devised for extracting the fiber
from the plant and the prepared sisal commanded a higher
price than its Mexican rival.[74] The yield was, however,

[70] "The Henequen Industry," in *Mexican Review*, February, 1918, p. 18;
Publications of the Comisión Reguladora del Mercado de Henequen de
Yucatan. [The Mexican output in 1918 was 158,066 tons. *The Statesman's Year-Book*, 1921, p. 1077.]
[71] Paul Leutwein, "Siedelungs- und Plantagenkolonien," in *Weltverkehr*,
1914-15, pp. 207, 208.

[72] EXPORTS OF SISAL-HEMP FROM GERMAN EAST AFRICA

	Tons
1901	15
1905	1,400
1910	7,000
1911	10,090
1912	16,000

Rivista Coloniale, December 31, 1914, pp. 161, 162 [cf. also "Handbook
of German East Africa," p. 235].
[73] *Statistisches Jahrbuch*, 1915, p. 474.
[74] A. F. Calvert, "The German African Empire," pp. 132, 138-142; W. A.

small in comparison with that of Yucatan. Roughly, the
German output in 1912 was ten per cent of the total supply.[75] In 1913, 19,698 tons were exported, valued at 2.5
million dollars.[76] This German advance led to the introduction of the industry into British East Africa,[77] and into the
French colonies on the West Coast.[78] It is probably assured a prosperous future, as the African sisal is apparently
able to compete successfully with its Mexican rival. There
are, however, distinct limitations to the indefinite expansion
of the African output, both in the labor supply and in the
comparatively small demand for the product.

Cotton.—Far less hopeful is the outlook for cotton, to
which vastly greater attention has been paid. It was the
desire of the colonizing Powers to create new sources of
supply in Middle Africa to supplement the crops of the
United States, India, and Egypt, which were not increasing
as rapidly as was the world's demand. The United States
contributed between fifty and sixty per cent of the total
production and was by far the largest source of supply for

Crabtree, "Economic Resources of German Colonies," in *Journal of the African Society,* January, 1917, p. 132.

[75] In 1912, the Central American production was about 140,000 tons, and that of German East Africa, 17,000 tons, while about 10,000 tons were exported from the Bahamas, Java, and Mauritius. *Rivista Coloniale,* December 31, 1914, pp. 161, 162; R. V. Samele, "Coltivazione e Sfrutta-mento dell' Agave Sisalana," in *L'Esplorazione Commerciale,* 1917, p. 347. The Mexican exports in 1915 and 1916 increased to about 160,000 tons, but they fell in 1917 to 122,000. New York *Tribune,* April 26, 1918.

[76] *Statistisches Jahrbuch,* 1915, p. 465. [In 1918, the output was 7,954 tons, valued at £275,000. *The Statesman's Year-Book,* 1920, p. 181. In 1919-20, 16,744 tons, worth £436,000, were exported. *Ibid.,* 1921, p. 183.]

[77] W. A. Crabtree, *loc. cit.; The Statesman's Year-Book,* 1917, p. 184.

[78] G. François, "L'Aide de l'Afrique Occidentale à la Métropole," in *L'Afrique Française,* May and June, 1917, p. 196; René Chudeau, "Quelques Progrès en Afrique Occidentale," in *L'Afrique Française,* Octo-ber-December, 1916, Supplement, pp. 260 ff.

the European mills.[79]   To some this dependence was irksome in itself and, on the whole, it was deemed dangerous
since American consumption of the raw material was increasing rapidly.   Moreover, the fluctuations in the price
of raw cotton, whether natural or produced by such episodes
as Sully's famous corner of 1904, were deemed onerous as
they unsettled the European textile industry.   The situation was, in general, viewed quite seriously, and Dr. Paul
Leutwein's statement made in 1914 that it was "eine Lebens-
frage," a question of life and death, for Germany to secure
a source of supply under her own flag, was merely an
exaggeration of opinions widely held.[80]   Hence the systematic attempts of the European Governments, aided by
energetic private agencies, such as the British Cotton Growing Association, to stimulate the cultivation of cotton in
their African colonies.[81]   The plant is indigenous in many
parts of tropical Africa.   Before the products of the Lancashire looms had come to Africa, there was considerable
weaving of the native crop, but this had largely disappeared.   All efforts to expand African production so as
appreciably to increase the world's supply have failed.
Only very small quantities were exported from the German,
Portuguese, and French possessions and while the British
colonies—Nyasaland, Uganda, and Nigeria—were consid-

[79] The total crop of 1913-14 was 29,303,000 bales, of which the United
States contributed 14,610,000 (of 230 kg.); British India, 5,987,000 (of 180
kg.); Egypt, 966,000 (of 340 kg.); and Brazil, China, Russia, etc., all
together, 7,740,000 (of 135 kg.). *Statistisches Jahrbuch*, 1915, p. 30*.

[80] P. Leutwein, *op. cit.*, pp. 205, 206.

[81] Portugal granted a bonus to planters shipping more than five tons
of cotton from Angola and exempted all cotton grown there from export
duties in the colony and from import duties in Portugal. British Diplomatic and Consular Reports, No. 5402, p. 4.

erably more successful, still their outputs were in reality only a few drops in the bucket. The British colonies in Middle Africa exported in 1913 about 40,000 standard 500 pound bales [82] and their neighbors together about 16,000.[83] But at that time the world apparently required a yearly gain in the supply of as much as one million

[82] "Statistical Abstract of the British Empire," 1915, pp. 359-361.

[83] British Diplomatic and Consular Reports, No. 5147, p. 5; No. 5402, p. 7; *Statistisches Jahrbuch*, 1915, pp. 465, 468; François, *loc. cit.;* A. F. Calvert, *op. cit.,* pp. 132-137; *Journal of the African Society*, October, 1914, p. 44. *Bulletin of the Imperial Institute*, 1914, pp. 466, 467. The production of the Anglo-Egyptian Sudan (about 10,000 bales) and that of Eritrea (about 900 bales) are not included in the statement in the text. The output from the Sudan in 1909-13, in bales of 400 lbs. each, was as follows (J. A. Todd, "The World's Cotton Crops," pp. 200-201, London, 1915): 1909, 6,890; 1910, 15,370; 1911, 21,907; 1912, 14,487; 1913, 12,830 [and the estimated output in 1914-18 was (*The Statesman's Year-Book*, 1919, p. xxiii; 1920, p. xxiv): 1914, 10,000; 1915, 24,000; 1916, 16,200; 1917, 23,000; 1918, 12,000].

Similarly, the estimated cotton production in new African fields of the Empire is as follows:

Colony	1914	1915	1916	1917	1918
Gold Coast	100	100	100	100	100
Lagos	13,600	6,200	9,300	7,800	3,000
Southern Nigeria	150	100	100	100	100
Northern Nigeria	1,000	1,200	10,800	3,900	3,000
Total, West Africa	14,850	7,600	20,300	11,900	6,200
Uganda	42,000	25,200	25,100	24,000	23,000
British East Africa	500	300	200	200	200
Nyasaland and Rhodesia	8,000	9,000	8,500	6,500	5,000
Total, East Africa	50,500	34,500	33,800	30,700	28,200
Total, Africa (except Sudan)	65,350	42,100	54,100	42,600	34,400

[The value of the output from British East Africa (Kenya) in 1918 was £1,110,980, of which Uganda supplied £965,951; while the Tanganyika Territory exported 1,665,000 lbs., valued at £87,000. In 1919 Kenya exported cotton to the value of £1,100,980 (mostly from Uganda), Tanganyika Territory to the value of £62,000 (1,629,851 lbs.), and Uganda to the value of £1,209,633. For 1920 the corresponding figures were £3,195,261, £119,255, and £3,778,931. *The Statesman's Year-Book*, 1920, pp. 179, 181, 183; 1921, pp. 181, 183, 185; 1922, pp. 186, 188, 190.]

The distribution of output between the colonies of the various Powers

bales.[84]   Here again the main obstacle to a rapid increase in the African output is labor scarcity coupled, as in other cases, with inadequate transportation facilities.

Other Products.—Similar local successes of a pioneer character have also been scored with a number of other products—such as tobacco, sugar, and coffee. But no one of them was grown on a large scale. Angola exported a fair quantity of coffee and sugar.[85] Coffee was also sent from British East Africa and Uganda, and from the neighboring German colony.[86] Tobacco in appreciable quantity

in 1910-12 was as follows (L. Polier, "La Question du Prix du Coton," in *L'Egypte Contemporaine,* V [1914], p. 321):

Colonies	1910	1911	1912
British	32,300	44,500	58,000
German	4,400	6,400	11,000
Italian	2,400	3,600	4,800
French	1,400	1,900	2,700
Total	40,500	56,400	76,500

[See further "Manual of Belgian Congo," pp. 196-198; "Handbook of German East Africa," pp. 236-237.]

[84] Professor Todd sums up the situation as follows: "All the work of the European Associations, German, French, Italian and Portuguese as well as British in every part of Africa [Egypt excepted], had not up till 1913 succeeded in producing a total crop of 100,000 bales in a year, and the fact must be faced that while the capabilities of these areas have now been proved beyond doubt, there is still much to be done before these pioneer successes can be translated into terms of, say, a million bales of cotton." In his expert judgment, Nigeria offers the best prospects, but even there, he points out, many years must elapse before the crop can hope to reach 100,000 bales. J. A. Todd, "The Cotton Resources of the British Empire," in A. P. Newton, "The Staple Trades of the Empire," pp. 100, 106, 107. See also J. A. Todd, "The World's Cotton Crops," pp. 159-202, London, 1915.

[85] Angola exported in 1913 nearly 5 million kilos of coffee and nearly 4 million kilos of sugar. British Diplomatic and Consular Reports, No. 5402, p. 7.

[86] "Statistical Abstract of the British Empire," 1915, pp. 129, 131, 335; *Statistisches Jahrbuch,* 1915, pp. 464-467; Calvert, *op. cit.,* pp. 132, 161. [The value of the coffee exported from British East Africa (Kenya) in 1918 was £365,872, of which £105,009 came from Uganda, this figure rising to £574,884 in 1920. From the Shiré province of Nyasaland 131,390 lbs.

was likewise shipped from Nyasaland.[87]   In addition, such
native products as cola nuts and gum copal were exported.
The output of gum copal, which is used in making varnish,
was increasing rapidly in the Belgian Congo and had
reached, in 1912, 3,688 tons, valued at 6.4 million francs.[88]

were shipped in 1916-17, as were 420,685 lbs. of tea. The figures for coffee
output in 1917-18 were 2,774 lbs.; in 1918-19, 188,865 lbs.; and in 1920,
64,362 lbs.; and for tea, 155,338 lbs. in 1917-18; 700,455 lbs. in 1918-19;
and 496,836 lbs. in 1920. The value of the coffee exported from Uganda
in 1919-20 was £161,714, and in 1920, £90,362; from Tanganyika Territory
in 1919-20, £187,000 (78,530 cwts.), and in 1920-21, £88,683 (33,086 cwts.);
from the Ivory Coast in 1918, 75,159 francs, in 1919, 284,147 francs, and
in 1920, 86,328 francs. *The Statesman's Year-Book*, 1920, pp. 179, 183,
193, 883; 1921, pp. 183, 185, 195, 899; 1922, pp. 190, 188, 921. The sugar
output, in tons, of Natal and Mozambique in 1918-21 was (*ibid.*, 1921,
p. xxii):

Colony	1918-19	1919-20	1920-21
Natal	185,000	150,000	160,000
Mozambique	20,615	35,000	40,000

In German East Africa (Tanganyika Territory) the area under cultivation rose from 3,262 acres in 1909 to 5,808 in 1911 and the value in the
same years (only £4,817 in 1899 and £23,204 in 1908) from £47,111 to
£63,000. "Handbook of German East Africa," pp. 235-236.]
   [87] "Statistical Abstract of the British Empire," 1915, p. 369. [The tobacco
exported from Nyasaland after supplying the local demand amounted to
3,706,203 lbs. in 1915-16, 4,304,124 lbs. in 1916-17, 2,025,372 lbs. in 1917-18,
5,805,396 lbs. in 1918-19, and 4,963,130 lbs. in 1920. The tobacco acreage
in 1919 was 6,027, and in 1920, 14,218. *The Statesman's Year-Book*, 1920,
p. 193; 1921, p. 195; 1922, p. 200.]

[88] EXPORT OF GUM COPAL

	Tons
1909	807
1910	958
1911	2,100
1912	3,688
1913	4,613
[1914	6,993
1915	4,266
1916	8,719
1917	6,911
1918	3,611]

British Diplomatic and Consular Reports, No. 5240, p. 6; No. 5493,
p. 5 ["Manual of Belgian Congo," p. 269, cf. pp. 186-187; *The Statesman's
Year-Book*, 1920, p. 695. The output from German East Africa (Tanganyika Territory) is much less important, being only 209,987 lbs. in 1911,

From some of the colonies, such as Angola, Nigeria, and British East Africa, maize and pulse were shipped in noticeable quantities.[89] Furthermore, in the Lake Chad region and in the highlands of British and German East Africa, the number of cattle, goats, and sheep was increasing, as were the exports of hides and skins. A considerable future for this industry as a source both of skins and also of meats has been predicted.[90] Finally, the valuable woods of tropical Africa—ebony, mahogany, and cedar—were being shipped to Europe in ever larger quantities. The exports of lumber from French West Africa in 1913 amounted to about one million dollars and consisted mainly of okoumé, a pale, inferior mahogany used for cigar boxes and the internal parts of furniture. This was shipped principally

valued at £5,369. "Handbook of German East Africa," p. 238. The value of the kola nuts shipped from the Gold Coast was £239,134 in 1918, £350,249 in 1919, and £452,245 in 1920; from Sierra Leone, £321,105 in 1918, £417,378 in 1919, and £626,815 in 1920; from the Ivory Coast, £4,151 in 1918 and £2,148 in 1919. *The Statesman's Year-Book,* 1920, pp. 245, 247, 883; 1921, pp. 249, 251, 899; 1922, pp. 258, 261].

[89] British Diplomatic and Consular Reports, No. 5402, p. 7; "Statistical Abstract of the British Empire," 1915, p. 133; R. E. Dennett, "British and German Trade in Nigeria," in *United Empire Magazine,* December, 1914, p. 887.

[90] "Statistical Abstract of the British Empire," 1915, pp. 129, 133, 135, 375, 377; René Chudeau, *op. cit.,* pp. 258-260; "L'Élevage des Bovidés au Territoire du Tchad," in *L'Afrique Française,* March, 1917, Supplement, pp. 69-74; *L'Afrique Française,* May-June, 1917, p. 196. F. A. G. Pape, "Tropical Eastern Africa," in *United Empire Magazine,* 1916, pp. 393, 394; British Diplomatic and Consular Reports, No. 5441, p. 33; Karl Dove, "Die Grossen Wirtschaftsgebiete Afrikas," in *Weltwirtschaft,* 1915, p. 161. [In 1918, hides and skins to the value of £150,012 were exported from British East Africa, £77,000 from the Tanganyika Territory, £293,019 from Nigeria, and £51,528 from Gambia (*The Statesman's Year-Book,* 1920, pp. 179, 181, 242, 244. In 1919-20, the corresponding figures were: Tanganyika Territory, £256,000; Nigeria, £1,262,140; Gambia, £8,419; with £270,472 from Uganda; *ibid.,* 1921, pp. 183, 185, 245, 248. For 1920-21 they were, respectively, £96,478, £774,725, £21,125, £93,008. *Ibid.,* 1922, pp. 188, 254, 257, 190.]

to Germany. The exports of lumber in general from Nigeria and the Gold Coast together were valued at about twice this amount, two million dollars.[91]   The aggregate worth of all these miscellaneous exports was considerable. While they play a large part in the domestic life of the various colonies, apparently Africa's output of no one of them will within an appreciable time be an influential factor in the economic system of the world.

[91] "Statistical Abstract of the British Empire," 1915, pp. 145, 147; H. R. Tate, "British East Africa," in *United Empire Magazine,* 1917, pp. 544, 545; A. Girault, "The Colonial Tariff Policy of France," pp. 229, 230, 241, 242; British Diplomatic and Consular Reports, No. 5423, p. 10; No. 5494, p. 6; Address of Governor-General Merlin in *L'Afrique Française,* March, 1916, Supplement, p. 60.

In 1913, 42,000 tons of wood were shipped from the magnificent forests of the Ivory Coast (*L'Afrique Française,* July-August, 1918, p. 158). In this same year, the exports of woods, in tons, and their values, in francs, were ("Statistique du Commerce des Colonies Françaises," 1913, I, 1, pp. 643, 707, Paris, 1915):

Country	Tons	Value
France	22,108	1,500,000
Great Britain	29,517	2,000,000
Germany	67,169	3,500,000
Others	31,894	1,300,000
Total	150,688	8,800,000

Of this the chief items were:

Wood	Tons	Value
Acajou	10,081	1,300,000
Okoumé	134,223	6,400,000
Total	144,304	7,700,000

The shipments of woods from French Equatorial Africa amounted to 58,844 tons in 1910, 102,240 tons in 1911, and 95,767 tons in 1912. The output in 1911 was valued at 5,285,545 francs, and of the exports in this year, 91,540 tons were okoumé, worth 4,122,545 francs, thus representing ninety per cent of the quantity and eighty per cent of the value (G. Bruel, "L'Afrique Équatoriale Française," pp. 357, 462). The shipments of acajou from the Ivory Coast in 1912 were worth 2,900,000 francs, and in the following year, 5,000,000 francs ("Statistique du Commerce des Colonies Françaises," 1913, I, 1, p. 417, Paris, 1915. [The value of the mahogany shipped from the Ivory Coast in 1918 was 3,003,956 francs (*The Statesman's Year-Book,* 1920, p. 883), in 1919, 3,422,391 francs (*ibid.,* 1921, p. 899), and in 1920, 20,370,876 francs (*ibid.,* 1922, p. 921).]

CHAPTER III

THE MINERAL RESOURCES OF MIDDLE AFRICA

Their Wide Distribution and Unknown Extent.—While it is an established fact that Middle Africa contains mineral resources of considerable variety, relatively little is known as to their general extent and commercial value. The area as a whole has been only most superficially and incompletely investigated, largely because none but exceptionally rich and favorably located mines can be profitably worked under prevailing conditions of labor scarcity and inadequate transportation. Mineral deposits of varied nature are scattered throughout Middle Africa and are to be found in practically every colony. In Togoland, there is considerable good iron ore; while in German East Africa (Tanganyika Territory) are deposits of gold, coal, iron, and mica, and probably also of tin and copper.[1] Very little, however, had been done to develop these resources in the German colonies. Only small quantities of gold and mica were shipped from German East Africa.[2] French Equatorial Africa similarly exported a little copper.[3] In the Belgian

[1] A. F. Calvert, "The German African Empire," pp. 174-182, 226, 227; F. A. G. Pape, "Tropical Eastern Africa," in *United Empire Magazine,* 1916, pp. 395-397; *Bulletin of the Imperial Institute,* 1914, pp. 580-599. ["Handbook of German East Africa," pp. 243-245.]

[2] In 1913, German East Africa exported raw gold to the value of 678,000 marks, and mica to the value of 313,000 marks. *Statistisches Jahrbuch,* 1915, p. 465.

[3] A. Girault, "The Colonial Tariff Policy of France," pp. 243, 244; "Annuaire du Gouvernement Général de l'Afrique Équatoriale Française,"

Congo, leaving the Katanga copper belt out of consideration, diamonds were being successfully mined in the south-
east and gold was being produced on a small scale in the
Welle and Arawumi districts to the northeast.[4] But apart
from these minor enterprises, there were three regions in
which mining was conducted on a large scale; namely,
the Gold Coast, Nigeria, and the Katanga District of the
Belgian Congo.

The Katanga Copper Belt.—The Katanga District is an
extensive area in the Southern Congo adjoining Northern
Rhodesia, with which it is in close economic relations. The
mineral wealth of this region was proved by a British prospecting expedition acting on the behalf of the Tanganyika
Concessions Company, of which Mr. Robert Williams was

1912, I, p. 113. A railway from the Mindouli mines to Brazzaville, 163
kilometers due east, was completed in 1911, and in that year, 1,899 tons
of copper ore, yielding over forty-five per cent of metal, were shipped by
this route. In 1912, 1,968 tons were transported and in 1913, 1,275, with an
estimated value of 678,960 francs. During this period, other mining
enterprises were just getting under way. G. Bruel, "L'Afrique Équatoriale Française," pp. 386-391.
    [4] J. Renkin, "L'Avenir du Congo Belge," in *L'Afrique Française,* March,
1916, Supplement, p. 64. In 1912, the exports of gold from the Belgian
Congo amounted to 3.3 million francs. British Diplomatic and Consular
Reports, No. 5260, p. 19. In 1912, this quantity was 965 kilos and in
1913, 1,475. *Ibid.,* No. 5493. See also *L'Afrique Française,* 1914, p. 275.
In 1909, 1910, and 1911, the output was 657, 876, and 639 kilos respectively.
"Annuaire Statistique de la Belgique et du Congo Belge," 1913, p. 519.
[In 1917, it was 3,573 kilos; in 1918, 3,605; in 1919, 3,356, and in 1920,
3,324. *The Statesman's Year-Book,* 1920, p. 695; 1921, p. 701; 1922, p. 716;
cf. "Manual of Belgian Congo," pp. 209-211, 268. In 1918, 149,680 carats
of diamonds were exported, in 1919, 215,532 carats, and in 1920, 274,103
carats, as compared with 372,139 carats from the Protectorate of Southwest Africa in 1918, 462,181 carats in 1919, and 606,424 carats in 1920.
The Statesman's Year-Book, 1920, pp. 695, 237; 1921, pp. 701, 241; 1922,
pp. 716, 248; cf. "Manual of Belgian Congo," pp. 211-213.] In addition,
coal has been discovered at the mouth of the Lukuga, near the terminus
of the railroad at Albertville on Lake Tanganyika, and valuable oil-fields
have been located.

the guiding spirit.   The country is remarkably rich in
copper, and it also contains valuable deposits of diamonds,
gold, tin, and iron.   The work of development has been
undertaken chiefly by the Union Minière du Haut Katanga,
a Belgian company, 39.2 per cent of whose stock is owned
by the Tanganyika Concessions Company.   An extensive
plant has been erected, and preparations are being made to
use the local water power to supplement the coal imported
from Rhodesia.   The output of copper is rapidly reaching
large dimensions.   In 1917, it fell somewhat short of 30,000
tons.   If the output for 1918 should reach the estimate of
40,000 tons, then—as Mr. Williams has said—"the Union
Minière will be the largest copper producer outside of
America."   The aim of the management is to attain as
speedily as possible an annual production of 100,000 tons.[5]
The great obstacle to this goal is the difficulty of procuring
sufficient labor.   The local supply is not adequate and
workers have to be recruited in Rhodesia and Portuguese
Nyasaland.   The labor shortage was very great in 1917 and
is bound to be an important factor in the future.   If it can
be overcome, and 100,000 tons of copper can be mined, the
effect on the Belgian Congo will be marked; for at fifteen
cents a pound—a normal price in times of peace—the output
will amount to 33.5 million dollars, which is more than was
the entire volume of this colony's foreign commerce in
1913.   It should be noted, however, that an enterprise of

[5 The actual total output was 21,872 tons in 1916, 24,497 tons in 1917,
20,742 tons in 1918, 22,130 tons in 1919, and 18,924 tons in 1920, as compared with 7,500 tons from the mines in the Protectorate of Southwest
Africa in 1918 and 26,675 tons in 1919. *The Statesman's Year-Book*, 1919,
p. 699; 1920, pp. 695, 237; 1921, pp. 701, 241; 1922, p. 716.   For the
Katanga fields generally, see "Manual of Belgian Congo," pp. 202-207, 270.]

such character is relatively not so valuable to Africa as an industry like that of cocoa in the Gold Coast, where virtually the entire value of the output accrues to the natives. In the case of a mine, all above the cost of production and the expense of marketing belongs to the European stockholders.[6]

The Gold Coast.—As its name implies, the Gold Coast has auriferous deposits. In fact, it has been a more or less constant source of supply to Europe since the days of the Portuguese discoveries; and the gold imported from this region by the Royal African Company gave the name "guinea" to a seventeenth century English coin. The production reached its nadir in 1901, when only £22,187 worth of gold was exported. Since then, simultaneously with the growth of the cocoa industry, there has been a rapid development in mining. Before that time, the gold was derived from alluvial deposits, but since 1900-01, deep shafts have been sunk and heavy machinery has been introduced.[7] In 1913, the exports were somewhat over 8

[6] The cost of producing copper in 1917 was about six and one-half cents a pound. Addresses of Mr. Robert Williams, December 12, 1917, at the general meeting of the Tanganyika Concessions Company, Limited, and May 8, 1917, before the Royal Colonial Institute; British Diplomatic and Consular Reports, No. 5303, pp. 4, 8; No. 5520, pp. 3, 7; F. Rodriguez, "Congo-Katanga-Angola," in *Rivista Coloniale*, May, 1915, pp. 260-271; M. H. Weed, "Mines Handbook," Tuckahoe, New York, 1918. On the labor problem here, see "Bulletin de la Société Belge d'Études Coloniales," 1914, pp. 360-376, 415-465, 593-598; "Bulletin de la Société Royale Belge de Géographie," 1913, pp. 233-254. On the general resources of the northern and southern Katanga regions, see *ibid.*, 1913, pp. 143-146, 667-680.

[7] *Journal of the African Society*, 1916, pp. 242, 243; A. B. Keith, "West Africa," pp. 254, 324, 325. In addition, a large deposit of manganese has been discovered 33 miles north of Secondee. Exportation began in September, 1916, and in three months 4,338 tons were shipped. Washington Daily and Consular Trade Reports, 1917, No. 304, pp. 1210-1212. British

million dollars, which is an appreciable amount, though quite insignificant when compared with the production of the Union of South Africa, amounting to 185 million dollars.[8]

Nigeria Tin.—In Nigeria, the natives have worked metals —iron, tin, and lead—for centuries. In the northern section of the colony are important deposits of tin stretching over an extensive area. The development of these resources before the war was in reality an infant industry, but it was growing very rapidly. In 1913, the exports amounted to 4,194 tons, valued at £567,959. This is not an important quantity, but it was fifteen times as large as the output of 1909.[9] It is scarcely probable that anything

India, the great source of supply, produced in 1913 815,047 tons of manganese, valued at £1,211,034. For details about a new coalfield in Southern Nigeria, see *Bulletin of the Imperial Institute,* 1916, pp. 369-378.

[8] GOLD PRODUCTION OF GOLD COAST

1905	£ 596,583	[1915	£ 1,719,638
1907	1,163,516	1916	1,629,746
1912	1,499,468	1917	1,549,275
1913	1,648,770	1918	1,334,000
1914	1,744,498	1919	1,403,760
		1920	889,248]

"Statistical Abstract of the British Empire," 1915, pp. 382, 383; *The Statesman's Year-Book,* 1917, p. 245 [1921, p. 249; 1922, p. 258]. The West African output of gold in 1917 was 389,068 ounces, valued at £1,615,316, as against 368,168 ounces, valued at £1,529,977, in 1916 (*ibid.,* 1918, p. xliii). [The relative values for the production in the Gold Coast and in the Union of South Africa in 1919 were £1,403,760 and £35,390,609, and in 1920, £889,248 and £34,654,922. *Ibid.,* 1921, pp. 249, 220; 1922, pp. 258, 226.]

[9] TIN PRODUCTION OF NIGERIA

	Tons	Pounds Sterling
1909	269	38,165
1910	692	72,660
1911	1,530	181,759
1912	2,830	336,330
1913	4,194	567,959
1914	6,143	706,988
1915	6,535	723,480

like this rate of progress will be maintained and that Nigeria will ever overtake the Malay States which, with their annual production of 70,000 tons, are the world's chief source of supply.[10]

	Tons	Pounds Sterling
1916	7,054	859,603
1917	9,966	1,485,887
1918	8,294	1,770,003
[1919	7,685	1,324,074
1920	7,913	1,785,724]

"Blue Book of Nigeria," p. W 156, Lagos, 1916; cf. also British Colonial Reports, Nigeria, 1915, No. 920, p. 9, which gives somewhat higher figures: 6,143 tons for 1914 and 6,910 for 1915. See also A. F. Calvert, "Nigeria and Its Tin Fields." [For the tin fields of northern Katanga, see "Manual of Belgian Congo," pp. 208-209.]

[10] A. P. Newton, "The Staple Trades of the Empire," p. 134, London, 1917. [The output from the Federated Malay States in 1919 was 36,938 tons, with a value of £8,745,635, the figures for 1920 being 34,935 and 10,345,188 respectively. *The Statesman's Year-Book,* 1921, pp. 172, 173; 1922, pp. 176, 177.]

CHAPTER IV

THE TRANSPORTATION SYSTEM

Porterage.—Apart from the fundamental question of the labor supply, the development of the rich resources of Middle Africa will depend largely upon the adequacy of the transportation system to bring these products cheaply to the seaboard. This is a question of vital importance. The two primitive instruments of carriage in Africa are the native porter and the canoe with the native paddler. For long distances porterage is exceedingly costly and is commercially possible only in the case of commodities whose value is large in proportion to their bulk, such as ivory and rubber. It was a potent cause of the universal slavery of former times and led to infinite abuses, including great mortality among the impressed carriers, but it cannot be entirely eliminated until, at some future time, Africa is completely covered with a network of railroads and roads. Excellent highways of a very considerable mileage have been built in a number of the colonies, notably in Southwest Africa and in the French Congo,[1] and these will enable the motor truck to be of increasing importance in solving the transportation problem. Even before the war, the cocoa in the Gold Coast within an accessible distance from the ocean was largely collected in this manner. The native carrier, however, still

[1] J. du Plessis, "Thrice Through the Dark Continent," pp. 41, 125, London, 1917; Mary Gaunt, "Alone in West Africa" (3d ed.), p. 243.

plays his part and is the chief instrument in taking the cocoa of the interior to the railroad. Over 100,000 porters were used for this purpose in 1912 and since then the crop has greatly increased.[2] In fact, the very economic development that accompanies better communications is apt, for the time being, to increase the absolute, if not the relative, use of carriers.

Rivers.—The vast network of rivers [3] in Middle Africa provides a natural highway, from which great advantages were expected by those who first opened up the continent. There are, however, two serious drawbacks that largely impair the value of this system. In the first place, these rivers do not give access from the ocean to the interior, because the plateaus are cut off from the coastal lowlands by cataracts and rapids that cannot be passed by ships. The Niger, Gambia, and Senegal are important exceptions to this general rule. In the second place, many of the rivers run very low during the dry season and the shoals then render navigation either very difficult or altogether impossible. Besides, long reaches of the Congo [4] and the Niger are at all times out of the question for fair-sized craft. In general, the system

---

[2] John H. Harris, "Dawn in Darkest Africa," pp. 3, 4. These carriers receive good wages. *Ibid.*, pp. 45, 46.

[[3] On the freedom of river navigation, see *infra*, pp. 206-211.]

[4] As regards the Congo, the navigable sections are ("Annuaire Statistique de la Belgique et du Congo Belge," 1913, p. 539):

Léopoldville to Stanleyville	1,685 km.
Ponthierville to Kindu	315
Kongolo to Bukama	640
	2,640

The length of waterways in the Belgian Congo for boats of 500 tons is 1,685 km.; for those of 150 tons, 3,140; for those of 22 tons, 7,730; and for those of less than 22 tons, 12,213. [For a full description of the Congo and its affluents, see "Manual of Belgian Congo," pp. 235-247.]

of river communications has been a disappointment. Not only is the native paddler still essential, but, at nearly the other extreme of locomotion, extensive railroads have had to be built and many more have been planned. In 1914, including the Rhodesian lines (2,481 miles), there were in operation or nearing completion, in Middle Africa, somewhat over 9,000 miles of railroad.[5] Since then, despite the war, the mileage has somewhat increased.

Supplementary Railroads. — The railroads of Middle Africa fall into three general categories: First, those whose purpose is to supplement river communications; second, local lines to open the immediate hinterland; third, intercolonial railroads connected with more or less vague transcontinental projects. The supplementary lines fulfil various functions. That from Matadi on the lower Congo, 110 miles from the Atlantic, to Léopoldville on Stanley Pool (248 miles), whence the navigable Congo stretches a thousand odd miles to Stanleyville, was essential in order to gain access to the central plateau. Then, to bridge the non-navigable part of the river beyond Stanleyville, a railroad had to be built to Ponthierville (78 miles), while, farther on, another line was for the same reason constructed from Kindu

		Miles
[5] British	....	4,736
German	....	1,473
French	....	1,389
Belgian	....	880
Portuguese	....	809

"Statistical Abstract of the British Empire," 1915, p. 303; *Statistisches Jahrbuch*, 1915, p. 459; Evans Lewin, "The Germans and Africa," p. 299; *The Statesman's Year-Book*, 1917, pp. 884-886; British Diplomatic and Consular Reports, No. 5402, p. 6; No. 5493, p. 9. For the origins of these railroads, see E. A. de Renty, "Les Chemins de Fer Coloniaux en Afrique," 3 vols.

to Kongolo (220 miles). A similar supplementary railroad in French West Africa connects the Senegal at Kayes with the Niger at Kulikoro and gives relatively quick access from France to Timbuktu.[6] A more expeditious route is, however, nearing completion, if it has not already reached that state.

Local Railroads.—Many of the railroads, on the other hand, are independent of river systems and have been constructed to bring the products of the interior to the seaboard. Thus, the Usambara line (220 miles) from Tanga, in the northeast of the Tanganyika Territory, to New Moshi serves as an outlet for the fertile Kilimanjaro-Meru district where some Germans had settled. The two railroads in the Gold Coast, from Sekondi to Kumasi, and from Akra to Tafo, afford access to the colony's gold mines and cocoa fields. Similar purely regional lines tapping the hinterland are those from Loanda to Malanje and from Mossamedes to Lubango in Angola, and the railroads in Sierra Leone, Dahomey, the Ivory Coast, the Cameroons, and Togoland.

Intercolonial Railways.—Other lines, in addition to meeting local needs, stretch farther inland—sometimes to the borders of other colonies— and are designed both to serve as outlets for remoter districts and to form links in larger projects. Thus, the railroads of Senegal and French Guinea

---

[6] As the Senegal is not navigable in the dry season, the route was found very inconvenient during the war for bringing Senegalese troops to France. Accordingly, a railroad from Thiès to Kayes (215 miles), which was already under construction, will soon be completed and will connect the Upper Niger with the Ocean. *The Statesman's Year-Book,* 1917, p. 884; *L'Afrique Française,* 1915, pp. 125, 201. At the beginning of 1918, 422 kilometers were open, leaving 245 to be completed. Colonies et Marine, 1918, I, p. 276. [In April, 1920, the situation was practically unchanged. *Le Temps,* May 16, 1920.]

and the Nigerian system not only tap the Western Sudan, but are ultimately to be connected with the future Trans-Saharan railroad. Similarly, the Uganda Railway serves as an outlet for the Victoria Nyanza district, and the Tanganyika line, completed just before the outbreak of the war, is intended to open up the area around that lake. On the western side of Lake Tanganyika, the Belgians have since the war finished their railroad from Albertville on the lake to Kabalo on the Congo (170 miles). From the south, the Rhodesian lines reach the Belgian frontier and in connection with the Belgian railroads supply an outlet for the products of the Katanga district. Finally, from Lobito Bay in Angola, the finest harbor in West Africa and one of the best in the world, the Benguella Railway is being pushed to Katanga.[7]

[7 In 1921 the railroads of Middle Africa were as follows (*The Statesman's Year-Book*, 1922, pp. 186, 188, 190, 201, 207, 249-250, 254, 259, 262, 717, 909, 916, 919, 920, 921, 922, 923, 1049, 1228, 1229):

Colony	Line	Miles
Kenya	Mombasa-Victoria	618
Tanganyika Territory	Tanga-New Moshi	220
	Dar-es-Salaam-Kigoma	780
Uganda	Jinja-Namasagali	62
	Port Bell-Kampala	7½
Nyasaland	Blantyre-Portuguese boundary	174
Basutoland	Maseru-Marseilles Station	16
Southwest Africa		1,163
Nigeria		1,126
Gold Coast	Sekondi-Kumasi	168
	Tarquah-Prestea	19
	Inchaban-Inchaban Junction	5
	Akra-Anyinam	85
Sierra Leone	Freetown-Pendembu	227½
	Boia Junction-Kamabai	104
Congo	Matadi-Léopoldville	248
	Boma-Chela	90
	Stanleyville-Ponthierville	78
	Kindu-Kongolo	220
	Kabalo-Albertville	170
	Bukama-Elisabethville-Rhodesian frontier	451
	Others	1,396

Transcontinental Projects.—Nearly all these lines are potential parts of more or less inchoate transcontinental

Colony	Line	Miles
Senegal	Dakar-Rufisque-St. Louis	165
	Thiès-Kayes (open portion)	350
Togo	Lome-Anecho	27
	Lome-Atakpame	103
	Lome-Palime	74
Cameroons	....	359
French Guinea	Konakri-Kankan	412
Ivory Coast	Abijean-Bouaké	197
Dahomey	Kotonu-Savé	156
	Branches to Whydah and Segborué	20
	Porto Novo-Pobé	50
French Sudan	Kayes-Kulikoro	344
Eritrea (and Abyssinia)	Jibuti-Addis Abeba	485
	Massawah-Asmara	74
Angola	Loanda-Lucalla-Malanje	375
	Canhoca-Golungo Alto	9
	Lobito-Chinguar (Benguella line)	323
	Mossámedes-Chela Mountains	111
Mozambique	Delagoa Bay-Rhodesian frontier	57
	Lourenço Marques-Swaziland frontier (open portion)	44
	Chai Chai-Manjacaze (open portion) ...	32
	Mutamba-Inharrime (open portion)	25
	Beira Railway	204
Total	....	11,424

The total mileage in the various colonies is:

Kenya	618
Tanganyika Territory	1,000
Uganda	69½
Nyasaland	174
Basutoland	16
Southwest Africa	1,163
Nigeria	1,126
Gold Coast	277
Sierra Leone	331½
Congo	2,653
Senegal	515
Togo	204
Cameroons	359
French Guinea	412
Ivory Coast	197
Dahomey	226
French Sudan	344
Eritrea (and Abyssinia)	559
Angola	818
Mozambique	362
Total	11,424

projects. The French had planned a railroad from Jibuti in French Somaliland through Abyssinia to the West Coast, but the arrangements made with England after Fashoda (1898) rendered this impossible.[8] Sir Edwin Arnold, as early as 1876, and, later, Sir Harry H. Johnston and Cecil Rhodes—the last preëminently—had outlined "the Cape to Cairo" road, but the project was blocked by France and Germany in 1894. Similar ambitions had also been attributed to Germany and they fit in with what is known of her plan to create a vast Mid-African Empire.[9] However much

Divided according to Powers, this mileage is:

British	4,775
Belgian	2,653
French	2,257
Italian (including Abyssinian line)	559
Portuguese	**1,180**
Total	11,424

The following railways, among others, are either planned or under construction (*The Statesman's Year-Book,* 1922, pp. 186, 201, 250, 259, 262, 908, 919, 921, 1049, 1228, 1229):

Colony	*Line*
Kenya	Nakuru-Tuobo
Nyasaland	Chindio-Beira
Southwest Africa	Windhuk-Gobabis
Gold Coast	Akra-Kumasi (surveys in hand)
Sierra Leone	Kamabai-Baga (under consideration)
French Equatorial Africa	Brazzaville-Pointe Noire
Senegal	Thiès-Kayes (350 out of 435 miles open)
Ivory Coast	Extension northward from Bouaké (under contract)
Dahomey	Savé-Chaoru (future intention)
Eritrea	Asmara-Keren and Asmara-Agordat (under construction)
Angola	Lucalla-Malanje to be linked with Central African Railway
Mozambique	Lourenço Marques-Swaziland frontier (44 miles open), Chai Chai-Manjacaze (32 miles open), Mutamba-Inharrime (25 miles open), Beira-Zambezi (to be constructed).]

[8] It was only in 1915 that the railroad from Jibuti reached Addis Abeba, the capital of Abyssinia. *L'Afrique Française,* 1916, pp. 107, 108.

[9] *L'Afrique Française,* June and July, 1915, Supplement, pp. 127-130.

these grandiose projects may have appealed to the imagination, they lost some of their hold when the facts were carefully scrutinized. During the past fifteen years, little had been heard in England of the Cape to Cairo scheme, in so far as it implied a railroad running entirely through British territory and broken only by the international waters of Lake Tanganyika. The Rhodesian section had been deflected westwards from Tanganyika by the mineral discoveries in Katanga. Though it might have some minor strategic and political advantages,[10] the project was from the economic standpoint thoroughly unsound. Africa does not need transcontinental railroads. The traffic will normally be from the center outwards, not from the Indian to the Atlantic Ocean, nor from Egypt to the Cape. The rivalry will be to secure the transportation from the interior to the coast. Thus, the economic aim of the Trans-Saharan project is to obtain for the French Mediterranean ports the output from the Northern Congo and the Central Sudan. Here there is a distinct rivalry between the Mediterranean and West Africa.[11] But the real economic hub of Middle Africa is Katanga and hence it is to this center that the railways are extending from all points of the compass. When these radiating roads are joined together at this focus, various transcontinental routes will be established.

[10] "We might take a line, say the proposed railway line from the Cape to the head of the Nile (approximating to the meridian of 30° East Longitude), and it is along that line, spreading east and west in irregular extension, that we find the white man's land. . . . It is for us to see to it that the great central line which may hereafter link up the white Colonies of Africa remains in strong and friendly hands." Sir Thomas H. Holdich, "Political Frontiers and Boundary Making," pp. 229, 230, London, 1916.

[11] Giuseppe Piazza, "Le Nostre Rivendicazioni Libiche," in *Rivista Coloniale,* March, 1917.

The Benguella Railway.—The line that is admittedly the most favorably situated to secure this central traffic, which now goes over the Rhodesia-Katanga Junction Railway to Beira, is the Benguella Railway, which is being built from Lobito Bay to Katanga. The concession was obtained from Portugal in 1902 by Mr. Robert Williams,[12] but as adequate capital was secured only in 1906, construction was delayed. Further difficulty was encountered in reaching the plateau from the coast, and thus in 1914 only 320 miles were in operation. The war, for the time being, put a virtual stop to further construction, but the railroad will probably be rushed to completion as soon as conditions are again favorable. The finished section is already paying its way from the local traffic in Angola—mainly in mealies, beans, and flour—and the enterprise promises to be a brilliant financial success after the Katanga mineral belt is reached.[13] It has two distinct advantages over the competing routes on the East Coast: in the first place, Lobito Bay is much nearer Europe; in the second place, ships from that port for Europe escape payment of the Suez Canal tolls. The relative distances from Katanga to London by the various routes are as follows: Lobito Bay, 6,457 miles; Cape Town, 8,480; Beira through Broken Hill and Ayrshire, 8,890; Lake

[12] See *supra*, pp. 107-108. [On this railway, and on the other Congolese lines, see "Manual of Belgian Congo," pp. 217-235.]

[13] British Diplomatic and Consular Reports, No. 5402, p. 6; No. 5497, pp. 4-6; Evans Lewin, "Railways in Africa," in *United Empire Magazine*, February and March, 1917, pp. 98, 172; Robert de Caix, in *L'Afrique Française*, 1913, pp. 317-319, 373, 374; Franz Baltzer, "Die Eisenbahnen in den Portugiesischen Kolonien," in *Weltverkehr*, 1913-14, pp. 247-249; Extracts from Report of Benguella Railway Company in the Report of the Tanganyika Concessions, Limited, December 12, 1917, pp. 10-24. Louis Habran, "Le Chemin de Fer de Lobito," in "Bulletin de la Société Belge d'Études Coloniales," 1913, pp. 701-715, 837-857; 1914, pp. 348-357.

Tanganyika and Dar-es-Salaam, 8,937; Beira through Bulawayo, 9,514.[14] The Dar-es-Salaam line is in the worst position to compete, as, apart from all else, four trans-shipments are required before goods can be embarked on vessels for Europe.[15]

Other Projects.—The Congo River route to Matadi is likewise impossible, on account of the numerous changes from steamer to railroad and back again. The Belgian authorities are planning to rectify this by building a line from Stanley Pool direct to Katanga, cutting across the colony. They also have in view a railroad from Stanleyville to Lake Albert, which will connect the Anglo-Egyptian Sudan and Egypt with their own possessions.[16] As these undertakings, especially the former, will necessitate a heavy outlay,[17] their future is problematical. The scarcity of capital resulting from the prolonged hostilities will also be a factor in the future of the Trans-Saharan railroad and may likewise lead to the postponement of the construction of the lines in the French Congo which had been authorized before the war. One of these two railroads was to have connected Stanley Pool with the coast.[18] It would have

[14] British Diplomatic and Consular Reports, No. 5497, pp. 4-6. From Southampton to Lobito Bay the distance is 4,900 miles; thence to the Belgian frontier it is 803 miles and Kambove is 527 miles farther.

[15] *Weltverkehr,* 1914-15, p. 82.

[16] J. Renkin, "L'Avenir du Congo Belge," in *L'Afrique Française,* March, 1916, Supplement, pp. 66, 67.

[17] "Les Communications au Congo Belge," in "Bulletin de la Société Belge d'Études Coloniales," 1912, pp. 297-345.

[18] British Diplomatic and Consular Reports, No. 5249, p. 10; No. 5494, p. 5; *L'Afrique Française,* March, 1915, Supplement, p. 34; "Annales de Géographie," 1915, No. 131, p. 407. The railroad to the coast was to have run from Brazzaville to Pointe Noire (G. Bruel, "L'Afrique Équatoriale Française," pp. 412-413; for other proposed lines in French Equatorial Africa, see *ibid.,* pp. 413-417).

been a serious competitor of the Belgian Matadi line, which, however, was already much congested with freight.[19] While the war, temporarily at least, stopped these projects and others in British Nigeria [20] and in German East Africa,[21] military considerations led to the construction of a connecting link between the Uganda Railway and the Usambara line in the adjoining German colony.[22] In general, the future of railroad enterprise in Middle Africa [23] will depend upon the speed of post-bellum recuperation and upon the extent to which the German menace shall have been eliminated in Africa and throughout the world.

[19] John H. Harris, "Dawn in Darkest Africa," pp. 211, 212.

[20] The construction of the new trunk railroad from Port Harcourt in Nigeria (550 miles) was discontinued on account of the war after reaching the Udi coalfields (151 miles). *The Statesman's Year-Book,* 1917, p. 242.

[21] In 1914, Germany authorized the construction of a railroad from Tabora, in the center of German East Africa, northwards (481 kilometers). Its object was to open up the Ruanda region, into which the Germans had as yet virtually not penetrated. Calvert, "German African Empire," pp. 129, 130. On the inability of this railroad to compete with the Uganda line for the traffic of the Victoria Nyanza district, see *Weltverkehr,* 1913-14, pp. 245 ff. [On the railway system of Tanganyika Territory, see "Handbook of German East Africa," pp. 271-282.]

[22] F. A. G. Pape, "Tropical Eastern Africa," in *United Empire Magazine,* 1916, pp. 395, 396. The first line constructed in Africa during the war was from Prieska, on the Orange River, to Upington, on the same river near the border, a distance of 142 miles. It was completed by November 20, 1914. The line of 170 miles between Upington and Kalkfontein was laid in 105 days (H. Burton, "Railways in South Africa," in *Journal of the African Society,* October, 1918, p. 6).

[23] A railroad has been suggested to connect Beira with the Zambezi and with Nyasaland. Beira would serve as the port for Nyasaland and also for part of Northern Rhodesia. *Journal of the African Society,* October, 1918, p. 70 [*The Statesman's Year-Book,* 1921, p. 196; 1922, p. 201].

CHAPTER V

AFRICA AS A MARKET

Cotton Textiles.—The position of Africa as a market is dependent both upon the value of her exports and upon the amount of foreign capital required for railroads, mines, and other enterprises. These investments from without will continue to demand an increasing amount of equipment and machinery. But, apart from such imports for reproductive works, Africa's wants in general will be limited only by the native's ability to pay. For some indefinite, but long, period his purchases will continue to be chiefly for personal consumption and will increase *pari passu* with the growth of native production. Among all primitive peoples emerging from savagery, the first and foremost demand is for clothing. Middle Africa supplies a comparatively large and expanding market for cotton textiles. They constitute one quarter of the goods shipped to this section of the continent. The value of the cotton goods brought into the British African colonies was in 1913 approximately twenty million dollars out of total imports of ninety-one millions. The corresponding figures for the French colonies were eleven out of thirty-four and those for the German colonies six out of twenty-five.[1] Of these cotton goods, amounting

[1] "Statistical Abstract of the British Empire," 1915, pp. 125-145; British Diplomatic and Consular Reports, No. 5423, pp. 11, 19-44; No. 5249, p. 6; *Statistisches Jahrbuch*, 1915, pp. 464, 465.

to more than thirty-six million dollars in value, a very large portion came from Great Britain, where cotton manufacturing had been longest and most extensively established.[2]

International Regulation of Imports.—At one time it was currently believed that trade was in itself a civilizing influence and that the African would gradually emerge from savagery by commercial intercourse with the Western world. It was, however, slowly realized that this view was entirely erroneous and that, if left to himself, the native would buy goods that were most injurious to him, while for his part the European trader would be entirely willing to supply them. Instead of civilizing the aborigines, unregulated commercial intercourse with the outside world led to their deterioration and very frequently to that of the foreigner as well. This mutual demoralization made it essential for the Western world to control these commercial relations and this

[2] Of total imports of cotton textiles in 1912 into the Cameroons, amounting to 6.2 million marks, 3.6 came from Germany and 2.3 from England. For Togoland the corresponding figures were, total 2.7, England, 1.4, Germany, 0.8.   For East Africa the total was 10, of which Germany's share was 2.2, England's 1.2, Zanzibar's 1.1, and British India's 2.9. "Die Deutschen Schutzgebiete," 1914, *Statistischer Teil*, pp. 142-145, 236, 276. Apparently, about two thirds of the imports from British India were of that country's produce. "Statistical Abstract of British India," 1915, p. 179. For the state of affairs in the French colonies, see the details in Girault, "Colonial Tariff Policy of France," pp. 230-232, 241, 242. [The figures for the principal colonies in 1918 were as follows (*The Statesman's Year-Book*, 1920, pp. 179, 181, 242, 244, 245, 247, 695, 883):   British East Africa, £912,467; Tanganyika Territory, £485,000; Nigeria, £2,804,379; Gambia, £429,367; Gold Coast, £675,218; Sierra Leone (1917), £445,447; Congo, £408,925; Ivory Coast, £265,967.   For 1919 the values were (*ibid.*, 1921, pp. 183, 245, 248, 249, 251, 899): Tanganyika Territory, £554,000; Nigeria, £3,262,933; Gambia, £335,570; Gold Coast, £1,981,120; Sierra Leone, £461,098; Ivory Coast, £184,965, and for 1920 (*ibid.*, 1922, pp. 188, 254, 257, 258, 261, 920), £762,923, £6,101,580, £861,765, £3,801,835, £875,462, and £476,160 respectively.]

necessity is the chief moral justification for progressive extension of European and American rule over backward peoples.[3] No other course was feasible except the absolute prohibition of commercial connections, which would have meant the abandonment of the continent to continuing savagery. The fact that in Africa the colonies of the various Powers were juxtaposed rendered it impossible, however, for any one of them to control the situation effectively without the coöperation of the others. Important steps of this character were taken by the Anti-Slavery Conference that met at Brussels in 1889. In addition to devising elaborate measures for the extirpation of the slave trade, this international assembly reached an agreement for the restriction of the importation both of arms and ammunition and also of spirituous liquors in Africa between the latitudes of 22° South and 20° North.[4] Very detailed provisions were adopted prohibiting the admission, except for governmental purposes, of modern firearms of precision and of ammunition for them.[5]

---

[3] P. H. Kerr, "Political Relations Between Advanced and Backward Peoples," in "An Introduction to the Study of International Relations" (by Grant, Greenwood, Hughes, Kerr, and Urquhart), pp. 141-179. This sequence is plain in the case of Samoa. "The rival interests of several powers served as counterpoises and for many years protected the islands from seizure or control by any one. Unhappily, there was no protection of the islanders from the malign influences of dishonest and immoral traders, and there appeared the characteristic corruption which too often results from the contact of selfish civilization with unsophisticated primitive society." W. F. Johnson, "America's Foreign Relations," II, p. 136, New York, 1916. Similarly, in his book on "Imperialism," Mr. J. A. Hobson writes: "The contact with white races cannot be avoided, and it is more perilous and injurious as it lacks governmental sanction and control."

[4] Brussels Act of July 2, 1890, in Hertslet, "The Map of Africa by Treaty" (3d ed.), pp. 488-517 ["Trattati . . . relativi all'Africa," pp. 268-297; Malloy, "Treaties," pp. 1964-1992. See also map facing page 198.]

[5] Articles 8-14. On the problem of regulating trade in arms and ammunition, see *infra*, pp. 230-237.

These regulations appear, in general, to have worked quite satisfactorily.[6] As a result of the Brussels Protocol of July 22, 1908, signed by the Plenipotentiaries of the Congo Free State, France, Germany, Great Britain, Portugal, and Spain, and prohibiting the importation of arms and ammunition for a period of four years from February 15, 1909,[7] the traffic, hitherto rather flourishing, came to an end. Nevertheless, denunciation of this Protocol might result in revival of the trade in certain districts fixed by the Contracting Parties.[8]

[During the Peace Conference one of the three Conventions drawn up by the Commission appointed to consider revision of the General Act of Berlin and the General Act

[6] Thus, Sir Alfred Sharpe (one of the administrators of the Companhia de Moçambique) writes: "I can speak with some authority on this matter, as I have spent over 20 years in Nyasaland, and have paid lengthy visits to the Belgian Congo, Portuguese East Africa, Uganda, British East Africa, German East Africa, the Sudan, and Rhodesia. So far from there being any indiscriminate introduction of arms and ammunition in these territories, the importation or purchase is absolutely prohibited. . . . I have never met this person [the gun-runner], nor, within what I may call modern times, have I ever heard of him. As a matter of fact, he does not now exist in any British territory, nor, so far as I have seen, in any other territory administered by a European Power in the eastern half of Central Africa." London *Daily Mail*, February 6, 1918. On gun-running from Abyssinia into the Southern Sudan and on the relation of Jibuti to this traffic, see Sir Reginald Wingate, Memorandum on the Sudan, 1914, pp. 3, 6, 7; *Egypt*, No. 1 (1912), pp. 44, 65; 1914, p. 62; Sir H. H. Johnston, "Common Sense in Foreign Policy," p. 34, London, 1913. The value of the arms imported into Senegal in 1913 was 68,922 francs, and of trade powder 20,855 francs ("Statistique du Commerce des Colonies Françaises," 1913, I, i, p. 60, Paris, 1915). In the same year, the total importations of arms and ammunition into French Somaliland were valued at 4,060,797 francs, divided as follows: from France, 1,666,817; from Germany, 380,025; from Belgium, 1,899,925; from other countries, 114,030. Of the total amount 3,861,705 were arms and munitions of war, and only 199,092 for other purposes (*ibid.*, pp. 1100-1103). [Arms imported into the Belgian Congo amounted to only £647 in 1917, and to still less—£604—in 1918; but in 1919 the figure rose to £33,409 (*The Statesman's Year-Book*, 1920, p. 695; 1922, p. 716).]

[7] "Trattati," Supplemento, pp. 182-184.
[8] Bruel, "L'Afrique Équatoriale Française," p. 457.

and Declaration of Brussels, and signed at Saint-Germain-en-Laye, September 10, 1919, further restricted the traffic in arms and ammunition. These may not be exported into any part of the Continent of Africa, except Algeria, Libya, and the Union of South Africa unless the High Contracting Parties grant, through their own authorities, export licenses after ascertaining that the arms and ammunition in question "are not intended for export to any destination, or for disposal in any way, contrary to the provisions of this Convention." Further, manufacture or assembling of arms or ammunition is forbidden, except in government arsenals, and arms may be repaired only at arsenals or establishments licensed for this purpose by the local administration. Finally, elaborate provision is made for the prevention of gun-running. This Convention may be revised at the end of a period of seven years in the light of the experience gained "if the Council of the League of Nations, acting if need be by a majority, so recommends." [9]]

The provisions regulating the importation of liquor had worked less satisfactorily.

The Brussels Act and the Liquor Trade.—The Brussels Act of 1890 [10] forbade the importation and distillation of spirituous liquors in those regions in which, whether for religious or other reasons, their use did not as yet exist or had not as yet developed. To each Power was left the determination of the bounds of these prohibition areas. They cover the major portion of Africa between 22° South and 20°

[9] For the complete text of this Convention, see Annex E; and cf. Article 3, Paragraph 2, of the Mandate for German Southwest Africa, Annex L.]

[10] Brussels Act, Chapter VI, Articles 90-95. See further *infra,* pp. 222-223.

North and, in general, have been greatly extended since 1890. Thus, the prohibition sphere in the Belgian Congo has been gradually pushed closer and closer to the littoral.[11] There has been some smuggling from the open into the closed zones,[12] but, in the main, this prohibition has been effective.[13] In the open areas, the Brussels Act provided that the Powers should impose import duties or equivalent excises of 15 francs a hectoliter (about 11 cents a gallon) on liquors at 50 degrees Centigrade. These taxes were only the minimal rates, each Power reserving the right to levy customs and excises in excess of them. These duties of 15 francs were to remain in effect for three years, when they could be increased to 25 francs for another three years. After the expiration of these six years, they might be revised in the light of the experience gained. In 1899, the Brussels Conference increased these duties to 70 francs a hectoliter (53 cents a gallon) on liquors at 50 degrees Centigrade, with propor-

[11] John H. Harris, "Dawn in Darkest Africa," p. 99. Similarly, the Portuguese in Angola abolished the distilleries, compensating the owners. Instead of being used in the manufacture of rum, the sugar was shipped to Portugal. *Ibid.*, and British Diplomatic and Consular Reports, No. 5402, pp. 3, 4. The tracts placed under the prohibition of the Brussels Act "include Northern Nigeria, the hinterland to the north of Togo and the Gold Coast, British Somaliland, British East Africa, Uganda, the Kamerun, Belgian Congo, German East Africa, German West Africa, part of Portuguese East Africa, Nyasaland, and Northern and Southern Rhodesia. In some of these areas the full policy of the Brussels Act has been enforced. In others it is being introduced gradually." Shortly before the war, the prohibition area was further extended to include "more than three-fifths of the Ivory Coast, part of the hinterland of Dahomey, the Koinadugu province in the hinterland of Sierra Leone, the northeastern corner of Southern Nigeria, the Portuguese province of Angola." A. J. Macdonald, "Trade, Politics, and Christianity in Africa and the East," p. 107. See Harcourt's statement, June 27, 1912, in Hansard, 40, p. 535.

[12] For instance, from Southern into Northern Nigeria.

[13] Sir Alfred Sharpe writes: "In the eastern half of Central Africa, so far as Great Britain is concerned, the sale or supply of alcohol to natives is absolutely prohibited." *Loc. cit.*

tional augmentation for each degree above 50 and proportional diminution for each degree below 50.[14] In 1906, the duties were raised to 100 francs (76 cents a gallon).[15] In 1912, the representatives of the Powers again met at Brussels for further consideration of this problem, but they were unable to come to any decision, despite the fact that these duties had not accomplished their purpose of diminishing the consumption of liquor in West Africa.

West Africa and the Liquor Problem.—The liquor question is practically confined to the coastal region of West Africa, whose natives have been accustomed to distilled beverages ever since the days of the slave trade, in which rum from the West Indies and New England played so notorious a part. In addition, the aborigines have also been used to domestic fermented beverages, such as native beer and wine made from the oil palm. These indigenous liquors are, however, generally less harmful than are the distilled importations from Europe. The problem was further complicated by the fact that a very large proportion of the colonial revenues, especially in Southern Nigeria, was derived from this traffic, and that its suppression would probably necessitate greatly increased direct taxation which, in turn, might have unfortunate political consequences. The situation was admittedly serious throughout West Africa. The importation of distilled liquors was growing rapidly. The increasingly heavy duties had not checked it, because they did not keep pace with the growing ability of the natives to

[14] Hertslet, *op. cit.*, II, pp. 528-531 ["Trattati," pp. 618-621]. Dahomey and Togoland were not obliged to raise their duties above 60 francs.

[15] Eritrea was not compelled to raise its duties above 70 francs ["Trattati," pp. 1247-1250].

pay higher prices for liquor. This was true of the German, French, and British colonies.[16] In the five years 1908 to 1912 inclusive, the importation of alcoholic drinks into French West Africa had doubled in quantity.[17] In Nigeria, the importations of gin, rum, and whiskey rose from 3.2

[16] The evil had reached greater dimensions in Togoland than in the Cameroons. J. K. Vietor, "Geschichtliche und Kulturelle Entwickelung Unserer Schutzgebiete," pp. 134-136. See also "Bulletin de la Société Belge d'Études Coloniales," 1913, pp. 314, 315.

[17] British Diplomatic and Consular Reports, No. 5423, pp. 5-7, 42, 44: L'Afrique Française, 1913, pp. 302, 304. Of the total imports into Senegal in 1913, valued at 8.8 million francs, wines and alcoholic beverages amounted to 2. each, beer to .3, and liqueurs to .1. The importation of alcohol had risen from 15,448 to 24,440 hectoliters and as the duty was increased the quality of the spirits, especially of the gin, deteriorated, this being particularly true of the German and Dutch beverages which the Woermann Line carried to the French colonies. It was felt that absolute prohibition was impossible for fiscal reasons, to say nothing of the dangers involved in native manufacture of spirits. "Statistique du Commerce des Colonies Françaises," 1913, I, i, pp. 59-60, Paris, 1915. Of the alcohol thus imported, only 920,118 francs' worth came from France, 1,074,379 from other countries. Ibid., p. 71. The revenue from alcohol in 1908-13, in millions of francs, is shown by the following figures (ibid., pp. 509-510):

	Total Revenue	From Alcohol	Percentage
1908	3.1	1.9	62.02
1909	5.	3.5	70.13
1910	6.7	5.	74.24
1911	7.2	5.1	71.19
1912	7.2	5.1	71.46
1913	5.8	4.	69.34

As a result of the extension of prohibition to practically all parts of French Equatorial Africa, imports of liquors in 1908 amounted to 202,000 francs and in 1909 to 158,000, as compared with 414,000 in 1907. Prohibition being lifted, the imports rose to 303,000 in 1910 and to 485,000 in 1911. [In 1918 the figures were 488,950 francs, in 1919, 636,484 francs, and in 1920, 1,021,600 francs for the Ivory Coast alone. The Statesman's Year-Book, 1920, p. 883; 1921, p. 899; 1922, p. 920.] Though this course was compelled by fiscal needs, the results were deplorable, since alcoholism worked terrible ravages among the coastal tribes who "diminish rapidly, in great part because of alcoholism, which helps decrease the birthrate or makes the offspring rachitic and malformed." The importation of wine had also increased, so that whereas the average value of imports for 1886-1900 was 135,000 francs and for 1907-11 was 561,000, that of 1911 alone was 765,000 francs. Bruel, "L'Afrique Équatoriale Française," pp. 457-459.

million gallons in 1908 to 4.5 in 1913. In the Gold Coast, the rate was approximately the same, but in Sierra Leone and Gambia it was far greater. In Sierra Leone, the quantity imported was relatively small, but it had gained over twofold in this period, while in Gambia the proportional increase was even more.[18]

Necessity for International Action. — The British Government had adopted strong measures to check this growing evil. For instance, in Nigeria and Sierra Leone the duties imposed stood before the war at nearly twice the minimum enjoined by the Brussels Conference of 1906. Furthermore, since the last abortive meeting of that Conference in 1911-12, the distillation of liquor in British West Africa has been prohibited.[19] During the war itself, the import duties in Nigeria were again greatly increased.[20] Similarly, the duties in French West Africa were raised in 1912.[21] There

[18] "Statistical Abstract of the British Empire," 1915, pp. 143-155. On this problem in the British colonies and in general in West Africa, see John H. Harris, "Dawn in Darkest Africa," pp. 99-105; A. J. Macdonald, "Trade, Politics, and Christianity in Africa and the East," pp. 62-126; A. B. Keith, "West Africa," pp. 210-215. [The value of the imports into Nigeria in 1918 was £163,616; into the Gold Coast in 1918, £166,842; into Sierra Leone in 1917, £46,378, in 1919, £60,940, and in 1920, £72,955; into Gambia in 1918, £6,795, in 1919, £12,295, and in 1920, £10,735; into British East Africa in 1918-19, £218,155; into the Tanganyika Territory in 1918-19, £34,000, in 1919-20, £55,000, and in 1920, £58,802; into the Belgian Congo in 1917, £76,847, in 1918, £104,322, and in 1919, £185,140. *The Statesman's Year-Book,* 1920, pp. 179, 181, 242, 244, 245, 247, 695; 1921, pp. 183, 248, 251; 1922, pp. 188, 257, 261, 716.]

[19] A. J. Macdonald, *op. cit.,* p. 109; Keith, *op. cit.,* p. 213.

[20] In 1916 the duty on trade spirits in Nigeria was 8s. 9d. per Imperial gallon, *i.e.,* roughly $2.18 as against the Brussels Conference minimum of 76 cents. *Anti-Slavery Reporter,* October, 1916, p. 74. In 1917 duties on spirits were increased in the Gold Coast, the excise on brandy, whisky, etc., being raised from 7s. 6d. to 8s. 6d. per gallon. *Board of Trade Journal,* May 9, 1918, p. 572.

[21] British Diplomatic and Consular Reports, No. 5423, pp. 5-7, 42, 44; *L'Afrique Française,* 1913, pp. 302, 304. In all French Equatorial Africa

is wide difference of opinion as to the extent of drunkenness in Africa, some contending that alcoholism is a potential rather than a real evil, and others, again, insisting that drink is undermining the moral and physical vigor of the native. Virtually all candid students agree, however, that the traffic needs stringent curbing. It is still a moot question whether the present system of high customs and excises should be maintained or whether total prohibition should be adopted. Whichever policy be chosen, international coöperation will be essential to make it effective. Unless there is a uniform policy in all the West African colonies, smuggling will inevitably occur across borders that in the present stage of African development cannot be closely watched. As a result, the high tariff or prohibition policy of one colony can be nullified by the low customs of its neighbor. As in the past, so in the future, international coöperation is imperative if the liquor traffic is to be diminished or abolished.

[*The Convention of 1919.*—The Commission entrusted by the Peace Conference with revision of the Berlin Act and the Brussels Act and Declaration drew up *inter alia* a Convention relating to the liquor traffic in Africa, which was signed at Saint-Germain-en-Laye on September 10, 1919, by the Plenipotentiaries of the United States, Belgium, Great Britain, France, Italy, Japan, and Portugal.[22] By this Convention "the importation, distribution, sale and possession of trade spirits of every kind, and of beverages mixed with these spirits," are forbidden throughout Africa, with the ex-

---

the duties are 200 francs per hectoliter of pure alcohol plus a "consommation" tax of 50 francs, which will be increased to 100 francs. Bruel, "L'Afrique Équatoriale Française," pp. 423-424.

[22] For the complete text of this Convention, see Annex F.

ception of Algeria, Tunis, Morocco, Libya, Egypt, and the Union of South Africa. The prohibition extends likewise to "distilled beverages containing essential oils or chemical products which are recognized as injurious to health, such as thujone, star anise, benzoic aldehyde, salicylic ethers, hyssop and absinthe." Distilled liquors other than those absolutely forbidden may be imported into those parts of the prohibited area where their use has already developed, but they are subject to a minimum duty of 800 francs per hectoliter of pure alcohol (600 francs in Italian colonies).[23] Similar restrictions are imposed (except in the Italian colonies) on the manufacture of distilled liquors and on "the importation, distribution, sale and possession of stills and of all apparatus or portions of apparatus suitable for distillation of alcohol and the rectification or redistillation of spirits." The only important exception to these principles is the right to import and manufacture pharmaceutical alcohol and apparatus necessary for testing and making alcohol for pharmaceutical, scientific, and commercial purposes, though even here special permission must first be obtained from the local authorities. This Convention may after five years receive such modifications as may prove necessary and each High Contracting Party must submit an annual report to a Central International Office established as part of the organization of the League of Nations, while provision is also made for arbitration of disputes which cannot be settled by negotiation. Finally, the last paragraph of Article 3 of the Mandate for

[23] By Article 4, "the above prohibition can be suspended only in the case of limited quantities destined for the consumption of non-native persons, and imported under the system and conditions determined by each 'Government."

Southwest Africa states that "the supply of intoxicating spirits and beverages to the natives shall be prohibited.[24]]

[24] See Annex L, similarly, by Article 4 of the Draft Mandate for Togoland (British), "the mandatory . . . will exercise a strict control over the traffic in arms and ammunition and the sale of spirituous liquors."

CHAPTER VI

THE DEVELOPMENT OF AFRICAN CIVILIZATION

The Negro's Limitations and Possibilities.—The negro race has hitherto shown no capacity for progressive development except under the tutelage of other peoples. In America, the African has imitatively, and very imperfectly, acquired alien civilization—the Latin in the South and the English-speaking in the North—while, in his native home, the civilizing influences have also come from extraneous sources—Hamitic, Arabic, and European. Moreover, according to many scientists, it is an established physiological fact that the cranial sutures of the negro close at an early age, which condition, it has been contended, prevents organic intellectual progress thereafter. Hence, many have denied the capacity of the negro to advance far on the path of civilization. Even if this gloomy view be fully admitted—many reject it altogether—it is of little immediate significance, however great its ultimate importance may be. The essential fact to-day is that the African's existing stage of civilization is far below his real potentialities for progress. The situation is well summarized by Ambassador Reinsch, who said:

"The difference between the average negro and the average European does not explain, nor is it at all commensurate to, the difference between their respective civilizations. . . . Should favorable conditions for the existence and develop-

179

ment of permanent societies in Africa be brought about, it then would admit of little doubt that the negro race would develop in civilization—a civilization proper to it, rather than an imitation of the European type." [1]

The Essentials of Sound Progress.—It should be the prime function of the colonizing Powers to develop and establish these favorable conditions. The preëminent consideration in colonial administration must be the welfare of the native. The outside world can in the long run gain no benefit from Africa unless its evolution is on a firm and sound economic basis. Such a foundation cannot be reached if Middle Africa is viewed merely as a huge plantation on which the negro toils as a helot for the advantage of Europe. [2] Wherever the colonizing Powers have tried this system of exploitation, it has proved disastrous. It is not only abominably selfish, but it is stupidly suicidal. It has led to the depopulation of Middle Africa in the last thirty years; and, as the native is the chief asset, this decrease has meant a serious impairment of the country's resources. The experience of these years has conclusively shown that wherever the negro is deprived of his land and is forced to work for European masters, the output is small and the population diminishes. On the other hand, the record in British West Africa has fully demonstrated that if the native is assured of his personal freedom and of adequate land, great progress may be attained. The two pillars of sound

[1] P. S. Reinsch, "Colonial Government," pp. 59, 60, New York, 1905. For a valuable discussion of this theory of arrest in mental development, see C. T. Lorham, "The Education of the South African Native," pp. 209, 224, London, 1917.

[2 For what may be construed as at least a suggestion of a desire to return to this point of view, see Antonelli, "L'Afrique et la Paix de Versailles," p. 256, quoted *infra*, p. 279.]

colonial administration must be an equitable land system and a liberal and humane labor policy.

Land Policy.—It is generally agreed that a sound land policy implies that sufficient ground should be reserved for the present and prospective needs of the aborigines and that the African should not be allowed to alienate this recklessly either to Europeans or to a privileged native land-owning class [3] the native having no conception of private rights to land. According to the customary tenure in West Africa, the ownership was vaguely vested in the community, every member of which was entitled to its use. Hence, land could not be permanently alienated and the native had no intention of doing so, no matter what might be the wording of the European title-deeds.[4] Moreover, in a number of instances, the colonizing Powers had granted huge tracts without any regard to native rights. This was notoriously the case in the Belgian Congo and in the Cameroons. Furthermore, insurrections in the German possessions led to the wholesale confiscation of native soil. Just as the Hereros, in German Southwest Africa, became in this manner a landless people, so the Bakwiri, in the Cameroons, were deprived of the fertile areas that were then made into German cocoa plantations. The *fait accompli* of dispossession in the German colonies could not be rectified, but so far as the remaining unoccupied land was concerned, the condition had been largely remedied as regarded the future by a change in Ger-

---

[3] On this entire section cf. also *infra,* pp. 255-258.
[4] S. D. Morel, "Africa and the Peace of Europe," pp. 52-56; J. K. Vietor, "Geschichtliche und Kulturelle Entwickelung Unserer Schutzgebiete," pp. 122, 123. [For the native theory, see A. H. Post, "Afrikanische Jurisprudenz," II, pp. 166-175, Oldenburg, 1887.]

man policy.[5]   Yet, just before the war, the Duala, in the
Cameroons, were being deprived of their homes.   In the
Belgian Congo also the Leopoldian principles had been discarded and the land system inaugurated in 1909 was based
upon the principle that the native had the first title and
right to the soil.   Important areas were reserved for his
use, and he was not permitted to alienate them.   Furthermore, he was allowed to harvest the fruits of all unoccupied
lands.[6]   This reformed system followed that of the British
colonies, in which native rights were most carefully and
effectively protected.   In Nigeria, for instance, the acquisition of land by non-natives from natives was forbidden
without the consent of the colonial authorities, and the
negro's customary rights of occupation and use were amply
safeguarded.[7]   As African civilization cannot develop along
sound lines unless these principles are generally adopted, it
would be highly advisable to secure an international agreement embodying them.   But, since conditions vary in the
different colonies, such an agreement may have to be so
vague in character as to be equivalent to no more than a
pious wish.[8]   Further, its enforcement might create grave

[5] J. K. Vietor, *op. cit.*, pp. 86, 87, 122-126.
[6] J. Renkin, "L'Avenir du Congo Belge," in *L'Afrique Française,* March,
1916, Supplement, p. 62. [Cf. also "Manual of Belgian Congo," pp. 285-
287.]
[7] A. B. Keith, "West Africa," pp. 165, 198-204, 221. Similar land systems
were established in Sierra Leone and in the Gold Coast. *Ibid.*, pp. 227,
230-232. See also Émile Baillaud, "La Politique Indigène de l'Angleterre
en Afrique Orientale," pp. 144-152, 187-216.
[8 At the session of the Commission for the Revision of the Berlin and
Brussels Acts on August 1, 1919, the Italian Delegation proposed, as part
of an article to replace Article 9 of the Draft Convention (the basis of
the present Article 11), the following clauses: "Au nom de la civilisation,
les méthodes colonisatrices contraires à l'existence, au bien-être et à la
graduelle élévation des populations indigènes sont à jamais bannies. En

problems, if it should involve international inspection of, and interference in, a matter that is usually deemed to be exclusively a domestic concern. Possibly less difficulty may be encountered in establishing international control over the labor situation.

Labor Question.—Even more important for the future of Africa than an equitable land system is the maintenance of the native's personal freedom.[9] It is not generally realized that Middle Africa is very sparsely populated, and that the prevailing scarcity of labor has been due essentially to this

conséquence, la législation concernant la propriété foncière devra respecter autant que possible les coutumes en vigueur dans les territoires et les intérêts des populations indigènes. Les terrains et les droits réels appartenant à des indigènes ne pourront être transférés à des non-indigènes sans le consentement du Gouvernement local et aucun droit sur lesdits terrains ne pourra être créé au profit de non-indigènes sans le même consentement." To this, Mr. Strachey, the British Delegate, objected that these provisions would find proper place in the Mandates, but that they could not be extended to "pays de pleine souveraineté"; and M. de Peretti de la Rocca, French Delegate and President of the Commission, added that his Government could not permit an International Convention to impose principles which that Government's legislation already recognized. The Italian proposal accordingly failed of adoption. "Procès-Verbaux et Rapport de la Commission pour la Revision des Actes Généraux de Berlin et de Bruxelles," p. 123. In harmony with the view set forth by Mr. Strachey, the "B" Mandates include the following Article (*e.g.*, Article 5 of the Draft Mandate for Togoland [British]): "In the framing of laws relating to the holding or transference of land, the mandatory will take into consideration native laws and customs, and will respect the rights and safeguard the interests of the native population. No native land may be transferred, except between natives, without the previous consent of the public authorities, and no real rights over native land in favour of non-natives may be created except with the same consent." In Mandates of the "C" type, no such provision is necessary since by Article 22, Paragraph 6, of the Covenant of the League of Nations mandated territories of the "C" class "can be best administered under the laws of the Mandatory as integral portions of its territory." For the three types of Mandates, see Annexes B, H, I, L.]

[9] On the labor question see P. S. Reinsch, *op. cit.*, pp. 358-391; A. J. Macdonald, "Trade, Politics, and Christianity in Africa and the East," pp. 11-61; John H. Harris, "Dawn in Darkest Africa," pp. 45, 46, 131-163.

fact rather than to the more or less accentuated indolence of the negro. It is true that in some sections the native has shown marked industry, especially when he has received the full reward of his toil and has not been obliged to work in unfamiliar surroundings, cut off from family and community. Unhappiness, it is claimed, plays as much physical havoc with the African negro as do the most virulent diseases. The economic history of Nigeria and the Gold Coast since 1900 furnishes complete proof of the African's ability to develop the resources of his native soil. But, in general, his needs are as yet undeveloped and those which are urgent are freely supplied by a bountiful nature. As a rule, therefore, the negro is unwilling to leave his home to work for a white master on plantations and in mines. In order to overcome this disinclination, various methods of compulsion have been employed. Forced labor in Africa was of three kinds: (1) that on works of public necessity, such as building of roads and bridges and the clearing of the waterways; (2) that on the construction of railroads and other reproductive public utilities; (3) that on private undertakings. Forced labor in the first category is legitimate, provided abuses are not allowed to creep in. On the other hand, it is of more than doubtful expediency in the second class; while in the third, it is wholly vicious and is a virtual return to the slavery of the past. Some of the indirect means used to oblige the natives to work, such as the hut and poll taxes which he cannot pay unless he earns something, are not objectionable, but direct constraint for private enterprises is absolutely inadmissible. Such compulsion prevailed throughout broad sections of Middle Africa. It was a characteristic feature of the Leopoldian Congo and of the Portuguese cocoa islands before the reforms introduced in the present decade. For a time also French Equatorial Africa was cursed with this indefensible system.[10] In the German colonies, the method was less openly one of coercion, but the full authority of the Government was used to compel a supply of labor for the European plantations. As the Organizing Secretary of the Aborigines' Protection Society said, the means employed were those of a military despotism.[11] The British record, on the whole, is by far the best. But conditions even in the British colonies, mainly in East Africa, were not wholly above criticism, chiefly because the authorities were not always able to prevent abuses on the part of the planters.[12]

The Contract System.—In general, the system of labor in Middle Africa has been one of contracts ranging from three months to periods of five years. The method is not objectionable in itself provided the agreements are of reasonable duration, are free from compulsion, and have their clauses fully and explicitly brought within the restricted

[10] H. A. Gibbons, "The New Map of Africa," pp. 344, 345.

[11] John H. Harris, *op. cit.*, pp. 141, 142. In German East Africa the chiefs were ordered by the Government to supply certain quantities of labor for the different plantations, public works, etc. *Idem,* "Germany's Lost Colonial Empire," pp. 23, 24. Regarding German West Africa, Mr. Harris writes: "The abject fear exhibited by the natives whenever the white man approaches is too eloquent to be mistaken. Moreover, the whip is carried by the planters as openly as a man in Europe carries a walking-stick. Whips and free contracts seldom go together" ("Dawn in Darkest Africa," p. 262).

[12] In British East Africa the contracts were carefully supervised by the Government and the natives were protected from frauds and surprises in them. C. Paladini, "L'Africa Orientale Inglese," in *Rivista Coloniale,* March, 1915, pp. 135, 136. Despite this vigilance, some abuses occurred. See Norma Lorimer, "By the Waters of Africa," pp. 43, 66, 67, 119, 120, 148, 205.

understanding of the native. Moreover, the conditions of employment and the facilities for repatriation must be such that the negro is not practically obliged to renew his contract at its expiration. This system cannot be abandoned. It has been found essential even in the native industries in the Gold Coast and Nigeria. It should be noted, however, that the Africans there were not hampered by the prevailing scarcity of workers and generally had little difficulty in securing the labor that they needed. In addition to the native enterprises, railroads will have to be constructed, mineral resources must be developed, and apparently some products—such as sisal-hemp and the finer grades of tobacco—cannot do without the expert supervision of the European plantation system.[13]   The alternative to native contract labor is the importation of Chinese coolies, which had been suggested in connection with the Katanga mines and those in the Gold Coast, but which would indubitably introduce an element hostile to the development of a sound and stable African civilization.[14]

The International Element in the Problem.—The labor problem will become very urgent after the war, because there is danger that the world-wide scarcity of raw mate-

[13 By the "B" Mandates (*e.g.*, Article 4 of the Draft Mandate for Togoland [British]), "the mandatory . . . (iii) Will prohibit all forms of forced or compulsory labour, except for essential public works and services, and then only in return for adequate remuneration.   (iv) Will protect the natives from abuse and measures of fraud and force by the careful supervision of labour contracts and the recruiting of labour." Similarly in the "C" Mandates (*e.g.*, Article 3 of the Mandate for German Southwest Africa), "the mandatory shall see . . . that no forced labour is permitted, except for essential public works and services, and then only for adequate remuneration."]
[14 This suggestion is radically different from that of using East Africa as a land for permanent settlement by East Indians (see *supra*, pp. 61-64).]

rials will lead to attempts to stimulate production by illegitimate means. Hence, the need for adequate protection of the native. The question is by no means purely local. It is in actual practice partly international, since in some instances workers had already to be brought from outside the colony's frontiers and this necessity will increase as development proceeds. Thus the Spanish cocoa island of Fernando Po procured its labor from Liberia. Similarly, the Katanga mines rely upon workers recruited in Rhodesia and Portuguese East Africa and will probably draw upon Angola when the Benguella Railway is completed.[15] An international agreement regarding the labor problem could start from the basis of controlling this international migration and should include other matters. According to the matured opinion of lifelong students of the problem who are wholly disinterested advocates of native interests, such an agreement should at the very least provide for the abolition of all forced toil for private profit. It should further establish a maximum term for labor contracts—six months in mining and three years in agriculture—and should provide that only civil penalties, after trial by the authorities, should be inflicted for breach of these terms. Moreover, in the case of workers recruited across the borders, special provisions for repatriation should be made and the official protectors of such labor, whose duty it is to see that the terms of the contract are kept and that the working conditions are satisfactory, should be appointed by the Government of the place of recruitment.[16]

[15] Camille Martin, "La Main d'Œuvre au Katanga," in *L'Afrique Française*, 1913, pp. 288-290.

[16] Memorial to the Foreign Office of January 22, 1917, from the Anti-

Slavery and Aborigines' Protection Society and from the Edinburgh and Glasgow Committees for the Protection of Native Races, in the *Anti-Slavery Reporter,* April, 1917, pp. 3-6; John H. Harris, "Native Races and Peace Terms" (reprinted from the *Contemporary Review*) and his article, "Tropical Colonies and International Government," in *The Fortnightly Review,* November, 1917. [Cf. also "Manual of Belgian Congo," pp. 298, 302-304.]

PART III

MIDDLE AFRICA: PROBLEMS OF INTER-NATIONAL COÖPERATION AND CONTROL

(Written for THE INQUIRY. Finished October 31, 1918.)

PART III: MIDDLE AFRICA: PROBLEMS OF INTERNATIONAL COÖPERATION AND CONTROL

EXPLANATORY NOTE

INTRODUCTION

CHAPTER I
THE REGULATION OF FOREIGN TRADE

CHAPTER II
FREEDOM OF NAVIGATION ON RIVERS

CHAPTER III
THE PROBLEM OF THE OPEN DOOR

CHAPTER IV
REGULATION OF THE LIQUOR TRADE

CHAPTER V
REGULATION OF THE TRAFFIC IN ARMS

CHAPTER VI
PRESERVATION OF WILD ANIMALS AND THE CONTROL OF
SLEEPING SICKNESS

CHAPTER VII
PROTECTION OF NATIVE RIGHTS : LABOR AND LAND

CHAPTER VIII
NEUTRALIZATION

CHAPTER IX
MILITARIZATION

CHAPTER X
CONCLUSIONS

MIDDLE AFRICA: PROBLEMS OF INTERNATIONAL COOPERATION AND CONTROL

EXPLANATORY NOTE

The purpose of this memorandum is to give brief accounts both of the acts of all the international conferences that dealt with the affairs of tropical Africa, beginning with the Berlin Conference of 1884-85, and also of the various treaties and agreements made by two or more of the colonizing Powers with the object of securing coöperation in dealing with some common problem. Their purpose was twofold in nature. On the one hand, the aim was to diminish European rivalries by creating equality of commercial opportunity in Middle Africa. On the other hand, their object was both to further the welfare of the natives and to adopt joint measures against evils of more than local scope. In pursuit of the former end, freedom of commerce, limited only by low and non-discriminatory customs for revenue purposes, was established in a wide area of Middle Africa, and likewise freedom of navigation was secured on its two chief rivers, the Congo and Niger. These principles were further extended by a number of special treaties between the colonizing Powers (Chapters I-III).

In order to protect the natives from manifest evils, steps were taken to prohibit and to restrict the importation and distillation of alcoholic liquors (Chapter IV). Similar control was exercised over the traffic in arms (Chapter V). Furthermore, there was some coöperation in the matter of preserving Africa's great animal wealth from indiscriminate slaughter, and the scourge of sleeping sickness also came under international action (Chapter VI). The slave trade was one of the first objects of comprehensive treatment by the Powers acting in concert, but very little had been done internationally with the difficult problems of protecting the native from forced labor and of securing to him an adequate share of the land (Chapter VII). A timid attempt had been made to protect a large section of Middle Africa from the ravages of extraneous wars by a neutralization that was either incomplete or entirely optional (Chapter VIII).

This comprehensive system of coöperation and control is analyzed with the object of showing where and why it failed, what were its successes, and what its shortcomings. Upon past experience must be based the international control of the future. New problems arising from new conditions, such as that of the militarization of Africa, are also discussed (Chapter IX). Finally, in the "Conclusions," some measures are proposed that, in the opinion of the writer, will both make far more effective the mechanism of international control and also establish the international character of Mid-African colonization in accordance with the spirit of the Berlin Conference of 1884-85 (Chapter X).

INTRODUCTION

It is not generally appreciated to what an extent the affairs of tropical Africa have been a matter of international concern and regulation. The European diplomacy of the past half-century was almost continuously occupied in preventing the friction generated by the partition of Africa from bursting into the flames of a European war, and it is the greatest achievement of that diplomacy that the political map of tropical Africa as it existed in 1914 had been actually established by the peaceful processes of negotiation. Moreover, no other region had called forth more international coöperation or had been subjected to more comprehensive international control. This was the inevitable result both of the conditions in Middle Africa and of the attitude of the outside world towards that vast area.

The lack of effective natural barriers in tropical Africa was unfavorable to the development of indigenous civilizations and left the entire interior in virtually a single level of primitive savagery. This essential unity could not be fundamentally altered by the political boundary lines which the colonizing Powers drew and redrew in their many treaties and agreements. Mid-African problems transcended these artificial frontiers and necessitated international coöperation if effective remedies were to be applied. Tropical diseases, the slave trade, alcoholism, and other questions were not local in character, and it was futile to attempt to treat them as such. Hence the necessity for international coöperation and regulation which have been marked features in Europe's connection with Middle Africa since the Berlin Conference of 1884-85. At the time of that Conference, the outside world was determined that no one Power or group of Powers should secure uncontrolled possession of the Mid-African center and thus be able to use it for self-regarding economic aggrandizement. Hence measures were adopted to secure equal opportunities for all trade. A knowledge of this varied movement of coöperation and control in the past, together with an understanding of the shortcomings of the system, must serve as the basis of future action.

CHAPTER I

THE REGULATION OF FOREIGN TRADE

The Provisions of the Berlin Act, 1885.—The chief purpose for which the International Conference of Berlin met in 1884 was to establish freedom of commerce in the mouth and basin of the Congo,[1] whose potential resources had just been revealed to the world, in the main by the epoch-making discoveries of Stanley. Each of the Powers was interested in preventing its fellows, either singly or in combination, from securing special commercial privileges in a region whose riches loomed unwarrantedly large, not only in the popular imagination but also in the minds of explorers and statesmen.[2] In his speech on the opening day of the Conference, November 15, 1884, Bismarck said that any Power that exercised sovereign rights in this region was "to allow free access thereto to all flags, without distinction," and was "not to grant any monopolies, or to introduce any discriminating usage." [3] In its final shape, the

---

[1] Senate Executive Document, No. 196, 49th Congress, 1st Session, pp. 9, 11. In deference largely to the suggestion of Stanley ("The Congo," II, p. 395, London, 1885), the principles of free trade were extended more widely than had perhaps primarily been contemplated by the Powers (Keith, "The Belgian Congo and the Berlin Act," p. 59, Oxford, 1919).

[2] For the diplomatic history leading up to the summoning of this Conference, at the original suggestion of Portugal, see J. Scott Keltie, "The Partition of Africa" (2d ed.), pp. 136-148.

[3] Senate Executive Document, No. 196, p. 26.

General Act of the Conference provided that the trade of all nations should enjoy complete freedom, that all flags should have free access to the whole of the coast line, as well as to the Congo and its affluents, that no import or transit duties should be levied, and that no "monopoly or favor of any kind in matters of trade" should be granted.[4] At first, it was intended to establish this system of freedom of commerce only in the Congo Basin, but the American delegate, Mr. John A. Kasson, who enjoyed the invaluable assistance of Stanley, proposed the extension of the zone to the Indian Ocean. This suggestion was adopted. Owing to Portugal's objections,[5] however, a reservation was inserted which kept the Portuguese colony of Mozambique outside the free zone, in spite of the fact that the northern half of this colony was actually within its bounds.[6] This zone, generally known as the Conventional Basin, was carefully defined. In addition to the Belgian Congo, under the territorial division of Africa existing in 1914, it included on the West Coast portions of the German Cameroons and also parts of both Portuguese Angola and of French Equatorial Africa. Within its borders on the East Coast were British

[4] Berlin Act of February 26, 1885, Articles I to V. Hertslet, "The Map of Africa by Treaty" (3d ed.), II, pp. 471-473 ["Trattati . . . relativi all'Africa," pp. 107-109].

[5] Senate Executive Document, No. 196, p. 66. Sir E. Malet, on December 23, 1884, wrote to Earl Granville: "Special reservation, however, was made of all existing sovereign rights; consequently, the Mozambique Colony, the territory of the Sultan of Zanzibar and that of other independent States, cannot be affected by the Declaration without the assent of the Rulers." *Ibid.*, p. 306; *Africa*, No. 2 (1885), p. 1.

[6] Article I, last paragraph: "It is expressly recognized that in extending the principle of free trade to the eastern zone, the Conference Powers only undertake engagements for themselves, and that in the territories belonging to an independent Sovereign State this principle shall only be applicable in so far as it is approved by such State."

East Africa, Uganda, Nyasaland, and a part of Rhodesia, as well as German East Africa [now Tanganyika Territory] and the southern section of Italian Somaliland.

The Brussels Act of 1890.—In this vast region not only were all differential customs dues prohibited, but all import duties whatsoever. The system was to be one of complete free trade. As the Independent State of the Congo, which came into existence at the time of the Berlin Conference, found itself financially embarrassed without this source of revenue, the International Conference of Brussels in 1890 reconsidered the question and permitted the imposition of import duties up to ten per cent *ad valorem* in the Conventional Basin.[7] Since it was highly inadvisable to impose a general tariff of this maximum rate and since there was need for uniformity in policy among the many contiguous jurisdictions in the Conventional Basin, the interested Powers made further arrangements. On December 22, 1890, Great Britain, Germany, and Italy signed a protocol as to the duties to be imposed in the eastern zone.[8] Two years later, France, Portugal, and the Congo Free State likewise reached an agreement about the customs on imports and exports in the western zone.[9] This arrangement was, however, denounced by France in 1911 and, in the following year, an independent tariff was established for French Equatorial Africa.[10]

[7] Declaration of July 2, 1890. Hertslet, *op. cit.*, II, pp. 517, 518 ["Trattati," pp. 296-297].

[8] Hertslet, *op. cit.*, II, pp. 518, 519 ["Trattati," pp. 330-331].

[9] Protocol of Lisbon, April 8, 1892. "British and Foreign State Papers, 1891-1892," Vol. LXXXIV (1898), pp. 447, 448 ["Trattati," pp. 368-369].

[10] A. Girault, "The Colonial Tariff Policy of France," pp. 113, 114; Georges Bruel, "L'Afrique Équatoriale Française," pp. 423, 424.

The Berlin Act in Practice.—1.   Belgian Congo.—It was the expectation of the Berlin Conference that the regulations adopted would give to all nations equal commercial opportunities in Middle Africa.[11]   These expectations were, however, not realized.   The spirit of the Act was ignored and its provisions were interpreted literally.   Equality of trade was almost completely nullified in the Congo Basin through the system of exploitation adopted by the Independent State and by France.[12]   The former declared that all land not actually occupied by the natives, together with its products, was state property.   The Government itself proceeded to exploit these resources in some districts, and in others it granted the sole right of development to large concessionary companies.   As a consequence, the native had nothing to sell to the private merchant and, in turn, could not buy his wares.   The entire trade was controlled by the Government and by those companies and, furthermore, it inevitably centered in Belgium.[13]   Foreign merchants had no opportunity in the Belgian Congo and naturally kept

[11 For further details of the subject considered in this entire section, see *supra,* pp. 76-110.]

[12] From the purely legal standpoint the defenders of the concessionaire system had a strong case, since the official report made to the Berlin Conference on the significance of Article V, which prohibited monopolies or favors of any kind in matters of trade, stated: "There exists no doubt in the strict and literal sense it should be necessary to assign to the terms 'in commercial matters' [matters of trade], as concerns exclusively traffic, the unlimited power for each to sell and buy, to import and to export, products and manufactures.   No privileged situation can be created under this condition.   The situation remains open without restriction to free concurrence [competition] upon the grounds of commerce, but the obligations of the local governments do not go beyond."   Senate Executive Document, No. 196, p. 76.

[13 For the various commercial companies operating in the Congo, see "Manual of Belgian Congo," pp. 304-312.]

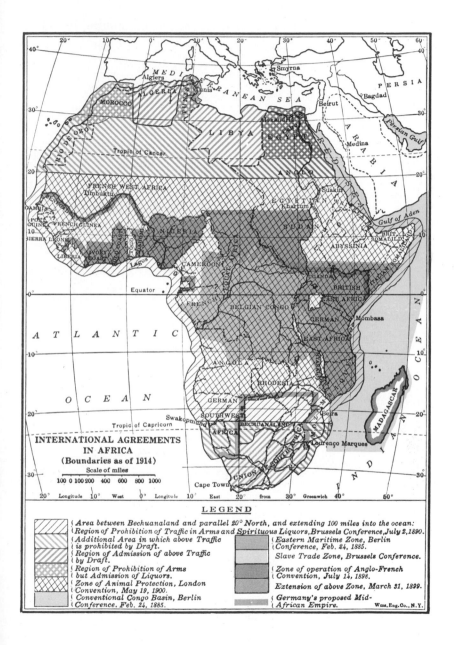

INTERNATIONAL AGREEMENTS
IN AFRICA
(Boundaries as of 1914)
Scale of miles
100 0 100 200   400   600   800 1000

LEGEND

{ Area between Bechuanaland and parallel 20° North, and extending 100 miles into the ocean:
{ Region of Prohibition of Traffic in Arms and Spirituous Liquors, Brussels Conference, July 2, 1890.

{ Additional Area in which above Traffic
{ is prohibited by Draft.
{ Region of Admission of above Traffic
{ by Draft.

{ Region of Prohibition of Arms
{ but Admission of Liquors.

{ Zone of Animal Protection, London
{ Convention, May 19, 1900.

{ Conventional Congo Basin, Berlin
{ Conference. Feb. 24, 1885.

{ Eastern Maritime Zone, Berlin
{ Conference, Feb. 24, 1885.

Slave Trade Zone, Brussels Conference.

{ Zone of operation of Anglo-French
{ Convention, July 14, 1898.

Extension of above Zone, March 31, 1899.

{ Germany's proposed Mid-
{ African Empire.

Wms. Eng. Co., N.Y.

away. The British Government for years protested against a system that nullified the commercial equality stipulated in the Berlin Act.[14]   In 1908, Sir Edward Grey insisted that, "so long as the Concessions are worked upon the same conditions as at present, it is difficult to see how the complete freedom of trade, which is guaranteed under Article I of the Berlin Act, can possibly exist."[15]   Thanks largely to these objections, to which the United States also gave their support in 1908 and in 1909,[16] reforms were rapidly introduced after 1908, when Belgium annexed the Congo. In 1915 Émile Vandervelde was able to say that the natives had the right to the natural products of the soil, that monopolies had been suppressed, and that "freedom of commerce, complete and entire, exists throughout the whole extent of the Congo."[17]   But, as a consequence in the main of the old monopolistic system, the commerce of the Belgian Congo continued in spite of these reforms to run in the established

[14] On August 8, 1903, the Foreign Secretary, Lord Lansdowne, sent a circular dispatch to the British representatives at Paris, Rome, and other capitals, in which, among other matters, it was pointed out that the system of trade in the Independent State was not in harmony with the Berlin Act. He wrote: "With the exception of a relatively small area on the lower Congo, and with the further exception of the small plots actually occupied by the huts and cultivation patches of the natives, the whole territory is claimed as the private property either of the State or of holders of land concessions. Within these regions the State or, as the case may be, the concession-holder alone may trade in the natural produce of the soil. The fruits gathered by the natives are accounted the property of the State, or of the concession-holder, and may not be acquired by others. In such circumstances, His Majesty's Government are unable to see that there exists the complete freedom of trade or absence of monopoly in trade which is required by the Berlin Act." *Africa*, No. 14 (1903), pp. 2, 3.
[15] *Africa*, No. 3 (1908), p. 3.
[16] *American Journal of International Law*, III, Supplement, pp. 94-96, 140-143.
[17] *Journal of the African Society*, April, 1915, p. 268.

national channels. In 1912, out of imports of 53.9 million francs 35.8 came from Belgium and 53.9 out of total exports of 59 million francs had that destination.[18]

2. The French Congo.—Owing to her absorption in other interests, France had neglected the vast territories on the Congo and Ubangi that she had secured during the "scramble" for Africa in the 'eighties. In 1899, however, she most precipitately introduced the Belgian concessionary system and in one year divided up the major part of the French Congo among a number of companies. The same abuses followed as had developed in the Belgian Congo— forced labor and gross maltreatment of the natives, together with the closed door to foreign trade.[19] There ensued a prolonged diplomatic controversy with Great Britain,[20] thanks to which, as well as to other factors, the rights of the large companies were greatly curtailed in 1910-12 and a wider field was opened to the activities of private traders, foreign as well as French.[21] The evils of the old system were, however, not completely eradicated, for the fact that the companies still retained large tracts of land worked against equality of commercial opportunity.

[18] *The Statesman's Year-Book*, 1915, p. 734. [In 1911-12, the percentages were ("Manual of Belgian Congo," p. 272):

	Belgium	United Kingdom	France	Germany	Rhodesia and South Africa
1911	65	12	4.5	5	3
1912	66	10	2	8	6]

[19] Georges Bruel, *op. cit.*, pp. 428-435; Sir H. H. Johnston, "The History of the Colonization of Africa by Alien Races," pp. 230-234; Charles Humbert, "L'Œuvre Française aux Colonies," pp. 48-54.

[20] André Tardieu, "Le Mystère d'Agadir," pp. 209-245, 255-257, 260-285 *et seq.*

[21] Georges Bruel, *op. cit.*, pp. 439-442; Humbert, *op. cit.*, pp. 54-65; "Annuaire du Gouvernement Général de l'Afrique Équatoriale Française," 1912, II, pp. 223-322.

The Area Outside the Conventional Basin.—From the foregoing brief summary, it is apparent that the provisions of the Berlin Act for equality of commercial opportunity in the Congo Basin were really abortive and that the aim of those who desired the Conference to establish "a great state, whose organization and administration shall afford a guarantee that it is to be held for all time, as it were, in trust for the benefit of all peoples" [22] was completely frustrated by nationalistic forces. In fact, there was far more equality of trade conditions in the unrestricted portion of Middle Africa outside the Conventional Basin than there was within it. This outer region is very large and includes some of the richest and most populous colonies. Such are: British West Africa with an area of 444,842 square miles and a population of twenty millions, and French West Africa with an area of 1,478,000 square miles and a population of between eleven and twelve and one-half millions. In this unregulated region also are Togoland and the greater part of the Cameroons; Portuguese East Africa and half of Angola, together with Portuguese Guinea; Liberia, Spanish Rio Muni, and a section of French Equatorial Africa. The total foreign commerce of Middle Africa in 1913 amounted to about 350 million dollars, of which only somewhat more than one quarter was the share of the Conventional Basin.

Tariff Policies in This Area.—The tariff policies in this unrestricted area differed widely. Commercially, by far the most important colonies are the British, with a foreign trade

---

[22] Secretary Frelinghuysen to John A. Kasson, October 17, 1884. Senate Executive Document, No. 196, p. 14.

of 152 million dollars in 1913. In them, Great Britain naturally applied her traditional free trade and there were no discriminatory duties either in imports or in exports in favor of the Mother Country. Germany, likewise, pursued this policy in her oversea possessions, though less from a conviction of its inherent soundness than from fear that any other course would lead to dreaded retaliation on the part of Great Britain.[23] On the other hand, both Portugal and France had systems by which their own goods were favored in the colonial markets, and the colonial products, in turn, received preferential treatment in the metropolis. On account of the long, unguarded frontiers in Africa and the fact that any very marked divergence in duties would lead to smuggling from low-tariff neighbors,[24] France could not in West Africa go to the extreme of discrimination that she did elsewhere. In fact, she was obliged by inexorable geographical facts to conclude treaties that allowed foreign goods to enter some of her colonies on the same terms as did her own.

Franco-German Agreements of 1894 and 1908. — In 1894[25] and 1908,[26] France and Germany concluded agreements regarding their territories in the basins of the Benué,

[23] See the discussion of December 1, 1913, in the Reichstag on Germany's commercial relations with the British Empire. *Verhandlungen des Reichstags, Stenographische Berichte,* 291, pp. 6096-6106.

[24] In 1894, an interesting experiment was tried when Great Britain and Germany concluded a treaty establishing a customs union between Togoland and the Gold Coast east of the Volta River. There was to be no intervening customs barrier between them and uniform duties for both were established. Convention of Berlin, February 24, 1894. Treaty Series, 1894, No. 16; Hertslet, *op. cit.,* III, p. 915 ["Trattati," Supplemento, pp. 30-32]. Upon its denunciation by Germany, the Convention was terminated in 1904.

[25] Hertslet, *op. cit.,* II, p. 659 ["Trattati," pp. 418-423].

[26] Hertslet, *op. cit.,* III, p. 1219 ["Trattati," Supplemento, pp. 162-172].

the Shari, the Logone, and their tributaries, and also in the French Chad areas south of 13° North, to the effect that, in the matter of taxes and customs, there should be no differential treatment of the merchants of either nation. Economically, these arrangements were of little significance, as France had not established any custom houses in the areas affected, the frontiers being too long, so that merchandise passed to and fro duty free.[27] Far more important were the Anglo-French arrangements of 1898 and 1899.

Anglo-French Arrangements of 1898 and 1899.—In 1898, during the negotiations for settling some boundary disputes in Africa, especially the Nigerian frontier, Lord Salisbury proposed that the two Governments should establish an identical tariff in all their West African possessions. M. Hanotaux reserved his reply until the question had been studied, and also stated that France would have to take into account the sacrifices necessitated by the establishment of the colonies in West Africa.[28] In the end, a compromise was reached and the concluded treaty provided that for thirty years from the date of its ratification (June 13, 1899) British and French persons and goods should enjoy equality of treatment as regards river navigation, commerce, tariffs, and taxes in a region embracing French Dahomey and the Ivory Coast as well as British Nigeria and the Gold Coast.[29]

[27] Georges Bruel, *op. cit.*, p. 425; Karl Kuckleutz, "Das Zollwesen der Deutsche Schutzgebiete," p. 33. A similar clause is found in Article V of the Anglo-German Agreement of July 1, 1890. ["Trattati," pp. 264-265.]

[28] *Documents Diplomatiques, Correspondance et Documents Relatifs à la Convention Franco-Anglaise du 14 Juin* 1898, pp. 25, 26, 30, Paris, 1899.

[29] Article IX. Treaty Series, 1899, No. 15, p. 11 and map; Hertslet, *op. cit.*, II, pp. 789, 790 ["Trattati," p. 599].

By a subsequent declaration made in 1899,[30] this agreement was extended to include large sections of both French Equatorial Africa and the Anglo-Egyptian Sudan.[31]   As a result of the favored-nation clause, the equality of treatment provided for in these conventions was also accorded to all countries.[32]

Inadequacy of These Regulations.—Granted that equality of commercial opportunity in Middle Africa for all people is a desirable goal, the defects of the arrangements as they existed in 1914 are patent.   In the first place, the Conventional Basin covered only a portion of Middle Africa and, furthermore, the spirit of the Berlin Act could be, and was, evaded by a narrow, but literally correct, interpretation of its terms.   In the third place, only a part of the area outside this Basin came within the scope of the Anglo-German and Anglo-French arrangements and thus Spain, Portugal, and France were free to impose preferential systems in this unrestricted region.   Moreover, the Anglo-French agreements are of limited duration.   Finally, as attention was settled on Middle Africa as a market and as there was no dearth of raw materials, the problem of

[30] The Declaration of 1899 applied the agreement of 1898 to the territories situated south of 14° 20′ N. and north of 5° N., between 14° 20′ East of Greenwich and the course of the Upper Nile.   Treaty Series, 1899, No. 15, p. 20; Hertslet, *op. cit.*, II, p. 796 ["Trattati," pp. 613-614]; *Documents Diplomatiques, Correspondance Concernant la Déclaration Additionelle du 21 Mars 1899*, and the annexed map, Paris, 1899.

[31] Article VI of the Anglo-Egyptian Treaty of January 19, 1899, had already provided that in matters of liberty of trade, residence, and holding of property, "no special privileges shall be accorded to the subjects of any one or more Power." Hertslet, *op. cit.*, II, p. 621 ["Trattati," p. 611].

[32] Pierre Pégard, "Le Régime Douanier Colonial," in *Revue des Sciences Politiques,* 28 (1912), p. 229.

their control had not arisen. In the future, however, equality of commercial opportunity must also imply that to the trading nations also shall be secured the opportunity to obtain these supplies at practically identical prices.

[By the Convention for revision of the Berlin and Brussels Acts, signed at Saint-Germain-en-Laye, September 10, 1919,[33] complete commercial equality in the Conventional Basin, as defined in Article I of the Berlin Act, is secured to nationals of the Signatory Powers (the United States, Belgium, the British Empire, France, Italy, Japan, and Portugal) and to nationals of States, Members of the League of Nations, which may adhere to the Convention. Merchandise belonging to such nationals is exempt from all differential treatment, "the transit remaining free from all duties, taxes or dues, other than those collected for services rendered."]

[33 Articles 1-3; see Annex G. For criticism of the principle of complete commercial equality in colonies, see Antonelli, "L'Afrique et la Paix de Versailles," pp. 254-255.]

CHAPTER II

The Navigation of the Congo and Niger.—The question of freedom of navigation on the rivers of Africa is intimately connected with that of the open door in general. One of the three specific objects for which the Berlin Conference met in 1884 was the "application to the Congo and the Niger of the principles adopted by the Vienna Congress with a view to sanctioning free navigation on several international rivers, which principles were afterwards applied to the Danube." [1] These essentials were that navigation should be open on equal terms to all merchantmen and that there should be no undue tolls and local charges.[2] The Berlin Conference adopted this program and its General Act provided that the navigation of the Congo [3] and of the Niger,[4] as well as of their affluents, should "remain free for the merchant ships

---

[1] Senate Executive Document, No. 196, 49th Congress, 1st Session, p. 7.

[2] *Ibid.*, p. 11. The same principles were embodied in 1853, in the treaties of Great Britain, France, and the United States with Argentina for the navigation of the Paraná and Uruguay. *Ibid.*, pp. 26, 108-110; Malloy, "Treaties," pp. 18-20. For the texts of Articles 108-116 of the Treaty of Vienna of 1815 and of Article 15-19 of the Treaty of Paris of 1856, see *ibid.*, pp. 106, 107, 110, 111; Hertslet, "The Map of Europe by Treaty" (3d ed.), I, pp. 75-92, 269-272; II, pp. 1257-1259.

[3] Chapter IV, Articles 13-16. Senate Executive Document, No. 196, pp. 300-301; *Africa,* No. 3 (1886); Hertslet, "The Map of Africa by Treaty," II, p. 468 ["Trattati . . . relativi all'Africa," pp. 111-113].

[4] Chapter V, Articles 26-32.

of all nations equally, whether carrying cargo or ballast, for the transport of goods or passengers" and that "in the exercise of this navigation the subjects and flags of all nations shall in all respects be treated on a footing of perfect equality, not only for the direct navigation from the open sea to the inland ports of the Congo [and the Niger] and *vice versa,* but also for the great and small coasting trade, and for boat traffic on the course of the river." Transit dues and tolls were prohibited and only "taxes or duties having the character of an equivalent for services rendered to navigation itself," such as harbor, pilot, and lighthouse fees, were permitted. In addition, provision was made for an international commission to execute these stipulations regarding the Congo; [5] but, as the foundation of the Independent State seemed to render this cumbersome machinery superfluous, it was never established.

Extension of the Principle to the Zambezi and Shiré.— The British Government were desirous that this principle be extended also to the other great rivers of Africa, such as the Senegal and Zambezi.[6] Sir Edward Malet, the British delegate at the Conference, was, however, unable to effect this. Both France and Portugal declined, the latter on the ground that the question of the Zambezi was not one of the subjects for discussion by the Conference, although her delegate pointed out at the same time that the navigation of the river was actually free.[7] As a matter of fact, Portugal was

[5] Chapter IV, Articles 17-24.
[6] Earl Granville to Sir E. Malet, November 7, 1884. *Africa,* No. 8 (1884), p. 2.
[7] Senate Executive Document, No. 196, pp. 134, 306, 309; *Africa,* No. 2 (1885), pp. 2, 5.

already committed to this course [8] and the Anglo-Portuguese Treaties of 1890 and 1891 definitely established it for the Zambezi and Shiré rivers with their tributaries.[9]

Other Applications of the Principle.—In addition, the principle of free navigation was adopted in a number of other instances in a limited form in order to meet local needs of intercolonial trade. By the Franco-German conventions of 1894 and 1908, the Benué, Mayo-Kebbi, Shari, Logone, and Sanga were brought under the system of the Berlin Act, in so far as the territories of the signatories were concerned.[10] The "Entente Cordiale" of 1904 between Great Britain and France gave to the latter country freedom of navigation on the Gambia River, which jutted into French West Africa, Great Britain agreeing that the conditions should be at least as favorable as those in effect on the Congo and Niger.[11] The arrangement of 1906 between Great Britain and the Independent State of the Congo provided that ships flying the Congolese or Belgian flag should have the

[8] Article III of the abortive Anglo-Portuguese Treaty of February 26, 1884. Hertslet, *op. cit.*, III, p. 1005. For accounts of this Treaty, see J. Scott Keltie, "The Partition of Africa" (2d ed), pp. 143 ff.; A. B. Keith, "The Belgian Congo and the Berlin Act," pp. 50 ff. On December 15, 1882, Lord Granville intimated to Portugal that he was willing to consider an arrangement which would promote freedom of commerce for all nations, free navigation of the Congo and Zambezi, with their affluents, etc.

[9] Hertslet, *op. cit.*, III, pp. 1014-1016 ["Trattati," pp. 350-358].

[10] Hertslet, *op. cit.*, II, pp. 658, 659; III, pp. 1218, 1219 ["Trattati," pp. 420-421; Supplemento, pp. 167-168]. As affluents respectively of the Niger and the Congo, the Benué and Sanga were within the provisions of the Berlin Act. As a tributary of the Benué, so was the Mayo-Kebbi. On this entire subject see also the Franco-German Agreement of November 4, 1911. Debidour, "Histoire Diplomatique de l'Éurope, 1904-1916," pp. 336-340; R. Pinon, "France et Allemagne, 1870-1913," pp. 291-298, Paris, 1913.

[11] Hertslet, *op. cit.*, II, p. 817 ["Trattati," p. 715].

right of navigating the waters of the Upper Nile, and that no distinction as regards mercantile facilities should be made between them and British or Egyptian trading vessels.[12] Similarly, a number of agreements were concluded regulating the navigation on boundary rivers and on adjacent waters.[13]

Additional Arrangements.—Moreover, in order to render such freedom of navigation effective and to facilitate intercolonial trade, tracts of land on rivers were leased for nominal sums by one Government to the other.   In 1892, Great Britain rented from Portugal some ground at the Chinde mouth of the Zambezi River "for the landing, storage, and transshipment of goods" and, simultaneously, Portugal secured on the same terms a tract on Lake Nyasa from Great Britain.[14]   In 1903, according to the Anglo-French Treaty of 1898, Great Britain likewise leased to France two small areas on the Niger, one at the mouth and the other at the beginning of navigation.[15]   Similarly, in 1905, Great Britain rented to the Italian Government a plot of land on

---

[12] Hertslet, *op. cit.*, II, p. 586 ["Trattati," p. 1194].

[13] Tendo and Ahy Lagoons, the River Tendo, the Ajarra and the Addo River—Anglo-French Treaty, August 10, 1889 (Hertslet, *op. cit.*, II, pp. 731, 732 ["Trattati," pp. 229-230]).   River Campo—Franco-German Treaty, December 24, 1885 (Hertslet, *op. cit.*, II, p. 653 ["Trattati," p. 150]).   River Cavally—Franco-Liberian Treaty, December 8, 1892 (Hertslet, *op. cit.*, III, pp. 1134, 1141 ["Trattati," p. 386]).   Cross River—Anglo-German Treaty of 1913 (Treaty Series, 1913, No. 13).   Manoh River—Anglo-Liberian Treaty of 1913 (*ibid.*, No. 6, and *American Journal of International Law,* VII, Supplement, pp. 177-179; Hertslet, *op. cit.*, III, pp. 1140 ff.)   By Article III of the Franco-Liberian Agreement of September 18, 1907, "la navigation sur les cours d'eau formant la frontière sera libre et ouverte au trafic et aux citoyens et protégés français ainsi qu'aux sujets et citoyens libériens" ["Trattati," Supplemento, p. 128].

[14] Hertslet, *op. cit.*, III, pp. 1025, 1026 ["Trattati," pp. 370-375].

[15] Hertslet. *op. cit.*, II, pp. 789-792, 812-814 ["Trattati," pp. 700-701].

the British side of the Juba River near Kismayu for the erection of a bonded warehouse and pier.[16]   Finally, as part of the Agadir crisis settlement of 1911, Germany agreed to make a lease to France of some river-front lands in the Cameroons on the same lines as the Anglo-French arrangement of 1903 in Nigeria.[17]

Possible Future Extension of Freedom of Navigation.— From this summary account it is apparent that there was a marked will to coöperate in this matter and that very much had been done to establish freedom of navigation on the African rivers.   The situation in this respect was certainly up to the level of the most advanced practice in other continents and was, in general, excellent according to the standards that prevailed in 1914.   The question arises whether it will be equally satisfactory in the future when the trade of Middle Africa becomes more important than it now is. Free navigation of international rivers is not as yet a recognized rule of the Law of Nations and, in addition, in the absence of treaties to the contrary, every State can exclude foreign vessels from the rivers that are wholly within its bounds.[18]   In view of the fact that Middle Africa should be administered in an international spirit and not for the self-regarding national advantages of the colonizing Powers, the time seems to be ripe for a more advanced principle there. It would appear to be advisable to adopt and apply the principle that the navigation of all African rivers that have con-

[16] Hertslet, *op. cit.*, III, pp. 958-960 ["Trattati," pp. 745-748].

[17] "Contrat de Bail" of November 4, 1911. Debidour, *op. cit.*, pp. 342-344.

[18] L. F. L. Oppenheim, "International Law" (2d ed.), I, pp. 239-243, London, 1912; H. Bonfils, "Manuel de Droit International Publique" (7th ed.), pp. 347-359, Paris, 1914.

nection with the high seas should be free to all flags on
equal terms, regardless of whether or no these rivers are
entirely within the jurisdiction of one State or of two adjacent ones. Such a further extension of freedom of navigation would apparently be a valuable supplement to any regulations securing the open door.

[*Transit Dues and Railroad Rates.*—Like problems arise
in connection with transit dues and railroad rates.[19]   By
the Treaty of December 11, 1875,[20] between Portugal and
the Transvaal, no fees could be levied on goods and agricultural products in transit across Mozambique to or from the
Transvaal. Similar products from Middle Africa were, however, subject to harbor dues, etc., and certain classes of merchandise destined for the Transvaal were required to pay an
import duty. By Article XI of the Anglo-Portuguese Convention of June 11, 1891,[21] transit dues might not exceed
for twenty-five years three per cent, and like freedom was
accorded "across the Zambesi, and through the districts
adjoining the left bank of the river situated above the confluence of the Shiré, and those adjoining the right bank of
the Zambesi situated above the confluence of the river Lu-
enha (Ruanga)." The Italo-Franco-British Agreement of
December 13, 1906, regarding Abyssinia provides in Articles
6-7 [22] that the nationals of the three countries shall enjoy
in all matters of trade and transport absolute equality of
treatment on the railroad and in the port of Jibuti, as well

---

[19] This section has been prepared in accordance with a manuscript note
of Mr. Beer: "Include a brief statement about *(a)* transit dues; *(b)*
equality of railroad rates."
[20] Articles 3, 5, 7-12. "Trattati," pp. 902, 903-905.
[21] *Ibid.*, pp. 353-354; Hertslet, *op. cit.*, III, pp. 1016-1025.
[22] "Trattati," pp. 1254-1255; Treaty Series, 1907, No. 1.

as on all railroads which may be built in Abyssinia by British or Italian companies, and in British or Italian ports from which such lines may start. These benefits are to be extended to the nationals of all other countries and merchandise cannot be subjected to any fiscal transit duties for the benefit of French, British, or Italian colonies or treasuries. Article 14 of the Franco-German Agreement of November 4, 1911,[23] stipulates that "equality of treatment for transportation of passengers and goods shall be assured to the nationals of the two nations on the railroads within their possessions in the Congo and the Cameroons."

The most important document in this connection, however, is the Berlin Act. This provides [24] that all railroads constructed "with the special object of obviating the innavigability or correcting the imperfection of the river route" of the Congo and Niger, and of their affluents, branches, outlets, etc., shall give equality of treatment to the traffic of all nations. "Only tolls calculated on the cost of construction, maintenance, and management, and on the profits due to the promoters" may be levied and in this respect "foreigners and the natives of the respective territories shall be treated on a footing of perfect equality." Finally, this freedom is to be maintained even in time of war. The only real change in the Convention for the Revision of the Berlin and Brussels Acts [25] is that equality of treatment is restricted to "nationals of the Signatory Powers, and to those of States, Members of the League of Nations, which may adhere to the present Convention."]

[23] Pinon, op. cit., p. 298; Debidour, op. cit., p. 340.
[24] Articles 16, 29, 33.
[25] Article 7.

CHAPTER III

Trade and the Flag.—The general effect of the methods of development in the Belgian Congo and of the preferential systems established in the Portuguese and in some of the French possessions was that colonial trade tended to center in the Mother Country.[1] Thus, approximately, one half of the total foreign commerce of the French territories in Middle Africa was with France.[2] This condition was, however, even more marked in the British and German colonies, where there were no discriminatory duties to influence the course of traffic. Of the total trade of the British possessions in this region, fifty-five per cent in 1913-14 was with the United Kingdom.[3] In the case of the German colonies, the percentage was higher still; sixty-three per cent of their foreign commerce in 1912 was with the Mother Land.[4] In the Cameroons, this figure reached all but eighty-two per cent which was somewhat larger than even the abnormally high

[1] For a fuller discussion of this question see *supra,* pp. 96-110.
[2] British Diplomatic and Consular Reports, No. 5249, pp. 5, 11; No. 5494, pp. 8-14; No. 5423, pp. 17, 25-43; A. Girault, "The Colonial Tariff Policy of France," pp. 227, 231, 232, 239-242; Georges Bruel, "L'Afrique Équatoriale Française," pp. 452-454; A. Messimy, "Notre Œuvre Coloniale," p. 297; Charles Humbert, "L'Œuvre Française aux Colonies," p. 38.
[3] "Statistical Abstract of British Self-Governing Dominions," 1915, pp. 230-247.
[4] "Die Deutschen Schutzgebiete," 1914, p. xix; *Statistisches Jahrbuch,* 1915, pp. 463-467.

percentage in the Belgian Congo.[5]   The close commercial relations of metropolis and colony are not merely the effect of preferential systems.   That trade tends to follow the flag is largely inherent in the colonial status and is the result of many forces.

The Factor of Transportation.—One of these forces is the system of transportation.   The political relations between the governing and dependent country necessitate regular communications and these, in turn, facilitate the interchange of commodities.   The shipping of the metropolis tends to be predominant in the colony.   In some instances, furthermore, protective legislation and direct and indirect subsidies had established a virtual monopoly for vessels plying under the national flag.   This was the case in Portuguese West Africa.[6]   Similarly, the German East Africa Line received a considerable subsidy from the Government which strengthened the monopolistic hold of Germany on the colonial trade.[7]   Such predominance of the national shipping in the ports of the oversea possessions inevitably increased the commercial interdependence of transmarine territory and metropolis.

The Personal and National Factors.—Other factors are equally, if not more, important in establishing these closer ties.   The personal equation played a large part.   It was naturally easier for a Frenchman than for a German to do business in a French colony and *vice versa*.   Apart from all else, difference of language is a barrier and, besides, greater

[5 See *supra*, pp. 96-99.]
[6] "Annuário Colonial da 1916," p. 151; British Diplomatic and Consular Reports, No. 5402, pp. 6, 8.
[7] W. Ross, "Die Entwicklung der Schiffahrt nach den Deutschen Kolonien," in *Weltverkehr*, 1914-15, pp. 87-90.

confidence is generally placed in a fellow national than in an alien. Moreover, public authorities and those in charge of transportation and docking facilities are prone, at times purposely, but also unconsciously, to favor their fellow citizens. No regulation or legislation, no solemn international covenant, can eliminate this factor of sympathy and prejudice which must enter largely into the question of establishing the open door in dependent and backward countries. So long as there are distinct and sharply segregated nations and states, and so long as men regard themselves primarily as Americans, Englishmen, Frenchmen, and Germans, the full attainment of this goal is impossible. Until national feelings are eradicated, until there is a universal language in common usage, and until the State is no longer generally viewed as carrying on trade through its individual members, commerce is bound to follow the flag to a more or less marked extent. Whether this is regrettable or not is beside the mark; the actuality must be faced.

The Commercial Aspect of the Open Door.—On account of these fundamental facts, it is at present impossible to establish absolute equality of opportunity in the spheres of exploitation, investment, and commerce in Middle Africa. In its commercial aspect, the open door means essentially that all individuals, regardless of nationality, shall have the same facilities in trade with backward and undeveloped countries. This implies four things:

1. That goods of every origin and imported on any vessels should enter the colony on equal terms;

2. That colonial products may be freely shipped to any destination without discrimination;

3. That there should be complete freedom of navigation on rivers; [8]

4. That foreign merchants and traders should have unrestricted access to such colonies and also full freedom to settle there and to hold property.

The first three conditions can be secured, provided it is deemed advisable to do so. It would be in itself a comparatively simple matter to extend the Conventional Basin of the Berlin Act to cover all of Middle Africa. It would be more difficult to draw the line between legitimate public and private concessions necessary for economic development and those that tend to nullify equality of commercial opportunity.[9] On the other hand, it will be practically impossible to provide that foreign merchants shall be welcomed in the various colonies.[10] It is largely inevitable that the business of each possession should be controlled by national firms.

[8] Closely connected with this question is that of transit dues through a coastal region to a foreign hinterland, as from Portuguese Mozambique to British Rhodesia and British Nyasaland. See the Anglo-Portuguese Treaty of June 11, 1891. Hertslet, "The Map of Africa by Treaty" (3d ed.), III, pp. 1016-1025 ["Trattati . . . relativi all'Africa," pp. 350-358, and cf. *supra*, pp. 211-212].

[9] "The prohibition of the grant of any monopoly or favour in matters of trade [in the Berlin Act] is so widely worded as to be capable of becoming, if strictly observed, a menace to the safety of the State. The prohibition is at once too wide, and by its non-application to the Government itself too narrow, and it will be necessary to replace it by some formula which permits of the grant or exercise of a monopoly in trade matters by the State only when necessary in the interest of public health and security or otherwise (as in the case of a railway concession) unavoidable: the security for a just interpretation of the clause must rest in the right of recourse to an arbitral tribunal." A. B. Keith, "The Revision of the Berlin Act," in *Journal of the African Society*, July, 1918, pp. 253, 254.

[10] It will also be difficult to guard against indirect shipping subsidies, government purchase and control of raw materials, and drawbacks of colonial export duties paid by manufacturing countries in order to attract raw materials.

This, however, does not mean that the imports into the colony and the exports thence must follow national trade routes. As a matter of fact, a very considerable proportion of the output from British West Africa went directly to Germany and France and a marked share of the imports of cotton textiles into the German and French colonies came directly or indirectly from England.

The Financial Aspect of the Open Door.—In addition to commercial equality, the full open door further implies that all, irrespective of nationality, shall have equal opportunity:

1. To secure contracts for public works and to furnish governmental supplies;

2. To obtain concessions for the development of the country's resources.

The first has to-day little actuality in so far as Middle Africa is concerned, but in time it will probably become of importance. The Algeciras Act of 1906 provided that in Morocco such contracts should be awarded upon the basis of public international tender and this was confirmed by the Franco-German Morocco Treaty of 1911.[11] In applying the principle to Middle Africa great care will have to be exercised that the colonial authorities are not hampered in the choice of the best method in executing works of public utility and also that they are able to retain full control over

[11] Act of Algeciras, April 7, 1906, Chapter IV, Articles 105-119 ["Trattati," pp. 1178-1180; Malloy, "Treaties," pp. 2178-2180]; Franco-German Morocco Agreement, November 4, 1911, Article VI [Debidour, "Histoire Diplomatique de l'Europe, 1904-1916," p. 333]. On the significance of these clauses and on the Franco-German Consortium of 1909, see A. Tardieu, "Le Mystère d'Agadir," Chapters I and II, and pp. 483-487, 508-517, 565-576.

them. Thus, in British Nigeria, it was found that railways
were built most expeditiously and cheaply by the Director
of Public Works and Railways of the colony.[12] Furthermore, an absolutely rigid system of public tender for supplies is impracticable. The authorities must have some
freedom of decision. Accordingly, Lord Cromer wrote in
1905, in connection with the system of public tenders used
for the purchase of supplies required by the Egyptian Railways:

"I do not doubt that, generally speaking, that system, if
carefully applied, is the best, which in the public interests
can be adopted. But it requires careful application. More
especially it has to be remembered, in dealing with railway
material, that price is only one of the factors to be considered in deciding the points at issue." [13]

In other words, such questions as durability and economy of
operation have also to be taken into account.

Private Concessions.—The question of equal opportunity
for all in securing private concessions for the exploitation
of Middle Africa's resources likewise bristles with difficulties.
[Nevertheless, an attempt was made to meet the problem
in the Convention of September 10, 1919, for the Revision
of the Berlin and Brussels Acts. Article 4 of this document
states that "each State reserves the right to dispose freely
of its property and to grant concessions for the development
of the natural resources of the territory, but no regulations
on these matters shall admit of any differential treatment

---

[12] A. B. Keith, "West Africa," pp. 238-242.
[13] *Egypt*, No. 1 (1905) (Cromer), p. 37. For a discussion of these other
factors, see Correspondence Respecting the Comparative Merits of British, Belgian, and American Locomotives in Egypt, Commercial Series,
1902, No. 1.

between the nationals of the Signatory Powers and of States, Members of the League of Nations, which may adhere to the present Convention." [14]   The Berlin Act, on the other hand, declared in its fifth Article that "No Power that exercises or that shall hereafter exercise sovereign rights in the above-mentioned regions shall be allowed to grant therein a monopoly or favour of any kind."]

Could the problem be divorced from its overwhelming political features, it would be comparatively simple. In fact, the question is not primarily economic. Financiers were not really competing to invest in Africa. Capital needed considerable coaxing before it could be induced to venture into such a speculative field as tropical Africa. It took a number of years for Mr. Robert Williams to secure funds for the construction of the railway from Lobito Bay in Angola to the Katanga mining district. Yet this is the most promising enterprise of its kind in tropical Africa. Germany's annoyance when Mr. Williams secured this concession in 1902 and her attempts in 1914 to secure control of the railway proceeded primarily from the fact that such domination might be used to secure political influence over Portuguese Angola and the Belgian Congo.[15]   In the past, there was constant dread on the part of the weaker colonizing Powers that foreign investments in their possessions might be but the prelude to the transfer of these territories to the

[[14] Cf. also paragraph 3 of Article 7 of the Draft Mandate for (British) East Africa and of Article 6 of the Draft Mandates for British Togoland and the British Cameroons, reproduced in Annexes I and J.]

[15] Robert Williams, "The Milestones of African Civilization," in *United Empire Magazine*, July, 1917, pp. 446-457, and his address, "Peaceful Penetration in Central Africa," in *The Times* (London), weekly ed., July 5, 1918.

flag of the peaceful penetrator. Fears of such nature kept Portugal, especially, from welcoming German capital in the past. There can be no doubt that, with non-restoration of the German colonies and with loss of physical German foothold in Africa, there will be more opportunities for the investment of German capital in the Belgian and Portuguese colonies than if Germany were to remain an African Power. The crux of the problem is to eliminate the political motive. That effected, the real difficulty will not consist in giving equal investment opportunities to private capital of all nations, but in securing adequate funds for Africa's needs.

CHAPTER IV

REGULATION OF THE LIQUOR TRADE

Native Interests at the Berlin Conference.—In his instructions to the British delegate at the Berlin Conference of 1884-85, Lord Granville wrote:

"Commercial interests should not, in the opinion of Her Majesty's Government, be looked upon as exclusively the subject of deliberation; while the opening of the Congo markets is to be desired, the welfare of the natives should not be neglected; to them it would be no benefit, but the reverse, if freedom of commerce, unchecked by reasonable control, should degenerate into licence." [1]

Lord Granville referred especially to two evils, the slave trade and the importation of spirituous liquors, regarding both of which, as he wrote, there was "a strong feeling" in England.[2] The Conference adopted some very general resolutions against the slave trade and in favor of promoting the welfare of the natives,[3] but declined to treat these questions directly. Concerning the proposed restrictions on the liquor traffic, the American delegate, Mr. John A. Kas-

[1] Earl Granville to Sir E. Malet, November 7, 1884. *Africa*, No. 8 (1884), p. 1.

[2] Earl Granville to Sir E. Malet, November 12, 1884. *Africa*, No. 3 (1885), p. 2.

[3] Chapter I, Article 6; Chapter II, Article 9. Hertslet, "The Map of Africa by Treaty" (3d ed.), II, pp. 473, 474 ["Trattati . . . relativi all'Africa," pp. 109, 110]. See also Sir E. Malet to Earl Granville, February 21, 1885. *Africa*, No. 2 (1885), pp. 6, 7.

son, wrote to Secretary Frelinghuysen that it was "alleged by Holland and Germany that in portions of this region commerce is dependent on the exchange of such liquors for the native goods; and further that it could not be prohibited without involving a right of search of foreign vessels by the local authorities." [4]   This matter was, however, regulated a few years later by the Brussels Conference of 1889-90, which also dealt with the slave trade and the importation of arms.

The Brussels Act of 1890.—The Brussels Act of July 2, 1890,[5] established an arbitrary zone in Africa between 22° South and 20° North and reaching from ocean to ocean. Within this vast region, the signatories agreed to .prohibit the importation and distillation of spirituous liquors in those parts thereof in which, whether for religious or other reasons, their use did not as yet exist or had not developed. To each state was left the determination of the bounds of these forbidden areas. In the open zones, the Brussels Act provided that the various Powers should impose minimum import duties or equivalent excises of 15 francs a hectoliter (about 11 cents for the American gallon) on liquors up to 50 degrees Centigrade. These fees were to remain in effect for three years and could then be increased to 25 francs for another period of three years, at the expiration of which they were to be revised in the light of the experience gained. Lord Vivian, the British representative, insisted that these duties were far too low to check the traffic and urged that

---

[4] Senate Executive Document, No. 196, p. 136. See also Protocol V, *ibid.*, pp. 126, 132-134.

[5] Chapter VI, Articles 90-95. Hertslet, *op. cit.*, II, pp. 514, 515; Treaty Series, 1892, No. 7 ["Trattati," pp. 293-294].

a much higher rate be imposed. In this, he was supported by France. The opposition of the Dutch and German delegates could not, however, be overcome.[6]

The Brussels Convention of 1899.—A few years' experience conclusively demonstrated that these duties were too low to prevent the importation of liquor in the open zones, which were mainly on the West African coast. On account of the number of juxtaposed colonies in that region and the impossibility of watching closely their long frontiers, it was futile for one Power alone to increase its duties heavily, since this would merely lead to smuggling from the adjacent jurisdictions. As the British Government was unable during the course of protracted negotiations to induce France and Germany to augment their duties, Lord Salisbury decided to call another international conference.[7] The Brussels Convention of June 8, 1899,[8] adopted by this Conference, raised the minimum duties and excises to 70 francs at 50 degrees Centigrade. The rates were to be proportionately

[6] *Documents Diplomatiques, Conférence Internationale de Bruxelles,* pp. 80-83, 281, 282, 291, 293, 391, 392, Paris, 1891. See also *Correspondance Diplomatique,* pp. 57, 58, *et passim* (annexed to these *Documents Diplomatiques*): "The British Representatives at the Conference were instructed by Her Majesty's Government to propose the imposition of a duty upon imported spirits which would have amounted to approximately 10s. a gallon. It appeared, though, that so high a rate as this was not acceptable to the other members of the Conference, and, after discussion, a duty of about 1s. 10d. a gallon was suggested; but in the end, the utmost that could be obtained was a minimum duty of about 6½d. a gallon. It does not appear that up to the present time the resolutions of the Conference have had any very material effect so far as the trade on the West Coast is concerned." Memorandum from the British Colonial Office, March 10, 1896. Liquor Trade in West Africa (Cd. 8480, 1897), p. 2.
[7] Liquor Trade in West Africa (Cd. 8480, 1897), pp. 48, 55, 56, 59, 60.
[8] The normal rate was placed at 60 francs in the cases of Togoland and Dahomey. Hertslet, *op. cit.* (3d ed.), II, pp. 529-531; Treaty Series, 1900, No. 13 ["Trattati," pp. 618-621].

lower or higher as the strength varied from this norm; and they were to remain in effect for six years, when they were to be subject to revision. At the last session of the Conference, the British representative, Sir F. R. Plunkett, read a declaration to the effect that the British Government, "in accepting the minimum rate of duty agreed to by the Conference for a term of six years, by no means admit that that rate is sufficient" and they "sincerely regret that it has not been possible to obtain the assent of the Conference to a higher rate." [9]

The Brussels Conference of 1906.—In due course another international conference met at Brussels in 1906. The British representative, Sir Arthur Hardinge, stated that despite the fact that the British proposal of a duty of 100 francs had been rejected in 1899 in favor of one of 70 francs, yet the duties in British Gambia and Sierra Leone had been raised to 110 francs, those in Lagos and Southern Nigeria to 96 francs, and those in the Gold Coast west of the Volta River to 124 francs.[10] He then proposed that the Conference should adopt this Gold Coast rate of 124 francs as the

---

[9] *Africa*, No. 7 (1899), p. 9. The United States did not take part in the Brussels Conferences subsequent to that of 1890, but they adhered to the acts adopted by them. In 1899, Secretary John Hay officially wrote that the rate of 70 francs was believed to be scarcely adequate. "American Foreign Relations, 1899," p. 83.

[10] Between 1906 and 1912, the duties were raised from 110 to 115 francs in Gambia, from 110 to 138 in Sierra Leone, from 80 to 100 in the Gold Coast east of the Volta, from 124 to 152 in the same colony west of the Volta, and from 96 to 138 in Southern Nigeria. "Actes de la Conférence pour la Revision du Régime des Spiritueux en Afrique, 1912," pp. 29-30, Brussels, 1912. The duties in force in 1910 were as follows (*ibid.*, pp. 84-85): 80 marks in Togo and the Cameroons; 400 marks in German Southwest Africa; 100 rupees in German East Africa; 100 francs in the Belgian Congo, Ivory Coast, Dahomey, and French Equatorial Africa; 100 francs and 30 per cent on fermented products in French West Africa; 250 francs in Fernando Po; 125 francs in Rio Muni and Elobe;

normal one. Considerable opposition was manifest. Portugal objected to an increase; Germany conditionally consented; Italy raised some difficulties on account of the
special circumstances in Eritrea. The Belgian Congo was
ready to agree to an increase to 90 or 100 francs and even
more. France had already raised the duties to 90 francs in
a part of her equatorial colony and thought that this should
be the limit, but she was willing to go even further.[11] In
the end, a compromise was reached and 100 francs was established as the normal rate for duties and excises.[12]

The Abortive Conference of 1912.—Even this rate was
insufficient to check the importation of spirits into West

115 francs in Gambia; 138 francs in Sierra Leone; 152 francs in the Gold
Coast; and 138 francs in Southern Nigeria. Absolute prohibition was
enforced in Northern Nigeria, Rhodesia, Nyasaland, Uganda, British
Somaliland, British East Africa, and Zanzibar.
  [11] *Archives Diplomatiques*, 112 (1909), pp. 163-170.
  [12] Brussels Act of November 3, 1906. *Ibid.*, pp. 236-239 ["Trattati,"
pp. 1247-1250]; *Africa*, No. 2 (1906); "American Foreign Relations, 1907,"
Part I, pp. 80-83. On account of the special circumstances in Eritrea,
a rate of 70 francs was allowed there. The Portuguese Government also
was permitted to deduct 30 francs from the 100 francs normal excise,
in order to facilitate the transformation of the distilleries in Angola into
sugar factories. Between 1906 and 1910 the increase in the importation
of liquor into British West Africa was 40 per cent, the customs receipts
being 23.7 million francs in 1906, and 37.6 in 1910. Imports into Togo
and the Cameroons were likewise gaining. "Actes de la Conférence pour
la Revision du Régime des Spiritueux en Afrique, 1912," pp. 30-31, Brussels, 1912. [At the Brussels Conference of 1908-09, the German delegate,
Graf von Wallwitz, sought to bring up the question of revision of the
liquor agreement and proposed a duty of 120 marks per hectoliter at
fifty degrees Centigrade; but the Belgian representative, M. Capelle,
held that this matter was not within the competence of the assembly.
Nevertheless, it was considered in the sessions of December, 1909, when
the following statistics on the importation of trade brandy into the
Congo were presented:

1893	1,400,054 liters	}	15 francs duty
1898	1,229,582 "		
1902	467,764 "	}	70 " "
1905	494,472 "		
1908	187,659 "		100 " "

Africa and accordingly another congress, in which **Germany,
Belgium, Spain, France, Great Britain, Italy, Liberia, the
Netherlands, Portugal, and Russia** were represented, met
at Brussels on January 4, 1912, for a fresh regulation of the
problem. The two principal aims were to increase the duties
and to delimit the prohibited zone. Great Britain and Germany stood sponsors for a jointly regulated project, according to which the rate was to be raised on January 1, 1913,
from 100 to 150 francs and then augmented by yearly increases of ten francs until the limit of 200 francs was
reached. Nevertheless, the Powers reserved the right to levy
higher duties and to maintain such tariffs if they already
existed. Furthermore, the zone of prohibition was to be
delimited by the simplest possible lines in all colonies as it
had been in those of Great Britain, Belgium, and Germany,
with the idea that this area should constitute one solid
block. The French delegate felt that the latter measure
would profoundly modify Article 91 of the Brussels Act and
further restrict territorial sovereignty in Africa. He accordingly held that local authorities should be given a free
hand in determining the prohibition areas, that all projects
for increasing duties should be determined circumspectly,
and that the Powers should especially devote their attention
to checking local manufacture of liquors. He was, however,
willing to accept the proposal for Somaliland and a minimum
of 110 francs (possibly 120 francs after January 1, 1915),
but must adhere to the *status quo* in French Equatorial

The French delegate had, however, received no instructions which would
permit him to take part in the discussion of this matter, and the problem
was not considered further. "Actes de la Conférence pour la Revision du
Régime des Armes en Afrique, 1908-1909," pp. 7-10, 308-309, Brussels, 1909.]

Africa; and though he later agreed to 120 francs for both these colonies, he could not assent to a zone of prohibition in North Dahomey. The controversy turned, in great part, on the meaning to be given to Article 91 of the Brussels Act, which France interpreted as optional, Germany as binding. Great Britain and Germany felt themselves unable to assent to the French counter-proposals and, since no satisfactory solution of the deadlock could be reached, the Conference adjourned February 5.[13]

The Nature of the Problem.—This problem [14] is predominantly confined to West Africa. The prohibition areas cover the major portion of Africa between 22° South and 20° North and, in general, they have been greatly extended since 1890, when this system was instituted. Thus, in the Belgian Congo, the forbidden zone has been pushed ever closer to the coast until, in 1916, it embraced the entire colony.[15] There has been some smuggling from the open into the closed areas, and there have also been some lapses in certain

[13] *La Vie Internationale,* I (1912), pp. 93-96; Statement of Dr. Gleim, April 25, 1913, in the *Verhandlungen des Reichtags, Stenographische Berichte,* 289, p. 5106. See also Dr. Solf's statement on March 6, 1913. *Ibid.,* 288, p. 4338. Officially, France's attitude was based in part upon a belief that this policy would not suppress alcoholism among the natives, since they would merely increase their domestic production of alcoholic beverages, if deprived of the imported stock, and would ruin the oil palms, the chief resource of the country, in preparing toddy from them. "Bulletin de la Société Belge d'Études Coloniales," 1913, p. 314. Fiscal reasons likewise entered and it is also assumed that the influence of the disti.lers in France was a factor. On the whole subject of this Conference, see "Actes de la Conférence pour la Revision du Régime des Spiritueux en Afrique, 1912," Brussels, 1912.
[14] For further details, see *supra,* pp. 171-178 [and cf. John H. Harris, "Africa: Slave or Free?", pp. 153-161].
[15] The Belgian law permits the sale of beverages containing a low percentage of alcohol to the natives. For this law, see J. Geerincks, "Guide Commercial de Congo Belge," published by the Belgian Ministère des Colonies.

outlying jurisdictions,[16] but, in the main, the prohibition
has been effective.   In West Africa, on the other hand, the
natives have been accustomed to distilled liquors for several
centuries.   In addition, they make their own fermented
beverages.   These are, however, generally less harmful than
those which are imported.   The situation was admittedly
serious throughout West Africa, as the importation of distilled liquors was growing rapidly.[17]   The increasingly heavy
duties did not keep pace with the expanding ability of the
natives to pay higher prices for spirits.

International Coöperation Essential.—The British Government had adopted strong measures to check this growing
evil.[18]   After the failure of the Brussels Conference in 1912,
the distillation of liquor in West Africa was prohibited and
the import duties have been successively raised until they
stand at a very high level, far in excess of those stipulated
at the Brussels Conference of 1906.[19]   There is a wide difference of opinion as to the extent of drunkenness in Middle
Africa, some contending that alcoholism is a potential rather
than a real evil and others insisting that drink is undermining the moral and physical vigor of the native.   Virtually all
candid students agree, however, that the traffic needs stringent curbing.   But, whether the present system of high customs and excises should be maintained and increased, or

[16] See Sir H. H. Johnston, "Alcohol in Africa," in *The Nineteenth Century and After,* September, 1911, p. 476.
[17] See especially Report on the Liquor Trade in Southern Nigeria and
the Minutes of Evidence (Cd. 4906 and 4907, 1909).   Cf. also Georges
Bruel, "L'Afrique Équatoriale Française," pp. 457-459.
[18] A. J. S. MacDonald, "Trade, Politics, and Christianity in Africa and
the East," p. 109; A. B. Keith, "West Africa," p. 213.   See also the
statement of Mr. L. Harcourt of June 27, 1912.   Hansard, 40, p. 535.
[19] *Anti-Slavery Reporter,* October, 1916, p. 74; *Board of Trade Journal,*
May 9, 1918, p. 572.

whether total prohibition of distilled liquors should be enforced, is a moot question. In any event, unless there is a virtually uniform policy in all the West African colonies, smuggling will inevitably occur across the long borders that, in the present stage of African development, cannot be closely watched. As a result, the high tariff or prohibition policy of one colony can be nullified by the low customs of its neighbor. As in the past, so in the future, international coöperation is imperative if the liquor traffic is to be abolished or diminished.[20]

[[20] For the provisions of the Convention of September 10, 1919, on this matter, see *supra*, pp. 176-178.]

CHAPTER V

The Brussels Act of 1890.—The international conference which met at Brussels in 1890, on the invitation of Belgium in agreement with Great Britain, was convoked particularly to deal with the slave trade and the general welfare of the native. Experience had shown "the pernicious and preponderating part" played by firearms in the slave traffic and in inter-tribal warfare. Accordingly, the signatories to the General Act of July 2, 1890, agreed to prohibit in their respective jurisdictions within the areas between 20° North and 22° South the sale to natives of rifles and improved weapons, as well as of ammunition for them. Only flintlock, unrifled guns and common powder, known as "poudre de traité," could be sold to the negroes. Elaborate provisions were drawn up to make it impossible for the aborigines to procure any arms of precision, such as rifles, magazine-guns, or breech-loaders and their ammunition.[1]

The Protocol of 1908.—In 1908, Great Britain, the Congo Free State, France, Germany, Portugal, and Spain signed a further treaty suspending for a period of four years the importation of all kinds of firearms and ammunition destined for natives, as well as their sale to them within a large zone

[1] Chapter I, Articles 8-14. Hertslet, "The Map of Africa by Treaty" (3d ed.), II, pp. 494-497 ["Trattati . . . relativi all'Africa," pp. 273-276]; see also A. B. Keith, "The Belgian Congo and the Berlin Act," pp. 79-80, for a clear outline of these provisions.

in Eastern Equatorial Africa.   It was distinctly understood
that in exceptional cases the local authorities should have
power to depart from this rigid rule.[2]   This agreement was,
however, not continued after 1913 and the regulation of the
importation of antiquated, slow-firing arms for the use of
natives was left to the local authorities.[3]   In order not to
hamper them an agreement was reached in 1910 permitting
import duties on arms and ammunition in the Conventional
Basin in excess of the ten per cent rates authorized by the
Brussels Declaration of 1890.[4]   The natives require these
obsolete weapons for hunting and for protection against wild
animals and the trade in them is considerable.[5]   As it is
carefully supervised by the authorities,[6] very little, if any,
serious harm has resulted from it.

[*The Abortive Conference of 1908-09.*—This Protocol
marked the medial point of a Brussels conference which sat
from April 28 to July 20, 1908, and from December 14 to
December 30, 1909.[7]   The Powers represented were Ger-

[2] Protocol of Brussels, July 22, 1908.   Treaty Series, 1908, No. 29;
Archives Diplomatiques, 108, p. 262 ["Trattati," Supplemento, pp. 182-184].
   [3] Georges Bruel, "L'Afrique Équatoriale Française," p. 457.
   [4] Declaration of Brussels, June 15, 1910.   Treaty Series, 1912. No. 5;
A. B. Keith, *op. cit.*, p. 322.
   [5] Thus, in the second half-year of 1913, after the denunciation of the
Protocol of 1908, the quantities authorized to be imported into Gabun
and the Middle Congo in French Equatorial Africa were 6,500 guns, 22
tons of powder, and 222,000 caps.   Georges Bruel, *op. cit.*, p. 457.
   [6] For the regulations in the Belgian Congo, see J. Geerincks, "Guide
Commercial de Congo Belge," pp. 132-136.   For those in French West
Africa, see "Annuaire du Gouvernement Général de l'Afrique Occidentale
Française," 1915-1916, pp. 527-536.
   [7] This Protocol was prepared during, but independently of, the Conference for revision of the arms traffic, held at Brussels in 1908-09.   "Actes
de la Conférence pour la Revision du Régime des Armes en Afrique,
1908-09," pp. 253-254.   These Actes should be consulted for an account
of all the proceedings of the Conference.   Cf. also *Annuaire de la Vie*

many, Belgium, Spain, the Congo, the United States, France, Great Britain, Italy, Liberia, the Netherlands, Portugal, Russia, Sweden, Persia, and Turkey. The purpose of the assembly, convened by Belgium at the request of Great Britain, was to increase the duties on arms and ammunition, to strengthen the stipulations of Articles 8-14 of the Brussels Act, to extend the zones of prohibition and supervision established by that Act, and to provide for international control of the traffic. The German delegate, Graf von Walwitz, proposed, as regarded Article 9 of the Brussels Act, to reserve to the Governments exclusive sale and delivery of arms and ammunition to natives, stressing the dangerous possibilities of the increasing entry of weapons on the West Coast as contrasted with conditions on the East Coast, where this traffic was forbidden to individuals. Liberia objected to this plan as out of harmony with her needs. The Italian delegate desired the area of prohibition to include all Africa, the Red Sea, the Gulf of Oman, and the Persian Gulf, but this met with objection from Great Britain and France. Sir Arthur Hardinge proposed the creation of two bureaus on the East Coast and of one bureau on the West Coast, modeled on the International Maritime Office established at Zanzibar by Articles 74-80 of the Brussels Act. At the session of May 20, Germany presented a revision of Articles 8-9 of the Brussels Act along lines which her delegate had already set forth. Spain agreed in principle, as did the Congo, Great Britain, Italy, Persia, and Turkey; France, the Netherlands, Portu-

Internationale, 1910-11, pp. 251-260. The summary here given has been condensed from notes inserted in the author's manuscript.

gal, and Sweden made reservations; the United States delegate was without instructions. At the following session, the French delegate submitted a draft to strengthen Article 9 of the Brussels Act. Subsequently, the Italian delegate proposed a maritime police which on the high seas should have the right to search only native vessels.[8]

On June 30 the Italian delegation presented an elaborate draft in fourteen Articles. The zone in which the importation of arms and ammunition was to be prohibited was to extend from 22° South to 20° North and was to be so drawn as to include Tunis and Egypt, as well as Arabia from Suez to the southern boundary of Hadramaut. Within this area, all imported arms and ammunition must be deposited in public warehouses under the care of the State. No arms of precision might be sold to natives and the sale of flintlock, unrifled guns and of trade powder was to be carefully regulated. In the prohibited zone, manufacture of arms and ammunition was reserved to the State. All loading, unloading, and transshipment of arms were prohibited within that area for vessels of less than 500 tons' burden unless they "were engaged in the coasting trade between different ports of the same Colony or Protectorate." Provision was also made for transit trade in arms and for minimum duties. Each State was to exercise supervision in the territorial waters along its possessions and for a distance of 100 miles from shore men-of-war of the Contracting Powers were to have rights of search in case of native vessels flying the flag of any State which had ratified the entire Brussels Act. Any other suspected native vessel might, however, be visited to

[8] Cf. Articles 30 ff. of the Brussels Act.

determine whether she was flying her true colors. By the concluding Article, the International Bureau at Zanzibar and two other bureaus, one of which was to be at Aden, were to exercise the supervision required by these stipulations.

As regards import duties, Great Britain proposed increases which would amount to twenty-five per cent for arms of precision, to sixty per cent for flintlocks, and to four hundred per cent for powder and percussion caps, pointing out that the duty in Southern Rhodesia was one pound per gun and so, generally speaking, in Sierra Leone, the Gold Coast, and Gambia. Germany imposed twenty marks on breech-loaders and France, in Gabun, twenty francs on guns for hunting and fifty on magazine-guns. Subsequently, the British delegate consented to reduce the duties to twenty francs for breech-loaders, ten for muzzle-loaders, and five for flintlocks.

When the sessions were resumed on December 14, 1909, it was found that Belgium, the Congo, the United States, Great Britain, Italy, Persia, Portugal, Russia, and Sweden were agreed in principle and on condition that all gave assent; Germany, Spain, France, the Netherlands, and Turkey adhered with reservations; Liberia was no longer represented. By December 30, all were willing to sign except France. The latter, however, felt able to assent only to the first paragraph of Article 1 and to Articles 2-5, 14-21. Neither Italy nor Great Britain could accept this position, holding that Articles 1, 6, and 8-13 were vital portions of the document. The conference accordingly adjourned without reaching a successful conclusion.]

The System Generally Satisfactory.—In general, the system of international regulation and local control has produced the desired results. In East Africa especially, conditions have been most satisfactory. Sir Alfred Sharpe, who has had exceptional experience as a colonial official, as a traveler, and as an administrator of the Mozambique Company, writes as follows:

"I can speak with some authority on this matter, as I have spent over twenty years in Nyasaland, and have paid lengthy visits to the Belgian Congo, Portuguese East Africa, Uganda, British East Africa, German East Africa, the Sudan, and Rhodesia. So far from there being any indiscriminate introduction of arms and ammunition in these territories, the importation or purchase is absolutely prohibited. . . . I have never met this person [the gun-runner] nor, within what I may call modern times, have I ever heard of him. As a matter of fact, he does not now exist in any British territory, nor, so far as I have seen, in any other territory administered by a European Power in the eastern half of Central Africa." [9]

Gun-Running from Abyssinia.—The situation was, however, far from gratifying in Northeast Africa. Although within the zone drawn by the Brussels Act of 1890, Abyssinia was not a party to this agreement and accordingly in 1906 the adjacent Powers, Great Britain, France, and Italy, concluded a treaty regarding the importation of arms and ammunition into that country.[10] The signatories agreed to exercise a rigorous supervision over the entry of arms into their colonies, to stop their exportation to unauthorized persons in Abyssinia, and to prevent smuggling by the trading

[9] London *Daily Mail,* February 6, 1918.
[10] Agreement of London, December 13, 1906. Treaty Series, 1907, No. 2 ["Trattati," pp. 1258-1260] ; Albin, "Les Grands Traités Politiques," p. 412.

"dhows." Apparently, in the main, because France would not permit these small craft to be searched outside of territorial waters when flying the French flag, this agreement was largely ineffective.[11] In his report on the Sudan for 1913, Lord Kitchener wrote:

"The only part of the country where the situation cannot be described as altogether satisfactory is the south-eastern frontier, where an extensive trade in arms and ammunition is carried on between Abyssinia and the Nuer country. . . . The political situation at Adis Ababa, and the apparent inability of the Abyssinian Government to put a stop to the smuggling of arms from the coast, also makes for unrest in the outlying districts bordering on the Sudan." [12]

The Governor-General of the Anglo-Egyptian Sudan, Sir Reginald Wingate, was even more explicit in his report for 1914. The steady influx of arms and ammunition from Abyssinia, he said, caused unrest in the Nuer country and the situation was profoundly unsatisfactory, since disaffection was growing. It was idle to hope that Abyssinia would soon be able to control this traffic, as arms were being continually introduced in large quantities into Abyssinia by way of the French port of Jibuti.[13]

[No further steps were taken to regulate the traffic in arms and ammunition until a Convention for the control of this trade was signed at Saint-Germain-en-Laye on Sep-

[11] Sir H. H. Johnston, "Common Sense in Foreign Policy," p. 34, London, 1913.

[12] *Egypt*, No. 1 (1914) (Kitchener), p. 62. See also *ibid.*, 1912, pp. 44, 65.

[13] Sir Reginald Wingate, "Memorandum on the Sudan 1914," pp. 3, 6, 7. [This trade by way of Jibuti had aroused British anxiety in 1908, when the Mad Mullah was so disturbing a factor. "Actes de la Conférence pour la Revision du Régime des Armes en Afrique, 1908-1909," pp. 112-114, Brussels, 1909.]

tember 10, 1919.[14] By this, arms and ammunition may not be imported into any part of Africa except Algeria, Libya, and the Union of South Africa, unless authorities of the High Contracting Parties grant special export licences. Similarly, manufacture and assembling of arms and ammunition are forbidden, except in government arsenals, and even the repair of weapons is permitted only in duly licensed establishments. Elaborate provision is made to prevent gunrunning. After seven years, the Convention may be revised in the light of experience "if the Council of the League of Nations, acting if need be by a majority, so recommends."]

[14 Cf. *supra*, pp. 170-171, and, for the complete text of the Convention, see Annex E; see also the Mandate for German Southwest Africa, Article 3, paragraph 2, *infra*, Annex L. For the details of the drawing up of this Convention, see "Procès-Verbaux et Rapport de la Commission pour la Revision des Actes Généraux de Berlin et de Bruxelles," pp. 6-77, 136, 144-146.]

CHAPTER VI

PRESERVATION OF WILD ANIMALS AND THE CONTROL OF
SLEEPING SICKNESS

The London Conference of 1900.—Obviously the question of the preservation of wild animals in Africa is intimately connected with the regulation of the traffic in arms. To a certain extent, they are the positive and negative sides of the same problem. The more freely guns are permitted to be imported and sold, the less easy will it be to check the ruthless slaughter of Africa's varied fauna. Moreover, both are markedly international questions and require comprehensive international agreements if the measures adopted are to be effective in a country of many jurisdictions like Africa. In the 'nineties of the last century this came to be realized in England, where there was in a number of circles real concern at the indiscriminate killing of "big game" and other animals in Africa, portending the disappearance of some valuable species.[1] The matter was taken up by Great Britain and in 1897, with a view to an international agreement, she approached the German Government. Upon the recommendation of the distinguished traveler and administrator, Hermann von Wissmann, Germany tentatively advised that an international conference be assembled.[2]

[1] Correspondence Relating to the Preservation of Wild Animals in Africa (Cd. 3189, 1906), pp 1-29, 81, *et passim*.
[2] *Ibid.*, pp. 30, 34-36.

238

The British Government adopted this suggestion and proposed that, after agreeing with Germany upon the exact bases of discussion, invitations should be issued for sessions to be held in London in the spring or early summer of 1898.[3] The German Government concurred, but suggested a postponement of the conference until their expert, von Wissmann, had returned from Africa.[4] The following year, 1899, the British Government again raised the question and, after having secured the support of the German Government, issued with their accord invitations to the interested Powers for a conference to sit in London early in 1900.[5] The invitation was generally accepted.

The Convention of 1900.—This assembly adopted an elaborate convention,[6] modeled in general upon the bases antecedently drawn up by the British and approved by the German Government. The zone in which the agreement was to apply was bounded laterally by the shores of the continent, on the north by the parallel of 20° North, and on the south by the northern boundary of German Southwest Africa and the Zambezi River. Except in the south, its delimitations thus coincided with those of the sphere demarcated by the Brussels Act of 1890. Within this area the following regulations were to be put into effect by the local authorities:

[3] Cd. 3189 (1906), pp. 42, 45.
[4] *Ibid.*, pp. 51, 52.
[5] *Ibid.*, pp. 56, 62, 71.
[6] Convention of London, May 19, 1900, *ibid.*, pp. 86-89; *Africa*, No. 5 (1900); "British and Foreign State Papers, 1900-1901," Vol. XCIV, pp. 715-722; *Annuaire de la Vie Internationale*, 1908-09, pp. 107-112 ["Trattati . . . relativi all'Africa," pp. 632-638]. The signatories were Great Britain, France, Germany, Italy, Portugal, Spain, and the Congo Free State.

a. Prohibition to kill animals of utility and rarity, such as vultures, giraffes, and gorillas;

b. Prohibition to kill young animals of certain species, such as elephants, rhinoceroses, and buffaloes;

c. Prohibition to kill the females of these species when accompanied by their young;

d. Prohibition to kill, except in limited numbers, such animals and birds as elephants, rhinoceroses, small monkeys, ostriches, marabous, and egrets;

e. Establishment of large animal reserves;

f. Establishment of close seasons and of licences for hunting;

g. Restrictions on the use of nets and traps in hunting and prohibition of the employment of explosives and poison in fishing;

h. Imposition of export duties on the hides of such animals as giraffes and antelopes and on such articles as rhinoceros horns and hippopotamus tusks.

i. Prohibition of killing young elephants and the confiscation of all tusks weighing less than five kilos;

j. Measures for an adequate reduction of the number of dangerous animals, such as lions, leopards, crocodiles, and snakes;

k. Protection of ostrich eggs.

Difficulties in Operation.—Difficulties immediately arose from the fact that the zone did not include the British self-governing possessions of South Africa—Natal and the Cape Colony—whom the British Government, according to constitutional practice, could not bind by treaty in questions necessitating domestic legislation. For this reason and because of the exclusion of German Southwest Africa, Portugal signed the convention with a reservation that her ratification would be delayed until such accession had been secured.[7] Steps were immediately taken to gain the adhesion of Natal and the Cape Colony, both of whom promptly acceded.[8] At the same time, instructions were sent to the British colonies in the zone to carry out the provisions of the treaty, which was likewise promptly done, and in the course of a few years elaborate systems were established.[9] For years Natal and the Cape, however, failed to pass the necessary laws. Similarly, while some of the other Powers proceeded to execute the stipulations, in general they also lagged behind.[10] The situation in 1908-09 was that, in consequence of the failure of a number of the signatories to ratify the Convention of 1900, it was not deemed binding upon the others and hence there was no uniformity in the measures adopted. In 1908, it was the opinion of the British Colonial Secretary that almost any form of international agreement was "preferable to the present chaotic state of affairs." All the Powers concerned, with the exception of Germany and Portugal, had expressed their willingness to ratify. Portugal's ratification was made contingent upon all the colonies in South Africa, including German Southwest, enacting appropriate legislation.[11] Of this there was every

---

[7] Correspondence Relating to the Preservation of Wild Animals in Africa (Cd. 3189, 1906), pp. 92, 93, 121. This Blue Book and those enumerated below contain the essential facts about this question. Further Correspondence, etc., Cd. 4472 (1909); do. Cd. 5136 (1910); do. Cd. 5775 (1911); do. Cd. 6671 (1913).

[8] Cd. 3189 (1906), pp. 109, 125-127.

[9] Ibid., pp. 109, 112, 115 et seq.

[10] Ibid., pp. 251, 305, 306, et passim.

[11] Cd. 5136 (1910), pp. 1, 7, 8, 9, 27.

prospect. On the other hand, the attitude of Germany was not favorable. Shortly before this, the Governor of the Cameroons had reduced the minimum weight for trade in elephant tusks from five kilos, as specified in the treaty, to two kilos and was sustained by the home authorities.[12]

The Sleeping Sickness Factor.—While this question was thus unsettled, it was further complicated by the introduction of a new factor. For several years it had been surmised that there was some connection between wild beasts and sleeping sickness and that the tsetse fly which carried the virus of this disease to man obtained it from the animals.[13] As yet this was largely an hypothesis.[14] In 1910-11, there was an alarming increase in sleeping sickness in Nyasaland, and a fair case was made for the theory that game constituted a reservoir whence the tsetse fly derived the trypanosomes with which man was subsequently infected. This immediately altered the entire aspect of animal preservation and led to a demand that the wild beasts should be exterminated. Ordinary prudence demanded, however, that before such a reversal of policy was instituted, the exact facts be ascertained and accordingly in 1911 a commission was appointed to investigate the question.[15] These experts reported that certain wild animals in Rhodesia were by nature infected with trypanosomes and might, therefore, be a

[12] Cd. 5136 (1910), p. 25. With reference to this question, the German Colonial Secretary stated in 1909 that an effective means of preventing the extermination of elephants would be found both in the enforcement of the Brussels Agreement of 1908 prohibiting the importation of arms and in moving "the Spanish, French, and Belgian Governments to join in raising the minimum export weight of tusks." *Ibid.,* p. 50.

[13] Cd. 3189 (1906), pp. 144, 148, 151.

[14] Cd. 5136 (1910), pp. 74, 90.

[15] Cd. 5775 (1911), pp. 13, 16, 28-32.

reservoir from which sleeping sickness could be transmitted to man by the tsetse fly. Upon this, demands arose that active measures be taken for an extensive destruction of game. As the evidence was not decisive and as the conclusions were contested by other experts, the British Government decided that further inquiry was necessary and appointed a committee for this purpose.[16] In the spring of 1914, this body reported on its extensive investigations.

The Report of 1914 on Sleeping Sickness.—Sleeping sickness was first recognized as a specific disease about one hundred years ago, but its serious character as affecting man was not fully appreciated until, in 1901, it was found to be epidemic in Uganda. The mortality there assumed enormous proportions. It is estimated that the disease caused 200,000 deaths from 1898 to 1906. About 1903 it was discovered that the cause of the disease was a trypanosome carried by a species of tsetse fly (*Glossina palpalis*) that did not live far from the water. The epidemic in Uganda was effectually checked in 1907 by the removal of all natives from the shores of Lake Victoria. In 1908-10, cases of sleeping sickness (trypanosomiasis) were detected in Rhodesia and Nyasaland and, upon investigation, it was found that the

[16] Cd. 6671 (1913), pp. 4, 9, 15, 31, 35-54; Report of the Inter-Departmental Committee on Sleeping Sickness, Cd. 7349 (1914), p. 3. In 1912, the Secretary of State for the Colonies gave the following summary of the situation in the House of Commons: "It might well happen then that, as a result of exterminating or greatly reducing the game, the tsetse, unable to obtain blood from these animals, would attack man and the domestic animals to a yet greater extent than it does at present, and that if, as is probable, these domestic animals harbour the human trypanosome, human beings would become infected in increased proportion owing to close association with their flocks and herds. I do not maintain that this would happen, but I am advised that it undoubtedly might, and such a possibility should make us pause before taking decisive action on the evidence before us." Cd. 6671 (1913), p. 55.

carrier here was a different tsetse fly (*Glossina morsitans*), which was not limited to the neighborhood of water. Thus there are two distinct types of sleeping sickness, known respectively as *Trypanosoma rhodesiense,* which occurs south of 10° South Latitude, and *Trypanosoma gambiense,* which is widely distributed throughout Middle Africa north of this parallel. In Rhodesia, Nyasaland, and the adjacent regions, the disease is of a very virulent character and is always fatal, but it is only endemic there, few people in the aggregate having been infected. The northern type is less acute and is more amenable to treatment, but unless guarded against, it may become epidemic as it was in Uganda and the Congo.[17] In the opinion of the committee, the exact relation between human and animal trypanosomiasis in Nyasaland and Rhodesia was not fully established, but they added that "the evidence indicates that game may serve as a reservoir of the human disease." At the same time, they rejected as unproved the contention that wild game in this region constituted the main, if not the only, source from which the tsetse fly derived his infectivity.[18] As regards the Uganda type, they decided that wild animals played a minor part as reservoirs in comparison with infected human beings.[19] Finally, the committee stated as one of their general conclusions that:

"Knowledge of the disease, its cause and its remedies, is still in the making, and hasty and imperfectly considered action of a drastic character such as the attempt to effect a general destruction of wild animals is not justified by the evidence before your Committee. On the other hand, your

[17] Cd. 7349 (1914), pp. 1-6.
[18] *Ibid.,* pp. 3, 14.
[19] *Ibid.,* p. 12. Cf. pp. 2, 4, 5.

committee recommend that until direct means of checking the fly have been discovered, the food supply of the fly and the chances of infection should be lessened in the vicinity of centres of population and trade routes by the removal of wild animals, and that for this purpose freedom be granted both to settlers and natives to hunt and destroy the animals within prescribed areas and subject to prescribed conditions." [20]

This inconclusive report left the question of preservation or destruction of wild animals in an undecided state. International coöperation will be equally essential whether the policy be one of partial destruction or of preservation, for infected migratory animals are no respecters of the boundaries set by man. Moreover, such collaboration is necessary to secure the fuller knowledge upon which alone sound policy can be based and by which alone can best results be gained for all concerned.[21] An unsuccessful attempt of this nature had already been made.

Sleeping Sickness Conference of 1907.—In 1907, representatives of Great Britain, France, Germany, Italy, Portugal, the Congo, and the Sudan participated in an international conference at London on the problem of sleeping sickness.[22] In his opening address, Lord Fitzmaurice proposed the convocation every year, or every two years, of dele-

[20] Cd. 7349 (1914), p. 21.

[21] Thus the committee advised that entomological research be undertaken in the bionomics of the tsetse flies and "that endeavours should be made to obtain the co-operation in this work of Foreign Powers in their African Possessions." *Ibid.,* p. 22. Considerable invaluable scientific information on sleeping sickness is available in the annual reports of the Advisory Committee for the Tropical Diseases Research Fund, 1907 to 1915.

[22] Proceedings of the First International Conference on the Sleeping Sickness at London, June, 1907 [Miscellaneous, No. 4 (1907) (Cd. 3778)]; *Archives Diplomatiques,* 108, pp. 268-315.

gates from the different countries interested in the fight against the disease; and the founding of a central bureau to distribute all the new literature on the subject and to direct the work of scientific research by partitioning it among certain nations and individuals. In default of such common action, he said, the British Government were convinced that labor and time would be lost in duplicating scientific research and that it would be impossible to establish a system of quarantine and regulations concerning the circulation of natives most exposed to the disease.[23]   The Conference approved of this program and adopted a resolution that a central bureau should be set up at London and national bureaus in each country; that the central bureau should collect all papers concerning sleeping sickness, should take the initiative in every question of an international character, should communicate whenever it thought fit with the national bureaus, and "should decide the date and place of subsequent International Conferences." [24]   In addition, it was agreed that the local authorities in Africa should make every effort to prevent natives from passing out of contaminated districts into neighboring foreign jurisdictions; that the administrative officials and doctors near the frontiers should exchange information, especially about new cases; and, finally, that the governments in Africa should communicate as soon as possible the results of the measures adopted by them "so that each country may profit by the experiments made throughout the whole of tropical Africa." [25]

[23] Cd. 3778 (1907), pp. 1-3, 6, 7.
[24] *Ibid.*, pp. 36, 37.
[25] *Ibid.*, pp. 41, 43.

The Abortive Conference of 1908.—Apparently there was every prospect of effective international coöperation, but the aspect of affairs changed quickly. In 1908 the Conference met again in London, mainly to embody in a general act or convention the resolutions adopted the preceding year. The draft that was drawn up in accordance with these conclusions proved unacceptable to the French and Italian delegates on what was apparently a very minor point, the location of the central bureau. They were unwilling to abide by the resolution that this be established at London and proposed that the work connected with sleeping sickness be taken over by the hygienic bureau which was to be created at Paris. As time was an essential factor and as London was already prepared to function, while the hygienic bureau at Paris was not set up or organized, this proposed change in the accepted program aroused opposition. The final result was that the Conference dissolved without accomplishing anything.[26]

Anglo-German Agreements of 1908 and 1911.—Shortly after the unfortunate wreck of this project, the British and German Governments concluded an agreement for coöperation against sleeping sickness.[27] They determined to take such steps as were practicable to prevent natives of their territories who were or might be suffering from the disease from crossing the frontier; and to segregate and detain all negroes who had evaded these measures. The treaty contained further clauses of a similar character and, in addition, an agreement to destroy crocodiles and other migratory ani-

[26] *The British Medical Journal,* 1908, I, p. 701.
[27] London Agreement and Protocol of October 27, 1908. Treaty Series, 1908, No. 28 ["Trattati," Supplemento, pp. 185-186].

mals that might reasonably be suspected of being a source of food for the *Glossina palpalis* type of tsetse fly. A second Anglo-German agreement made in 1911 referred solely to Togoland and the Gold Coast and provided for thorough investigation into the extent of sleeping sickness in these colonies and a mutual exchange of all the information acquired. The two parties further agreed to give medical treatment to every sufferer from this disease in those territories and to adopt preventive measures. The two Governments finally recognized each other's right to turn back at the frontiers native subjects of the other Power proved or suspected to be suffering from the malady and, further, to impose such restrictions on the frontier traffic as might be deemed necessary to prevent the spread of sleeping sickness.[28]

[28] Berlin Agreement of August 17, 1911. Treaty Series, 1911, No. 22.

CHAPTER VII

PROTECTION OF NATIVE RIGHTS: LABOR AND LAND

The Slave Trade and the Brussels Act.—The great scourge of Africa at the time of the Berlin Conference of 1884-85 was the slave trade, which was rampant throughout the tropical belt. This could not be ignored nor could it be eradicated except by the coöperation of the colonizing States. The Brussels Conference was called especially to deal with this question and adopted elaborate measures to extirpate the evil.[1] In the ensuing crusade, great activity was shown by the various Powers and, in addition, there was considerable collaboration among them. As a result thereof, the slave trade was reduced to comparatively insignificant proportions. It has never been entirely suppressed and presumably never will be until there is a more effective administrative occupation of all tropical Africa. In addition, slavery itself has not been entirely eliminated. This is especially true of domestic bondage, which is an institution deeply rooted in Mohammedan society and which not infrequently persists despite the absence of legal protection and even in face of positive prohibition.[2]

[1] General Act of the Brussels Conference, July 2, 1890, Articles 1-89. Hertslet, "Map of Africa by Treaty" (3d ed.), II, pp. 490-514 ["Trattati," pp. 271-293].
[2] For the native rules governing slavery, see A. H. Post, "Afrikanische Jurisprudenz," I, pp. 89-112, Oldenburg, 1887, and for brief outlines of Mohammedan principles concerning it, see T. P. Hughes, "Dictionary of Islam," pp. 596-600, London, 1885. For the Belgian Congo, see "Manual of Belgian Congo," pp. 112-114. Cf. also L. Vignon, "Un

Domestic Slavery in German East Africa.—In Zanzibar, slavery was gradually abolished under British rule. The decree of 1909 prohibited the courts from recognizing its status in any case.[3] On the other hand, in the neighboring German colony in East Africa, domestic bondage still continued, but the institution there was not the generally mild servitude of Mohammedan society. It was used as a means of fresh enslavement and to procure labor for the insatiable needs of the German-owned plantations. This was done in spite of the regulations to the contrary. The law of 1901 prohibited the creation of fresh bondmen by self-sale, by debts, or by any other means, and provided that domestic slaves could work two days for their own account and that they could purchase their freedom for comparatively small sums. Furthermore, it was enacted in 1905 that all children born of domestic slaves after that year should be free. In 1912, Mathias Erzberger, who had constantly manifested great interest in colonial questions, stated in the Reichstag that the town of Tabora, in the center of the colony, counted from 15,000 to 20,000 bondmen among its 35,000 to 40,000 inhabitants. Here, he said, could be found slaves from tribes that had never known servitude and who in some manner or other were forcibly dragged away from their villages and sold into bondage. He further stated that certain individuals owned as many as 500 to 800 slaves and he insisted that the institution be abolished by 1920.[4] The Reichstag

Programme de Politique Coloniale" (2d ed.), pp. 374-380, Paris, 1919; John H. Harris, "Africa: Slave or Free?", pp. 65-71.]

[3] *Africa*, No. 3 (1909); H. A. Gibbons, "The New Map of Africa," pp. 36, 37.

[4] *Verhandlungen des Reichstags, Stenographische Berichte*, 284, pp. 1529-1531.

passed a resolution to this effect, but the colonial authorities virtually ignored it.[5] Obviously, this is not domestic slavery as the term is generally understood. The number of such bondmen in German East Africa was approximately 180,000 [6] and not a few of them were hired or purchased by the German planters for use in the field.[7] Since the conquest of this colony, there has been a demand in England that these slaves be immediately emancipated. Legally, such action cannot be taken until the future sovereignty of this region is determined.[8] When that is decided, and possibly as a part of the settlement, provision should be made for the gradual, if not immediate, liberation of these slaves.[9]

[5] *Verhandlungen des Reichstags, Stenographische Berichte,* 291, p. 7913.
[6] *Ibid.,* 291, p. 7927.
[7] Frank Weston (Bishop of Zanzibar), "The Black Slaves of Prussia," pp. 15-16.
[8] *The Spectator,* July 13, 1918, pp. 39, 40; Memorial of the Anti-Slavery and Aborigines' Protection Society, August 19, 1918, to Secretary Long (*ibid.,* August 24, 1918).
[[9] Article 5 of the Draft Mandate for British East Africa (Tanganyika Territory) stipulates that "the mandatory (i) shall provide for the eventual emancipation of all slaves and for as speedy an elimination of domestic and other slavery as social conditions will allow; (ii) shall suppress all forms of slave trade; (iii) shall prohibit all forms of forced or compulsory labour, except for essential public works and services, and then only in return for adequate remuneration; (iv) shall protect the natives from abuse and measures of force and fraud by the careful supervision of labour contracts and the recruiting of labour." See Annex I. The same requirement is contained in the Draft Mandates for British Togoland and the British Cameroons. See Annex J. This problem was considered on August 1, 1919, by the Commission for the Revision of the Berlin and Brussels Acts, when the Italian Delegation presented draft Articles of essentially this content for inclusion in the Convention then being drawn up. It was felt, however, that the requirement more properly belonged, as Mr. Strachey, the British Delegate, pointed out, in the Mandates than in the Convention, and this view prevailed. "Procès-Verbaux et Rapport de la Commission pour la Revision des Actes Généraux de Berlin et de Bruxelles," pp. 122-123.]

Forced Labor.—The line of demarcation between slavery and forced labor is very tenuous.[10]   Forced labor in Africa was of three kinds: first, that on works of public necessity, such as building roads and bridges and clearing waterways; second, that on constructing railroads and other reproductive public utilities; third, that on private undertakings. Forced labor in the first category is probably legitimate, provided that abuses are not allowed to creep in.[11]   It is, however, of more than doubtful expediency in the second class; while in the third it is wholly vicious and is a virtual reversion to slavery.[12]   Compulsory work on private undertakings at one time prevailed throughout broad sections of Middle Africa.   It was a characteristic feature of the Leopoldian Congo and of the Portuguese cocoa islands before the reforms introduced in the present decade.[13]   For a time, French Equatorial Africa also was cursed with this indefensible system.   In German East Africa and the Cameroons there were laws to protect the native worker, but they were disregarded and the authority of the Government was freely used to compel a supply of labor for the European plantations.[14]   In the Reichstag debate of 1914, it was shown conclusively that the conditions in these two colonies were appalling.   Natives were dragged by force and

[10] On this and the following matters, see also *supra,* pp. 183-188.

[11] John H. Harris, *op. cit.,* pp. 71-74.]

[12] By the first paragraph of Article 3 of the Mandate for German Southwest Africa (a Mandate of the "C" type), "the mandatory shall see that the slave trade is prohibited, and that no forced labour is permitted, except for essential public works and services, and then only for adequate remuneration." See Annex L.]

[13] John H. Harris, *op. cit.,* pp. 92-99.]

[14] *Verhandlungen des Reichstags, Stenographische Berichte,* 288, pp. 4257, 4304, 4305, 4347, 4348. [Cf. "Handbook of German East Africa," p. 240; John H. Harris, *op. cit.,* pp. 75-91.]

fraud from their villages and were kept in virtual servitude on the plantations. Though the labor contracts were of limited duration, they were for the most part much prolonged by the planters in a purely arbitrary and dishonest manner. Moreover, the mortality on the plantations and their constant demand for workers were depopulating considerable areas.[15] [In the Cameroons, negroes in debt to the Treasury were required by Orders of November 11, 1904, and January 20, 1906, to discharge their obligations at the rate of twenty pfennigs a day. On slight pretexts natives were punished by heavy fines which they obviously could not pay, but must work out. Thus a fine of 150 marks, by no means an uncommon sum, virtually obliged a negro to 750 days of forced labor, which might easily be prolonged by additional sentences in the course of this period.[16]]

The Contract System.—In general, the form of labor in Middle Africa was one of contracts ranging from three months to periods of five years. The system is not objectionable in itself provided that the agreements are of reasonable duration, that they are free from compulsion, and that their terms are made perfectly clear to the native. Moreover, the conditions of employment and the facilities for repatriation must be such that the laborer is not practically obliged to renew his contract at its expiration.

International Regulation.—This method cannot be abandoned, but it requires careful supervision and control. The

[15] *Verhandlungen des Reichstags, Stenographische Berichte,* 291, pp. 7903, 7904, 7910-7912. [The contracts were for one year, with a margin for days when no work was done. About half returned home at the expiration of the agreement. "Handbook of German East Africa," *loc. cit.*]

[[16] *Journal Officiel de la République Française,* November 8, 1918, p. 9632.]

labor problem in Africa may become very urgent after the war because there is grave danger that the world-wide scarcity of raw materials will lead to attempts to stimulate production at the expense of the native's welfare. The question is by no means purely local. In actual practice it is already partly international, since labor in a number of instances has had to be recruited outside the colony's frontiers. Thus the Spanish cocoa island of Fernando Po procured laborers from Liberia. Similarly, the Katanga mines obtained workmen from Rhodesia and Portuguese East Africa and will probably draw upon Angola when the Benguella Railway is completed. Such conditions had already led to instructive international arrangements. Following the lines of a similar agreement in 1897, the Convention of April 1, 1909, between the Transvaal and Mozambique regulated in detail the methods of securing Portuguese natives for the Rand gold mines and provided for the appointment of a Portuguese official as "Curator for Portuguese natives in the Transvaal." [17]   In 1913, a similar arrangement was made between Portugal and the British South Africa Company regarding Portuguese negroes recruited for Rhodesia. The Curator provided for in this case was also to give assistance to Portuguese aborigines in the Katanga district of the Belgian Congo.[18] An international convention regarding labor could start from the basis of regulating such intercolonial recruiting somewhat on the lines of those arrangements. They should, however, include other matters as well. According to the matured opinion of life-long stu-

[17] *Transvaal*, 1909 (Cd. 4587); *American Journal of International Law*, III, Supplement, pp. 309-321; "Annuário Colonial da 1916," pp. 357-360.
[18] "Annuário Colonial da 1916," pp. 360, 361.

dents of the problem, who are wholly disinterested advocates of native interests, such an agreement should at the very least provide for the abolition of all forced work for private profit. It should further establish a maximum term for labor contracts—six months in mining and three years in agriculture—and should provide that only civil penalties, after trial by the authorities, should be inflicted for breach of these documents. Moreover, in the case of labor recruited across the borders, special stipulations for repatriation should be made.[19] Provided the local authorities strictly enforced such an agreement, it would greatly improve conditions. Upon these officials must fall the ultimate responsibility, since the world is apparently not ripe for any supernational inspection of what are deemed to be the internal affairs of the State.

Land Policy.—The two pillars of sound colonial administration must be a liberal and humane labor régime and an equitable land system. It is generally agreed that a just land policy implies that amply sufficient areas should be reserved for the native's present and prospective needs and that the African should not be allowed to alienate this territory recklessly either to Europeans or to a privileged land-owning class. In general, the negro has no conception of private occupation of ground. According to the customary tenure in West Africa, the ownership was vaguely vested in the community, every member of which was entitled to its use. Hence, land could not be permanently alienated and the

---

[19] Memorial to the Foreign Office of January 22, 1917, from the Anti-Slavery and Aborigines' Protection Society, etc., in the *Anti-Slavery Reporter*, April, 1917, pp. 3-6. [Regarding measures for the protection of natives, see also "Manual of Belgian Congo," pp. 298, 302-304.]

native had no intention of doing so, no matter how explicit were the words of the European title-deeds.[20] Moreover, in a number of instances the colonizing Powers had arbitrarily granted huge tracts without any regard to aboriginal rights. This was notoriously the case in the Belgian Congo and the Cameroons. Furthermore, insurrections in the German colonies led to the wholesale confiscation of native areas. Just as the Hereros of Southwest Africa became in this way a landless people, so the Bakwiri in the Cameroons were deprived of the fertile territories that were subsequently turned into European cocoa plantations. The accomplished fact of dispossession in the German colonies could not be rectified, but concerning the remaining unoccupied land, the condition had been largely remedied as regards the future by a change in German policy.[21] In the Belgian Congo also the Leopoldian principles had been discarded and the system inaugurated in 1909 was based upon the principle that the native had first title and right to the soil. Important areas were reserved for his use and he was not permitted to alienate them. Furthermore, he was allowed to harvest the fruits of all unoccupied lands.[22] This reformed system followed that of the British colonies, in which native rights were very carefully guarded and effectively protected.[23] As African civilization cannot develop along

[20] For the native African views concerning tenure of land, see Post, op. cit., II, pp. 166-175.]

[21] J. K. Vietor, "Geschichtliche und Kulturelle Entwickelung Unserer Schutzgebiete," pp. 86, 87, 122-126.

[22] J. Renkin, "L'Avenir du Congo Belge," in L'Afrique Française, March, 1916, Supplement, p. 62. [See further "Manual of Belgian Congo," pp. 285-287.]

[23] Émile Baillaud, "La Politique Indigène de l'Angleterre en Afrique Orientale," pp. 68-81, 144-152, 187-216; A. B. Keith, "West Africa," pp

sound lines unless these principles are strictly adhered to, it would be highly advisable to secure an international convention embodying them. But since conditions vary so greatly in the different colonies, such an agreement might have to be of so vague a character as to be merely a pious wish.

[*The Problem before the Peace Conference.*—This problem received full consideration at the Paris Peace Conference. At a session of the Commission for the Revision of the Berlin and Brussels Acts on August 1, 1919, the Italian Delegation presented, among other matters which they desired incorporated in the new Convention, the following draft clause: [24]

"Legislation regarding landed property shall respect as far as possible customs in force in the territories and the interests of the native populations.

"Land and real rights belonging to natives cannot be transferred to non-natives without the consent of the local Government and no claim to the said lands can be created for the benefit of non-natives without like consent."

It was felt, however, by the other Delegates that these stipulations should not be extended to territories under the full sovereignty of the Powers, and that they had proper place only in the Mandates. Accordingly, in the Mandates of the "B" type the following stipulation appears: [25]

"The mandatory shall in the framing of laws relating to the holding or transference of land take into consideration

165, 198-204, 221, 227, 230-232. [Cf. also, on this whole subject, John H. Harris, *op. cit.*, pp. 113-141.]

[24] "Procès-Verbaux et Rapport de la Commission pour la Revision des Actes Généraux de Berlin et de Bruxelles," pp. 123-124.

[25] Draft Mandate for East Africa (British). See Annex I.

native laws and customs, and shall respect the rights and safeguard the interests of the native population.

"No native land may be transferred, except between natives, without the previous consent of the public authorities, and no real rights over native land in favour of non-natives may be created except with the same consent.

"The mandatory will promulgate strict regulations against usury."]

CHAPTER VIII

NEUTRALIZATION

The Neutralization Provisions of the Berlin Act of 1885.—
In addition to providing for freedom of trade and navigation
in the Conventional Basin, the Berlin Conference adopted
some provisions for the neutralization of this area. The
subject was introduced by Mr. John A. Kasson, the principal
delegate of the United States, who urged that there was no
adequate motive to make the interior of Africa "a scene for
the struggle of foreign governments in their wars with each
other." His underlying idea was that Middle Africa should
not be drawn into purely European conflicts and that this
vast area should be spared "the destructive effects of foreign wars." Accordingly, he proposed that, in case of hostilities between two or more of the signatories of the proposed international act, each should agree to treat as neutral
territory the entire Conventional Basin and that no act of
warfare in this region should be committed by the belligerents.[1] This broad outlook met with a generally favorable
reception, but practical difficulties arose from the fact that
both France and Portugal already possessed colonies which
were partly within and partly without the Conventional
Basin. As these obstacles were real,[2] the plan had to be
modified.

[1] Senate Executive Document, No. 196, 49th Congress, 1st Session, pp.
43, 61-64, 70, 87, 136, 137, 177, 178, 121, 122.
[2] On February 21, 1885, Sir Edward Malet wrote from Berlin to Lord
Granville that some difficulty had been encountered in giving effect

(1)   The Neutrality of the Independent State of the Congo.—In its final form, the Berlin Act of 1885 provided, in the first place, that any state exercising "the rights of sovereignty or Protectorate" over territories within this area should have the option of declaring such territory neutral; and the signatories to the Act, on their part, bound themselves to respect such neutrality.[3] This clause was specifically framed to meet the case of the Independent State of the Congo, which was in process of formation and which

to the general wish that the Conventional Basin should be exempted from the evils of war. The main obstacle was the fact that portions of French and Portuguese Africa were both within and without the Basin "and that it would not be easy to secure the absolute neutrality of given portions of the territories of a belligerent Power." The British Government, he continued, were anxious to extend the benefits of neutrality, "but they felt it to be absolutely necessary to insist on such provisions as should secure that, if parts of the territories of a belligerent were to be respected as enjoying immunity from hostilities, they should in no sense and in no degree be capable of serving as a base of operations for the forces of such belligerent." The French and Portuguese delegates admitted that it was natural that such provisions be demanded, but "felt that it would be inconsistent with sovereign rights to accept them." It was found impossible to reconcile these contending views. Senate Executive Document, No. 196, pp. 308, 309; *Africa*, No. 2 (1885), p. 4.

[3] General Act of the Berlin Conference, February 26, 1885, Chapter III, Article X. "In order to give a new guarantee of security to trade and industry, and to encourage, by the maintenance of peace, the development of civilization in the countries mentioned in Article I, and placed under the free trade system, the High Signatory Powers to the present Act, and those who shall hereafter adopt it, bind themselves to respect the neutrality of the territories, or portions of territories, belonging to the said countries, comprising therein the territorial waters, so long as the Powers which exercise or shall exercise the rights of sovereignty or Protectorate over those territories, using their option of proclaiming themselves neutral, shall fulfil the duties which neutrality requires." Hertslet, "The Map of Africa by Treaty" (3d ed.), II, pp. 474, 475 ["Trattati," p. 110]. It should be noted that this neutrality could be either temporary or perpetual. For an exposition of the purpose of the Article, see the report of Courcel and Lambremont to the Conference. *Documents Diplomatiques, Affaires du Congo et de l'Afrique Occidentale,* pp. 274-276; Senate Executive Document, No. 196, pp. 246-247, 276.

availed itself of this option, on August 1, 1885, by declaring
itself to be "perpetually neutral." [4] Though the right extended over the whole area, no other state took this course.
The situation thus established was in no sense guaranteed.
The signatories of the Berlin Act agreed to respect this neutrality, but did not assume any obligation to prevent its
violation. As Mr. Kasson explained, in such an eventuality,
"any of the other signatory powers would have the option
to call them to account for a breach of their engagements." [5]
This was tantamount to saying that, in case of violation of
neutrality, each party to the Act had merely an unquestion-
able right of intervention, but that no Power actually bound
itself to take any action.

(2) Optional Neutral Status.—In the second place, the
Berlin Act provided that if a state "exercising rights of
sovereignty or Protectorate" should become involved in war,
then the signatories bound themselves to use their good
offices in order that the territories in question in the Conventional Basin should "by the common consent of this Power
and of the other belligerent or belligerents" be considered
neutral during the war. [6] As the British representative at
the Conference, Sir Edward Malet, wrote: "The result of
the provision is that opportunity is given to provide for
special neutralization, but that the rights of the Sovereign
State and freedom of the belligerent Power are fully re-

---

[4] Hertslet, *op. cit.,* II, p. 552 ["Trattati," pp. 137-138].

[5] Kasson to Secretary Frelinghuysen, February 23, 1885. Senate Executive Document, No. 196, pp. 180-181. As the report to the Conference
on this clause stated, the obligation was assumed towards all the signatories who "acquièrent ainsi le droit d'en demander le respect" (*ibid.,*
pp. 246-247).

[6] Chapter III, Article XI. Hertslet, *op. cit.,* II, p. 475 ["Trattati," pp.
110-111].

served." [7] As this clause was purely optional, each belligerent had complete liberty of action.

These Provisions during the War.—Thus, at the outbreak of the war in 1914, the Belgian Congo alone had been declared neutral and the belligerents were entirely free to decide as to the neutrality of the rest of the Conventional Basin.[8] The Belgian Government early in August sent instructions to the Governor General of the Congo to take defensive measures on the frontiers of the Cameroons and German East Africa, but to abstain from all offensive action against these colonies. They further expressed a desire not to extend hostilities to Middle Africa and inquired of the French and British Governments whether they intended to avail themselves of Article XI of the Berlin Act "to neutralise such of their colonies as are contained in the conventional basin of the Congo." [9] At first, the French Government was inclined to take this course, but soon reached the conclusion that Germany should be attacked wherever this was possible.[10] The British Government had from the

[7] Senate Executive Document, No. 196, pp. 308-309; *Africa,* No. 2 (1885), p. 4.

[8] In addition, Articles 25 and 33 of the Berlin Act stipulated that the provisions for the freedom of the navigation of the Congo and the Niger, including their affluents, should remain in force during time of war. Hertslet, *op. cit.,* II, pp. 481, 484 ["Trattati," pp. 116, 118-119]. These articles were drawn up without any regard for reality and are so inherently impracticable that they should be canceled [as has since been done, see p. 268]. Cf. A. B. Keith, "The Revision of the Berlin Act," in *Journal of the African Society,* July, 1918, p. 260. Furthermore, the exact legal effect of Belgium's annexation of the Congo in 1908 upon the colony's neutral status was not entirely clear. Cf. F. W. Baumgartner, "The Neutralization of States," pp. 14, 15, Kingston, Canada, 1917; L. F. L. Oppenheim, "International Law" (2d ed.), I, pp. 153, 154, London, 1912.

[9] "First Belgian Grey Book," Nos. 57, 58.

[10] *Ibid.,* Nos. 61, 74.

outset been firmly of this opinion.[11] In view of the fact
that there was complete freedom of action under the Berlin
Act, any other decision would, under the circumstances,
have been most unwise.[12] In the meanwhile, acts of hostility had been committed in both East and West Africa by
the German, British, and French forces. Finally, on August
22, 1914, the Germans attacked Lukuga on the Belgian side
of Lake Tanganyika, thus violating the neutrality of the
Belgian Congo.[13] Prior to this action, the Belgian authorities had scrupulously maintained the neutrality of the
Colony, but they were now at liberty to coöperate with their
allies and they proceeded to do so.[14] Up to this point, the
German Government had taken no action regarding this
question, but on August 22, the very day on which the neutrality of the Belgian Congo was violated, the German
Under-Secretary of State, Zimmermann, wrote to Ambassador Gerard and, after referring to the prominent part taken
by John A. Kasson in the formulation of the third Chapter
of the Berlin Act, invoked the good offices of the American
Government in securing the neutralization of the Conven-

[11] "First Belgian Grey Book," No. 75.
[12] In fact, the Committee of Imperial Defence, whose function it was
to coördinate naval and military policy and to advise on technical questions of defence, had already in 1898 and 1911 advocated such action
in the event of war. Hansard, 5th Series (1915), Vol. 75, pp. 327, 328,
1657. On the organization and functions of this Committee, see W.
Basil Worsfold, "The Empire on the Anvil," pp. 45-49, London, 1916;
Richard Jebb, "The Britannic Question," pp. 43-50, London, 1913. For
a full discussion of the question, see L'Afrique Française, 1916, pp. 61-66;
and for a bitter attack on British policy, consult R. C. Hawkin, "The
Belgian Proposal to Neutralise Central Africa during the European
War," in The Grotius Society, I (1916), pp. 67-85.
[13] "First Belgian Grey Book," No. 76.
[14] "Second Belgian Grey Book," No. 39.

tional Basin.[15]   Whatever their opinion as to the problem
may have been, the American Government were virtually
prevented from complying, because they had in 1885 deliberately refused to ratify the Berlin Act.[16]   Accordingly,
Ambassador Gerard wrote to Zimmermann on August 31
that, as the United States were not parties to the document,
they could not accede to his request.[17]   A fortnight later, the
German Government, however, made a fresh appeal, which
the American Government, acting solely "as a medium of
communication," transmitted to the belligerents without
making any comments.[18]   They all naturally rejected [19] a
proposal which would have been of great advantage to

[15] *L'Afrique Française*, March, 1916, Supplement, p. 71.   The diplomatic
documents concerning the question were published here from a German
source.
[16] When the United States was invited to attend the Berlin Conference,
Secretary Frelinghuysen inquired of John A. Kasson whether such participation would "harmonize with the policy adopted by the United States
Government of non-interference."   Kasson replied that "it was not contemplated that the Governments represented should be bound by the
conclusions of the Conference, but could refuse or accept them at their
will."   The United States participated in the Conference on this distinct
understanding.   Senate Executive Document, No. 196, pp. 9-13.   During
the course of the Conference, considerable opposition was manifest in
Congress and in the press at the part played by the United States, on
the ground that it was a distinct departure from the traditional policy.
President Cleveland was apparently also of this opinion, for he refrained
from submitting the Berlin Act to the Senate for their approval.   In
his Annual Message of December 8, 1885, he stated that in his opinion
"an engagement to share in the obligation of enforcing neutrality in
the remote valley of the Congo would be an Alliance whose responsibilities
we are not in a position to assume."   On April 16, 1886, Secretary
Bayard wrote to the German Minister at Washington, Mr. von Alvensleben,
that the United States had participated in the Conference "in a merely
consultative capacity" and were "unprepared to join in the responsible
political engagements in so remote and undefined a region as that of
the Congo Basin."   *Ibid.*, pp. 321-322.
[17] *L'Afrique Française*, March, 1916, Supplement, p. 72.
[18] "Second Belgian Grey Book," No. 54.   See also Nos. 66, 67.
[19] *L'Afrique Française*, March, 1916, Supplement, pp. 72, 73, 77.

Germany, in that it would have enabled her to retain a part of the Cameroons and all of German East Africa. The latter, furthermore, might have been used as a base for raiders upon Allied commerce.

The Question of Future Neutralization.—The defects in the neutrality articles of the Berlin Act are patent. The neutralization of the Congo Free State was incomplete, no one of the signatories being obligated to prevent its violation; in the rest of the Conventional Basin, neutralization was entirely optional. A joint and several guaranty on the part of the signatories to the future peace, explicitly defined,[20] covering the whole Conventional Basin and possibly even all Middle Africa—that is, both Central and West Africa—would be the obvious remedy. It would apparently remove this entire area from the range of the rivalries of the colonizing Powers and it would free the region from the ravages of wars due to extraneous causes. At first glance, this proposal has a definite attractiveness, but on closer examination serious doubts arise as to its advisability and necessity. In the first place, Germany's invasion of Belgium has brought the entire process of neutralization into considerable disfavor. Reliance upon Germany's honesty did actually create a dangerous atmosphere of false security and history may repeat itself in other climes. Then, neutralization would probably overstabilize conditions in Middle Africa, as it would virtually be equivalent to a perpetual

[20] While all existing treaties of guarantee are quite definite as to the obligation of the signatories not to violate neutrality themselves, they are generally very vague as to the obligation assumed to prevent others from committing such an act. On this subject, see C. P. Sanger and H. T. J. Norton, "England's Guarantee to Belgium and Luxemburg," London, 1915.

guarantee of existing boundary lines and those to be established at the Peace Conference. The interests of Africa may in the future well demand some important territorial readjustments. Even more vital than these considerations are the questions whether neutralization will be necessary when a League of Nations is established and whether it is not in a measure inconsistent with the fundamental democratic purpose of the war.[21] Neutralization of Africa would deprive the future League of Nations of a valuable means of coercion against aggressive states, as their African colonies would be secure from attack. It would be equivalent to an emasculation of the League's power. On the other hand, the use of this weapon for such a purpose implies that Africa might still become the scene of extraneous wars. But the interests of the native are likely to be vitally affected in such conflicts, because they determine his future. Certainly many of the negroes in the German colonies have consciously been deeply concerned in being freed from the ruthless rule of Germany. Provided the welfare of the African aborigines be fully considered, it is not unjustifiable to wage such wars in Africa. But it is ignoble to use Africa merely as a pawn and to purchase security elsewhere at the expense of the native.[22] Moreover, as the aim of the League of Nations is to prevent future hostilities, its establishment would

[21] There is also the question whether neutralization might not be so arranged as to apply only in wars unauthorized by the League of Nations, but not in hostilities authorized by that body.

[22] Late in 1917, the question of the possible return of "German East Africa" was discussed by some students from that colony in St. Andrew's College, Zanzibar. Their final word was: "If the English mean to give us back to the Germans, why did they bring the war to our land in the beginning? If they don't want to keep it, why did they want to take it? We shall all have suffered, and so many of our brothers will have died in

greatly diminish, if not altogether eliminate, the danger of
Africa becoming the scene of foreign struggles. Finally,
there is one very important practical consideration. The
man power of Africa has been used extensively in Europe
during the war, especially by France. As neutralization
would prevent this, serious objections to such a proposal
would in all probability arise in France,[23] unless it were
strictly confined to a limited area in Middle Africa. Thus,
on the whole, it appears that the desired aims can best be
attained by an effective League of Nations giving its sanction, but not its perpetual guarantee, to the rights of
sovereignty and protectorate exercised in Middle Africa and
providing that no areas can change flags without its consent.[24] Under such an eventuality, neutralization would

vain if the only result of the fighting is to lay up for us a German
revenge." In connection with this, the Principal of the College, Rev.
Ernest F. Spanton, wrote:
"And I could not but feel the justice of this contention. If the unfortunate African should be used by the English as a mere counter with
which to gain the better some diplomatic end in Europe, then, indeed,
England would have a heavy charge to meet at the bar of humanity.
After having induced these people to help her fight the Germans, believing, as they have done, that by their sufferings they were winning freedom
for themselves and their children, if at last we were to wash our hands
of them, and, with cynical remarks about justice and generosity, to hand
them over to Germany to wreak her vengeance upon them, we should,
indeed, deserve some of the harsh things said of us lately by the German
Press." *The Times* (London), March 11, 1918.

[23 See *infra*, pp. 276-277, 278.]

[24] Before the war, the practical situation was that the territorial arrangements within the Conventional Basin were under the sanction of
the parties to the Berlin Act and that no extensive areas could be transferred without their consent, either formal or tacit. In 1884, France
secured the right of preëmption of the Belgian Congo and this was confirmed by a number of subsequent treaties. Hertslet, *op. cit.*, II, pp. 562,
563, 567, 570, 571; III, p. 1226. In 1911, Germany unsuccessfully endeavored to secure this privilege from France, but an agreement was reached
that, in case the territorial status within the entire Conventional Basin
were to be modified, France and Germany would confer with one another
and with the other signatories of the Berlin Act. Franco-German Treaty,
November 4, 1911, Article 16. Debidour, "Histoire· Diplomatique de

appear to be superfluous.   [This view was held, in fact, by the Commission appointed during the Peace Conference to consider revision of the Berlin and Brussels Acts and in the resultant Convention [25] signed at Saint-Germain-en-Laye, September 10, 1919, the neutrality articles of Berlin were among those considered as abrogated.]

l'Europe, 1904-1916," p. 340; *American Journal of International Law*, VI, Supplement, pp. 62-65. This was a virtual waiver of France's prior rights, but, as M. Tardieu correctly points out, these prerogatives were more theoretical than practical and the agreement really subjected all future territorial changes within the Conventional Basin to the final consent of the parties to the Berlin Act. A. Tardieu, "Le Mystère d'Agadir," pp. 528-530.

[[25] Article 13.]

CHAPTER IX

MILITARIZATION

Native Troops before the War.—It is quite obvious that the problem of the militarization of Middle Africa is intimately connected with the question of neutralization. Before the war it was customary to recruit natives for the military and police in all the tropical African colonies. In no case were these forces large. Thus, in 1914, German East Africa had 2,472 natives in the military and 2,140 in the police.[1] An even smaller number of troops, called the King's African Rifles, was maintained in the adjoining British Protectorates.[2] Similarly, the West African Frontier Force in British West Africa was a small body. The Belgian and French levies were considerably larger. The "Force Publique" of the Belgian Congo numbered 17,800 men and French West Africa in 1912 had an armed force of 20,804, of whom 7,459 were in the police.[3] In general, there was

[1] GERMAN EAST AFRICA, 1914

	Military	Police
Germans	260	67
Natives	2,472	2,140

CAMEROONS, 1914

	Military	Police
Germans	205	47
Natives	1,650	1,450

Statistisches Jahrbuch, 1915, p. 457.

[2] *The Statesman's Year-Book,* 1915, pp. 183, 186. At the outbreak of the war, this force consisted of three battalions of about 2,000 men in all.

	[3] Troops	Police	Total
French West Africa, 1912	13,345	7,459	20,804
French Equatorial Africa, 1912	7,125	1,972	9,097

Georges Bruel, "L'Afrique Équatoriale Française," p. 480.

269

little difficulty in raising these troops, as the natives of the warlike tribes were anxious to serve with the colors. The primary function of these forces, furthermore, was to preserve order within the colony. They were not established for the purpose of aggression against their neighbors, or even for the purpose of defense against them. Two broad facts, however, should be noted. In the German colonies, as in Germany herself, the militaristic system prevailed. Not only were the military forces incompletely controlled by the civil authorities,[4] but a soldier caste was established. The natives who were enrolled in the *Schutztruppen* were encouraged to regard themselves as superior to their civilian fellows. From this proceeded some of the most flagrant abuses in the German possessions. Another noteworthy fact is that France had for a long time regarded her African empire as a source of man power in case of war and that, with this eventuality in view, steps had already been taken before 1914 to raise a much larger force in French West Africa than the needs of the colony itself demanded.[5]

The Lessons of the War.—(1) Native Troops in Africa.— The experiences of the war have emphasized two fundamen-

[4] On March 6, 1913, in the Reichstag, Erzberger criticized this diarchy, insisting that the commander of the military forces should be subordinate to the Governor. The Governor, he said, was an official, but the Commander was not and hence was not responsible. "Der ist Offizier, hat keinen Beamteneid geleistet und kennt nur eine Verantwortung gegenüber der Kommandogewalt." He maintained that this dualism was more or less accentuated in all of Germany's African colonies. *Verhandlungen des Reichstags, Stenographische Berichte,* 288, pp. 4307, 4308. The Colonial Secretary, Solf, was unable to refute Erzberger's charge and virtually had to admit that in practice this dualism existed. *Ibid.,* p. 4336.

[5] Twenty thousand additional troops were to be raised in four years. Louis Sonolet, "L'Afrique Occidentale Française," pp. 89-91. See also Mangin, "La Force Noire"; *Questions Diplomatiques et Coloniales,* 34 (1912), p. 652; 36 (1913), pp. 334, 395; 37 (1914), pp. 65, 290.

tal facts—the military possibilities of the African native in
his own continent and his importance as a combatant and
non-combatant in Europe. Large forces were raised by the
Allies for operations against the German colonies and by
the Germans in defense of them. Over 10,000 combatants
and 10,000 porters were sent from British West Africa for
the campaign against German East Africa. In British East
Africa [Kenya], the King's African Rifles were expanded
from 2,000 to over 20,000 men. In addition, a very large
number of carriers were employed. In the East African
Protectorate no less than 150,000 porters were recruited.
In Uganda, 40,000 carriers were raised for service with the
British and Belgian troops; and in Nyasaland, the number
of natives employed for various military purposes exceeded
100,000.[6] It is not quite clear how many negroes the Germans in East Africa recruited during the entire campaign,
but the maximum strength of their forces at any one time
was apparently 2,309 Europeans and 11,621 natives, together with at least an equal number of porters.[7] The pro-

[6] Statement of Mr. W. H. Long, Secretary of State for the Colonies,
January 28, 1918, in *Geographical Journal*, March, 1918, p. 148. Cf. "The
Times [London] History of the War," XIII, pp. 411, 412.
[7] J. H. V. Crowe, "General Smuts' Campaign in East Africa," pp. 32-35,
278-280. See also "The Times [London] History of the War," X, pp. 130-
132; XII, p. 80.
[By September, 1915, the German forces in German East Africa were
estimated to comprise:

European troops	2,200
Native Protectorate troops	2,472
Former police (military training)	2,140
Former carriers (some military training)	600
Discharged native soldiers and police	2,000
Recruits	3,888
Native irregulars	3,000
Total	16,300

"Handbook of German East Africa," pp. 197-198; for details of the irregu-

longed resistance of the German colony and the large number of troops raised in Africa for local purposes have made necessary a reconsideration of the Middle African situation in the light of these facts.

(2)   The Native in the European Field.—In addition, Africa's man power has been extensively drawn upon for war work in Europe, especially by France. Only a small labor corps was recruited by the British in South Africa for this purpose, but France was able to secure large numbers from West Africa both for combatant and non-combatant purposes.[8] In the first year of the war, 70,000 troops—*tirailleurs*—were raised in French West Africa,[9] and the numbers were steadily increased by more intensive recruiting.[10] Up to 1918, French West Africa had supplied France with over 120,000 *tirailleurs*.[11] Subsequent levies yielded about 64,000 more.[12] According to the statement made by the French Colonial Minister, M. Henry Simon, in the Senate on July 9, 1918, the French colonies, including North

lars, Protectorate Force (*Schutztruppe*), pre-war distribution of troops and police, tribes capable of use as irregulars, etc., see "Handbook of German East Africa," pp. 198-211.]

[8] The Union of South Africa objected to the use of South African natives for purely military purposes, fearing that this might lead to subsequent troubles at home. Had it not been for this opposition a considerable force could in all probability have been raised. Many of the native laborers that went to France were graduates of the mission schools and careful measures were taken to secure their welfare in the unfamiliar surroundings behind the battle line. *The Round Table,* December, 1916, pp. 182, 183; *The Spectator,* December 15, 1917, p. 713; *Journal of the African Society,* April, 1918, pp. 199-211. According to R. V. Dolbey, "Sketches of the East Africa Campaign," pp. 9-10, the Cape Corps was an experiment in recruiting which "many of us were at first inclined to condemn," but the men covered themselves with distinction in fighting on the Rufiji.

[9] *L'Afrique Française,* 1916, p. 56.   [10] *Ibid.,* p. 406.

[11] *Ibid.,* 1917, p. 195; 1918, p. 157.

[12] *Ibid.,* 1918, pp. 26, 27. See also *ibid.,* 1918, Supplement, pp. 28 ff.

Africa, had furnished 918,000 men, of whom 680,000 were combatants and 238,000 laborers.[13]

Solf's Views on Militarization.—This extensive use of native man power both in Africa and in Europe has raised the question of the militarization of Africa. The Germans were especially impressed by the prolonged resistance of their colony in East Africa and hence they demanded a redistribution of Africa, so that Germany might have a compact empire reaching from the Indian Ocean to the Atlantic and capable of defending itself even if communications with Germany were cut. At the same time, the Germans were considerably disturbed at the use which France made of Africa's man power in Europe. In his address of December 21, 1917,[14] the German Colonial Secretary, Dr. Solf, stated

[13] *L'Afrique Française,* 1918, p. 192. The recruitment of African natives during the war was:

Colony	1914-15	1916	1917	1918	Total
French West Africa	34,055	51,913	13,831	63,208	163,007
French Equatorial Africa	3,766	—	—	14,164	17,930
Madagascar	1,097	6,852	32,406	1,000	41,355
Somalis	—	1,560	418	466	2,444
Total	38,918	60,325	46,655	78,838	224,736

At the time of the Armistice there were on all fronts ninety-two battalions of Senegalese *tirailleurs,* ten Malagasy, and one Somali. In May, 1919, the negro effectives numbered 133,000, of whom 63,000 were in France. The Government intended to maintain a permanent force of 63,000, which, if the duration of service should be two years, would require an annual recruitment of 15,000 (*Le Temps,* May 4, 1919). The losses during the war were 31,700 (24,400 killed, 7,300 missing) (*Le Matin,* July 3, 1919).

[For North Africa, the figures for the entire war were (*Le Temps,* May 7, 1919):

Colony	Combatants	Killed	Wounded
Algeria	177,800	56,000	82,000
Tunis	50,400	15,000	30,000
Morocco	34,500	9,000	17,000
Total	262,700	80,000	129,000]

[14] *Kölnische Zeitung,* December 22, 1917. The same argument has been

that it was necessary to stop this new danger which France had created and that the best way to do so would be to reapportion Africa in such a manner that there would be an equilibrium of power there. Then, in case of a European war, no State would be able to send native troops to Europe without losing its African colonies. It is obvious that Solf's scheme, which he again explained on several occasions, contemplated the establishment of a separate and distinct balance of power in Africa and that not alone would it not effect its ostensible purpose, but that it would really lead to the militarization of the entire continent. Its fundamental aim was to prevent the use of African troops in Europe and thus to gain a military advantage for Germany.

Smuts's Views.—The protracted campaign in German East Africa aroused considerable anxiety in South Africa and this feeling was greatly intensified by the aims widely expressed in Germany, of demanding at the Peace Conference both the return of her colonies in Middle Africa and also an extension of their area.[15] The German plan of creating a compact Mid-African empire which would be

developed by Friedrich Hupfeld, the author of "Das Deutsche Kolonialreich der Zukunft." See *The New Europe*, May 23, 1918, No. 84.

[15 In their "Remarques sur les Conditions de Paix," the German Delegation at Paris protested strongly against the Articles (119 ff.) of the Versailles Treaty concerning renunciation of all of Germany's oversea possessions, but did not claim any colonial extension. Their arguments were rejected by the Allied and Associated Powers, who, as they declared in the Covering Letter of their Reply to the German Observations, were "satisfied that the native inhabitants of the German colonies are strongly opposed to being again brought under Germany's sway, and the records of German rule, the traditions of the German Government and the use to which these colonies were put as bases from which to prey upon the commerce of the world, make it impossible for the Allied and Associated Powers to return them to Germany, or to entrust to her the responsibility for the training and education of their inhabitants."]

self-sufficient in a military sense [16] naturally implied that South Africa would also have to keep armed. This would mean an enormous aggravation of the already difficult racial problem in South Africa, where a heterogeneous white population of one and one-half millions is attempting to establish a stable democracy in the midst of six million natives. Any necessity of arming the natives would imperil the delicately balanced fabric. General Smuts was the natural spokesman of this sentiment and perhaps the clearest of his utterances regarding it was that of May 22, 1917, when he said:

"I must say that my experience in East Africa has opened my eyes to many very serious dangers that threaten the future not only of Southern Africa, but also of Europe. We have seen, what we have never known before, what enormously valuable military material lay in the Black Continent. You are aware of the great German scheme which existed before the war, and which no doubt is still in the background of many minds in Germany, of creating a great Central African Empire which would embrace not only the Cameroons and East Africa, but also the Portuguese Colonies and the Congo—an extensive area which would have a very large population and would not only be one of the most valuable tropical parts of the world, but in which it would be possible to train one of the most powerful black armies of the world. We were not aware of the great military value of the natives until this war. This war has been an eye-opener in many new directions. It will be a serious question for the statesmen of the Empire and Europe, whether they are going to allow a state of affairs like that to be possible, and to become a menace not only to Africa, but perhaps to Europe itself. I hope that one of the results of this war will be some arrangement or convention among the nations interested in Central Africa by

[16] See *supra,* pp. 55-56, and map facing page 198; and cf. Edwyn Bevan's Introduction to E. Zimmermann, "The German Empire of Central Africa," pp. vii-lxii.

which the military training of natives in that area will be prevented, as we have prevented it in South Africa." [17]

In order to obviate such militarization of the natives, General Smuts urged not only an international agreement to this effect, but also that the conquered German colonies be not returned to Germany. In February of 1918, he wrote:

"With German East Africa restored to the Kaiser at the end of the war, and a large Askari army recruited and trained from its 8,000,000 natives, the conquest or forced acquisition of the Congo Free State, Portuguese East and West Africa, and perhaps even the recovery of the Kameroons may be only a matter of time. In this way this immense tropical territory, with almost unlimited economic and military possibilities, and provided with excellent submarine bases on both the Atlantic and Indian seaboards, might yet become an important milestone on the road to World-Empire." [18]

The Question of an International Agreement.—Thus the question has arisen whether an international agreement of this nature is advisable and feasible. It is obvious that France would not consent to such a measure if it included West Africa, because it would deprive her of valuable man power. Moreover, the theory and to some degree also the practice of French colonization are that the colonies are an extension of the French State and that their inhabitants are ultimately to become Frenchmen with all the rights and obligations of their fellow citizens in France, including the duty to serve in the Army.[19] Hence, the agreement would

[17] J. C. Smuts, "War-Time Speeches," p. 82, London, 1917.
[18] J. H. V. Crowe, *op. cit.*, p. xvi.
[19] By the decree of May 25, 1912, every French subject in French West Africa may upon the fulfillment of certain conditions become a French

in all probability have to be limited to Middle Africa. It is apparent upon analysis that a denial of right of military service to the natives is really in conflict with democratic principles, since it implies that the negro is permanently to take no part in matters that vitally affect him. In the present stage of African civilization this consideration is, however, of little practical moment. It is, as a matter of fact, most advisable that after the war the armed forces in Middle Africa should be on approximately the same scale as they were in 1914. To meet the situation an international regulation would not only have to limit the actual military and police establishments to a maximum percentage of the population, but it would also have to restrict the quantity of warlike stores to be imported as well as the proportion of men permitted to be trained in arms. It might be difficult to determine a maximum low enough to prevent militarization and at the same time high enough to cope with all possible disturbances within the colony. This obstacle should not, however, be insurmountable. Granted good faith, such a regulation would apparently be both advisable and feasible. Without honesty of purpose on the part of all, it would be futile and possibly even dangerous.

[The problem was not considered by the Peace Conference, and, outside the ex-German colonies, conditions remain unchanged. Within those areas, however, "the military training of the natives, otherwise than for purposes of internal police and the local defence of the territory shall be

citizen. "Annuaire du Gouvernement Général de l'Afrique Occidentale Française," 1915-1916, pp. 525, 526. On the obligation of the natives of French West and Equatorial Africa to serve, see *L'Afrique Française*, 1918, Supplement, pp. 28 ff.

prohibited.   Furthermore, no military or naval bases shall be established or fortifications erected in the territory." [20]]

[20] Mandate for German Southwest Africa, Article 4.   Article 4 of the Draft Mandate for East Africa (British) is similar: "The mandatory shall not establish any military or naval bases, nor erect any fortifications, nor organise any native military force in the territory except for local police purposes and for the defense of the territory."   See further R. S. Baker, "Woodrow Wilson and World Settlement," I, pp. 422-432, Garden City, N. Y., 1922; and for the French view, maintaining the right to raise troops in territories placed under French Mandate, see *ibid.*, pp. 426-432.]

CHAPTER X

CONCLUSIONS

Need for Enlarged International Regulation.—From the foregoing survey, it is apparent that very much has been accomplished in the way of international control and co-operation in Middle Africa. The failures should not obscure the actual progress registered. On the other hand, it is also plain that much still remains to be done to eliminate the subordination of native interests to those of some of the colonizing Powers, and to emphasize the fact that the administration of tropical Africa is essentially an international trust, primarily for the benefit of the aboriginal peoples and only secondarily for the welfare of the outside world.[1] While certain well devised projects were wrecked owing to honest divergences of opinion, in some instances at least, the main reef was the self-regarding nationalism of the colonizing Powers. But, in addition, there were defects both in the old machinery and also in the legislative output.

[1 That this view is not yet universally held would seem to follow from such statements as one recently made by Antonelli, "L'Afrique et la Paix de Versailles," p. 256, that "les nations possessionnées d'Afrique entre-prenaient une mise en exploitation économique active et intensive de leurs territoires. Alors dans l'accroissement rapide du volume des échanges économiques, ces nations pourraient trouver, à bref délai, les compensa-tions de leurs sacrifices, sans avoir besoin de réserver ces marchés à leurs nationaux pendant de longues périodes. Mais ce n'est pas en réalisant l'aménagement de l'Afrique par tranches d'emprunt de vingt-cinq millions qu'on obtiendra ce résultat. Il faudra y jeter tout de suite, dans un délai de 20 ans, une partie des milliards que l'Europe a jetés en fumée et en acier meutrier, à la guerre, pendant 4 ans."]

There is urgent need to apply remedies. It is admitted on all sides that the measures existing now need considerable revision.

Membership of the Conference.—Very many, if not all, of the numerous African problems that necessitate international regulation demand highly specialized and expert knowledge if they are to be settled satisfactorily. One need cite only the land and liquor questions, or the control of sleeping sickness. Hence it has been argued that the Peace Conference will have neither qualifications to deal with such technical matters nor time to devote to all the phases of this vast subject. Its part, then, would be to adopt certain general lines and to provide for the convocation of a special African Conference to embody these principles in legislation. It might, however, be highly disadvantageous to defer the settlement of these questions and there is no real reason why the Peace Conference could not, after disposing of the more urgent problems elsewhere, devote its attention to tropical Africa. Whichever plan be adopted, it would be distinctly reactionary to exclude from a voice in these arrangements those Powers that hold no territory in Middle Africa. The Berlin Conference of 1884-85 was composed in a genuinely international spirit and contained representatives of virtually the entire commercial world. The same principle obtained in the Brussels Conference of 1889-90 but was unfortunately gradually allowed to lapse at the subsequent Brussels Conferences dealing with the liquor traffic. That the welfare of Africa is a concern of the entire outside world requires fresh affirmation. This is so essential and so important that it completely outweighs the disadvantage of the fact that, the larger the membership, the more difficult it is to secure the unanimity necessary for effective action by any international conference. While the *liberum veto* of the sovereign state frequently necessitates sterile compromises, it is far better to accept this drawback than to proceed upon the reactionary principle that the affairs of Middle Africa are solely the concern of those exercising rights of government there.[2]

Periodic Conferences.—During the course of the preceding pages many of the flaws and deficiencies of the existing arrangements have been examined and it has been suggested in a broad way how they might be remedied. But, in addition, there were certain defects in the machinery through which international control was exercised over Middle Africa. Entirely apart from the necessity of unanimity inherent in the theory of the equality of all sovereign states, the practice of convoking conferences at irregular intervals for specific purposes of more or less restricted scope did not attract wide attention to them. Hence, the wholesome effect of publicity was lost and whatever opinion on these questions there was throughout the world was not brought to bear effectively upon the assemblies. Moreover,

[2] Sir H. H. Johnston has pointed out that across the short sea passage separating Brazil from Africa there was growing up prior to 1915, almost unnoticed by Europe, a considerable traffic in sailing boats entirely manned by natives of Africa and transporting to Brazil large quantities of African produce. These inconspicuous vessels contained as supercargoes or merchants representatives of that strange aristocratic, half-white indigene of West Africa, the Mohammedan Fula who, of late, has been spreading Islam in Brazil. Hence, Johnston contends that "in the future International Council that sits at Lisbon or Paris, London or Rome, and discusses the management and development of negro Africa, it will be hard to deny Brazil and Argentine due representation." Sir H. H. Johnston, "Africa and South America," in *The Nineteenth Century and After*, July, 1918, p. 187.

the interested Powers could always refuse their assent to the convocation of a fresh conference and continued insistence by one Power upon the advisability of such sessions might be considered an unfriendly act, which again might imperil other and broader interests. Thus the welfare of Africa might be sacrificed to considerations entirely alien to it. During the prolonged controversy from 1902 to 1910 with France about the concessionary system in French Equatorial Africa, Great Britain at various times offered to submit the question at issue to arbitration and in 1905 suggested the convocation of an international conference to determine the meaning of the term "freedom in matters of commerce" as used in the Berlin Act. France refused to join in such an invitation. Britain could, of course, have proceeded to issue the call on her own responsibility, but such action would have verged on the unfriendly and was out of the question if only because the clouds of the first Morocco crisis had not as yet disappeared from the European skies. The matter was temporarily settled otherwise.[3] It is quite plain that this difficulty would not have arisen if it had been provided that the Berlin Conference was to reassemble automatically at regular intervals. Apparently it is highly advisable that there be established as a permanent institution an international conference for African matters meeting at fixed intervals of possibly three years. There is need for periodic readjustment of international regulations to meet conditions that are constantly changing.[4]

[3] A. Tardieu, "Le Mystère d'Agadir," pp. 235-246 ff.

[[4] The Powers signatory to the Convention revising the Berlin and Brussels Acts, signed at Saint-Germain-en-Laye, September 10, 1919, "will

Obligatory Arbitration.—The Berlin Act of 1885 contained a quite ineffective clause according to which, in cases of disputes, the Powers reserved to themselves "the option of having recourse to arbitration." [5] In the Anglo-French controversy, to which reference has just been made, France refused to arbitrate the point at issue.[6] A few years later, in 1908, during the course of a similar dispute about conditions in the Belgian Congo, Great Britain proposed that Belgium should agree "to refer in the last resort to arbitra-

reassemble at the expiration of ten years from the coming into force of the present Convention, in order to introduce into it such modifications as experience may have shown to be necessary" (Article 15). By Article 9 of the Liquor Convention of like date, the period after which "by common agreement . . . such modifications as may prove to be necessary" may be introduced is five years. Seven years is the time set by the Preamble to the Arms Convention, also of September 10, 1919, for "revision in the light of the experience gained, if the Council of the League of Nations, acting if need be by a majority, so recommends."]

[5] Article XII. Hertslet, "The Map of Africa by Treaty" (3d ed.), II, p. 475 ["Trattati . . . relativi all'Africa," p. 111].

[6] In 1904, M. Delcassé even maintained that the land system in the French Congo was not a subject for diplomatic discussion since it would infringe the State's internal sovereignty, into which the Berlin Conference had refused to penetrate. Tardieu, *op. cit.*, p. 242. Similarly, in 1906, the Congo Government contended "that the internal affairs of the Congo State, as of every other independent State, concerned itself alone." In reply Sir Edward Grey stated that the British Government "have in no way modified the view held by them and their predecessors that the Powers parties to the Berlin Act have every right to take such steps as they may consider called for with a view to the due observance by the Independent State of its obligations under that Act." The position taken by the Congo Independent State was that no foreign Power or even the signatories of the Berlin Act collectively could interfere with the internal administration of the Congo Free State, though the British Government might intervene on behalf of its nationals if commercial or other rights guaranteed to them by the Berlin Act were violated. But in regard to the obligations for the furtherance of native welfare assumed by the parties to the Berlin Act, it was maintained that the other parties to it "could not legally interfere, and that the engagements . . . were a declaration of general principles and intentions as regarded the treatment of the native populations rather than a binding obligation which the remaining Signatories, or any one of them, had a right to enforce." *Africa*, No. 1 (1906), pp. 17-19.

tion any differences of view as to the meaning of those Articles in the Treaties binding the Congo State which bear on commercial questions, should an agreement between the two Governments respecting them be unattainable by ordinary diplomatic methods." [7]   Belgium, however, declined to admit that they, "alone among the Powers which signed the said [Berlin] Act, should give to one of those Powers a general undertaking which differs as regards arbitration from the principle laid down in Article 12." [8]   Furthermore, they contended that "recourse to arbitration could only take place if the other Powers having possessions in the conventional basin had consented beforehand to intervene in the proceedings or to accept for their possessions the interpretation given by the award." [9]   A general agreement to arbitrate all differences arising from the interpretations and application of the measures of international control adopted for Middle Africa would, it is self-evident, obviate much diplomatic friction and would automatically dispose of these questions.[10]   Such disputes might be referred to the Hague Tribunal or to the organs of a League of Nations,[11] but there are many reasons why it would be preferable to create

[7] *Africa*, No. 4 (1908), p. 3.

[8] *Ibid.*, p. 9.

[9] *Ibid.*, No. 2 (1909), p. 9.

[10] Much in the same way, although the procedure and machinery were entirely different, the establishment of Mixed Tribunals in Egypt in 1876 eliminated diplomatic friction, since the claims of foreigners against the Egyptian Government were in due course decided by these courts.   Milner, "England in Egypt" (7th ed.), pp. 43-46.

[[11] The Arms Convention (Article 24), the Liquor Convention (Article 8), and the Convention revising the Berlin and Brussels Acts (Article 12) stipulate that any unnegotiable dispute arising between the Signatory Powers relating to the application of these agreements "shall be submitted to an arbitral tribunal in conformity with the provisions of the Covenant of the League of Nations."]

a special international court for the affairs of Middle Africa. Above all, it is essential that its members should have a deep understanding of African problems, so that the decisions might not be based solely upon narrow legal considerations.

A Central Bureau.—In addition, it would apparently be most useful to establish as an adjunct to the African Conference a permanent central bureau on the lines of that proposed by the International Sleeping Sickness Conference of 1907.[12] Its scope should, of course, be much broader and would naturally include the entire field of administration in Africa, as well as the scientific work that is required to guide it along sound channels. In the technical field its functions would not be merely to centralize and to coördinate the labors of the various national agencies. Its usefulness would be greatly increased if it also undertook upon its own initiative comprehensive and exhaustive studies of such questions as tropical diseases, native land tenures, and alcoholism—problems which transcend the bounds of the local jurisdictions. In this manner there could be collected a mass of accurate information both to direct the periodic International Conferences and also to assist the local authorities in the actual work of administration in Africa.[13]

[12 Central International Offices, "placed under the control of the League of Nations," are to be established by the Arms and Liquor Conventions (Articles 5 and 7 respectively) "for the purpose of collecting and preserving documents of all kinds exchanged by the High Contracting Parties" with reference to the matters dealt with by these agreements.]

[13 A Pan-African Congress held at Paris, February 19-21, 1919, under the presidency of M. Diagne, Deputy for Senegal, adopted, among other resolutions, the following: (1) the Allied and Associated Powers should establish a code of international protection for the natives; (2) a permanent secretariat within the League of Nations should be set up especially for the execution of all political, social, and economic measures for the welfare of the natives. "The negroes of the world demand that, henceforth, the natives of Africa and the peoples of African descent be governed by the following principles wherever such are not already applied": (a) land and natural resources to be reserved and protected for the natives; (b) concessions, to be controlled by the State and to be only temporary, not to be permitted to exploit the natives or to exhaust natural resources; some part of the proceeds to be devoted to the moral and material advancement of the aborigines; (c) slavery and corporal punishment to be abolished; forced labor to be permitted only as punishment for crime; an official regulation of labor to be promulgated; (d) all negro children to be instructed both in their native tongue and in the language of the tutelary Power; professional education also to be given them; (e) the State to be responsible, without prejudice to missionary and personal initiative, for sanitary conditions and supervision, medical and hospital services being established by the Government; (f) the African natives shall be admitted to share in the conduct of public affairs in progressive proportion to their intellectual development, in virtue of the principle that governments exist for peoples, and not peoples for governments. *Le Temps,* February 23, 1919.]

PART IV

EGYPTIAN PROBLEMS

(Written for THE INQUIRY. Finished August 9, 1918.)

PART IV: EGYPTIAN PROBLEMS

CHAPTER I
THE HISTORICAL AND ECONOMIC BACKGROUND

CHAPTER II
THE GOVERNMENT OF EGYPT

CHAPTER III
RESTRICTIONS ON EGYPTIAN AUTONOMY

CHAPTER IV
EGYPTIAN QUESTIONS AT THE PEACE CONFERENCE

CHAPTER V
EGYPT DURING AND AFTER THE WAR

Explanatory Note

One Pound Egyptian (£E) equals £1-0-6.154 or £T1.139.
One Pound Sterling (£) equals £T1.111.
One Pound Turkish (£T) equals 18 shillings sterling.
One Kantar equals 99.05 pounds.
One Feddan equals 1.038 acres.

EGYPTIAN PROBLEMS

CHAPTER I

1. Great Britain and Egypt

The Roots of Western Civilization.—The historical roots of Western civilization reach far back into the semi-legendary past and the deepest are those that took firm hold some six thousand years ago in the river valleys of Egypt and Mesopotamia. In addition to their abiding historical interest, both of these regions have an immediate practical importance, since they lie across the two shortest roads connecting the West and the East—the highly developed sea-route through the Suez Canal and the almost finished rail-route to the Persian Gulf. While the course of the late war brought the future of these regions within its scope, the extent to which they will be affected by it must differ radically. Only the faint traces of Mesopotamia's ancient prosperity remain, and hence the whole region requires drastic regeneration from the very foundations up. Egypt, on the other hand, has for a full generation enjoyed the benefits of an honest and enlightened administration. In the case of Mesopotamia, the Peace Conference has to decide both the question of emancipation from Turkish misrule and also the future status, while internationally recognized and firmly established facts had already before the war deter-

289

mined the general position of Egypt in the world. Yet there are a number of important Egyptian questions that need settlement at the Peace Conference and others whose adjustment by the established authorities requires international confirmation and, possibly, some modifications before the full sanction of such recognition is accorded.

Egypt and Europe.—Egypt came first prominently within the range of modern international politics in 1798, when Napoleon induced the French Government to undertake an eastern expedition that "would menace her [Britain's] trade with the Indies." [1] He was instructed to seize Egypt, to have the Isthmus of Suez cut, and "to assure the free and exclusive possession of the Red Sea to the French Republic." [2] Although Napoleon speedily conquered Egypt, his ambitious plans against the British Empire were equally quickly frustrated by Nelson's destruction of the French fleet at Aboukir Bay in 1798. Since that time, however, British statesmen have been keenly alive to the strategic position of Egypt and have kept their weather eye on events there. Overtures by other Powers to Great Britain to assume actual control were, nevertheless, firmly rejected.[3]

---

[1] J. H. Rose, "Life of Napoleon I," I, p. 161, London, 1913.

[2] *Ibid.,* p. 166.

[3] On February 22, 1853, Sir G. H. Seymour wrote from Petrograd to Lord John Russell: "The Emperor went on to say that in the event of the dissolution of the Ottoman Empire, he thought it might be less difficult to arrive at a satisfactory territorial arrangement than was commonly believed. . . . As to Egypt [he said] I quite understand the importance to England of that territory. I can then only say, that if, in the event of a distribution of the Ottoman succession upon the fall of the Empire, you should take possession of Egypt, I shall have no objection to offer." To this suggestion the Earl of Clarendon replied on March 23, 1853: "England desires no territorial aggrandizement, and could be no party to a previous arrangement from which she was to derive any such benefit." "Parliamentary Papers," LXXI (1884), pp. 11, 12, 19.

In 1857, Napoleon III suggested a general partition of North Africa, of which England's share was to be Egypt, on the theory that these valuable regions were rendered useless to humanity and civilization by their abominable governments.[4] In this connection, Lord Palmerston, then Prime Minister, wrote:

"It is very possible that many parts of the world would be better governed by France, England, and Sardinia than they are now. . . . How could England and France, who have guaranteed the integrity of the Turkish Empire, turn around and wrest Egypt from the Sultan? A coalition for such a purpose would revolt the moral feelings of mankind, and would certainly be fatal to any English Government that was a party to it. Then as to the balance of power to be maintained by giving us Egypt. In the first place, we don't want to have Egypt. What we wish about Egypt is that it should continue attached to the Turkish Empire, which is a security against its belonging to any European Power. We want to trade with Egypt, and to travel through Egypt, but we do not want the burthen of governing Egypt." [5]

When, in 1869, the dreams of the first Napoleon were realized and the Suez Canal was opened, this policy was emphasized and it became a cardinal maxim of British statesmanship not to allow this essential link in the communications between East and West to come under the exclusive control of any one of the Great Powers. In view of the magnitude of the interests at stake, any other attitude would have been suicidally short-sighted. As Bismarck said in 1882:

"Egypt is of the utmost importance to England on account of the Suez Canal, the shortest line of communication be-

[4] O. E. Ollivier, "L'Empire Libéral," III, p. 418, Paris, 1895 ff.
[5] E. Ashley, "Life of H. J. Temple, Viscount Palmerston," II, p. 124, London, 1876.

tween the eastern and western halves of the Empire. That
is like the spinal cord which connects the backbone with
the brain." [6]

Ismail Pasha's Spendthrift Career.—After the opening
of the Suez Canal, events in Egypt moved rapidly towards
making imperative outside interference. The prosperity
anticipated from the Canal did not accrue to Egypt, which
was preëminently a way station on a main-traveled route,
but the spendthrift Khedive, Ismail Pasha, was not deterred by this fact in his orgy of reckless extravagance.
Corruption was rampant. When, in 1863, Ismail succeeded
his father, Said, the Egyptian debt amounted to only
£3,292,800, but towards the end of 1876 it had reached
the enormous total of £91 million and the tide was still
rising. About £16 million had been spent on the Suez
Canal,[7] but the greater part of the £91 million had been
squandered on non-productive works of little or no public
utility.[8] This "profligate debt," to use Lord Morley's expressive term,[9] was an intolerable burden on the shoulders

[6] M. Busch, "Bismarck," II, pp. 321, 322, London, 1898.

[7] At the present time Egypt derives no income from the Suez Canal,
as the Khedive's shares were sold in 1875 to Great Britain and the fifteen
per cent of the net profits from the Canal reserved to Egypt were disposed of in 1880 to the Crédit Foncier. But, according to the charter,
the Canal in 1969 becomes the property of Egypt. The negotiations of
1910 to extend the charter for forty years were abortive. *Annuaire Statistique,* 1914, p. 268; 1916, p. 255.

[8] In his report of March 23, 1876, on the financial condition of Egypt,
Mr. Stephen Cave wrote: "Egypt may be said to be in a transition state,
and she suffers from the defects of the system out of which she is passing,
as well as from those of the system into which she is attempting to enter.
She suffers from the ignorance, dishonesty, waste, and extravagance of
the East, such as have brought her Suzerain to the verge of ruin, and at
the same time from the vast expense caused by hasty and inconsiderate
endeavours to adopt the civilization of the West." *Egypt,* No. 7 (1876),
p. 1.

[9] J. Morley, "Life of William Ewart Gladstone," III, p. 73, London, 1903.

of an oppressed peasantry, subjected to forced labor and governed by the lash and corruption. Furthermore, even if well governed, Egypt would not have been able to pay the high rate of interest stipulated in the loans, generally seven per cent, but in some instances as much as nine per cent. It was the expert judgment of Mr. Stephen Cave, who investigated the financial situation in 1875-76, that "Egypt is well able to bear the charge of the whole of her present indebtedness at a reasonable rate of interest." [10] The only possible outcome was a declaration of bankruptcy followed by a composition with the creditors. The position of Egypt differed radically from that of other debtor states, in that there had just been established in Egypt international tribunals—the Mixed Courts—in which foreign creditors could sue the Government. Accordingly, when in 1876 the Khedive suspended payment of the Treasury Bills, he was obliged by the circumstances of his exceptional case immediately to start negotiations with the foreign creditors.

The Egyptian Debt.—Some of the earlier Egyptian loans had been entirely legitimate financial transactions, but as Egypt's credit sank to ever lower levels, they became increasingly dubious in character. Many were purely speculative ventures on the part of the lenders, in which not only was the interest rate high, but far less than the face value of the loans was actually paid into the Treasury. Thus the great £32 million seven per cent loan of 1873 yielded to the Treasury only £20,740,000.[11] In general, however, the

[10] *Egypt*, No. 7 (1876), p. 12.

[11] *Ibid.*, pp. 6, 7. In addition, Ismail was consistently swindled in his expenditure of the funds thus secured. "Reference has already been made to the large sums required to meet preposterous claims brought

legality of the loans was not open to question and, furthermore, among the creditors were many innocent holders
whose rights could neither be ignored nor distinguished
from the investments of those who had wantonly encouraged
Ismail in his prodigal course.   The entire episode furnishes
a distinctly unsavory page in financial history, but one that
has many parallels.   Such situations are bound to recur
when rulers of backward countries are subjected to the temp-
tations of modern finance.[12]   Up to now, the only effective
way of preventing such abuses has been the assumption
by the progressive states of some measure of control over
the finances of backward countries as, for instance, was done

against Ismail by foreign adventurers, to whom his speculativeness, his
trickery, and his unbusinesslike character gave ample opportunities for
extortion.   And even when he could afford to spend some of his borrow-
ings upon himself or upon the country, he always contrived to get the
least possible value for his money.   The contracts entered into by the
'Daira' [the Khedive's private estate] or the Government were monu-
ments of wastefulness.   The prices paid in hard cash for material obtained
from Europe were on the scale of those at which a fashionable tailor
supplies goods upon credit to young men of large prospects but no
immediate income."   Lord Milner, "England in Egypt" (7th ed.), p. 179.
Lord Cromer wrote in 1904: "The greater portion of the present Egyptian
debt is a dead weight on the country, because the money borrowed was,
for the most part, wasted."   *Egypt*, No. 1 (1904) (Cromer), p. 3.   See
also *Egypt*, No. 1 (1903) (Cromer), pp. 12, 13.

[12] "The maximum amount of harm is probably done when an Oriental
ruler is for the first time brought in contact with the European system
of credit.   He then finds that he can obtain large sums of money with
the utmost apparent facility.   His personal wishes can thus be easily
gratified.   He is dazzled by the ingenious and often fallacious schemes
for developing his country which European adventurers will not fail to
lay before him in the most attractive light.   He is too wanting in fore-
sight to appreciate the nature of the future difficulties which he is creating
for himself.   The temptation to avail himself to the full of the benefits,
which a reckless use of credit seems to offer to him, are too strong to be
resisted.   He will rush into the gulf which lies open before him, and
inflict an injury on his country from which not only his contemporaries
but future generations will suffer.   This is what Ismail Pasha did."
Cromer, "Modern Egypt," I, pp. 58, 59.

in the case of Cuba by the United States.[13] The necessity of correcting and obviating such financial abuses, and even greater ones in the commercial field, has led to the gradual extension of European and North American control over the less progressive sections of the world. Such also was to be the ultimate outcome of the financial chaos in Egypt and the disorder springing from it.

International Financial Control.—Shortly after the suspension of payments in 1876, the Khedive instituted on May 2d of that same year a Commission of the Public Debt (Caisse de la Dette Publique), whose members were to act as representatives of the bondholders.[14] A French, an Italian, and an Austrian Commissioner were nominated at the instance of their respective Governments, but the British Government refused to select a Commissioner because of unwillingness to interfere in the internal affairs of Egypt. Accordingly, when in 1877, Captain Evelyn Baring, the future Earl of Cromer, was appointed, his nomination proceeded from the British bondholders, not from the British Government. In the meanwhile, these bondholders and those of the other countries had in 1876 reached an agreement with the Egyptian Government, by which the interest on the debt was somewhat reduced. At the same time, also, a British and a French Controller-General were appointed to supervise respectively the revenues and the

[13] On the insistence of the United States, Cuba in 1901 adopted the Platt Amendment, giving the United States a conditional right of intervention and binding Cuba not to contract any debt that could not be defrayed out of the ordinary revenue. J. H. Latané, "America as a World Power," p. 179, New York, 1907 [cf. also Malloy, "Treaties," pp. 362-363].
[14] "British and Foreign State Papers 1875-1876," Vol. LXVII (1883), pp. 1014-1016.

expenditure, while other officials of the same nationalities together with Egyptian associates were put in charge of the railways, of the telegraphs, and of the port of Alexandria, whose revenues were allocated to the payment of the interest on the debt. The essential defect in the financial arrangement of 1876 was that the reduction in interest was not sufficiently drastic. Egypt, suffering from a low Nile and involved in the Russo-Turkish War with its accompanying expenditure and commercial disturbance, could only at the cost of much suffering meet her liabilities in 1877-78. The French Government did not believe that the inability claimed was genuine and energetically pressed for payment. Hitherto the British Government had adhered to the traditional policy of the Foreign Office as established by Lord Palmerston [15] and had refrained from such action on behalf of the British bondholders. Only unofficial assistance was given to them. The Foreign Secretary, Lord Derby, declined "to accept any responsibility" for the Brit-

[15] British policy in this regard was established in 1848 by Lord Palmerston in a circular dispatch, in which he stated that hitherto it had been thought undesirable that British subjects should take part in loans to foreign governments instead of investing in profitable enterprises at home, and "with a view to discourage hazardous loans to foreign governments, who may be either unable or unwilling to pay the stipulated interest thereupon, the British Government has hitherto thought it the best policy to abstain from taking up as international questions the complaints made by British subjects against foreign governments which have failed to make good their engagements in regard to such pecuniary transactions." He further stated that this policy was entirely discretionary and that if the loss were large, it might become the duty of the British Government to make the matter the subject of diplomatic negotiation. W. E. Hall, "A Treatise on International Law" (7th ed., A. Pearce Higgins), pp. 290-291, Oxford, 1917. It is rather curious that Palmerston should popularly be considered the innovator of a policy just the opposite of that which he established in the Foreign Office. H. N. Brailsford, "The War of Steel and Gold," pp. 54, 245, London, 1915.

ish officials appointed by the Egyptian Government in 1876 and held that they were merely Englishmen in the employ of the Egyptian Government.[16] His successor in the Foreign Office, Lord Salisbury, was induced by various considerations to depart from this established policy and supported the French policy of pressure.[17] The inevitable result was a fresh crisis in Egyptian finances.

The Liquidation of 1880.—No really accurate information as to Egypt's resources was available. It was futile to grope further in the dark. Accordingly, in 1878, an expert Commission, mainly European in membership, was appointed to make an exhaustive examination of the financial condition of Egypt.[18] It was becoming more and more clear not only that a radical cut in the interest was necessary, but that even the reduced amount could not be paid unless the corrupt and wasteful administrative system was thoroughly

[16] *Egypt*, No. 8 (1876), pp. 1, 2, 36, 40, 65; *Egypt*, No. 2 (1879), pp. 1, 2, 5, 22, 33, 38, 44, 45.

[17] The British Government thus became in a certain degree responsible for the oppression which necessarily accompanied the collection of the taxes. Moreover, the step taken at this moment involved a departure both from the local Egyptian policy, which the British Government had hitherto pursued, and also from their general policy in such matters. As regards local policy, the British had never espoused the cause of the bondholders as warmly as had the French Government. On the contrary, a just consideration for the interests of the Egyptian people had always tempered any support given to the foreign creditors. As regards general policy, it had for years been the tradition of the London Foreign Office that British subjects who invested their money in a foreign country must do so at their own risk. They could not rely on any energetic support in the enforcement of their claims. There was evidently some special reason for so brusque a departure from the principles hitherto adopted. The reason is not far to seek. The Berlin Congress was then about to sit, to regulate the situation arising from the recent Russo-Turkish War. Egyptian interests had to give way to broader diplomatic considerations. It was necessary to conciliate the French. The French initiative was, therefore, followed. Cromer, "Modern Egypt," I, pp. 37, 38.

[18] *Documents Diplomatiques, Affaires d'Égypte*, 1880, pp. 5 *et seq.*

overhauled. The latter result could not, however, be effected without the genuine coöperation of the Khedive. Instead of assisting, Ismail thwarted the work of reform and planned to rid himself of European intervention. As a consequence, the British and French Governments resorted to his Suzerain, the Sultan of Turkey, who in 1879 deposed Ismail and appointed his son Tewfik to be his successor as Khedive.[19] Shortly thereafter, in 1880, the Law of Liquidation was promulgated with the approval of the Powers. The interest on the debt was very extensively reduced and, while the burden was still very onerous, it was not beyond Egypt's real strength.[20] In addition, British and French officials had in 1879 been put in control of the finances with general supervision over the entire administrative machinery. As these officials were not removable except with the consent of their own Government, this arrangement amounted to a virtual Anglo-French condominium.[21] Af-

---

[19] *Egypt*, No. 3 (1879).

[20] After the passage of the Law of Liquidation, the Egyptian Debt stood as follows:

Privileged Debt 5%	£22,629,800
Unified Debt 4%	58,043,326
Daira Loan 4%	9,512,804
Domains Loan 5%	8,500,000
	£98,685,930

Milner, "England in Egypt" (7th ed.), p. 181; Sir Auckland Colvin, "The Making of Modern Egypt" (3d ed.), pp. 102, 103. See also *Egypt*, No. 1 (1881), p. 2.

[21] Granville, in his note to Waddington of June 16, 1884, described the difference between the arrangements of 1876 and the Dual Control of 1879: "Although the powers of investigation conferred on these two officers [the British and the French Controllers General] were limited to financial matters, at the same time the fact that they had a right to be present at the meetings of the Council of Ministers virtually gave to them the right of interference in all questions connected with the administration of the country. They were no longer, as before, purely financial

fairs seemed to be on the high-road to permanent improvement, but there were ominous clouds on the horizon.

The Arabist Rebellion.—The gross maladministration of Ismail and the oppressive taxation which it involved had led to marked discontent. At the outset, the feeling was directed mainly against the Turkish ruling class and found chief expression in the army, where there was great dissatisfaction among the officers over the non-payment of their salaries and the placing of many on half-pay before they had received their arrears. In 1879 a serious mutiny occurred, in which the officers carried their point and thus realized the power that they could wield. The discontent in the army was not allayed and found a leader in Colonel Ahmed Arabi, an Egyptian of fellah origin. In 1881, the mutinous army succeeded in securing the dismissal of the Minister of War and soon Arabi was the virtual ruler of Egypt. The movement also became much broader. It linked up with those elements that were hostile to Turkish rule, to European interference, and also to Christian influences in general. As Sir Auckland Colvin wrote at the time, "the movement, though in its origin anti-Turk, is in itself an Egyptian national movement." It was

officers. Important political functions were conferred upon them." *Documents Diplomatiques, Affaires d'Égypte,* 1884, p. 23. During the discussion of this matter in the House of Commons in 1882, Mr. Gladstone correctly said: "What is a political control? I assert that this was not a political control then [*i.e.,* prior to 1879] because the [British] Government were not concerned in it. The fact that the Egyptians chose to establish foreign Controllers . . . was not necessarily an arrangement entailing foreign interference, because they retained the right to dismiss the Controllers, but in the year 1879, in depriving them of that right, you brought foreign intervention into the heart of the country, and established, in the strictest sense of the phrase, a 'political control.'" Cromer, "Modern Egypt," I, pp. 160, 161.

a genuine revolt against misgovernment which, as Lord
Cromer said in 1905, excusably assumed an anti-European
character,[22] intensified by resentment at France's occupation of Tunis at this very time.[23]   In the spring of 1882, the
Revolution was in full sway.   The military and national
parties were united, with the former dominant.   A considerable following was secured among the peasants and
small farmers, the fellaheen, whose vision had hitherto
been limited to their fields.   Grave disorders ensued.   In
the eyes of the uneducated natives, the movement meant
"that the Christians were going to be expelled from Egypt,
that they were to recover the land bought by Europeans or
mortgaged to them, and that the National Debt would be
canceled." [24]   On June 11, 1882, some fifty Europeans were
massacred by the mob in Alexandria and many others were
severely wounded.   It was no longer a question of safeguarding European financial interests in Egypt, but of protecting
the very lives of the considerable European population, of
saving the country from anarchy, and of ensuring the safety
of the Suez Canal.   The fabric of Egyptian society was tot-
tering.   An exodus of the European residents began.

The Question of Armed Intervention.—British and
French statesmen had never reached an agreement as
to what should be done in case active intervention
should eventually become necessary.   Such a course was
in the extreme distasteful to the British Premier, Gladstone, whose aversion to the use of force and to foreign

---

[22] *Egypt,* No. 1 (1905), p. 2. See also Sir Auckland Colvin, "The Making of Modern Egypt," pp. 10-15.
[23] The page of copy on which footnotes 23-31, inclusive, appeared has,
unfortunately, been lost.

intervention verged on pacificism. At the beginning of the year 1882, when it became evident that some action would probably be necessary, the British Foreign Secretary, Lord Granville, "felt strong objections to all the modes of intervention," [25] but the least objectionable to his mind was Turkish. The French Prime Minister, Gambetta, would not, however, listen to this suggestion, mainly because he feared that a strengthening of Turkish influence in Egypt might prove dangerous to France's position in Algeria and Tunis. Instead, he urged an Anglo-French occupation. This possibility was, however, soon removed as Gambetta's Ministry fell early in 1882 and his timid successor, Freycinet, disapproved of such joint intervention. Freycinet's attitude was very irresolute, but on the whole he favored action by the European Concert. The French ships took no part in the reduction of the Arabist fortifications at Alexandria in July by the British fleet, but left the scene of action. The Chamber of Deputies was afraid of the threatening state of Europe itself and, by an overwhelming vote, even refused to sanction an expedition solely for the restricted purpose of protecting the Suez Canal.[26] Clemenceau's specch demanding that France reserve her freedom of action in Europe was decisive. Turkey, characteristically, backed and filled; and could not be induced to undertake the task of restoring order under terms that were satisfactory until the necessity for action had passed, Britain having already suppressed the rebellion. Italy, especially, was asked to coöperate, but declined.[27] No one of the Powers was willing to assume the responsibility. The International Conference that had been convoked at Constantinople especially to consider the problem shirked the job. In Bismarck's eyes, this Conference was merely a device of France and England to get "the rest of Europe to help them out of their difficulty." "The rest of us would not coöperate in a military sense," he said, "as for the present the question is one of comparative indifference to us, and it is no business of ours to pull the chestnuts out of the fire for other people, particularly for the English." [28] Satiated with Prussia's extensive conquests of 1866 at the expense of the other German States and with Germany's annexation of Alsace-Lorraine in 1871, Bismarck desired freedom from foreign complications, in order to digest these territorial acquisitions and to complete the process of German unification. It served his purposes well if Germany's neighbors pursued extra-European enterprises, especially if such a course led to friction between them. "We must look on quietly," he said in the autumn of 1882 to the German Ambassador to France, "should the French and English locomotives happen to collide." [29]

The British Occupation, 1882.—Under these circumstances and in view of the fact that the British Government was firmly and honestly convinced that no stable and progressive government could possibly emerge from the Arabist movement, the only alternative was isolated intervention. A small expeditionary force was sent to Egypt "in support of the authority of His Highness the Khedive, as established by the Firmans of the Sultan and existing international engagements, to suppress a military revolt in that country." [30] After a brilliant campaign of a scant month's duration, the Arabist army was shattered at Tel-el-Kebir on

September 13, 1882, and the rebellion almost instantly collapsed.[31] Thus Great Britain was placed in a position of control in Egypt by the force of circumstances and against her own volition. Lord Morley's statement that "Mr. Gladstone and his Cabinet fought as hard as they could, and for good reasons, against single-handed intervention by Great Britain," [32] is not open to serious discussion. While it is unquestionably true that Mr. Gladstone's estimate of the Arabist movement as an exclusively military rebellion was erroneous, on the other hand, the sanest and soundest opinion of that day and of subsequent times agreed with him that Egypt's regeneration could not have proceeded from Ahmed Arabi and that, in actuality, the only alternatives were intervention or anarchy. The murders in Alexandria, the pillaging and the burning of the town at the time of the reduction of the fortifications by the British fleet had been an ominous portent. British intervention would naturally not have occurred if British interests had not been involved. But the debt was a minor consideration in comparison with the lives of the European population, and behind all loomed the compelling fact that anarchy in Egypt

[32] J. Morley, "Life of William Ewart Gladstone," III, p. 80, London, 1903. Lord Cromer vividly summarized the attitude of the British in the following words: "British diplomacy, which may at times have been mistaken, but which was certainly honest, did its best to throw off the Egyptian burden. But circumstances were too strong to be arrested by diplomatic action. Egypt was to fall to Kinglake's Englishman. Moreover, it was to fall to him, although some were opposed to his going there, others were indifferent as to whether he went or not, none much wished him to go, and, not only did he not want to go there himself, but he struggled strenuously and honestly not to be obliged to go." Cromer, "Modern Egypt," I, p. 130. See also S. L. Gwynn and G. M. Tuckwell, "Life of the Rt. Hon. Sir Charles W. Dilke," I, p. 454 n., London, 1917; Baron Fitzmaurice, "Life of Granville George Leveson-Gower, second Earl Granville," II, pp. 258 ff., London, 1905.

would have imperiled the safety of the Suez Canal, especially since, in 1875, the British Government had purchased the Khedive's shares in the Canal Company. As Lord Salisbury said in 1879, England could not leave Egypt to its fate; "the geographical situation of Egypt, as well as the responsibility which the English Government have in past times incurred for the actual conditions under which it exists as a state" made this impossible.[33] The inevitable result of the occupation was that within a few months the Anglo-French Dual Control of 1879 was abolished and Great Britain assumed the task of reform.

Duration of the Occupation.—When the British Government thus reluctantly occupied Egypt, it was their firm intention to evacuate the country as soon as order had been restored. Various official declarations to this general effect were made. But a policy of reform and one of speedy evacuation were irreconcilable.[34] There was at the time no real understanding of the situation and no appreciation of the extent to which the country needed reorganization. The Egyptian army was a lamentably ineffective and undisciplined force; gross corruption and extreme inefficiency prevailed in all the administrative branches; the finances were disordered and required careful handling; the irrigation system upon which Egypt depended for existence was in decay and needed thorough overhauling and further extension. In addition, the rise of the Mahdi in the Sudan and

[33] Lord Salisbury to Mr. Lascelles, June 18, 1879. *Egypt*, No. 3 (1879), p. 11. On Great Britain's vital interest in the Suez Canal, as viewed at that time, see Sir D. Mackenzie Wallace, "Egypt and the Egyptian Question," pp. 450-501.

[34] *Egypt*, No. 1 (1905) (Cromer), p. 2.

the successful rebellion there against Egyptian rule brought up the serious possibility of an invasion of Egypt from that quarter. Egypt could not be deemed secure while the Sudan was in hostile hands. The flow of the life-giving Nile might be disastrously curtailed. One important problem after another arose and thus the evacuation was gradually postponed until the term of the occupation became indefinite. With very few exceptions, British statesmen and administrators did not regard British rule as a permanent institution, but all of those who were most intimately acquainted with the situation were firmly convinced that the laboriously constructed fabric would quickly fall into decay if the guiding hand and watchful eye of Britain were removed. British policy was clear and consistent. Sir Eldon Gorst, Lord Cromer's successor, defined it in 1909 as follows:

"Since the commencement of the occupation, the policy approved by the British Government has never varied and its fundamental idea has been to prepare the Egyptians for self-government, while helping them in the meantime to enjoy the benefits of good government. The gradual evolution during the past quarter of a century of a sound system of administration has not only effected the latter purpose, but has, at the same time, constituted a valuable school of training for the higher Egyptian officials." [35]

There were but few traces of the view which is now gaining ground that Egypt will ultimately become an autonomous unit in "the Commonwealth of Nations" into which the British Empire is gradually developing. The process of schooling the Egyptian character and mind for self-gov-

[35] *Egypt,* No. 1 (1909) (Gorst), p. 48. [For a summary of the history of the occupation up to the outbreak of the war, see Chirol, "The Egyptian Problem," pp. 65-119.]

ernment was under the supervision of British officials, whose
authority was sustained by the Army of Occupation. This
was at no time a large force and it varied in size according
to circumstances.[36]　In 1914, before the outbreak of the
war, the British garrison consisted of 6,067 men of all ranks
and services, including one company at Cyprus and the
British troops stationed in the Anglo-Egyptian Sudan.[37]

2.　The Development of Egypt, 1882-1914

The Nile Country.—The part played by geographical facts
in historical development is possibly more dominant, and
certainly more obvious, in the Nile Valley than anywhere
else.[38]　The words of the Greek historian, Herodotus, "The
Nile is Egypt and Egypt is the Nile," were not only descrip-
tive of the three thousand years under the Pharaohs that
preceded his age, as well as of the many millennia of unre-
corded history that lie behind the first Egyptian dynasty,
but are equally applicable to the present. As Sir William
Willcocks, the engineer who has done so much to increase
the usefulness of the waters that descend from Equatorial
Africa, has said, "Egypt is nothing more than the deposit left

---

[36] Thus, in 1893, when the youthful Khedive, Abbas Hilmi, was trying
to dispense with British advice, the garrison was somewhat increased and
the increase had its desired moral effect. Cromer, "Abbas II," pp. 37-39.

[37] The Egyptian Government contributed £150,000 towards the cost of
these troops. Their total cost, according to the Army Estimates for 1914-
15, was £547,900. *The Statesman's Year-Book,* 1915, pp. 98, 257, 258. The
amount contributed by Egypt was based in the arrangement of 1885 upon
the extra cost of maintaining these British troops in Egypt above their
cost in England. In 1904, the British force was 3,500 men and Egypt's
contribution £100,000. *Egypt,* No. 1 (1905) (Cromer), p. 26.

[38] J. H. Breasted, "A History of the Ancient Egyptians," pp. 3-13, New
York, 1913.

by the Nile in flood." [39]   The nominal area of Egypt is large, about 350,000 square miles, but this includes vast expanses of hopelessly arid and useless desert. The cultivable and inhabitable portion covers only 12,226 square miles.[40]   North of Cairo is Lower Egypt, the triangular area which the Greeks graphically called the Delta, comprising 7,782 square miles of exceptionally rich agricultural land. South of Cairo, reaching to Wadi Halfa, some 750 miles distant, is the narrow valley of the Nile with an excrescence to the west, the Fayoum District, where the Nile has succeeded in breaking through the rocky walls of the desert. The area of this region, called Upper Egypt, is 4,362 square miles. This narrow strip of alluvial soil along the Nile, together with the Delta, made by like deposits, comprises practically all of Egypt that is of use to man for habitation and cultivation.[41]

Irrigation.—The first and essential function of government in Egypt is to see that the cultivable land receives neither too much nor too little water. At the time of the British occupation, the irrigation system was in a state of decay. Expert engineers were immediately brought from

[39] D. G. Hogarth ("The Nearer East," p. 77, London, 1902) describes the Egyptian Plain as "bisected by the valley of a single mighty stream, which derives neither its origin nor any of its waters from it, but, itself an alien, has laid down a ribbon of alien soil and fenced the sea from the northern edge of the Plain with a large deltaic tract."

[40] *The Statesman's Year-Book,* 1917, pp. 252, 253; *Annuaire Statistique,* 1914, p. 2. "Egypt, as a geographical expression, is two things—the Desert and the Nile. As a habitable country, it is only one—the Nile." Milner, "England in Egypt" (7th ed.), p. 221. For details, see Sir W. Willcocks and J. I. Craig, "Egyptian Irrigation," II, pp. 449-518, London, 1913; Report of Sir William Garstin on the Basin of the Upper Nile, *Egypt,* No. 2 (1904).

[41] The deserts harbor a small nomadic population and they also contain some mineral deposits, such as potash and petroleum.

British India and under their guidance the path was entered that has led to a vast improvement and extension of the irrigation and drainage systems. Further developments are being planned, but as a result of those already in effect, considerable territory has been reclaimed and the cultivable area greatly increased. Furthermore, a large portion of the land was thereby enabled to produce two and even three crops annually, when only one was possible before. As a result, the gross agricultural output increased rapidly and simultaneously also the number of inhabitants.

Increase in Population.—The census of 1882 showed a population of 6,830,000; that of 1897, one of 9,730,000; and that of 1907, one of 11,290,000.[42] The full figures of the 1917 census are not yet available, but the provisional ones indicate about 12,731,551 inhabitants, which is somewhat below previous official estimates.[43] It is generally agreed that the enumeration of 1882, which was taken during the confusion of the Arabist Rebellion, understated the real figures; yet, making full allowance for this fact, the increase during the British Occupation has been most remarkable. Population statistics are a fundamental, but not an infallible, criterion of material progress. The fact that the same land now supports in comparative well-being almost twice as many people as a generation ago lived there in penury is irrefutable proof of good administration. Even according to the standards of highly industrialized countries, Egypt

---

[42] *The Statesman's Year-Book*, 1915, p. 250; *Annuaire Statistique*, 1914. pp. xxiii, 22, 23.

[43] *The Near East*, June 1, 1917, p. 83; *Annuaire Statistique*, 1916, p. xviii. [The actual figures for this census were 12,750,918. *The Statesman's Year-Book*, 1921, p. 259.]

would be exceptionally densely populated. Its density is over three times that of Germany and about one half greater than that of Belgium and England. But Egypt is an agricultural country, where such density of population is rare. It can be compared in this respect only with Bengal, with its proverbial teeming millions. Yet the Egyptian density exceeds that of the East Indian Province by considerably over one half. Compared with British India as a whole, the Egyptian population is more than five times as dense.[44]

Expansion of Foreign Trade.—Even more rapid has been the simultaneous expansion of foreign trade. The average total of imports and exports for the years 1885-89 was £E18.9 million, or about ninety-five million dollars. The average for the period 1900-04 was £E34.6 million, and that for 1905-09 was £E47.8 million.[45] In 1913, Egypt's foreign commerce aggregated £E59.6 million, which was more than three times the amount during the first decade of the British Occupation.[46] It should also be noted that the imports increased considerably more rapidly than did the exports,

[44] *Statistisches Jahrbuch,* 1915, pp. 3*-6*; *Egypt,* No. 1 (1909) (Gorst), pp. 7, 8; R. J. M. Cressaty, "L'Égypte d'Aujourd'hui," p. 59.

[45] EGYPT'S FOREIGN TRADE
AVERAGES OF FIVE-YEAR PERIODS
(*in millions of £E*)

	1885-89	1890-94	1895-99	1900-04	1905-09
Imports	7.9	8.9	10.3	16.3	23.8
Exports	11.	12.9	13.3	18.3	24.

Annuaire Statistique, 1914, pp. 290, 291.

[46] *Corresponding Figures for*

	1910	1911	1912	1913	1914	1915	1916	1917	1918	1919	1920	1921
Imports	23.6	27.2	25.9	27.9	21.7	19.3	30.9	33.2	51.1	47.4	101.9	55.5
Exports	28.9	28.6	34.6	31.7	24.1	27.	37.5	41.1	45.4	75.9	85.5	36.4
£E	52.5	55.8	60.5	59.6	45.8	46.3	68.4	74.3	96.5	123.3	187.4	91.9

which indicated the growing prosperity of the country and
the relatively decreasing weight of the foreign debt. For
purposes of comparison, it should be noted that in amount
Egypt's foreign commerce was only slightly less than that
of Cuba and that the entire foreign trade of Middle Africa
exceeded it by only about seventeen per cent.

Radical Improvement in the Finances.—When the Egyptian debt was liquidated in 1880, the interest charge was
very onerous and bore heavily on the country. It absorbed
thirty-seven per cent of the public revenue. In 1913, the
proportion had fallen to twenty-two per cent. This favorable development was due entirely to a large gain in revenue, which had risen from £E9,584,000 in 1880 to £E17,705,-
000 in 1913.[47] The expansion, it should be noted, was not the
result of increased taxation, but solely of economic growth.
In fact, the taxes were not only equalized but they were
actually reduced. Moreover, forced labor, an indirect form
of taxation of a most burdensome character, was abolished.
As a consequence of this expansion, the recurring deficits
of the 'seventies gave way in the 'eighties to a period of
strenuous efforts to make both sides of the ledger balance
and this era of careful supervision and rigid economy led to

---

[47] PUBLIC DEBT CHARGES AND TOTAL REVENUE

(in thousands of £E)

1880	3,529	9,584
1890	4,227	11,892
1900	3,674	11,867
1910	3,922	16,337
1912	3,924	17,848
1913	3,925	17,705

Annuaire Statistique, 1914, pp. 406, 418. [In 1920, the charges on the
public debt were £E3,552,266 and the total revenue was £E33,677,401.
The Statesman's Year-Book, 1921, pp. 264, 265.]

a period of increasing surpluses until, towards 1900, the margin of safety became more than adequate and the Egyptian finances were and remained thoroughly sound. In the years before the war a considerable surplus over the ordinary expenditures was always available.[48] Large sums were spent out of current revenues for works of great public utility, especially on the irrigation system and the railroads, whose cost in other countries is generally defrayed in the main by loans. As a consequence, Egypt now owns a valuable railroad system from which a considerable income is derived.[49] The public debt itself has been reduced by about

[48] EGYPTIAN FINANCES

(*in millions of £E*)

	Receipts	Ordinary Expenditures	Extraordinary Expenditures
1909	15.9	13.6	3.3
1910	16.3	13.8	3.1
1911	17.2	14.1	2.9
1912	17.8	14.8	2.7
1913	17.7	14.9	2.8

Egypt, No. 1 (1914) (Kitchener), p. 16.

[For 1914-21 the figures were:

	Receipts	Expenditures	Balance
1914	17.4	15.7	1.7
1915	15.4	16.8	—1.4
1916	17.7	16.6	1.1
1917	19.9	17.2	2.7
1918	23.1	22.5	.6
1919	27.7	23.4	4.3
1920	33.7	29.	4.7
1921	46.4	62.1	—15.7]

[49] The total length of the Egyptian railroads was, in 1913, 3,667 kilometers, valued at £E30,109,000. Of these, the State owned 2,391 kilometers, valued at £E27,491,430. *Annuaire Statistique,* 1914, pp. xxvi, xxvii, 166, 168. The gross receipts in 1913 were £E3.8 million, the expenses, £E2.2 million, leaving a net revenue of £E1.6 or equivalent to 5.97 per cent on the capital value. *Egypt,* No. 1 (1914) (Kitchener), p. 26. According to Lord Kitchener, some £30 million had been spent by Egypt on public works and railways since 1883 without recourse to foreign capital. *Egypt,* No. 1 (1913) (Kitchener), p. 3. [In 1920, the total length of the railroads was 4,913 kilometers, of which the State owned 3,752. The gross receipts were £E7.0 million, the expenses £E5.1

£10 million since 1880. While, on the one hand, the
loans which were secured by Khedive Ismail's ill-gotten
private estates were paid off by the sale of these lands, on
the other, there was fresh borrowing for sorely needed public
improvements. The £9 million loan of 1885 at three
per cent was guaranteed by Great Britain, France, Italy,
Russia, Germany, and Austria-Hungary.[50] Similarly, in
1890, some new money was obtained, but at the same time
the interest rate on the Privileged Debt was reduced from
five to three and one-half per cent. This brings up an important point. The security resulting from the British Occupation greatly enhanced Egypt's credit and thus not only
permitted this conversion, but made it possible to obtain
abundant capital at moderate rates for Egypt's private enterprises. It is the same story in all backward countries
that have come under the ægis of the progressive Powers,
and is a vital fact that is usually ignored in discussions of
this many-sided question. The great bulk of the foreign
capital invested in the Egyptian debt and in private enterprises is French and British.[51] Frenchmen, apparently,

million, and the net revenue was £E1.9 million. *The Statesman's Year-
Book*, 1921, pp. 270-271. In 1921, the corresponding figures were: £E8 million, 7.9 million, and .1 million. *Ibid.*, 1922, p. 279.]

[50] *Annuaire Statistique*, 1914, p. 483. For details of this and other fresh
loans, see *Egypt*, No. 1 (1907) (Cromer), pp. 55, 56. The nominal amount
borrowed in order to obtain £9,000,000 in 1885 was £9,424,000 and, as the
interest rate was only three per cent and £315,000 was set aside yearly
for the service of the loan, it will gradually be paid off out of the surplus
of this annuity. The actual interest paid on the loan was, thus, about
three and one-eighth per cent. Milner, *op. cit.*, p. 186. The text of the
London Agreement of March 17, 1885, is in Noradounghian, "Recueil
d'Actes Internationaux de l'Empire Ottoman," IV, pp. 354, 355; *Egypt*,
No. 7 (1885), pp. 1-5.

[51] It was claimed in 1905 that France held about two-thirds of the Egyptian Debt, that is 1,580,000,000 out of 2,340,000,000 francs. Of the Unified

have the preponderant share and it is even claimed that their investments in Egypt have exceeded those made by them in any other country except Russia.[52] The aggregate amount of such foreign interests in Egypt was considerable, but it can be only approximately estimated. The total of the Government Debt, mainly held by foreigners, is of course an open fact. On December 31, 1913, the amount in the hands of the public was, all told, £88.7 million.[53]

Mineral Resources and Industry.—While Egypt is predominantly an agricultural country, it does not wholly lack either mineral resources or industry. The inhospitable Sinai Peninsula, so sparsely peopled as to be virtually uninhabited, contains some indefinite quantities of phosphates, manganese, copper, and iron. In the Arabian Desert, between the Nile and the eastern border along the Gulf of Suez and the Red Sea, are to be found emeralds, gold, copper, lead, zinc, sulphur, phosphates,[55] and petroleum.[54] The only commercially significant developments, however, are the

Debt, France owned sixty per cent. André Tardieu, "Questions Diplomatiques de l'Année 1904," pp. 37, 38, Paris, 1905.
[52] R. J. M. Cressaty, "L'Égypte d'Aujourd'hui," p. 5.

[53] STATE OF THE DEBT, DECEMBER 31, 1913

(in millions of pounds sterling)

	Total	In Public Hands
Guaranteed Loan 3%	7.1	7.
Privileged Loan 3½%	31.1	28.7
Unified Loan 4%	56.	53.
	£94.2	£88.7

Annuaire Statistique, 1914, p. 486.
[54] For the location of these resources, see the map in the *Annuaire Statistique* of 1914, reproduced as map facing page 314. Lord Cromer in 1906 stated that the estimated population of the Sinai Peninsula was 30,000. *Egypt,* No. 1 (1906) (Cromer), p. 13.
[55] See first note on page 314.

potash and petroleum enterprises near the Suez and Red Sea littorals.[55] But, as yet, these are not important and it is extremely doubtful if they will ever play a large part in the world economy. Nor is there any considerable industrial development. In the aggregate, however, a large number of people were employed in industries for local needs, such as building, carpentry, dressmaking, and metal working, and in small special handicrafts, such as weaving of cotton and silks, or the manufacture of shawls, pottery, and baskets. In addition, there were also some larger-scale industries, such as cotton spinning, refining of petroleum, and crushing and even refining of sugar.[56] The cotton itself was ginned and some oil and cake were also made from the cotton-seed. As yet, this development had not attained very significant proportions. From the standpoint of the outside world, unquestionably the chief industry was the manufacture of cigarettes, for which Egypt is justly so well and so widely known.

The Cigarette Industry.—Curiously, and contrary to the general impression, the Egyptian cigarette is not made from

	[55] *Phosphates*	*Petroleum*
		(in tons)
1910	2,397	....
1911	6,425	3,391
1912	69,958	27,522
1913	101,311	12,586
1914	72,000	100,000
1915	83,000	30,000

Annuaire Statistique, 1914, p. 8; 1916, p. xvii; British Diplomatic and Consular Reports, No. 5474 (Port Said, 1914), p. 12.

[56] *The Near East,* June 7, 1918, p. 471. The manufacture of sugar and the decortication of rice employ a number of factories in Upper Egypt (Mohammed Sourour Bey, "Egypt," in "Papers on Inter-Racial Problems: First Universal Races Congress, 1911," ed. G. Spiller, p. 173).

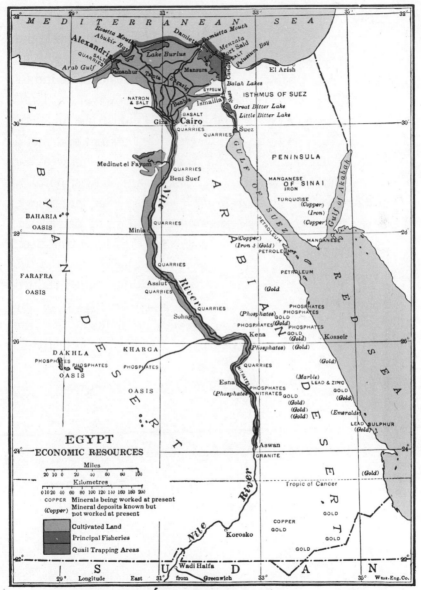

EGYPT
ECONOMIC RESOURCES

Miles
20 10 0   20   40   60   80   100

Kilometres
0 10 20 40 60 80 100 120 140 160 180 200

COPPER   Minerals being worked at present
(Copper) Mineral deposits known but
          not worked at present

          Cultivated Land
          Principal Fisheries
          Quail Trapping Areas

From "Annuaire Statistique de l'Égypte." 1914.

native tobacco, but exclusively from imported leaf. In fact, the cultivation of tobacco in Egypt was absolutely forbidden by the decrees of 1890 and 1892.[57] This prohibition was due, on the one hand, to fiscal reasons, as a large part of the Egyptian customs revenue is derived from the tobacco duties, and, on the other, to a desire to sustain the reputation of the Egyptian cigarette by preventing the use of the inferior tobacco grown in Egypt.[58] It is interesting to note that this measure was an application of a policy established in Great Britain in the seventeenth century, when the American Colonies began to grow tobacco on a large scale. It is a far cry from colonial Virginia to modern Egypt, but the lineal descent of the policy is indisputable and is one of the many proofs of the real unity of history. The tobacco imported into Egypt was derived from Turkey, Macedonia, Greece, and Russia; and amounted in value annually to somewhat less than six million dollars.[59] The greater part of this was consumed locally and the remainder was exported in the form of cigarettes. The annual value

[57] *Egyptian Government Almanac,* 1913, p. 74, Cairo, 1912. Sir Auckland Colvin, "The Making of Modern Egypt," p. 171.

[58] Tobacco constituted in 1913 only five per cent of the total imports, but furnished nearly one-half of the customs revenue. Achille Sékaly, "La Culture du Tabac," in *L'Égypte Contemporaine,* V (1914), pp. 345, 346.

[59] IMPORTS OF TOBACCO, ETC.

(*in £E*)

	Total	From Turkey	From Greece	From Russia
1910	1,155,000	596,000	313,000	93,000
1911	1,190,000	544,000	331,000	123,000
1912	1,214,000	523,000	378,000	181,000
1913	1,082,000	412,000	364,000	234,000

Annuaire Statistique, 1914, p. 310. See also British Diplomatic and Consular Reports, No. 5296 (Russia, 1913), p. 29.

of these shipments was, however, only two million dollars.[60] This surprisingly low total is due to the fact that most European and American states have either established tobacco monopolies or have placed almost prohibitive import duties on cigarettes. As a result, the Egyptian export industry is completely at the mercy of foreign governments. In 1900-04 the average shipments to Germany were £E184,144, but in 1903 they had fallen to £E87,986.[61] In the case of America, the tariff barriers are so high that a number of the most famous Egyptian brands, such as the Nestor and the Melachrino cigarettes, are manufactured in the United States itself.

The Dominant Position of Cotton.—There is a marked similarity between the economic situation of Egypt and that of Cuba. Each one produces commodities, cigarettes and cigars, respectively, that are famous throughout the world as standards of perfection, yet in both cases these play a relatively insignificant part in the country's economic sys-

[60] EXPORTS OF CIGARETTES

Average of Five-Year Periods	*Amounts in £E*
1885-89	82,315
1890-94	156,709
1895-99	239,727
1900-04	425,922
1905-09	428,903
Year Periods	
1910	379,128
1911	407,123
1912	422,666
1913	397,978

Annuaire Statistique, 1914, p. 310.

[61] In 1913, the exports of cigarettes to the British Empire amounted to £E111,169; to Germany, £E87,986, and to the United States, £E14,465. *Ibid.*

tem. In 1912, sixty-nine per cent of Cuba's exports consisted of sugar [62] and, in 1915, this share had risen to seventy-seven per cent.[63] In Egypt, raw cotton occupied an even more important position, constituting over eighty per cent of the exports.[64] This predominance would be still further emphasized if cotton seed and cotton-seed products were included in the percentage. The only other crop which Egypt exports on an appreciable scale is sugar, the cultivation of which was extensively fostered by Ismail Pasha during the crisis resulting from the severe fall in the price of cotton after the American Civil War.[65] The

[62] *The Statesman's Year-Book*, 1915, p. 821.
[63] *Ibid.*, 1917, p. 803.

[64] EXPORTS

(*in millions of £E*)

	Total	Cotton
1910	28.9	24.2
1911	28.6	23.
1912	34.6	27.5
1913	31.7	25.5
	123.8	100.2

[For 1914-21 the corresponding figures were:

	Total	Cotton
1914	24.1	18.7
1915	27.	19.1
1916	37.5	29.8
1917	41.1	33.5
1918	45.4	38.
1919	75.9	65.4
1920	85.5	75.1
1921	36.4	28.4]

Annuaire Statistique, 1914, pp. 290, 291, 308. See also I. G. Lévi, "Le Commerce Extérieur de l'Égypte," in *L'Égypte Contemporaine*, V (1914), pp. 413-418. In 1917, Egypt's exports amounted to £E41,049,612, of which cotton contributed £E33,495,193; cotton seed £E1,818,257; and cotton-seed cake, £E587,691. Department of State, Weekly Reports on Near Eastern Affairs, April 25, 1918, pp. 22, 23.

[65] Milner, "England in Egypt" (7th ed.), pp. 176, 177.

attempt was, on the whole, a failure.   Before 1914, sugar
production was on a declining scale [66] and the crop was
completely dwarfed by cotton, the exports of which exceeded
the value of that of sugar by more than a hundredfold.[67] As
Lord Kitchener said, in 1914, cotton was "the main source
of the riches of the country." [68]   To such an extent was
interest concentrated upon this crop that Egypt, which in
ancient times was an important granary for the outside
world, had to import foodstuffs in increasing measure.[69]

[66] SUGAR OUTPUT IN SACKS OF 100 KILOS

1900-01	920,950
1903-04	665,557
1906-07	416,640
1909-10	553,346

Egypt, No. 1 (1912) (Kitchener), p. 18.

[67] PRODUCTION OF SUGAR CANE IN TONS

1910-11	49,403
1911-12	54,960
1912-13	75,420
1913-14	69,368
1914-15	75,738

EXPORT OF SUGAR CANE

	(*in kantars*) (equal to 99.05 lbs.)	(*in £E*) (equal to $5.00)
1914	13,335,056	229,711
1915	26,734,493	573,610

Annuaire Statistique, 1916, pp. 144, 264.
[68] *Egypt,* No. 1 (1914) (Kitchener), p. 1.

[69] AREA UNDER MAIZE, WHEAT, RICE, ETC.

	Feddans *	Imports of Foodstuffs (*£E*)
1898-99	4,192,000	1,002,000
1912-13	4,248,000	4,242,000

* One feddan equals 1.038 acres.

Annuaire Statistique, 1914, p. xxx. See also *Bulletin of the Imperial
Institute,* 1915, p. 13.

Such absolute dependence upon one staple crop is usually hazardous, but the peril in Egypt's case is reduced almost to a minimum by the fact that the world's potential demand for cotton is increasing faster than is the actual supply, and the Egyptian type of cotton is especially sought after.

The Egyptian Type of Cotton.—The Egyptian cotton industry was established in the early decades of the nineteenth century and received a great impetus during the cotton famine of the American Civil War, when Lancashire was cut off by the blockade from the crop of the Southern States. The hold that Egyptian cotton then gained has never been lost. On the contrary, it has grown stronger as improved spinning methods have rendered possible the manufacture of finer yarns and finer fabrics. Egyptian cotton is of a distinctive type as regards length and strength of fiber, fine quality, and silky texture. The supply of the long-staple West Indian and Sea Island cotton was very small and the Egyptian variety, which ranked next in length of fiber, became increasingly required for the finer products.[70] The revival of mercerizing, some twenty years ago, and the rise of new industries, such as that of automobile tires, which needed strong fabrics, still further increased the demand and raised the price of Egyptian cotton far above that of the American standard type. In 1910, its price was sixty-seven per cent higher than that of American "Middling," and the average excess in the years preceding

[70] John A. Todd, "The World's Cotton Crops," pp. 236-240, London, 1915; Cressaty, *op. cit.*, pp. 38, 39.

the war was fifty-one per cent.[71] The Egyptian crop did
not constitute a large share of the total world supply—only
1,537,000 bales of 500 pounds out of 25,703,000 in 1913-14 [72]
—but the peculiar qualities of the Egyptian staple gave it
almost a monopoly value.[73] While Egyptian cotton has to
face certain dangers, such as the pink boll-worm, its position
and prospects are, on the whole, probably fully as satisfactory as are those of any other crop in the world.[74]

[71] EGYPTIAN COTTON CROP

	Feddans (1.038 acres)	Kantars (99.05 lbs.)	Price in pence	Percentage above American "Middling"
1886	874,615	2,872,000	6.56	28
1896-97	1,050,749	5,879,750	5.31	26
1909-10	1,597,055	5,000,772 *	13.12	67
1910-11	1,642,610	7,573,537	10.75	35
1911-12	1,711,241	7,424,208	9.56	57
1912-13	1,721,815	7,532,920	9.82	46

* A year of flood.

John A. Todd, "The World's Cotton Crops," pp. 294, 295, London, 1915.
[72] *Idem*, "The Cotton Resources of the British Empire," in A. P. Newton.
"The Staple Trades of the Empire," p. 113, London, 1917.
[73] During the first decade of the British Occupation, the cotton crop
increased in size, but the price fell. The crop of 1894 realized no more
than that of 1883, though production had nearly doubled in the interval.
A definite upward tendency set in after 1900, which in a few years doubled
the value of Egypt's exports. The result was considerable inflation and
speculation accompanied by an influx of foreign capital. *Egypt*, No. 1
(1913) (Kitchener), pp. 2, 3.

EXPORTS OF COTTON

Yearly Average	Quantity in Kantars	Value in £E
1899-1901................	6,076,000	12,157,000
1911-13	7,306,000	25,343,000
Increase	20%	109%

Alfred Eid, "La Guerre et ses Conséquences Économiques pour l'Égypte,"
in *L'Égypte Contemporaine*, VII, p. 76. In the *Vossische Zeitung* of
August 5, 1918, Dr. W. Goetze emphasized the dependence of Germany's
textile industry on long-fibered Egyptian cotton, "which is absolutely
essential for the manufacture of a number of the finer kinds of cotton
goods." *The New Europe*, No. 97 (August 22, 1918), p. 138.
[74] The first effect of the war was to cause a severe decline in the price
of cotton which, in turn, led to a decreased output in 1914-15. Despite

[Oil.—The existence of petroleum [75] along the western coast of the Gulf of Suez has long been known, but at the

the subsequent enormous rise in prices, the ante-bellum crops have not been equaled, mainly because the Government adopted measures to decrease the output of cotton and to increase that of grain.

EGYPTIAN COTTON CROP IN BALES OF 500 POUNDS

1913-14	1,537,000
1914-15	1,298,000
1915-16	961,000
1916-17	1,022,000
1917-18	1,300,000

But the rise in prices more than compensated for the deficiency in quantity and raised the value of Egypt's exports to unprecedented heights.

EGYPT'S FOREIGN TRADE

(in millions of £E)

	Imports	*Exports*
August 31, 1913-August 31, 1914	28.3	32.6
" " 1914- " " 1915	15.3	22.6
" " 1915- " " 1916	27.5	29.9
" " 1916- " " 1917	30.	44.6

The shortage of shipping and the submarine campaign in 1917 made it difficult to get this cotton to market. Accordingly, the British and Egyptian Governments bought the entire 1917-18 crop at prices equivalent to double the pre-war values. No one but the Government could buy or export cotton. Arrangements were made so that American manufacturers could secure what they needed, but the British War Trade Board in June, 1918, revoked all the outstanding licenses for the importation of Egyptian cotton in general, though it permitted the importation of the longest staple types up to a total of 80,000 bales in 1918. In this connection, it should be noted that the Egyptian type of cotton is now being produced in Arizona and the neighboring states. In 1916, the American production was 3,331 bales; in 1917, it was 16,000 and the acreage was 35,000. The crop of 1918, on an acreage of 80,000, was estimated at between 40,000 and 50,000 bales. John A. Todd, in A. P. Newton, *op. cit.,* pp. 113, 116; Annual Meeting of the National Bank of Egypt, April 25, 1918, in *The Times* (London), weekly ed., May 10, 1918; *The Near East,* March 22, May 3, August 16, 1918; New York *Evening Sun,* July 20, 1918; *The New York Times,* June 5, 1918; Sir Malcolm McIlwraith, "Egypt in Wartime," in *The Fortnightly Review,* August, 1917, pp. 222-224; see also *The Commercial and Financial Chronicle,* June 22, 1918.

[75] This paragraph has been prepared by the Editor from a memorandum intercalated by the Author in his manuscript.

beginning of the war the sole survivor of the various companies formed to search for it was the Anglo-Egyptian Oilfields, Ltd., founded in 1911, as an offshoot of the Shell Group, to take over the assets of an earlier organization for working a number of additional prospecting claims obtained from the Egyptian Government and for establishing a refinery at Suez. Until 1914, the only important finds were at Gemsa, where several gushers had been struck, but the formation of the field proved very irregular and none of the wells gave a permanent yield. In 1914, however, another field was discovered at Hurghada, and its output, in a singularly regular formation, steadily increased until, in the second half of 1918, it was approximately 200,000 barrels of crude oil per month.[76] To meet the demands of local consumption it is estimated that a daily production of 7,500 barrels is required, thus necessitating the operation of at least 300 wells. Technical experts believe, however, that the Hurghada anticlinal, so far as it has been proved, could barely

---

[76] The total annual production of this field is as follows:

	Barrels
1915	239,827
1916	383,600
1917	941,500
1918 (first six months)	952,000

The three principal wells brought in in 1915-16, Nos. 7. 9, and 13, averaged respectively 1,300, 6,180, and 8,000 barrels weekly. The largest, No. 19, brought in on June 23, 1918, gave a daily flow of 31,000 barrels, but was soon allowed to become choked with sand, the Company claiming that it was impossible to handle all the oil being obtained from the field. It is believed, however, that this well will eventually decline to a flow of about 200 barrels daily and the same is probably true of No. 3, which, after a fair yield since 1916, came in on July 7, 1918, with a daily flow of 11,900 barrels from the deeper level.

support this number. Hence the Company has made urgent representations to the Egyptian Government to be permitted to find, if possible, further territories in which permanent exploitation may be developed. The Company holds exploration rights over large areas, but has been unable to carry out prospecting because of the exceptional conditions which have prevailed, especially as the Egyptian Government desired every effort to be concentrated on production at Hurghada during the period of the war.[77] The Company's refinery at Suez, the only one in Egypt, was so enlarged that by January 1, 1918, it had a capacity of 7,000 barrels daily. It is hoped that in the near future as much oil will be available for internal consumption as can be dealt with by the existing transport facilities of the country and, in consequence, most of the public utilities companies in Egypt have now converted their plants so as to burn petroleum residue. When oil was struck for the first time in great quantities at Hurghada, the Company, believing, with good reason, that a large production would ensue, suggested the use of liquid fuel to the Egyptian State Railways and proposed a contract which should be subject to two years' notice on either side, relying on the holdings of associated companies in other fields, in case the Egyptian supply should fail to materialize. The offer was not accepted, however, the railroads still being operated by coal. Nevertheless, the Egyptian Government is interested in the Company to the

[77] Production was further restricted by lack of storage facilities and shipping, although the situation was somewhat ameliorated when the resources of all the Shell Group were placed at the disposal of the Anglo-Egyptian Oilfields.

extent that it receives sixteen per cent of the profits.[78] Furthermore, all tank cars in the country are the property of the State Railways.[79] The annual consumption (exclusive of the requirements of the Egyptian Expeditionary Force) is 194,200 tons.[80]]

Land Ownership.—Despite the fact that recourse was had to foreign capital in the expensive operation of reclaiming land made available for cultivation by the extension and improvement of the irrigation system, there was little absentee landlordism in Egypt. Most of the country was owned by natives. In 1913, foreigners held only thirteen

[78] The following facilities for storing oil in bulk are to be found in Egyptian ports:

Alexandria
{
6 tanks with a capacity of 35,000 barrels each
1 tank " " " " 32,200 "
1 tank " " " " 28,000 "
3 tanks " " " " 21,000 " "
4 tanks " " " " 1,855 " "
3 tanks " " " " 700 " "
}

Port Said
{
1 tank " " " " 30,489 "
1 tank " " " " 28,555 "
1 tank " " " " 5,939 "
1 tank " " " " 2,644 "
2 tanks " " " " 255 " "
2 tanks " " " " 126 " "
2 tanks " " " " 30 " "
}

Suez
{
20 tanks " " " " 28,000 " "
4 tanks " " " " 7,000 " "
2 tanks " " " " 285 " "
}

[79] These cars are divided as follows:

Capacity	Number for Transporting Refined Oil	Number for Transporting Fuel Oil	Total Number
15 tons	4	21	25
19 "	16	24	40
25 "	38	3	41
30 "	8	4	12
Total	66	52	118

[80] I.e., 2,200 tons of gasoline, 117,000 tons of refined oil, and 75,000 tons of fuel oil.

per cent of the total. The Egyptian peasant-farmer, the *fellah*, has an intense love of the soil and is very keen upon owning the property that he cultivates. Between 1902 and 1913 the number of native landed proprietors increased from 1,019,941 to 1,548,519.[81] The result of this gain has been a corresponding growth in the number of small holdings. In 1913, 1,411,000 proprietors owned less than five *feddans* (about five acres), and of these, 942,000 owned less than one *feddan*.[82] This preponderance of small holdings has its dangers. Improvements in agricultural methods cannot be

[81] EGYPTIAN LAND OWNERSHIP

1902

1,026,081	proprietors owned	5,164,388	feddans
1,019,941	Egyptians owned	4,581,890	feddans
6,140	foreigners owned	582,498	feddans

1913

1,556,310	proprietors owned	5,472,930	feddans
1,548,519	Egyptians owned	4,770,250	feddans
7,791	foreigners owned	702,680	feddans

[1919

1,806,647	proprietors owned	5,511,259	feddans
1,799,238	Egyptians owned	4,883,673	feddans
7,409	foreigners owned	627,586	feddans

1920

1,866,761	proprietors owned	5,535,352	feddans
1,859,745	Egyptians owned	4,982,081	feddans
7,016	foreigners owned	553,271	feddans]

Annuaire Statistique, 1916, pp. 106, 107. [*The Statesman's Year-Book*, 1921, p. 266; 1922, p. 274.]

[82]	Owners of Less than Five Feddans	Owners of Less than One Feddan
1912	1,340,000	871,000
1913	1,411,000	942,000

"Il se produit donc en Égypte un morcellement de plus en plus grand de la propriété foncière." *Annuaire Statistique*, 1914, pp. xxxi, xxxii; *ibid.*, 1916, p. xxii.

[In 1919, however, the number of natives owning less than five *feddans* had fallen to 494,791, while those owning less than one *feddan* had risen to 1,158,681. In 1920, the figures were 504,341 and 1,205,642 respectively. *The Statesman's Year-Book*, 1921, p. 266; 1922, p. 274.]

so readily and so quickly introduced, as the *fellah* has all
the conservatism of both the rustic and the illiterate. Moreover, the small proprietor has generally little reserve financial strength and is apt to be at the mercy of the usurious
money lender. The Egyptian Government, in 1912, adopted
several measures to protect these small holders. Of these,
"the Five Feddan Law" was the most important. It was
based upon East Indian, American, and other precedents
and provided that no holding less than this size was subject
to seizure for mortgage debts. It gave protection to the
small cultivator "against expropriation of his land, house,
and farming utensils for debt" and was aimed against the
petty foreign usurers that had preyed upon the *fellah*.[83]

Handicaps.—While the material development of Egypt
since 1882 has been strikingly rapid and sound, there is
a dark side to the picture. So great an increase in population has marked drawbacks. The Malthusian Law still holds
true for many Eastern countries, such as India and Egypt,
and the fact that the inhabitants tend to increase almost
as rapidly as the means of subsistence renders it exceedingly
difficult to raise the general standard of life. Every addition
to the aggregate social income tends to stimulate the growth
of population in almost equal measure. Hence, while as
an entity Egypt's condition has been virtually transformed
since 1882, the improvement in the case of the individual
Egyptian is decidedly less marked. The *fellah* has been
freed from onerous and uncertain taxation, from tyrannical
and corrupt misgovernment; his general welfare has been

---

[83] *Egypt*, No. 1 (1913) (Kitchener), pp. 4, 23, 49-51; John A. Todd, "The
World's Cotton Crops," pp. 296, 297, London, 1915.

greatly improved, but his standard of life is still very low according to the standpoint of the West. It is quite easy to state the facts' but surpassingly difficult to find the remedy. It may possibly consist in a more widespread and thorough system of education. Since Egypt has been placed upon a sound economic and financial basis, more and more attention has been paid to the general education of the people. The number of schools and of pupils has increased rapidly. But much still remains to be done, as general illiteracy is very marked.[84] The path is, however, not without serious thorns, nor is the remedy a sovereign one. Extensive education is in a measure futile if it leaves the *fellah* with no other prospect than that of his daily task in the field. In all probability, Egypt will continue to be, in the main, a land of comparatively poor and ignorant, but

[84] *The Statesman's Year-Book*, 1917, pp. 254-256 [1921, pp. 260-262; 1922, pp. 268-270]; *Annuaire Statistique*, 1914, p. xxiv; 1916, pp. 49-56; 1917, pp. 22, 23, 24-25. In 1914-15, the number of native (*maktab*) and foreign schools in Egypt, with their pupils, was as follows:

	Number	Boys	Girls	Total
Maktabs	7,590	339,900	42,240	382,140
Other	1,130	117,797	37,333	155,130
Total	8,720	457,697	79,573	537,270

The educational estimates for 1918-19 were £E578,733, an increase of £E110,975 over the pre-war level. *The Near East*, June 14, 1918, p. 472. [Lord Milner's mission found that "another contributory cause of the general discontent [in Egypt] was the manifest insuccess of educational policy resulting in the production of an unnecessarily large and ever-increasing number of candidates for official posts, provided with examination certificates, but destitute of any real educational culture. . . . Education, for which there is a real and crying demand among the people, remains atrophied. The mass of the population is not only still illiterate, but without social or moral training. . . . In spite of these criticisms, however, it must be admitted that the general level of instruction has greatly advanced since the early years of the Occupation, and that the number of those taking an intelligent interest in public affairs is very much larger to-day." *Egypt*, No. 1 (1921), pp. 9, 10.]

fairly comfortable and contented, peasants until, at some future time, modern industries are introduced and Egypt begins to spin some of the cotton that it produces. That time is apparently not at hand and will be near only when the world's supply of cotton approaches the potential demand. So long as Egyptian cotton commands a high price, it will be more remunerative to raise the raw product and to exert every energy to increasing the size of the crop. In the meanwhile, however, an ever greater amount is being spent on technical education, and a movement is on foot to stimulate industry by enlarging such training and by establishing protected duties.[85]

[85] See the Report of the Commission of Commerce and Industry created in March, 1916, under the presidency of Ismail Sidky Pasha. In addition to reforms in the tariff, an extension of professional education, the exemption of Egyptian industries from all excises unless countervailing customs were imposed on similar imported goods, the reduction of transportation rates on Egyptian manufactures, this commission recommended increased industrial and technical education. *The Near East,* June 7, 1918, p. 471; July 5, 1918, p. 552; July 26, 1918, p. 613.

CHAPTER II

1. Internal System

The Khedive and the Ministers.—The head of the Egyptian Government was the Khedive, whose position theoretically was that of an absolute monarch. In practice, however, his powers of administration were limited by the fact that he ruled through Ministers, who were responsible for his acts. Apart from the British control, the Khedive's freedom of choice of these Ministers was to some considerable extent restricted by public opinion. As in nearly all modern States, the administration was divided into departments—Interior, Finance, Education, Justice, Agriculture, Pious Foundations, Public Works, and War—and at the head of each was a Minister.[1] While executive and legislative authority resided in the Khedive and the Ministers, representative institutions had been introduced in both the local and the central governments.

The Legislative Council and General Assembly.—Representative bodies of a consultative nature had existed before the British Occupation. As Lord Kitchener pointed out in his valuable Report for 1913, the villages from time immemorial had elected their Sheikhs and in all matters of

---

[1] The Departments of Agriculture and Pious Foundations (*Wakfs*) were established only in 1913. *Egypt*, No. 1 (1914) (Kitchener), p. 1.

internal economy had been governed by them.[2] In Mehemet
Ali's reign (1811-48), a Council of Village Sheikhs and other
provincial notables was created. This fell into decline, but
under Ismail Pasha, the Chamber of Notables was revived.
Shortly after the British Occupation, a distinguished diplomat and statesman, Lord Dufferin, was sent to Egypt to
report on the measures that were necessary in order that
"the administration of affairs should be reconstructed on a
basis which would afford satisfactory guarantees for the
maintenance of peace, order, and prosperity in Egypt, for
the stability of the Khedive's authority, for the judicious
development of self-government, and for the fulfillment of
obligations towards the Powers."[3] Dufferin realized that
the Arabist movement had distinctly popular and national
elements in it. He eloquently expressed this view in his
famous dispatch, advocating the establishment of a Legislative Council and a General Assembly.[4] These bodies were

[2] *Egypt*, No. 1 (1914) (Kitchener), pp. 2-6.
[3] Cromer, "Modern Egypt," I, pp. 340, 341. On Dufferin's Mission, see
Sir A. C. Lyall, "Life of the Marquis of Dufferin and Ava," II, pp. 31-51,
London, 1905; D. Mackenzie Wallace, "Egypt and the Egyptian Question,"
pp. 419-450; W. S. Blunt, "Secret History of the English Occupation of
Egypt," pp. 460-480; Sir Auckland Colvin, "The Making of Modern
Egypt," pp. 24-37.
[4] On February 6, 1883, Dufferin wrote to Lord Granville: "Though obliged
to admit that those infirmities of character which have been the chief
notes of their past still cling to the Egyptian masses, we need not be too
much disheartened. The metamorphic spirit of the age, as evoked by the
inventions of science, intercourse with European countries, and other
invigorating influences, have already done something to inspire the fellah
with the rudiments of self-respect, and a dim conception of hitherto un-
imagined possibilities. Nor, like his own Memnon, has he remained
irresponsive to the beams of the new dawn. His lips have trembled, if
they have not articulated, and in many indirect and half unconscious
ways he has shown himself not only equal to the discharge of some of
those functions of which none but the members of the most civilized
communities were thought capable, but unexpectedly appreciative of his
legitimate political interests and moral rights." *Egypt*, No. 6 (1883), p. 42.

accordingly created. By manhood suffrage the villagers elected representatives who, in turn, elected Provincial Councils. These, then, elected fourteen men who, together with twelve members nominated by the Khedive on the advice of his Ministers, constituted the Legislative Council. This Council had the right to examine the budget and legislative projects and to give its opinion on them, but the Government was not bound to accept this advice. In other words, this Legislative Council was merely an advisory body. The General Assembly, established also in 1883, consisted of eighty members—eight Ministers, the twenty-six members of the Legislative Council, and forty-six other delegates elected by the representatives of the villages. This body had nothing to do with legislation, but no public loans could be contracted and no fresh general taxes could be imposed without its concurrence.

The Organic Law of 1913.—These institutions were, in the opinion of all parties, a failure. As Lord Cromer said, they did not prove a success either as "factors in the government of the country or [as] efficient instruments to help in administrative and fiscal reform." [5] Hence, in 1913, a revised Organic Law was promulgated, establishing in the place of these two bodies a new Legislative Assembly on a fresh electoral basis, which provided a more equally distributed and more comprehensive representation of the people.[6] This new Assembly consisted

[5] Cromer, "Modern Egypt," I, p. 343.
[6] *Egypt,* No. 3 and No. 3a (1913), contain the French text and the English translation of this law, which to some extent lessened the opposition of the Nationalists to the British Occupation. *Revue des Sciences Politiques,* 33 (1915), p. 320.

of eighty-nine members, of whom sixty-six were elected. The Cabinet Ministers belonged to it by virtue of their office and the Government also nominated seventeen members in order to give certain classes and races a minimum representation. Thus, the Copts were always to have four members; the Bedouins three; the merchants and doctors each two; and the engineers one. The sixty-six elected representatives were selected by indirect suffrage. The new registry included two million voters, who, in blocks of fifty, chose delegates. These, then, elected the members of the new Assembly. The legislative powers of this body were, however, restricted. It was empowered to initiate projects of law, but the Ministry was free to reject them. On the other hand, all enactments emanating from the Executive had to be laid before the Assembly by the Ministry. If the Assembly disapproved, a conference had to be held, and if there were no agreement, the law could again be submitted after an interval of fifteen days. If then again there was no agreement, the Government might either dissolve the Assembly or promulgate the law in dispute, but only after explaining to the Assembly the reasons for such action. Thus, the ultimate word still rested with the Khedive and the laws were still Khedivial decrees.[7]

Constitutional Development.—This development of representative institutions in Egypt was intimately connected with the movement against autocratic government in neighboring Mohammedan countries during the first decade of the twentieth century. In fact, the whole Eastern world—

---

[7] *Egypt*, No. 1 (1914) (Kitchener), pp. 6, 7; Sir Sidney Low, "Egypt in Transition," pp. 265-268.

China, India, and the Philippines—not alone Turkey and
Persia, was demanding more popular government and was
trying constitutional experiments. Public opinion in Egypt
was deeply affected. The great mass of the people, it is
true, continued engrossed in their wonted agricultural pur-
suits and remained profoundly unconcerned with political
issues, but it was decidedly otherwise among the better
educated classes, who had manifested increasing interest in
questions of government and administration. In this connection, Sir Eldon Gorst, who in 1907 succeeded Lord
Cromer as British Agent and Consul-General, wrote in
1909:

"This class aspires, quite rightly, to help in bringing
about the day when Egypt will be able to govern herself
without outside assistance. This is also the end to which
British policy is directed, and there need, therefore, be no
antagonism of principle between the Egyptian and English
reforming elements." [8]

Gorst, who fully sympathized with these aspirations, concluded, however, that Egypt was not as yet ripe for constitutional and parliamentary government, and this is also
the general opinion of all careful students of the problem.
It is impossible as yet to determine the success or the failure
of the constitutional experiment of 1913.[9] But the question
arises as to whether it would not be a better training

---

[8] *Egypt,* No. 1 (1909) (Gorst), p. 1. [For an excellent survey of Egyptian nationalism in all its shades and manifestations, see the Report of
Lord Milner's Mission, *Egypt,* No. 1 (1921), pp. 15-18.]
[9] The Legislative Assembly opened in January, 1914, and passed several
measures dealing with administrative reform and questions of economy.
As a result of the war, its operations were suspended. George Peel,
"Egypt," in *The New Europe,* No. 68 (January 31, 1918), pp. 84, 85.

towards ultimate complete self-government to adopt the policy that is now being considered in connection with British India [10] and to give the Egyptian Legislature complete control over some departments of administration with the idea of ultimately extending these powers until they include the whole field of government. The Egyptian problem differs greatly from that of India, but in both cases it is true that only by the assumption of full responsibility for measures can those qualities of character and mind be developed that are essential to efficient self-government.[11] This question is largely, almost entirely, independent of whether Egypt shall ultimately become one of the numerous small sovereign states so disturbing to the peace of the world or shall evolve into a completely self-governing unit in the British Commonwealth of Nations that is being established.

2. British Control

The Authority of the British Agent.—While the final legislative and executive authority rested with the Khedive

[10] Report of Mr. E. S. Montagu and Lord Chelmsford on Indian Constitutional Reforms, April 22, 1918 (Cd. 9109); Lionel Curtis, "Letters to the People of India on Responsible Government," London, 1918.

[11] There has also been a considerable extension of local self-government in Egypt. The Organic Law of 1883 suppressed the five local Agricultural Councils of 1871 and substituted for them Provincial Councils which consisted of the Governor of the Province as President, the Irrigation Officer of the Province *ex officio* and one representative of each District. Their functions were, however, not important and in 1909 they were reorganized. Under the new system they raise local taxes and have elevated the educational standards in the elementary schools. The establishment of adequate municipal institutions has been rendered very difficult by the fact that the consent of the foreign Powers is necessary to measures imposing taxation upon their citizens and subjects resident in Egypt. In 1890, however, their consent was obtained to the creation of the municipality of Alexandria. *Egypt*, No. 1 (1914) (Kitchener), pp. 4, 5. In 1918, village councils were established. *The Near East*, March 4, April 19, 1918.

acting through his Ministers, the real power behind the throne was the -British Government. Beyond the small British garrison and the comparatively few Englishmen in the Egyptian Civil Service and in the Egyptian Army, no external indications of this fact were evident. Judged by surface appearances and by outward forms, the British Agent and Consul-General was merely one among the many foreign diplomatic representatives at Cairo. He had no precedence over his fellows in the diplomatic corps, and took his place among them according to seniority of appointment. In reality, he was the actual ruler of the country. The basis for this control was established early in the Occupation. On January 3, 1883, the British Foreign Secretary, Lord Granville, informed the Great Powers that, although for the present a British force remained in Egypt to preserve public tranquillity, yet the British Government were desirous of withdrawing it as soon as the state of the country permitted. In the meantime, he added, upon the British Government was imposed

"the duty of giving advice, with the object of securing that the order of things to be established shall be of a satisfactory character, and possess the elements of stability and progress." [12]

A year later, when the Khedive and his Ministry manifested some disinclination to follow the counsel of the British representatives, Lord Granville gave a vigorous interpretation of the word "advice" and made it virtually synonymous with "command." On January 4, 1884, he wrote officially to Sir Evelyn Baring, the future Lord Cromer:

[12] Milner, "England in Egypt" (7th ed.), p. 27.

"I hardly need point out that in important questions, where the administration and safety of Egypt are at stake, it is indispensable that Her Majesty's Government should, so long as the provisional occupation of the country by English troops continues, be assured that the advice which, after full consideration of the views of the Egyptian Government, they may feel it their duty to tender to the Khedive, should be followed. It should be made clear to the Egyptian Ministers and Governors of provinces, that the responsibility which for the time rests on England obliges Her Majesty's Government to insist on the adoption of the policy which they recommend, and that it will be necessary that those Ministers and Governors who do not follow this course should cease to hold their offices." [13]

Nine years later, in 1893, when the young Khedive, Abbas Hilmi, shortly after his accession, dismissed his Prime Minister without consulting the British Agent, this principle was again explicitly enunciated. Lord Rosebery telegraphed as follows to Lord Cromer:

"Her Majesty's Government expect to be consulted in such important matters as a change of Ministers. No change appears to be at present necessary or peremptory. We cannot, therefore, sanction the proposed nomination of Fakhry Pasha." [14]

Authoritative Advice.—Thus the counsel given by the British Government could not be ignored. As Sir Sidney Low has aptly said, the British control was "government

---

[13] *Egypt*, No. 1 (1884), p. 176; *Egypt*, No. 1 (1893), p. 11; Milner, *op. cit.*, p. 27; Colvin, "The Making of Modern Egypt," p. 49.

[14] *Egypt*, No. 1 (1893), p. 4; Cromer, "Abbas II," p. 24. The reappointment of the dismissed Prime Minister was not insisted on, but the Khedive, as one of the conditions of the settlement, signed a declaration dictated by Lord Cromer that "he would always most willingly adopt the advice of Her Majesty's Government on all questions of importance in the future." *Ibid.*, p. 27. See also Lord Rosebery's dispatch to Lord Cromer, February 16, 1893. *Egypt*, No. 2 (1893).

by inspection and authoritative advice." [15] This "authoritative advice," a phrase of Lord Rosebery, was, however, limited to important measures and policies and was not meddlesome in character. The actual administration was left predominantly in Egyptian hands. The heads of the governmental sections were all Egyptians, but in the chief departments were placed British advisers, whose function it was to see that the administration was efficient and honest. Of these officials, the most important was the financial adviser, who was distinguished from his colleagues by having a seat in the Council of Ministers. Though he had no vote there, yet as the British Government had laid down the rule that "no financial decision should be taken without his consent," he had a power of veto over nearly everything. In the words of Lord Milner, "the financial adviser is the corner-stone of English influence inside the Egyptian Administration." [16] The smooth working of this system depended largely upon the personal qualities of these British advisers and their chiefs. The suggestions of the advisers were not invariably adopted and not infrequently the initiative proceeded from the nominal head of the department. In case of disagreement, the adviser might yield, but if the matter were of importance he could appeal to the British Agent who, provided that in the light of all the facts he deemed it desirable, would step in and secure the execution of the measure in dispute. In this aspect, the

---

[15] Sir Sidney Low, "Egypt in Transition," p. 233. The phrase, "authoritative advice" was used by Lord Rosebery in his dispatch of January 17, 1893, to Lord Dufferin, regarding Lord Granville's dispatch of January 4, 1884. *Egypt*, No. 1 (1893), p. 5.

[16] Milner, *op. cit.*, p. 86. See also Cromer, "Modern Egypt," II, pp. 286 ff.

system was one of "authoritative advice." Its authoritative character naturally varied under the three successive British Agents and Consuls-General.[17]

Inspection.—In addition, there were a number of British inspectors attached to the Ministries of Finance and the Interior, whose function it was to travel throughout the country in order to see that the measures of the central government were actually executed and that well conceived projects were not nullified by the local authorities. Besides these British Advisers and Inspectors—comparatively few all told—a number of British subjects were employed in various departments, especially in the irrigation and railroad administrations where technical skill was required. As all of these officials were employees of the Egyptian Government, they occupied a somewhat anomalous position. As Egyptian officials, they were bound by the immunities that the Christian Powers had secured in Egypt and as Christians themselves they had to be most careful in dealing with matters that in any way affected the religion of Islam.[18]

---

[17] Under Lord Cromer's successor, Sir Eldon Gorst, "British guidance was reduced to a minimum, and the Egyptian Ministers, as also their principal subordinates, were made to feel that they must act on their own responsibility and to the best of their judgment." A serious dislocation ensued and some abuses were revived. "As events turned out," Lord Cromer wrote, "the general result of the experiment was to put back the hands of the political clock. Egyptian autonomy, far from gaining, rather lost ground. . . . It soon became apparent that it would be necessary to revert to the system of vigilant and active British supervision, and more direct interference on the part of the representative of the British Government." A reaction set in under Lord Kitchener and the government became more personal than at any time since 1882. Cromer, "Abbas II," pp. xiv-xvi. See also Cromer, "Political and Literary Essays 1908-1913," pp. 253 ff., London, 1913.

[18] "Lord Cromer and the staff of British officials are thus blocked re-

The Number of British Officials.—The total of these British officials was not large and their numbers were not increasing disproportionately to the expansion of governmental activities.[19] In 1896, the Egyptian Civil Service contained 286 British officials, and in 1906, 662. The increase was mainly in the railway administration. At the former date, the Civil Service included 9,134 employees all told; at the latter, 13,279.[20] In this connection, it should be noted that the employment of Europeans in Egypt was not the result of the British Occupation, but had been extensively resorted to by Mehemet Ali and his successors in their attempts to modernize Egypt.[21] In 1906, in addition to 662 British officials in the Civil Service, there were 590 other Europeans. The situation has apparently not

spectively by the Capitulations and the Shariyeh, and find themselves, in nautical parlance, between the devil and the deep sea." Colvin, *op. cit.,* p. 238.

[19] "The English staff, in most Egyptian Ministries, is a comparatively small proportion of the whole. The guiding principle of British civilian administration in Egypt has, indeed, always been merely to leaven the mass of native officials with a comparatively small number of picked Englishmen." Sir Malcolm McIlwraith, "Egypt in Wartime" in *The Fortnightly Review,* August, 1917, p. 228.

[20] EGYPTIAN CIVIL SERVICE

	1896		1906	
Egyptians		8,444		12,027
Europeans:				
British	286		662	
Others	404		590	
		690		1,252
Totals		9,134		13,279

Egypt, No. 1 (1907) (Cromer), pp. 36 ff.; Cromer, "Modern Egypt," II, pp. 294, 295.

[21] In 1882, there were in the service of the Egyptian Government 1,325 Europeans and Americans, of whom 348 were Italians, 326 French, 174 British and 94 British protégés, 115 Greeks, and 101 Austrians. *Egypt,* No. 4 (1882), p. 2. For further details, see also *Egypt,* No. 6 (1882).

altered appreciably since that time.[22] Lord Cromer, in
an illuminating and characteristic passage about modern
British Imperialism, has pointed out that the Englishman

[22] George Peel, "Egypt," in *The New Europe*, No. 68 (January 31, 1918),
p. 86. Exact figures for more recent years are not available at the time of
writing. In addition, the Commander-in-Chief of the Egyptian Army,
the Sirdar, was British and a number of British officers served in it. In
1916, the Egyptian Army was constituted as follows:

Officers:

British	155
Egyptian	750
	905
Other Ranks	17,679
Total	18,584

Annuaire Statistique, 1916, p. 34. There were in all Egypt 8,290 police-
men with 434 officers; and of the officers only sixty-two were British.
Sir Sidney Low, *op. cit.*, p. 244.

[In 1920, omitting the seven ministerial posts, the staff of the Sultan's
Cabinet, the Council of Ministers, the Legislative Assembly, and the
Ministry of *Wakfs* (Pious Foundations), in which the offices were held
almost exclusively by Egyptians, natives had 86 per cent of the positions
and drew 71 per cent of the salaries, British held 6 per cent and drew
19 per cent, others held 8 per cent and drew 10 per cent. Of posts between
£E240 and £E499, Egyptians held about two-thirds; of those between
£E500 and £E799, a little over one-third; between £E800 and £E3,000,
less than one-quarter. The Egyptian share in posts between £E1,200
and £E1,499 is over one-third, due to the fact that the Ministries of
Interior and Justice provide *Mudirs* (Provincial Governors) and Judges.
The higher posts of the Ministries of Finance, Education, Public Works,
Agriculture and Communications, however, had only thirty-one Egyptians
as against one hundred and sixty-eight British and thirty-two others
holding posts over £E800. "Doubtless in these particular Ministries
there are many higher posts requiring special technical qualifications
which it is impossible at the moment to find Egyptians qualified to fill.
If, however, Egyptians are to be responsible for the internal administration of their country, it is essential that better provision should be made
for training them to occupy such higher posts. . . . In the total of posts
the Egyptian element has grown from 45.1 per cent in 1905 to 50.5 per
cent in 1920. Egyptians in lower posts have also increased from 48.4
per cent of the total in 1905 to 55 per cent in 1920. But in the higher
posts their number has declined from 27.7 per cent in 1905 to only 23.1
per cent in 1920, while in the same category the British share of posts
has increased from 42.2 per cent to 59.3 per cent of the total." *Egypt*,
No. 1 (1921) (Milner), p. 30, note.]

"is in truth always striving to attain two ideals, which are apt to be mutually destructive—the ideal of good government, which connotes the continuance of his own supremacy, and the ideal of self-government, which connotes the whole or partial abdication of his supreme position. Moreover, although after rather a dim, slipshod, but characteristically Anglo-Saxon fashion, he is aware that empire must rest on one of two bases—an extensive military occupation or the principle of nationality—he cannot in all cases quite make up his mind which of the two bases he prefers." [23]

During his own twenty-four years of virtual rule in Egypt, Cromer sought to keep the British staff down to a minimum, despite the recognized fact that it was clearly at the expense of full efficiency.[24] In some cases, in pursuance of the principle that the Egyptians must themselves be led to learn by experience the problems of government, serious abuses were even allowed to continue until public opinion realized their gravity and was prepared for the necessary reforms.[25]

[23] Cromer, "Ancient and Modern Imperialism," p. 118, London, 1910.
[24] *Idem*, "Modern Egypt," II, pp. 294, 295. In 1906, Brodrick told Morley that Cromer had said that "in Egypt with him a standing principle had been to employ a Native wherever it was at all possible, in spite of the fact that the Native was comparatively inefficient, and that a European would do it a vast deal better." Morley, "Recollections," II, p. 169, London, 1917.
[25] There was very marked irregularity in the management of the religious and charitable endowments, the estates of minors, etc., known as *Wakfs*, until Kitchener took the matter out of the hands of the Khedive. The administration of some of these trust funds by Abbas Hilmi was highly corrupt and his financial transactions since his deposition in 1914 show that he had inherited from his grandfather the financial ineptitude and irresponsibility that allowed Ismail Pasha to become the prey of plausible adventurers. Cromer, "Abbas II," pp. 70 ff.; Sir Malcolm McIlwraith, "The Mohammedan Law-Courts of Egypt," in *The Nineteenth Century and After*, October, 1916, pp. 747, 748; Aldo Cassuto, "An Eastern Rabagas," in *The New Europe*, No. 79 (April 18, 1918); *The New York Times*, July 5, 1918. [For a criticism of the whole system of administration, see Chirol, "The Egyptian Problem," pp. 206-220.]

3. Basis of the Occupation in International Law

The Treaties of 1885 and 1887.—From the standpoint of international law, the position of Great Britain in Egypt was decidedly anomalous. There was no avowed protectorate, but in reality a very effective one had been established. Whatever purely legal basis the British Occupation had was derived from its indirect acknowledgment by Turkey in 1885 and from a similar recognition on the part of France and other Great Powers in 1904. In 1885, Great Britain concluded a treaty with the Porte, by which it was provided that, after the safety of the frontiers and the stability of the Egyptian Government had been assured, a future agreement regarding the withdrawal of the British troops should be drawn up. Such a treaty was negotiated in 1887 and provided for evacuation at the end of three years, if conditions were then satisfactory. But as this document recognized Great Britain's right of reëntry in case of fresh disorder, France and Russia strongly objected and succeeded in inducing the Porte to withhold final signature.[26] The essential legal point is that by the Treaty of 1885 [27] Egypt's suzerain, Turkey, recognized the British Occupation. As the British diplomat, Sir H. Drummond Wolff, who negotiated this agreement, stated, it was the only official document that regulated Great Britain's rela-

---

[26] Milner, "England in Egypt" (7th ed.), pp. 117-125; Colvin, "The Making of Modern Egypt" (3d ed.), pp. 143-157.

[27] The text of the Convention of October 24, 1885, is in *Egypt,* No. 1 (1886), pp. 37-39 [and in Noradounghian, "Recueil d'Actes Internationaux de l'Empire Ottoman," IV, pp. 364-366]. That of the Treaty of 1887 is in Noradounghian, IV, pp. 426-429.

tions with Egypt.[28]   At the time of its negotiation, he wrote
to Lord Salisbury that this Convention

"recognizes and adopts the fact of our occupation with
the same publicity, and the Sultan as Sovereign of Egypt
and Caliph of his religion thus solemnly calls on his temporal and spiritual subjects to concur in the measures which
will be jointly recommended.   Both the legitimate sovereignty and the *de facto* occupation are acknowledged, and
the forces of both are to be utilized for the purposes of a
permanent settlement." [29]

The argument is not entirely convincing.   Nubar Pasha,
one of modern Egypt's two eminent statesmen, it is true,
considered this treaty "the title-deed" of the British Occupation, but it unquestionably was not a flawless one in
law.

The Declarations of 1904.—The European Powers also
had a legal voice in this matter, both because they had
guaranteed the integrity of the Ottoman Empire and also
because they had secured Egypt's administrative independence from Turkey in 1841.[30]   The Treaty of 1885 had met
with their approval,[31] and they were to some extent bound
by it.   But as the ultimate evacuation proposed in it was
constantly postponed, France showed her annoyance at
Great Britain's continued occupation of Egypt and sought

---

[28] Sir H. D. Wolff, "Rambling Recollections," II, p. 287, London, 1908.
[29] Wolff to Salisbury, October 24, 1885. *Egypt,* No. 1 (1886), p. 39.
[30] For the Firman of February 13, 1841, conferring the hereditary government of Egypt on Mehemet Ali, see Noradounghian, *op. cit.,* II, pp.
320-323; for that of even date conferring on him the administration of
Nubia, Darfur, Kordofan, and Sennar, *ibid.,* pp. 323-334; for that of May 13,
1841, replacing the Firman of three months earlier, *ibid.,* pp. 335-337; and
for that of May 23, 1841, fixing the amount of the Egyptian tribute, *ibid.,*
p. 338.]
[31] Wolff, *op. cit.,* II, p. 288.

by every means to hamper her action there. This situation continued until the establishment of the Entente Cordiale in 1904. All the outstanding Anglo-French difficulties, including the Egyptian one, were then settled. In the Declaration of April 8, 1904, the British Government stated "that they had no intention of altering the political status of Egypt" and the French Government, on their side, agreed not to "obstruct the action of Great Britain in that country by asking that a limit of time be fixed for the British Occupation or in any other manner." [32] Subsequently in this year, declarations to the same effect were made by Russia, Italy, Germany, and Austria-Hungary.[33] This unquestionably constituted recognition, even though its character was negative. More was impossible, in view of the fact that Great Britain was not prepared to sever the ties binding Egypt to Turkey by establishing a formal protectorate.

The Anglo-Egyptian Sudan.—The legal irregularity of the British position in Egypt was further emphasized, but at the same time also its practical foundations were strengthened, by the reconquest of the Sudan. When, in 1898, this country was freed from Dervish barbarism by joint British and Egyptian military forces and at the expense of both exchequers,[34] its future status had to be determined. If the Sudan had been incorporated in Egypt, the

---

[32] Article I of Declaration of April 8, 1904. Treaty Series, 1905, No. 6 ["Trattati . . . relativi all'Africa," pp. 1116-1131]. See also Lord Lansdowne's explanatory dispatch of April 8, 1904, to Sir E. Monson. *France,* No. 1 (1904).

[33] Hansard, 1904, pp. 1351, 1352; *Egypt,* No. 1 (1905) (Cromer), p. 4.

[34] The reconquest of the Sudan cost £E2,354,354, of which the British Government contributed £E725,641. Included in this total cost were £E1,181,372 spent on railroads, £E154,934 on gunboats and £E21,825 on telegraphs. Colvin, *op. cit.,* p. 285.

Capitulations would immediately have applied there. But the British administrators desired above all things to avoid this, as they had had unfortunate experience with the hampering effect of these foreign immunities in Egypt. Hence Lord Cromer conceived the idea of attaching the Sudan jointly to the British Empire and to Egypt. The project was worked out in suitable legal phraseology by Sir Malcolm McIlwraith and was accepted by Lord Salisbury, who, according to Lord Cromer, "joyfully agreed to the creation of a hybrid state of a nature eminently calculated to shock the susceptibilities of international jurists." [35] The Treaty of 1899 between Great Britain and Egypt provided that "the British and Egyptian flags shall be used together, both on land and water, throughout the Sudan." The supreme military and civil command in the Sudan was entrusted to an officer, called the Governor General, who was to be appointed by the Khedive on the recommendation of the British Government and who was to be removable by the Khedive only with the consent of that Government.[36] It is impossible to define the exact status of the Anglo-Egyptian Sudan according to this agreement. Legally, it is under the joint sovereignty of Great Britain and Egypt. It is thus more than a mere condominium.

[35] Cromer's Introduction to Sir Sidney Low's "Egypt in Transition," pp. xii, xiii.

[36] Hertslet, "The Map of Africa by Treaty" (3d ed.), II, pp. 620-622. Suakin was at first excepted from this joint arrangement, but on July 10, 1899, it was removed from the Egyptian to the Anglo-Egyptian jurisdiction. *Ibid.*, p. 622. [See also "Trattati . . . relativi all'Africa," pp. 610-612, 622. By Article 113 of the Treaty of Sèvres, "the High Contracting Parties declare and place on record that they have taken note" of these documents; and by Article 114, "Soudanese shall be entitled when in foreign countries to British diplomatic and consular protection."]

But as Egypt was a part of the Ottoman Empire, the Sudan legally formed a portion both of this Empire and of the British Empire. Actually, it had no political connection with Turkey. It was administered like a British Crown Colony, in its own interests, but in subordination to the imperative need of Egypt for the waters of the Nile. The very fact, however, that it was a joint colony of Great Britain and Egypt further strengthened the political ties between these two countries and reinforced the British position in Egypt itself.[37]

[After careful study of the problem, the Milner Commission of 1920 reached the conclusion that, whatever the ultimate political status of the Sudan might be, it must not be subject to its northern neighbor, from which it is entirely distinct both in character and in constitution. Unlike Egypt, whose population is relatively homogeneous, the Sudan is divided ethnically between Arabs and Negroids, its tribes differing widely and often being mutually antagonistic. Political bonds connecting the two regions have always been fragile and the Sudan has never really been conquered by Egypt, much less amalgamated with her. The present system of administration, which is virtually in British hands, has won the approval of the Sudanese and has made for their progress in all respects; but a centralized bureaucratic government is eminently unsuitable, especially as the country's immediate need is material development. Every measure must be taken to prevent any such diversion of the waters of the Nile in their long course through the

[37 For the status fixed by the Peace Conference, recognizing "the Protectorate proclaimed over Egypt on December 18, 1914," see *infra*, p. 445.]

Sudan as might diminish either the cultivable or the re-claimable areas in Egypt; but while the contiguity of the two countries and their common interest in the Nile make some political nexus desirable, the Sudan, for which the Egyptian Government should be relieved of all financial responsibility, "is capable of and entitled to independent development in accordance with its own character and re-quirements."] [38]

[[38] *Egypt,* No. 1 (1921), pp. 32-34.]

CHAPTER III

1. Relations with the Porte

Legal Status of Egypt.—In itself, this combination of a visible Egyptian Government with an effective British control in the background was quite a complicated system, but it was rendered even more involved by the fact that Egyptian autonomy was greatly curtailed both by the suzerainty of the Porte and by foreign immunities and jurisdictions within its confines. Jurists have never been able to agree whether Egypt was a simple province of the Ottoman Empire under the administration of an hereditary government, or a semi-sovereign state, or a distinct state, though one that was vassal and tributary to Turkey. Most jurists, as well as most publicists, have adhered to the third view.[1] The discussion was largely academic, the essential point being that in actual fact Egypt was, in the words of Nubar Pasha, not a real government at all. This distinguished Egyptian statesman of Armenian origin frequently said: "Ce n'est pas un gouvernement; c'est une administration." [2] Entirely apart from the fact of British control,

---

[1] Constant Dahan, "La Question de la Nationalité en Égypte," in *L'Égypte Contemporaine*, VII, pp. 355-357. Sir Malcolm McIlwraith, "The Declaration of a Protectorate in Egypt and its Legal Effects," in *Journal of Society of Comparative Legislation*, November, 1917, pp. 249, 250.

[2] Lord Cromer's comment on this statement reads as follows: "This is

Egypt's freedom of action in both external and internal affairs was greatly restricted. In neither field did she enjoy anything like full sovereignty.

Turkish Suzerainty.—In 1840, when the Porte's unruly vassal, Mehemet Ali, who had successfully established his power in Egypt, appeared to be on the point of overthrowing the Ottoman Empire itself, a group of the European Powers—Great Britain, Russia, Austria, and Prussia—interfered and forced a settlement. France at first held aloof, but in 1841 adhered to this arrangement.[3] Its details were not dictated by the Concert of Europe, but they were prepared under their supervision and amended to suit their wishes, and its general principles were an expression of their will.[4] This agreement was embodied in a Firman issued by the Porte in 1841 to Mehemet Ali, constituting Egypt a Pashalic or Viceroyalty, hereditary in his family. In return, the country was bound to pay to the Porte a fixed yearly tribute of £T400,000, or about £360,000. This action was taken under the sanction of the Powers, who thus became the moral sponsors for the new status of Egypt. Without their consent, the rights granted to Egypt could not be in-

---

quite true. The Khedive is deprived by the Egyptian constitutional charter of all rights of external sovereignty, neither does he possess to the full those rights of internal sovereignty which are inherent in the rulers of all independent, and even of some semi-independent states." Cromer, "Modern Egypt," II, p. 262.

[3] C. de Freycinet, "La Question d'Égypte," pp. 61-93; A. S. White, "The Expansion of Egypt," pp. 54-56.

[4] The successive changes in the arrangements of 1840-41 can be followed in the documents printed in Noradounghian, "Recueil d'Actes Internationaux de l'Empire Ottoman," II, pp. 303-338. See also *Egypt,* No. 4 (1879), pp. 1, 2. This Parliamentary Paper gives the text of the Firmans from 1841 to 1873, together with the British diplomatic correspondence regarding them.

fringed or lessened.[5] Thus the country in 1841 became in an administrative sense largely independent of Turkey. Subsequently, this measure of autonomy was greatly increased, but never to the extent of severing Egypt from the Ottoman Empire.

International Status.—As a part of the Ottoman Empire, Egypt had no independent international standing. Turkey represented her in international affairs with one very important exception. The Firmans of 1867 [6] and 1873 [7] gave Egypt the right to conclude non-political treaties, such as commercial conventions. Similarly, the Egyptian Army was theoretically a part of the Ottoman Army and, if Turkey were at war, Egypt automatically became involved in it. Thus she had contributed contingents in the Crimean War (1853-56) and in the Russo-Turkish War (1877-78). In practice, however, this custom had fallen into disregard. During the Turco-Greek War of 1897, Egypt contented herself with severing diplomatic relations with Greece.[8] In the Turco-Italian War of 1911 and in the Balkan Wars of 1912-13, she did even less, and maintained a strict neutrality despite the widespread sympathy with

[5] "En résumé, l'Égypte est placée sous le contrôle et la garantie du concert européen." De Freycinet, *op. cit.,* pp. 93, 94. Though in the form of unilateral grants, these Firmans were "international instruments, being concerted among the Powers chiefly interested, and then imposed by them upon a more or less recalcitrant Suzerain." McIlwraith, *loc. cit.,* pp. 244, 245. See also J. H. Scott, "The Law Affecting Foreigners in Egypt," pp. 141 ff.

[6] Noradounghian, *op. cit.,* III, pp. 261, 262; P. Albin, "Les Grands Traités Politiques," pp. 381, 382.

[7] Noradounghian, *op. cit.,* III, pp. 347-350. These non-political treaties had to be submitted to the Porte before promulgation, but the Porte's assent to them was not necessary. *Ibid.,* IV, pp. 227, 228. [See also "Trattati . . . relativi all'Africa," pp. 876-880.]

[8] McIlwraith, *loc. cit.,* p. 246.

Turkey.[9] Under the British Occupation it was inevitable that Turkish suzerainty should actually mean less than it had done, even though Great Britain was careful that Egypt paid scrupulous regard to her explicit legal obligations to the suzerain power. While not a matter of very great moment, Turkish suzerainty was, however, not a mere diplomatic expression. It was manifest in many ways, of which some were merely formal, none beneficial, and virtually all superfluous and irksome.

The Firman of Investiture.—Although by the Firman of 1841 the administration of Egypt was made hereditary in the family of Mehemet Ali, and although by the Firman of 1867 [10] the title of Khedive—a word of Persian origin, denoting somewhat vaguely a minor sovereign [11] —was conferred on the rulers of Egypt, it was held that they could not legally succeed to their position without a Firman of investiture from the Sultan. These Firmans could not derogate essentially from those previously issued, since they "constituted international agreements between Turkey and the Powers themselves." [12]

On two occasions, Turkey tried to use this power of investiture to curtail Egypt's rights. In 1879, when Tewfik succeeded Ismail, such an attempt was in part frustrated

[9] *Egypt*, No. 1 (1912) (Kitchener), p. 1; A. E. P. B. Weigall, "A History of Events in Egypt from 1798 to 1914," pp. 239-257, 272; Sir Thomas Barclay, "The Turco-Italian War and its Problems," pp. 87-94, London, 1912; Arminjon and Perret, "Die Rechtslage Aegyptens Während der Balkankriege," in *Jahrbuch des Völkerrechts*, II (1914), pp. 425-438; N. Bentwich, "Aegypten," *ibid.*, pp. 673 ff.

[10] Noradounghian, *op. cit.*, III, pp. 261, 262.

[11] Sir H. D. Wolff, "Rambling Recollections," II, p. 293 [P. Horn, "Grundriss der Neupersischen Etymologie," p. 104, Strassburg, 1893].

[12] McIlwraith, *loc. cit.*, pp. 244, 245.

by the joint action of Great Britain and France.[13] Again in 1892, when Abbas II followed Tewfik, Turkey tried to diminish Egypt's territorial limits, but Great Britain effectively thwarted the plan.[14] Under more propitious circumstances, it is, however, probable that the Firman of Investiture might have been used to encroach upon Egyptian autonomy.

The Tribute.—The origin of the tribute paid by Egypt to the Ottoman Empire goes back to the Turkish Conquest in 1517.[15] Its modern history, however, dates from 1841, when Egypt was made an hereditary administrative entity and the tribute was fixed at £T400,000 annually.[16] In general, in return for grants of greater autonomy, but more particularly in consideration of the fact that Turkey agreed in 1866 to change the rule of Khedivial succession from the Mohammedan one to that of primogeniture in the male line, Ismail Pasha in that year agreed to raise the tributes to £T750,000 yearly.[17] It afterwards remained virtually at this sum, equivalent to about £675,000.[18] While the tribute

---

[13] In 1873, Ismail Pasha had obtained four concessions from the Sultan in return for large sums of money: 1, the Mohammedan law of succession was set aside in favor of primogeniture; 2, the right to conclude commercial conventions was conceded to Egypt; 3, full power was granted to the Khedive to contract foreign loans; 4, the Khedive was permitted to determine the size of the Egyptian Army without limits being set. In 1879, the Porte wished to withdraw all four of these concessions. France opposed in every case, Great Britain only in the first. In the end, the Porte carried its point regarding the last two. Cromer, "Modern Egypt," I, pp. 155, 158; Noradounghian, *op. cit.*, IV, pp. 226-229; *Egypt*, No. 1 (1880), *passim*.

[14] Cromer, "Modern Egypt," II, pp. 267-269.

[15] De la Jonquière, "Histoire de l'Empire Ottoman," I, p. 145.

[16] Noradounghian, *op. cit.*, II, p. 338.

[17] *Ibid.*, III, p. 254.

[18] From 1881 to 1888, the tribute was £E678,000 yearly. In that year, the tribute of Zeila ceased and thereafter the yearly payment was

was thus largely the result of conquest and of dynastic considerations, it may perhaps more truly be regarded as the ransom paid by Egypt for emancipation from Turkish rule.

The Egyptian Army.—The Firmans restricted the size of the Egyptian Army to 18,000 men,[19] and this limit was carefully observed.[20]   Moreover, these troops were considered as forming part of the Ottoman forces.   The Khedive was not permitted to appoint any officers above the rank of Colonel.[21]   In practice, this restriction was evaded by procuring from Constantinople signed commissions in blank.   The forms were carefully regarded.   The badges of the officers bore the Turkish insignia and the words of command were in the Turkish language.   Thus, it was the custom in what Milner happily called "the Land of Paradox" that the British officers in the Egyptian Army issued their orders in Turkish to Arabic-speaking soldiers.

The Forms of Turkish Suzerainty.—The outward forms of Turkish suzerainty were duly observed in other respects as well.   The people of Egypt were the Sultan's legal sub-

---

£E665,000.   *Annuaire Statistique,* 1914, p. 423.   In 1903, Lord Cromer wrote that "the payment of this sum involves political issues into which I need not now enter.   It is well known that, in return for certain concessions made by the Porte, the amount of the Tribute was largely increased during the Khedivate of Ismail Pasha."   *Egypt,* No. 1 (1903) (Cromer), pp. 12, 13.   [It is wholly renounced by Turkey in Article 112 of the Sèvres Treaty.]

[19] The construction of armored vessels was also forbidden.

[20] THE EGYPTIAN ARMY IN 1913

British Officers	136
Egyptian and Sudanese Officers	721
Other Ranks	17,137
	17,994

Egyptian Government Almanac, 1913, p. 132, Cairo, 1912.

[21] Firman of 1892.   Noradounghian, *op. cit.,* IV, pp. 505-507.

jects and the taxes were levied in the Sultan's name. The Turkish flag floated over Egypt and the Consuls of the European Powers in Egypt received their *exequaturs* from Constantinople. Similarly, the Egyptian coins bore the Turkish insignia. The Khedive was not allowed to bestow orders of distinction beyond those of a low grade. And, finally, he was not permitted to make civil appointments of a higher rank than that of *bey* or *sanieh*,[22] though this again was overcome by securing from Constantinople blank brevets of appointment.

The Grand Cadi.—Most of these rights were merely the futile trappings of an outworn temporal suzerainty, but, in addition, the Sultan as Caliph was the spiritual head of orthodox Islam.[23] Consequently, he had close relations with the religious powers in Egypt, such as the Grand Mufti, whose duty it is to pronounce opinions on doubtful points of the Sacred Law.[24] The most important of the Sultan's rights as Caliph was that the appointment of the Grand Cadi belonged to him. The Cadi was the head of the Mekhkemeh Sher'ieh, the religious courts that deal with all affairs concerning the personal status of Mohammedans, such as marriage, divorce, and inheritance, as well as with all trust funds. These important and far-reaching matters are governed by the Sacred Law of Islam and any intrusion by the secular authorities was resented. These courts were characterized by disorder and lack of justice, but the

[22] Firman of 1892. Noradounghian, *op. cit.*, IV, pp. 505-507.

[23] Since 1538, the Sultan of Turkey has been *de facto* Caliph of the greater part of orthodox Islam. Stanley Lane-Poole, "A History of Egypt in the Middle Ages," pp. 354, 355.

[24] Cromer, "Modern Egypt," II, pp. 174, 175; Constant Dahan, *loc. cit.*, pp. 355-357.

British authorities could not interfere. Nor could the Egyptian Government, as the Grand Cadi resolutely refused to admit that they had any right of surveillance over him.[25]

2. International Restrictions

The Capitulations in Egypt.—In addition to the limitations upon her sovereignty arising from her connection with the Ottoman Empire, Egypt had further to submit to others of a far more important character, both because of this very connection and also on account of the peculiar circumstances of her case. As a result of the financial chaos under Ismail Pasha, various international administrations were established in the country and constituted real *imperia in imperio*. With the financial regeneration, these have either disappeared or have been rendered harmless. Further, as a part of the Ottoman Empire, Egypt was bound by Turkish treaties and came within the scope of the Capitulations, through which foreigners had acquired extensive immunities from Ottoman jurisdiction and positive extraterritorial rights in Turkey. The Capitulations are based partly upon established custom, partly upon specific treaties. The latter reach back to the age of the Crusades, but the fundamental ones are those with Venice of 1454, with France of 1535 and 1740, and with England of 1675.[26] By favored-nation clauses

[25] Sir Malcolm McIlwraith, "The Mohammedan Law-Courts of Egypt," in *The Nineteenth Century and After*, October, 1916, pp. 740-742, 751; Cromer, "Abbas II," pp. 71-74; J. H. Scott, *op. cit.*, pp. 250-254, 266-268.

[26] J. H. Scott, "The Law Affecting Foreigners in Egypt," pp. 31-54, *et passim;* P. M. Brown, "Foreigners in Turkey—Their Juridical Status," pp. 15-17, 28-41. The texts of the French Treaties of 1535 and 1740 are in Noradounghian, "Recueil d'Actes Internationaux de l'Empire Ottoman," I. pp. 83-87, 295; that of the English Treaty of 1675 is in G. de Bern-

the privileges conferred by these documents were enjoyed by all Western foreigners. Custom and the interpretation of treaties also played their parts. In the case of Turkey, a comparatively strong government was able to offer some resistance to foreign encroachments. Egypt was not so fortunate. Hence the system of Capitulations in Egypt differed in many respects from that in Turkey, and especially in that foreigners had secured more extensive immunities and privileges.[27]

Foreign Immunities.—(a) Freedom from Taxation.— By specific international agreements, foreigners in Egypt paid the customs duties and the taxes on houses and land, but no fresh levies could be imposed upon them without the consent of the sixteen European and American States enjoying the benefits of the Capitulations.[28] In point of fact, the natives actually paid no imposts to which foreigners were not also subject, but this inability to broaden the scope of taxation was a distinct handicap to the Egyptian Government.[29] In especial, it prevented the establishment

hardt, "Handbook of Commercial Treaties between Great Britain and Foreign Powers," pp. 947-970, London, 1912 [that of the Venetian Treaty of 1454 is in Aristarchi, "Législation Ottomane," IV, p. 234, Constantinople, 1873-87; Noradounghian, I, p. 17, observes that neither the original nor any copy is to be found in the Turkish or Venetian archives].

[27] G. Pélissié du Rausas, "Le Régime des Capitulations dans l'Empire Ottoman," I, p. 129; II, pp. 177, 178; Cromer, "Modern Egypt," II, pp. 426-428; Milner, "England in Egypt" (7th ed.), pp. 39-41.

[28] These States were: in Europe, Great Britain, France, Russia, Italy, Germany, Austria-Hungary, the Netherlands, Spain, Sweden, Norway, Denmark, Belgium, Portugal, Greece; and in the Americas, the United States and Brazil.

[29] In 1885, the six Great Powers of Europe conceded the principle that their nationals should pay the Egyptian taxes, but the only result was that they were made liable to the house tax. No further agreement could be reached. Noradounghian, *op. cit.,* IV, pp. 354, 355; Cromer, "Modern Egypt," II, pp. 435, 436; Milner, *op. cit.,* pp. 49, 50.

of municipalities with local powers of raising revenue, like that of Alexandria, to which the Powers had given their consent in 1890.[30] As Sir Eldon Gorst pointed out in 1908, this was a serious matter, because local institutions must be developed if the Egyptians are ever to become proficient in the art of self-government.[31]

(b) Freedom from Arrest.—Under the Capitulations, foreigners further enjoyed freedom from arrest by the local authorities. In Egypt, this immunity had acquired a very extensive interpretation.[32] The clearest enunciation of this principle is in the Treaty of 1830 between the United States and Turkey which, by the most-favored-nation clause, is applicable to all the Capitulation Powers. It provides that:

"Citizens of the United States of America, quietly pursuing their commerce, and not being charged or convicted of any crime or offence, shall not be molested; and even when they may have committed some offence they shall not be arrested and put in prison by the local authorities, but they shall be tried by their Minister or Consul, and punished according to their offence, following, in this respect, the usage observed towards other Franks." [33]

Turkey was able to resist the full execution of this provision, but in Egypt it was obeyed to the letter.[34]

[30] *Egyptian Government Almanac*, 1913, pp. 46, 47, Cairo, 1912.
[31] *Egypt*, No. 1 (1908) (Gorst), p. 1.
[32] Du Rausas, II, pp. 179-184.
[33] W. M. Malloy, "Treaties," II, p. 1319.
[34] In Egypt the French version of this provision read that citizens of the United States, "si même ils avaient commis quelque délit, ils ne seront ni arrêtés ni mis en prison par les autorités locales, mais ils seront jugés par leur Ministre ou consul, et punis suivant leur délit et suivant la coutume établie à l'égard des Francs." *Egypt*, No. 2 (1913), p. 3. While Egypt

(c) Inviolability of Domicile.—The fundamental principle of inviolability of domicile is most clearly laid down in the French Treaty of 1740, a document which provides that,

"Les gens de justice et les officiers de ma Sublime-Porte, de même que les gens d'epée, ne pourront sans nécessité entrer par force dans une maison habitée par un Français; et lorsque le cas requerra d'y entrer, on en avertira l'ambassadeur ou le consul, dans les endroits ou il y en aurait, et l'on se transportera dans l'endroit en question, avec les personnes qui auront été commies de leur part." [35]

Method of Arrest and Search.—Thus, none of the privileged foreigners could be arrested in Egypt without the consent of his consul, unless he were taken red-handed. In the latter case, the consul concerned in the seizure had to be informed at once and the prisoner had to be handed over to him within twenty-four hours. In addition, the Egyptian police could not enter a foreign domicile to make an arrest unless the consul were present.[36] Even if an alien were

accepted this French version, which agrees absolutely with the English one, the Porte insisted upon a radically different French version, which gave it the power to arrest and to try Americans. During the protracted dispute about this question, the United States had the better of the argument, but in practice Turkey maintained her claims. J. B. Moore, "Digest of International Law," II, pp. 668-711, Washington, 1906; P. M. Brown, *op. cit.*, pp. 76-79. [The régime of Capitulations in Egypt is renounced by Germany (Versailles Treaty, Article 147), Austria (Saint-Germain-en-Laye Treaty, Article 102), and Hungary (Trianon Treaty, Article 86).]

[35] Noradounghian, *op. cit.*, I, p. 295; *Egypt*, No. 2 (1913), p. 3. For the English version, see P. M. Brown, *op. cit.*, p. 40.

[36] Such domiciliary visits were permitted if they were the result of criminal proceedings within the competence of the Mixed Courts. Their jurisdiction in this respect was, however, very limited. *Egypt*, No. 1 (1907) (Cromer), p. 13. In 1917, Sir William Willcocks related the following episode in his experiences as an irrigation official. A Greek trader had built a shop at a regulator on a canal head and no regulation could be performed without his consent. "As he had a roof over his head, he was protected by the

seen committing the crime, in plain *flagrante delicto,* and if he had then taken refuge in a foreigner's house, the police were not permitted to enter it until his consul had appeared on the scene.   In case the fugitive and the occupant of the house were of different nationalities, the presence of both consuls was necessary.   As Lord Kitchener tersely remarked in 1913, "the effect of such restrictions on police work can easily be imagined." [37]

The Consular Jurisdiction.—The essential point is that under the Capitulations foreigners were generally not subject to Egyptian statutes but only to the law of their own lands.   Thus, when arrested, the foreigner was turned over to his own consul for trial.   In addition, though there is no actual mention of this right in the Capitulations, the consuls were by established usage accustomed to call upon the police to arrest foreigners designated by them.   In three-quarters of these cases there was no mention of the charge.   The Egyptian police simply made the requested arrest and delivered the prisoner to the consul.   As few of the consulates had prisons, the usual procedure then was to turn the accused over to the local department of prisons and to keep him at the disposal of the consul.   The consul might subsequently either try, dismiss, or punish the prisoner; or he might deport him for trial in his own country.   The last course was usually followed in the case of grave crimes by

Capitulations and the people were helpless. I went to the place, built a masonry wall three metres high, on the public land right round his shop, and starved him into surrender." "This is but one instance," adds Willcocks, "of the hundreds of thousands of worries and humiliations the *fellahin* have had to submit to, owing to abuses of the Capitulations." *The Grotius Society,* III (1918), p. 77.

[37] *Egypt,* No. 2 (1913).

all countries except Greece, which had an Assize Court in Egypt.[38]

Some Results of This System.—It is quite plain that such a system is inherently vicious and lends itself to grave abuses. In his report of 1913 on this question, Lord Kitchener said:

"A person incarcerated at the request of his consul in an Egyptian prison may also be detained there indefinitely without the Egyptian Government having any say in the matter, the consul being only amenable to his own laws on the subject, of which the local authorities have no cognisance."

Thus, in 1913, one Alexander Adamovitch, accused of being a well-known Russian revolutionary leader, who had instigated strikes at Odessa, was arrested at Alexandria on the application of the Russian consul and was kept in prison at his disposal. This case aroused considerable public interest in Great Britain and induced Lord Cromer to break the six years of silence on Egyptian affairs that he had maintained since his retirement in 1907. He pointed out that the arrest of Adamovitch revealed to public knowledge

---

[38] FOREIGNERS IMPRISONED BY THEIR CONSULS IN EGYPTIAN PRISONS IN THE YEAR 1912-13:

Italians	142		
French	55		
Greeks	35	Places:	
Russians	28	Alexandria	159
Austrians	13	Cairo	84
Germans	6	Port Said	40
Rumanians	2		
Dutch	1		283
Americans	1		
	283		

Egypt, No. 2 (1913).

the fact that a country occupied and administered by Great Britain was no safe place for a political refugee. The merits of the case—the nature of the accusation, the innocence or guilt of the accused—he added, were beside the question because "the legal obligation of the Egyptian Government to comply with the request that the man should be handed over to the Russian Consular authorities would have been precisely the same if he had been accused of no offence at all." [39]

Its Evils.—This system lent itself as well to many minor abuses, which the Egyptian Government was powerless to correct. Immunity from arrest and from domiciliar visit protected the foreign smuggler, foreign keepers of dives and gambling dens, and foreign venders of opiates. It made an effective control over druggists and liquor dealers impossible. In general, it prevented the passage of the most ordinary and necessary police regulations for securing public morals and health. [40]

The Mixed Tribunals.—In addition to their criminal competence, the Consular Courts had jurisdiction in all civil suits between foreigners of the same nationality except those concerning real estate. Originally, this consular power in civil cases had been much more extensive, [41] but in 1875 all

[39] Cromer, "The Capitulations in Egypt," in *The Nineteenth Century and After,* July, 1913, p. 1. [See also Chirol, "The Egyptian Problem," pp. 57-64.]

[40] Cf. Sir William Brunyate's memorandum in *Egypt,* No. 1 (1905) (Cromer), pp. 90-97. As the author of that memorandum stated in 1917, conditions had considerably improved during the interval. *The Near East,* August 17, 1917, p. 304. For a sympathetic account of Cromer's proposals in 1904 and 1905, see "Les Projets de Réforme des Capitulations en Égypte," by Gilbert Gidel in *Revue Générale de Droit International Public,* XIII (1906), pp. 408-423.

[41] Du Rausas, *op. cit.,* II, pp. 243-270. See likewise Nubar Pasha's report

the Treaty Powers, except Brazil, which had no interests involved, gave their assent to Nubar Pasha's scheme for the establishment of Mixed Tribunals.[42] Three courts of first instance and one of appeal were created and began to function in 1876.[43] Foreign and native judges were appointed to sit in these courts. Primarily there were to have been only nineteen foreign and thirteen native judges, but owing largely to pressure of business their number was in the course of time increased to forty-one and twenty-three, respectively.[44] All the Signatory Powers were entitled to representation in these courts. It was provided in the original agreement that the nomination and choice of the foreign judges should belong to the Egyptian Government, but that this Government would non-officially [45] communicate with the proper authorities of the Signatory Powers concerned and would not engage persons without their acquiescence and authorization.[46] This was virtually equiv-

(pp. 77-83) and the other documents in "Les Capitulations en Égypte," in *Documents Diplomatiques*, XIII, pp. 77-145, Paris, 1869.

[42] Du Rausas, *op. cit.*, II, pp. 271-298; Colvin, "The Making of Modern Egypt" (3d ed.), pp. 53 ff.; Morcos Sadek, "La Constitution de l'Égypte," pp. 193-196; J. H. Scott, *op. cit.*, pp. 210 ff.

[43] The Court of Appeal was at Alexandria and the courts of first instance at Alexandria, Cairo, and Mansourah.

[44] *Annuaire Statistique*, 1914, pp. 111, 120; *Egyptian Government Almanac*, 1913, p. 113, Cairo, 1912. *The Times* (London), January 2, 1915. The international mandate for these courts had to be renewed every five years. On its expiration in 1915, they were continued by yearly renewals. *The Near East*, December 29, 1916 and August 17, 1917. On the foreign personnel of these courts in 1882, see *Egypt*, No. 6 (1882), pp. 20-23. Of the Treaty Powers, Brazil and Portugal alone had no representatives in 1882.

[45] There is no exact English equivalent for the French term used, "*officieusement*," which means something less formal than "official" and something more authoritative than "non-official."

[46] Article V of *Règlement* for the Mixed Tribunals. "British and Foreign State Papers, 1874-1875," Vol. LXVI (1882), pp. 593-603. Originally the United States, Great Britain, France, Italy, Russia, Germany, and Austria-

alent to giving the foreign government the real choice and in many cases this was actually the practice.[47]   These Mixed Tribunals have civil and commercial jurisdiction:

1.   In all cases between natives and foreigners;

2.   In all cases not involving questions of personal status between foreigners of different nationalities;

3.   In cases involving real estate between foreigners of the same nationality;

4.   In cases of bankruptcy, provided the bankrupt or one of his creditors is a foreigner.

In addition, these courts have criminal jurisdiction in cases arising from infractions of their own ordinances and rules, and from violations of the bankruptcy law.[48]

Legislation by Diplomacy.—The system that these tribunals applied was that formulated in the Mixed Codes, but any change in it required the consent of each of the Treaty Powers.   In addition, it was a general principle of the Capitulations that no legislation affecting foreigners could be passed unless all these Powers had agreed thereto.[49]

Hungary were each represented by one judge in the Court of Appeal, the other four judges being natives.

[47] Cromer. "Modern Egypt," II, p. 318.   In 1916, Great Britain, France, and Italy had four representatives on the Mixed Courts.   *The Near East,* April 21, 1916.   At the present time, the United States has three representatives: Sommerville P. Tuck, Court of Appeal; William G. Van Horne, Alexandria Court of First Instance; Pierre Crabitès, Cairo Court of First Instance.   On the United States and the Mixed Courts, see J. B. Moore, *op. cit.,* pp. **722-727.**

[48] *Annuaire Statistique,* 1914, p. 111; *Egypt,* No. 1 (1907) (Cromer), p. 13.

[49] "Une conséquence des capitulations qui complique le droit civil Ottoman se trouve dans le droit d'intervention, et même de veto, en toute législation intéressant les étrangers, que les Missions considèrent leur appartenant en vertu de ces capitulations."   George Young, "Corps de Droit Ottoman," I, p. xi.   For details, see *ibid.,* pp. 251-303.   For the special situation in Egypt, consult Du Rausas, *op. cit.,* II, pp. 431-457; A. Debono,

The result was what Lord Cromer termed "legislative impotence." In some cases, highly essential measures were
blocked for purely political purposes and Egypt was the
innocent victim of the rivalries of the Powers in quite remote
regions.[50] Even when these motives were absent, it was
difficult in the extreme to obtain the consent of fifteen different Governments to new projects. Thus, Sir Eldon Gorst
pointed out in 1910 that it was

"a labour of Hercules to get the assent of fifteen Powers to
any alteration in the Mixed Codes and, until some change
is effected in the existing method of legislating, foreigners
resident, or having interests, in Egypt must continue to bear
with resignation the imperfections and deficiencies of the
law." [51]

At that time, two harmless measures for improving the
system of registering land titles which had been passed in
1903 were in abeyance pending the assent of France and
Russia.[52] Many essential reforms—child labor, building
laws, fraudulent weights and measures, trade-marks, pat-
ents, and copyright—could not be executed.[53] Lord Cromer
observed that Egyptian autonomy was out of the question
as long as no important law could be made applicable to
European residents in Egypt without the consent of all
the Treaty Powers, and he quoted on at least two occasions
with distinct relish Lord Salisbury's remark to him that the
system was like the *liberum veto* of the old Polish Diet

"Du Système Législatif, de l'Organisation Judiciaire . . . en Égypte," pp.
111-118, Paris, 1908.
  [50] Colvin, *op. cit.*, pp. 300, 301.
  [51] *Egypt*, No. 1 (1910) (Gorst), p. 4.
  [52] *Ibid.*, p. 39.
  [53] *Ibid.*, 1908, p. 1.

"without being able to have recourse to the alternative of striking off the head of any recalcitrant voter." [54] The great defect in the method was that Egypt had no machinery for general legislation where Europeans were concerned. To some extent the situation was improved by the establishment in 1911 of a new Legislative Assembly, with power to legislate for foreigners.[55] This body is composed of the judges of the Mixed Courts, each of the Treaty Powers being represented on it. A two-thirds majority is required for the adoption of any measure proposed by the Government, and, furthermore, any one of the Treaty Powers may within three months of the project's passage require that it be resubmitted to the Assembly.[56] Under this anomalous system the same persons are both the makers and the interpreters of the law. The Law of 1911, however, unquestionably improved conditions—1912 was a year of great legislative activity [57]—but Egypt was still far from enjoying

[54] Cromer, "The Capitulations in Egypt," in *The Nineteenth Century and After,* July, 1913, pp. 3, 9. In 1905, Lord Cromer said of this system that "it goes far to produce a condition of legislative importance." *Egypt,* No. 1 (1905) (Cromer), pp. 6, 7, 14. See also Cromer, "Modern Egypt," II, pp. 318, 319.

[55] In 1889, after great trouble, the Powers agreed to allow Egypt to pass legislation on such minor matters as the maintenance of dykes and canals, the establishment of drinking shops and places of amusement, and the right to carry arms, which usually in advanced countries are regulated by by-laws of subordinate bodies. All such Egyptian regulations had, however, to have the approval of a special commission of the judges of the Mixed Courts, and the penalties permitted were limited to fines of £E1 or one week's imprisonment, obviously too low to be effective deterrents. Cromer, "Modern Egypt," II, pp. 433, 434; *Egypt,* No. 1 (1908) (Gorst), p. 1; Debono, *op. cit.,* pp. 111-113; J. H. Scott, *op. cit.,* pp. 277-279.

[56] *Egypt,* No. 1 (1912) (Kitchener), pp. 42, 43; *Egyptian Government Almanac,* 1913, p. 113, Cairo, 1912. The scheme was originally proposed in 1905 and modified in 1909. *Egypt,* No. 1 (1910) (Gorst), p. 40.

[57] *L'Égypte Contemporaine,* IV (1913), p. 113; *Egypt,* No. 1 (1914)

the degree of legislative autonomy to which she was fully
and clearly entitled by reason of the advanced state of her
political civilization.

The Commission of the Debt.—Egypt was at one time
burdened with a number of other international administrations, of which the chief was the Commission of the Debt.
The foreign management of the Khedivial estates disappeared automatically when the loans for which they were
pledged as security were paid off. Likewise, with the improvement of Egypt's finances, the control of the railroads,
telegraphs, and port of Alexandria was handed over to the
Egyptian Government. All of these international administrations had worked badly.[58] In 1914, the only one of the
bodies arising out of Egypt's former financial difficulties
still in existence was the Commission of the Debt. Originally constituted in 1876 with extensive control over Egyptian finances and with power to veto fresh public borrowing,
it remained up to 1904 a veritable "International Cer-
berus," [59] to use Sir Auckland Colvin's expressive designa-
tion. By the agreement of that year it was shorn of all its
powers of interference in administrative affairs, and thereafter the Commission merely performed the essentially
clerical work of taking care of the revenue of that portion
of the land-tax which was allocated to the debt.[60] The Com-

(Kitchener), pp. 56, 57; N. Bentwich, "Aegypten," in *Jahrbuch des
Völkerrechts,* II (1914), p. 677, also in I (1913), pp. 1144-1148.
    [58] Colvin, *op. cit.,* pp. 318, 319; Cromer, "Modern Egypt," II, pp. 311, 312.
    [59] Colvin, *op. cit.,* pp. 97, 98. [Cf. also Chirol, *op. cit.,* pp. 52, 56-57, 82,
89-90.]
    [60] Anglo-French Treaty of April 8, 1904, with annexed Khedivial Decree.
Treaty Series, 1905, No. 6 ["Trattati . . . relativi all'Africa," pp. 1116-1131];
Egypt, No. 1 (1905) (Cromer), p. 10; Colvin, *op. cit.,* pp. 340-345; Cromer,
"Modern Egypt," II, pp. 304-310.

mission is a useless relic of a bankrupt past and one whose cost of retention is by no means insignificant.[61]

Tariff Restrictions.—(a) The Turkish System in Egypt.— As a part of the Ottoman Empire, Egypt was bound by the treaties limiting Turkey's right to impose customs duties beyond a fixed maximum.   The Venetian Treaty of 1454 provided for a levy of two per cent on all goods sold by Venetians in Turkish ports.   In this connection Professor P. M. Brown writes:

"In thus including import duties in a solemn treaty agreement, Turkey brought on itself in the course of centuries a most unfortunate situation, such that it cannot today change its customs tariffs without first obtaining the consent of all nations with whom it has treaties.   As this consent in each case can only be obtained as a rule by the concession of a substantial *quid pro quo*, a virtual servitude of a singularly harsh nature was .thus innocently established by these early treaties of the Porte." [62]

The English Treaty of 1675 limited the duties to three per cent.[63]   Similar agreements were likewise made with the other European Powers and, as the favored-nation clause was also gradually established, the result was that all Euro-

[61] EXPENSES OF THE CAISSE DE LA DETTE

1913-14 .... £E34,917	1917-18 ... £E35,000
1914-15 .... £E34,366	1918-19 ... £E38,617
1915-16 .... £E34,948	1920-21 ... £E41,446
[1916-17 .... £E34,985	1921-22 ... £E39,470 (estimated)]

Annuaire Statistique, 1916, p. 297.

[By Article 151 of the Versailles Treaty, "Germany consents to the abrogation of the decree issued by His Highness the Khedive on November 28, 1904, relating to the Commission of the Egyptian Public Debt, or to such changes as the Egyptian Government may think it desirable to make therein." This stipulation is repeated in the Austrian and Hungarian Treaties (Articles 106 and 90 respectively).]

[62] P. M. Brown, *op. cit.,* p. 30.

[63] Article 58. De Bernhardt, *op. cit.,* pp. 947-970.

pean goods paid import fees of a uniformly low rate. The
most favorable agreement from the standpoint of the foreign
countries was the one that applied to all the Treaty
Powers.[64]　Until recently this was the Franco-Ottoman
Treaty of 1861 which, in general, permitted import duties
up to a maximum of eight per cent *ad valorem*.[65]　This arrangement applied also automatically in Egypt.[66]　In the
meanwhile, the Firmans of 1867 and 1873 [67] had conferred
upon the Khedive authority to negotiate separate commercial conventions.　An elaborate Egyptian tariff was framed,
but the Powers, being quite satisfied with the Franco-Ottoman eight per cent arrangement of 1861, were unwilling to
enter upon less favorable agreements with Egypt.　As,
however, the Treaty of 1861 expired in 1889, when it was
continued year by year provisionally, and as it was apparent
that Turkey would probably secure the right to increase the
customs duties, the Egyptian situation assumed a different
aspect.[68]　Any rise in the Turkish customs would apply
automatically to Egypt unless special conventions had been
concluded with her.[69]

[64] The Turkish duties had been raised in 1838 from three per cent to
five per cent. Du Rausas, *op. cit.*, I, pp. 187, 188. See also George Young,
op. cit., III, pp. 221-227.

[65] Noradounghian, *op. cit.*, III, pp. 130-135, 169-171.

[66] See agreement between Turkey and Egypt of 1890. George Young,
op. cit., III, p. 414.

[67] Noradounghian, *op. cit.*, III, pp. 261-262, 347-350.

[68] It was only in 1907 that the Turkish customs were raised from eight
per cent to eleven per cent. Protocol, April 25, 1907, in Treaty Series, 1909,
No. 1; De Bernhardt, *op. cit.*, p. 976; J. Grunzel, "Economic Protectionism," pp. 55, 56, London, 1916. One of the leading features of the abortive
Bagdad Railway settlement of 1913-14 was that Turkey was to be allowed
to increase the customs to fifteen per cent. Speech of Viscount (Sir
Edward) Grey, June 29, 1914, in Hansard, 64, pp. 115 ff.

[69] In 1884, Greece concluded such a treaty. Article IV thereof provided

(b) The Egyptian Commercial Treaties.—In 1889, Great Britain negotiated such a treaty which limited to ten per cent the customs on a long list of goods in which she was especially interested and otherwise gave Egypt a free hand.[70] Most of the remaining Powers followed suit along the same lines, with the result that the schedule of enumerated articles restricted to ten per cent grew constantly, while Egypt's open field became more and more circumscribed.[71] By 1902, France and Russia were the only two important commercial countries that had not signed such conventions. In that year, however, France concluded a treaty which provided that, in general, the maximum duties should be eight per cent, which was also the existing limitation. But in the case of alcohol below fifty per cent proof, refined sugar, and wood, the rate might go to ten per cent; and in the case of alcohol above fifty per cent proof, petroleum, and live stock, customs up to fifteen per cent might be imposed.[72] Of all these commercial treaties, this was the most

---

for a fixed duty of eight per cent *ad valorem,* except that the Egyptian Government reserved the right to raise the customs on "distilled beverages, wines and fancy articles" up to sixteen per cent *ad valorem.* Certain commodities, notably tobacco, were excluded from this general limitation by Article V. The United States, in 1885, by a special treaty adhered to this Greek Treaty. Malloy, *op. cit.,* I, pp. 442-465.

[70] De Bernhardt, *op. cit.,* p. 285.

[71] *Egypt,* No. 1 (1903) (Cromer), pp. 28, 29; Du Rausas, *op. cit.,* II, pp. 185-189; Henri Lamba, "Le Statut Politique de l'Égypte au Regard de la Turquie," in *Revue Générale de Droit International Public,* XVII (1910), pp. 46, 47; J. H. Scott, *op. cit.,* pp. 162-169. Cromer (*loc. cit.*) stated specifically that, with the exception of France and Russia, all the Powers having commercial conventions with Turkey had concluded similar agreements with Egypt. As a matter of fact, Denmark, Norway, and Sweden had not, but their trade with Egypt was insignificant.

[72] *Egypt,* No. 1 (1903) (Cromer), pp. 28, 29. G. P. du Rausas, "Régime des Capitulations dans l'Empire Ottoman," II, 185-189, on French Treaty of 1902, on customs duties in Egypt.

unfavorable to Egypt and the most advantageous to the foreign Powers. Hence, under the most-favored-nation clause, it of course applied to all of them, but it could not go into effect until Russia had also made a similar agreement. This was done only in 1909, when Russia signed a treaty following in all essentials the French Convention of 1902.[73] During these protracted negotiations, the Turkish eight per cent schedule continued to be in force in Egypt.[74] In fact, it was only in 1915 that Egypt availed herself of the very restricted freedom she had secured and raised the import duties on alcoholic drinks, alcoholic extracts, and perfumeries to ten per cent.[75] Thus, the same international shackles that prevent Egypt from passing laws of a general character also deprive her of autonomy in fiscal matters. So long as these restrictions remain it will be impossible for her to stimulate native industries by a protective tariff.

[73] Treaty $\frac{\text{March 13}}{\text{February 28}}$ 1909, in *Staatsarchiv*, 78, p. 63, No. 14048.

[74] Up to 1914, a special schedule applied to tobacco and its products, from which a considerable revenue was collected, and eight per cent *ad valorem* was imposed on all other articles, except that a few commodities like coal and meat paid only four per cent. The export duties were one per cent. *Annuaire Statistique*, 1914, p. 283.

[75] *Annuaire Statistique*, 1916, p. 258; Kelly's "Customs Tariffs of the World," 1916, p. 138.

CHAPTER IV

EGYPTIAN QUESTIONS AT THE PEACE CONFERENCE

1. The British Protectorate

Effect of Turkey's Entrance into the War.—The anomalies of Egypt's international status were brought into high relief by the war. On its outbreak in August, 1914, no action could legally be taken, since Egypt was a part of the Ottoman Empire. The British authorities refused, however, to be hampered by these technical niceties and induced the Egyptian Government to regard itself as in a state of war with Germany and Austria-Hungary. Their diplomatic representatives were dismissed and, further, the subjects of the Central Empires were either expelled or put under restraint [1] in order to stop their intrigues. [2] Technically, this was an act of rebellion on the part of Egypt against her suzerain. [3] On her part, Turkey endeavored to

[1] Correspondence Respecting Events Leading to the Rupture of Relations with Turkey, Miscellaneous, No. 13 (1914) (Cd. 7628), No. 118. See also "L'Égypte et les Débuts du Protectorat," in *Revue des Sciences Politiques,* 33 (1915), pp. 311-331; Sir Malcolm McIlwraith, "Legal War Work in Egypt," in *The Grotius Society,* III (1918), pp. 73 ff.

[2] According to the Report of 1913 in the "French Yellow Book," the Germans, before the war, used as their chief field of intrigue the Egyptian religious university which had great prestige in the Mohammedan world. "French Yellow Book," 1914, No. 2, enclosure, Part II; "The Times Documentary History of the War," I, pp. 271, 272, London, 1917; "Collected Diplomatic Documents Relating to the Outbreak of the European War," p. 132, London, 1915.

[3] A. E. P. B. Weigall, "A History of Events in Egypt from 1798 to 1914," pp. 272-290.

stir up trouble in Egypt and prepared for military operations against the Suez Canal.[4] When in the autumn of 1914 Turkey became an actual belligerent, the situation was even more irregular. Legally, Turkey's entrance into hostilities meant that Egypt was also at war with all of Turkey's enemies, including Great Britain.

The Declaration of the British Protectorate.—The situation was impossible and could be regularized only by making the law conform to the facts and declaring Egypt's political independence. On December 18, 1914, the British Government issued a proclamation which stated that,

"in view of the state of war arising out of the action of Turkey, Egypt is placed under the protection of His Majesty, and will henceforth constitute a British Protectorate. The suzerainty of Turkey over Egypt is thus terminated." [5]

On the following day, a further proclamation announced the deposition from the Khediviate of Abbas Hilmi, who had adhered to the enemy, and the accession of Prince Hussein Kamel Pasha to that dignity, with the title of Sultan of Egypt.[6] In the dispatch covering this proclamation, the

[4] Cd. 7628, Nos. 44, 66, 85, 89-92, 94, 97, 109, 125, 136, 155, 160, 164, 166, 169, 172, 176.

[[5] "The mere abolition of Turkish suzerainty by an act of war would have deprived Egypt of any definite status and left her in the position of a former Turkish dependency in the hands of Great Britain. This difficulty might, of course, have been summarily disposed of by the annexation of Egypt to the British Empire, but the British Government deliberately chose a less drastic course, which would afford security to Egypt, while leaving the principle of an Egyptian national entity unimpaired. This was to place Egypt under the protection of Great Britain." *Egypt,* No. 1 (1921) (Milner), p. 7. For a criticism, see Chirol, "The Egyptian Problem," pp. 123-125.]

[6] Hussein Kamel was a son of Ismail Pasha and thus the uncle of Abbas Hilmi. On Hussein's death in 1917, his youngest brother, Ahmed Fuad,

British Government declared that they regarded themselves as trustees of the newly acquired, as well as of the established, British rights for the inhabitants of Egypt. They further reasserted their purpose,

"while working through and in the closest association with the constituted Egyptian authorities, to secure individual liberty, to promote the spread of education, and, in such measure as the degree of enlightenment of public opinion may permit, to associate the governed in the task of government."

Real Significance of This Step.—Protectorates are of varying degrees and kind, but there is one feature that is common to all of them. The Protecting State invariably controls the foreign relations of the Protectorate. Accordingly, this dispatch declared that,

"as regards foreign relations, His Majesty's Government deem it most consistent with the new responsibilities assumed by Great Britain that the relations between Your Highness's Government and the Representatives of Foreign Powers should, henceforth, be conducted through His Majesty's Representative in Cairo." [7]

The divergencies in this form of political relation arise in the extent of control over the internal affairs of the Protectorate. In practice, the term "Protectorate" is very loosely

succeeded him. [In April, 1922, a Royal Rescript established succession to the throne by primogeniture; but if the King has no male issue, he is succeeded by his eldest brother. Each King will secretly nominate three persons as pro-regent, but Parliament has the right of approval or change.]

[7] Sir Malcolm McIlwraith, "The Declaration of a Protectorate in Egypt," *loc. cit.*, pp. 238-241; *The Times* (London), December 19, 1914. The British Agent and Consul-General was replaced by a High Commissioner. Sir Henry McMahon was the first appointee. After two years, he was succeeded by Sir Reginald Wingate, the highly successful Governor-General of the Sudan. [Since October, 1919, the High Commissioner has been Field-Marshal Viscount Allenby.]

used in the British Empire, and it contains many different
varieties of this general type. But the technical distinction is that, while the soil of a Colony is British and its inhabitants are British subjects, the same is not true of a
Protectorate.[8]

Its International Recognition.—The effect of the declaration of the Protectorate was to abolish all the formal indications of Egypt's political connection with Turkey. Thus,
the Turkish was displaced by an Egyptian flag, and new
coins were used instead of those with the Ottoman insignia.
Even the Turkish appointee, the Grand Cadi, was removed.
These changes did not, however, affect fundamentals, for
the essential point was that Great Britain for over thirty
years had actually exercised a virtual Protectorate.[9] What
was done in 1914 was merely a formal proclamation of a
state of affairs already in existence.[10] The Protectorate,

[8] Sir C. P. Lucas, "The Meaning of Protectorate," in *History,* January,
1918, pp. 241-243.

[9] "We have had a Protectorate *in fact* for some five and thirty years
(recognized by France and other Powers in 1904), and the essential characteristics and needs of the country will not be fundamentally altered
by a diplomatic document." Sir Malcolm McIlwraith, "Egypt in War-
time," in *The Fortnightly Review,* August 1, 1917, p. 232. See also A.
Morel, "La Condition Internationale de l'Égypte," in *Revue Générale de
Droit International Public,* XIV (1907), pp. 405-417.

[10] "It is this superimposition of a formal Protectorate on the previous
long-established occupation—officially recognized by the Great Powers
since 1904—which distinguishes this Protectorate from all others, and
furnishes the key to the solution of the various legal problems which
may arise. The rights of Great Britain in Egypt are primarily founded
not upon general doctrines of international law applicable to any Protectorate which a Great Power may be pleased to declare, but on the
specific and fundamental fact that she rescued the country in 1882, by
force of arms, from anarchy and bankruptcy, and saved from destruction
the dynasty of Mohammed Ali, from one member of whose family she
has now transferred the rule to another." Sir Malcolm McIlwraith, "The
Declaration of a Protectorate in Egypt," *loc. cit.,* pp. 241, 242.

however, requires international recognition. In the first place, the relations between Egypt and the Porte were established in 1841 by the Concert of Europe and, in the second place, various international treaties, notably those of 1856, guaranteed the integrity of the Ottoman Empire.[11] The consent of the Powers is therefore required and the question must come up before the Peace Conference. The matter is essentially a formal one. A number of states, all of which are Great Britain's allies, have already recognized the Protectorate,[12] but it is probable that the Central Empires and Turkey may raise difficulties and try to make their recognition dependent upon compensations to themselves in other directions.[13]

The Question of the Tribute.—Regarded as an abstract question, apart from the peculiar features of the case, it would seem to be self-evident that the annual tribute paid by Egypt to Turkey, £675,000, would automatically cease

[11] Treaties of March 30, Article VII (between Great Britain, Austria, France, Prussia, Russia, Sardinia, and Turkey), and April 15, 1856, Article I (between Great Britain, Austria, and France), in E. Hertslet, "The Map of Europe by Treaty" (3d ed.), II, pp. 1254, 1280; J. H. Scott, "The Law Affecting Foreigners in Egypt," pp. 141, 142; de Freycinet, "La Question d'Égypte," pp. 93, 94. For a discussion of the nature of this guarantee under the treaties of 1856, see C. P. Sanger and H. T. J. Norton, "England's Guarantee to Belgium and Luxemburg," pp. 33-35, 51 ff., London, 1915; Sir E. M. Satow, in *The English Historical Review,* XXXIII (1918), p. 411.

[12] According to *The Statesman's Year-Book,* 1917, p. 251, France, Russia, Belgium, Norway, Serbia, Greece, and Portugal have recognized this Protectorate. The 1918 edition of this Annual (p. 240) omits Norway from the list [as do the editions of 1919 (p. 245), 1920 (p. 252), 1921 (p. 256), and 1922 (p. 264)].

[13 Recognition of this Protectorate is required of Germany by Article 147 of the Versailles Treaty, of Austria by Article 102 of the Treaty of Saint-Germain-en-Laye, of Hungary by Article 86 of the Trianon Treaty, and of Turkey by Article 101 of the Sèvres Treaty. None of the Enemy Powers, not even Turkey, raised any objection to the stipulation.]

with the severance of the political ties between the two countries. As has already been pointed out,[14] this originated in the Turkish conquest and was continued and increased partly for dynastic reasons, but partly also in order to secure emancipation from Turkish rule. The tribute had some measure of international sanction as well, as its amount was determined in 1841 at £360,000 under the auspices of the European Concert. But even more important actually is the fact that Egypt and Turkey are not the only interested parties. For Turkey pledged the tribute as security for monies borrowed abroad and those who made the loans did so on the legitimate assumption that the tribute could not be canceled, at least not until these loans had been repaid. The rights of these bondholders should not be lightly disregarded. Before the war, there were outstanding Turkish loans to the amount of somewhat more than £16 million secured by the Egyptian tribute.[15] In fact, this tribute was not paid to Constantinople at all, but by an arrangement to which the Egyptian Government was a party, it was remitted directly to financial institutions in London for the payment of interest on these loans. As the amount of the tribute exceeds the interest requirements,

---

[14] *Supra*, p. 352.

[15] AMOUNT OUTSTANDING

		1916	1917
I.	1855 Guaranteed Loan 4%	£3,815,200	
II.	1891 Egyptian Tribute 4%	5,246,920	£5,104,920
III.	1894 Egyptian Tribute 3½%	6,996,160	6,910,520
		£16,058,280	£12,015,440

Thomas Skinner, "The Stock Exchange Year-Book," 1914 (London), pp. 151, 152; Fitch "Record of Government Debts," p. 301, New York, 1917; F. C. Mathieson, "Stock Exchange Ten-Year Record," p. 176, London, 1916; *Investor's Monthly Manual*, February 4, 1918, p. 7.

there is a balance for amortization and in the normal course the major part of these loans would be paid off towards the middle of the century. These are the bald facts of the case. No decision has as yet been reached.[16] It raises some fine points, upon which conflicting views are bound to be held. It is of some significance that the prices of the Turkish Egyptian tribute securities have ruled far higher than those of the unsecured Turkish loans, though somewhat below those of the Egyptian loans themselves.[17] This indicates plainly that the holders of the former bonds expect that they will be protected. How this is to be done is another problem. Possibly the most equitable solution would be the continuation of the payment of the tribute in its present manner until these loans are extinguished, when the tribute shall automatically cease.

[*The Final Solution.*—The settlement of the problem as finally reached by the Treaty of Sèvres [18] was as follows:

[16] In the Egyptian financial statements for 1915-16, there is a blank under the entry "tribute," but a new column has been inserted called "Emprunts Divers," in which the amount of the tribute, £E664,826, is inserted. *Annuaire Statistique*, 1916, p. 297. The 1891 loan will be automatically paid off by the sinking fund in 1951, and the 1894 loan in 1955. Fitch, "Record of Government Debts," p. 176; *Investor's Monthly Manual*, February 4, 1918, p. 7.

		1913	1914	1915	1916	1917
[17] Turkish Egyptian Tribute Loan 4% of 1891:	High ...	99¾	99½	88	80¾	81½
	Low ...	89¼	92	80¾	74	70
Turkish Unified 4%:	High ...	88¾	87	62	57¼	57
	Low ...	81⅝	77	47½	44½	49¾
Turkish 4% of 1908:	High ...	75⅞	74¼	55¼	41	38¾
	Low ...	67	64	35	34	33¾
Turkish 4% of 1909:	High ...	80⅝	74½	47¹�ⁿ₁₆	39⅛	38½
	Low ...	65½	69½	30	29⅞	35¼
Egyptian Unified 4%:	High ...	101⅛	101¾	91⅝	81⅞	84½
	Low ...	95	95	73	73	77¼

F. C. Mathieson, *op. cit.*, p. 76; *Investor's Monthly Manual*, February 4, 1918, p. 7.
[18] Article 112.]

"Turkey renounces all claim to the tribute formerly paid by Egypt. Great Britain undertakes to relieve Turkey of all liability in respect of the Turkish loans secured on the Egyptian tribute. . . . The sums which the Khedives of Egypt have from time to time undertaken to pay over to the houses by which these loans were issued will be applied as heretofore to the interest and the sinking funds of the loans of 1894 and 1891 until the final extinction of those loans. The Government of Egypt will also continue to apply the sum hitherto paid towards the interest on the guaranteed loan of 1855. Upon the extinction of these loans of 1894, 1891, and 1855, all liability on the part of the Egyptian Government arising out of the tribute formerly paid by Egypt to Turkey will cease."]

2. The Future of the Capitulations

Their Validity under the Protectorate.—The severance of the political ties binding Egypt to the Ottoman Empire did not of itself diminish the rights of the Treaty Powers in Egypt, nor would the recognition of the British Protectorate affect the legal validity of the Capitulations. But the added security and stability implied by the new régime reduced to a vanishing quantity, if they did not entirely remove, the need for the further continuance of these extraterritorial rights and immunities.[19] The successive British Agents and Consuls-General in Egypt—Cromer, Gorst, and

[19] In 1907, Viscount (Sir Edward) Grey stated officially that the British Government "recognize that the maintenance and development of such reforms as have hitherto been effected in Egypt depend upon the British occupation. This consideration will apply with equal strength to any changes effected in the régime of the Capitulations. His Majesty's Government, therefore, wish it to be understood that there is no reason for allowing the prospect of any modifications in that régime to be prejudiced by the existence of any doubt as to the continuance of the British occupation of the country." Cromer, "The Capitulations in Egypt," in *The Nineteenth Century and After,* July, 1913, p. 7. This article is reprinted in Cromer, "Political and Literary Essays, 1908-1913," pp. 156-174, London, 1913.

Kitchener—pointed out year after year the hampering effect of the Capitulations and, for some time, the British Government had been preparing the diplomatic ground for their ultimate eradication. In 1904, France agreed not to oppose future measures designed to cure Egypt's "legislative impotence" [20] and, in 1912, Italy also made a similar agreement with Great Britain.[21] When, in December, 1914, the Protectorate was declared, the British Government stated officially that "the system of treaties known as the Capitulations . . . are no longer in harmony with the development of the country," but that, in their opinion, "the revision of those treaties may most conveniently be postponed until the end of the present war." As the subject was, however, very complicated, a strong Commission was appointed in Egypt in 1917, to study the reforms which the

[20] In the articles of the Anglo-French Declaration of April 8, 1904, which were not made public at the time, the British Government declared that they had no present intention of proposing to the Powers any changes in the Capitulations or in the judicial organization of Egypt, but it was agreed that, "in the event of their considering it desirable to introduce in Egypt reforms tending to assimilate the Egyptian legislative system to that in force in other civilized countries, the Government of the French Republic will not refuse to entertain any such proposals, on the understanding that His Britannic Majesty's Government will agree to entertain the suggestions that the Government of the French Republic may have to make to them with a view of introducing similar reforms in Morocco." Treaty Series, 1911, No. 24; *American Journal of International Law*, VI, Supplement, p. 29.

[21] On April 16, 1916, the Foreign Minister, Baron Sonnino, stated in the Italian Chamber that an *entente* had been concluded with Great Britain by which Italy consented in principle to the eventual cessation of the Capitulations in Egypt, to which she was pledged in 1912 when Great Britain recognized Italian sovereignty in Tripoli and Cyrenaica. He added that they had agreed to the transformation of the Mixed Tribunals. *L'Afrique Française*, 1916, pp. 147, 148. It was subsequently rumored in Cairo, in 1917 and 1918, that the consent of France and Italy to a change in the judicial system had been secured by promising to appoint a Frenchman and an Italian to the bench of judges in the projected new Court of Cassation. Cf. *The Near East*, April 21, 1916, p. 671.

prospective abolition of the Capitulations would necessitate in judicial organization, in legislative machinery, and in general administration.[22]

[22] The Commission was composed of Youssef Pasha Wahba, Minister of Finance; Adly Yeghen Pasha, Minister of Education; Abd el Khalek Saroit Pasha, Minister of Justice; Mr. Lindsay, Acting Financial Adviser; Sir William Brunyate, Judicial Adviser; Mr. Haines, Adviser of the Interior; M. Laloë, Vice-President of the Mixed Court of Appeal, and Sig. Piola Caselli, Counsel to the Sultan. *Journal of Society of Comparative Legislation*, November, 1917, pp. 279-281. In Egypt, there are five distinct bodies of law and five separate sets of courts—the Mixed, the Native, the Consular, the Mehkemeh, and the Patriarchal—all mutually independent, but overlapping and causing conflicts of jurisdiction. In 1875, when the Mixed Tribunals were instituted, six codes (civil, commercial, maritime, penal, civil procedure, and criminal procedure) were framed, embodying the law which these courts were to apply. These codes were founded upon those of Napoleon and, to a minor extent, upon Italian models, but of late years, as a result of legislative changes, they had become increasingly British in form and substance. In general, however, they were antiquated, as the machinery adopted for modifying them proved unworkable in practice in consequence of the necessity of securing the consent of the Treaty Powers to changes in them. J. H. Scott, "The Law Affecting Foreigners in Egypt," pp. 269-279; N. Bentwich, "Aegypten," in *Jahrbuch des Völkerrechts*, I (1913), pp. 1144-1148; Sir Malcolm McIlwraith in *The Grotius Society*, III (1918), p. 77, and *The Near East*, May 31, 1918, p. 441. This, in brief, was the problem that confronted this Commission. Their preliminary report of April 1, 1918, contained an elaborate project for a system of unified courts to take over the jurisdictions exercised by the Native, Mixed, and Consular Courts. In matters of personal status of Mohammedans, the existing jurisdiction of the religious tribunals was retained and the consular courts were also, though only provisionally, to keep their jurisdiction in questions of personal status regarding the subjects of the Capitulation Powers. Foreigners were to be protected by having the right to have their civil and criminal cases tried by foreign judges. In addition, new codes were to be promulgated. *The Near East*, May 3, 1918, p. 357; May 17, 1918, p. 395. [The first draft code published by the Commission was the Penal Law. This was a comprehensive revision of the old Penal Code in the light of experience gained since the Egyptian was adapted from the French Code in 1883. The Native Code was taken as the basis, the Mixed Code never having been in general use. Various other sources were also utilized—the Draft Penal Code drawn up for the International Zone of Tangier, the Indian and Sudan Penal Codes, the Tunisian Code of 1913, the Siamese Code of 1908, and Italian, Dutch, Swiss, and Belgian Codes. A number of new provisions were likewise introduced. Although the form and much of the substantive law of the French Code were

General Principles of the Reforms.—It would be useless at present to attempt to forecast the details of the final report of this Commission. Certain general principles —clearly recognized by the authorities—will, however, have to be taken into account. In the first place, Egypt is a country of a heterogeneous population; and, in the second place, there are a large number of foreigners in her Civil Service. These are fundamental facts. There were in Egypt in 1907 about 150,000 foreigners, of whom the greater part were permanently domiciled there.[23] They are not mere birds of passage and are entitled to full consideration. Thus, as Egypt is to this degree a cosmopolitan country, it is generally recognized that it will never develop, even if such were the wish, into a British India or Ceylon.

retained, the Commission held that the new law should be harmonized, so far as possible, with the spirit and principles of English Criminal Law. But, in view of the long-continued French influence in Egypt, and in consideration of the nationality of the majority of the foreigners in the country, efforts were made to exclude English concepts in conflict with legal principles generally admitted on the Continent. *The Times* (London), February 6, 1919.]

[23] FOREIGN POPULATION IN EGYPT IN 1907

Greeks	62,973
Italians	34,926
British	20,653
French	14,591
Austrians	7,704
Russians	2,410
Germans	1,847
Spaniards	797
Swiss	637
Belgians	340
Dutch	185

In 1897, there were only 38,204 Greeks and 24,454 Italians. *Annuaire Statistique,* 1914, p. 25. Among the British subjects were 6,292 Maltese; and furthermore, among the foreigners in general were included a considerable number of Egyptians and Levantines who had adopted a European allegiance in order to benefit by the Capitulations. Pierre Arminjon, "La Situation Économique et Financière de l'Égypte," p. 145.

These foreigners have a legitimate stake in Egypt.[24] They
are entitled to a voice in framing its measures and they
must be protected from possible miscarriage of justice by
purely native courts.[25] This can, however, be accomplished
by less clumsy methods than are the present ones, which
hamper progress and block reforms.[26] In addition, the

[24] "Now, the dominating fact of that situation is that Egypt can never
become autonomous in the sense in which that word is understood by
the Egyptian nationalists. It is, and will always remain, a cosmopolitan
country. The real future of Egypt, therefore, lies not in the direction
of a narrow nationalism, which will only embrace native Egyptians, nor
in that of any endeavour to convert Egypt into a British possession on
the model of India or Ceylon, but rather in that of an enlarged cosmo-
politanism, which, whilst discarding all the obstructive fetters of the
cumbersome old international system, will tend to amalgamate all the
inhabitants of the Nile Valley and enable them all alike to share in the
government of their native or adopted country." Cromer, "The Capitulations in Egypt," in *The Nineteenth Century and After*, July, 1913, p. 8.
[25] Lord Cromer insisted upon the abolition of the jurisdiction of the
Consular Courts, as there were other means of giving ample protection
to the subjects of the Treaty Powers. *Egypt*, No. 1 (1907) (Cromer), pp.
14, 15. In 1913, he wrote: "Capitulations or no Capitulations, the
European charged with a criminal offence must be tried either by
European judges or an European jury. All matters connected with the
personal status of any European must be judged by the laws in force
in his own country. Adequate safeguards must be contrived to guard
against any abuse of power on the part of the police." Cromer, "The
Capitulations in Egypt," in *The Nineteenth Century and After*, July, 1913,
p. 5.
[26] During the last years of his tenure of office, Lord Cromer proposed
that the principle of modification should be that "the Powers should
transfer to Great Britain the legislative functions which they now collectively possess." In this connection, he further suggested the creation
of a legislature out of the European elements in Egypt and proposed
that this body should take part in the enactment of laws applicable to
Europeans. *Egypt*, No. 1 (1905) (Cromer), pp. 6-9; No. 1 (1906), pp.
1-11; No. 1 (1907), pp. 13-26. This proposal he continued to advocate
in 1913-15, though not dogmatically insisting that it was the only possible
solution of the problem. Cromer, "The Capitulations in Egypt," in *The
Nineteenth Century and After*, July, 1913, pp. 6-8; Cromer's Introduction
to Sir Sidney Low's "Egypt in Transition," pp. x-xiii; Cromer, "Abbas
II," p. xix. The introduction to Low's book is reprinted in Cromer,
"Political and Literary Essays: Second Series," pp. 214, 215, London, 1914.
After Cromer's retirement, the campaign was carried on by his successors,

European element in the Civil Service must continue and this element cannot lose its cosmopolitan character and become altogether British. Such is not the aim.[27] The purpose is to abolish the remaining vestiges of the right of the Treaty Powers to appoint Egyptian officials. The practice is inherently vicious, as it injected into purely Egyptian affairs entirely irrelevant foreign rivalries.[28] It should be comparatively easy to reach an agreement on these underly-

Gorst and Kitchener, but, writes Sir Malcolm McIlwraith, "as they did not agree entirely with all his views, they discontinued the discussion of the matter in public, and confined themselves to setting forth their own opinions and plans in their private despatches to the Foreign Office." *The Grotius Society*, III (1918), p. 87.

[27] The Anglo-French Declaration of 1904, to which Russia, Italy, Austria-Hungary, and Germany agreed, provided that "officials of those nationalities now in the Egyptian service shall not be placed under conditions less advantageous than those applying to British officials in the same service." Hansard, 1904, pp. 1351, 1352. [Cf. also *Egypt*, No. 1 (1921) (Milner), pp. 29-31.]

[28] In his Annual Report of 1905, Cromer objected to the transfer of the consular jurisdiction to the Mixed Tribunals. "I venture to assert," he wrote, "that any extension of the international principle—at all events, in so far as judicial and administrative questions are concerned—is not in the true interests either of the Egyptians or of the European residents in Egypt; and that reform, if it be undertaken at all, should move rather in the counter-direction, namely, that of gradually freeing Egypt from such international shackles as now exist." In support of this position, he pointed out that Egyptian autonomy was the ultimate goal and that the proposed step was in the opposite direction. Furthermore, he emphasized that it was almost impossible to free international judicial or financial administrations from the political taint which should be alien to them. In conclusion, Lord Cromer distinguished between international institutions in whose working individuals of various nationalities are employed, and those by which foreign Governments have by treaty a direct or indirect power of interference in the internal government and administration of Egypt. He objected to international institutions of the latter character. *Egypt*, No. 1 (1905) (Cromer), pp. 8, 9. "The system which I wish to condemn," he wrote subsequently, "is that under which executive officials are practically nominated by foreign Governments and become, as experience in Egypt has abundantly proved, the political agents of their countries of origin." There was no objection, in fact it was an advantage in his opinion, that Egypt should choose her foreign officials from all nations. To an even greater extent was this

ing principles. The chief difficulty will consist in devising the institutions to fit so complex a situation.

[*Solution Proposed by Lord Milner's Commission.*—Lord Milner's Commission in 1920 gave very careful consideration to the question of the Capitulations, their conclusions being: [29]

"It is, and always has been, the policy of Great Britain to get rid of the Capitulations and to substitute for them a system which, while protecting all legitimate foreign interests, would put an end to the indefensible privileges which foreigners now enjoy. Negotiations to secure that object have for some time been going on between Great Britain and the other Powers who have capitulatory rights in Egypt. But the Powers in question cannot be expected to give up these rights unless they are assured that their nationals can rely on obtaining justice and fair treatment in the future. In order to be able to give them that assurance, Great Britain must be put into a position enabling her to implement it. Thus it is in Egypt's own interest to empower Great Britain to act as the protector of such of the privileges as it is just and reasonable to maintain. It is in this sense that the recognition in the recent Peace Treaties [30] of Great Britain's special position in Egypt should be interpreted."

The Capitulations would accordingly be abolished and a Treaty to be negotiated between Great Britain and Egypt [31] should make provision for the right of the former "to intervene in legislation affecting foreigners and to exercise a cer-

---

true of the judiciary. Thus, he added that "European judges for the Egyptian law-courts should continue, as at present, to be chosen from various nationalities." Cromer, "Modern Egypt," II, pp. 440-442.

[29] *Egypt*, No. 1 (1921), p. 20; for alternative proposals to be incorporated in an Anglo-Egyptian Treaty, see Annex M.

[30] Versailles Treaty, Article 147; Saint-Germain-en-Laye Treaty, Article 102; Trianon Treaty, Article 86; Sèvres Treaty, Article 101.

[31] See Annex M; cf. Annex O.

tain measure of control over those branches of the administration which most directly affect foreign interests." [32]]

3. The Open Door

Anglo-Egyptian Commerce.—Ever since the Industrial
Revolution and especially since the opening of the Suez
Canal, the economic ties between Great Britain and Egypt
have been very close and important. British economic interests in Egypt far exceeded those of every other state.
Great Britain had a predominant share in the foreign trade
of Egypt and British vessels passing through the Suez Canal
greatly outnumbered those of any other nation. In the
years preceding the war, sixty per cent of the traffic on this
narrow highway was British.[33] Similarly, over forty per
cent of the shipping entering Egyptian ports in 1913 flew
the British flag.[34] In the same year, 30.5 per cent of Egypt's

[32] *Egypt*, No. 1 (1921), pp. 38-39. Portugal, by a treaty of December 9,
1920 (Treaty Series, 1921, No. 23; reprinted as Annex P), has formally
assented, so far as she is concerned, to such abolition.

[33] TONNAGE OF VESSELS PASSING THROUGH THE SUEZ CANAL
(in millions of net tons)

	Total	British
1910	16.6	10.4
1911	18.3	11.7
1912	20.3	12.9
1913	20.	12.

Annuaire Statistique, 1914, pp. 272, 273. See also *ibid.*, pp. 258, 259,
where the tonnage is figured differently.

[34] TOTAL ENTRIES IN ALL PORTS OF EGYPT, 1913, 5,656,906 NET TONS

British	2,470,386
Austro-Hungarian	702,433
French	540,437
German	536,849
Russian	495,744
Italian	443,210
Greek	133,791

Ibid., pp. 258, 259.

imports came from the United Kingdom and 43.1 per cent of the exports had that destination.[35] This predominant position was not due to the British Occupation. It existed before 1882. In fact, Egypt is one of the instances in which trade did not follow the virtual hoisting of the flag. While British commerce with Egypt has increased greatly in size since 1882, the United Kingdom's proportion of the total

[35] TRADE STATISTICS IN MILLIONS OF £E

	Total Exports	To the United Kingdom	Percentage
1910	28.9	14.3	49.6
1911	28.6	14.	48.8
1912	34.6	16.	46.3
1913	31.7	13.6	43.1

	Total Imports	From the United Kingdom	Percentage
1910	23.6	7.3	31.
1911	27.2	8.5	31.4
1912	25.9	8.	30.8
1913	27.9	8.5	30.5

Annuaire Statistique, 1914, pp. 290, 291, 294.
[For 1914-21 the corresponding figures were:

	Total Exports	To the United Kingdom	Percentage
1914	24.1	10.4	43.15
1915	27.	13.9	51.5
1916	37.5	19.9	53.1
1917	41.	24.4	59.5
1918	45.4	30.5	67.2
1919	75.9	40.2	52.9
1920	85.5	36.3	42.4
1921	36.3	17.	46.8

	Total Imports	From the United Kingdom	Percentage
1914	21.7	7.1	32.7
1915	19.3	8.7	45.1
1916	30.9	15.1	48.86
1917	33.2	14.1	42.47
1918	51.2	27.1	52.9
1919	47.4	21.5	45.3
1920	101.9	37.9	37.1
1921	55.5	16.9	30.45]

volume has steadily fallen.[36]   In the years preceding the
Occupation, this percentage stood at fifty-seven.   By 1913,
it had sunk to thirty-seven.[37]   That Great Britain was able
to hold so large a share was chiefly due to the fact that the
British and Egyptian economic systems are largely complementary.   Thanks to a variety of circumstances—a damp
climate, highly skilled workmen, and extreme specialization
—England has an undoubted supremacy in the manufacture of the finest cotton yarns and in the finest woven
fabrics as well.[38]   Now, it is just in the manufacture of these
finer grades that the long-staple cotton of Egypt is essential.   Even in 1913, which was an abnormally low year,
forty-three per cent of the entire cotton crop of Egypt
found a market in Great Britain.[39]   On the other hand, the
chief imports into Egypt are cotton textiles in which, again,

[36] PERCENTAGE OF TRADE WITH THE UNITED KINGDOM, AVERAGE OF
FIVE-YEAR PERIODS

	1885-89	1890-94	1895-99	1900-04	1905-09
Imports	37.5	34.7	33.8	36.	32.1
Exports	62.8	59.6	51.4	52.1	52.6

Annuaire Statistique, 1914, p. 294.

[37] Milner, "England in Egypt" (7th ed.), p. 215.

[38] F. W. Taussig, "Some Aspects of the Tariff Question," pp. 290, 291,
Boston, 1915.

[39] COTTON EXPORTS

(in millions of £E)

	1910	1911	1912	1913
Totals	24.2	23.	27.5	25.5
To Great Britain	12.2	11.	12.6	11.
Percentage	50.4	47.7	45.7	43.

Annuaire Statistique, 1914. p. 308.   Great Britain also used large quantities of Egyptian cotton seed from which fodder and oil were made.
Erwin W. Thompson, Department of Commerce, Special Agents' Series,
No. 84, pp. 49, 50; No. 89, p. 5.   In 1913, the total exports of cotton seed
from Egypt amounted to £E3.3 million, of which £E1.7 went to the
United Kingdom and £E1.5 to Germany. *Egypt,* No. 1 (1914) (Kitchener), p. 61.

Lancashire has, in general, a considerable advantage over its competitors.[40]

The Open Door.—The general principle of the open door, which had been scrupulously regarded in all parts of the British Empire under the control of the London Parliament, was, of course, also the rule in Egypt. It was even more rigid here on account of the special circumstances of the case. In 1892, the present Lord Milner wrote:

"So far from unduly favouring the commercial interests of their own countrymen, the British administrators in Egypt err, if anything, on the other side; so intense is the anxiety, that in the position of trust which they occupy they should be above the least suspicion of partiality. Neither directly nor indirectly has Great Britain drawn from her predominant position any profit at the expense of other nations."[41]

In 1904, when France and the other Great Powers of Europe formally recognized the British Occupation, this general principle was embodied in the agreement. In the Anglo-French Treaty of that year, the two Governments declared that they would not, either in Egypt or in Morocco, "countenance any inequality either in the imposition of customs duties or other taxes, or of railway transport charges." This mutual agreement was to be binding for thirty years.[42] On the one hand, the question now arises why there should be

[40] The value of the cotton tissues imported in 1913 was £E3.7 mill.on, of which £E3 came from the United Kingdom. *Egypt,* No. 1 (1913) (Kitchener), pp. 58, 59.

[41] Milner, *op. cit.,* p. 215.

[42] Article IV, containing this agreement, further provided that both Governments reserved to themselves "the right to see that concessions for roads, railways, ports, etc., are only granted on such conditions as will maintain intact the authority of the State over these great undertakings of public interest." Treaty Series, 1905, No. 6; De Bernhardt,

any limitation of time; and, on the other, why, in case of necessity, Great Britain should be hampered in using a not insignificant economic weapon against the Central Empires and their allies. Egypt imported considerable merchandise from Turkey and Austria-Hungary,[43] and Germany needs Egyptian long-staple cotton. As this type is not produced in Russia,[44] the control of the Egyptian supply by the Allies is one among many of the economic arms that can be used with effect by the Allies at the Peace Conference.[45]

Tariff Autonomy.—Closely connected with this question is that of tariff autonomy for Egypt. Very obviously, the

"Handbook of Commercial Treaties between Great Britain and Foreign Powers," p. 338 ["Trattati . . . relativi all'Africa," p. 1117]; M. P. Price, "The Diplomatic History of the War," p. 275, London, 1914.

[43] IMPORTS INTO EGYPT

(*in millions of £E*)

	1912	1913
Turkey	2.8	2.7
Austria-Hungary	1.7	1.9
Germany	1.4	1.6

Egypt, No. 1 (1914) (Kitchener), p. 58.

[44] A considerable part of the Russian crop in Turkestan and Transcaucasia "is about American quality, but the native varieties are more like the inferior grades of Indian cotton." J. A. Todd, "The Cotton Resources of the British Empire," in A. P. Newton, "The Staple Trades of the Empire," p. 102, London, 1917. In fact, Russia in 1913 imported from Egypt cotton to the value of £E2,200,000. On the Russian cotton crop, especially in Ferghana in Turkestan, see A. Woeikof, "Le Turkestan Russe," Paris, 1914; ["Werner Daya" (pseudonym of W. Karfunkelstein), "Der Aufmarsch im Osten: Russisch-Asien als Deutsches Kriegs- und Wirtschaftsziel," pp. 109-118, Dachau-bei-München, n.d.].

[45] According to the Egyptian statistics, Egypt exported in 1913 cotton to Germany valued at £E2.4 million, or 9.54 per cent of the total crop. *Annuaire Statistique*, 1914, p. 308; *Egypt*, No. 1 (1914) (Kitchener), p. 61. The German statistics value these imports at 73 million marks and, according to other authorities, the German consumption of Egyptian cotton in 1912-13 was 102,241 bales (each of 750 lbs.) as against 201,000 for the United States and 351,406 for Great Britain. *Statistisches Jahrbuch*, 1915, pp. 185, 30*.

economic weapon cannot be used if Egypt is to be bound
by the existing commercial conventions, with their favored-
nation clauses. But entirely apart from this, the problem
demands serious consideration. It is an indefensible policy
to restrict the economic freedom of countries like China and
Egypt in the interest of the commerce of foreign states. Up
to the present, Egypt has not suffered much on this score,
but the time will probably come when it will be desirable
to use the tariff to establish industries in Egypt. Nationalism in the East, as well as elsewhere, tends to assume an
economic aspect. The experience in British India is instructive. There is really no sound reason why Egypt should
not enjoy the same tariff autonomy as does that country and
why there should not be full freedom to impose protective
duties, if such a course should in itself seem to be advisable
or if public opinion should insistently demand it.

4.   Possible Territorial Changes

The Question of the Gulf of Akaba.—In 1914, there were
a number of boundary problems that concerned Egypt and
the Anglo-Egyptian Sudan, but no one of these had any
political importance. The question between Great Britain
and France as to the frontier between Darfur and Wadai,
which had been left open in the agreement of 1899, had been
referred to The Hague for arbitration.[46] A rectification of

[46] On September 8, 1919, an Anglo-French agreement (not as yet published) was reached concerning this boundary by which the region of
Dar Tama was attached to Wadai, and Dar Massalit to Darfur (*Le
Temps,* February 14, 1920).] For the Anglo-French Agreement of 1899,
see Hertslet, "Map of Africa by Treaty" (3d ed.), II, pp. 796, 797
[Trattati . . . relativi all'Africa," pp. 613-614]. Cf. *L'Afrique Française,*
1918, p. 116.

the British Uganda-Sudan boundary had likewise been proposed. The delimitation of the Sudan-Congo frontier was also to have been taken in hand early in 1915, but this was postponed.[47] The war, however, raised some territorial questions. The use of submarines for the destruction of merchantmen directed attention to the strategic position of the Gulf of Akaba, to the east of the Sinai Peninsula, since a submarine base there could be a source of great danger to traffic through the Red Sea. This boundary had been determined only recently. After a rather acrimonious dispute, the Turco-Egyptian frontier was clearly defined in 1906.[48] The agreement left in Turkish hands the head and the eastern shore of the Gulf of Akaba. The question has arisen of pushing Egypt's frontier farther to the east as a defensive measure, so as to include at least the head of the Gulf. The advisability of this step must, of course, depend upon the outcome of the war. If the present Kingdom of Hedjaz remains as an established institution, free from Turkish and German domination, there will apparently be no real need of changing the established boundary.[49]

Italian Colonial Ambitions.—Far more important and extensive are likely to be the territorial changes resulting from the agreement made previous to Italy's entrance into the war. Article XIII of the Treaty of London of April 26, 1915, reads:

"In the event of an extension of the French and British colonial possessions in Africa at the expense of Germany,

[47] Sir Reginald Wingate, "Memorandum on the Sudan, 1914," p. 8.
[48] *Egypt*, No. 2 (1906), pp. 6-36; Hertslet, *op. cit.,* III, pp. 1199-1203 ["Trattati," pp. 1244-1246].
[49 The Boundary remains unchanged.]

France and Great Britain recognize to Italy in principle the right of demanding for herself certain compensations, in the form of an extension of her possessions in Eritrea, Somaliland, Libya, and the colonial districts bordering on French and British colonies." [50]

Since then, there has been a widespread discussion in Italy by influential bodies, like the Istituto Coloniale Italiano, the Società Africana d'Italia, the Società Italiana di Esplorazioni, and the Istituto Orientale di Napoli, and by a number of publicists.[51] It should be remembered, of course, that these are non-official views. Some of the claims are undoubtedly exaggerated,[52] and have been criticized by

[50] *The New Europe*, No. 66 (January 17, 1918), p. 27. *L'Afrique Française*, Nos. 1, 2, 3 (1918), p. 40 gives the French text, cf. *infra*, p. 463 [*The Times* (London) of April 30, 1920, contains the official English translation].

[51] Report of National Colonial Conference at Naples, April 26-28, 1917, in *L'Esplorazione Commerciale*, May 31, 1917, pp. 133-139; Ghibellino, "La Guerra Europea e la Politica Coloniale Italiana" in *Rivista Coloniale*, 1915, pp. 15-18; Mario Corsi, "La Nostra Pace Coloniale," *ibid.*, 1917, pp. 251-256; Giuseppe Piazza, "Le Nostre Rivendicazioni Libiche," *ibid.*, 1917, pp. 93-106, and "La Nostra Pace Coloniale," Rome, 1917. See also the account of Piazza's report as secretary of a committee of the Istituto Coloniale Italiano in the New York *Bollettino della Sera*, August 5, 1918 and "Relazione del Comitato per gl'Interessi Coloniali Italiani e per Quelli in Oriente," in *Rivista Coloniale*, April 30, 1918, pp. 138-146. For French opposition to this extensive program, see *L'Afrique Française*, July-August, 1917, and September-November, 1917, also Nos. 1, 2, 3 (1918), pp. 40, 41. On the broad aspects of the question from the Italian standpoint, see G. A. Colonna di Cesarò, "Aspetti Coloniali della Guerra," in *La Vita Italiana*, June 15, 1918.

[52] Thus the Istituto Orientale of Naples, at its meeting on January 24, 1917, demanded among other things that the coast of Yemen from Confuda to Sheikh Said be recognized as within the Italian sphere, on the ground that the eastern coast of the Red Sea has the same importance for Eritrea as the eastern coast of the Adriatic has for Italy herself. In fact, Sheikh Said has relatively about the same strategic importance as Valona. "The favoured passage for ships passing into and out of the Red Sea lies through the narrow strait between Perim and Sheikh Said, and there is no doubt that the possession of this place, if it were fortified with modern artillery, would be a most serious menace to British and other shipping." Sir H. H. Johnston, "Common Sense in Foreign Policy," pp. 99, 100, London, 1913. See also A. M. Murray, "Imperial Outposts from a Strategical and Commercial Aspect," pp. 38-53, London, 1907. There

Italians themselves, but there is substantial unanimity on the main points.

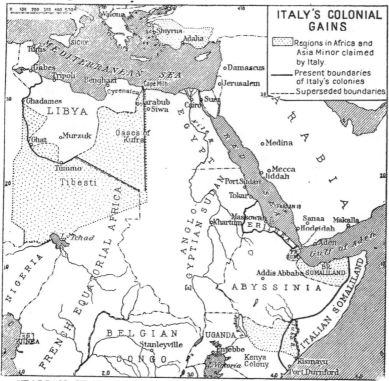

ITALIAN CLAIMS AND ACQUISITIONS IN NORTH AFRICA
From I. Bowman, "The New World: Problems in Political Geography." Copyright, 1921 by World Book Company, Yonkers-on-Hudson, New York.

A Hinterland for Libya.—Before the war the Italians had been dissatisfied because Tripoli and Cyrenaica, generally designated as Italian Libya, lacked a hinterland. The securing of such an *arrière-pays* now became the chief item in the comprehensive program of the Italian colonial party.

is apparently no substantial basis for this claim on the part of Italy. For even more exaggerated claims, consult Giovanni Graziani, "La Guerra Europea e l'Avvenire Coloniale Italiano," in *La Geografia*, May-June, 1915, pp. 168 ff. [Cf. also Antonelli, "L'Afrique et la Paix de Versailles," pp. 201-205.]

The general argument was that the natural outlet for a
large part of the Sudanese trade is through Libya, but that
this traffic had been attracted to Algeria and Tunis and
that it had also been diverted either to the West Coast by
the British Nigerian and the French Senegalese and Guinea
railroads or to the Red Sea by the railroads in the Anglo-
Egyptian Sudan.   Libya was thus left high and dry.   In
order to redress this situation in favor of Mediterranean
ports and to make Libya prosperous, it was contended that
the hinterland must be extended to Lake Chad. This would
involve the cession of considerable territory by France and
Egypt. The proposed new boundary on the west, as drawn
by the colonial party, would run almost directly from
Ghadames to Ghat, cutting off the unjustifiable French
wedge between these two places. From Ghat the line would
then proceed roughly along the 9th degree of east longitude
to Nigeria. On the east, the proposed new boundary would
start, as at present, from the Bay of Sollum, but would
pass south along the 25th degree of east longitude so as to
include the Oasis of Jarabub and thence by the heights of
Ennedi, to Lake Chad. This proposal would give all of
Borku and Tibesti to Italy and also access to Lake Chad,
leaving Wadai to France. While some details of this proposal were highly indefensible,[53] its main principle, that

---

[53] This proposed western boundary is apparently inadmissible since it
gratuitously interposes an Italian wedge between French territory and
prevents direct communication *via* Lake Chad between important French
colonies. By deflecting the line from Ghat to the east so that it runs
to Lake Chad, Italy would still have access to this region without unnecessarily thwarting French development. See also Frank R. Cana, "The
Northwest Frontier of Egypt," in *Geographical Journal*, February, 1916,
p. 132, *et passim*.

Libya should have an adequate hinterland, was sound.[54] The details of whatever may be effected will probably be arranged by direct negotiations between Great Britain (acting on behalf of Egypt and the Anglo-Egyptian Sudan), France, and Italy. If such an arrangement is carried out, Italy will have a hard road to travel, as the regions to be added to Libya are the center of the powerful Senussi sect.[55]

Kassala.—In addition, the Italian colonial party has desired an extension of the boundaries of Eritrea at the expense of the Anglo-Egyptian Sudan. In 1891, when the Dervishes under the Mahdi's successor, the Khalifa, had nearly complete control over the Sudan, a treaty was concluded between Great Britain and Italy, by which the latter country was allowed, in case of military necessity, to occupy Kassala and the adjoining country up to the Atbara River.

Camille Fidel, "Le Programme Colonial Italien," in *L'Afrique Française,* September-October, 1918, pp. 270-275, desires a full discussion to reconcile French and Italian aims. He refers to an article by Dr. Angelo Nicola in *L'Esplorazione Commerciale* of May-June, 1918, and to a report by Giuseppe Piazza in *Rivista Coloniale,* April, 1918, both agreeing on the necessity of extending Libya to Lake Chad (in 1914, Great Britain recognized Italy's rights to the Oasis of Kufra). The main criticism is directed against the Italian charges that the French title is illegal and that Italy succeeded to Turkish rights, which were full and complete in the hinterland. The editorial of the Royal Colonial Institute in *United Empire Magazine* for May, 1918, is also hostile to the Italian program.

[54] The hinterland for Libya proposed by Sir Harry H. Johnston ran considerably farther to the East and did not give access to Lake Chad. *Geographical Journal,* April, 1915, pp. 274 ff. [For the solution reached in the Franco-Italian notes of September 12, 1919, see *infra,* p. 451.]

[55] The Senussi are the most powerful Mohammedan sect in Northeast Africa. Up to 1915, they had been friendly with Egypt, but their leader, Sidi Ahmed, had fought for many years against the extension of French authority in the Central Sudan and he was, when the war broke out, conducting a campaign against the Italians in Cyrenaica. By the end of 1914, the Senussi held the whole interior of Cyrenaica, and the Italian garrisons had all been withdrawn to the coast. "The Times [London] History of the War," IX, pp. 281-292.

It was provided, however, that such temporary measures should not abrogate Egypt's rights, which should "only remain in suspense until the Egyptian Government shall be in a position to reoccupy the district in question." [56]   Italy, accordingly, took control of the Kassala region in 1894, but after the disastrous defeat at Adowa in 1896 at the hands of the Abyssinians, a reaction against colonial adventures set in and Rome decided to withdraw.   Great Britain, however, requested Italy to delay the evacuation until Anglo-Egyptian troops could be sent to hold that important station.[57] This was formally effected in 1897.[58]   The Italian colonial party's program now includes the retrocession of Kassala to Eritrea, presumably with the boundaries as defined in the Treaty of April 15, 1891.   This region is one of the most fertile parts of the Anglo-Egyptian Sudan and is well adapted for the cultivation of cotton.[59]   If the Italian claim is conceded, as it might well be under certain eventualities, adequate safeguards will have to be provided that the waters of the Atbara River shall not be used to an extent prejudicial to Egypt.[60]

[56] Protocol of April 15, 1891. Hertslet, op. cit., III, pp. 949, 950 ["Trattati," pp. 341-342].

[57] J. H. Rose, "The Development of the European Nations, 1870-1900," II, pp. 203, 204, London, 1905.

[58] Act of Cession by Italy to Egypt of Fort of Kassala, December 25, 1897. Hertslet, op. cit., III, pp. 1109, 1110 ["Trattati," pp. 568-569]. See also the boundary agreements of 1900 and 1902. Hertslet, op. cit., pp. 433, 460 ["Trattati," pp. 639-640, 686-690].

[59] Colvin, "The Making of Modern Egypt" (3d ed.), p. 386. It is said to contain 120,000 acres of land suitable for cotton. J. A. Todd, "The World's Cotton Crops," p. 305, London, 1915.

[60] Article III of the Anglo-Italian Protocol of April 15, 1891, reads: "The Italian Government engages not to construct on the Atbara, in view of irrigation, any work which might sensibly modify its flow into the Nile."

Control of the Juba River.—In addition, this program provides for better means of approach to the Italian colony of Somaliland, which is divided from British East Africa by the Juba River. By a special treaty, made in 1891, it was agreed that the port of Kismayu with its territory on the right bank of the Juba River should be British.[61] By a subsequent agreement drawn up in 1905 a plot of ground at Kismayu was leased for a nominal sum to Italy for the purpose of erecting a bonded warehouse with a special pier leading to it.[62] It is now claimed that the possession of the port of Kismayu is necessary to the development of Italian Somaliland. In order to pass definite judgment on this question, detailed knowledge of local conditions is essential.[63]

British and French Somaliland.—These three claims—a vast hinterland for Libya, the Kassala region, and the port of Kismayu—command the unanimous support of the colonial party. But in addition, there are also far more ambitious projects which have many champions. "The grandeur that was Rome" stimulates the imagination of the modern Italian, who considers himself ancient Rome's direct heir. Many colonial enthusiasts demand the cession to Italy of both French and British Somaliland. It has been pointed out to them by the more moderate of their associates that Jibuti is the only French coaling station between Marseilles and Madagascar and the Far East, and

[61] Protocol of March 24, 1891. Hertslet, *op. cit.*, III, p. 948 ["Trattati," p. 340].

[62] Agreement of January 13, 1905. Hertslet, *op. cit.*, pp. 958-960 ["Trattati," pp. 745-748].

[[63] Thus far, the only increment of Italian territory in Africa has been the additional area attached to Libya.]

that, in view of the completion of the French railroad from
Jibuti to Addis Abeba, the capital of Abyssinia, it is scarcely
likely that France would cede this colony. The cession of
British Somaliland, which has never been pacified, presents
fewer obstacles, but there is this difficulty, that much of this
coastal region is required for the provisioning of Aden.

Abyssinia.—The cession of French and British Somaliland
to Italy would more than half surround Abyssinia by Italian
territory. Those who urge these claims have also in mind
a revival of Italy's former attempts to establish a protectorate over Abyssinia, which came to a sanguinary end at
Adowa in 1896.[64] Since then, Great Britain, France, and
Italy have by formal treaty in 1906 guaranteed the integrity
of Abyssinia and the *status quo* there.[65] Italy's colonial
enthusiasts now urge that this agreement be virtually canceled. It is, of course, impossible to predict exactly what
will be the outcome of the disturbances in Abyssinia since
the death of King Menelik in 1913, but on its face, this
Italian project is highly indefensible and should not be
countenanced unless the condition of Abyssinia were to
become really hopeless.

[64] Sir H. H. Johnston, "History of the Colonization of Africa by Alien
Races," pp. 395, 396.

[65] Hertslet, *op. cit.*, II, pp. 436-444 ["Trattati," pp. 1251-1257]; Albin,
"Les Grands Traités Politiques," pp. 408-412; *American Journal of Inter-
national Law*, I, Supplement, pp. 226-230. For a study of this treaty, see
Pierre Alype, "L'Éthiopie," pp. 99-110.

CHAPTER V

EGYPT DURING AND AFTER THE WAR

[*Attitude Towards the Two Groups of Belligerents.*— With the proclamation of the British Protectorate on December 18, 1914, Egypt was in a state of war with her former suzerain, Turkey. Nevertheless, it could not be said that she was wholeheartedly on the side of the Allies. Bonds of a common religion and a common civilization linked her with Constantinople; the growth of a nationalistic spirit made her desire to exchange vassalage for independence rather than for the status of a Protectorate; and discontent was fostered not only by enemy agents, but by British measures dictated by military exigencies. The spirit of resistance already smoldering ill-concealed among the Egyptian *intelligenzia* spread to the *fellahin,* who had hitherto shown more interest in their cotton crops than in their political status.[1]

Discontent of the Higher Classes.—In common with all other belligerent countries, Egypt became subject to the restrictions of censorship and military constraint. If these measures were necessary in lands unanimous in their

---

[1] The history of Anglo-Egyptian relations from 1879 to the end of 1920 is conveniently summarized by H. J. Carman, "England and the Egyptian Problem," in *Political Science Quarterly,* 36, pp. 51-78. See also for a history of events since the outbreak of the war, Sir Valentine Chirol, "The Egyptian Problem," pp. 120-141, 177-205, 243-259; and for a survey of Egyptian nationalism, *ibid.,* pp. 94-97, 150-155.

support of the side for which they fought, whether for the Allies or for the Central Powers, they were doubly requisite in a country divided within itself. Naturally such restraints proved highly irksome to those who had already been restive under the Occupation, and the resentment of the Nationalists increased, especially as the legislative bodies were not permitted to assemble or to take any part in the measures adopted by Government for the prosecution of the war. The absolute necessity of this course is self-evident; but it was capable of sinister distortion by those interested in misrepresenting the reason for its adoption.

Dissatisfaction of the Fellahin.—Among the *fellahin* also a restive spirit grew up. This was due not merely to incitement from Nationalist agitators and enemy agents, but likewise to facts arising immediately from measures taken by the British in Egypt. The chief of these, as enumerated by Lord Milner's Commission,[2] were: (*a*) the controlled price of cotton, denying the cultivator the advantage of competing in foreign markets, while the rent of his land continued to increase; and, more obviously, (*b*) recruiting for the Egyptian Labour and Camel Transport Corps; (*c*) requisition of domestic animals; (*d*) requisition of cereals; (*e*) collection for the Red Cross Fund. Yet even here, "in each case it was not so much the measures themselves that were resented as the manner in which they were carried out." As a matter of fact, it would appear that such abuses as existed were committed in the main by unscrupulous *Omdehs* (administrative officers serving without pay in the

[2] *Egypt*, No. 1 (1921), pp. 11-12.

country districts) and other native officials, whom, under the exceptional conditions then prevailing, the British were unable adequately to supervise. In addition to all this, there was an unprecedented and progressive rise in prices, especially for the necessities of life, and stories of outrages committed on native women by British soldiers and of murderous attacks on villages were widely circulated.

The Peace Conference.—On the termination of hostilities the Nationalists thought that the hour was come for Egypt's complete independence and that they might now press for abolition of the Protectorate. Unfortunately for themselves, they, like certain other groups, mistook the purpose of the Peace Conference, which was not intended to be a court for hearing all conceivable complaints and adjudicating all conceivable claims, but was convened for the purpose of framing treaties with the ex-Enemy Powers and of determining the status and the relations of new States arising within the territory of those Powers.[3] By the proclamation of the Protectorate, Egypt had ceased, on December 18, 1914, to form part of the Ottoman Empire in any sense whatever and was not, consequently, a subject for consideration by the Conference. If, therefore, the memorials

[3] The sole deviations (more apparent than real) from this principle were the attribution of the *terrae nullius* of Spitsbergen and Bear Island, in both of which Germany had shown keen interest, to Norway, in consideration of her losses in the Allied cause during the war through German activities (for a convenient survey of the diplomatic history of the Spitsbergen problem, see L. H. Gray, "Spitsbergen and Bear Island," Washington, 1919); the three Conventions relating to Africa (see Annexes E, F, and G) arising from revision of the Berlin and Brussels Acts, to both of which Austria, Germany, and Turkey had been signatory; and the Convention for the Regulation of Aerial Navigation of October 13, 1919.

presented to the Conference by the Egyptian Delegation met with no response, and if the Delegation were granted no official audience, it was not because of prejudice against Egypt, and implied no decision, whether favorable or the reverse, concerning her claims. The same position was taken towards other Delegations in like case. The Conference held it to be beyond its competence to rule upon the claims of non-belligerent countries or to receive Delegations of ethnic or political factions from within the territories of the Allied and Associated Powers.

Outbreak of March, 1919.—The position taken by the British Government in declining to receive at London either the advanced Nationalist group, who desired to put forward a program of "complete autonomy" for Egypt, or the Prime Minister, Rushdi Pasha, who wished to discuss Egyptian affairs, particularly the precise extent of the Protectorate,[4] resulted in increased unrest. Early in March, 1919, it was deemed necessary to deport to Malta Saad Zaghlul, the leader of the advanced Nationalists, and three of his most prominent associates. This caused an outbreak of such gravity that Lord Allenby was sent to Egypt. Out-

---

[4] The Foreign Office felt that "no useful purpose would be served by allowing Nationalist leaders to come to London," and that, since both the Foreign Secretary and the other Ministers would be absent from London because of the Peace Negotiations, they "would not be able to devote sufficient time and attention to problems of Egyptian internal reform." In this connection the Milner Report adds (*Egypt,* No. 1 [1921], pp. 13-14): "There were no doubt obvious difficulties in the way of discussing such questions with the Egyptian Ministers at a moment of high political pressure, when the Peace Conference was about to open, but it would appear that, in spite of the insistence with which the High Commissioner [Sir Reginald Wingate] appealed for their reception, the real urgency of dealing with the Egyptian problem at that critical moment had not been realised."

ward tranquillity was restored; steps were taken to remove the sources of discontent; and the best class of Egyptians showed themselves willing to coöperate in the cause of order. On April 7, the deportation of Zaghlul Pasha and his colleagues was revoked, and their freedom of movement being unrestricted, they proceeded to Paris to represent their party at the Peace Conference.

The Milner Commission.—Notwithstanding all attempts at conciliation, the Egyptians continued to be sullen and restive. In view of this, in May, 1919, a Commission "to enquire into the causes of the late disorders in Egypt, and to report on the existing situation in the country and the form of the Constitution which, under the Protectorate, will be best calculated to promote its peace and prosperity, the progressive development of self-governing institutions, and the protection of foreign interests" was sent, with Lord Milner as Chairman, to Egypt,[5] although it was not until December 7 that the Mission actually arrived at Cairo. Throughout its stay in Egypt, until the end of the first week of March, 1920, the Mission was confronted with an attitude of studied reserve on the part of the official world and with active opposition from the native public and the native press, although many educated Egyptians, even some advanced Nationalists, did not approve this course. So severe was the pressure of intimidation exercised by the Nationalists, however, that it overshot its mark, "for it was impossible not to come to the conclusion that, if the Egyptians were really so unanimous as we were intended to think, we

[5] A full account of the Mission is contained in *Egypt*, No. 1 (1921); cf. also Chirol, *op. cit.*, pp. 260-273.

should have been left to find that out for ourselves by going about the country without let or hindrance." [6]

The Commission's Conclusions.—The views of the Commission as to the best course to be pursued in regard to the future relations of Great Britain and Egypt involved considerable modification of the policy hitherto adopted and were so momentous that they merit quotation in full.[7]

"We gradually came to the conclusion that no settlement could be satisfactory which was simply imposed by Great Britain upon Egypt, but that it would be wiser to seek a solution by means of a bilateral agreement—a Treaty—between the two countries. In no other way did it appear possible to release Egypt from the tutelage to which Egyptians so vehemently object, without endangering any of the vital interests which we are bound to safeguard. All necessary safeguards, as it seemed to us, could be provided in the terms of a Treaty of Alliance by which Egypt, in return for Great Britain's undertaking to defend her integrity and independence, would agree to be guided by Great Britain in her foreign relations and would at the same time confer upon Great Britain certain definite rights in Egyptian territory. The rights we contemplated were of a twofold character. Firstly, in order to protect her special interest in Egypt—the safety of her Imperial communications—Great Britain was to have the right to maintain a military force on Egyptian soil; and secondly, for the protection of all legitimate foreign interests, she was to have a certain measure of control over Egyptian legislation and administration, as far as they affected foreigners. The former privilege was no more than what Egypt could honourably concede to an ally who undertook to defend her against all external dangers, and whose strength and security were therefore of vital importance to Egypt herself. And the latter privilege would involve no greater infringement of Egyptian independence than that to which, by

[6] *Egypt*, No. 1 (1921), p. 5.
[7] *Ibid.*, pp. 19, 20; cf. also pp. 38-39.

virtue of the Capitulations, Egypt has always been exposed. Indeed, by substituting a single Power, Great Britain, for the thirteen foreign Powers which have hitherto enjoyed capitulatory rights in Egypt, it would tend to enlarge rather than to curtail that independence. Moreover, it was part of our scheme, as it has always been a feature of British policy in Egypt, to confine the special privileges enjoyed by foreigners under the Capitulations within more reasonable limits, and by so doing to make Egypt much more the mistress in her own house than she is to-day. But this could only be done if Egypt was prepared to recognise Great Britain as the protector of these foreign privileges when reduced to reasonable proportions. . . . These, in broad outline and reserving details for later explanation, are the main features of the settlement by which we had come to think that the relations between Great Britain and Egypt might in future be regulated. And when we began to discuss them with those Egyptians, all of more or less advanced Nationalist opinions, with whom we were in friendly contact, it was encouraging to find that our suggestions met with a large measure of sympathy. No doubt the idea of a Treaty, of a settlement arrived at by agreements between equals, not by dictation from above, appealed strongly to their sense of being a distinct people, to their national self-respect. For evidently that idea involved the recognition, in principle, of the independence of Egypt and was inconsistent with the theory of her being a British possession. And when they came to consider the conditions which in our proposal were attached to this recognition, they were ready to admit that, however unacceptable to extreme Nationalists, these conditions were nevertheless such as they could themselves justify to their countrymen, as being compatible with their status as a nation. For that status could only be maintained in fact by the support of Great Britain and Great Britain was entitled to a reasonable *quid pro quo* for this indispensable support. That she should claim to control the foreign policy of Egypt and should have the right to maintain, for her own Imperial purposes, a force on Egyptian soil, was no more than such a *quid pro quo*. As regards her domestic affairs, Egypt would be completely self-governing except in respect of the privileges of foreigners. And the restrictions upon the full exercise of Egyptian sovereignty which the maintenance of some of these privileges involved were no greater but less, and far less irksome, than the restrictions which had always existed. In view of these practical considerations, it could not be denied that the proposed arrangement was conceived in the interests, not only of Great Britain, but of Egypt, and could be defended as a fair and reasonable basis for future co-operation."

The Milner-Zaghlul Agreement.—After the Commission's return to England, its work still continued. Zaghlul Pasha and seven other members of the Paris Delegation came to London in June and until the middle of August discussed with Lord Milner and his colleagues the bases of an Anglo-Egyptian Treaty along the lines of the conclusions just recorded.[8] The result was the Memorandum of August 18, 1920, known as the "Milner-Zaghlul Agreement," [9] its essence being Paragraph 3 (i):

"As between Egypt and Great Britain a Treaty will be entered into, under which Great Britain will recognise the independence of Egypt as a constitutional monarchy with representative institutions, and Egypt will confer upon Great Britain such rights as are necessary to safeguard her special interests and to enable her to furnish the guarantees which must be given to foreign Powers to secure the relinquishment of their capitulatory rights."

Furthermore, provision was made for representation of Egypt in foreign countries, defense of imperial communications, British officials in the Egyptian service, and reservations for the protection of foreigners.[10]

[8] For a summary of these conversations, see *Egypt,* No. 1 (1921), pp. 22-23.
[9] For the complete text of the Agreement (given *ibid.,* pp. 24-26) see Annex M.
[10] See *ibid.,* pp. 26-32 for the reasons underlying these provisions.

Reception in Egypt.—On the close of the conversations culminating in the Milner-Zaghlul Agreement, the Egyptian Delegation returned to Paris, sending four of their number to Egypt to sound the feeling of their fellow-countrymen. The reception was, generally speaking, favorable, so that, for instance, forty-seven of the fifty-one remaining members of the Legislative Assembly voted for the proposals, two abstained from expressing their opinion, and only two recorded themselves as opposed.[11]   At the same time, further interpretation of certain points was desired, and a number of modifications were requested, particularly "a limitation of the functions of the Financial Adviser and of the British official in the Ministry of Justice; the abandonment of the provision of Article 5 of the memorandum —that the coming into force of the contemplated Treaty between Great Britain and Egypt should be dependent upon the previous conclusion of agreements with the Powers for necessary modifications in the régime of the Capitulations; and, above all, the formal abolition of the Protectorate." [12]

The Present Status.—While the Commission were most anxious to meet all possible Egyptian desires, they were obviously incompetent to bind their Government. As Lord Milner pointed out in his closing address to the Delegation on November 9, 1920:

"The memorandum never professed to do more than indicate the general lines on which an agreement could be arrived at.   In any case, as we have always foreseen, the

[11] *Egypt,* No. 1 (1921), p. 25.
[12] *Ibid.,* p. 36.

agreement itself, if it is decided to proceed with it, will have to be the outcome of formal negotiations between duly accredited representatives of the British and Egyptian Governments. . . . What is far more important at the present stage than any further discussion of details is to influence opinion both here and in Egypt in a sense favourable to a settlement on the lines which we both favour, and above all to cultivate and strengthen by every means the spirit of friendship and mutual confidence which our conversations here have helped to engender, but which must become general on both sides if our efforts are to lead to the desired result." [13]

On November 10, 1921, after extended conversations, a draft Convention was handed by Lord Curzon to the Egyptian Delegation.[14] In its main outlines, this followed the Milner-Zaghlul Agreement; but the Delegation objected to it on the ground that it was restrictive of Egypt's complete independence. In view of this attitude, Lord Allenby, on December 3, addressed a communication to the Sultan [15] discussing in full the problem of Anglo-Egyptian relations; but this likewise failed to gain Nationalist approval. During the latter part of the month, agitation aroused by Zaghlul attained such proportions that he, with several of his adherents, was deported to Ceylon, later to the Seychelles, and finally to Gibraltar, where he remained until his release in March, 1923. Meanwhile, Lord Allenby more than once had advised termination of the Protectorate; [16] and on February 28, 1922, the following Declaration was made: [17]

[13] *Egypt*, No. 1 (1921), p. 36.
[14] *Ibid.*, No. 4 (1921), pp. 3-6; reprinted as Annex O.
[15] *Ibid.*, pp. 10-14.
[16] *Ibid.*, No. 1 (1922), pp. 8, 19-20, 24.
[17] Cf. *ibid.*, pp. 29-30.

"Whereas His Majesty's Government, in accordance with their declared intentions, desire forthwith to recognise Egypt as an independent sovereign State; and

"Whereas the relations between His Majesty's Government and Egypt are of vital interest to the British Empire;

"The following principles are hereby declared:—

"1. The British Protectorate over Egypt is terminated, and Egypt is declared to be an independent sovereign State.

"2. So soon as the Government of his Highness shall pass an Act of Indemnity with application to all inhabitants of Egypt, martial law as proclaimed on the 2nd November, 1914, shall be withdrawn.

"3. The following matters are absolutely reserved to the discretion of His Majesty's Government until such time as it may be possible by free discussion and friendly accommodation on both sides to conclude agreements in regard thereto between His Majesty's Government and the Government of Egypt:—

"*(a.)* The security of the communications of the British Empire in Egypt;

"*(b.)* The defence of Egypt against all foreign aggression or interference, direct or indirect;

"*(c.)* The protection of foreign interests in Egypt and the protection of minorities;

"*(d.)* The Soudan.

"Pending the conclusion of such agreements, the *status quo* in all these matters shall remain intact."

This was officially proclaimed at Cairo on March 16, 1922, and on the same day Sultan Ahmed Fuad Pasha became King. Some mob hostility was manifested by irreconcilable elements on this occasion; but, on the whole, the country remained quiet, and on April 19, 1923, King Fuad signed the new Egyptian Constitution. The future of Egypt, it would seem, now depends upon the Egyptians themselves.]

PART V

THE FUTURE OF MESOPOTAMIA

(Written for THE INQUIRY. Finished January 1, 1918.)

THE FUTURE OF MESOPOTAMIA

Strategic Importance of Mesopotamia and the Persian Gulf.—It was not due to mere military expediency, to a desire to strike a fresh enemy in a weak spot, that, shortly after Turkey's entrance into the war in the autumn of 1914, a force was thrown from British India into the region at the head of the Persian Gulf and a campaign was inaugurated against the Turks in Mesopotamia.[1] For not only is Mesopotamia potentially one of the richest of the world's undeveloped regions, but the head of the Persian Gulf commands a very valuable trade route and is one of the world's chief strategic points. As the outlet for a rich hinterland, it is destined to have some of the importance of a Trieste or an Odessa and, because of its situation upon a potentially great world route, it may in the distant future rank with a Panama and a Suez. But even under conditions existing before the war, its value was great. In 1902, Admiral Mahan wrote that "the control of the Persian Gulf by a foreign state of considerable naval potentiality, a 'fleet in being' there based upon a strong military port . . . would flank all the routes to the Farther East, to India, and to Australia." [2]

[1] All notes in this Part are by the Editor.
For accounts of this campaign, see C. Stiénon, "Les Campagnes d'Orient et les Intérêts de l'Entente," pp. 61-153, Paris, 1916; "The Times [London] History of the War," III, pp. 91-98; X, pp. 201-240; XII, pp. 391-416; XIII, pp. 253-288; XVII, pp. 253-288.
[2] A. T. Mahan, "The Persian Gulf and International Relations," in *The National Review,* XL (1902), pp. 27-45, reprinted in his "Retrospect

British Policy and German Methods.—British statesmen fully realized this and, while establishing no naval base of their own in the Persian Gulf, they steadfastly refused to permit any other Power to do so. The English had first begun the task of policing these waters and of suppressing piracy on them some three hundred years ago, considerably before the Turkish wave of conquest had reached the Persian Gulf; and this work is being continued at the present day with great advantage to all the world. While British policy put no obstacles whatsoever in the way of purely economic developments on the part of other nations, it resolutely opposed the establishment of naval stations connected with transcontinental railroads under foreign, and possibly hostile, control. As a result, there was at one period considerable friction with Russia, whose expansionists aimed to reach these warm waters; and, later, there was even more trouble with Germany over the projected Bagdad Railway and the German attempts to gain a footing in the Persian Gulf. For a number of years, Germany persistently tried to establish herself in these waters and, as in Morocco, her method was to employ what were apparently business men whose varied activities were in some way or other to furnish the pretext for official intervention and the hoisting of the German flag.[3] The process was not that of

and Prospect," pp. 209-251, Boston, 1902. See also Rouire, "La Question du Golfe Persique," in *Revue des Deux Mondes,* V, xvi (1903), pp. 889-917; xvii (1903), pp. 349-375; L. Fraser, "Some Problems of the Persian Gulf," London, 1908.

[3] Cf. E. Lewin, "The German Road to the East," ch. iv, London [1916]; G. Demorgny, "La Question Persane et la Guerre," pp. 229-284, Paris, 1916; R. Machray, "The Germans in Persia," in *The Fortnightly Review,* CV (1916), pp. 342-353.

"capitalistic imperialism," in which the business man is supposed to drag his country's standard into paths of territorial aggression, but its very opposite.

Germany's Fundamental Purpose.—This British policy was based upon valid reasons and in no way interfered with the development of Germany's legitimate economic interests in Turkey. But Germany's most cherished aims were not fundamentally economic. They were distinctly political and imperialistic. In ultimate analysis, they were aimed at the predominant position that English-speaking peoples have acquired by centuries of laborious pioneer work throughout the world, and, as a means to this end, they determined to establish themselves through Turkey on the flanks of the British Commonwealth and to imperil its continued existence. As Professor Kurt Wiedenfeld of Halle wrote: "All economic measures we may take in Turkey are only a means to an end, not an end in themselves." Similarly, Paul Rohrbach, the chief exponent of the Bagdad Railway and of German expansion in general, but especially in China and Africa, wrote on May 25, 1916, in *Die Hilfe:*

"Unless we make ourselves a strong colonial people, the world will end by becoming Anglo-Saxon. In this way even our policy in the Near East is only the preliminary of German colonial policy in the sense of a policy with a world-wide outlook. Nothing is more wrong than to represent the Near East Idea and the Colonial Idea as rivals; it is a question of both."

In addition to their economic aims, German railroad enterprises in Turkey had the fundamental and imperialistic purpose of imperiling British communications with India and Australia by a constant threat to Suez and by the establishment of a naval base at the terminus of the other branch of the railway in the Persian Gulf. Thus Rohrbach wrote in his widely read book on this project, published some years before the war:

"England can be attacked and mortally wounded by land from Europe only in one place—Egypt. The loss of Egypt would mean for England not only the end of her dominion over the Suez Canal and of her connections with India and the Far East, but would probably entail also the loss of her possessions in Central and East Africa." [4]

The 1914 Agreement about the Bagdad Railway.—England had no legitimate means of checking the construction of the Hedjaz Railway, close to the Egyptian frontier, but she was able to prevent the extension under German control of the railway to the Persian Gulf and the establishment of a German naval station there. After protracted negotiations, this matter was finally settled by an agreement in the summer of 1914, just before the outbreak of the war.[5]

While this treaty recognized Britain's predominant position in the Persian Gulf, it permitted Germany to prolong the Bagdad Railway to Basra, a deep-water port some sixty miles from the head of the Persian Gulf proper. No further extension was to be undertaken except by future agreement. Furthermore, Germany was to share fully in the economic

[4] "Die Bagdadbahn," Berlin, 1902, quoted in "Conquest and Kultur," p. 66, Washington, 1918. See also M. Jastrow, "The War and the Bagdad Railway," ch. iii, New York, 1917.
[5] The Lichnowsky Memorandum, ed. and tr. Munroe Smith, in *International Conciliation*, No. 127, June, 1918, p. 71; the terms of this agreement are given *ibid.*, pp. 174-175, following S. S. McClure, "Obstacles to Peace," pp. 41-42, New York [1917].

development of Mesopotamia which had hitherto been predominantly in British hands.

The War Has Created a Clean Sheet.—With many other things, this agreement of 1914 has been nullified by the war. The British conquest has erased it and established a clean sheet. The question has been raised anew and must be reconsidered in the fresh light derived from the conclusive demonstration of the aggressive nature of Germany's policy. In general, the chief interests to be considered are, first, those of the natives and, secondly, those of British India, whose real concern in this region outweighs that of the European peoples. British policy in the entire Middle East has largely been dictated by India, not by London. Under the circumstances, this is but natural and is in harmony with the general spirit of the British Commonwealth of Nations, which insists that the local opinion of the constituent peoples should be carefully regarded, in so far as it is consistent with the larger interests of the political entity as a whole.

Turkish Rule and the Arabs.—The region which is popularly known as Mesopotamia [6] and which has in great part been conquered by the British Indian Army is a very considerable area of approximately 143,000 square miles with

[6] For a comprehensive outline of the physical and political geography, political history, social and political conditions, and economic conditions, see "Mesopotamia" (No. 63 of the Handbooks published under the Direction of the Historical Section of the Foreign Office, in "Peace Handbooks issued by the Historical Section of the Foreign Office," XI, London, 1920). See also I. Bowman, "The New World: Problems in Political Geography," pp. 72-76, Yonkers, 1921. A large amount of valuable information is contained in Review of the Civil Administration of Mesopotamia (1920) (Cd. 1061), prepared by Miss Gertrude L. Bell.

an estimated population of roughly two millions.[7] The inhabitants are of various races, but the predominant element, especially in the south, is Arab.[8] In general, the Turk is only the ruling and official class. Despite the fact that this region was once a garden spot, its population is now very sparse, especially in Lower Mesopotamia and Irak.[9] This has been the result of permitting the irrigation system of the past to fall into decay. Added to this, there have been constant misrule and extortion on the part of the Turkish officials. In some sections brigandage is rampant and, generally, extreme poverty prevails. Whatever economic development has taken place south of Bagdad has been due to British enterprise, which shortly before the war completed an important irrigation project and which furnished adequate steamship facilities on the Tigris and the Euphrates. The Arabs cherished bitter feelings towards their Turkish overlords on account of their oppressive misrule, and these sentiments were aggravated by the Turkish nationalist movement's hostility towards Arabic civilization. In general, the Arabs welcomed the British conquest as a relief from grievous oppression. If considerations of justice alone were to enter into the settlement of

[7] By the Census of 1920, the figures are:

Sanjak	Square Miles	Population
Mosul	35,130	703,378
Bagdad	54,540	1,360,304
Basra	53,580	785,600
Total	143,250	2,849,282

The Statesman's Year-Book, 1921, p. 1350.

[8] See especially "The Arab of Mesopotamia," Basra, 1918.

[9] By the Census of 1920, the population per square mile in Mosul was 20, in Bagdad, 25; in Basra, 14; in all Mesopotamia, 20. This figure is lower than for any other Vilayet or Sanjak of the former Ottoman Empire except Zor (3) and Yemen (10).

this problem, absolutely no valid argument could be advanced for the return of this region to the blasting tyranny of the Turk.   If compelling forces were to permit of no other course, it would be a grievous tragedy.

Economic Possibilities from Irrigation.—It is generally admitted by engineers and by geographers who have carefully investigated the question that it is quite feasible to reclaim this land for civilization and to restore its former prosperity by an effective system of irrigation.   The soil itself is most fertile and is suited to the production of wheat and cotton.   In addition, the region is believed to be rich in petroleum which has as yet not been developed.[10] How large a population it could support is a subject of debate among experts.   But even if only the least sanguine estimates were realized, this region, and especially the southern portion, Lower Mesopotamia or Irak, could sustain in civilized conditions a far greater number of inhabitants than at present exists there in penury.   European settlers are out of the question, as the climate bars them definitely. It would be folly to spend a large sum of money on an irrigation project—that elaborated by Sir William Willcocks in 1910 involved the expenditure of 26 million pounds—if there were not labor sufficient to till the soil.   The present population is manifestly inadequate and not enough immigrants can be obtained from the neighboring Arab communities.   All plans for reclaiming Mesopotamia have con-

---

[10] The Anglo-Persian Oil Company, which supplies fuel on a large scale to the British Navy, operates in adjoining Persian territory.   Cf. also Correspondence between His Majesty's Government and the United States Ambassador respecting Economic Rights in Mandated Territories.   Miscellaneous, No. 10 (1921) (Cd. 1226).

templated the necessity of securing settlers from either Egypt or India, preferably from the latter.

The Problem of Over-Population in India.—The great problem of the future will be to meet the demands of the Asiatic peoples for more land. Their numbers are gaining rapidly. This is markedly true of British India, whose population increased in the ten years between 1901 and 1911 from 294 to 315 millions. Indian opinion demands some satisfaction for its vital economic needs in return for its sacrifices during the war, and hopes to find an outlet for its surplus people in East Africa and Mesopotamia where the native populations are sparse. The Moslems in India could furnish many valuable settlers who should be able to live in harmony with the native Arabs of Mesopotamia. Moreover for centuries close commercial relations have been established between India and the countries bordering on the Persian Gulf.

The Disposition of Mesopotamia: the Possibility of a New Arabia.—While it would be unfortunate in the extreme were this maltreated country to be restored to Turkish misrule, the question inevitably arises as to what shall be its future political fate. It has been suggested by some that it should form part of an independent New Arabia which should include the bulk of the four to seven million Arabs within the Turkish Empire or on its borders.[11] Although of

[11] By Article 27 of the Sèvres Treaty, Turkey no longer has sovereignty over any portion of Arabia and by Article 98 the Hedjaz is recognized as "a free and independent State." No New Arabia as a whole has yet been formed and the peninsula is at present divided into the Kingdom of Hedjaz, the Emirate of Nejd and Hasa, the Emirate of Jebel Shammar, the Principate of Asir, the Imamate of Yemen, the British Protectorate of Aden, the Sultanate of Oman, the Sultanate of Koweit, and the

a distinctly virile and able stock, the Arabs are apparently still too uneducated politically for so extensive a project. If left to themselves, they would continue to live in dread of a reimposition of the Turkish yoke and this possibility would become a certainty were the Russian Empire to disintegrate and its sixteen millions of Turkish-speaking peoples to join a political union with their fellows in the Ottoman Empire.[12] Moreover, it is most doubtful if, under the unstable conditions that would exist even without this latter possibility, the capital would be forthcoming from Europe and America for the reclamation of Mesopotamia.

An International Protectorate in the Light of Past Experience.—Another suggestion that has found wide favor, primarily because it apparently seems to diminish the risks of war by eliminating rivalry among the Great Powers, is that this region should be placed under an international protectorate. What is intended by this project is that its political administration and also its economic development should be under direct international control. Former experiments of this nature, such as those in Samoa, in the New Hebrides, and in Egypt, do not hold out much promise

Emirate of Kerak. For the difficulties—both external and internal—in the way of creation of a unified Arabia, see Bowman, *op. cit.*, pp. 68-70.

[12] On the possibilities and aims of a Pan-Turanian movement, see "A Manual on the Turanians and Pan-Turanianism," London, 1921; "Turkey, Russia, and Islam," in *The Round Table*, VIII (1918), pp. 100-138; Tekin Alp (*nom de plume* of M. Cohen), "Türkismus und Pantürkismus," Weimar, 1915 (English translation, "The Turkish and Pan-Turkish Ideal," London, 1916); Mary Czaplicka, "The Turks of Central Asia," pp. 9-18, 118-120, Oxford, 1918. The course of events since the Russian *débâcle* and the defeat of Turkey has not as yet led to a Pan-Turanian union and the likelihood of such an event seems to grow increasingly remote.

of success.[13] They have always fostered intrigues and rivalries among the governors, who have never been able to forget the special interests of their own states. Among the governed, this system fomented faction and led to disorder and even to anarchy. During the Anglo-French condominium in Egypt, from 1879 to 1882, the French and British Consuls-General interpreted an important instruction from Europe differently and the knowledge of this divergence of views encouraged the nationalistic party in its projects and led to the outbreak that caused the British occupation.[14] In connection with the tripartite protectorate over Samoa, Cleveland said in 1894: "The present Government has failed to correct, if indeed it has not aggravated, the very evils it was intended to prevent." Five years later, owing to the anarchic conditions, a Joint High Commission representing the United States, Great Britain, and Germany was sent to Samoa to investigate and report. They concluded that no wholly satisfactory arrangement was possible so long as the tripartite control continued and they insisted that the only natural plan of government, and the only system that could ensure tranquillity and prosperity, was rule by a single power.

[13] For the Samoan condominium (terminated by the Anglo-German-American Treaty of December 2, 1899), see the Anglo-German-American Treaty of June 14, 1889, in Malloy, "Treaties," pp. 1576-1589; J. B. Henderson, "American Diplomatic Questions," pp. 205-286, New York, 1901. Regarding the New Hebrides, see the Franco-British Convention of October 20, 1906 (text in *American Journal of International Law,* I, Supplement, pp. 179-200); "France and England in the New Hebrides: The Anglo-French Condominium," Melbourne, 1914; and the Anglo-French Protocol Respecting the New Hebrides of August 6, 1914 (Treaty Series, 1922, No. 7).

[14] A. Debidour, "Histoire Diplomatique de l'Europe, 1878-1904," pp. 56-59.

Lord Cromer on Administrative Internationalism.—On this point there is no more valuable testimony than that of Lord Cromer, whose success as a ruler of backward peoples is unsurpassed and who has had ample opportunity to estimate the value of international administrative agencies. The following pregnant and somewhat sarcastic words from his pen merit the most careful consideration:

"Semi-civilized countries, in which the rulers are sometimes only possessed of incomplete sovereign rights, open up a wide field for development of internationalism. . . . But alas! however much exclusiveness may in appearance be expelled by the cosmopolitan pitchfork, it but too often comes back again to its natural resting-place. The experiment of administrative internationalism has probably been tried in the No Man's Land [Egypt] of which this history treats to a greater extent than in any other country. The result cannot be said to be encouraging to those who believe in the efficacy of international action in administrative matters. What has been proved is that international institutions possess admirable negative qualities. They are formidable checks to all action, and the reason why they are so is that, when any action is proposed, objections of one sort or another generally occur to some member of the international body. Any action often involves a presumed advantage accorded to some rival nation, and it is a principle of internationalism, which is scornfully rejected in theory and but too often recognized as a guide for practical action, that it is better to do nothing, even though evil may ensue, than to allow good to be done at the expense of furthering the interests, or of exalting the reputation of an international rival."

Reasons for Attachment to the British Commonwealth of Nations.—One of the most unfortunate results of the war has been a great intensification of national feelings and it would be hazardous to risk the fate of any people on the assumption that in any future collaboration by the present belligerents there will be less rivalry than there was in the past. The suspicions, jealousies, antipathies, and hatreds engendered by this war cannot be dispelled quickly. An international protectorate over Mesopotamia would not solve the question. It would probably lead to renewed friction if the work of regeneration were seriously attempted or it might paralyze all action. What is required in such cases is concentration of responsibility. Under modern political conditions, apparently the only way to determine the problem of politically backward peoples, who require not only outside political control but also foreign capital to reorganize their stagnant economic systems, is to entrust the task of government to that state whose interests are most directly involved. In the case of Mesopotamia, this state would inevitably be the British Commonwealth on account of, first, the predominant commercial interests of British India and of the United Kingdom in the Persian Gulf and in Lower Mesopotamia; second, the part that British officials have for centuries taken in suppressing piracy in the Persian Gulf; third, the facts that British capital had already before the war been employed in irrigating Mesopotamia and in providing transportation on the Tigris and Euphrates and that since the war very considerable work has been done in draining, in building embankments, and wharfs, and in constructing railroads; fourth, the fact that British India needs an outlet for its swarming millions and has in its surplus Moslem peoples a suitable source of settlers.

Provision to Safeguard the Open Door.—If, however, such backward regions are entrusted by international mandate to one state, there should be embodied in the deed of trust most rigid safeguards both to protect the native population from exploitation and also to ensure that the interests of other foreign states are not injured either positively or negatively. Provision should be made for the full open door, so that not only should all merchandise enter upon the same terms and that railroad rates should be equal, but also that complete opportunity should be given to all nations to participate on an equal basis in the economic development of the country. The latter desideratum can probably never be fully attained, but some more or less close approximation to it can be reached by an arrangement like that of the Six-Powers Group in China and that of the Algeciras Act of 1906. In order to render this fully effective, it would presumably be necessary for the parties to the agreement to bind themselves to submit to arbitration any disputes connected with it and to agree to abide by the decision.

The Necessity of Protecting the Natives from Exploitation.—But far more important than any arrangement of this character to secure the interests of the European and American states in such backward countries is the necessity of clearly defined provisions to protect the natives from exploitation. If foreign capital is to reap the bulk of the benefits from the reclamation of Mesopotamia, the project is not an alluring one. It was this that Colonel Sir Mark Sykes had in mind when recently, in connection with Zionism, he said:

"What did the Arab fear? He feared financial corporations pivoted on Palestine controlling Syria and Mesopotamia. He feared the soil of Palestine would be bought by companies and that he would become the proletariat working on the soil."

There is grave danger of such a development if, in the impatience for quick results, foreign capital is allowed to secure a great part of the soil and then to sell it or to rent it to the natives and immigrants after irrigation has greatly enhanced its value. Such an unfortunate outcome can and should be prevented. The native must be protected from his own ignorance and cupidity by strict land laws. The capitalistic penetration must be rigidly supervised and controlled, so that the result of Mesopotamia's reclamation may not be merely a vastly large population scarcely elevated from its former state of penury and a considerable accession of wealth to London, New York, Paris, and Berlin.

[*Great Britain Made Mandatory for Mesopotamia.*—By the Treaty of Sèvres, signed August 10, 1920, Turkey "renounces in favour of the Principal Allied Powers all rights and title which she could claim on any ground over or concerning" Mesopotamia and other regions "outside her frontiers as fixed by the present Treaty," binding herself, moreover, "to recognise and conform to the measures which may be taken now or in the future by the Principal Allied Powers, in agreement where necessary with third Powers, in order to carry the above stipulation into effect." [15] This document defines the northern boundary of Mesopotamia: [16]

[15] Article 132.
[16] Article 27, II (3). By the last paragraph of Article 64, this boundary may be modified in case of creation of a Kurdish State by "the voluntary adhesion to such an independent Kurdish State of the Kurds inhabiting that part of Kurdistan which has hitherto been included in the Mosul Vilayet."

the eastern frontier presumably marches with Persia, but the western and southern limits are still to be drawn by the Principal Allied Powers.[17]   By Article 94, Mesopotamia is provisionally recognized as an independent State, subject to the rendering of administrative advice and assistance by a Mandatory until such time as it may be able to stand alone. This Mandatory is to be chosen by the Principal Allied Powers, who will also formulate the terms of the Mandate, which must be submitted to the Council of the League of Nations for approval.[18]   In accordance with these provisions, the Mandate for Mesopotamia has been given to Great Britain; [19] and on October 10, 1922, a treaty was signed between Great Britain and Irak whereby the latter Kingdom ceases to be a mandated territory and becomes a sovereign state, though still, in considerable degree, under the guidance of Great Britain.[20]]

[17] Article 94.
[18] Articles 94, 96. For provisions of option for Mesopotamian nationality, see Article 125.
[19] For the text of this document, see Annex H.
[20] For the text of this Treaty, see Annex Q.

PART VI

THE COLONIAL QUESTIONS

(Written for THE INQUIRY. Undated.)

PART VI: THE COLONIAL QUESTIONS

INTRODUCTION

CHAPTER I
TROPICAL AFRICA

CHAPTER II
GERMAN SOUTHWEST AFRICA

CHAPTER III
NORTH AFRICA

CHAPTER IV
THE PACIFIC ISLANDS

THE COLONIAL QUESTIONS

INTRODUCTION

In the settlement of the colonial questions,[1] the primary consideration must be the welfare of the native populations. In second place only come the interests of the outside world. These demand preëminently equality of economic opportunity. In order to carry these principles into effect, the administration of the derelict territories and peoples freed from German and Turkish rule must, in general, be entrusted to different states acting as mandatories of the League of Nations. These mandates cannot, however, be uniform, but must vary with the circumstances of the dif-

[1] By Article 119 of the Versailles Treaty, "Germany renounces in favour of the Principal Allied and Associated Powers all her rights and titles over her oversea possessions." On May 7, 1919, the Supreme Council of the Peace Conference allotted the ex-German territories in Africa to be mandated areas as follows: German East Africa (now Tanganyika Territory), about one-quarter of Togoland, and a small portion of the Cameroons to Great Britain; the remainder of Togoland and of the Cameroons to France. Belgium and Portugal subsequently received parts of German East Africa. By Articles 94-96 of the Sèvres Treaty, the High Contracting Parties agree that Syria, Mesopotamia, and Palestine be placed under Mandatories to be selected by the Principal Allied Powers. Great Britain has been chosen for Mesopotamia and Palestine, and France for Syria. The Mandates, in conformity with Article 22, paragraphs 4-6, of the Covenant of the League of Nations, fall into three classes, termed "A," "B," and "C" respectively (see Annexes H, I, and L). Cf. *infra*, Annex B, and see, for some account of the history and theory of the Mandate-Concept, "The League of Nations Starts," pp. 101-120, London, 1920; R. S. Baker, "Woodrow Wilson and World Settlement," I, pp. 261 ff., Garden City, N. Y., 1922. For adverse views, see R. Lansing, "The Peace Negotiations," pp. 149-161, Boston, 1921; Antonelli, "L'Afrique et la Paix de Versailles," pp. 226-235.

431

ferent cases. Since the factors of national power and prestige, as well as those of national economic advantage, cannot be wholly eliminated by such arrangements, the selection of mandatories in one region cannot be separated from the choice made in other areas. In fact, all the territorial problems are interwoven and must be viewed as a whole. Thus the solution in Africa must depend upon that in Asiatic Turkey and *vice versa*. There are also other considerations that at the moment make impossible a final decision as to the colonial settlement. Not only the form, but the satisfactory nature, of the territorial arrangements in Africa and Asiatic Turkey are largely dependent upon whether or no the United States is willing to assume any mandates of administration in these regions. Furthermore, in case events in Liberia and Abyssinia render international control essential there, the mandatory stipulations in other areas might advantageously be altered to meet these contingencies.

CHAPTER I

1. Territorial

A. Togoland

It is recommended:

That this area be divided along ethnic lines and transferred to France and Great Britain on condition that the Anglo-French agreements of 1898 and 1899 [2] providing for reciprocal equality in import duties,

> *a.* should include in their scope export duties also and should embrace this transferred area as well;
>
> *b.* should extend indefinitely beyond their present time limit, 1929; and that
>
> *c.* the benefit of this equality of commercial treatment should accrue directly to all states and not indirectly, as is now the case in consequence of the most-favored-nation clause.

Discussion

This recommendation is made because the population belongs ethnically, in about the proportion of two to one, to the adjacent colonies of French Dahomey and the British Gold Coast.[3] The mandatory system, in so far as it im-

---

[1] All notes in this Part are by the Editor.

[2] "Trattati . . . relativi all'Africa," pp. 594-599, 613-614.

[3] See insert map between pages 66 and 67, where the final partition of Togoland between France and Great Britain is also indicated.

plies the maintenance of administrative integrity, would hamper the development of this small area. The essential features of the mandatory principle would, however, be secured by the measures suggested in connection with the Anglo-French treaties of 1898 and 1899, especially as Togoland is already within the scope of all the international agreements regarding Tropical Africa, except the Berlin Act of 1885 establishing the Conventional Basin of the Congo.[4]

Provision would also have to be made for the protection of personal and property rights of Germans in this area.[5]

[4] Both Togoland and the Cameroons are now mandated territories of the "B" type. For the text of the Draft Mandates for the British portion of these two areas, see Annex J, where the Anglo-French Declarations respecting the boundaries of Togoland and the Cameroons, signed at London, July 10, 1919, and the Joint Recommendation of the British and French Governments as to the future of these ex-German colonies, signed December 17, 1920, are also given. See further Antonelli, "L'Afrique et la Paix de Versailles," p. 245; and especially G. L. Beer, in "A History of the Peace Conference of Paris," II, pp. 241-242, London, 1920. Consult also Report on the British Mandated Sphere of Togoland for 1920-1921 (1922) (Cd. 1698).

[5] By Article 122 of the Versailles Treaty, applicable to all ex-German colonies, "the Government exercising authority over such territories may make such provisions as it thinks fit with reference to the repatriation from them of German nationals and to the conditions upon which German subjects of European origin shall, or shall not, be allowed to reside, hold property, trade or exercise a profession in them" (cf. also Articles 121, 123). The original form of this Article, as proposed by the British Delegation at the first session of the Commission on African Colonies, April 24, 1919, was: "La Puissance mandataire pourra prendre telles dispositions qu'elle jugera bonnes en ce qui regarde la nationalité et le rapatriement des ressortissants allemands hors de ce territoire." The French Delegation felt, however, that this did not cover the case of German nationals who had taken refuge in neutral territory, particularly Germans of European birth and natives belonging to German auxiliary forces who had fled from the Cameroons to the Spanish colonies of Fernando Po and Rio Muni. They accordingly presented the sixth Article of their draft, with two slight amendments: "Dès la mise en vigueur du présent Traité, le Gouvernement allemand rapatriera à ses frais ceux de ses ressortissants européens qui se sont réfugiés dans les colonies espagnoles du Golfe de Guinée. De même, les indigènes des colonies allemandes réfugiés dans lesdites colonies espagnoles seront libres de regagner leur pays d'origine

B. The Cameroons

It is recommended:

1. That the areas added to this colony in 1911 at the expense of French Equatorial Africa be returned to France.[6]

Discussion

The restoration of the regions that France was forced to cede in 1911 under threat of war is partly a point of honor

sans être soumis, à cet égard, à aucun empêchement ou entrave de la part des autorités allemandes." To this, Mr. Beer objected that repatriation from neutral territory could scarcely be required, particularly as some refugees might intend to settle permanently in their new homes; and Mr. Payne, of the British Delegation, also called attention to possible derogation to the sovereign rights of Spain. The French Delegate, M. de Peretti de la Rocca, who was President of the Commission, maintained his Government's point of view, holding that this repatriation was in harmony with the interests of Spain herself, but he expressed willingness to withdraw the Article since negotiations looking towards repatriation had already been opened at Madrid by Great Britain and France. At the second session of the Commission (April 25), the present Article 122 was presented in the following form: "Le Gouvernement exerçant l'autorité peut prendre telles dispositions qu'il juge nécessaires relativement à la nationalité, au rapatriement des nationaux allemands et aux conditions dans lesquelles les sujets allemands d'origine européenne seront autorisés à posséder, résider, faire le commerce ou exercer une profession dans le territoire en question." Here the mention of nationality gave rise to discussion by the French Delegation. M. Duchêne feared that this might imply the right of "the Government exercising authority" to deny German nationality to a German established in the ceded territory, to which Sir Herbert Read answered that the Government could not retain German nationals in ceded territories. M. Merlin felt that all proper freedom of action would be ensured by dropping reference to nationality and inserting "ou non" after "seront." The Article thus assumed its final form. The French Draft Article was then presented anew, but although different phrasings were proposed, the danger of infringing Spanish rights of sovereignty was felt to be so great that the entire Article was finally dropped. "Procès-Verbaux et Rapport de la Commission des Colonies Allemandes," pp. 12-14, 23-27.

[6] See *supra*, pp. 65-66 and insert maps between pages 66 and 67. For an outline of the controversy resulting in this cession, see A. Debidour, "Histoire Diplomatique de l'Europe, 1904-1916," pp. 147-151, 159-161, 166-172. For the text of the Franco-German Convention of November 4, 1911, regarding Equatorial Africa, see *ibid.*, pp. 336-340.

which should be recognized, while, in addition, the present boundaries of French Equatorial Africa are in the extreme unnatural and inconvenient.

2. That some territory also be transferred to British Nigeria in order to make the boundary conform in a general way to ethnic and tribal facts.[7]

Discussion

The present boundary between Nigeria and the Cameroons is purely diplomatic and arbitrarily cuts into vital native institutions, social and political.

3. That the remainder of the Cameroons be transferred to a mandatory of the League of Nations, under stringent and explicit conditions securing native rights and ensuring equality of economic opportunity to the outside world.[8]

Discussion

For many reasons, the United States would be the most satisfactory mandatory. Hitherto, the efforts of Great Britain to secure the open door in Tropical Africa, to obtain adequate international agreements about the liquor traffic, and, in general, to promote essential international coöperation, have been hampered by opposition from one or more of the other colonizing Powers.[9] The exercise by the United

[7] See insert map between pages 66 and 67, where the partition of the Cameroons between France and Great Britain as mandatories is also indicated.

[8] For the final decision regarding the division of the Cameroons, see *supra*, Introduction, Note 1; and cf., for the Cameroons and Togoland, the Draft Mandates for their British portions, given in Annex J. See also *Le Temps*, January 30, May 12, July 2, 1919. The French took formal possession of Togoland on October 1, 1920 (*ibid.*, September 21, October 6, 9, 1920), and of the Cameroons on October 30, 1920 (*ibid.*, November 4, 1920).

[9] This opposition, it may be hoped, will be eliminated by the provisions of the "B" type of Mandates and, for the portion of the Cameroons

States of a mandate in the Cameroons would be a powerful factor in gaining adequate protection for native rights. In case this solution is impossible, either from unwillingness on the part of the United States to accept such a mandate or on that of France to offer it, France should be selected as the mandatory.

4. That, if France is chosen as the mandatory, one of the conditions of the mandate should, if possible, be that all existing and future international agreements about equality of economic opportunity and the freedom of navigation of rivers should apply not only to all the Cameroons, but also to all French Equatorial and West Africa.

Discussion

In large sections of French Tropical Africa, French imports are favored by differential duties. To the extent that it is possible, this system should be abolished and the issuance of a mandate to France for the administration of the Cameroons should be used to secure equality of economic opportunity not only in this area but also elsewhere.[10]

5. That, in case France is selected as the mandatory, the retention of the administrative integrity of the Cameroons be made optional, but that all such changes must have the approval of the League of Nations.[11]

within the Conventional Basin of the Congo, by the Conventions of September 10, 1919, relating to the liquor traffic in Africa and revising the General Acts of Berlin and Brussels (see Annexes F and G).

[10] So far as Togoland and the Cameroons are concerned, by Article 6 of the Draft Mandate, "the mandatory will ensure to all nationals of States, Members of the League of Nations, on the same footing as to his own nationals, freedom of transit and navigation, and complete economic, commercial and industrial equality."

[11] This matter is covered by Articles 9-11 of the Draft Mandates.

Discussion

In view of the fact that the Cameroons and French Equatorial Africa are adjacent, an administrative reorganization of the entire region would probably be found to be advantageous now or in the future. The development of the area should not be hampered by rigid restrictions.

6.   That the personal and property rights of Germans in the Cameroons be duly safeguarded.[12]

[12] See *supra,* Note 5. By Article 124 of the Versailles Treaty, "Germany hereby undertakes to pay, in accordance with the estimate to be presented by the French Government and approved by the Reparation Commission, reparation for damage suffered by French nationals in the Cameroons or the frontier zone by reason of the acts of the German civil and military authorities and of German private individuals during the period from January 1, 1900, to August 1, 1914." This Article had its origin in the eighth article of the French Draft: "Le Gouvernement allemand prend à sa charge, suivant l'évaluation qui sera présentée par le Gouvernement français, la réparation des dommages subis par les ressortissants français dans la colonie du Cameroun ou dans les contrées limitrophes du fait des actes des autorités civiles et militaires allemandes et des particuliers allemands, tant avant la délimitation de la frontière franco-allemande par le Traité du 18 avril 1908 que pendant la période postérieure et pendant celle des hostilités." In presenting this text, M. de Peretti de la Rocca stated that certain damages caused French nationals by German nationals in consequence of cessions in virtue of the Franco-German Treaty of 1911 were still pending, and since, when signing that Treaty, France had not asked of Germany reparation for such damages, his Government was charged with them. He expressed the conviction that the time had come for settlement of the question, that pre-war damages were not within the domain of the Reparation Commission, that the best place for the stipulation was in the Colonial Clauses, and that this matter was not in the same category as other controversies pending between France and Germany at the outbreak of the war. Taken up anew at the second session of the Commission, M. Merlin, for France, presented details and estimated the damages, in 1910, at about three million francs, although he felt it unnecessary to insert any specific amount in the Treaty text. He further proposed 1900 as the *terminus a quo,* and Mr. Beer suggested insertion of the words "and approved by the Reparation Commission." Thus the Article reached its final form. "Procès-Verbaux et Rapport de la Commission des Colonies Allemandes," pp. 15-16, 28-30.

C. German East Africa

It is recommended:

1.   That this area be entrusted by mandate to the British Empire as a place of settlement for British East India.[13]

Discussion

There is a widespread demand in India for a country in which the rapidly increasing population may freely settle.[14] The relations between India and East Africa have long been very close and there is a real need of such a colony for immigration. Whether this region [now called the Tanganyika Territory] should be administered by the Indian or by the British Government is predominantly a question that concerns the British Empire domestically.[15] The essential thing is that India's need of a country for unrestricted settlement be met.

2.   That, in the event of this recommendation being adopted,

    a.   the northeastern section of German East Africa, which contains a number of white settlements, be excluded from the mandate and be attached to British East Africa; [16]

[13] For the text of the Draft Mandate for this territory, see Annex I. There is nothing in its terms to prevent Indian immigration on any desirable scale. On this latter problem, see John H. Harris, "Africa: Slave or Free?", pp. 100-110. See further *supra,* pp. 61-64, and especially Correspondence Regarding the Position of Indians in East Africa (Kenya and Uganda), 1921 (Cd. 1311), and Report by Sir Benjamin Robertson, Dated 4th August, 1920, Regarding the Proposed Settlement of Indian Agriculturists in Tanganyika Territory, etc., 1921 (Cd. 1312).

[14] See *supra,* pp. 61-64, 420, 424.

[15] The Mandate is actually given to Great Britain.

[16] This failed of adoption. For the final settlement, see *supra,* Introduction, Note 1.

b. the northwestern section, containing the densely populated native areas of Ruanda and Urundi, be similarly excluded and attached to British Uganda.[17]

Discussion

The effect of these exclusions would be largely to eliminate the racial difficulties and would leave a large, compact, and very sparsely populated country for Indian settlement.

3. That the personal and property rights of Germans be safeguarded.[18]

2. International Control

It is recommended that there be established, as a part of the organization of the League of Nations,

a. a special international conference for Tropical Africa, meeting periodically at fixed intervals not exceeding three years;

[17] This region was placed under Belgian Mandate (*supra,* p. 23; see also *Le Temps,* May 9, 12, July 19, 1919; Antonelli, *op. cit.,* pp. 247-248). By an Agreement of June, 1920, Belgium obtained, in consideration of British retention of small portions on the eastern boundary to have a practicable route for a Tanganyika-Uganda railroad, "(1) A free outlet for the produce of the east-central portion of the Belgian Congo by way of Lake Tanganyika to Dar es Salaam on the Indian Ocean. (2) Concession areas at Kigoma (on Lake Tanganyika) and Dar es Salaam on the eastern coast for the storage of goods. (3) The right to transport merchandise from Lake Tanganyika to the Indian Ocean in Belgian freight cars." I. Bowman, "The New World: Problems in Political Geography," pp. 125, 126, Yonkers, 1921; cf. *Le Temps,* June 23, 1920. The texts of these agreements have not yet been published. On this Belgian Mandate Mr. Beer has expressed the judgment that "Belgium was not entrusted with the care of these populous districts, solely with a view to native interests. Other considerations were also allowed to enter. For instance, no one wanted to refuse the insistent claim of a state which had suffered so seriously from Germany's aggression in Europe, and had done so much to break Germany's power in East Africa." "A History of the Peace Conference of Paris," II, p. 243, London, 1920.

[18] See *supra,* Note 5.

b. a special African court, having jurisdiction over all cases involving the interpretation of international acts regarding Tropical Africa and violations thereof;

c. a permanent central bureau for the collection, correlation, and study of all the data upon which these international agreements must be based.[19]

Discussion

The international agreements regarding Africa, as the Berlin Act of 1885 and the Brussels Act of 1890, covering such questions as equality of trade, freedom of navigation, the arms traffic, and the liquor trade, admittedly need revision and amplification, both as to content and as to area covered.[20] Additional arrangements are necessary for the protection of native rights to land for the elimination of all forms of compulsory labor except on essential administrative works.[21] The question of tropical diseases and that of the preservation of wild animals must be handled interna-

[19] Special Central International Offices under the control of the League of Nations are to be established "for the purpose of collecting and preserving documents of all kinds exchanged by the High Contracting Parties" with reference to the traffic in liquor and arms (Convention relating to the Liquor Traffic in Africa, Article 7; Convention for the Control of the Trade in Arms and Ammunition, Article 5). The special International Conference, the African Court, and the Permanent Central Bureau are still to be created. These should obviously be placed under the jurisdiction of the League of Nations by Article 24 of the Covenant.

[20] These matters have been regulated by the Peace Conference in the Conventions, signed September 10, 1919, for revision of the Berlin and Brussels Acts, control of the trade in arms and ammunition, and regulation of the liquor traffic. For the texts of these documents, see Annexes G, E, and F, and for the areas concerned, see map facing page 198.

[21] These problems are covered by the provisions of the several Mandates. See Articles 5-6 of the Draft Mandate for British East Africa, Articles 4-5 of the Draft Mandates for British Togoland and the Cameroons, and Article 3 of the Mandate for German Southwest Africa (Annexes I, J, L).

tionally.[22]   There is an urgent immediate need for fresh agreements.   But, as new conditions are constantly arising, continuous international coöperation is essential and provision must be made so that international legislation can automatically cope with the changing situation.

[22] See *supra,* pp. 238-248, and cf. Article 23 (*f*) of the Covenant: "Subject to and in accordance with the provisions of international conventions existing or hereafter to be agreed upon, the Members of the League . . . will endeavour to take steps in matters of international concern for the prevention and control of disease." See further "Public Health, the League, and the Red Cross," in "The League of Nations Starts," pp. 155-169, and cf. Article 9 of the Draft Mandate for British East Africa (Annex I).

CHAPTER II

It is recommended:

1. That this region be transferred to the British Empire for incorporation in the self-governing Dominion of South Africa.

2. That the personal and property rights of Germans be protected.[1]

Discussion

For various valid reasons, the mandatory principle is inadvisable and really inapplicable in this case. In other areas, we are concerned mainly with derelict peoples, here essentially with land. This vast, inhospitable region of 322,450 square miles had in 1913 only a native population variously estimated at from 231,000 to 281,000 and a white population of no more than 14,830, including the relatively large German military and administrative staffs. Deducting the latter and also the foreign elements, there were in the colony only 9,597 Germans.[2] The development of this territory would be gravely handicapped if it were administered

---

[1] See *supra,* Ch. I, n. 5.

[2] In 1919, despite the deportation of 6,350 Germans, the white population was estimated at 16,000 or 17,000, the increase being chiefly South Africans in search of farms. *The Statesman's Year-Book,* 1921, p. 239. According to the census of 1921, the white population is 19,237, of whom between 7,000 and 8,000 are Germans. *Ibid.,* 1922, p. 246.

entirely apart from the adjoining Union of South Africa with distinct native, fiscal, and railroad policies and systems.[3]

[3] Southwest Africa now constitutes a mandated territory of the "C" type with the Union of South Africa as mandatory. For the text of the Mandate, see Annex L.

CHAPTER III

A. *Egypt*

It is recommended:

1. That the absolute political separation of Egypt from Turkey should be recognized, and concurrently also the British Protectorate.[1]

Discussion

Turkey's rights in Egypt were merely the futile trappings of an outworn suzerainty and served no purpose but to hamper Egypt's development. They should be abolished. But, as Egypt is not able to stand alone politically, the virtual protectorate exercised by Great Britain since 1882, which received indirect international recognition in 1904,[2] should be formally recognized.

2. That the Treaty-Powers should relinquish their extraterritorial rights under the Capitulations, upon the es-

[1] By Article 147 of the Versailles Treaty, Article 102 of the Treaty of Saint-Germain-en-Laye, Article 86 of the Trianon Treaty, and Article 101 of the Sèvres Treaty, Germany, Austria, Hungary, and Turkey recognize the British Protectorate; and Turkey renounces, as from November 5, 1914, "all rights and title in or over Egypt." The Protectorate has also been recognized by France, Russia, Belgium, Serbia, Greece, Portugal, and the United States (and, by implication, by all Powers signatory to the Peace Treaties with Germany, Austria, Hungary, and Turkey).

[2] Anglo-French Declaration of April 8, 1904. "Trattati," pp. 1116-1118; *American Journal of International Law,* VI, Supplement, pp. 26-30 (including the secret Articles).

tablishment of satisfactory safeguards for the European population.[3]

Discussion

Under the present system, Egypt has neither legislative nor judicial autonomy and is unable to cope with many evils, social and political. In view of the stable and civilized government now existing in the country, foreigners do not require these special prerogatives.

3. That the present treaty restrictions which render it impossible for Egypt to impose customs duties according to her wants and needs be abandoned and that full tariff autonomy be established.

Discussion

Under the existing régime, which prevents Egypt from levying other than moderate customs, her interests are subordinated to those of the outside manufacturing world and she is unable to stimulate native industries by means of protective duties. The system is wholly indefensible.[4]

4. That the existing obligation of Great Britain to preserve equality for all in customs, other taxes, and railway charges, which expires in 1934,[5] be extended indefinitely.

[3] The Capitulations are renounced by Germany, Austria, and Hungary (Versailles Treaty, Article 147; Saint-Germain-en-Laye Treaty, Article 102; Trianon Treaty, Article 86). See also the proposals in paragraphs 4 (v) (with alternative), 7-8 of the Milner-Zaghlul Memorandum of August 18, 1920, regarding transfer of Capitulation rights to Great Britain, and Article 9 of the suggested Anglo-Egyptian Convention of November 10, 1921. Annexes M, O. Cf. also the Anglo-Portuguese Treaty of December 9, 1920, relating to the suppression of the Capitulations in Egypt. Annex P.

[4] This matter still remains *in statu quo.*

[5] Anglo-French Declaration of April 8, 1904, Article 4. This question also is still unsettled.

Discussion

A complete and formal obligation to maintain the open door should be made a condition of consenting to the abolition of the Capitulations.

5.   That the rights of the holders of the Turkish loans secured by the Egyptian tribute be fully safeguarded.

Discussion

Probably the most equitable manner to accomplish this is to continue the payment of the Egyptian tribute until those Turkish loans are entirely paid off. But, whether this is done or whether Great Britain herself assumes the obligation is not primarily an international, but a British, concern.[6]

B. Morocco

It is recommended:

1.   That no obstacles be placed in the way of any French attempts to secure by negotiation with Spain the partial or entire withdrawal of that Power from the protectorate zone assigned to her.[7]

[6] By Article 112 of the Sèvres Treaty, "Turkey renounces all claim to the tribute formerly paid by Egypt. Great Britain undertakes to relieve Turkey of all liability in respect of the Turkish loans secured on the Egyptian tribute. . . . Upon the extinction of these loans of 1894, 1891 and 1855, all liability on the part of the Egyptian Government arising out of the tribute formerly paid by Egypt to Turkey will cease."

[7] Cf. the Franco-Spanish Declaration of October 3, 1904, and the secret Agreements of April 8, 1904, and September 1, 1905. Texts in Debidour, op. cit., p. 9; P. Albin, "Le 'Coup' d'Agadir," pp. 371-384, Paris, 1912. By Article 141 of the Versailles Treaty, Germany "undertakes not to intervene in any way in negotiations relating to Morocco which may take place between France and the other Powers." The same stipulation is contained in the Treaty of Saint-Germain-en-Laye, Article 96, and in the Trianon Treaty, Article 80. For a brief summary of the history and present problems of the Moroccan situation, see Bowman, "The New World: Problems of Political Geography," pp. 105-111, Yonkers, 1921.

Discussion

The existing artificial division of Morocco into three zones —the International, the Spanish, and the French—is admittedly unsatisfactory in all respects.[8] The soundest solution would be for Spain to relinquish her protectorate entirely or, at least, the western section thereof so as to secure unbroken physical connection under French control between the French zone and Tangier, the natural commercial inlet into Morocco.

2. That the present ill-defined status of Tangier should be terminated and that the administration of this city together with its surrounding area be entrusted under a mandate of the League of Nations to France, with explicit provision securing both the rights of the inhabitants and also economic equality to all outside nations.[9]

Discussion

The existing international administration is a center of intrigue and has paralyzed the development of this advantageously situated port.

[8] The French Protectorate was recognized by the Franco-Moroccan Treaty of Fez, March 30, 1912 (*American Journal of International Law,* VI, Supplement, pp. 207-209), and the delimitation of the French, Spanish, and International zones was regulated by the Franco-Spanish Treaty of Madrid, November 27, 1912 (*ibid.,* VII, Supplement, pp. 81-99). Germany recognizes this Protectorate (Versailles Treaty, Article 142), as do also Austria, Hungary, Bulgaria, and Turkey (Saint-Germain-en-Laye Treaty, Article 97; Trianon Treaty, Article 81; Neuilly Treaty, Article 62; Sèvres Treaty, Article 118).

[9] The question of Tangier was not specifically considered by the Peace Conference, but "la France a accepté que Tanger soit soumise dans l'avenir à un régime spécial." "Procès-Verbaux et Rapport de la Commission du Maroc," p. 15; cf. also pp. 11-12, 16. It is, however, implied by Article 141, paragraph 2, of the Versailles Treaty, which is identical, except for drafting changes, with that proposed by the French Delegation to the Commission on Morocco. *Ibid.,* p. 12.

From "The Statesman's Year-Book," 1913.

The great extension of French influence proposed in the two foregoing recommendations should be fully used to abate French claims which have been made elsewhere in Africa and in Asiatic Turkey [10] and they should, moreover, be contingent upon an equitable settlement of other territorial problems.

3. That the foreign consular jurisdictions, together with the connected system of taking natives under foreign protection, be abandoned.[11]

[10] As already observed (*supra*, Introduction, Note 1), France is mandatory for Syria. Further, by Article 5 (1) of the Anglo-Franco-Italian Agreement of August 10, 1920, an area of large extent north of Syria is delimited "in which the special interests of France are recognised."

[11] By the Treaties of Versailles (Articles 142, 143), Saint-Germain-en-Laye (Articles 97, 98), the Trianon (Articles 81, 82), and Neuilly (Article 62), Germany, Austria, Hungary, and Bulgaria renounce the régime of the capitulations in Morocco, and German, Austrian, and Hungarian protected persons cease "to enjoy the privileges attached to their status and shall be subject to the ordinary law." These same changes are implied in Article 118 of the Treaty of Sèvres. The Moroccan capitulations have also been renounced by Belgium, Bolivia, Costa Rica, Denmark, Greece, Haiti, Italy, Japan, Luxemburg, Paraguay, Portugal, Russia, Spain, Sweden, Uruguay, and Venezuela. "Annuaire Générale de la France et de l'Étranger," 1920-21, p. 622. The earliest form of the present Versailles Article 142 was: "Le Gouvernement allemand, qui a reconnu l'établissement du protectorat de la France sur le Maroc, déclare en accepter toutes les conséquences, dont la principale est l'abrogation des capitulations." It was discussed at length in the opening session of the Commission on Morocco (March 31, 1919), as was the first draft of what is now Article 143, paragraph 1, which was then widely different. Both Articles were reserved and at the second session (April 3) they were again considered. M. de Peretti de la Rocca finally proposed what is essentially the present form of Article 142, and Mr. Beer replaced the French draft of the present Article 143, paragraph 1, by the formula: "Le Gouvernement allemand reconnaît que la France a une entière liberté d'action pour régler le statut et les conditions de l'établissement des Allemands au Maroc." This was adopted with M. de Peretti de la Rocca's substitution of "le Gouvernement chérifien" for "la France," since the Sultan of Morocco, not France, rules Tangier. Paragraph 2 of Article 143 is identical with Article 11 of the French Draft. "Procès-Verbaux et Rapport de la Commission du Maroc," pp. 10-12, 13-14, 21-23, 27-28, 32.

Discussion

In view of the high character of the established French courts, there is no reason for the further maintenance of these extraterritorial rights. The United States has not yet consented to the proposed abolition. Nor has Great Britain, presumably because the matter is to be treated in conjunction with the abolition of the Capitulations in Egypt which is not yet in shape for final settlement.

4. That the complicated series of international agreements about Morocco from 1904 to 1912, especially the Algeciras Act of 1906, be revised, but that this process should leave fully intact,

    a. those classes [12] providing equality of economic opportunity for all nations in Morocco;

    b. the agreements of 1904 prohibiting the erection of fortifications on the northern coast of Morocco, except in the preëxisting Spanish possessions, notably Ceuta and Melilla.[13]

Discussion

It would be a decidedly reactionary step to permit the internationally established open door in Morocco to be shut and to allow this region to be enclosed within the French tariff barriers. Similarly, it would work against the peace of the world if France were permitted to fortify the northern littoral of Morocco. It would arouse great uneasiness in

[12] Anglo-French Declaration of April 8, 1904, Article 4; Franco-Spanish Treaties of September 1, 1905, Article 3, and November 27, 1912, Article 1.
[13] Anglo-French Declaration of April 8, 1904, Article 7; Franco-Spanish Treaty of November 27, 1912, Article 6.

Spain and would fundamentally alter the formally established *status quo* in the Western Mediterranean and the adjacent Atlantic.

C. Italian Libya

It is recommended:

1. That an adequate hinterland be given to Libya, so as to provide access to the Sudan and its trade.

Discussion

The Treaty of London, April 26, 1915, recognized in principle Italy's right to compensation in Africa, in case British and French colonial possessions there were extended at the expense of Germany.[14] Among the many colonial claims advanced unofficially on behalf of Italy, this one is the most reasonable and logical.[15] It should, however, be recognized

[14] Article 13: "Dans le cas où la France et la Grande-Bretagne augmenteraient leurs domaines coloniaux d'Afrique aux dépens de l'Allemagne, ces deux Puissances reconnaissent en principe que l'Italie pourrait réclamer quelques compensations équitables, notamment dans le règlement en sa faveur des questions concernant les frontières des colonies italiennes de l'Érythrée, de la Somalie et de la Libye et des colonies voisines de la France et de la Grande-Bretagne."

[15] For the extreme unofficial claim, see map on page 393 and Antonelli, *op. cit.*, pp. 201-205. By an exchange of notes (not yet published), September 12, 1919, France ceded to Italy the two reëntrant angles south of Tripoli, one between Gadames and Ghat, the other between Ghat and Tummo. Italy received the oases of Fehut and El-Baeka (near Ghat). This rectification does not affect the French line of communication between Fort Polignac and Janet. Further, equal fiscal treatment is to be applied in Tunisia to sales of real estate without regard to nationality. Italian private schools will there have the same rights as French and the French regulations in Morocco as to labor accidents are extended to Italians in Tunisia. *Le Temps*, February 24, 1920; cf. *ibid.*, May 16, 29, June 6, 1919. On September 8, 1919, an Anglo-French Agreement (not yet published) was reached concerning the boundary to be drawn between Wadai and Darfur, attaching the region of Dar Tama to the former and Dar Massalit to the latter. *Ibid.*, February 14, 1920. This delimitation had remained in suspense since the Anglo-French Declaration of March 21, 1899 ("Trattati," pp. 613-614). An Anglo-Italian Agreement,

only if it is confined to limits that will not hamper the development of the French colonial domain and of the Anglo-Egyptian Sudan.

2.   That, if possible, the principle of commercial and economic equality should be established, not only in the ceded area, but throughout Libya.

Discussion

The tariff of 1914 gives very marked preferential treatment to Italian goods—cottons, woolens, and sugar—imported into Libya.

also unpublished as yet, was reached in May, 1920, by which, according to the Italian press, the Gulf of Solum on the Mediterranean is left to Egypt, while Italy receives all the territory west of 25° with the oases of Jarabub and Kufra. In East Africa, Italy obtains almost all of Jubaland in Kenya (about 100,000 square kilometers). Antonelli, *op. cit.*, pp. 246-247; cf. *The Statesman's Year-Book*, 1921, pp. 1029, 1030. By Article 121 of the Sèvres Treaty, "Turkey definitely renounces all rights and privileges which under the Treaty of Lausanne of October 18, 1912, were left to the Sultan in Libya." For the text of this Lausanne Treaty, see *American Journal of International Law*, VII, Supplement, pp. 58-62.

CHAPTER IV

THE PACIFIC ISLANDS

Note.—As these former German islands will, in general, have to be disposed of on the same basis as has already been set forth with regard to the other ex-German possessions, it is highly important that the Peace Conference determine first the fate of those which Japan is occupying, because it is far more essential to establish safeguards in them than in those which are now occupied by Australia and New Zealand.[1]

---

[1] By decision of the Supreme Council at Paris, May 7, 1919, Mandates, all of the "C" type, were allotted for these islands as follows: north of the Equator, to Japan; south of the Equator, except ex-German Samoa and Nauru, to the Commonwealth of Australia; ex-German Samoa, to New Zealand; Nauru, to the British Empire. For the Japanese reservation concerning this type of Mandate, see the following note; for a type of "C" Mandate, see that for German Samoa, Annex K. By Article 1 of the Four-Power Treaty of December 13, 1921, it would appear that this allocation of Mandates is virtually recognized by the United States, though not yet a member of the League of Nations: "The High Contracting Parties [the United States, the British Empire, France, and Japan] agree as between themselves to respect their rights in relation to their insular possessions and insular dominions in the region of the Pacific Ocean." Formal recognition is, nevertheless, withheld by an American reservation of even date: "That the treaty shall apply to the mandated islands in the Pacific Ocean; provided, however, that the making of the treaty shall not be deemed to be an assent on the part of the United States of America to the mandates and shall not preclude agreements between the United States of America and the mandatory powers respectively in relation to the mandated islands." According to an Associated Press dispatch of December 12, 1921, an agreement has been reached between the United States and Japan by

A. The Marianne, Pelew, Caroline, and Marshall Islands

It is recommended:

That these islands be entrusted to Japan under a mandate of the League of Nations containing the following conditions:

a. the islands to remain unfortified and no naval bases to be established upon them;

b. differential import and export duties to be prohibited and equality of economic opportunity to be assured in other respects;

c. native rights to land to be safeguarded;

d. compulsory labor, direct or indirect, to be prohibited, except on essential public works;

e. freedom of activity to be allowed to Christian missions;

f. personal and property rights of Germans to be protected.[2]

Discussion

These islands have been occupied by Japan since the autumn of 1914. They have but slight importance, except

which the former has certain definite rights, including cable privileges, as to the island of Yap, while the latter has control over the island and over the other ex-German islands north of the Equator, observing the mandate conferred by the Supreme Council. Negotiations for a similar agreement between the United States and Great Britain are said to be contemplated regarding the islands allotted as mandated areas to the British Empire, Australia, and New Zealand. On the question of Yap see also R. S. Baker, "Woodrow Wilson and World Settlement," II, pp. 247, 467, 470-471, 480-481; and for the Anglo-Japanese exchange of notes in February, 1917, regarding the partition of German possessions in the Pacific, see *ibid.,* I, pp. 59-61.

[2] By the terms of the "C" Mandates (cf. Annex K), conditions *a, d,* and *e* are covered; condition *f* is governed by Article 122 of the Versailles Treaty, combined with Article 22, paragraph 6, of the Covenant

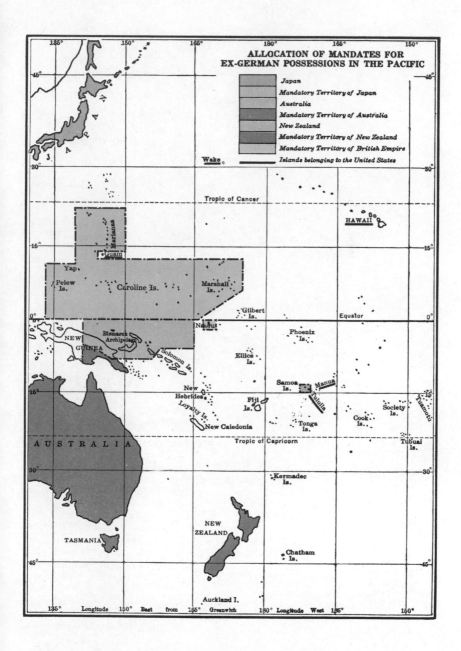

**ALLOCATION OF MANDATES FOR
EX-GERMAN POSSESSIONS IN THE PACIFIC**

Japan
Mandatory Territory of Japan
Australia
Mandatory Territory of Australia
New Zealand
Mandatory Territory of New Zealand
Mandatory Territory of British Empire
Islands belonging to the United States

Wake

135° 150° 165° 180° 165° 150°

45° 45°

30° 30°

Tropic of Cancer

HAWAII

15° 15°

Marianas

Guam

Yap

Pelew
Is. Caroline Is. Marshall
Is.

0° Equator 0°

Gilbert
Is.

Nauru

NEW Bismarck Phoenix
GUINEA Archipelago Is.

Solomon Is.

Ellice
Is.

Samoa Manua
Is. Tutuila

15° New 15°
Hebrides Fiji
Loyalty Is. Is. Society
Is. Tuamotu

New Caledonia Cook
Is.

Tonga

AUSTRALIA Tropic of Capricorn Tubuai
Is.

30° 30°

Kermadec
Is.

NEW
ZEALAND

TASMANIA Chatham
Is.

45° 45°

Auckland I.

135° Longitude 150° East from 165° Greenwich 180° Longitude West 165° 150°

possibly from the strategic standpoint. Their total population in 1913 was about 70,000 natives and 459 whites, of whom 259 were Germans.[3] Their foreign trade amounted to only $2,500,000 annually and there is little prospect of any very substantial expansion since labor is wanting to increase the two chief exports, copra and phosphates. Moreover, their aggregate area is very small. The Caroline and Pelew Islands contain 560 square miles, the Marianne 250. Their strategic value is possibly greater, but in view of the experiences of the present war even this is doubtful. In addition, this phase of the question must be considered in the light of the establishment of the League of Nations and the probable strict regulation of the future use of submarines. The United States has absolutely no legitimate right to these islands [4] and to advance such a claim would not only be considered a gratuitous affront by Japan, but would undermine the moral influence of the United States in the settlement of other questions.

of the League of Nations (see Ch. I, n. 5); condition *b* is intentionally omitted (see Covenant, *loc. cit.*), thus giving occasion for a Japanese reservation; condition *c* is not covered, except as it may be construed to come under the "prohibition of abuses" required by the Covenant in Mandates of the "B" and "C" types. Cf. *e.g.*, the Mandate for German Samoa, Annex K.

[3] According to *The Statesman's Year-Book*, 1922, p. 1080, the population is:

Island Groups	Native	Japanese	European and Chinese	Total
Marianne	3,638	1,754	——	5,392
Caroline	34,917	644	30	35,591
Marshall	8,901	102	5	9,008
Total	47,456	2,500	35	49,991

[4] The Senate of the United States strongly objected to the inclusion of Yap, in the western Carolines, under Mandate to Japan, in view of its importance as a cable station. For the present status of the controversy, see *supra*, Note 1.

B. *German Samoa*

It is recommended:

That these islands be entrusted on the same terms to the British Empire with the understanding that New Zealand is to execute the mandate.[5]

Discussion

Without offending Japan it would be impossible to discriminate between her and New Zealand. Not to permit New Zealand to exercise the mandate would, on the other hand, be deeply resented by a people who have made many sacrifices to win a remote war. Finally, it may confidently be assumed that no more trustworthy mandatory than New Zealand could be found. The interests involved are not large, as the native population is only about 35,000 and the trade approximately $2,500,000 a year.[6]

C. *The Bismarck Archipelago and the German Solomon Islands*

It is recommended:

That these islands be entrusted on the same terms to the

[5] As has already been observed (Note 1), the island of Nauru was detached from this group and placed under a Mandate exercised by the British Empire, New Zealand similarly administering ex-German Samoa (now called Territory of Western Samoa).

[6] By the census of 1917, the population was: natives, 37,223; coolies, 2,237; whites, 1,668; total, 41,128. The revenue collected in 1919-20 was £95,022 (chiefly customs—£58,729) and the expenditure was £96,314. The excess of assets over liabilities on March 31, 1920, was £28,030. In 1919, imports (exclusive of supplies for the troops) amounted to £291,368 and exports to £532,500; total trade, £823,868.—*The Statesman's Year-Book*, 1921, p. 439. By the census of 1921, the population was: natives, 32,953; other islanders, 758; coolies, 1,314; whites, 2,026; total, 37,051. Some 7,500 natives died in consequence of an epidemic of influenza in 1918. The revenue collected in 1921 was £149,027 (chiefly

British Empire with the understanding that Australia is to execute the mandate.[7]

Discussion

The return of these islands to Germany would be bitterly resented by Australia where a policy akin to the Monroe Doctrine has become firmly rooted in the popular mind. A strong feeling prevails against permitting any European power to gain a foothold south of the Equator, and the original establishment of Germany was resented as an intrusion.

D. German New Guinea

It is recommended:

1.   That this area be transferred to the British Empire on the understanding that it is to be added to Papua, the Australian section of New Guinea;

2.   That this transfer be made on condition that no differential import or export duties be imposed either in the ceded part of the island or in that already under Australian rule.[8]

Discussion

While the area of this part of New Guinea is large, 70,000 square miles, and its native population considerable, 531,000, the mandatory principle is not advisable on account of the fact that it adjoins Australian Papua.   To preserve the

customs—£92,905) and the expenditure was £149,327, the excess of liabilities being £27,329.   In 1920 imports amounted to £561,193 and exports to £947,780. *The Statesman's Year-Book*, 1922, p. 449.

[7] This was done. See *supra*, Note 1.

[8] This region was, however, placed under Australian Mandate and the second recommendation failed of adoption because of the scheme formulated for all "C" Mandates (cf. *supra*, Note 2).

administrative integrity of this section would serve no really useful purpose, but would artificially handicap its development by unnecessarily multiplying governmental machinery.

ANNEXES

ANNEXES

ANNEX A

AFRICAN QUESTIONS AT THE PEACE CONFERENCE.*

[NOTE. All notes in this Section are by the Editor.]

From the geographical and cultural standpoints, Africa falls into three distinct classes of territory. This division has determined the nature and extent of modern European intervention in that vast continent.

The first class is limited to Northern Africa, where, in countries like Morocco, Algeria, Tunis, and Egypt, there is a fairly dense native population with quite definite civilizations. Although climatic conditions in great sections of this region are not opposed to European immigration and settlement, the numerical strength of the natives and their established economic systems render it virtually impossible, as well as highly inadvisable, to substitute for the present owners of the soil a large European element.

The second class comprises those areas in which the aboriginal population is both comparatively sparse and is also in a low state of civilization and where Europeans can live and rear families under conditions similar to those in Europe and in North America. Considerable territory of this nature is to be found within the tropics, but the suitable highlands and plateaus are there scattered like

---

* Apparently written for Mr. Beer's own guidance and merely as a skeleton outline.

islands in a huge tropical lake. The great bulk of land suitable for white colonization forms a compact mass south of the Zambezi and Kunene rivers and includes Southwest Africa and the Union of South Africa, as well as parts of Rhodesia, and also some portions of the Portuguese territories on the East and West Coasts.[1]

The third class includes the tropical parts of Africa, where Europeans cannot thrive as manual laborers and where they are unable to settle for long periods and bring up healthy families. In "white man's" Africa, a civilization of the Western European type is evolving. In Northern Africa, the European is controlling and directing already established civilizations; in Middle Africa, his prime function is to found order and justice and to promote the rudiments of civilization among peoples who are in general only slightly advanced from a savage state. His secondary duty here is to develop the vast resources of these fertile regions and, subject to the rights of the natives, to obtain the raw materials required by the diversified needs of advanced and progressive peoples throughout the world.

In accordance with these great divisions of Africa, this continent presents three distinct groups of problems, some of which will come before the Peace Conference.

A. Problems of Northern Africa

In general, the political status of this region and also the boundaries of the different areas under European protectorates had been clearly determined before 1914 by a series of international agreements. Two matters will, however, in all probability require further regulation.

---

[1] For the areas suitable for white settlement, see map facing p. 118.

I. The southern boundary of Tripoli and Cyrenaica (Libia Italiana) has never been satisfactory to the Italians, as it did not give -them access to the Sudan. One of the conditions of Italy's entrance into the war in the spring of 1915 was that, in case France and Great Britain retained any of the conquered German colonies in Africa, Italy should receive compensation.[2] Presumably, this will be an extension of the southern frontiers of Tripoli and Cyrenaica at the expense of the Anglo-Egyptian Sudan and of the French Sudan. If any such arrangement be made, it will probably be concluded by the three Powers directly interested and will not come before the Peace Conference for discussion.[3] The new status of Egypt, however, requires international recognition.

II. On December 18, 1914, after Turkey's entrance into the war, a British Protectorate over Egypt was declared and all political connection with Turkey was severed. As this new status merely expressed a condition of affairs that had already been in existence under full international recognition, there is apparently no objection to giving international validity to the formal British Protectorate. But several other matters intimately associated with this changed position will probably require settlement.

1. Under the old régime, Egypt paid an annual tribute to Turkey of £692,350, which, in turn, had been hypothe-

[2] Pact of London, April 26, 1915, Article 13: "Dans le cas où la France et la Grande-Bretagne augmenteraient leurs domaines coloniaux d'Afrique aux dépens de l'Allemagne, ces deux puissances reconnaissent en principe que l'Italie pourrait réclamer quelques compensations équitables, notamment dans le règlement en sa faveur des questions concernant les frontières des colonies italiennes de l'Erythrée, de la Somalie et de la Libye et des colonies voisines de la France et de la Grande-Bretagne."

[3] For the changes actually effected, see *supra*, pp. 451-452.

cated by Turkey as security for a loan of £T17,981,106. This involves some thorny ethical questions.

2. The Capitulations, which exempt foreigners from the jurisdiction of the local tribunals, are by many considered unnecessary in a country so well governed as is Egypt and for years considerable opposition to their continuance has been manifest.[4]

3. Egypt has inherited from Turkey the old agreements with the European Powers limiting the customs duties on imports to eight per cent *ad valorem*. The continuance of this condition down to the year 1934 is assured by the Anglo-French declaration of April 8, 1904, by which Britain also agrees not to give preferential treatment within that period to British goods.[5] The problem arises whether or no Egypt should not have full tariff autonomy and also whether or no the pledge of equality of treatment should not in return be extended beyond 1934, if not indefinitely. The answer to the latter question depends largely upon the nature of the peace and the situation in Central Europe, which will determine the necessity of holding economic weapons in reserve to combat Teutonic autocracy in the future.

[4] The British Protectorate is recognized by the Treaties with Germany (Article 147), Austria (Article 102), Hungary (Article 86), and Turkey (Article 101). It has also been recognized by France, Russia, Belgium, Serbia, Greece, Portugal, and the United States. By Article 112 of the Sèvres Treaty, "Turkey renounces all claim to the tribute formerly paid by Egypt. Great Britain undertakes to relieve Turkey of all liability in respect of the Turkish loans secured on the Egyptian tribute." The Capitulations are renounced by Germany (Versailles Treaty, Article 147), Austria (Treaty of Saint-Germain-en-Laye, Article 102), and Hungary (Trianon Treaty, Article 86).

[5] "Trattati . . . relativi all'Africa," p. 1117. The other Egyptian problems here noted have thus far remained undecided.

4. One other matter in connection with Egypt must also be considered. The question arises whether or no the eastern frontier of Egypt should be slightly advanced so as to include both shores of the Gulf of Akabah. The establishment of a submarine base here by a hostile Power would very grievously imperil the communications of the British Commonwealth. The real advisability of such an extension of Egypt's boundary will, however, largely depend upon the future status of Palestine and upon that of the new Kingdom of Hedjaz.[6]

B. German Southwest Africa

In that part of Africa primarily suited for white colonization, the important problem will be the determination of the future of German Southwest Africa, which was conquered by the forces of the Union of South Africa. In settling this question in accordance with justice, the interests of the comparatively small native population, the rights of the few German settlers, and the claims of the Anglo-Dutch Dominion, which is the paramount civilizing force in South Africa, must have more weight than either the wishes of Germany or those of Great Britain.[7]

   I. Germany's acquisition of this region. Attitude of the British Government and of Cape Colony.
  II. Its physical characteristics and natural resources.
 III. The natives and the Herero War.
 IV. Its economic development and white immigration.
  V. The discovery of diamonds and of copper.

  [6] The terms of the arrangements with Palestine have rendered unnecessary any change in the Egyptian frontier.
  [7] For the text of the Mandate placing this territory under the control of the Union of South Africa, see Annex L.

VI. Its actual economic worth to Germany and its potential future value.
VII. The conquest of the colony. German methods of warfare.
VIII. Germany's desire to retain it. Economic and political reasons and also those of national prestige and honor.
IX. With British statesmen, the position of the Union of South Africa is the most important factor. Analysis of this attitude:
   1. The desire to be free from European interference and intrigues—an inchoate African "Monroe Doctrine";
   2. National pride in retaining what their prowess has won. Compare with attitude of New England in 1748 towards Louisbourg and that of the American Colonies in 1761-63 towards the retention of Canada;
   3. The aim to unite in one inclusive political system practically all of "white man's" Africa south of the Zambezi and Kunene.

C. MIDDLE AFRICA.[8]

I. General physiography of tropical Africa. The river communications. Natural resources. The native races. Arabic and Mohammedan influences. The distribution of the highlands suitable for white settlement.
II. Modern European intervention.
   1. The Portuguese navigators.
   2. Rivalry of the maritime powers in the seventeenth and eighteenth centuries. The chief interest in Africa was that it formed the reservoir of slave labor for the plantations in the West Indies and on the American continents. At that time, West Africa was economically a part of America.
   3. With the abolition of the slave trade and of negro slavery, Europe's concern in Africa declined. Interest was, however, kept alive by:
      a. The constantly growing trade with Africa;
      b. The efforts of missionaries to civilize the natives;
      c. The activities of a series of intrepid explorers in revealing the geographical features of Africa, the barbarism of the indigenes, and the potential wealth of its soil. In all of these activities British pioneers were most conspicuous, but the Government avoided, as far as possible, the responsibilities connected with the annexations of vast territories. This timid policy could not be maintained when, in the 'eighties of the past century, it became apparent that other European Powers were ready to place under their flags areas in which British commercial

[8] For the elaboration of this scheme, see Parts II and III.

interests were paramount. Reasons for this marked revival of interest by Europe. The economic factor and others.

III. The Partition of Africa, 1884-1912. The division of this vast continent among the European Powers without war is the greatest feat of diplomacy. Rivalry between Britain, Germany, France, Portugal, and Belgium. All difficulties were settled by negotiation and embodied in treaties. In 1914, the only independent states in Africa were Liberia and Abyssinia. Notes on:

1. The relations of the United States and Liberia.
2. The status of Abyssinia.

IV. The British Colonies and Protectorates.

1. Their history.
2. British policy towards the natives.
3. Free trade policy and the open door.
4. Economic development.

V. The French Colonies and Protectorates.

1. Their history.
2. The French preferential system of trade.
3. Economic development.
4. Native policy in West Africa and on the Congo.

VI. The Belgian Congo.

1. The old régime of Leopold.
2. The new system.

VII. The German Colonies.

1. History and economic development.
2. Native policy.

VIII. The Portuguese Colonies.

IX. The Italian Colonies.

X. The Spanish Colonies.

XI. A comparison of the policies of the European Powers towards the natives.

XII. A comparison of their systems of administration.

XIII. A comparison of the economic development of the several colonies.

XIV. A comparison of the different interests of the various European countries in the trade with Central Africa.

XV. The function of tropical colonization in the economy of Europe.

1. Middle Africa as a market.
2. Middle Africa as a source of supplies.
3. Both are intimately connected with the policy towards the natives. Markets and supplies can be evolved only by civilizing the negroes. Necessity of developing their needs, not their wants, so that they will demand wares conducive

to their uplift and will be willing to work in return for them. Extreme urgency of restricting traffic in spirits.

4. Up to 1914, the total commerce of Middle Africa was very small and played a minor part in the foreign trade of Great Britain, Germany, and France. Their respective shares in it.

XVI. The political situation in 1914.

Although the possessions of the European Powers were determined by treaties, Germany did not regard the distribution as definitive and was distinctly dissatisfied. Germany's aim to secure by negotiation or otherwise the greater part of the Portuguese and Belgian Colonies. The argument that Portugal and Belgium did not have sufficient resources in men and in capital to develop their vast possessions.

1. International status of the Belgian Congo. French rights and their waiver in 1911.

2. Anglo-German agreement of 1898 about the Portuguese colonies and Britain's subsequent guarantee of the integrity of the Portuguese possessions.

3. Negotiations between Britain and Germany about a redistribution of Africa, 1912 to 1914. Sir Edward Grey's attitude. The abortive agreement of 1914, whose terms have not been announced.

XVII. The political situation as altered by the war.

1. The revelation of German aims.

2. The German plan to train the natives of Africa into a potent military force.

3. Germany's conduct of the war, especially in East Africa.

4. The guarantee to Belgium of her African possessions.

XVIII. The economic situation as altered by the war.

The world-wide scarcity of raw materials. Hence the temporary enhancement of the value of Middle Africa as a reservoir. The ensuing danger that the natives may be coerced to work.

XIX. The decision of the territorial questions.

This, if based solely upon considerations of justice, would have to take into account primarily and predominantly the welfare and wishes of the negroes and only secondarily the needs of the European Powers. Attitude of the natives towards Germany. But the settlement in a fallible world will be based largely upon the European military situation and the *fait accompli* in Africa itself. In all probability also agreements between France and England will provide for some redistribution of their territories in West Africa as between themselves and likewise for a partition of the German colonies there, contingent upon the verdict of the Peace Conference.

XX. France's claims.

The desire to retain the territories in French Equatorial Africa, which France was obliged under threat of war to cede to Germany in 1911. Combined with this is the wish to oust an unfriendly neighbor from the Cameroons and to give to France a vast, compact territorial empire from the Congo to the Mediterranean.

XXI. Germany's aims.

An analysis of the expression of opinion since 1914. Necessity of distinguishing between the interests of minor groups and the nation as a whole. To the nation as a whole, the German colonial movement has been a pecuniary loss, though it has benefited some merchants and ship owners. In addition, the restoration of the colonies involves questions of prestige and national honor that reach deep. No need of the nation is satisfied by the possession of African territories, but imperative wants urge their return and even their extension.

XXII. The attitude of the British Commonwealth.

    1. In Great Britain there is no desire to retain the German colonies for themselves, but the opinious of the other members of the Commonwealth must be considered. In addition, there is the negative wish to have the British Protectorates freed from the menace of an aggressive neighbor and there is the positive anxiety to retain at least sufficient territory to make possible the Cape-to-Cairo railroad. This could be gratified by the cession of a small strip between Uganda and Lake Tanganyika, as had been arranged in 1894, when Germany and France vetoed the project. But South Africa and India would not be satisfied with so slight a readjustment.

    2. Attitude of the Union of South Africa.

Statements of General Smuts. Analysis of local opinion.

    3. Attitude of British India.

        a. The problem of over-population in India, and emigration.

        b. Attitude of the self-governing Dominions towards East Indian immigration, with special reference to the situation in Natal and South Africa.

        c. German East Africa for India's surplus population. Statement of the Indian Government. The testament of the nationalist leader, Gokhale. Analysis of Indian opinion. This question is intimately connected with the ultimate disposition of Mesopotamia and Irak, which may also be retained for East Indian colonization.

XXIII. The possibilities of international control of Middle Africa.

        a. Obstacles in the way of direct government by a league of nations.

ANNEX B *

THE MANDATE ARTICLE OF THE COVENANT OF THE LEAGUE OF NATIONS.

ARTICLE 22.

To those colonies and territories which as a consequence of the late war have ceased to be under the sovereignty of the States which formerly governed them and which are inhabited by peoples not yet able to stand by themselves under the strenuous conditions of the modern world, there should be applied the principle that the well-being and development of such peoples form a sacred trust of civilisation and that securities for the performance of this trust should be embodied in this Covenant.

The best method of giving practical effect to this principle is that the tutelage of such peoples should be entrusted to advanced nations who by reason of their resources, their experience or their geographical position can best undertake this responsibility, and who are willing to accept it, and that this tutelage should be exercised by them as Mandatories on behalf of the League.

The character of the mandate must differ according to the stage of the development of the people, the geographical situation of the territory, its economic conditions and other similar circumstances.

Certain communities formerly belonging to the Turkish Empire have reached a stage of development where their existence as independent nations can be provisionally recognised subject to the rendering of administrative advice and assistance by a Mandatory until such time as they are able to stand alone. The wishes of these communities must be a principal consideration in the selection of the Mandatory.

Other peoples, especially those of Central Africa, are at such a stage that the Mandatory must be responsible for the administration of the territory under conditions which will guarantee freedom of conscience and religion, subject only to the maintenance of public order and morals, the prohibition of abuses such as the slave trade, the arms traffic and the liquor traffic, and the prevention of the establishment of fortifications or military and naval bases and of military training of the natives for other than police purposes and the defence of territory, and will also secure equal opportunities for the trade and commerce of other Members of the League.

* All Parliamentary Papers are reproduced exactly as printed by the British Government.

There are territories, such as Southwest Africa and certain of the South Pacific Islands, which, owing to the sparseness of their population, or their small size, or their remoteness from the centres of civilisation, or their geographical contiguity to the territory of the Mandatory, and other circumstances, can be best administered under the laws of the Mandatory as integral portions of its territory, subject to the safeguards above mentioned in the interests of the indigenous population.

In every case of mandate, the Mandatory shall render to the Council an annual report in reference to the territory committed to its charge.

The degree of authority, control, or administration to be exercised by the Mandatory shall, if not previously agreed upon by the Members of the League, be explicitly defined in each case by the Council.

A permanent Commission shall be constituted to receive and examine the annual reports of the Mandatories and to advise the Council on all matters relating to the observance of the mandates.

ANNEX C

COLONIAL AND AFRICAN ARTICLES OF THE VERSAILLES TREATY.*

ARTICLE 119.

Germany renounces in favour of the Principal Allied and Associated Powers all her rights and titles over her oversea possessions.

ARTICLE 120.

All movable and immovable property in such territories belonging to the German Empire or to any German State shall pass to the Government exercising authority over such territories, on the terms laid down in Article 257 of Part IX (Financial Clauses) of the present Treaty. The decision of the local courts in any dispute as to the nature of such property shall be final.

* The relation of these Articles to those in the Peace Treaties with Austria and Hungary is shown by the following table:

Versailles	Saint-Germain	Trianon
119-125	. . . . . .	. . . . . .
126	373	356
127, 138-140	. . . . . .	. . . . . .
141-154	96-109	80-93

As regards the Treaty with Bulgaria, Article 126 of the Versailles Treaty here appears as Article 290 and Morocco and Egypt are covered by Articles 62-63:

ARTICLE 62.

Bulgaria declares that she recognizes the French Protectorate in Morocco, and that she will make no claim on behalf of herself or her nationals to the benefits or immunities derived from the régime of the capitulations in Morocco. All treaties, agreements, arrangements and contracts concluded by Bulgaria with Morocco are regarded as abrogated as from October 11, 1915.

Moroccan goods entering Bulgaria shall enjoy the treatment accorded to French goods.

ARTICLE 63.

Bulgaria declares that she recognises the Protectorate proclaimed over Egypt by Great Britain on December 18, 1914, and that she will make no claim on behalf of herself or her nationals to the benefits or immunities derived from the régime of the capitulations in Egypt. All treaties, agreements, arrangements and contracts concluded by Bulgaria with Egypt are regarded as abrogated as from October 11, 1915.

Egyptian goods entering Bulgaria shall enjoy the treatment accorded to British goods.

473

ARTICLE 121.

The provisions of Sections I and IV of Part X (Economic Clauses) of the present Treaty shall apply in the case of these territories whatever be the form of Government adopted for them.

ARTICLE 122.

The Government exercising authority over such territories may make such provisions as it thinks fit with reference to the repatriation from them of German nationals and to the conditions upon which German subjects of European origin shall, or shall not, be allowed to reside, hold property, trade or exercise a profession in them.

ARTICLE 123.

The provisions of Article 260 of Part IX (Financial Clauses) of the present Treaty shall apply in the case of all agreements concluded with German nationals for the construction or exploitation of public works in the German oversea possessions, as well as any sub-concessions or contracts resulting therefrom which may have been made to or with such nationals.

ARTICLE 124.

Germany hereby undertakes to pay, in accordance with the estimate to be presented by the French Government and approved by the Reparation Commission, reparation for damage suffered by French nationals in the Cameroons or the frontier zone by reason of the acts of the German civil and military authorities and of German private individuals during the period from January 1, 1900, to August 1, 1914.

ARTICLE 125.

Germany renounces all rights under the Conventions and Agreements with France of November 4, 1911, and September 28, 1912, relating to Equatorial Africa. She undertakes to pay to the French Government, in accordance with the estimate to be presented by that Government and approved by the Reparation Commission, all the deposits, credits, advances, etc., effected by virtue of these instruments in favour of Germany.

ARTICLE 126.

Germany undertakes to accept and observe the agreements made or to be made by the Allied and Associated Powers or some of them with any other Power with regard to the trade in arms and spirits, and to the matters dealt with in the General Act of Berlin of February 26, 1885, the General Act of Brussels of July 2, 1890, and the conventions completing or modifying the same.

ARTICLE 127.

The native inhabitants of the former German oversea possessions shall be entitled to the diplomatic protection of the Governments exercising authority over those territories.

ARTICLE 138.

Germany renounces all rights and privileges arising from the arrangements of 1911 and 1912 regarding Liberia, and particularly the right to nominate a German Receiver of Customs in Liberia.

She further renounces all claim to participate in any measures whatsoever which may be adopted for the rehabilitation of Liberia.

ARTICLE 139.

Germany recognizes that all treaties and arrangements between her and Liberia terminated as from August 4, 1917.

ARTICLE 140.

The property, rights and interests of Germans in Liberia shall be dealt with in accordance with Part X (Economic Clauses) of the present Treaty.

ARTICLE 141.

Germany renounces all rights, titles and privileges conferred on her by the General Act of Algeciras of April 7, 1906, and by the Franco-German Agreements of February 9, 1909, and November 4, 1911. All treaties, agreements, arrangements and contracts concluded by her with the Sherifian Empire are regarded as abrogated as from August 3, 1914.

In no case can Germany take advantage of these instruments and she undertakes not to intervene in any way in negotiations relating to Morocco which may take place between France and the other Powers.

ARTICLE 142.

Germany having recognized the French Protectorate in Morocco, hereby accepts all the consequences of its establishment, and she renounces the régime of the capitulations therein.

This renunciation shall take effect as from August 3, 1914.

ARTICLE 143.

The Sherifian Government shall have complete liberty of action in regulating the status of German nationals in Morocco and the conditions in which they may establish themselves there.

German protected persons, semsars and "associés agricoles" shall be considered as having ceased, as from August 3, 1914, to enjoy the privileges attached to their status and shall be subject to the ordinary law.

Article 144.

All property and possessions in the Sherifian Empire of the German Empire and the German States pass to the Maghzen without payment.

For this purpose, the property and possessions of the German Empire and States shall be deemed to include all the property of the Crown, the Empire or the States, and the private property of the former German Emperor and other Royal personages.

All movable and immovable property in the Sherifian Empire belonging to German nationals shall be dealt with in accordance with Sections III and IV of Part X (Economic Clauses) of the present Treaty.

Mining rights which may be recognised as belonging to German nationals by the Court of Arbitration set up under the Moroccan Mining Regulations shall form the subject of a valuation, which the arbitrators shall be requested to make, and these rights shall then be treated in the same way as property in Morocco belonging to German nationals.

Article 145.

The German Government shall ensure the transfer to a person nominated by the French Government of the shares representing Germany's portion of the capital of the State Bank of Morocco. The value of these shares, as assessed by the Reparation Commission, shall be paid to the Reparation Commission for the credit of Germany on account of the sums due for reparation. The German Government shall be responsible for indemnifying its nationals so dispossessed.

This transfer will take place without prejudice to the repayment of debts which German nationals may have contracted towards the State Bank of Morocco.

Article 146.

Moroccan goods entering Germany shall enjoy the treatment accorded to French goods.

Article 147.

Germany declares that she recognises the Protectorate proclaimed over Egypt by Great Britain on December 18, 1914, and that she renounces the régime of the Capitulations in Egypt.

This renunciation shall take effect as from August 4, 1914.

Article 148.

All treaties, agreements, arrangements and contracts concluded by Germany with Egypt are regarded as abrogated as from August 4, 1914.

In no case can Germany avail herself of these instruments and she undertakes not to intervene in any way in negotiations relating to Egypt which may take place between Great Britain and the other Powers.

Article 149.

Until an Egyptian law of judicial organization establishing courts with universal jurisdiction comes into force, provision shall be made, by means of decrees issued by His Highness the Sultan, for the exercise of jurisdiction over German nationals and property by the British Consular Tribunals.

Article 150.

The Egyptian Government shall have complete liberty of action in regulating the status of German nationals and the conditions under which they may establish themselves in Egypt.

Article 151.

Germany consents to the abrogation of the decree issued by His Highness the Khedive on November 28, 1904, relating to the Commission of the Egyptian Public Debt, or to such changes as the Egyptian Government may think it desirable to make therein.

Article 152.

Germany consents, in so far as she is concerned, to the transfer to His Britannic Majesty's Government of the powers conferred on His Imperial Majesty the Sultan by the Convention signed at Constantinople on October 29, 1888, relating to the free navigation of the Suez Canal.

She renounces all participation in the Sanitary, Maritime, and Quarantine Board of Egypt and consents, in so far as she is concerned, to the transfer to the Egyptian Authorities of the powers of that Board.

Article 153.

All property and possessions in Egypt of the German Empire and the German States pass to the Egyptian Government without payment.

For this purpose, the property and possessions of the German Empire and States shall be deemed to include all the property of the Crown, the Empire or the States, and the private property of the former German Emperor and other Royal personages.

All movable and immovable property in Egypt belonging to German nationals shall be dealt with in accordance with Sections III and IV of Part X (Economic Clauses) of the present Treaty.

Article 154.

Egyptian goods entering Germany shall enjoy the treatment accorded to British goods.

ANNEX D

AFRICAN, MANDATE, AND HEDJAZ ARTICLES OF THE SÈVRES TREATY.*

ARTICLE 94.

The High Contracting Parties agree that Syria and Mesopotamia shall, in accordance with the fourth paragraph of Article 22, Part I (Covenant of the League of Nations), be provisionally recognised as independent States subject to the rendering of administrative advice and assistance by a Mandatory until such time as they are able to stand alone.

A Commission shall be constituted within fifteen days from the coming into force of the present Treaty to trace on the spot the frontier line described in Article 27, II (2) and (3). This Commission will be composed of three members nominated by France, Great Britain and Italy respectively, and one member nominated by Turkey; it will be assisted by a representative of Syria for the Syrian frontier, and by a representative of Mesopotamia for the Mesopotamian frontier.

The determination of the other frontiers of the said States, and the selection of the Mandatories, will be made by the Principal Allied Powers.

ARTICLE 95.

The High Contracting Parties agree to entrust, by application of the provisions of Article 22, the administration of Palestine, within such boundaries as may be determined by the Principal Allied Powers, to a Mandatory to be selected by the said Powers. The Mandatory will be responsible for putting into effect the declaration originally made on November 2, 1917, by the British Government, and adopted by the other Allied Powers, in favour of the establishment in Palestine of a national home for the Jewish people, it being clearly understood that

* The relation between the Sèvres and the Versailles Treaties is shown by the following table, divergencies of note being indicated by an asterisk :

Sèvres	Versailles
94-100	....
101	*147
102-105	....
106	150
107	....
108	154
109-110	152-153
111-114	....
118	*141
119	146

nothing shall be done which may prejudice the civil and religious rights of existing non-Jewish communities in Palestine, or the rights and political status enjoyed by Jews in any other country.

The Mandatory undertakes to appoint as soon as possible a special Commission to study and regulate all questions and claims relating to the different religious communities. In the composition of this Commission the religious interests concerned will be taken into account. The Chairman of the Commission will be appointed by the Council of the League of Nations.

ARTICLE 96.

The terms of the mandates in respect of the above territories will be formulated by the Principal Allied Powers and submitted to the Council of the League of Nations for approval.

ARTICLE 97.

Turkey hereby undertakes, in accordance with the provisions of Article 132, to accept any decisions which may be taken in relation to the questions dealt with in this Section.

ARTICLE 98.

Turkey, in accordance with the action already taken by the Allied Powers, hereby recognises the Hedjaz as a free and independent State, and renounces in favour of the Hedjaz all rights and titles over the territories of the former Turkish Empire situated outside the frontiers of Turkey as laid down by the present Treaty, and comprised within the boundaries which may ultimately be fixed.

ARTICLE 99.

In view of the sacred character attributed by Moslems of all countries to the cities and the Holy Places of Mecca and Medina, His Majesty the King of the Hedjaz undertakes to assure free and easy access thereto to Moslems of every country who desire to go there on pilgrimage or for any other religious object, and to respect and ensure respect for the pious foundations which are or may be established there by Moslems of any countries in accordance with the precepts of the law of the Koran.

ARTICLE 100.

His Majesty the King of the Hedjaz undertakes that in commercial matters the most complete equality of treatment shall be assured in the territory of the Hedjaz to the persons, ships and goods of nationals of any of the Allied Powers, or of any of the new States set up in the territories of the former Turkish Empire, as well as to the persons, ships and goods of nationals of States, Members of the League of Nations.

ARTICLE 101.

Turkey renounces all rights and title in or over Egypt. This renunciation shall take effect as from November 5, 1914. Turkey declares that in conformity with the action taken by the Allied Powers she recognises the Protectorate proclaimed over Egypt by Great Britain on December 18, 1914.

ARTICLE 102.

Turkish subjects habitually resident in Egypt on December 18, 1914, will acquire Egyptian nationality *ipso facto* and will lose their Turkish nationality, except that if at that date such persons were temporarily absent from, and have not since returned to, Egypt they will not acquire Egyptian nationality without a special authorisation from the Egyptian Government.

ARTICLE 103.

Turkish subjects who became resident in Egypt after December 18, 1914, and are habitually resident there at the date of the coming into force of the present Treaty may, subject to the conditions prescribed in Article 105 for the right of option, claim Egyptian nationality, but such claim may in individual cases be refused by the competent Egyptian authority.

ARTICLE 104.

For all purposes connected with the present Treaty, Egypt and Egyptian nationals, their goods and vessels, shall be treated on the same footing, as from August 1, 1914, as the Allied Powers, their nationals, goods and vessels, and provisions in respect of territory under Turkish sovereignty, or of territory detached from Turkey in accordance with the present Treaty, shall not apply to Egypt.

ARTICLE 105.

Within a period of one year after the coming into force of the present Treaty persons over eighteen years of age acquiring Egyptian nationality under the provisions of Article 102 will be entitled to opt for Turkish nationality. In case such persons, or those who under Article 103 are entitled to claim Egyptian nationality, differ in race from the majority of the population of Egypt, they will within the same period be entitled to opt for the nationality of any State in favour of which territory is detached from Turkey, if the majority of the population of that State is of the same race as the person exercising the right to opt.

Option by a husband covers a wife and option by parents covers their children under eighteen years of age.

Persons who have exercised the above right to opt must, except where authorised to continue to reside in Egypt, transfer within the ensuing twelve months their place of residence to the State for which they have opted. They will be entitled to retain their immovable property in Egypt, and may carry with them their movable property of every description. No export or import duties or charges may be imposed upon them in connection with the removal of such property.

ARTICLE 106.

The Egyptian Government shall have complete liberty of action in regulating the status of Turkish subjects in Egypt and the conditions under which they may establish themselves in the territory.

ARTICLE 107.

Egyptian nationals shall be entitled, when abroad, to British diplomatic and consular protection.

ARTICLE 108.

Egyptian goods entering Turkey shall enjoy the treatment accorded to British goods.

ARTICLE 109.

Turkey renounces in favour of Great Britain the powers conferred upon His Imperial Majesty the Sultan by the Convention signed at Constantinople on October 29, 1888, relating to the free navigation of the Suez Canal.

ARTICLE 110.

All property and possessions in Egypt belonging to the Turkish Government pass to the Egyptian Government without payment.

ARTICLE 111.

All movable and immovable property in Egypt belonging to Turkish nationals (who do not acquire Egyptian nationality) shall be dealt with in accordance with the provisions of Part IX (Economic Clauses) of the present Treaty.

ARTICLE 112.

Turkey renounces all claim to the tribute formerly paid by Egypt.

Great Britain undertakes to relieve Turkey of all liability in respect of the Turkish loans secured on the Egyptian tribute.

These loans are:

The guaranteed loan of 1855;
The loan of 1894 representing the converted loans of 1854 and 1871;
The loan of 1891 representing the converted loan of 1877.

The sums which the Khedives of Egypt have from time to time undertaken to pay over to the houses by which these loans were issued will be
applied as heretofore to the interest and the sinking funds of the loans
of 1894 and 1891 until the final extinction of those loans. The Government of Egypt will also continue to apply the sum hitherto paid towards
the interest on the guaranteed loan of 1855.

Upon the extinction of these loans of 1894, 1891 and 1855, all liability
on the part of the Egyptian Government arising out of the tribute formerly
paid by Egypt to Turkey will cease.

ARTICLE 113.

The High Contracting Parties declare and place on record that they
have taken note of the Convention between the British Government and
the Egyptian Government defining the status and regulating the administration of the Soudan, signed on January 19, 1899, as amended by the
supplementary Convention relating to the town of Suakin signed on
July 10, 1899.

ARTICLE 114.

Soudanese shall be entitled when in foreign countries to British diplomatic and consular protection.

ARTICLE 118.

Turkey recognizes the French Protectorate in Morocco, and accepts all
the consequences thereof. This recognition shall take effect as from
March 30, 1912.

ARTICLE 119.

Moroccan goods entering Turkey shall be subject to the same treatment as French goods.

ARTICLE 120.

Turkey recognizes the French protectorate over Tunis and accepts all
the consequences thereof. This recognition shall take effect as from
May 12, 1881.

Tunisian goods entering Turkey shall be subject to the same treatment
as French goods.

ANNEX E

[Translation.]

CONVENTION FOR THE CONTROL OF THE TRADE IN ARMS AND AMMUNITION, AND PROTOCOL, SIGNED AT SAINT-GERMAIN-EN-LAYE,* SEPTEMBER 10, 1919.†

THE United States of America, Belgium, Bolivia, the British Empire, China, Cuba, Ecuador, France, Greece, Guatemala, Haiti, the Hedjaz, Italy, Japan, Nicaragua, Panama, Peru, Poland, Portugal, Roumania, the Serb-Croat-Slovene State, Siam and Czecho-Slovakia;

Whereas the long war now ended, in which most nations have successively become involved, has led to the accumulation in various parts of the world of considerable quantities of arms and munitions of war, the dispersal of which would constitute a danger to peace and public order;

Whereas in certain parts of the world it is necessary to exercise special supervision over the trade in, and the possession of, arms and ammunition;

Whereas the existing treaties and conventions, and particularly the Brussels Act of July 2, 1890, regulating the traffic in arms and ammunition in certain regions, no longer meet present conditions, which require more elaborate provisions applicable to a wider area in Africa and the establishment of a corresponding régime in certain territories in Asia;

Whereas a special supervision of the maritime zone adjacent to certain countries is necessary to ensure the efficacy of the measures adopted by the various Governments both as regards the importation of arms and ammunition into those countries and the export of such arms and ammunition from their own territory;

And with the reservation that, after a period of seven years, the present Convention shall be subject to revision in the light of the experience gained, if the Council of the League of Nations, acting if need be by a majority, so recommends;

---

* Some of the signatures were affixed in Paris and some at Saint-Germain-en-Laye.

† Treaty Series, 1919, No. 12.

Have appointed as their Plenipotentiaries:

The President of the United States of America:
 The Honourable Frank Lyon Polk, Under-Secretary of State;
 The Honourable Henry White, formerly Ambassador Extraordinary and Plenipotentiary of the United States at Rome and Paris;
 General Tasker H. Bliss, Military Representative of the United States on the Supreme War Council;

His Majesty the King of the Belgians:
 M. Paul Hymans, Minister for Foreign Affairs, Minister of State;
 M. Jules van den Heuvel, Envoy Extraordinary and Minister Plenipotentiary of His Majesty the King of the Belgians, Minister of State;
 M. Emile Vandervelde, Minister of Justice, Minister of State;

President of the Republic of Bolivia:
 M. Ismail Montes, Envoy Extraordinary and Minister Plenipotentiary of Bolivia at Paris;

His Majesty the King of the United Kingdom of Great Britain and Ireland and of the British Dominions Beyond the Seas, Emperor of India:
 The Right Honourable Arthur James Balfour, O.M., M.P., His Secretary of State for Foreign Affairs;
 The Right Honourable Andrew Bonar Law, M.P., His Lord Privy Seal;
 The Right Honourable Viscount Milner, G.C.B., G.C.M.G., His Secretary of State for the Colonies;
 The Right Honourable George Nicoll Barnes, M.P., Minister without Portfolio.

 And

for the Dominion of Canada:
 The Honourable Sir Albert Edward Kemp, K.C.M.G., Minister of the Overseas Forces;

for the Commonwealth of Australia:
 The Honourable George Foster Pearce, Minister of Defence;

for the Union of South Africa:
 The Right Honourable Viscount Milner, G.C.B., G.C.M.G.;

for the Dominion of New Zealand:
 The Honourable Sir Thomas Mackenzie, K.C.M.G., High Commissioner for New Zealand in the United Kingdom;

for India:
 The Right Honourable Baron Sinha, K.C., Under-Secretary of State for India;

The President of the Chinese Republic:
 M. Lou Tseng-Tsiang, Minister for Foreign Affairs;
 M. Chengting Thomas Wang, formerly Minister of Agriculture and Commerce;

The President of the Cuban Republic:
M. Antonio Sanchez de Bustamante, Dean of the Faculty of Law in the University of Havana, President of the Cuban Society of International Law;

The President of the Republic of Ecuador:
M. Dorn y de Alsua, Envoy Extraordinary and Minister Plenipotentiary of Ecuador at Paris;

The President of the French Republic:
M. Georges Clemenceau, President of the Council, Minister of War;
M. Stephen Pichon, Minister for Foreign Affairs;
M. Louis-Lucien Klotz, Minister of Finance;
M. André Tardieu, Commissary-General for Franco-American Military Affairs;
M. Jules Cambon, Ambassador of France;

His Majesty the King of the Hellenes:
M. Nicolas Politis, Minister for Foreign Affairs;
M. Athos Romanos, Envoy Extraordinary and Minister Plenipotentiary to the French Republic;

The President of the Republic of Guatemala:
M. Joaquim Mendez, formerly Minister of State for Public Works and Public Instruction, Envoy Extraordinary and Minister Plenipotentiary of Guatemala at Washington, Envoy Extraordinary and Minister Plenipotentiary on Special Mission at Paris;

The President of the Republic of Haiti:
M. Tertullien Guilbaud, Envoy Extraordinary and Minister Plenipotentiary of Haiti to Ecuador;

His Majesty the King of the Hedjaz:
M. Rustem Haidar;
M. Abdul Hadi Aouni;

His Majesty the King of Italy:
The Honourable Tommaso Tittoni, Senator of the Kingdom, Minister for Foreign Affairs;
The Honourable Vittorio Scialoja, Senator of the Kingdom;
The Honourable Maggiorino Ferraris, Senator of the Kingdom;
The Honourable Guglielmo Marconi, Senator of the Kingdom;
The Honourable Silvio Crespi, Deputy;

His Majesty the Emperor of Japan:
Viscount Chinda, Ambassador Extraordinary and Plenipotentiary of H.M. the Emperor of Japan at London;
M. K. Matsui, Ambassador Extraordinary and Plenipotentiary of H.M. the Emperor of Japan at Paris;
M. H. Ijuin, Ambassador Extraordinary and Plenipotentiary of H.M. the Emperor of Japan at Rome;

The President of the Republic of Nicaragua:
M. Salvador Chamorro, President of the Chamber of Deputies;

The President of the Republic of Panama:
  M. Antonio Burgos, Envoy Extraordinary and Minister Plenipotentiary
  of Panama at Madrid;

The President of the Republic of Peru:
  M. Carlos G. Candamo, Envoy Extraordinary and Minister Plenipotentiary of Peru at Madrid;

The President of the Polish Republic:
  M. Ignace J. Paderewski, President of the Council of Ministers,
  Minister for Foreign Affairs;
  M. Roman Dmowski, President of the Polish National Committee;

The President of the Portuguese Republic:
  Dr. Affonso da Costa, formerly President of the Council of Ministers;
  Dr. Augusto Luiz Vieira Soares, formerly Minister for Foreign
  Affairs;

His Majesty the King of Roumania:
  M. Nicolas Misu, Envoy Extraordinary and Minister Plenipotentiary
  of Roumania at London;
  Dr. Alexander Vaida-Voevod, Minister without Portfolio;

His Majesty the King of the Serbs, the Croats, and the Slovenes:
  M. N. P. Pachitch, formerly President of the Council of Ministers;
  M. Ante Trumbic, Minister for Foreign Affairs;
  M. Ivan Zolger, Doctor at Law;

His Majesty the King of Siam:
  His Highness Prince Charoon, Envoy Extraordinary and Minister
  Plenipotentiary of H.M. the King of Siam at Paris;
  His Serene Highness Prince Traidos Prabandhu, Under-Secretary of
  State for Foreign Affairs;

The President of the Czecho-Slovak Republic:
  M. Charles Kramàř, President of the Council of Ministers;
  M. Edouard Beneš, Minister for Foreign Affairs;

Who, having communicated their full powers found in good **and** due
form,
Have agreed as follows:

CHAPTER I.

Export of Arms and Ammunition.

ARTICLE 1.

The High Contracting Parties undertake to prohibit the export of the
following arms of war: artillery of all kinds, apparatus for the discharge
of all kinds of projectiles explosive or gas-diffusing, flame-throwers, bombs,
grenades, machine-guns and rifled small-bore breech-loading weapons

of all kinds, as well as the exportation of the ammunition for use with such arms. The prohibition of exportation shall apply to all such arms and ammunition, whether complete or in parts.

Nevertheless, notwithstanding this prohibition, the High Contracting Parties reserve the right to grant, in respect of arms whose use is not prohibited by International Law, export licences to meet the requirements of their Governments or those of the Government of any of the High Contracting Parties, but for no other purpose.

In the case of firearms and ammunition adapted both to warlike and also to other purposes, the High Contracting Parties reserve to themselves the right to determine from the size, destination, and other circumstances of each shipment for what uses it is intended and to decide in each case whether the provisions of this Article are applicable to it.

Article 2.

The High Contracting Parties undertake to prohibit the export of firearms and ammunition, whether complete or in parts, other than arms and munitions of war, to the areas and zone specified in Article 6.

Nevertheless, notwithstanding this prohibition, the High Contracting Parties reserve the right to grant export licences on the understanding that such licences shall be issued only by their own authorities. Such authorities must satisfy themselves in advance that the arms or ammunition for which an export licence is requested are not intended for export to any destination, or for disposal in any way, contrary to the provisions of this Convention.

Article 3.

Shipments to be effected under contracts entered into before the coming into force of the present Convention shall be governed by its provisions.

Article 4.

The High Contracting Parties undertake to grant no export licences to any country which refuses to accept the tutelage under which it has been placed, or which, after having been placed under the tutelage of any Power, may endeavour to obtain from any other Power any of the arms or ammunition specified in Articles 1 and 2.

Article 5.

A Central International Office, placed under the control of the League of Nations, shall be established for the purpose of collecting and preserving documents of all kinds exchanged by the High Contracting Parties with regard to the trade in, and distribution of, the arms and ammunition specified in the present Convention.

Each of the High Contracting Parties shall publish an annual report showing the export licences which it may have granted, together with the quantities and destination of the arms and ammunition to which the export licences referred. A copy of this report shall be sent to the Central International Office and to the Secretary-General of the League of Nations.

Further, the High Contracting Parties agree to send to the Central International Office and to the Secretary-General of the League of Nations full statistical information as to the quantities and destination of all arms and ammunition exported without licence.

CHAPTER II.

Import of Arms and Ammunition. Prohibited Areas and Zone of Maritime Supervision.

ARTICLE 6.

The High Contracting Parties undertake, each as far as the territory under its jurisdiction is concerned, to prohibit the importation of the arms and ammunition specified in Articles 1 and 2 into the following territorial areas, and also to prevent their importation and transportation in the maritime zone defined below:

1. The whole of the Continent of Africa with the exception of Algeria, Libya and the Union of South Africa.

Within this area are included all islands situated within a hundred nautical miles of the coast, together with Prince's Island, St. Thomas Island and the Islands of Annobon and Socotra.

2. Transcaucasia, Persia, Gwadar, the Arabian Peninsula and such continental parts of Asia as were included in the Turkish Empire on August 4, 1914.

3. A maritime zone, including the Red Sea, the Gulf of Aden, the Persian Gulf and the Sea of Oman, and bounded by a line drawn from Cape Guardafui, following the latitude of that cape to its intersection with longitude 57° east of Greenwich, and proceeding thence direct to the eastern frontier of Persia in the Gulf of Oman.

Special licences for the import of arms or ammunition into the areas defined above may be issued. In the African area they shall be subject to the regulations specified in Articles 7 and 8 or to any local regulations of a stricter nature which may be in force. In the other areas specified in the present Article, these licences shall be subject to similar regulations put into effect by the Governments exercising authority there,

CHAPTER III.

Supervision on Land.

ARTICLE 7.

Arms and ammunition imported under special licence into the prohibited areas shall be admitted only at ports designated for this purpose by the Authorities of the State, Colony, Protectorate or territory under mandate concerned.

Such arms and ammunition must be deposited by the importer at his own risk and expense in a public warehouse under the exclusive custody and permanent control of the Authority and of its agents, of whom one at least must be a civil official or a military officer. No arms or ammunition shall be deposited or withdrawn without the previous authorisation of the administration of the State, Colony, Protectorate or territory under mandate, unless the arms and ammunition to be deposited or withdrawn are intended for the forces of the Government or the defence of the national territory.

The withdrawal of arms or ammunition deposited in these warehouses shall be authorised only in the following cases:—

1. For despatch to places designated by the Government where the inhabitants are allowed to possess arms, under the control and responsibility of the local Authorities, for the purpose of defence against robbers or rebels.

2. For despatch to places designated by the Government as warehouses and placed under the supervision and responsibility of the local Authorities.

3. For individuals who can show that they require them for their legitimate personal use.

ARTICLE 8.

In the prohibited areas specified in Article 6, trade in arms and ammunition shall be placed under the control of officials of the Government and shall be subject to the following regulations:

1. No person may keep a warehouse for arms or ammunition without a licence.

2. Any person licensed to keep a warehouse for arms or ammunition must reserve for that special purpose enclosed premises having only one entry, provided with two locks, one of which can be opened only by the officers of the Government.

The person in charge of a warehouse shall be responsible for all arms or ammunition deposited therein and must account for them on demand. For this purpose all deposits or withdrawals shall be entered in a special register, numbered and initialled. Each entry shall be supported by references to the official documents authorising such deposits or withdrawals.

3. No transport of arms or ammunition shall take place without a special licence.

4. No withdrawal from a private warehouse shall take place except under licence issued by the local Authority on an application stating the purpose for which the arms or ammunition are required, and supported by a licence to carry arms or by a special permit for the purchase of ammunition. Every arm shall be registered and stamped; the Authority in charge of the control shall enter on the licence to carry arms the mark stamped on the weapon.

5. No one shall without authority transfer to another person either by gift or for any consideration any weapon or ammunition which he is licensed to possess.

ARTICLE 9.

In the prohibited areas and zone specified in Article 6 the manufacture and assembling of arms or ammunition shall be prohibited, except at arsenals established by the local Government or, in the case of countries placed under tutelage, at arsenals established by the local Government, under the control of the mandatory Power, for the defence of its territory or for the maintenance of public order.

No arms shall be repaired except at arsenals or establishments licenced by the local Government for this purpose. No such licence shall be granted without guarantees for the observance of the rules of the present Convention.

ARTICLE 10.

Within the prohibited areas specified in Article 6, a State which is compelled to utilise the territory of a contiguous State for the importation of arms or ammunition, whether complete or in parts, or of material or of articles intended for armament, shall be authorised on request to have them transported across the territory of such State.

It shall, however, when making any such request, furnish guarantees that the said articles are required for the needs of its own Government, and will at no time be sold, transferred or delivered for private use nor used in any way contrary to the interests of the High Contracting Parties.

Any violation of these conditions shall be formally established in the following manner:—

(a) If the importing State is a sovereign independent Power, the proof of the violation shall be advanced by one or more of the Representatives accredited to it of contiguous States among the High Contracting Parties.

After the Representatives of the other contiguous States have, if necessary, been informed, a joint enquiry into the facts by all these Representatives will be opened, and if need be, the importing State will be called upon to furnish explanations. If the gravity of the case should so require, and if the explanations of the importing State are considered unsatisfactory, the Representatives will jointly notify the importing State that all transit licences in its favour are suspended and that all future requests will be refused until it shall have furnished new and satisfactory guarantees.

The forms and conditions of the guarantees provided by the present Article shall be agreed upon previously by the Representatives of the contiguous States among the High Contracting Parties. These Representatives shall communicate to each other, as and when issued, the transit licences granted by the competent authorities.

(b) If the importing State has been placed under the mandatory system established by the League of Nations, the proof of the violation shall be furnished by one of the High Contracting Parties or on its own initiative by the Mandatory Power. The latter shall then notify or demand, as the case may be, the suspension and future refusal of all transit licences.

In cases where a violation has been duly proved, no further transit licence shall be granted to the offending State without the previous consent of the Council of the League of Nations.

If any proceedings on the part of the importing State or its disturbed condition should threaten the public order of one of the contiguous States signatories of the present Convention, the importation in transit of arms, ammunition, material and articles intended for armament shall be refused to the importing State by all the contiguous States until order has been restored.

CHAPTER IV.

Maritime Supervision.

ARTICLE 11.

Subject to any contrary provisions in existing special agreements, or in future agreements, provided that in all cases such agreements comply with the provisions of the present Convention, the sovereign State or Mandatory Power shall carry out all supervision and police measures within territorial waters in the prohibited areas and zone specified in Article 6.

ARTICLE 12.

Within the prohibited areas and maritime zone specified in Article 6, no native vessel of less than 500 tons burden shall be allowed to ship, discharge, or transship arms or ammunition.

For this purpose, a vessel shall be considered as a native vessel if she is either owned by a native, or fitted out or commanded by a native, or if more than half of the crew are natives of the countries bordering on the Indian Ocean, the Red Sea, the Persian Gulf, or the Gulf of Oman.

This provision does not apply to lighters or barges, nor to vessels which, without going more than five miles from the shore, are engaged exclusively in the coasting trade between different ports of the same State, Colony, Protectorate or territory under mandate, where warehouses are situated.

No cargoes of arms or ammunition shall be shipped on the vessels specified in the preceding paragraph without a special licence from the territorial authority, and all arms or ammunition so shipped shall be subject to the provisions of the present Convention.

This licence shall contain all details necessary to establish the nature and quantity of the items of the shipment, the vessel on which the shipment is to be loaded, the name of the ultimate consignee, and the ports of loading and discharge. It shall also be specified thereon that the licence has been issued in conformity with the regulations of the present Convention.

The above regulations do not apply:

1. To arms or ammunition conveyed on behalf of the Government, provided that they are accompanied by a duly qualified official.

2. To arms or ammunition in the possession of persons provided with a licence to carry arms, provided such arms are for the personal use of the bearer and are accurately described on his licence.

ARTICLE 13.

To prevent all illicit conveyance of arms or ammunition within the zone of maritime supervision specified in Article 6 (3), native vessels of less than 500 tons burden not exclusively engaged in the coasting trade between different ports of the same State, Colony, Protectorate or territory under mandate, not going more than five miles from the shore, and proceeding to or from any point within the said zone, must carry a manifest of their cargo or similar document specifying the quantities and nature of the goods on board, their origin and destination. This document shall remain covered by the secrecy to which it is entitled by the law of the State to which the vessel belongs, and must not be examined during the proceedings for the verification of the flag unless the interested party consents thereto.

The provisions as to the above-mentioned documents shall not apply to vessels only partially decked, having a maximum crew of ten men, and exclusively employed in fishing within territorial waters.

Authority to fly the flag of one of the High Contracting Parties within the zone of maritime supervision specified in Article 6 (3) shall be granted only to such native vessels as satisfy all the three following conditions:

1. The owners must be nationals of the Power whose flag they claim to fly.

2. They must furnish proof that they possess real estate in the district of the authority to which their application is addressed, or must supply a solvent security as a guarantee for any fines to which they may become liable.

3. Such owners, as well as the captain of the vessel, must furnish proof that they enjoy a good reputation, and especially that they have never been convicted of illicit conveyance of the articles referred to in the present Convention.

The authorisation must be renewed every year. It shall contain the indications necessary to identify the vessel, the name, tonnage, type of rigging, principal dimensions, registered number, and signal letters. It shall bear the date on which it was granted and the status of the official who granted it.

The name of the native vessel and the amount of her tonnage shall be incised and painted in Latin characters on the stern, and the initial letters of the name of the port of registry, as well as the registration number in the series of the numbers of that port, shall be painted in black on the sails.

Article 15.

Native vessels to which, under the provisions of the last paragraph of Article 13, the regulations relating to the manifest of the cargo are not applicable, shall receive from the territorial or consular authorities, as the case may be, a special licence, renewable annually and revocable under the conditions provided for in Article 19.

This special licence shall show the name of the vessel, her description, nationality, port of registry, name of captain, name of owner and the waters in which she is allowed to sail.

Article 16.

The High Contracting Parties agree to apply the following rules in the maritime zone specified in Article 6 (3):—

1. When a warship belonging to one of the High Contracting Parties encounters outside territorial waters a native vessel of less than 500 tons burden flying the flag of one of the High Contracting Parties, and the commander of the warship has good reason to believe that the

native vessel is flying this flag without being entitled to do so, for the purpose of the illicit conveyance of arms or ammunition, he may proceed to verify the nationality of the vessel by examining the document authorising the flying of the flag, but no other papers.

2. With this object, a boat commanded by a commissioned officer in uniform may be sent to visit the suspected vessel after she has been hailed to give notice of such intention. The officer sent on board the vessel shall act with all possible consideration and moderation; before leaving the vessel the officer shall draw up a *procès-verbal* in the form and language in use in his own country. This *procès-verbal* shall state the facts of the case and shall be dated and signed by the officer.

Should there be on board the warship no commissioned officer other than the commanding officer, the above-prescribed operations may be carried out by the warrant, petty, or non-commissioned officer highest in rank.

The captain or master of the vessel visited, as well as the witnesses, shall be invited to sign the *procès-verbal,* and shall have the right to add to it any explanations which they may consider expedient.

3. If the authorisation to fly the flag cannot be produced, or if this document is not in proper order, the vessel shall be conducted to the nearest port in the zone where there is a competent authority of the Power whose flag has been flown and shall be handed over to such authority.

Should the nearest competent authority representing the Power whose flag the vessel has flown be at some port at such a distance from the point of arrest that the warship would have to leave her station or patrol to escort the captured vessel to that port, the foregoing regulation need not be carried out. In such a case, the vessel may be taken to the nearest port where there is a competent authority of one of the High Contracting Parties of nationality other than that of the warship, and steps shall at once be taken to notify the capture to the competent authority representing the Power concerned.

No proceedings shall be taken against the vessel or her crew until the arrival of the representative of the Power whose flag the vessel was flying or without instructions from him.

4. The procedure laid down in paragraph 3 may be followed if, after the verification of the flag and in spite of the production of the manifest, the commander of the warship continues to suspect the native vessel of engaging in the illicit conveyance of arms or ammunition.

The High Contracting Parties concerned shall appoint in the zone territorial or consular authorities or special representatives competent to act in the foregoing cases, and shall notify their appointment to the Central Office and to the other Contracting Parties.

The suspected vessel may also be handed over to a warship of the nation whose flag she has flown, if the latter consents to take charge of her.

ARTICLE 17.

The High Contracting Parties agree to communicate to the Central Office specimen forms of the documents mentioned in Articles 12, 13, 14 and 15, as well as a detailed list of the licences granted in accordance with the provisions of this Chapter whenever such licences are granted.

ARTICLE 18.

The authority before whom the suspected vessel has been brought shall institute a full enquiry in accordance with the laws and rules of his country in the presence of an officer of the capturing warship.

If it is proved at this enquiry that the flag has been illegally flown, the detained vessel shall remain at the disposal of the captor, and those responsible shall be brought before the courts of his country.

If it should be established that the use of the flag by the detained vessel was correct, but that the vessel was engaged in the illicit conveyance of arms or ammunition, those responsible shall be brought before the courts of the State under whose flag the vessel sailed. The vessel herself and her cargo shall remain in charge of the authority directing the inquiry.

ARTICLE 19.

Any illicit conveyance or attempted conveyance legally established against the captain or owner of a vessel authorised to fly the flag of one of the Signatory Powers or holding the licence provided for in Article 15 shall entail the immediate withdrawal of the said authorisation or licence.

The High Contracting Parties will take the necessary measures to ensure that their territorial authorities or their consuls shall send to the Central Office certified copies of all authorisations to fly their flag as soon as such authorisations shall have been granted, as well as notice of withdrawal of any such authorisation. They also undertake to communicate to the said Office copies of the licences provided for under Article 15.

ARTICLE 20.

The commanding officer of a warship who may have detained a vessel flying a foreign flag shall in all cases make a report thereon to his Government, stating the grounds on which he acted.

An extract from this report, together with a copy of the *procès-verbal* drawn up by the officer, warrant officer, petty or non-commissioned officer sent on board the vessel detained shall be sent as soon as possible to the Central Office and at the same time to the Government whose flag the detained vessel was flying.

ARTICLE 21.

If the authority entrusted with the enquiry decides that the detention and diversion of the vessel or the measures imposed upon her were irregular, he shall fix the amount of the compensation due. If the capturing officer, or the authorities to whom he is subject, do not accept the decision or contest the amount of the compensation awarded, the dispute shall be submitted to a court of arbitration consisting of one arbitrator appointed by the Government whose flag the vessel was flying, one appointed by the Government of the capturing officer, and an umpire chosen by the two arbitrators thus appointed. The two arbitrators shall be chosen, as far as possible, from among the diplomatic, consular or judicial officers of the High Contracting Parties. These appointments must be made with the least possible delay, and natives in the pay of the High Contracting Parties shall in no case be appointed. Any compensation awarded shall be paid to the person concerned within six months at most from the date of the award.

The decision shall be communicated to the Central Office and to the Secretary-General of the League of Nations.

CHAPTER V.

General Provisions.

ARTICLE 22.

The High Contracting Parties who exercise authority over territories within the prohibited areas and zone specified in Article 6 agree to take, so far as each may be concerned, the measures required for the enforcement of the present Convention, and in particular for the prosecution and repression of offences against the provisions contained therein.

They shall communicate these measures to the Central Office and to the Secretary-General of the League of Nations, and shall inform them of the competent authorities referred to in the preceding Articles.

ARTICLE 23.

The High Contracting Parties will use their best endeavours to secure the accession to the present Convention of other States Members of the League of Nations.

This accession shall be notified through the diplomatic channel to the Government of the French Republic, and by it to all the signatory or adhering States. The accession will come into force from the date of such notification to the French Government.

ARTICLE 24.

The High Contracting Parties agree that if any dispute whatever should arise between them relating to the application of the present Convention which cannot be settled by negotiation, this dispute shall be submitted to an arbitral tribunal in conformity with the provisions of the Covenant of the League of Nations.

ARTICLE 25.

All the provisions of former general international Conventions, relating to the matters dealt with in the present Convention, shall be considered as abrogated in so far as they are binding between the Powers which are Parties to the present Convention.

ARTICLE 26.

The present Convention shall be ratified as soon as possible.

Each Power will address its ratification to the French Government, who will inform all the other signatory Powers.

The ratifications will remain deposited in the archives of the French Government.

The present Convention shall come into force for each Signatory Power from the date of the deposit of its ratification, and from that moment that Power will be bound in respect of other Powers which have already deposited their ratifications.

On the coming into force of the present Convention, the French Government will transmit a certified copy to the Powers which under the Treaties of Peace have undertaken to accept and observe it, and are in consequence placed in the same position as the Contracting Parties. The names of these Powers will be notified to the States which accede.

In faith whereof the above-named Plenipotentiaries have signed the present Convention.

Done at Paris, the tenth day of September, one thousand nine hundred and nineteen, in a single copy which will remain deposited in the archives of the Government of the French Republic, and of which authentic copies will be sent to each of the Signatory Powers.

(L.S.)	FRANK L. POLK.
(L.S.)	HENRY WHITE.
(L.S.)	HYMANS.
(L.S.)	J. VAN DEN HEUVEL.
(L.S.)	E. VANDERVELDE.
(L.S.)	ISMAIL MONTES.
(L.S.)	ARTHUR JAMES BALFOUR.
(L.S.)	
(L.S.)	MILNER.
(L.S.)	GEO. N. BARNES.
(L.S.)	A. E. KEMP.

(L.S.)	G. F. PEARCE.
(L.S.)	MILNER.
(L.S.)	THOMAS MACKENZIE.
(L.S.)	SINHA OF RAIPUR.
(L.S.)	J. R. LOUTSENGTSIANG.
(L.S.)	CHENGTING THOMAS WANG.
(L.S.)	ANTONIO S. DE BUSTAMANTE.
(L.S.)	E. DORN Y DE ALSUA.
(L.S.)	G. CLEMENCEAU.
(L.S.)	S. PICHON.
(L.S.)	L. L. KLOTZ.
(L.S.)	ANDRÉ TARDIEU.
(L.S.)	JULES CAMBON.
(L.S.)	N. POLITIS.
(L.S.)	A. ROMANOS.
(L.S.)	M. RUSTEM HAIDAR.
(L.S.)	ABDUL HADI AOUNI.
(L.S.)	TOM. TITTONI.
(L.S.)	VITTORIO SCIALOJA.
(L.S.)	MAGGIORINO FERRARIS.
(L.S.)	GUGLIELMO MARCONI.
(L.S.)	S. CHINDA.
(L.S.)	K. MATSUI.
(L.S.)	H. IJUIN.
(L.S.)	SALVADOR CHAMORRO.
(L.S.)	ANTONIO BURGOS.
(L.S.)	I. J. PADEREWSKI.
(L.S.)	ROMAN DMOWSKI.
(L.S.)	AFFONSO COSTA.
(L.S.)	AUGUSTO SOARES.
(L.S.)	N. MISU.
(L.S.)	ALEX VAIDA VOEVOD.
(L.S.)	
(L.S.)	
(L.S.)	DR. YVAN ZOLGER.
(L.S.)	CHAROON.
(L.S.)	TRAIDOS PRABANDHU.
(L.S.)	D. KAREL KRAMAR.
(L.S.)	DR. EDUARD BENES.

PROTOCOL.

At the moment of signing the Convention of even date relating to the trade in arms and ammunition, the undersigned Plenipotentiaries declare in the name of their respective Governments that they would regard it as contrary to the intention of the High Contracting Parties and to the spirit of this Convention that, pending the coming into force of the Convention, a Contracting Party should adopt any measure which is contrary to its provisions.

Done at Saint-Germain-en-Laye,* in a single copy, the tenth day of September, one thousand nine hundred and nineteen.

FRANK L. POLK.
HENRY WHITE.
TASKER H. BLISS.
HYMANS.
J. VAN DEN HEUVEL.
E. VANDERVELDE.
ISMAIL MONTES.
ARTHUR JAMES BALFOUR.
MILNER.
GEO. N. BARNES.
A. E. KEMP.
G. F. PEARCE.
MILNER.
THOS. MACKENZIE.
SINHA OF RAIPUR.
J. R. LOUTSENGTSIANG.
CHENGTING THOMAS WANG.
ANTONIO S. DE BUSTAMANTE.
E. DORN Y DE ALSUA.
G. CLEMENCEAU.
S. PICHON.
L. L. KLOTZ.
ANDRÉ TARDIEU.
JULES CAMBON.
N. POLITIS.
A. ROMANOS.

M. RUSTEM HAIDAR.
ABDUL HADI AOUNI.
TOM. TITTONI.
VITTORIO SCIALOJA.
MAGGIORINO FERRARIS.
GUGLIELMO MARCONI.
S. CHINDA.
K. MATSUI.
H. IJUIN.
SALVADOR CHAMORRO.
ANTONIO BURGOS.
I. J. PADEREWSKI.
ROMAN DMOWSKI.
AFFONSO COSTA.
AUGUSTO SOARES.
N. MISU.
ALEX VAIDA VOEVOD.
DR. YVAN ZOLGER.
CHAROON.
TRAIDOS PRABANDHU.
D. KAREL KRAMAR.
DR. EDUARD BENES.

* Some of the signatures were affixed in Paris and some at Saint-Germain-en-Laye.

ANNEX F

CONVENTION RELATING TO THE LIQUOR TRAFFIC IN AFRICA, AND PROTOCOL.*

Signed September 10, 1919.

(Translation.)

THE UNITED STATES OF AMERICA, BELGIUM, THE BRITISH EMPIRE, FRANCE, ITALY, JAPAN AND PORTUGAL,

Whereas it is necessary to continue in the African territories placed under their administration the struggle against the dangers of alcoholism which they have maintained by subjecting spirits to constantly increasing duties;

Whereas, further, it is necessary to prohibit the importation of distilled beverages rendered more especially dangerous to the native populations by the nature of the products entering into their composition or by the opportunities which a low price gives for their extended use;

Whereas, finally, the restrictions placed on the importation of spirits would be of no effect unless the local manufacture of distilled beverages was at the same time strictly controlled;

Have appointed as their plenipotentiaries:

THE PRESIDENT OF THE UNITED STATES OF AMERICA:
The Honourable Frank Lyon Polk, Under-Secretary of State;
The Honourable Henry White, formerly Ambassador Extraordinary and Plenipotentiary of the United States at Rome and Paris;
General Tasker H. Bliss, Military Representative of the United States on the Supreme War Council;

HIS MAJESTY THE KING OF THE BELGIANS:
M. Paul Hymans, Minister for Foreign Affairs, Minister of State;
M. Jules van den Heuvel, Envoy Extraordinary and Minister Plenipotentiary of His Majesty the King of the Belgians, Minister of State;
M. Emile Vandervelde, Minister of Justice, Minister of State;

* Treaty Series, 1919, No. 19.

HIS MAJESTY THE KING OF THE UNITED KINGDOM OF GREAT BRITAIN AND IRELAND AND OF THE BRITISH DOMINIONS BEYOND THE SEAS, EMPEROR OF INDIA:

The Right Honourable Arthur James Balfour, O.M., M.P., His Secretary of State for Foreign Affairs;

The Right Honourable Andrew Bonar Law, M.P., His Lord Privy Seal;

The Right Honourable Viscount Milner, G.C.B., G.C.M.G., His Secretary of State for the Colonies;

The Right Honourable George Nicoll Barnes, M.P., Minister without portfolio;

And:

for the DOMINION of CANADA:

The Honourable Sir Albert Edward Kemp, K.C.M.G., Minister of the Overseas Forces;

for the COMMONWEALTH of AUSTRALIA:

The Honourable George Foster Pearce, Minister of Defence;

for the UNION of SOUTH AFRICA:

The Right Honourable Viscount Milner, G.C.B., G.C.M.G.;

for the DOMINION of NEW ZEALAND:

The Honourable Sir Thomas Mackenzie, K.C.M.G., High Commissioner for New Zealand in the United Kingdom;

for INDIA:

The Right Honourable Baron Sinha, K.C., Under-Secretary of State for India;

THE PRESIDENT OF THE FRENCH REPUBLIC:

M. Georges Clemenceau, President of the Council, Minister of War;

M. Stephen Pichon, Minister for Foreign Affairs;

M. Louis-Lucien Klotz, Minister of Finance;

M. André Tardieu, Commissary-General for Franco-American Military Affairs;

M. Jules Cambon, Ambassador of France;

HIS MAJESTY THE KING OF ITALY:

The Honourable Tommaso Tittoni, Senator of the Kingdom, Minister for Foreign Affairs;

The Honourable Vittorio Scialoja, Senator of the Kingdom;

The Honourable Maggiorino Ferraris, Senator of the Kingdom;

The Honourable Guglielmo Marconi, Senator of the Kingdom;

The Honourable Silvio Crespi, Deputy;

HIS MAJESTY THE EMPEROR OF JAPAN:

Viscount Chinda, Ambassador Extraordinary and Plenipotentiary of H.M. the Emperor of Japan at London;

M. K. Matsui, Ambassador Extraordinary and Plenipotentiary of H.M. the Emperor of Japan at Paris;

THE PRESIDENT OF THE PORTUGUESE REPUBLIC:
Dr. Affonso da Costa, formerly President of the Council of Ministers;
Dr. Augusto Luiz Vieira Soares, formerly Minister for Foreign Affairs;

Who, having communicated their full powers found in good and due form,
Have agreed as follows:

ARTICLE 1.

The High Contracting Parties undertake to apply the following measures for the restriction of the liquor traffic in the territories which are or may be subjected to their control throughout the whole of the continent of Africa, with the exception of Algiers, Tunis, Morocco, Libya, Egypt and the Union of South Africa.

The provisions applicable to the continent of Africa shall also apply to the islands lying within 100 nautical miles of the coast.

ARTICLE 2.

The importation, distribution, sale and possession of trade spirits of every kind, and of beverages mixed with these spirits, are prohibited in the area referred to in Article 1. The local Governments concerned will decide respectively which distilled beverages will be regarded in their territories as falling within the category of trade spirits. They will endeavour, as far as possible, to establish a uniform nomenclature and uniform measures against fraud.

ARTICLE 3.

The importation, distribution, sale and possession are also forbidden of distilled beverages containing essential oils or chemical products which are recognised as injurious to health, such as thujone, star anise, benzoic aldehyde, salicylic ethers, hyssop and absinthe.

The local Governments concerned will likewise endeavour to establish by common agreement the nomenclature of those beverages whose importation, distribution, sale and possession according to the terms of this provision should be prohibited.

ARTICLE 4.

An import duty of not less than 800 francs per hectolitre of pure alcohol shall be levied upon all distilled beverages, other than those indicated in Articles 2 and 3, which are imported into the area referred to in Article 1, except in so far as the Italian colonies are concerned, where the duty may not be less than 600 francs.

The High Contracting Parties will prohibit the importation, distribution, sale and possession of spirituous liquors in those regions of the area referred to in Article 1 where their use has not been developed.

The above prohibition can be suspended only in the case of limited quantities destined for the consumption of non-native persons, and imported under the system and conditions determined by each Government.

ARTICLE 5.

The manufacture of distilled beverages of every kind is forbidden in the area referred to in Article 1.

The importation, distribution, sale and possession of stills and of all apparatus or portions of apparatus suitable for distillation of alcohol and the rectification or redistillation of spirits are forbidden in the same area, subject to the provisions of Article 6.

The provisions of the two preceding paragraphs do not apply to the Italian colonies; the manufacture of distilled beverages, other than those specified in Articles 2 and 3, will continue to be permitted therein, on condition that they are subject to an excise duty equal to the import duty established in Article 4.

ARTICLE 6.

The restrictions on the importation, distribution, sale, possession and manufacture of spirituous beverages do not apply to pharmaceutical alcohols required for medical, surgical or pharmaceutical establishments. The importation, distribution, sale and possession are also permitted of:

1. Testing stills, that is to say, the small apparatus in general use for laboratory experiments, which are employed intermittently, are not fitted with rectifying heads, and the capacity of whose retort does not exceed one liter;

2. Apparatus or parts of apparatus required for experiments in scientific institutions;

3. Apparatus or parts of apparatus employed for definite purposes, other than the production of alcohol, by qualified pharmacists and by persons who can show good cause for the possession of such apparatus;

4. Apparatus necessary for the manufacture of alcohol for commercial purposes, and employed by duly authorised persons, such manufacture being subject to the system of control established by the local administrations.

The necessary permission in the foregoing cases will be granted by the local administration of the territory in which the stills, apparatus, or portions of apparatus are to be utilised.

ARTICLE 7.

A Central International Office, placed under the control of the League of Nations, shall be established for the purpose of collecting and preserving documents of all kinds exchanged by the High Contracting Parties with regard to the importation and manufacture of spirituous liquors under the conditions referred to in the present Convention.

Each of the High Contracting Parties shall publish an annual report showing the quantities of spirituous beverages imported or manufactured and the duties levied under Articles 4 and 5. A copy of this report shall be sent to the Central International Office and to the Secretary-General of the League of Nations.

ARTICLE 8.

The High Contracting Parties agree that if any dispute whatever should arise between them relating to the application of the present Convention which cannot be settled by negotiation, this dispute shall be submitted to an arbitral tribunal in conformity with the Covenant of the League of Nations.

ARTICLE 9.

The High Contracting Parties reserve the right of introducing into the present Convention by common agreement after a period of five years such modifications as may prove to be necessary.

ARTICLE 10.

The High Contracting Parties will use every effort to obtain the adhesion to the present Convention of the other States exercising authority over the territories of the African Continent.

This adhesion shall be notified through the diplomatic channel to the Government of the French Republic, and by it to all the signatory or adhering States. The adhesion will come into effect from the date of the notification to the French Government.

ARTICLE 11.

All the provisions of former general international Conventions relating to the matters dealt with in the present Convention shall be considered as abrogated in so far as they are binding between the Powers which are parties to the present Convention.

The present Convention shall be ratified as soon as possible.

Each Power will address its ratification to the French Government, who will inform all the other signatory Powers.

The ratifications will remain deposited in the archives of the French Government.

The present Convention will come into force for each signatory Power from the date of the deposit of its ratification, and from that moment that Power will be bound in respect of other Powers which have already deposited their ratifications.

On the coming into force of the present Convention, the French Government will transmit a certified copy to the Powers which under the

Treaties of Peace have undertaken to accept and observe it, and are in consequence placed in the same position as the Contracting Parties. The names of these Powers will be notified to the States which adhere.

In faith whereof the above-named Plenipotentiaries have signed the present Convention.

Done at Saint-Germain-en-Laye, the tenth day of September, one thousand nine hundred and nineteen, in a single copy which will remain deposited in the archives of the Government of the French Republic, and of which authenticated copies will be sent to each of the signatory Powers.

(L.S.)	FRANK L. POLK.
(L.S.)	HENRY WHITE.
(L.S.)	TASKER H. BLISS.
(L.S.)	HYMANS.
(L.S.)	VAN DEN HEUVEL.
(L.S.)	E. VANDERVELDE.
(L.S.)	ARTHUR JAMES BALFOUR.
(L.S.)	MILNER.
(L.S.)	GEO. N. BARNES.
(L.S.)	A. E. KEMP.
(L.S.)	G. F. PEARCE.
(L.S.)	MILNER.
(L.S.)	THOS. MACKENZIE.
(L.S.)	SINHA OF RAIPUR.
(L.S.)	G. CLEMENCEAU.
(L.S.)	S. PICHON.
(L.S.)	L. L. KLOTZ.
(L.S.)	ANDRÉ TARDIEU.
(L.S.)	JULES CAMBON.
(L.S.)	TOM. TITTONI.
(L.S.)	VITTORIO SCIALOJA.
(L.S.)	MAGGIORINO FERRARIS.
(L.S.)	GUGLIELMO MARCONI.
(L.S.)	S. CHINDA.
(L.S.)	K. MATSUI.
(L.S.)	AFFONSO COSTA.
(L.S.)	AUGUSTO SOARES.

PROTOCOL.

At the moment of signing the Convention of even date relating to the Liquor Traffic in Africa, the undersigned Plenipotentiaries declare in the name of their respective Governments that they would regard it as contrary to the intention of the High Contracting Parties and to the spirit of this Convention that pending the coming into force of the Convention a contracting Party should adopt any measure which is contrary to its provisions.

Done at Saint-Germain-en-Laye, in a single copy, the tenth day of September, one thousand nine hundred and nineteen.

> FRANK L. POLK.
> HENRY WHITE.
> TASKER H. BLISS.
> HYMANS.
> J. VAN DEN HEUVEL.
> E. VANDERVELDE.
> ARTHUR JAMES BALFOUR.
> MILNER.
> GEO. N. BARNES.
> A. E. KEMP.
> G. F. PEARCE.
> MILNER.
> THOS. MACKENZIE.
> SINHA OF RAIPUR.
> G. CLEMENCEAU.
> S. PICHON.
> L. L. KLOTZ.
> ANDRÉ TARDIEU.
> JULES CAMBON.
> TOM. TITTONI.
> VITTORIO SCIALOJA.
> MAGGIORINO FERRARIS.
> GUGLIELMO MARCONI.
> S. CHINDA.
> K. MATSUI.
> AFFONSO COSTA.
> AUGUSTO SOARES.

ANNEX G

CONVENTION REVISING THE GENERAL ACT OF BERLIN, FEBRUARY 26, 1885, AND THE GENERAL ACT AND DECLARATION OF BRUSSELS, JULY 2, 1890.*

Signed September 10, 1919.

(Translation.)

THE UNITED STATES OF AMERICA, BELGIUM, THE BRITISH EMPIRE, FRANCE, ITALY, JAPAN AND PORTUGAL;

Whereas the General Act of the African Conference, signed at Berlin on February 26, 1885, was primarily intended to demonstrate the agreement of the Powers with regard to the general principles which should guide their commercial and civilising action in the little known or inadequately organised regions of a continent where slavery and the slave trade still flourished; and

Whereas by the Brussels Declaration of July 2, 1890, it was found necessary to modify for a provisional period of fifteen years the system of free imports established for twenty years by Article 4 of the said Act, and since that date no agreement has been entered into, notwithstanding the provisions of the said Act and Declaration; and

Whereas the territories in question are now under the control of recognised authorities, are provided with administrative institutions suitable to the local conditions, and the evolution of the native populations continues to make progress;

Wishing to ensure by arrangements suitable to modern requirements the application of the general principles of civilisation established by the Acts of Berlin and Brussels,

Have appointed as their Plenipotentiaries:

THE PRESIDENT OF THE UNITED STATES OF AMERICA:

The Honourable Frank Lyon Polk, Under-Secretary of State;
The Honourable Henry White, formerly Ambassador Extraordinary and Plenipotentiary of the United States at Rome and Paris;
General Tasker H. Bliss, Military Representative of the United States on the Supreme War Council;

* Treaty Series, 1919. No. 18.

HIS MAJESTY THE KING OF THE BELGIANS:

M. Paul Hymans, Minister for Foreign Affairs, Minister of State;
M. Jules van den Heuvel, Envoy Extraordinary and Minister Plenipotentiary of His Majesty the King of the Belgians, Minister of State;
M. Émile Vandervelde, Minister of Justice, Minister of State;

HIS MAJESTY THE KING OF GREAT BRITAIN AND IRELAND AND OF THE BRITISH DOMINIONS BEYOND THE SEAS, EMPEROR OF INDIA:

The Right Honourable Arthur James Balfour, O.M., M.P., His Secretary of State for Foreign Affairs;
The Right Honourable Andrew Bonar Law, M.P., His Lord Privy Seal;
The Right Honourable Viscount Milner, G.C.B., G.C.M.G., His Secretary of State for the Colonies;
The Right Honourable George Nicoll Barnes, M.P., Minister without Portfolio;

And:

for the DOMINION of CANADA:

The Honourable Sir Albert Edward Kemp, K.C.M.G., Minister of the Overseas Forces;

for the COMMONWEALTH of AUSTRALIA:

The Honourable George Foster Pearce, Minister of Defence;

for the UNION of SOUTH AFRICA:

The Right Honourable Viscount Milner, G.C.B., G.C.M.G.;

for the DOMINION of NEW ZEALAND:

The Honourable Sir Thomas Mackenzie, K.C.M.G., High Commissioner for New Zealand in the United Kingdom;

for INDIA:

The Right Honourable Baron Sinha, K.C., Under-Secretary of State for India;

THE PRESIDENT OF THE FRENCH REPUBLIC:

M. Georges Clemenceau, President of the Council, Minister of War;
M. Stephen Pichon, Minister for Foreign Affairs;
M. Louis-Lucien Klotz, Minister of Finance;
M. André Tardieu, Commissary-General for Franco-American Military Affairs;
M. Jules Cambon, Ambassador of France;

HIS MAJESTY THE KING OF ITALY:

The Honourable Tommaso Tittoni, Senator of the Kingdom, Minister for Foreign Affairs;
The Honourable Vittorio Scialoja, Senator of the Kingdom;
The Honourable Maggiorino Ferraris, Senator of the Kingdom;
The Honourable Guglielmo Marconi, Senator of the Kingdom;
The Honourable Silvio Crespi, Deputy;

HIS MAJESTY THE EMPEROR OF JAPAN:

Viscount Chinda, Ambassador Extraordinary and Plenipotentiary of H.M. the Emperor of Japan at London;

M. K. Matsui, Ambassador Extraordinary and Plenipotentiary of H.M. the Emperor of Japan at Paris;

M. H. Ijuin, Ambassador Extraordinary and Plenipotentiary of H.M. the Emperor of Japan at Rome;

THE PRESIDENT OF THE PORTUGUESE REPUBLIC:

Dr. Affonso da Costa, formerly President of the Council of Ministers;

Dr. Augusto Luiz Vieira Soares, formerly Minister for Foreign Affairs;

Who, after having communicated their full powers recognised in good and due form,

Have agreed as follows:

ARTICLE 1.

The Signatory Powers undertake to maintain between their respective nationals and those of States, Members of the League of Nations, which may adhere to the present Convention a complete commercial equality in the territories under their authority within the area defined by Article 1 of the General Act of Berlin of February 26, 1885, set out in the Annex hereto, but subject to the reservation specified in the final paragraph of that article.

Annex.

Article 1 of the General Act of Berlin of February 26, 1885.

The trade of all nations shall enjoy complete freedom:

1. In all the regions forming the basin of the Congo and its outlets. This basin is bounded by the watersheds (or mountain ridges) of the adjacent basins, namely, in particular, those of the Niari, the Ogowé, the Shari, and the Nile, on the north; by the eastern watershed line of the affluents of Lake Tanganyika on the east; and by the watersheds of the basins of the Zambesi and the Logé on the south. It therefore comprises all the regions watered by the Congo and its affluents, including Lake Tanganyika, with its eastern tributaries.

2. In the maritime zone extending along the Atlantic Ocean from the parallel situated in 2° 30′ of south latitude to the mouth of the Logé.

The northern boundary will follow the parallel situated in 2° 30′ from the coast to the point where it meets the geographical basin of the Congo, avoiding the basin of the Ogowé, to which the provisions of the present Act do not apply.

The southern boundary will follow the course of the Logé to its source, and thence pass eastwards till it joins the geographical basin of the Congo.

3. In the zone stretching eastwards from the Congo Basin as above defined, to the Indian Ocean from 5° of north latitude to the mouth of the Zambesi in the south, from which point the line of demarcation will ascend the Zambesi to 5 miles above its confluence with the Shiré, and then follow the watershed between the affluents of Lake Nyassa and those

of the Zambesi, till at last it reaches the watershed between the waters of the Zambesi and the Congo.

It is expressly recognised that in extending the principle of free trade to this eastern zone, the Conference Powers only undertake engagements for themselves, and that in the territories belonging to an independent Sovereign State this principle shall only be applicable in so far as it is approved by such State. But the Powers agree to use their good offices with the Governments established on the African shore of the Indian Ocean for the purpose of obtaining such approval, and in any case of securing the most favourable conditions to the transit (traffic) of all nations.

ARTICLE 2.

Merchandise belonging to the nationals of the Signatory Powers, and to those of States, Members of the League of Nations, which may adhere to the present Convention, shall have free access to the interior of the regions specified in Article 1. No differential treatment shall be imposed upon the said merchandise on importation or exportation, the transit remaining free from all duties, taxes or dues, other than those collected for services rendered.

Vessels flying the flag of any of the said Powers shall also have access to all the coast and to all maritime ports in the territories specified in Article 1; they shall be subject to no differential treatment.

Subject to these provisions, the States concerned reserve to themselves complete liberty of action as to the customs and navigation regulations and tariffs to be applied in their territories.

ARTICLE 3.

In the territories specified in Article 1 and placed under the authority of one of the Signatory Powers, the nationals of those Powers, or of States, Members of the League of Nations, which may adhere to the present Convention shall, subject only to the limitations necessary for the maintenance of public security and order, enjoy without distinction the same treatment and the same rights as the nationals of the Power exercising authority in the territory, with regard to the protection of their persons and effects, with regard to the acquisition and transmission of their movable and real property, and with regard to the exercise of their professions.

ARTICLE 4.

Each State reserves the right to dispose freely of its property and to grant concessions for the development of the natural resources of the territory, but no regulations on these matters shall admit of any differential treatment between the nationals of the Signatory Powers and of States, Members of the League of Nations, which may adhere to the present Convention.

ARTICLE 5.

Subject to the provisions of the present chapter, the navigation of the Niger, of its branches and outlets, and of all the rivers, and of their branches and outlets, within the territories specified in Article 1, as well as of the lakes situated within those territories, shall be entirely free for merchant vessels and for the transport of goods and passengers.

Craft of every kind belonging to the nationals of the Signatory Powers and of States, Members of the League of Nations, which may adhere to the present Convention shall be treated in all respects on a footing of perfect equality.

ARTICLE 6.

The navigation shall not be subject to any restriction or dues based on the mere fact of navigation.

It shall not be exposed to any obligation in regard to landing, station, or depôt, or for breaking bulk or for compulsory entry into port.

No maritime or river toll, based on the mere fact of navigation, shall be levied on vessels, nor shall any transit duty be levied on goods on board. Only such taxes or duties shall be collected as may be an equivalent for services rendered to navigation itself. The tariff of these taxes or duties shall not admit of any differential treatment.

ARTICLE 7.

The affluents of the rivers and lakes specified in Article 5 shall in all respects be subject to the same rules as the rivers or lakes of which they are tributaries.

The roads, railways or lateral canals which may be constructed with the special object of obviating the innavigability or correcting the imperfections of the water route on certain sections of the rivers and lakes specified in Article 5, their affluents, branches and outlets, shall be considered, in their quality of means of communication, as dependencies of these rivers and lakes, and shall be equally open to the traffic of the nationals of the Signatory Powers and of the States, Members of the League of Nations, which may adhere to the present Convention.

On these roads, railways and canals only such tolls shall be collected as are calculated on the cost of construction, maintenance and management, and on the profits reasonably accruing to the undertaking. As regards the tariff of these tolls, the nationals of the Signatory Powers and of States, Members of the League of Nations, which may adhere to the present Convention, shall be treated on a footing of perfect equality.

ARTICLE 8.

Each of the Signatory Powers shall remain free to establish the rules which it may consider expedient for the purpose of ensuring the safety and control of navigation, on the understanding that these rules shall facilitate, as far as possible, the circulation of merchant vessels.

ARTICLE 9.

In such sections of the rivers and of their affluents, as well as on such lakes, as are not necessarily utilised by more than one riverain State, the Governments exercising authority shall remain free to establish such systems as may be required for the maintenance of public safety and order. and for other necessities of the work of civilisation and colonisation; but the regulations shall not admit of any differential treatment between vessels or between nationals of the Signatory Powers and of States, Members of the League of Nations, which may adhere to the present Convention.

ARTICLE 10.

The Signatory Powers recognise the obligation to maintain in the regions subject to their jurisdiction an authority and police forces sufficient to ensure protection of persons and of property and, if necessary, freedom of trade and of transit.

ARTICLE 11.

The Signatory Powers exercising sovereign rights or authority in African territories will continue to watch over the preservation of the native populations and to supervise the improvement of the conditions of their moral and material well-being. They will, in particular, endeavour to secure the complete suppression of slavery in all its forms and of the slave trade by land and sea.

They will protect and favour, without distinction of nationality or of religion, the religious, scientific or charitable institutions and undertakings created and organised by the nationals of the other Signatory Powers and of States, Members of the League of Nations, which may adhere to the present Convention, which aim at leading the natives in the path of progress and civilisation. Scientific missions, their property and their collections, shall likewise be the objects of special solicitude.

Freedom of conscience and the free exercise of all forms of religion are expressly guaranteed to all nationals of the Signatory Powers and to those under the jurisdiction of States, Members of the League of Nations, which may become parties to the present Convention. Similarly, missionaries shall have the right to enter into, and to travel and reside in, African territory with a view to prosecuting their calling.

The application of the provisions of the two preceding paragraphs shall be subject only to such restrictions as may be necessary for the maintenance of public security and order, or as may result from the enforcement of the constitutional law of any of the Powers exercising authority in African territories.

ARTICLE 12.

The Signatory Powers agree that if any dispute whatever should arise between them relating to the application of the present Convention which cannot be settled by negotiation, this dispute shall be submitted to an arbitral tribunal in conformity with the provisions of the Covenant of the League of Nations.

ARTICLE 13.

Except in so far as the stipulations contained in Article 1 of the present Convention are concerned, the General Act of Berlin of 26th February, 1885, and the General Act of Brussels of 2nd July, 1890, with the accompanying Declaration of equal date, shall be considered as abrogated, in so far as they are binding between the Powers which are Parties to the present Convention.

ARTICLE 14.

States exercising authority over African territories, and other States, Members of the League of Nations, which were parties either to the Act of Berlin or to the Act of Brussels or the Declaration annexed thereto, may adhere to the present Convention. The Signatory Powers will use their best endeavours to obtain the adhesion of these States.

This adhesion shall be notified through the diplomatic channel to the Government of the French Republic, and by it to all the Signatory or adhering States. The adhesion will come into force from the date of its notification to the French Government.

ARTICLE 15.

The Signatory Powers will reassemble at the expiration of ten years from the coming into force of the present Convention, in order to introduce into it such modifications as experience may have shown to be necessary.

The present Convention shall be ratified as soon as possible.

Each Power will address its ratification to the French Government, which will inform all the other Signatory Powers.

The ratifications will remain deposited in the archives of the French Government.

The present Convention will come into force for each Signatory Power from the date of the deposit of its ratification, and from that moment that Power will be bound in respect of other Powers which have already deposited their ratifications.

On the coming into force of the present Convention, the French Government will transmit a certified copy to the Powers which, under the

Treaties of Peace, have undertaken to accept and observe it. The names of these Powers will be notified to the States which adhere.

In faith whereof the above-named Plenipotentiaries have signed the present Convention.

Done at Saint-Germain-en-Laye, the 10th day of September, 1919, in a single copy, which will remain deposited in the archives of the Government of the French Republic, and of which authenticated copies will be sent to each of the Signatory Powers.

(L.S.)	FRANK L. POLK.
(L.S.)	HENRY WHITE.
(L.S.)	TASKER H. BLISS.
(L.S.)	HYMANS.
(L.S.)	J. VAN DEN HEUVEL.
(L.S.)	E. VANDERVELDE.
(L.S.)	ARTHUR JAMES BALFOUR.
(L.S.)	
(L.S.)	MILNER.
(L.S.)	G. N. BARNES.
(L.S.)	A. E. KEMP.
(L.S.)	G. F. PEARCE.
(L.S.)	MILNER.
(L.S.)	THOS. MACKENZIE.
(L.S.)	SINHA OF RAIPUR.
(L.S.)	G. CLEMENCEAU.
(L.S.)	S. PICHON.
(L.S.)	L. L. KLOTZ.
(L.S.)	ANDRÉ TARDIEU.
(L.S.)	JULES CAMBON.
(L.S.)	TOM. TITTONI.
(L.S.)	VITTORIO SCIALOJA.
(L.S.)	MAGGIORINO FERRARIS.
(L.S.)	GUGLIELMO MARCONI.
(L.S.)	S. CHINDA.
(L.S.)	K. MATSUI.
(L.S.)	H. IJUIN.
(L.S.)	AFFONSO COSTA.
(L.S.)	AUGUSTO SOARES.

ANNEX H

FINAL DRAFT OF THE MANDATE FOR MESOPOTAMIA FOR THE APPROVAL OF THE COUNCIL OF THE LEAGUE OF NATIONS.*

THE COUNCIL OF THE LEAGUE OF NATIONS.

Whereas by Article 132 of the Treaty of Peace signed at Sèvres on the tenth day of August, 1920, Turkey renounced in favour of the Principal Allied Powers all rights and title over Mesopotamia, and whereas by Article 94 of the said treaty the High Contracting Parties agreed that Mesopotamia should, in accordance with the fourth paragraph of Article 22 of Part I (Covenant of the League of Nations), be provisionally recognised as an independent State, subject to the rendering of administrative advice and assistance by a Mandatory until such time as it is able to stand alone, and that the determination of the frontiers of Mesopotamia, other than those laid down in the said treaty, and the selection of the Mandatory would be made by the Principal Allied Powers; and

Whereas the Principal Allied Powers have selected His Britannic Majesty as Mandatory for Mesopotamia; and

Whereas the terms of the Mandate in respect of Mesopotamia have been formulated in the following terms and submitted to the Council of the League for approval; and

Whereas His Britannic Majesty has accepted the Mandate in respect of the said territories and undertaken to exercise it on behalf of the League of Nations in conformity with the following provisions;

Hereby approves the terms of the said Mandate as follows:—

ARTICLE 1.

The Mandatory will frame within the shortest possible time, not exceeding three years from the date of the coming into force of this Mandate, an Organic Law for Mesopotamia, which shall be submitted to the Council of the League of Nations for approval, and shall, as soon as possible, be published by it. This Organic Law shall be framed in consultation with the native authorities, and shall take account of the rights, interests and wishes of all the populations inhabiting the mandated territory. It shall contain provisions designed to facilitate the progressive development of Mesopotamia as an independent State. Pending the coming into effect of

* Mandates (1921) (Cd. 1500).

the Organic Law, the administration of Mesopotamia shall be conducted in accordance with the spirit of this Mandate.

ARTICLE 2.

The Mandatory may maintain armed forces in the territories under his Mandate for the defence of these territories. Until the entry into force of the Organic Law and the re-establishment of public security, he may organise and employ local forces necessary for the maintenance of order and for the defence of these territories. Such local forces may only be recruited from the inhabitants of the territories under the Mandate.

The said local forces shall thereafter be responsible to the local authorities, subject always to the control to be exercised over these forces by the Mandatory. The Mesopotamian Government shall not employ them for other than the above-mentioned purposes, except with the consent of the Mandatory.

Nothing in this article shall preclude the Mesopotamian Government from contributing to the cost of the maintenance of any forces maintained by the Mandatory in Mesopotamia.

The Mandatory shall be entitled at all times to use the roads, railways, and ports of Mesopotamia for the movement of armed forces and the carriage of fuel and supplies.

ARTICLE 3.

The Mandatory shall be entrusted with the control of the foreign relations of Mesopotamia, and the right to issue exequaturs to consuls appointed by foreign Powers. It shall also be entitled to afford diplomatic and consular protection to citizens of Mesopotamia when outside its territorial limits.

ARTICLE 4.

The Mandatory shall be responsible for seeing that no Mesopotamian territory shall be ceded or leased to or in any way placed under the control of the Government of any foreign Power.

ARTICLE 5.

The immunities and privileges of foreigners, including the benefits of consular jurisdiction and protection as formerly enjoyed by Capitulation or usage in the Ottoman Empire, are definitely abrogated in Mesopotamia.

ARTICLE 6.

The Mandatory shall be responsible for seeing that the judicial system established in Mesopotamia shall safeguard (a) the interests of foreigners; (b) the law, and (to the extent deemed expedient) the jurisdiction now existing in Mesopotamia with regard to questions arising out of the religious beliefs of certain communities (such as the laws of Wakf and personal status). In particular the Mandatory agrees that the control and administration of Wakfs shall be exercised in accordance with religious law and the dispositions of the founders.

ARTICLE 7.

Pending the making of special extradition agreements with foreign Powers relating to Mesopotamia, the extradition treaties in force between foreign Powers and the Mandatory shall apply to Mesopotamia.

ARTICLE 8.

The Mandatory will ensure to all complete freedom of conscience and the free exercise of all forms of worship, subject only to the maintenance of public order and morals. No discrimination of any kind shall be made between the inhabitants of Mesopotamia on the ground of race, religion or language. Instruction in and through the medium of the native languages of Mesopotamia shall be promoted by the Mandatory.

The right of each community to maintain its own schools for the education of its own members in its own language (while conforming to such educational requirements of a general nature as the Administration may impose) shall not be denied or impaired.

ARTICLE 9.

Nothing in this Mandate shall be construed as conferring upon the Mandatory authority to interfere with the fabric or the management of the sacred shrines, the immunities of which are guaranteed.

ARTICLE 10.

The Mandatory shall be responsible for exercising such supervision over missionary enterprise in Mesopotamia as may be required for the maintenance of public order and good government. Subject to such supervision, no measures shall be taken in Mesopotamia to obstruct or interfere with such enterprise or to discriminate against any missionary on the ground of his religion or nationality.

ARTICLE 11.

The Mandatory must see that there is no discrimination in Mesopotamia against the nationals of any State member of the League of Nations (including companies incorporated under the laws of such State) as compared with the nationals of the Mandatory or of any foreign State in matters concerning taxation, commerce or navigation, the exercise of industries or professions, or in the treatment of merchant vessels or civil aircraft. Similarly, there shall be no discrimination in Mesopotamia against goods originating in or destined for any of the said States, and there shall be freedom of transit under equitable conditions across the mandated area.

Subject as aforesaid the Mesopotamian Government may on the advice of the Mandatory impose such taxes and customs duties as it may consider necessary and take such steps as it may think best to promote the development of the natural resources of the country and to safeguard the interests of the population.

Nothing in this article shall prevent the Mesopotamian Government on the advice of the Mandatory, from concluding a special customs arrangement with any State, the territory of which in 1914 was wholly included in Asiatic Turkey or Arabia.

ARTICLE 12.

The Mandatory will adhere on behalf of Mesopotamia to any general international conventions already existing or that may be concluded hereafter with the approval of the League of Nations respecting the slave traffic, the traffic in arms and ammunition, and the traffic in drugs, or relating to commercial equality, freedom of transit and navigation, laws of aerial navigation, railways and postal, telegraphic and wireless communication, or artistic, literary or industrial property.

ARTICLE 13.

The Mandatory will secure the co-operation of the Mesopotamian Government, so far as social, religious and other conditions may permit, in the execution of any common policy adopted by the League of Nations for preventing and combating disease, including diseases of plants and animals.

ARTICLE 14.

The Mandatory will secure the enactment within twelve months from the coming into force of this Mandate, and will ensure the execution of a Law of Antiquities, based on the contents of Article 421 of Part XIII of the Treaty of Peace with Turkey. This law shall replace the former Ottoman Law of Antiquities, and shall ensure equality of treatment in the matter of archæological research to the nationals of all States, members of the League of Nations.

ARTICLE 15.

Upon the coming into force of the Organic Law an arrangement shall be made between the Mandatory and the Mesopotamian Government for settling the terms on which the latter will take over Public Works and other services of a permanent character, the benefit of which will pass to the Mesopotamian Government. Such arrangement shall be communicated to the Council of the League of Nations.

ARTICLE 16.

Nothing in this Mandate shall prevent the Mandatory from establishing a system of local autonomy for predominantly Kurdish areas in Mesopotamia as he may consider suitable.

ARTICLE 17.

The Mandatory shall make to the Council of the League of Nations an annual report as to the measures taken during the year to carry out the provisions of the Mandate. Copies of all laws and regulations promulgated or issued during the year shall be communicated with the report.

ARTICLE 18.

The consent of the Council of the League of Nations is required for any modification of the terms of the present Mandate, provided that in the case of any modification proposed by the Mandatory such consent may be given by a majority of the Council.

ARTICLE 19.

If any dispute whatever should arise between the members of the League of Nations relating to the interpretation or the application of these provisions which cannot be settled by negotiation, this dispute shall be submitted to the Permanent Court of International Justice provided for by Article 14 of the Covenant of the League of Nations.

ARTICLE 20.

In the event of the termination of the Mandate conferred upon the Mandatory by this Declaration, the Council of the League of Nations shall make such arrangements as may be deemed necessary for securing under the guarantee of the League that the Mesopotamian Government will fully honour the financial obligations legally incurred by the Mandatory during the period of the Mandate, including the rights of public servants to pensions or gratuities.

The present copy shall be deposited in the archives of the League of Nations. Certified copies shall be forwarded by the Secretary-General of the League of Nations to all Powers Signatories of the Treaty of Peace with Turkey.

Made at   the   day of

ANNEX I

Draft Mandate for East Africa (British) (in the form in which the Council of the League of Nations will be invited to approve it).*

The Council of the League of Nations:

WHEREAS by article 119 of the Treaty of Peace with Germany signed at Versailles on the 28th June, 1919, Germany renounced in favour of the Principal Allied and Associated Powers all her rights over her oversea possessions, including therein German East Africa; and whereas, in accordance with the treaty of the 11th June, 1891,† between Her Britannic Majesty and His Majesty the King of Portugal, the River Rovuma is recognised as forming the northern boundary of the Portuguese possessions in East Africa from its mouth up to the confluence of the River M'Sinje; and

Whereas the Principal Allied and Associated Powers agreed that in accordance with article 22, Part 1 (Covenant of the League of Nations), of the said treaty a mandate should be conferred upon His Britannic Majesty to administer part of the former colony of German East Africa, and have proposed that the mandate should be formulated in the following terms; and

Whereas His Britannic Majesty has agreed to accept the mandate in respect of the said territory, and has undertaken to exercise it on behalf of the League of Nations in accordance with the following provisions;

Hereby approves the terms of the mandate as follows:—

ARTICLE 1.

The territory over which a mandate is conferred upon His Britannic Majesty (hereinafter called the mandatory) comprises that part of the territory of the former colony of German East Africa situated to the east of the following line:—

From the point where the frontier between the Uganda Protectorate and German East Africa cuts the River Mavumba a straight line in a south-easterly direction to point 1640, about 15 kilom. south-south-west of Mount Gabiro;

* Miscellaneous, No. 14 (1921) (Cd. 1284).
† ["Trattati . . . relativi all'Africa," pp. 350-358.]

Thence a straight line in a southerly direction to the north shore of
Lake Mohazi, where it terminates at the confluence of a river situated
about 2½ kilom. west of the confluence of the River Msilala;

If the *tracé* of the railway on the west of the River Kagera between
Bugufi and Uganda approaches within 16 kilom. of the line defined above,
the boundary will be carried to the west, following a minimum distance
of 16 kilom. from the *tracé*, without, however, passing to the west of the
straight line joining the terminal point on Lake Mohazi and the top of
Mount Kivisa (point 2100), situated on the Uganda-German East Africa
frontier about 5 kilom. south-west of the point where the River Mavumba
cuts this frontier;

Thence a line south-eastwards to meet the southern shore of Lake
Mohazi;

Thence the watershed between the Taruka and the Mkarange and continuing southwards to the north-eastern end of Lake Mugesera;

Thence the median line of this lake and continuing southwards across
Lake Sake to meet the Kagera;

Thence the course of the Kagera downstream to meet the western
boundary of Bugufi;

Thence this boundary to its junction with the eastern boundary of
Urundi;

Thence the eastern and southern boundary of Urundi to Lake Tanganyika.

The line described above is shown on the attached British 1: 1,000,000
map,* G.S.G.S. 2932, sheet Ruanda and Urundi.

ARTICLE 2.

Boundary Commissioners shall be appointed by His Britannic Majesty
and His Majesty the King of the Belgians to trace on the spot the line
described in article 1 above.

In case any dispute should arise in connection with the work of these
Commissioners, the question shall be referred to the Council of the League
of Nations, whose decision shall be final.

The final report by the Commissioners shall give the definite description of this boundary as it has been actually demarcated on the ground;
the necessary maps shall be annexed thereto and signed by the Commissioners. The report, with its annexes, shall be made in triplicate; one
copy shall be deposited in the archives of the League of Nations, one
shall be kept by the Government of His Majesty the King of the Belgians, and one by the Government of His Britannic Majesty.

ARTICLE 3.

The mandatory shall be responsible for the peace, order and good
government of the territory, and shall undertake to promote to the utmost

* Not reproduced.

the material and moral well-being and the social progress of its inhabitants. The mandatory shall have full powers of legislation and administration.

ARTICLE 4.

The mandatory shall not establish any military or naval bases, nor erect any fortifications, nor organise any native military force in the territory except for local police purposes and for the defence of the territory.

ARTICLE 5.

The mandatory—

(i.) Shall provide for the eventual emancipation of all slaves, and for as speedy an elimination of domestic and other slavery as social conditions will allow;

(ii.) Shall suppress all forms of slave trade;

(iii.) Shall prohibit all forms of forced or compulsory labour, except for essential public works and services, and then only in return for adequate remuneration;

(iv.) Shall protect the natives from abuse and measures of fraud and force by the careful supervision of labour contracts and the recruiting of labour;

(v.) Shall exercise a strict control over the traffic in arms and ammunition and the sale of spirituous liquors.

ARTICLE 6.

The mandatory shall in the framing of laws relating to the holding or transference of land take into consideration native laws and customs, and shall respect the rights and safeguard the interests of the native population.

No native land may be transferred, except between natives, without the previous consent of the public authorities, and no real rights over native land in favour of non-natives may be created except with the same consent.

The mandatory will promulgate strict regulations against usury.

ARTICLE 7.

The mandatory shall secure to all nationals of States Members of the League of Nations the same rights as are enjoyed in the territory by his own nationals in respect to entry into and residence in the territory, the protection afforded to their person and property, the acquisition of property, movable and immovable, and the exercise of their profession or trade, subject only to the requirements of public order, and on condition of compliance with the local law.

Further, the mandatory shall ensure to all nationals of States Members of the League of Nations, on the same footing as to his own nationals, freedom of transit and navigation, and complete economic, commercial and industrial equality; provided that the mandatory shall be free to organise essential public works and services on such terms and conditions as he thinks just.

Concessions for the development of the natural resources of the territory shall be granted by the mandatory without distinction on grounds of nationality between the nationals of all States Members of the League of Nations, but on such conditions as will maintain intact the authority of the local Government.

The rights conferred by this article extend equally to companies and associations organised in accordance with the law of any of the Members of the League of Nations, subject only to the requirements of public order, and on condition of compliance with the local law.

ARTICLE 8.

The mandatory shall ensure complete freedom of conscience, and the free exercise of all forms of worship which are consonant with public order and morality.

Missionaries of all such religions shall be free to enter the territory, and to travel and reside therein, to acquire and possess property, to erect religious buildings, and to open schools throughout the territory.

The mandatory shall, however, have the right to exercise such control as may be necessary for the maintenance of public order and good government, and to take all measures required for such control.

ARTICLE 9.

The mandatory shall apply to the territory any general international conventions already existing, or which may be concluded hereafter, with the approval of the League of Nations respecting the slave traffic, the traffic in arms and ammunition, the liquor traffic, and the traffic in drugs, or relating to commercial equality, freedom of transit and navigation, aerial navigation, railways, postal, telegraphic, and wireless communication, and industrial, literary and artistic property.

The mandatory shall co-operate in the execution of any common policy adopted by the League of Nations for preventing and combating disease, including diseases of plants and animals.

ARTICLE 10.

The mandatory shall be authorised to constitute the territory into a customs, fiscal and administrative union or federation, with the adjacent territories under his own sovereignty or control; provided always that the measures adopted to that end do not infringe the provisions of this mandate.

ARTICLE 11.

The mandatory shall make to the Council of the League of Nations an annual report to the satisfaction of the Council, containing full information concerning the measures taken to apply the provisions of this mandate.

A copy of all laws and regulations made in the course of the year and affecting property, commerce, navigation or the moral and material wellbeing of the natives shall be annexed to this report.

ARTICLE 12.

The consent of the Council of the League of Nations is required for any modification of the terms of this mandate; provided that in the case of any modification proposed by the mandatory such consent may be given by a majority.

ARTICLE 13.

If any dispute whatever should arise between the Members of the League of Nations relating to the interpretation or application of the present mandate, which cannot be settled by negotiations, this dispute shall be submitted to the Permanent Court of International Justice provided for by article 14 of the Covenant of the League of Nations.

States Members of the League of Nations may likewise bring any claims on behalf of their nationals for infractions of their rights under this mandate before the said court for decision.

The present copy shall be deposited in the archives of the League of Nations. Certified copies shall be forwarded by the Secretary-General of the League of Nations to all Powers signatories of the Treaty of Peace with Germany.

Made at   the   day of

ANNEX J

Draft Mandates for Togoland (British) and the Cameroons (British). (In the form in which the Council of the League of Nations will be invited to approve them.)*

No. 1.

Mr. Balfour to Earl Curzon.

(Extract.) *Paris, May 7, 1919.*

THE following agreement was reached this afternoon at a meeting between Mr. Lloyd George, M. Clemenceau, President Wilson, and Signor Orlando, and will be published at once:—

It is agreed that in the case of—

Togoland and Cameroons, France and Great Britain shall make a joint recommendation to the League of Nations as to their future. . . .

*   *   *   *   *   *   *

No. 2.

Joint Recommendation of the British and French Governments as to the Future of the Former Colonies of Togo and the Cameroons.

BY the terms of the decision of the Supreme Allied Council of the 7th May, 1919, France and Great Britain were charged with the duty of coming to an agreement upon the future of Togo and the Cameroons, which they would recommend the League of Nations to adopt.

With this end in view they fixed, first of all, the limits of the areas to be brought within their respective spheres; this preliminary measure was the subject of the declarations signed in London on the 10th July, 1919, copies of which are attached.

The two Governments have also devoted themselves to the question of the political and administrative system to be applied in Togo and the Cameroons. The decision of the Supreme Council stated specifically that all the territories comprised in the former German colonies other than Togo and the Cameroons should be the subject of mandates. The conclusion might, therefore, be drawn that Togo and the Cameroons were not to be subjected to this régime. On the other hand, article 22 of the

* Miscellaneous, No. 16 (1921) (Cd. 1350).

Treaty of Versailles, of the 28th June, 1919, appeared to apply the mandate system to all the German possessions outside Europe.

In view of this stipulation, the two Governments, animated with the desire to arrive at a mutual understanding, have come to the conclusion that the plan which they ought to recommend to the League of Nations is that the territories of Togo and the Cameroons should be placed under a mandate, but that the terms of the mandate should take into account, firstly, the interests of the natives, up till now artificially separated from the areas occupied by people of the same race, and, secondly, the peculiar features of the areas to which the mandates will apply, particularly the administrative difficulties which would be created by any attempt to constitute these areas into separate and distinct political units.

The Government of the French Republic, and the Government of His Britannic Majesty have, therefore, and in accordance with the spirit of article 22 of the Covenant of the League of Nations prepared the four accompanying drafts,* two of which apply to the Cameroons and two to Togoland.

They venture to hope that when the Council has taken note of them it will consider that the drafts have been prepared in conformity with the principle laid down in the said article 22, and will approve them accordingly.

December 17, 1920.

No. 3.

*Anglo-French Declaration respecting Togoland, signed at London,
July 10, 1919.*

THE Undersigned:

Viscount Milner, Secretary of State for the Colonies of the British Empire,

M. Henry Simon, Minister for the Colonies of the French Republic,

have agreed to determine the frontier, separating the territories of Togoland placed respectively under the authority of their Governments, as it is traced on the map (Sprigade 1/200,000) annexed to the present declaration,† and defined in the description in three articles also annexed hereto.

MILNER.
HENRY SIMON.

London, July 10, 1919.

---

* English texts only reproduced.
† The original 1/300,000 map is attached to the signed Declaration.

Description of the Franco-British Frontier marked on Sprigade's Map of Togoland, scale 1/200,000.

ARTICLE 1.

THE frontier will run eastwards from the pillar erected at the point of junction of the three colonies of Haute Volta, Gold Coast and Togoland in about latitude 11° 8′ 33″ to the unnamed watercourse shown on the map to the east of this pillar.

The frontier will run thence as follows:—

1. Along this unnamed watercourse to its confluence with the Kula-palogo;
2. Thence by the course of the Punokobo to its source;
3. Thence in a south-westerly direction to meet the river Biankuri, which downstream is named the Njimoant and the Mochole, which it follows to its confluence with the Kulugona.
4. From the confluence of the Mochole and the Kulugona the frontier will follow in a southerly direction a line to be fixed on the ground to point 390 near the junction of the streams Nabuleg and Gboroch;
5. Thence a line running in a south-easterly direction to the Manjo so as to leave the village of Jambule to France and that of Bungpurk to Great Britain;
6. Thence downstream the course of the Manjo to its confluence with the Kunkumbu;
7. Thence the course of the Kunkumbu to its confluence with the Oti;
8. Thence the course of the Oti to its confluence with the Dakpe;
9. Thence the Dakpe upstream to the boundary between the two old German districts of Mangu-Yendi and Sokode-Bassari.
10. The frontier will follow this administrative boundary south-west to regain the Oti;
11. Thence the course of the Oti to its confluence with the Kakassi;
12. Thence the course of the Kakassi upstream to its confluence with the Kentau;
13. Thence the course of the Kentau to its junction with the tribal boundary between the Konkomba and the Bitjem;
14. Thence southwards a line following generally this tribal boundary so as to leave the villages of Natagu, Napari, and Bobotiwe to Great Britain and those of Kujunle and Bisukpabe to France;
15. Following this boundary to a point situated about 1½ kilom. north of the confluence of the Kula and the Mamale;
16. Thence the Mamale upstream to its junction with the road from Nabugem to Bpadjebe;
17. Thence a line southwards to meet the river Bonolo so as to leave Bpadjebe to France;

18. Thence downstream the rivers Bonolo and Tankpa to the confluence of the latter with the Nabol;

19. Thence the river Nabol upstream to the junction of the tribal boundary between the Konkomba and the Bitjem;

20. Thence southwards a line following generally this tribal boundary to the summit of Kusangnaeli;

21. Thence a line to reach the confluence of the Tunkurma and the Mo, following generally the course of the Kuji and the Tunkurma;

22. Thence the course of the Mo (Mola) downstream, following the southern boundary of the Dagbon country to its junction with an unnamed affluent on the left bank at a point shown on the map near longitude 0° 20′ E;

23. Thence a line from this confluence running generally south-east to the confluence of the Bassa and Kue, following as far as possible the course of the Mo (Moo);

24. Thence the course of the Kue upstream to the bend formed by this river at a distance of about 2 kilom. south-west of Kueda;

25. Thence a line running southwards following the watershed between the Bunatje, the Tschai and the Dibom on the west and the Kue and the Asuokoko on the east to the hill situated about 1 kilom. west of the Maria Falls, leaving the village of Schiare to Great Britain and that of Kjirina to France and cutting the road from Dadiasse (which remains British) to Bismarckburg (which remains French) near point 760.

26. From the hill situated to the west of the Maria Falls a line to reach the Asuokoko, which it follows to its confluence with the river Balagbo;

27. Thence a line running generally southwards to Mount Bendjabe;

28. Thence a line following the crest which runs southwards; then cutting the Wawa reaches point 850 situated north of Kitschibo.

29. From point 850 a line running approximately southwards to the Tomito mountain;

30. Thence a line running south-south-westwards and cutting the river Onana reaches the watershed between the Odjabi and the Sassa, then continuing south-south-westwards, cutting the river Daji between the Odjabi and the Sassa, reaches the summit of Awedjegbe.

31. From this point it follows the watershed between the Ebanda or Wadjakli on the west and the Seblawu and Nubui on the east, then cuts the latter river at a point situated about 1 kilom. east of Apegame;

32. Thence a line to the watershed of the Agumassato hills which it follows to the Akpata hills;

33. Thence a line running south-west to the confluence of the Tsi and the Edjiri;

34. Thence a line following generally the southern tribal boundary of the Agome to a point situated on the watershed about 2 kilom. south of Moltke Peak;

35. Thence a line running generally southwards following the watershed to the Fiamekito hills which it leaves to reach the river Damitsi;

36. Thence the river Damitsi to its confluence with the Todschie (or Wuto);

37. Thence the river Todschie to the boundary of the lands of the village of Botoe, which it passes on the east so as to leave it wholly to Great Britain;

38. Thence the road from Botoe to Batome to the western limit of the latter village;

39. Thence the line passes south of Batome so as to leave this village in its entirety to France.

40. From south of Batome the boundary runs to the point of junction of the present boundary of the Gold Coast Colony (parallel 6° 20' north) and the river Magbawi;

41. Thence it follows, to the sea, the present frontier as laid down in the Anglo-German Convention of the 1st July, 1890. However, where the Lome-Akepe road by way of Degbokovhe crosses the present frontier south of latitude 6° 10' north and west of longitude 1° 14' east of Greenwich, the new frontier shall run 1 kilom. south-west of this road, so as to leave it entirely in French territory.

ARTICLE 2.

1. It is understood that at the time of the local delimitation of the frontier, where the natural features to be followed are not indicated in the above description, the Commissioners of the two Governments will, as far as possible, but without changing the attribution of the villages named in Article 1, lay down the frontier in accordance with natural features (rivers, hills, or watersheds).

The Boundary Commissioners shall be authorised to make such minor modifications of the frontier line as may appear to them necessary in order to avoid separating villages from their agricultural lands. Such deviations shall be clearly marked on special maps and submitted for the approval of the two Governments. Pending such approval, the deviations shall be provisionally recognised and respected.

2. As regards the roads mentioned in Article 1, only those which are shown upon the annexed map * shall be taken into consideration in the delimitation of the frontier.

* Annexed only to the original Declaration.

3. Where the frontier follows a waterway, the median line of the waterway shall be the boundary.

4. It is understood that if the inhabitants living near the frontier should, within a period of six months from the completion of the local delimitation, express the intention to settle in the regions placed under French authority, or inversely, in the regions placed under British authority, no obstacle will be placed in the way of their so doing, and they shall be granted the necessary time to gather in standing crops, and generally to remove all the property of which they are the legitimate owners.

ARTICLE 3.

1. The map to which reference is made in the description of the frontier is Sprigade's map of Togoland on the scale 1/200,000; of which the following sheets have been used:—

Sheet A 1. Sansane-Mangu; date of completion, July 1, 1907.
Sheet B 1. Jendi; date of completion, October 1, 1907.
Sheet C 1. Bismarckburg; date of completion, December 1, 1906.
Sheet D 1. Kete-Kratschi; date of completion, December 1, 1905.
Sheet E 1. Misahöhe; date of completion, June 1, 1905.
Sheet E 2. Lome; date of completion, October 1, 1902.

2. A map of Togoland, scale 1/1,500,000, is attached to illustrate the description of the above frontier.*

No. 4.

Anglo-French Declaration respecting the Cameroons, signed at London, July 10, 1919.

THE Undersigned:

Viscount Milner, Secretary of State for the Colonies of the British Empire,

M. Henry Simon, Minister for the Colonies of the French Republic, have agreed to determine the frontier, separating the territories of the Cameroons placed respectively under the authority of their Governments, as it is traced on the map (Moisel 1/300,000) annexed to the present declaration † and defined in the description in three articles also annexed hereto.

MILNER.
HENRY SIMON.

London, July 10, 1919.

* Annexed only to the original Declaration.
† The original 1/300,000 map is attached to the signed Declaration.

Description of the Franco-British Frontier, marked on the Map of the Cameroons, scale 1/300,000.

ARTICLE 1.

THE frontier will start from the meeting-point of the three old British, French and German frontiers situated in Lake Chad in latitude 13° 05′ N. and in approximately longitude 14° 05′ E. of Greenwich.

Thence the frontier will be determined as follows:—

1. A straight line to the mouth of the Ebeji;
2. Thence the course of the river Ebeji, which upstream is named the Lewejil, Labejed, Ngalarem, Lebeit and Ngada respectively, to the confluence of the rivers Kalia and Lebaiitt;
3. Thence the course of the river Kalia, or Ame, to its confluence with the river Dorma, or Kutelaha;
4. Thence the course of the latter, which upstream is named the Amjumba, the village of Woma and its outskirts remaining to France;
5. From the point where the river Amjumba loses itself in a swamp, the boundary will follow the median line of this swamp so as to rejoin the watercourse which appears to be the continuation of the Amjumba and which upstream is named Serahadja, Goluwa and Mudukwa respectively, the village of Uagisa remaining to Great Britain.
6. Thence this watercourse to its confluence with the river Gatagule;
7. Thence a line south-westwards to the watershed between the basin of the Yedseram on the west and the basins of the Mudukwa and of the Benue on the east; thence this watershed to Mount Mulikia;
8. Thence a line to the source of the Tsikakiri to be fixed on the ground so as to leave the village of Dumo to France;
9. Thence the course of the Tsikakiri to its confluence with the Mao Tiel near the group of villages of Luga;
10. Thence the course of the Mao Tiel to its confluence with the river Benue;
11. Thence the course of the Benue upstream to its confluence with the Faro;
12. Thence the course of the Faro to the mouth of its arm, the Mao Hesso, situated about 4 kilom. south of Chikito;
13. Thence the course of the Mao Hesso to boundary pillar No. 6 on the old British-German frontier;
14. Thence a straight line to the old boundary pillar No. 7; and thence a straight line to the old boundary pillar No. 8;

15. Thence a line south-westwards reaching the watershed between the Benue on the north-west and the Faro on the south-east, which it follows to a point on the Hossere Banglang, about 1 kilom. south of the source of the Mao Kordo;

16. Thence a line to the confluence of the Mao Ngonga and the Mao Deo, to be fixed on the ground so as to leave to France the village of Laro as well as the road from Bare to Fort Lamy;

17. Thence the course of the Mao Deo to its confluence with the Tiba;

18. Thence the course of the Tiba, which is named upstream Tibsat and Tussa respectively, to its confluence with a watercourse flowing from the west and situated about 12 kilom. south-west of Kontscha;

19. Thence a line running generally south-west to reach the summit of the Dutschi-Djombi;

20. Thence the watershed between the basins of the Taraba on the west and the Mao Deo on the east to a point on the Tchape Hills, about 2 kilom. north-west of the Tchape Pass (point 1541);

21. Thence a line to the Gorulde Hills, so as to leave the road from Bare to Fort Lamy about 2 kilom. to the east;

22. Thence successively the watershed between the Gamgam and the Jim, the main watershed between the basins of the Benue and the Sanaga, and the watershed between the Kokumbahun and the Ardo (Ntuli) to Hossere Jadji;

23. Thence a line to reach the source of the river Mafu;

24. Thence the river Mafu to its confluence with the river Mabe;

25. Thence the river Mabe, or Nsang, upstream to its junction with the tribal boundary between Bansso and Bamum;

26. Thence a line to the confluence of the rivers Mpand and Nun, to be fixed on the ground, so as to leave the country of Bansso to Great Britain and that of Bamum to France;

27. Thence the river Nun to its confluence with the river Tantam;

28. Thence the river Tantam and its affluent, which is fed by the river Sefu;

29. Thence the river Sefu to its source;

30. Thence a line south-westwards, crossing the Kupti, to reach near its source east of point 1300 the unnamed watercourse which flows into the Northern Mafi below Bali-Bagam;

31. Thence this watercourse to its confluence with the Northern Mifi, leaving to France the village of Gascho, belonging to the small country of Bamenjam;

32. Thence the Northern Mifi upstream to its confluence with the river Mogo, or Doshi;

33. Thence the river Mogo to its source;

34. Thence a line south-westwards to the crest of the Bambuto Moun-

tains and thence following the watershed between the basins of the Cross River and Mungo on the west and the Sanaga and Wuri on the east to Mount Kupe;

35. Thence a line to the source of the river Bubu;
36. Thence the river Bubu, which appears from the German map to lose itself and reappear as the Ediminjo, which the frontier will follow to its confluence with the Mungo;
37. Thence the course of the Mungo to the point in its mouth where it meets the parallel of latitude 4° 2′ 30″ north;
38. Thence this parallel of latitude westwards so as to reach the coast south of Tauben I.
39. Thence a line following the coast, passing south of Reiher I, to Mokola Creek, thus leaving Möwe Lake to Great Britain;
40. Thence a line following the eastern banks of the Mokola, Mbakwele, Njubanan-Jau and Matumal creeks, and cutting the mouths of the Mbossa-Bombe, Mikanje, Tende, Victoria, and other unnamed creeks to the junction of the Matumal and Victoria creeks;
41. Thence a line running 35° west of true south to the Atlantic Ocean.

ARTICLE 2.

1. It is understood that at the time of the local delimitation of the frontier, where the natural features to be followed are not indicated in the above description, the Commissioners of the two Governments will, as far as possible, but without changing the attribution of the villages named in Article 1, lay down the frontier in accordance with natural features (rivers, hills, or watersheds).

The Boundary Commissioners shall be authorised to make such minor modifications of the frontier line as may appear to them necessary in order to avoid separating villages from their agricultural lands. Such deviations shall be clearly marked on special maps and submitted for the approval of the two Governments. Pending such approval, the deviations shall be provisionally recognised and respected.

2. As regards the roads mentioned in Article 1, only those which are shown upon the annexed map * shall be taken into consideration in the delimitation of the frontier.

3. Where the frontier follows a waterway, the median line of the waterway shall be the boundary.

4. It is understood that if the inhabitants living near the frontier should, within a period of six months from the completion of the local delimitation, express the intention to settle in the regions placed under French authority, or inversely, in the regions placed under British authority, no obstacle will be placed in the way of their so doing, and they shall be granted the necessary time to gather in standing crops, and generally to remove all the property of which they are the legitimate owners.

* Annexed only to the original Declaration.

Article 3.

1. The map to which reference is made in the description of the frontier is Moisel's map of the Cameroons on the scale 1/300,000. The following sheets of this map have been used:—

Sheet A 4. Tschad; dated December 1, 1912.
Sheet B 4. Kusseri; dated August 1, 1912.
Sheet B 3. Dikoa; dated January 1, 1913.
Sheet C 3. Mubi; dated December 15, 1912.
Sheet D 3. Garua; dated May 15, 1912.
Sheet E 3. Ngaundere; dated October 15, 1912.
Sheet E 2. Banjo; dated January 1, 1913.
Sheet F 2. Fumban; dated May 1, 1913.
Sheet F 1. Ossidinge; dated January 1, 1912.
Sheet G 1. Buea; dated August 1, 1911.

2. A map of the Cameroons, scale 1/2,000,000, is attached to illustrate the description of the above frontier.*

No. 5.

Draft Mandate for Togoland (British).

(In the form in which the Council of the League of Nations will be invited to approve it.)

The Council of the League of Nations,

Whereas by article 119 of the Treaty of Peace with Germany signed at Versailles on the 28th June, 1919, Germany renounced in favour of the Principal Allied and Associated Powers all her rights over her oversea possessions, including therein Togoland; and

Whereas the Principal Allied and Associated Powers agreed that the Governments of France and Great Britain should make a joint recommendation to the League of Nations as to the future of the said territory; and

Whereas the Governments of France and Great Britain have made a joint recommendation to the Council of the League of Nations that a mandate to administer in accordance with article 22 of the Covenant of the League of Nations that part of Togoland lying to the west of the line agreed upon in the Declaration of the 10th July, 1919, referred to in article 1, should be conferred upon His Britannic Majesty; and

Whereas by the terms of the said joint recommendation the Governments of France and Great Britain have proposed that the mandate should be formulated in the following terms; and

* Annexed only to the original Declaration.

Whereas His Britannic Majesty has agreed to accept the mandate in respect of the said territory, and has undertaken to exercise it on behalf of the League of Nations in accordance with the following provisions;

Hereby approves the terms of the said mandate as follows:

ARTICLE 1.

The territory over which a mandate is conferred upon His Britannic Majesty comprises that part of the former colony of Togoland which lies to the west of the line laid down in the Declaration, signed on the 10th July, 1919, of which a copy is annexed hereto.

The delimitation on the spot of this line shall be carried out in accordance with the provision of the said declaration.

The final report of the Mixed Commission shall give the exact description of the boundary line as traced on the spot; maps signed by the Commissioners shall be annexed to the report. This report with its annexes shall be drawn up in triplicate, one of these shall be deposited in the archives of the League of Nations, one shall be kept by His Britannic Majesty's Government, and one by the Government of the French Republic.

ARTICLE 2.

The mandatory shall be responsible for the peace, order and good government of the territory, and for the promotion to the utmost of the material and moral well-being and the social progress of its inhabitants.

ARTICLE 3.

The mandatory shall not establish in the territory any military or naval bases, not erect any fortifications, nor organise any native military force except for local police purposes and for the defence of the territory.

ARTICLE 4.

The mandatory—

(i.) Will provide for the eventual emancipation of all slaves, and for as speedy an elimination of domestic and other slavery as social conditions will allow.

(ii.) Will suppress all forms of slave trade.

(iii.) Will prohibit all forms of forced or compulsory labour, except for essential public works and services, and then only in return for adequate remuneration.

(iv.) Will protect the natives from abuse and measures of fraud and force by the careful supervision of labour contracts and the recruiting of labour.

(v.) Will exercise a strict control over the traffic in arms and ammunition and the sale of spirituous liquors.

ARTICLE 5.

In the framing of laws relating to the holding or transference of land, the mandatory will take into consideration native laws and customs, and will respect the rights and safeguard the interests of the native population.

No native land may be transferred, except between natives, without the previous consent of the public authorities, and no real rights over native land in favour of non-natives may be created except with the same consent.

The mandatory will promulgate strict regulations against usury.

ARTICLE 6.

The mandatory will secure to all nationals of States, Members of the League of Nations, the same rights as are enjoyed in the territory by his own nationals in respect to entry into and residence in the territory, the protection afforded to their person and property, and acquisition of property, movable and immovable, and the exercise of their profession or trade, subject only to the requirements of public order, and on condition of compliance with the local law.

Further, the mandatory will ensure to all nationals of States, Members of the League of Nations, on the same footing as to his own nationals, freedom of transit and navigation, and complete economic, commercial and industrial equality; provided that the mandatory shall be free to organise essential public works and services on such terms and conditions as he thinks just.

Concessions for the development of the natural resources of the territory shall be granted by the mandatory without distinction on grounds of nationality between the nationals of all States, Members of the League of Nations, but on such conditions as will maintain intact the authority of the local Government.

The rights conferred by this article extend equally to companies and associations organised in accordance with the law of any of the Members of the League of Nations, subject only to the requirements of public order, and on condition of compliance with the local law.

ARTICLE 7.

Subject to the provisions of any local law for the maintenance of public order and public morals, the mandatory shall ensure in the territory freedom of conscience and the free exercise of all forms of worship, and shall allow all missionaries, nationals of any State, Member of the League of Nations, to enter into, travel and reside in the territory for the purpose of prosecuting their calling.

ARTICLE 8.

The mandatory shall apply to the territory any general international conventions applicable to his contiguous territory.

ARTICLE 9.

The mandatory shall have full powers of administration and legislation in the area subject to the mandate. This area shall be administered in accordance with the laws of the mandatory as an integral part of his territory and subject to the above provisions.

The mandatory shall therefore be at liberty to apply his laws to the territory subject to the mandate with such modifications as may be required by local conditions, and to constitute the territory into a customs, fiscal or administrative union or federation with the adjacent possessions under his sovereignty or control.

ARTICLE 10.

The mandatory shall make to the Council of the League of Nations an annual report to the satisfaction of the Council, containing full information concerning the measures taken to apply the provisions of the present mandate.

ARTICLE 11.

The consent of the Council of the League of Nations is required for any modification of the terms of the present mandate, provided that in the case of any modification proposed by the mandatory such consent may be given by a majority of the Council.

ARTICLE 12.

If any dispute whatever should arise between the Members of the League of Nations relating to the interpretation or application of this mandate which cannot be settled by negotiations, this dispute shall be submitted to the Permanent Court of International Justice provided for by article 14 of the Covenant of the League of Nations.

The present copy shall be deposited in the archives of the League of Nations. Certified copies shall be forwarded by the Secretary-General of the League of Nations to all Members of the League.

No. 6.

Draft Mandate for the Cameroons (British).

(In the form in which the Council of the League of Nations will be invited to approve it.)

THE Council of the League of Nations,

Whereas by article 119 of the Treaty of Peace with Germany signed at Versailles on the 28th June, 1919, Germany renounced in favour of the Principal Allied and Associated Powers all her rights over her oversea possessions, including therein the Cameroons; and

Whereas the Principal Allied and Associated Powers agreed that the Governments of France and Great Britain should make a joint recommendation to the League of Nations as to the future of the said territory; and

Whereas the Governments of France and Great Britain have made a joint recommendation to the Council of the League of Nations that a mandate to administer in accordance with article 22 of the Covenant of the League of Nations that part of the Cameroons lying to the west of the line agreed upon in the Declaration of the 10th July, 1919, annexed hereto, should be conferred upon His Britannic Majesty; and

Whereas by the terms of the said joint recommendation the Governments of France and Great Britain have proposed that the mandate should be formulated in the following terms; and

Whereas His Britannic Majesty has agreed to accept the mandate in respect of the said territory, and has undertaken to exercise it on behalf of the League of Nations in accordance with the following provisions;

Hereby approves the terms of the said mandate as follows:—

ARTICLE 1.

The territory over which a mandate is conferred upon His Britannic Majesty comprises that part of the former colony of the Cameroons which lies to the west of the line laid down in the Declaration, signed on the 10th July, 1919, of which a copy is annexed hereto.

The delimitation on the spot of this line shall be carried out in accordance with the provision of the said declaration.

The final report of the Mixed Commission shall give the exact description of the boundary line as traced on the spot; maps signed by the Commissioners shall be annexed to the report. This report with its annexes shall be drawn up in triplicate, one of these shall be deposited in the archives of the League of Nations, one shall be kept by His Britannic Majesty's Government, and one by the Government of the French Republic.

ARTICLE 2.

The mandatory shall be responsible for the peace, order and good government of the territory, and for the promotion to the utmost of the material and moral well-being and the social progress of its inhabitants.

ARTICLE 3.

The mandatory shall not establish in the territory any military or naval bases, not erect any fortifications, nor organise any native military force except for local police purposes and for the defence of the territory.

The mandatory—

(i.) Will provide for the eventual emancipation of all slaves, and for as speedy an elimination of domestic and other slavery as social conditions will allow.

(ii.) Will suppress all forms of slave trade.

(iii.) Will prohibit all forms of forced or compulsory labour, except for essential public works and services, and then only in return for adequate remuneration.

(iv.) Will protect the natives from abuse and measures of fraud and force by the careful supervision of labour contracts and the recruiting of labour.

(v.) Will exercise a strict control over the traffic in arms and ammunition and the sale of spirituous liquors.

ARTICLE 5.

In the framing of laws relating to the holding or transference of land, the mandatory will take into consideration native laws and customs, and will respect the rights and safeguard the interests of the native population.

No native land may be transferred, except between natives, without the previous consent of the public authorities, and no real rights over native land in favour of non-natives may be created except with the same consent.

The mandatory will promulgate strict regulations against usury.

ARTICLE 6.

The mandatory will secure to all nationals of States, Members of the League of Nations, the same rights as are enjoyed in the territory by his own nationals in respect to entry into and residence in the territory, the protection afforded to their person and property, and acquisition of property, movable and immovable, and the exercise of their profession or trade, subject only to the requirements of public order, and on condition of compliance with the local law.

Further, the mandatory will ensure to all nationals of States, Members of the League of Nations, on the same footing as to his own nationals, freedom of transit and navigation, and complete economic, commercial and industrial equality; provided that the mandatory shall be free to organise essential public works and services on such terms and conditions as he thinks just.

Concessions for the development of the natural resources of the territory shall be granted by the mandatory without distinction on grounds of nationality between the nationals of all States, Members of the League

of Nations, but on such conditions as will maintain intact the authority
of the local Government.

The rights conferred by this article extend equally to companies and
associations organised in accordance with the law of any of the Members
of the League of Nations, subject only to the requirements of public
order, and on condition of compliance with the local law.

ARTICLE 7.

Subject to the provisions of any local law for the maintenance of public
order and public morals, the mandatory shall ensure in the territory freedom of conscience and the free exercise of all forms of worship, and shall
allow all missionaries, nationals of any State, Member of the League of
Nations, to enter into, travel and reside in the territory for the purpose
of prosecuting their calling.

ARTICLE 8.

The mandatory shall apply to the territory any general international
conventions applicable to his contiguous territory.

ARTICLE 9.

The mandatory shall have full powers of administration and legislation
in the area subject to the mandate. This area shall be administered in
accordance with the laws of the mandatory as an integral part of his
territory and subject to the above provisions.

The mandatory shall therefore be at liberty to apply his laws to the
territory under the mandate subject to the modifications required by local
conditions, and to constitute the territory into a customs, fiscal or administrative union or federation with the adjacent possessions under his
sovereignty or control.

ARTICLE 10.

The mandatory shall make to the Council of the League of Nations an
annual report to the satisfaction of the Council, containing full information concerning the measures taken to apply the provisions of the present
mandate.

ARTICLE 11.

The consent of the Council of the League of Nations is required for
any modification of the terms of the present mandate, provided that in
the case of any modification proposed by the mandatory such consent
may be given by a majority of the Council.

ARTICLE 12.

If any dispute whatever should arise between the Members of the League of Nations relating to the interpretation or application of this mandate which cannot be settled by negotiations, this dispute shall be submitted to the Permanent Court of International Justice provided for by article 14 of the Covenant of the League of Nations.

The present copy shall be deposited in the archives of the League of Nations. Certified copies shall be forwarded by the Secretary-General of the League of Nations to all Members of the League.

ANNEX K

Mandate for German Samoa.*

The Council of the League of Nations:

Whereas by article 119 of the Treaty of Peace with Germany signed at Versailles on the 28th June, 1919, Germany renounced in favour of the Principal Allied and Associated Powers all her rights over her overseas possessions, including therein German Samoa; and

Whereas the Principal Allied and Associated Powers agreed that, in accordance with article 22, part I (Covenant of the League of Nations), of the said treaty, a mandate should be conferred upon His Britannic Majesty, to be exercised on his behalf by the Government of the Dominion of New Zealand, to administer German Samoa, and have proposed that the mandate should be formulated in the following terms; and

Whereas His Britannic Majesty, for and on behalf of the Government of the Dominion of New Zealand, has agreed to accept the mandate in respect of the said territory and has undertaken to exercise it on behalf of the League of Nations in accordance with the following provisions; and

Whereas, by the aforementioned article 22, paragraph 8, it is provided that the degree of authority, control or administration to be exercised by the mandatory, not having been previously agreed upon by the members of the League, shall be explicitly defined by the Council of the League of Nations:

Confirming the said mandate, defines its terms as follows:

ARTICLE 1.

The territory over which a mandate is conferred upon His Britannic Majesty for and on behalf of the Government of the Dominion of New Zealand (hereinafter called the mandatory) is the former German colony of Samoa.

ARTICLE 2.

The mandatory shall have full power of administration and legislation over the territory subject to the present mandate as an integral portion of the Dominion of New Zealand, and may apply the laws of the Dominion of New Zealand to the territory, subject to such local modifications as circumstances may require.

* Miscellaneous, No. 7 (1921) (Cd. 1203).

542

The mandatory shall promote to the utmost the material and moral well-being and the social progress of the inhabitants of the territory subject to the present mandate.

Article 3.

The mandatory shall see that the slave trade is prohibited, and that no forced labour is permitted, except for essential public works and services, and then only for adequate remuneration.

The mandatory shall also see that the traffic in arms and ammunition is controlled in accordance with principles analogous to those laid down in the convention relating to the control of the arms traffic, signed on the 10th September, 1919, or in any convention amending the same.

The supply of intoxicating spirits and beverages to the natives shall be prohibited.

Article 4.

The military training of the natives, otherwise than for purposes of internal police and the local defence of the territory, shall be prohibited. Furthermore, no military or naval bases shall be established or fortifications erected in the territory.

Article 5.

Subject to the provisions of any local law for the maintenance of public order and public morals, the mandatory shall ensure in the territory freedom of conscience and the free exercise of all forms of worship, and shall allow all missionaries, nationals of any State member of the League of Nations, to enter into, travel and reside in the territory for the purpose of prosecuting their calling.

Article 6.

The mandatory shall make to the Council of the League of Nations an annual report to the satisfaction of the Council, containing full information with regard to the territory, and indicating the measures taken to carry out the obligations assumed under articles 2, 3, 4 and 5.

Article 7.

The consent of the Council of the League of Nations is required for any modification of the terms of the present mandate.

The mandatory agrees that, if any dispute whatever should arise between the mandatory and another member of the League of Nations relating to the interpretation or the application of the provisions of the mandate, such dispute, if it cannot be settled by negotiation, shall be submitted to the Permanent Court of International Justice provided for by article 14 of the Covenant of the League of Nations.

The present declaration shall be deposited in the archives of the League of Nations. Certified copies shall be forwarded by the Secretary-General of the League of Nations to all Powers signatories of the Treaty of Peace with Germany.

Made at Geneva the 17th day of December, 1920.

Certified true copy.
ERIC DRUMMOND,
Secretary-General.

ANNEX L

Mandate for German Southwest Africa.[*]

The Council of the League of Nations:

Whereas by article 119 of the Treaty of Peace with Germany signed at Versailles on the 28th June, 1919, Germany renounced in favour of the Principal Allied and Associated Powers all her rights over her overseas possessions, including therein German South-West Africa; and

Whereas the Principal Allied and Associated Powers agreed that, in accordance with article 22, part I (Covenant of the League of Nations), of the said treaty, a mandate should be conferred upon His Britannic Majesty, to be exercised on his behalf by the Government of the Union of South Africa, to administer the territory aforementioned, and have proposed that the mandate should be formulated in the following terms; and

Whereas His Britannic Majesty, for and on behalf of the Government of the Union of South Africa, has agreed to accept the mandate in respect of the said territory and has undertaken to exercise it on behalf of the League of Nations in accordance with the following provisions; and

Whereas, by the aforementioned article 22, paragraph 8, it is provided that the degree of authority, control or administration to be exercised by the mandatory, not having been previously agreed upon by the members of the League, shall be explicitly defined by the Council of the League of Nations:

Confirming the said mandate, defines its terms as follows:

Article 1.

The territory over which a mandate is conferred upon His Britannic Majesty for and on behalf of the Government of the Union of South Africa (hereinafter called the mandatory) comprises the territory which formerly constituted the German Protectorate of South-West Africa.

Article 2.

The mandatory shall have full power of administration and legislation over the territory subject to the present mandate as an integral portion of the Union of South Africa, and may apply the laws of the Union of

[*] Miscellaneous, No. 8 (1921) (Cd. 1204).

South Africa to the territory, subject to such local modifications as circumstances may require.

The mandatory shall promote to the utmost the material and moral well-being and the social progress of the inhabitants of the territory subject to the present mandate.

ARTICLE 3.

The mandatory shall see that the slave trade is prohibited, and that no forced labour is permitted, except for essential public works and services, and then only for adequate remuneration.

The mandatory shall also see that the traffic in arms and ammunition is controlled in accordance with principles analogous to those laid down in the convention relating to the control of the arms traffic, signed on the 10th September, 1919, or in any convention amending the same.

The supply of intoxicating spirits and beverages to the natives shall be prohibited.

ARTICLE 4.

The military training of the natives, otherwise than for purposes of internal police and the local defence of the territory, shall be prohibited. Furthermore, no military or naval bases shall be established or fortifications erected in the territory.

ARTICLE 5.

Subject to the provisions of any local law for the maintenance of public order and public morals, the mandatory shall ensure in the territory freedom of conscience and the free exercise of all forms of worship, and shall allow all missionaries, nationals of any State member of the League of Nations, to enter into, travel and reside in the territory for the purpose of prosecuting their calling.

ARTICLE 6.

The mandatory shall make to the Council of the League of Nations an annual report to the satisfaction of the Council, containing full information with regard to the territory, and indicating the measures taken to carry out the obligations assumed under articles 2, 3, 4 and 5.

ARTICLE 7.

The consent of the Council of the League of Nations is required for any modification of the terms of the present mandate.

The mandatory agrees that, if any dispute whatever should arise between the mandatory and another member of the League of Nations relating to the interpretation or the application of the provisions of the mandate, such dispute, if it cannot be settled by negotiation, shall be submitted to the Permanent Court of International Justice provided for by article 14 of the Covenant of the League of Nations.

The present declaration shall be deposited in the archives of the League of Nations. Certified copies shall be forwarded by the Secretary-General of the League of Nations to all Powers signatories of the Treaty of Peace with Germany.

Made at Geneva the 17th day of December, 1920.

Certified true copy.

ERIC DRUMMOND,
Secretary-General.

ANNEX M

The Milner-Zaghlul Memorandum.*

1. In order to establish the independence of Egypt on a secure and lasting basis, it is necessary that the relations between Great Britain and Egypt should be precisely defined, and the privileges and immunities now enjoyed in Egypt by the capitulatory Powers should be modified and rendered less injurious to the interests of the country.

2. These ends cannot be achieved without further negotiations between accredited representatives of the British and Egyptian Governments respectively in the one case, and between the British Government and the Governments of the capitulatory Powers in the other case. Such negotiations will be directed to arriving at definite agreements on the following lines:—

3.—(i.) As between Egypt and Great Britain a Treaty will be entered into, under which Great Britain will recognise the independence of Egypt as a constitutional monarchy with representative institutions, and Egypt will confer upon Great Britain such rights as are necessary to safeguard her special interests and to enable her to furnish the guarantees which must be given to foreign Powers to secure the relinquishment of their capitulatory rights.

(ii.) By the same Treaty, an alliance will be concluded between Great Britain and Egypt, by which Great Britain will undertake to support Egypt in defending the integrity of her territory, and Egypt will undertake, in case of war, even when the integrity of Egypt is not affected, to render to Great Britain all the assistance in her power, within her own borders, including the use of her harbours, aerodromes and means of communication for military purposes.

4. This Treaty will embody stipulations to the following effect:—

(i.) Egypt will enjoy the right to representation in foreign countries. In the absence of any duly-accredited Egyptian representative, the Egyptian Government will confide its interests to the care of the British representative. Egypt will undertake not to adopt in foreign countries an attitude which is inconsistent with the alliance or will create difficulties for Great Britain, and will also undertake not to enter into any agreement with a foreign Power which is prejudicial to British interests.

* *Egypt,* No. 1 (1921), pp. 24-26.

(ii.) Egypt will confer on Great Britain the right to maintain a military force on Egyptian soil for the protection of her Imperial communications. The Treaty will fix the place where the force shall be quartered and will regulate any subsidiary matters which require to be arranged. The presence of this force shall not constitute in any manner a military occupation of the country, or prejudice the rights of the Government of Egypt.

(iii.) Egypt will appoint, in concurrence with His Majesty's Government, a Financial Adviser, to whom shall be entrusted in due course the powers at present exercised by the Commissioners of the Debt, and who will be at the disposal of the Egyptian Government for all other matters on which they may desire to consult him.

(iv.) Egypt will appoint, in concurrence with His Majesty's Government, an official in the Ministry of Justice, who shall enjoy the right of access to the Minister. He shall be kept fully informed on all matters connected with the administration of the law as affecting foreigners, and will also be at the disposal of the Egyptian Government for consultation on any matter connected with the efficient maintenance of law and order.

(v.) In view of the contemplated transfer to His Majesty's Government of the rights hitherto exercised under the régime of the Capitulations by the various foreign Governments, Egypt recognises the right of Great Britain to intervene, through her representative in Egypt, to prevent the application to foreigners of any Egyptian law now requiring foreign consent, and Great Britain on her side undertakes not to exercise this right except in the case of laws operating inequitably against foreigners.

Alternative:—

In view of the contemplated transfer to His Majesty's Government of the rights hitherto exercised under the régime of the Capitulations by the various foreign Governments, Egypt recognises the right of Great Britain to intervene, through her representative in Egypt, to prevent the application to foreigners of any Egyptian law now requiring foreign consent, and Great Britain on her side undertakes not to exercise this right except in the case of laws inequitably discriminating against foreigners in the matter of taxation, or inconsistent with the principles of legislation common to all the capitulatory Powers.

(vi.) On account of the special relations between Great Britain and Egypt created by the Alliance, the British representative will be accorded an exceptional position in Egypt and will be entitled to precedence over all other representatives.

(vii.) The engagements of British and other foreign officers and administrative officials who entered into the service of the Egyptian

Government before the coming into force of the Treaty may be terminated, at the instance of either the officials themselves or the Egyptian Government, at any time within two years after the coming into force of the Treaty. The pension or compensation to be accorded to officials retiring under this provision, in addition to that provided by the existing law, shall be determined by the Treaty. In cases where no advantage is taken of this arrangement existing terms of service will remain unaffected.

5. This Treaty will be submitted to the approval of a Constituent Assembly, but it will not come into force until after the agreements with foreign Powers for the closing of their Consular Courts and the decrees for the reorganisation of the Mixed Tribunals have come into operation.

6. This Constituent Assembly will also be charged with the duty of framing a new Organic Statute, in accordance with the provisions of which the Government of Egypt will in future be conducted. This Statute will embody provisions for the Ministers being responsible to the Legislature. It will also provide for religious toleration for all persons and for the due protection of the rights of foreigners.

7. The necessary modifications in the régime of the Capitulations will be secured by agreements to be concluded by Great Britain with the various capitulatory Powers. These agreements will provide for the closing of the foreign Consular Courts, so as to render possible the reorganisation and extension of the jurisdiction of the Mixed Tribunals and the application to all foreigners in Egypt of the legislation (including legislation imposing taxation) enacted by the Egyptian Legislature.

8. These agreements will provide for the transfer to His Majesty's Government of the rights previously exercised under the régime of the Capitulations by the various foreign Governments. They will also contain stipulations to the following effect:—

(a.) No attempt will be made to discriminate against the nationals of a Power which agrees to close its Consular Courts, and such nationals shall enjoy in Egypt the same treatment as British subjects.

(b.) The Egyptian Nationality Law will be founded on the *jus sanguinis*, so that the children born in Egypt of a foreigner will enjoy the nationality of their father, and will not be claimed as Egyptian subjects.

(c.) Consular officers of the foreign Powers shall be accorded by Egypt the same status as foreign Consuls enjoy in England.

(d.) Existing Treaties and Conventions to which Egypt is a party on matters of commerce and navigation, including postal and telegraphic Conventions, will remain in force. Pending the conclusion of special agreements to which she is a party, Egypt will apply the Treaties in force between Great Britain and the foreign Power concerned on questions affected by the closing of the Consular Courts, such as extradition Treaties, Treaties for the surrender of seamen deserters, &c., as also Treaties of a political nature, whether multilateral or bilateral, *e.g.,* arbitration Conventions and the various Conventions relating to the conduct of hostilities.

(*e.*) The liberty to maintain schools and to teach the language of the foreign country concerned will be guaranteed, provided that such schools are subject in all respects to the laws applicable generally to European schools in Egypt.

(*f.*) The liberty to maintain or organise religious and charitable foundations, such as hospitals, &c., will also be guaranteed.

The Treaties will also provide for the necessary changes in the Commission of the Debt and the elimination of the international element in the Alexandria Board of Health.

9. The legislation rendered necessary by the aforesaid agreements between Great Britain and the foreign Powers, will be effected by decrees to be issued by the Egyptian Government.

A decree shall be enacted at the same time validating all measures, legislative, administrative or judicial, taken under Martial Law.

10. The decrees for the reorganisation of the Mixed Tribunals will provide for conferring upon these Tribunals all jurisdiction hitherto exercised by the foreign Consular Courts, while leaving the jurisdiction of the Native Courts untouched.

11. After the coming into force of the Treaty referred to in Article 3, Great Britain will communicate its terms to foreign Powers and will support an application by Egypt for admission as a member of the League of Nations.

August 18, 1920.

ANNEX N

Franco-British Convention of December 23, 1920, on certain points connected with the Mandates for Syria and the Lebanon, Palestine and Mesopotamia.*

THE British and French Governments, respectively represented by the undersigned Plenipotentiaries, wishing to settle completely the problems raised by the attribution to Great Britain of the mandates for Palestine and Mesopotamia and by the attribution to France of the mandate over Syria and the Lebanon, all three conferred by the Supreme Council at San Remo, have agreed on the following provisions:—

ARTICLE 1.

The boundaries between the territories under the French mandate of Syria and the Lebanon on the one hand and the British mandates of Mesopotamia and Palestine on the other are determined as follows:—

On the east, the Tigris from Jeziret-ibn-Omar to the boundaries of the former vilayets of Diarbekir and Mosul.

On the south-east and south, the aforesaid boundary of the former vilayets southwards as far as Roumelan Koeui; thence a line leaving in the territory under the French mandate the entire basin of the western Kabur and passing in a straight line towards the Euphrates, which it crosses at Abu Kemal, thence a straight line to Imtar to the south of Jebul Druse, then a line to the south of Nasib on the Hedjaz Railway, then a line to Semakh on the Lake of Tiberias, traced to the south of the railway, which descends towards the lake and parallel to the railway. Deraa and its environs will remain in the territory under the French mandate; the frontier will in principle leave the valley of the Yarmuk in the territory under the French mandate, but will be drawn as close as possible to the railway in such a manner as to allow the construction in the valley of the Yarmuk of a railway entirely situated in the territory under the British mandate. At Semakh the frontier will be fixed in such a manner as to allow each of the two High Contracting Parties to construct and establish a harbour and railway station giving free access to the Lake of Tiberias.

On the west, the frontier will pass from Semakh across the Lake of

* Miscellaneous, No. 4 (1921) (Cd. 1195).

Tiberias to the mouth of the Wadi Massadyie. It will then follow the course of this river upstream, and then the Wadi Jeraba to its source. From that point it will reach the track from El Kuneitra to Banias at the point marked Skek, thence it will follow the said track, which will remain in the territory under the French mandate as far as Banias. Thence the frontier will be drawn westwards as far as Metullah, which will remain in Palestinian territory. This portion of the frontier will be traced in detail in such a manner as to ensure for the territory under the French mandate easy communication entirely within such territory with the regions of Tyre and Sidon, as well as continuity of road communication to the west and to the east of Banias.

From Metullah the frontier will reach the watershed of the valley of the Jordan and the basin of the Litani. Thence it will follow this watershed southwards. Thereafter it will follow in principle the watershed between the Wadis Farah-Houroun and Kerkera, which will remain in the territory under the British mandate, and the Wadis El Doubleh, El Aioun and Es Zerka, which will remain in the territory under the French mandate. The frontier will reach the Mediterranean Sea at the port of Ras-el-Nakura, which will remain in the territory under the French mandate.

ARTICLE 2.

A commission shall be established within three months from the signature of the present convention to trace on the spot the boundary line laid down in article 1 between the French and British mandatory territories. This commission shall be composed of four members. Two of these members shall be nominated by the British and French Governments respectively, the two others shall be nominated, with the consent of the mandatory Power, by the local Governments concerned in the French and British mandatory territories respectively.

In case any dispute should arise in connection with the work of the commission, the question shall be referred to the Council of the League of Nations, whose decision shall be final.

The final reports by the commission shall give the definite dèscription of the boundary as it has been actually demarcated on the ground; the necessary maps shall be annexed thereto and signed by the commission. The reports, with their annexes, shall be made in triplicate; one copy shall be deposited in the archives of the League of Nations, one copy shall be kept by the mandatory, and one by the other Government concerned.

ARTICLE 3.

The British and French Governments shall come to an agreement regarding the nomination of a commission, whose duty it will be to make a preliminary examination of any plan of irrigation formed by the Government of the French mandatory territory, the execution of which would be of a nature to diminish in any considerable degree the waters of the Tigris and Euphrates at the point where they enter the area of the British mandate in Mesopotamia.

ARTICLE 4.

In virtue of the geographic and strategic position of the island of Cyprus, off the Gulf of Alexandretta, the British Government agrees not to open any negotiations for the cession or alienation of the said island of Cyprus without the previous consent of the French Government.

ARTICLE 5.

1. The French Government agrees to facilitate by a liberal arrangement the joint use of the section of the existing railway between the Lake of Tiberias and Nasib. This arrangement shall be concluded between the railway administrations of the areas under the French and British mandates respectively as soon as possible after the coming into force of the mandates for Palestine and Syria. In particular the agreement shall allow the administration in the British zone to run their own trains with their own traction and train crews over the above section of the railway in both directions for all purposes other than the local traffic of the territory under the French mandate. The agreement shall determine at the same time the financial, administrative and technical conditions governing the running of the British trains. In the event of the two administrations being unable to reach an agreement within three months from the coming into force of the two above-mentioned mandates, an arbitrator shall be appointed by the Council of the League of Nations to settle the points as to which a difference of opinion exists and immediate effect shall be given as far as possible to those parts of the agreement on which an understanding has already been reached.

The said agreement shall be concluded for an indefinite period and shall be subject to periodical revision as need arises.

2. The British Government may carry a pipe line along the existing railway track and shall have in perpetuity and at any moment the right to transport troops by the railway.

3. The French Government consents to the nomination of a special commission, which, after having examined the ground, may readjust the above-mentioned frontier line in the valley of the Yarmuk as far as Nasib in such a manner as to render possible the construction of the British railway and pipe line connecting Palestine with the Hedjaz Railway and the valley of the Euphrates, and running entirely within the limits of the areas under the British mandate. It is agreed, however, that the existing

railway in the Yarmuk valley is to remain entirely in the territory under the French mandate. The right provided by the present paragraph for the benefit of the British Government must be utilised within a maximum period of ten years.

The above-mentioned commission shall be composed of a representative of the French Government and a representative of the British Government, to whom may be added representatives of the local Governments and experts as technical advisers to the extent considered necessary by the British and French Governments.

4. In the event of the track of the British railway being compelled for technical reasons to enter in certain places the territory under French mandate, the French Government will recognise the full and complete extra-territoriality of the sections thus lying in the territory under the French mandate, and will give the British Government or its technical agents full and easy access for all railway purposes.

5. In the event of the British Government making use of the right mentioned in paragraph 3 to construct a railway in the valley of the Yarmuk, the obligations assumed by the French Government in accordance with paragraphs 1 and 2 of the present article will determine three months after the completion of the construction of the said railway

6. The French Government agrees to arrange that the rights provided for above for the benefit of the British Government shall be recognised by the local Governments in the territory under the French mandate.

ARTICLE 6.

It is expressly stipulated that the facilities accorded to the British Government by the preceding articles imply the maintenance for the benefit of France of the provisions of the Franco-British Agreement of San Remo regarding oil.

ARTICLE 7.

The French and British Governments will put no obstacle in their respective mandatory areas in the way of the recruitment of railway staff for any section of the Hedjaz Railway.

Every facility will be given for the passage of employees of the Hedjaz Railway over the British and French mandatory areas in order that the working of the said railway may be in no way prejudiced.

The French and British Governments agree, where necessary, and in eventual agreement with the local Governments, to conclude an arrangement whereby the stores and railway material passing from one mandatory area to another and intended for the use of the Hedjaz Railway will not for this reason be submitted to any additional customs dues and will be exempted so far as possible from customs formalities.

ARTICLE 8.

Experts nominated respectively by the Administrations of Syria and Palestine shall examine in common within six months after the signature of the present convention the employment, for the purposes of irrigation and the production of hydro-electric power, of the waters of the Upper Jordan and the Yarmuk and of their tributaries, after satisfaction of the needs of the territories under the French mandate.

In connection with this examination the French Government will give its representatives the most liberal instructions for the employment of the surplus of these waters for the benefit of Palestine.

In the event of no agreement being reached as a result of this examination, these questions shall be referred to the French and British Governments for decision.

To the extent to which the contemplated works are to benefit Palestine, the Administration of Palestine shall defray the expenses of the construction of all canals, weirs, dams, tunnels, pipe lines and reservoirs or other works of a similar nature, or measures taken with the object of reafforestation and the management of forests.

ARTICLE 9.

Subject to the provisions of Articles 15 and 16 of the mandate for Palestine, of Articles 8 and 10 of the mandate for Mesopotamia, and of Article 8 of the mandate for Syria and the Lebanon, and subject also to the general right of control in relation to education and public instruction, of the local Administrations concerned, the British and French Governments agree to allow the schools which French and British nationals possess and direct at the present moment in their respective mandatory areas to continue their work freely; the teaching of French and English will be freely permitted in these schools.

The present article does not in any way imply the right of nationals of either of the two parties to open new schools in the mandatory area of the other.

The present convention has been drawn up in English and French, each of the two texts having equal force.

Done at Paris, the 23rd December, 1920, in a double copy, one of which will remain deposited in the archives of the Government of the French Republic, and the other in those of the Government of His Britannic Majesty.

HARDINGE OF PENSHURST.
G. LEYGUES.

ANNEX O

Memorandum of Clauses of Suggested Convention between Great Britain and Egypt, handed by the Marquess Curzon of Kedleston to Adly Yeghen Pasha on November 10, 1921.*

I.—*Termination of Protectorate.*

---

1. The Government of His Britannic Majesty agree, in consideration of the conclusion and ratification of the present treaty, to terminate the Protectorate declared over Egypt on the 18th December, 1914, and thenceforth to recognise Egypt as a Sovereign State under a constitutional monarchy.

There is hereby concluded, and there shall henceforth subsist, between the Government and people of His Britannic Majesty on the one hand, and the Government and people of Egypt on the other hand, a perpetual treaty and bond of peace, amity and alliance.

II.—*Foreign Relations.*

2. The foreign affairs of Egypt shall be conducted by the Egyptian Ministry of Foreign Affairs under a Minister so designated.

3. His Britannic Majesty's Government shall be represented in Egypt by a High Commissioner, who, in virtue of his special responsibilities, shall at all times be entitled to an exceptional position, and shall take precedence over the representatives of other countries.

4. The Egyptian Government shall be represented in London, and in any other capital in which, in the opinion of the Egyptian Government, Egyptian interests may require such representation, by diplomatic representatives enjoying the rank and title of Minister.

5. In view of the obligations which Great Britain has undertaken in Egypt, notably in respect of foreign countries, the closest relations shall exist between the Egyptian Ministry of Foreign Affairs and the British High Commissioner, who will render all possible assistance to the Egyptian Government in respect of diplomatic transactions or negotiations.

6. The Egyptian Government will not enter into any political agreement with foreign Powers without consultation with His Britannic Majesty's Government through the British High Commissioner.

* Reprinted from *Egypt,* No. 4 (1921), pp. 3-6.

7. The Egyptian Government will enjoy the right of appointing such consular representatives abroad as their interests may require.

8. For the general conduct of diplomatic relations, and the consular protection of Egyptian interests in places where no Egyptian diplomatic or consular representative is stationed, His Britannic Majesty's representatives will place themselves at the disposal of the Egyptian Government, and will render them every assistance in their power.

9. His Britannic Majesty's Government will continue to conduct the negotiations for the abolition of the existing Capitulations with the various capitulatory Powers, and accept the responsibility for protecting the legitimate interests of foreigners in Egypt. His Majesty's Government will confer with the Egyptian Government before formally concluding these negotiations.

III.—*Military Dispositions.*

10. Great Britain undertakes to support Egypt in the defence of her vital interests and of the integrity of her territory.

For the discharge of these obligations and for the due protection of British Imperial communications, British forces shall have free passage through Egypt, and shall be maintained at such places in Egypt and for such periods as shall from time to time be determined. They shall also at all times have facilities as at present for the acquisition and use of barracks, exercise grounds, aerodromes, naval yards and naval harbours.

IV.—*Employment of Foreign Officers.*

11. In view of the special responsibilities assumed by Great Britain and of the existing position in the Egyptian army and public services, the Egyptian Government undertake not to appoint any foreign officers or officials to any of those services without the previous concurrence of the British High Commissioner.

V.—*Financial Administration.*

12. The Egyptian Government will appoint, in consultation with His Britannic Majesty's Government, a Financial Commissioner, to whom shall be entrusted in due course the powers at present exercised by the Commissioners of the Debt, and who will more especially be responsible for the punctual payment of the following charges:—

(i.) The charges for the budget of the Mixed Courts.

(ii.) All pensions or other annuities payable to retired foreign officials and their heirs.

(iii.) The budgets of the Financial and Judicial Commissioners and their respective staffs.

13. For the proper discharge of his duties the Financial Commissioner shall be kept fully informed on all matters within the purview of the

Ministry of Finance, and shall at all times enjoy the right of access to the President of the Council of Ministers and to the Minister of Finance.

14. No external loan shall be raised nor the revenue of any public service be assigned by the Egyptian Government without the concurrence of the Financial Commissioner.

VI.—*Judicial Administration.*

15. The Egyptian Government will appoint, in agreement with His Britannic Majesty's Government, a Judicial Commissioner, who, in virtue of the obligations assumed by Great Britain, shall be charged with the duty of watching the administration of the law in all matters affecting foreigners.

16. For the proper discharge of his duties, the Judicial Commissioner shall be kept fully informed on all matters affecting foreigners which concern the Ministries of Justice and of the Interior, and shall at all times enjoy the right of access to the Egyptian Ministers of Justice and of the Interior.

VII.—*Soudan.*

17. The peaceful development of the Soudan being essential to the security of Egypt and for the maintenance of her water supply, Egypt undertakes to continue to afford the Soudan Government the same military assistance as in the past, or, in lieu thereof, to provide the Soudan Government with financial assistance to an extent to be agreed upon between the two Governments.

All Egyptian forces in the Soudan shall be under the orders of the Governor-General.

Great Britain further undertakes to secure for Egypt her fair share of the waters of the Nile, and to this end it is agreed that no new irrigation works on the Nile or its tributaries south of Wadi Halfa shall be undertaken without the concurrence of a Board of three conservators representing Egypt, the Soudan and Uganda respectively.

VIII.—*Tribute Loans.*

18. The sums which the Khedives of Egypt have from time to time undertaken to pay over to the houses by which the Turkish loans secured on the Egyptian tribute were issued, will be applied as heretofore by the Egyptian Government to the interest and sinking funds of the loans of 1894 and 1891 until the final extinction of those loans.

The Egyptian Government will also continue to apply the sum hitherto paid towards the interest of the guaranteed loan of 1855.

Upon the extinction of these loans of 1894, 1891 and 1855, all liability on the part of the Egyptian Government arising out of the tribute formerly paid by Egypt to Turkey will cease.

IX.—*Retirement and Compensation of Officials.*

19.   The Egyptian Government shall be entitled to dispense with the services of British officials at any time after the coming into force of this treaty on condition that such officials shall receive monetary compensation as hereafter provided, in addition to any pension or indemnity to which their conditions of service may entitle them.

On the like condition British officials shall be entitled to resign at any time after the coming into force of this treaty.

The scheme shall apply to pensionable and non-pensionable officials as well as to employees of municipalities, provincial councils or other local bodies.

20.   An official dismissed or retiring under the terms of the preceding clause shall receive in addition to compensation a repatriation allowance sufficient to cover the cost of transporting himself, his family and his household goods to London.

21.   Compensation and pensions shall be payable in Egyptian pounds at the fixed rate of 97½ piastres to the pound sterling.

22.   A table of compensation, (*a*) for permanent officials, (*b*) for temporary officials, shall be prepared by the president of the Society of Actuaries.

X.—*Protection of Minorities.*

23.   Egypt undertakes that the stipulations following shall be recognised as fundamental laws, and that no law, regulation or official action shall conflict or interfere with these stipulations, nor shall any law, regulation or official action prevail over them.

24.   Egypt undertakes to assure full and complete protection of life and liberty to all inhabitants of Egypt without distinction of birth, nationality, language, race or religion.

All inhabitants of Egypt shall be entitled to the free exercise, whether public or private, of any creed, religion or belief, whose practices are not inconsistent with public order or public morals.

25.   All Egyptian nationals shall be equal before the law, and shall enjoy the same civil and political rights without distinction as to race, language or religion.

Differences of religion, creed or confession shall not prejudice any Egyptian national in matters relating to the enjoyment of civil or political rights, as, for instance, admission to public employments, functions and honours or the exercise of professions and industries.

No restriction shall be imposed on the free use by any Egyptian national of any language in private intercourse, in commerce, in religion, in the press or in publications of any kind or at public meetings.

26.   Egyptian nationals who belong to racial, religious, or linguistic

minorities shall enjoy the same treatment and security in law and in fact as the other Egyptian nationals. In particular, they shall have an equal right to establish, manage and control, at their own expense, charitable, religious and social institutions, schools, and other educational establishments, with the right to use their own language and to exercise their religion freely therein.

ANNEX P

AGREEMENT BETWEEN GREAT BRITAIN AND PORTUGAL RELATING TO THE SUPPRESSION OF THE CAPITULATIONS IN EGYPT.*

Lisbon, December 9, 1920.

[*Ratifications exchanged at Lisbon, September 29, 1921.*]

THE Government of His Britannic Majesty and the Government of the Portuguese Republic,
Considering the moment opportune to give full effect to the special situation of Great Britain in Egypt,
Have decided to replace the régime at present in force there in matters relating to Portuguese subjects by the following arrangements:—

ARTICLE 1.

Portugal having recognised the protectorate in Egypt, promulgated by Great Britain on the 18th December 1914, renounces in her favour all the rights and privileges which she holds in Egypt under the Capitulations.

ARTICLE 2.

From the coming into force of the new judicial system in Egypt under the authority of Great Britain the Portuguese Consular Courts will cease to sit, except to dispose of current proceedings.

ARTICLE 3.

Portuguese nationals shall enjoy in Egypt, in regard to public liberties, the administration of justice, private rights, including landed property and mining rights, the liberal, industrial and commercial professions, and taxes and duties, the same treatment as British nationals.
Children born in Egypt of a father who is a Portuguese national enjoying there the privileges accorded to foreigners shall be entitled to Portuguese nationality; they shall not become Egyptian subjects.

* Reprinted from Treaty Series, 1921, No. 23.

ARTICLE 4.

The Consuls-General, Consuls, Vice-Consuls, and Consular Agents of Portugal in Egypt shall enjoy, from the closing of the Consular Courts, the same immunities as in Great Britain.

They shall continue to exercise in the interests of private persons, so far as is consistent with the laws of Egypt, all their non-judicial functions under the same conditions as formerly.

ARTICLE 5.

Pending the conclusion of special agreements relating to Egypt or between Portugal and Egypt, the treaties in force between Great Britain and Portugal will apply in Egypt.

In the execution of the treaty of the 17th October 1892 and of the protocol annexed, relating to the extradition of criminals, it is agreed that the prohibition attached by article 3 to the extradition of the nationals of the High Contracting Parties shall apply, in the case of refugees in Egypt, to the subjects of His Highness the Sultan as well as to all British nationals.

On condition of reciprocity, the regulations now applied in Portugal and in Egypt respectively to imports coming from the other country or to exports to the other country shall not be altered unless notice to that effect has been previously given twelve months in advance.

It is understood, however, that the present agreement shall not limit the right of the Portuguese Government and of the Egyptian Government to introduce into the régime in force between the two countries modifications which may be applicable to all other countries without distinction.

ARTICLE 6.

Portugal agrees that, subject only to the unanimous consent of the Powers concerned, all the rights and duties of the International Quarantine Commission in Egypt are transferred to the Anglo-Egyptian authorities.

ARTICLE 7.

The present agreement shall be ratified, and the ratifications thereof shall be exchanged at Lisbon as soon as practicable.

In faith whereof the respective Plenipotentiaries have signed the present agreement and have affixed thereto the seal of their arms.

Done at Lisbon, the 9th December, 1920.

[L.S.]   LANCELOT D. CARNEGIE,
His Britannic Majesty's Minister.
[L.S.]   DOMINGOS LEITE PEREIRA,
Minister for Foreign Affairs.

ANNEX Q *

TREATY BETWEEN HIS BRITANNIC MAJESTY AND HIS MAJESTY THE KING OF IRAQ.

HIS BRITANNIC MAJESTY of the one part: and HIS MAJESTY THE KING OF IRAQ of the other part:

Whereas His Britannic Majesty has recognised Feisal Ibn Hussein as constitutional King of Iraq: and

Whereas His Majesty the King of Iraq considers that it is to the interests of Iraq and will conduce to its rapid advancement that he should conclude a Treaty with His Britannic Majesty on the basis of alliance: and

Whereas His Britannic Majesty is satisfied that the relations between himself and His Majesty the King of Iraq can now be better defined by such a Treaty of Alliance than by any other means:

For this purpose the High Contracting Parties have appointed as their Plenipotentiaries:

HIS MAJESTY THE KING OF THE UNITED KINGDOM OF GREAT BRITAIN AND IRELAND AND OF THE BRITISH DOMINIONS BEYOND THE SEAS, EMPEROR OF INDIA:

> Sir Percy Zachariah Cox, G.C.M.G., G.C.I.E., K.C.S.I., High Commissioner and Consul-General of His Britannic Majesty in Iraq:

HIS MAJESTY THE KING OF IRAQ:

> His Highness Sir Saiyid 'Abd-ur-Rahman, G.B.E., Prime Minister and Naqib-al-Ashraf, Baghdad:

Who, having communicated their full powers, found in good and due order, have agreed as follows:—

ARTICLE I.

At the request of His Majesty the King of Iraq, His Britannic Majesty undertakes subject to the provisions of this Treaty to provide the State of Iraq with such advice and assistance as may be required during the period of the present Treaty, without prejudice to her national sovereignty. His Britannic Majesty shall be represented in Iraq by a High Commissioner and Consul-General assisted by the necessary staff.

* *Iraq*, 1922 (Cd. 1757).

ARTICLE II.

His Majesty the King of Iraq undertakes that for the period of the present Treaty no gazetted official of other than Iraq nationality shall be appointed in Iraq without the concurrence of His Britannic Majesty. A separate agreement shall regulate the numbers and conditions of employment of British officials so appointed in the Iraq Government.

ARTICLE III.

His Majesty the King of Iraq agrees to frame an Organic Law for presentation to the Constituent Assembly of Iraq and to give effect to the said law, which shall contain nothing contrary to the provisions of the present Treaty and shall take account of the rights, wishes and interests of all populations inhabiting Iraq. This Organic Law shall ensure to all complete freedom of conscience and the free exercise of all forms of worship, subject only to the maintenance of public order and morals. It shall provide that no discrimination of any kind shall be made between the inhabitants of Iraq on the ground of race, religion or language, and shall secure that the right of each community to maintain its own schools for the education of its own members in its own language, while conforming to such educational requirements of a general nature as the Government of Iraq may impose, shall not be denied or impaired. It shall prescribe the constitutional procedure, whether legislative or executive, by which decisions will be taken on all matters of importance, including those involving questions of fiscal, financial and military policy.

ARTICLE IV.

Without prejudice to the provisions of Articles XVII and XVIII of this Treaty, His Majesty the King of Iraq agrees to be guided by the advice of His Britannic Majesty tendered through the High Commissioner on all important matters affecting the international and financial obligations and interests of His Britannic Majesty for the whole period of this Treaty. His Majesty the King of Iraq will fully consult the High Commissioner on what is conducive to a sound financial and fiscal policy and will ensure the stability and good organisation of the finances of the Iraq Government so long as that Government is under financial obligations to the Government of His Britannic Majesty.

ARTICLE V.

His Majesty the King of Iraq shall have the right of representation in London and in such other capitals and places as may be agreed upon by the High Contracting Parties. Where His Majesty the King of Iraq is not represented he agrees to entrust the protection of Iraq nationals to His Britannic Majesty. His Majesty the King of Iraq shall himself issue exequaturs to representatives of Foreign Powers in Iraq after His Britannic Majesty has agreed to their appointment.

ARTICLE VI.

His Britannic Majesty undertakes to use his good offices to secure the admission of Iraq to membership of the League of Nations as soon as possible.

ARTICLE VII.

His Britannic Majesty undertakes to provide such support and assistance to the armed forces of His Majesty the King of Iraq as may from time to time be agreed by the High Contracting Parties. A separate agreement regulating the extent and conditions of such support and assistance shall be concluded between the High Contracting Parties and communicated to the Council of the League of Nations.

ARTICLE VIII.

No territory in Iraq shall be ceded or leased or in any way placed under the control of any Foreign Power; this shall not prevent His Majesty the King of Iraq from making such arrangements as may be necessary for the accommodation of foreign representatives and for the fulfilment of the provisions of the preceding Article.

ARTICLE IX.

His Majesty the King of Iraq undertakes that he will accept and give effect to such reasonable provisions as His Britannic Majesty may consider necessary in judicial matters to safeguard the interests of foreigners in consequence of the non-application of the immunities and privileges enjoyed by them under capitulation or usage. These provisions shall be embodied in a separate agreement, which shall be communicated to the Council of the League of Nations.

ARTICLE X.

The High Contracting Parties agree to conclude separate agreements to secure the execution of any treaties, agreements or undertakings which His Britannic Majesty is under obligation to see carried out in respect of Iraq. His Majesty the King of Iraq undertakes to bring in any legislation necessary to ensure the execution of these agreements. Such agreements shall be communicated to the Council of the League of Nations.

ARTICLE XI.

There shall be no discrimination in Iraq against the nationals of any State, member of the League of Nations, or of any State to which His Britannic Majesty has agreed by treaty that the same rights should be ensured as it would enjoy if it were a member of the said League (including companies incorporated under the laws of such State), as compared with British nationals or those of any foreign State in matters concerning taxation, commerce or navigation, the exercise of industries or professions, or in the treatment of merchant vessels or civil aircraft. Nor shall there be any discrimination in Iraq against goods originating in or destined for any of the said States. There shall be freedom of transit under equitable conditions across Iraq territory.

ARTICLE XII.

No measure shall be taken in Iraq to obstruct or interfere with missionary enterprise or to discriminate against any missionary on the ground of his religious belief or nationality, provided that such enterprise is not prejudicial to public order and good government.

ARTICLE XIII.

His Majesty the King of Iraq undertakes to co-operate, in so far as social, religious and other conditions may permit, in the execution of any common policy adopted by the League of Nations for preventing and combating disease, including diseases of plants and animals.

ARTICLE XIV.

His Majesty the King of Iraq undertakes to secure the enactment, within twelve months of the coming into force of this Treaty, and to ensure the execution of a Law of Antiquities based on the rules annexed to Article 421 of the Treaty of Peace signed at Sèvres on the 10th August, 1920. This Law shall replace the former Ottoman Law of Antiquities, and shall ensure equality of treatment in the matter of archæological research to the nationals of all States members of the League of Nations, and of any State to which His Britannic Majesty has agreed by treaty that the same rights should be ensured as it would enjoy if it were a member of the said League.

ARTICLE XV.

A separate agreement shall regulate the financial relations between the High Contracting Parties. It shall provide, on the one hand, for the transfer by His Britannic Majesty's Government to the Government of Iraq of such works of public utility as may be agreed upon and for the rendering by His Britannic Majesty's Government of such financial assistance as may from time to time be considered necessary for Iraq, and, on the other hand, for the progressive liquidation by the Government of Iraq of all liabilities thus incurred. Such agreement shall be communicated to the Council of the League of Nations.

ARTICLE XVI.

So far as is consistent with his international obligations His Britannic Majesty undertakes to place no obstacle in the way of the association of the State of Iraq for customs or other purposes with such neighbouring Arab States as may desire it.

ARTICLE XVII.

Any difference that may arise between the High Contracting Parties as to the interpretation of the provisions of this Treaty shall be referred to the Permanent Court of International Justice provided for by Article 14 of the Covenant of the League of Nations. In such case, should there be any discrepancy between the English and Arabic texts of this Treaty, the English shall be taken as the authoritative version.

ARTICLE XVIII.

This Treaty shall come into force as soon as it has been ratified by the High Contracting Parties after its acceptance by the Constituent Assembly, and shall remain in force for twenty years, at the end of which period the situation shall be examined, and if the High Contracting Parties are of opinion that the Treaty is no longer required it shall be terminated. Termination shall be subject to confirmation by the League of Nations unless before that date Article 6 of this Treaty has come into effect, in which case notice of termination shall be communicated to the Council of the League of Nations. Nothing shall prevent the High Contracting Parties from reviewing from time to time the provisions of this Treaty, and those of the separate Agreements arising out of Articles 7, 10 and 15, with a view to any revision which may seem desirable in the circumstances then existing, and any modification which may be agreed upon by the High Contracting Parties shall be communicated to the Council of the League of Nations.

The ratifications shall be exchanged at Baghdad.

The present Treaty has been drawn up in English and Arabic. One copy in each language will remain deposited in the archives of the Iraq Government, and one copy in each language in those of the Government of His Britannic Majesty.

IN WITNESS OF WHICH the respective Plenipotentiaries have signed the present Treaty and have affixed thereto their seals. Done at Baghdad in duplicate this tenth day of October, One thousand nine hundred and twenty-two of the Christian Era, corresponding with the nineteenth day of Safar, One thousand three hundred and forty Hijrah.

P. Z. COX,
His Britannic Majesty's High
Commissioner in Iraq.
'ABD-UR-RAHMAN,
Naqib-al-Ashraf of Baghdad and
Prime Minister of the Iraq
Government.

ANNEX R

THE SITUATION IN AFRICA AS DETERMINED BY EXISTING TREATIES, AGREEMENTS, ETC.

I. *Collections of Treaties, Agreements, etc., relating to Africa.*

Hertslet, Sir Edward, "The Map of Africa by Treaty." 3d ed., revised and completed to the end of 1908, by R. W. Brant and H. L. Sherwood. 3 vols. London, 1909.

"Trattati, Convenzioni, Accordi, Protocolli ed altri Documenti relativi all'Africa, 1825-1906." Published by the Direzione Centrale degli Affari Coloniali for the Ministero degli Affari Esteri. 3 vols. Rome, 1906. Supplemento, 1884-1908. Rome, 1909.

(Further literature both on the documents here mentioned and on other treaties, etc., relating to Africa may be found in "Catalogue of Treaties, 1814-1918," published by the United States Department of State. Washington, 1919.)

II. *Chief Treaties, etc., providing for Equality of Commercial Treatment and of Navigation, Neutralization, Arbitration, Control of the Importation of Alcoholic Liquors, Suppression of the Slave Trade and the Traffic in Arms, Protection of Wild Animals, Railroad Construction, etc.*

1. General Act of the Berlin Conference, February 26, 1885. Hertslet, pp. 468-487; "Trattati," pp. 104-120; Albin, "Les Grands Traités Politiques," pp. 388-406; *American Journal of International Law*, III, Supplement, pp. 7-25.

2. General Act of the Brussels Conference, July 2, 1890. Hertslet, pp. 488-528; "Trattati," pp. 268-297; Malloy, "Treaties," pp. 1964-1992; *American Journal of International Law*, III, Supplement, pp. 29-60.

3. Brussels International Conventions of June 8, 1899, and November 3, 1906. Hertslet, pp. 528-534; "Trattati," pp. 618-621, 1247-1250; Malloy, pp. 1993-1995, 2205-2208.

4. Treaty between the United States and the Congo Free State, January 24, 1891. "Trattati," Supplemento, pp. 22-28; Malloy, pp. 328-333; *American Journal of International Law*, III, Supplement, pp. 62-68.

5. Anglo-French Treaty of June 14, 1898 (Article IX), and Declaration of March 21, 1899. Hertslet, pp. 789, 790, 796; "Trattati," pp. 594-603, 613-614.

6. Anglo-French Agreement of April 8, 1904, regarding equality of commerce in Egypt and Morocco. Hertslet, pp. 820-822; "Trattati," pp. 1116-1118; *American Journal of International Law,* I, Supplement, pp. 6-8.

7. Algeciras Act of April 7, 1906. Debidour, "Histoire Diplomatique de l'Europe, 1904-1916," pp. 293-319; "Trattati," pp. 1150-1184; Malloy, pp. 2157-2183; *American Journal of International Law,* I, Supplement, pp. 47-77.

8. Franco-German Agreement of November 4, 1911. Debidour, pp. 336-340; *American Journal of International Law,* VI, Supplement, pp. 4-9.

9. Treaty of May 19, 1900, between Great Britain, France, Italy, Germany, Spain, Congo, and Portugal for the protection of wild animals. "Trattati," pp. 632-638.

10. Treaty of December 13, 1906, between Great Britain, France, and Italy regarding the traffic in arms in Abyssinia and Somaliland. "Trattati," pp. 1258-1260; Albin, pp. 412-414; *American Journal of International Law,* I, Supplement, pp. 230-231. Also the Treaty of the same date regarding the railroad situation. Hertslet, pp. 436-444; "Trattati," pp. 1251-1257; Albin, pp. 408-412; *American Journal of International Law,* I, Supplement, pp. 226-230.

11. Suez Canal Convention of October 29, 1888. "Trattati," pp. 952-956; Albin, pp. 382-387; *American Journal of International Law,* III, Supplement, pp. 123-126.

12. Convention of April 1, 1909, between Mozambique and the Transvaal on recruitment of laborers. *American Journal of International Law,* III, Supplement, pp. 309-321.

13. Franco-Spanish Declaration of October 3, 1904, regarding Morocco. "Trattati," p. 1134; Albin, p. 331; *American Journal of International Law,* I, Supplement, pp. 8-9; VI, Supplement, p. 30.

14. Anglo-German Agreement of August 17, 1911, on sleeping sickness. *American Journal of International Law,* VI, Supplement, p. 10.

15. Anglo-Liberian Agreement of April 10, 1913, regarding navigation of the Manoh River. *American Journal of International Law,* VII, Supplement, pp. 177-179.

16. Anglo-French Convention of April 8, 1904 (Article V regarding navigation of the Gambia River). "Trattati," p. 715; *American Journal of International Law,* I, Supplement, p. 11.

17. Anglo-Italian Agreement of January 13, 1905 (Article III on British right of preëmption on the Benadir Coast). Hertslet, III, p. 955; "Trattati," pp. 742, 744. Cf. also Article V of the Treaty of October 26, 1896, between Italy and Abyssinia. Hertslet, II, p. 459; "Trattati," p. 509.

18. Anglo-Portuguese Treaty of June 11, 1891 (Article VII on mutual

rights of preëmption to territories south of the Zambezi). "Trattati," pp. 352-353.

19. Agreement of December 11, 1875, between Portugal and the Transvaal regarding Delagoa Bay. Hertslet, III, pp. 993-996; "Trattati," pp. 901-906.

III. *Treaties regarding the Present and Future Status of Some Areas.*

1. Morocco: Algeciras Treaty of April 7, 1906, and Franco-German Treaty of November 4, 1911. Also the Anglo-French Agreement of April 8, 1904. Albin, pp. 326-328; *American Journal of International Law*, VI, Supplement, pp. 26-29; secret articles, *ibid.*, pp. 29-30; Albin, "Le 'Coup' d'Agadir," pp. 369-370. Convention of Madrid, July 3, 1880, and Franco-German Declaration of February 9, 1909. "Trattati," pp. 923-929; Albin, pp. 315-320, 374-375; Malloy, pp. 1220-1227; *American Journal of International Law*, VI, Supplement, pp. 18, 24, 31. Franco-German Declaration of February 9, 1909. Albin, "Les Grands Traités Politiques," pp. 374-375; *American Journal of International Law*, VI, Supplement, p. 31. See further the Franco-Moroccan Treaty of March 30, 1912, and the Franco-Spanish Treaties of October 3, 1904, September 1, 1905, November 27, 1912, and October 3, 1914. *American Journal of International Law*, VI, Supplement, pp. 207-209; Albin, "Le 'Coup' d'Agadir," pp. 371-378, and *American Journal of International Law*, VI, Supplement, pp. 116-120; Albin, pp. 378-383; *American Journal of International Law*, VII, Supplement, pp. 81-99; *ibid.*, I, Supplement, pp. 8-9. Cf. also the Franco-Italian Agreements of 1900-02 on Morocco and Tripoli. *Documents Diplomatiques*, Paris, 1920.

2. Egypt: Convention of October 24, 1885 (Hertslet, "The Map of Europe by Treaty," IV, pp. 3274-3276, London, 1891), and the Anglo-French Agreement of April 8, 1904.

3. Abyssinia: Agreement of December 13, 1906, between Great Britain, France, and Italy. Hertslet, "The Map of Africa by Treaty," pp. 436-444; "Trattati," pp. 1258-1260; Albin, "Les Grands Traités Politiques," pp. 408-412; *American Journal of International Law*, I, Supplement, pp. 226-230.

4. Liberia: Agreements, etc., defining the status of the United States in Liberia, notably the Treaty of October 21, 1862. Malloy, pp. 1050-1052.

5. Portuguese Colonies: Anglo-German Agreement of 1898, Anglo-Portuguese Agreement of 1899, and the uncompleted Anglo-German Agreement of 1914. Memorandum of Prince Lichnowsky, ed. and tr. Munroe Smith, in *International Conciliation*, No. 127, June, 1918, pp. 57-69.

6. Belgian Congo: France's right of preëmption by the Franco-Congolese Agreements of April 23-24, 1884, April 22, 29, 1887, and February 5,

1895, and by the Franco-Belgian Treaty of December 23, 1908. Hertslet, pp. 562, 563, 567, 570, 571, 1226; "Trattati," pp. 71-72, 170-171, 447-478; Albin, pp. 406-407; *American Journal of International Law*, III, Supplement, pp. 293-296. Virtual waiver of the rights by the Franco-German Agreement of November 4, 1911. Anglo-Belgian Treaty of February 3, 1915, respecting boundaries in East Africa from Mount Sabinio to the Congo-Nile watershed. Treaty Series, 1920, No. 2.

7. Spanish Colonies: France's right of preëmption under the Franco-Spanish Treaty of June 27, 1900. Hertslet, pp. 1165-1167; "Trattati," Supplemento, pp. 33-37. Cession of this right to Germany in the Notes annexed to the Franco-German Treaty of November 4, 1911. Debidour, pp. 345-350.

8. Tunis: French Protectorate by Treaty of Bardo, or Casr Said, May 12, 1881, and Convention of La Marsa, June 8, 1883. Albin, pp. 291-294.

9. Agreement between France, Spain, and Great Britain of May 16, 1907, regarding the territorial *status quo* in the West Mediterranean and the adjacent Atlantic. "Trattati," Supplemento, pp. 110-113; Albin, pp. 121-123; *American Journal of International Law*, I, Supplement, p. 425.

IV. *Treaties, Conventions, Mandates, etc., in Consequence of Territorial Changes Arising from the War.*

1. Anglo-Portuguese Agreement of May 6, 1920, respecting the boundaries in South-East Africa. Treaty Series, 1920, No. 16.

2. Convention of September 10, 1919, revising the General Act of Berlin, February 26, 1885, and the General Act and Declaration of Brussels, July 2, 1890. Treaty Series, 1919, No. 18. Reprinted as Annex G.

3. Convention of September 10, 1919, relating to the Liquor Traffic in Africa. Treaty Series, 1919, No. 19. Reprinted as Annex F.

4. Convention of September 10, 1919, for the Control of the Trade in Arms and Ammunition. Treaty Series, 1919, No. 12. Reprinted as Annex E.

5. Tripartite Agreement of August 10, 1920, between the British Empire, France, and Italy respecting Anatolia. Treaty Series, 1920, No. 12.

6. Draft Mandate for East Africa (British). Miscellaneous, No. 14 (1921) (Cd. 1284). Reprinted as Annex I.

7. Draft Mandates for Togoland (British) and the Cameroons (British). Miscellaneous, No. 16 (1921) (Cd. 1350). Reprinted as Annex J.

8. Mandate of December 17, 1920, for German South-West Africa. Miscellaneous, No. 8 (1921) (Cd. 1204). Reprinted as Annex L.

9. Final Drafts of the Mandates for Mesopotamia and Palestine. Mandates, 1921 (Cd. 1500). Mesopotamian Draft Mandate reprinted as Annex H.

10. Franco-British Convention of December 23, 1920, on Certain Points connected with the Mandates for Syria and the Lebanon, Palestine and Mesopotamia. Miscellaneous, No. 4 (1921) (Cd. 1195). Reprinted as Annex N.

11. Mandate of December 17, 1920, for German Samoa. Miscellaneous, No. 7 (1921) (Cd. 1203). Reprinted as Annex K.

12. Mandate of December 17, 1920, for German Possessions in the Pacific Ocean situated south of the Equator other than German Samoa and Nauru. Miscellaneous, No. 5 (1921) (Cd. 1201).

13. Mandate of December 17, 1920, for Nauru. Miscellaneous, No. 6 (1921) (Cd. 1202).

14. Anglo-Portuguese Agreement of December 9, 1920, relating to the suppression of Capitulations in Egypt. Treaty Series, 1921, No. 23. Reprinted as Annex P.

15. Treaty of October 10, 1922, between Great Britain and Iraq. *Iraq*, 1922 (Cd. 1757). Reprinted as Annex Q.

A number of agreements arising from territorial changes due to the war are still unpublished, *e.g.*, the Anglo-Belgian Agreement of June, 1920, Franco-Italian Notes of September 12, 1919, Anglo-French Agreement of September 8, 1919, and Anglo-Italian Agreement of May, 1920. *Le Temps*, June 23, February 24, May 6, 29, June 6, 1919; February 14, 1920; Antonelli, "L'Afrique et la Paix de Versailles," pp. 246-247.

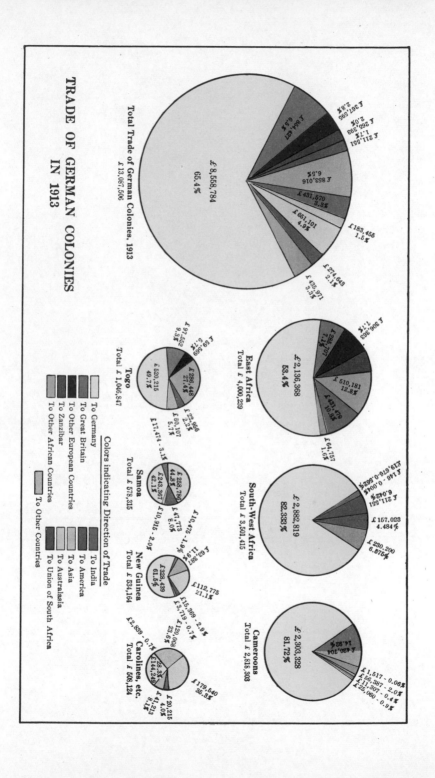

TRADE OF GERMAN COLONIES
IN 1913

Total Trade of German Colonies, 1913
£ 13,087,506

Total Trade of German Colonies, 1913
£ 13,087,506

£ 8,558,784
65.4%

£ 367,396
2.8%
£ 266,398
2.0%
£ 211,661
1.7%
£ 854,427
6.5%
£ 853,910
6.5%
£ 431,570
3.3%
£ 183,455
1.5%
£ 274,649
2.1%
£ 435,971
3.3%

East Africa
Total £ 4,000,239

£ 2,136,368
53.4%
£ 306,362
7.7%
£ 285,701
7.1%
£ 610,181
12.8%
£ 431,479
10.5%
£ 64,757
1.6%

South-West Africa
Total £ 3,501,415

£ 2,882,819
82.333%
£ 13,816-0.005%
£ 146-0.004%
£ 211,661
6.042%
£ 157,028
4.484%
£ 230,200
6.876%

Cameroons
Total £ 2,816,303

£ 2,303,328
81.72%
£ 430,704
14.82%
£ 1,517 - 0.05%
£ 66,387 - 2.0%
£ 11,307 - 0.4%
£ 22,080 - 7.9%
£ 20,215
£ 41,213
4.0%
8.1%

Togo
Total £ 1,046,847

£ 520,215
49.7%
£ 286,448
27.4%
£ 97,552
9.3%
£ 69,569
6.7%
£ 22,966
2.2%
£ 60,107
5.7%
£ 11,474 - 3.1%

Samoa
Total £ 578,315

£ 253,780
43.9%
£ 243,367
42.1%
£ 47,773
8.0%
£ 10,911 - 2.0%
£ 10,475 - 1.9%

New Guinea
Total £ 554,164

£ 328,439
61.5%
£ 112,775
21.1%
£ 63,397
11%
£ 15,369 - 2.9%
£ 3,719 - 0.7%

Carolines, etc.
Total £ 508,124

£ 179,640
36.3%
£ 144,249
28.3%
£ 120,008
23.6%

Colors indicating Direction of Trade

To Germany
To Great Britain
To Other European Countries
To Zanzibar
To Other African Countries

To India
To America
To Asia
To Australasia
To Union of South Africa

To Other Countries

BIBLIOGRAPHY

ADAM, J., "L'Angleterre et l'Égypte," Paris, 1922.
ALBIN, P., "Les Grands Traités Politiques," Paris, 1911.
———, "Le 'Coup' d'Agadir," Paris, 1912.
ALYPE, PIERRE, "La Provocation Allemande aux Colonies," Paris, 1915.
———, "L'Éthiopie et les Ambitions Allemandes," Paris, 1916.
ANTONELLI, ÉTIENNE, "L'Afrique et la Paix de Versailles," Paris, 1921.
ARCHER, WILLIAM, "Five Hundred and One Gems of German Thought," London, 1917.
ARMINJON, P., "La Situation Économique et Financière de l'Égypte," Paris, 1911.

BAILLAUD, ÉMILE, "La Politique Indigène de l'Angleterre en Afrique Orientale," Paris, 1912.
BAKER, R. S., "Woodrow Wilson and World Settlement," Garden City, N. Y., 1922.
BERNHARDT, G. DE, "Handbook of Commercial Treaties between Great Britain and Foreign Powers," London, 1912.
BLUNT, W. S., "Secret History of the English Occupation of Egypt," London, 1907.
BOWMAN, I., "The New World: Problems in Political Geography," Chapter XXXIII, "African Colonies of the European Powers," Yonkers, New York, 1921.
BROWN, P. M., "Foreigners in Turkey: Their Juridical Status," Princeton, 1914.
BRUEL, GEORGES, "L'Afrique Équatoriale Française," Paris, 1918.

CADBURY, W. A., "Labour in Portuguese West Africa," London, 1910.
CALVERT, A. F., "Nigeria and Its Tin Fields," London, 1910.
———, "The German African Empire," London, 1916.
———, "The Cameroons," London, 1917.
CHALLAYE, F., "Le Congo Français: La Question Internationale du Congo," Paris, 1909.
CHIROL, SIR VALENTINE, "The Egyptian Problem," London, 1920.

CHRISTY, C., "African Rubber Industry and Funtuimia Elastica," London, 1911.
CIORICEANU, G., "Les Mandats Internationaux," Paris, 1921.
COLVIN, SIR AUCKLAND, "The Making of Modern Egypt" (3d ed.), London, 1906.
"Conférence de la Paix, Procès-Verbaux et Rapports des Commissions du Maroc, des Colonies Allemandes et pour la Revision des Actes Généraux de Berlin et de Bruxelles" [Paris], 1919.
CRESSATY, R. J. M., "L'Égypte d'Aujourd'hui," Paris, 1912.
CROMER, EARL OF, "Modern Egypt" (2 vols.), London, 1908.
———, "Abbas II," London, 1915.
CROWE, J. H. V., "General Smuts' Campaign in East Africa," London, 1918.

DAWSON, W. H., "The Evolution of Modern Germany," London, 1911.
DEBIDOUR, A., "Histoire Diplomatique de l'Europe, 1878-1904," Paris, 1917.
———, "Histoire Diplomatique de l'Europe, 1904-1916," Paris, 1918.
DEBONO, A., "Du Système Législatif, de l'Organisation Judiciare . . . en Égypte," Paris, 1908.
DOLBEY, R. V., "Sketches of the East Africa Campaign," London, 1918.

FREYCINET, C. DE, "La Question d'Égypte," Paris, 1905.

GAUNT, MARY, "Alone in West Africa" (3d ed.), London, 1913.
GIBBONS, H. A., "The New Map of Africa," New York, 1917.
GIRAULT, A., "The Colonial Tariff Policy of France," London, 1916.
GORGES, E. H. M., Report on the Natives of Southwest Africa and their Treatment by Germany, Cd. 9146 (1918).
GRUMBACH, S., "Das Annexionistische Deutschland," Lausanne, 1917.

"Handbook of German East Africa," London, 1920.
HARRIS, J. H., "Dawn in Darkest Africa," London, 1912.
———, "Portuguese Slavery: Britain's Dilemma," London, 1913.
———, "Germany's Lost Colonial Empire," London, 1917.
———, "Africa: Slave or Free?" London, 1919.
HARRIS, N. D., "Intervention and Colonization in Africa," Boston, 1914.

HAUSER, HENRI, "Le Problème Colonial," Paris, 1915.
HERTSLET, SIR E., "The Map of Africa by Treaty" (3d ed.), (3 vols.), London, 1909.
HOBSON, J. A., "Imperialism," London, 1902.
HORNBECK, S. K., "Contemporary Politics in the Far East," New York, 1916.
HOURWICH, I. A., "Immigration and Labor," New York, 1912.
HUMBERT, C., "L'Œuvre Française aux Colonies," Paris, 1913.
HUPFELD, F., "Das Deutsche Kolonialreich der Zukunft," Berlin, 1917.

IRELAND, A., "Tropical Colonization," New York, 1899.

JOHNSTON, SIR H. H., "The History of the Colonization of Africa by Alien Races" (new ed.), Cambridge, 1913.
———, "The Black Man's Part in the War," London, 1917.

KEITH, A. B., "West Africa" (Lucas, Sir C. P., "Historical Geography of the British Colonies," vol. III), Oxford, 1913.
———, "South Africa," vol. III (Lucas, op. cit., vol. IV, part III), Oxford, 1913.
———, "The Belgian Congo and the Berlin Act," Oxford, 1919.
KELLER, A. G., "Colonization: A Study of the Founding of New Societies," Boston, 1908.
KELTIE, J. SCOTT, "The Partition of Africa" (2d ed.), London, 1895.
KUCKLEUTZ, K., "Das Zollwesen der Deutschen Schutzgebiete," Berlin, 1914.

LABRY, M., "La Révolution Égyptienne," Paris, 1922.
LA JONQUIÈRE, A. DE, "Histoire de l'Empire Ottoman" (revised ed.), (2 vols.), Paris, 1914.
LANE-POOLE, S., "A History of Egypt in the Middle Ages," London, 1901.
LEROY-BEAULIEU, P., "De la Colonisation chez les Peuples Modernes" (5th ed.) (2 vols.), Paris, 1902.
LEWIN, EVANS, "The Germans and Africa," London, 1915.
LORAM, C. T., "The Education of the South African Native," London, 1917.
LORIMER, NORMA, "By the Waters of Africa," London, 1917.
LOW, SIR SIDNEY, "Egypt in Transition," New York, 1914.
LUGARD, SIR F. D., "The Dual Mandate in British Tropical Africa," London, 1922.

MacDonald, A. J. S., "Trade, Politics, and Christianity in Africa and the East," London, 1916.
Mangin, C. M. E., "La Force Noire," Paris, 1910.
"Manual of Belgian Congo," London, 1920.
Maurice, L., "La Politique Marocaine de l'Allemagne," Paris, 1916.
"Mesopotamia" (Handbooks Prepared under the Direction of the Historical Section of the Foreign Office, No. 63, in Peace Handbooks, XI.), London, 1920.
Messimy, A., "Notre Œuvre Coloniale," Paris, 1910.
Milner, Lord, "England in Egypt" (7th ed.), London, 1899.
Morel, E. D., "Affairs of West Africa," London, 1902.
———, "The British Case in French Congo," London, 1903.
———, "Africa and the Peace of Europe," London, 1917.

Noradounghian, G. E., "Recueil d'Actes Internationaux de l'Empire Ottoman" (4 vols.), Paris, 1903.

Payen, E., "Belgique et Congo," Paris, 1917.
Pritchard, S. M., "Report on Tour to Ovamboland," Pretoria, 1915.

Rausas, G. Pélissié du, "Le Régime des Capitulations dans l'Empire Ottoman" (2 vols.), Paris, 1902-05.
Renty, E. A. de, "Les Chemins de Fer Coloniaux en Afrique" (3 vols.), Paris, 1903-05.
Rohrbach, Paul, "Das Deutsche Kolonialwesen," Leipzig, 1911.
———, "Zum Weltvolk Hindurch!", Stuttgart, 1914.
———, "Germany's Isolation," Chicago, 1915.
Roscher, W., and Jannasch, J., "Kolonien, Kolonialpolitik und Auswanderung" (3d ed.), Leipzig, 1885.

Sadek, Morcos, "La Constitution de l'Égypte," Paris, 1908.
Scott, J. H., "The Law Affecting Foreigners in Egypt," Edinburgh, 1907.
Sonolet, Louis, "L'Afrique Occidentale Française," Paris, 1913.

Tardieu, A., "Le Mystère d'Agadir," Paris, 1912.
"The League of Nations Starts" (an Outline by its Organisers), London, 1920.

Vietor, J. K., "Geschichtliche und Kulturelle Entwickelung Unserer Schutzgebiete," Berlin, 1913.
Vignon, Louis, "Un Programme de Politique Coloniale: Les Questions Indigènes," Paris, 1919.

WACK, H. W., "The Story of the Congo Free State," New York, 1905.
WALLACE, D. M., "Egypt and the Egyptian Question," London, 1883.
WEIGALL, A. E. P. B., "A History of Events in Egypt from 1798 to 1914," Edinburgh, 1915.
WESTON, F., "The Black Slaves of Prussia," London [1918].
WHITE, A. S., "The Expansion of Egypt," London, 1899.
WILLCOCKS, SIR W., and CRAIG, J. I., "Egyptian Irrigation" (3d ed.) (2 vols.), London, 1913.
WINGATE, SIR REGINALD, "Memorandum on the Sudan, 1914," London, 1915.

YOUNG, G., "Corps de Droit Ottoman" (7 vols.), Oxford, 1905-06.

ZIMMERMANN, A., "Geschichte der Deutschen Kolonialpolitik," Berlin, 1914.
ZIMMERMANN, E., "The German Empire of Central Africa," London, 1918.

INDEX

PART I: THE GERMAN COLONIES IN AFRICA

NOTE. References to notes are indicated in this Index by superior numbers.

PART II: MIDDLE AFRICA: THE ECONOMIC ASPECTS OF THE PROBLEM

PART III: MIDDLE AFRICA: PROBLEMS OF INTERNATIONAL COÖPERATION AND CONTROL

PART IV: EGYPTIAN PROBLEMS

PART V: THE FUTURE OF MESOPOTAMIA

PART VI: THE COLONIAL QUESTIONS